LANGUAGE

By the same Author

ESSENTIALS OF ENGLISH GRAMMAR
THE PHILOSOPHY OF GRAMMAR
A MODERN ENGLISH GRAMMAR
(*in seven volumes*)
HOW TO TEACH A FOREIGN LANGUAGE
AN INTERNATIONAL LANGUAGE
NOVIAL LEXIKE
CHAPTERS ON ENGLISH
MANKIND, NATION AND INDIVIDUAL
SELECTED WRITINGS OF OTTO JESPERSEN

LANGUAGE

ITS NATURE, DEVELOPMENT
AND ORIGIN

by

OTTO JESPERSEN

London
GEORGE ALLEN & UNWIN LTD
RUSKIN HOUSE   MUSEUM STREET

FIRST PRINTED IN JANUARY 1922
SECOND IMPRESSION FEBRUARY 1923
THIRD IMPRESSION AUGUST 1925
FOURTH IMPRESSION FEBRUARY 1928
FIFTH IMPRESSION MAY 1933
SIXTH IMPRESSION JANUARY 1934
SEVENTH IMPRESSION 1947
EIGHTH IMPRESSION 1949
NINTH IMPRESSION 1950
TENTH IMPRESSION 1954
ELEVENTH IMPRESSION 1959
TWELFTH IMPRESSION 1964

PRINTED IN GREAT BRITAIN BY
UNWIN BROTHERS LTD., WOKING AND LONDON

TO

VILHELM THOMSEN

Glæde, når av andres mund
  jeg hørte de tanker store,
Glæde over hvert et fund
  jeg selv ved min forsken gjorde.

PREFACE

THE distinctive feature of the science of language as conceived nowadays is its historical character : a language or a word is no longer taken as something given once for all, but as a result of previous development and at the same time as the starting-point for subsequent development. This manner of viewing languages constitutes a decisive improvement on the way in which languages were dealt with in previous centuries, and it suffices to mention such words as ' evolution ' and ' Darwinism ' to show that linguistic research has in this respect been in full accordance with tendencies observed in many other branches of scientific work during the last hundred years. Still, it cannot be said that students of language have always and to the fullest extent made it clear to themselves what is the real essence of a language. Too often expressions are used which are nothing but metaphors—in many cases perfectly harmless metaphors, but in other cases metaphors that obscure the real facts of the matter. Language is frequently spoken of as a ' living organism ' ; we hear of the ' life ' of languages, of the ' birth ' of new languages and of the ' death ' of old languages, and the implication, though not always realized, is that a language is a living thing, something analogous to an animal or a plant. Yet a language evidently has no separate existence in the same way as a dog or a beech has, but is nothing but a function of certain living human beings. Language is activity, purposeful activity, and we should never lose sight of the speaking individuals and of their purpose in acting in this particular way. When people speak of the life of words—as in celebrated books with such titles as *La vie des mots*, or *Biographies of Words*—they do not always keep in view that a word has no ' life ' of its own : it exists only in so far as it is pronounced or heard or remembered by somebody, and this kind of existence cannot properly be compared with ' life ' in the original and proper sense of that word. The only unimpeachable definition of a word is that it is a human habit, an habitual act on the part of one human individual which has, or may have, the effect of evoking some idea in the mind of another individual. A word thus may be rightly compared with such an habitual act as taking off one's hat or raising one's fingers to one's cap : in both cases we have a certain set of muscular activities which, when seen or heard by somebody else, shows him what is passing in the mind of the original agent or what he desires to bring to the consciousness of the other man (or men). The act is individual, but the interpretation presupposes that the individual forms part of a community with analogous habits, and a language thus is seen to be one particular set of human customs of a well-defined social character.

It is indeed possible to speak of ' life ' in connexion with language even from this point of view, but it will be in a different sense from that in which the word was taken by the older school of linguistic science. I shall try to give a biological or biographical science of language, but it will be through sketching the linguistic biology or biography of the speaking individual. I shall give, therefore, a large part to the way in which a child learns his mother-tongue (Book II) : my conclusions there are chiefly based on the rich material I have collected during many years from direct observation of many Danish children, and particularly of my own boy, Frans (see my book *Nutidssprog hos börn og voxne*, Copenhagen, 1916). Unfortunately, I have not been able to make first-hand observations with regard to the speech of English children ; the English examples I quote are taken second-hand either from notes, for which I am obliged to English and American friends, or from books, chiefly by psychologists. I should be particularly happy if my remarks could induce some English or American linguist to take up a systematic study of the speech of children, or of one child. This study seems to me very fascinating indeed, and a linguist is sure to notice many things that would be passed by as uninteresting even by the closest observer among psychologists, but which may have some bearing on the life and development of language.

Another part of linguistic biology deals with the influence of the foreigner, and still another with the changes which the individual is apt independently to introduce into his speech even after he has fully acquired his mother-tongue. This naturally leads up to the question whether all these changes introduced by various individuals do, or do not, follow the same line of direction, and whether mankind has on the whole moved forward or not in linguistic matters. The conviction reached through a study of historically accessible periods of well-known languages is finally shown to throw some light on the disputed problem of the ultimate origin of human language.

Parts of my theory of sound-change, and especially my objections

to the dogma of blind sound-laws, date back to my very first
linguistic paper (1886) ; most of the chapters on Decay or Progress
and parts of some of the following chapters, as well as the theory
of the origin of speech, may be considered a new and revised
edition of the general chapters of my *Progress in Language* (1894).
Many of the ideas contained in this book thus are not new with
me ; but even if a reader of my previous works may recognize
things which he has seen before, I hope he will admit that they
have been here worked up with much new material into something
like a system, which forms a fairly comprehensive theory of
linguistic development.

Still, I have not been able to compress into this volume the
whole of my philosophy of speech. Considerations of space have
obliged me to exclude the chapters I had first intended to write
on the practical consequences of the ' energetic ' view of language
which I have throughout maintained ; the estimation of linguistic
phenomena implied in that view has bearings on such questions
as these : What is to be considered ' correct ' or ' standard ' in
matters of pronunciation, spelling, grammar and idiom ? Can (or
should) individuals exert themselves to improve their mother-tongue
by enriching it with new terms and by making it purer, more precise,
more fit to express subtle shades of thought, more easy to handle
in speech or in writing, etc. ? (A few hints on such questions may
be found in my paper " Energetik der Sprache " in *Scientia*, 1914.)
Is it possible to construct an artificial language on scientific principles for international use ? (On this question I may here briefly
state my conviction that it is extremely important for the whole
of mankind to have such a language, and that Ido is scientifically
and practically very much superior to all previous attempts,
Volapük, Esperanto, Idiom Neutral, Latin sine flexione, etc. But
I have written more at length on that question elsewhere.) With
regard to the system of grammar, the relation of grammar to
logic, and grammatical categories and their definition, I must refer
the reader to *Sprogets Logik* (Copenhagen, 1913), and to the first
chapter of the second volume of my *Modern English Grammar*
(Heidelberg, 1914), but I shall hope to deal with these questions
more in detail in a future work, to be called, probably, *The Logic
of Grammar*, of which some chapters have been ready in my
drawers for some years and others are in active preparation.

I have prefixed to the theoretical chapters of this work a short
survey of the history of the science of language in order to show
how my problems have been previously treated. In this part
(Book I) I have, as a matter of course, used the excellent works
on the subject by Benfey, Raumer, Delbrück (*Einleitung in das
Sprachstudium*, 1st ed., 1880 ; I did not see the 5th ed., 1908, till

my own chapters on the history of linguistics were finished), Thomsen, Oertel and Pedersen.   But I have in nearly every case gone to the sources themselves, and have, I think, found interesting things in some of the early books on linguistics that have been generally overlooked ; I have even pointed out some writers who had passed into undeserved oblivion.   My intention has been on the whole to throw into relief the great lines of development rather than to give many details ; in judging the first part of my book it should also be borne in mind that its object primarily is to serve as an introduction to the problems dealt with in the rest of the book.   Throughout I have tried to look at things with my own eyes, and accordingly my views on a great many points are different from those generally accepted ; it is my hope that an impartial observer will find that I have here and there succeeded in distributing light and shade more justly than my predecessors.

Wherever it has been necessary I have transcribed words phonetically according to the system of the *Association Phonétique Internationale*, though without going into too minute distinction of sounds, the object being, not to teach the exact pronunciation of various languages, but rather to bring out clearly the insufficiency of the ordinary spelling.. The latter is given throughout in italics, while phonetic symbols have been inserted in brackets [ ]. I must ask the reader to forgive inconsistency in such matters as Greek accents, Old English marks of vowel-length, etc., which I have often omitted as of no importance for the purpose of this volume.

I must express here my gratitude to the directors of the Carlsbergfond for kind support of my work.   I want to thank also Professor G. C. Moore Smith, of the University of Sheffield : not only has he sent me the manuscript of a translation of most of my *Nutidssprog*, which he had undertaken of his own accord and which served as the basis of Book II, but he has kindly gone through the whole of this volume, improving and correcting my English style in many passages.   His friendship and the untiring interest he has always taken in my work have been extremely valuable to me for a great many years.

OTTO JESPERSEN.

University of Copenhagen,
June 1921.

CONTENTS

BOOK I

HISTORY OF LINGUISTIC SCIENCE

BOOK II

THE CHILD

BOOK III

THE INDIVIDUAL AND THE WORLD

BOOK IV

DEVELOPMENT OF LANGUAGE

ABBREVIATIONS OF BOOK TITLES, ETC.

Bally LV = Ch. Bally, *Le Langage et la Vie*, Genève 1913.
Benfey Gesch = Th. Benfey, *Geschichte der Sprachwissenschaft*, München 1869.
Bleek CG = W. H. I. Bleek, *Comparative Grammar of South African Languages* London 1862–69.
Bloomfield SL = L. Bloomfield, *An Introduction to the Study of Language*, New York 1914.
Bopp C = F. Bopp, *Conjugationssystem der Sanskritsprache*, Frankfurt 1816.
    AC = *Analytical Comparison* (see ch. ii, § 6).
    VG = *Vergleichende Grammatik*, 2te Ausg., Berlin 1857.
Bréal M = M. Bréal, *Mélanges de Mythologie et de Linguistique*, Paris 1882.
Brugmann VG = K. Brugmann, *Grundriss der Vergleichenden Grammatik*, Strassburg 1886 ff., 2te Ausg., 1897 ff.
    KG = *Kurze Vergleichende Grammatik*, Strassburg 1904.
ChE = O. Jespersen, *Chapters on English*, London 1918.
Churchill B = W. Churchill, *Beach-la-Mar*, Washington 1911.
Curtius C = G. Curtius, *Zur Chronologie der indogerm. Sprachforschung*, Leipzig 1873.
    K = *Zur Kritik der neuesten Sprachforschung*, Leipzig 1885.
Dauzat V = A. Dauzat, *La Vie du Langage*, Paris 1910.
    Ph = *La Philosophie du Langage*, Paris 1912.
Delbrück E = B. Delbrück, *Einleitung in das Sprachstudium*, Leipzig 1880; 5te Aufl. 1908.
    Grfr = *Grundfragen der Sprachforschung*, Strassburg 1901.
E. = English.
EDD = J. Wright, *The English Dialect Dictionary*, Oxford 1898 ff.
ESt = *Englische Studien*.
Feist KI = S. Feist, *Kultur, Ausbreitung und Herkunft der Indogermanen*, Berlin 1913.
Fonetik = O. Jespersen, *Fonetik*, Copenhagen 1897.
Fr. = French.
Gabelentz Spr = G. v. d. Gabelentz, *Die Sprachwissenschaft*, Leipzig 1891.
    Gr = *Chinesische Grammatik*, Leipzig 1881.
Ginneken LP = J. v. Ginneken, *Principes de Linguistique Psychologique*, Amsterdam, Paris 1907.
Glenconner = P. Glenconner, *The Sayings of the Children*, Oxford 1918.
Gr. = Greek.
Greenough and Kittredge W = J. B. Greenough and G. L. Kittredge, *Words and their Ways in English Speech*, London 1902.
Grimm Gr. = J. Grimm, *Deutsche Grammatik*, 2te Ausg., Göttingen 1822.
    GDS = *Geschichte der deutschen Sprache*, 4te Aufl., Leipzig 1880.

GRM = *Germanisch-Romanische Monatsschrift.*

GS = O. Jespersen, *Growth and Structure of the English Language,* 3rd ed. Leipzig 1919.

Hilmer Sch = H. Hilmer, *Schallnachahmung, Wortschöpfung u. Bedeutungs-wandel,* Halle 1914.

Hirt GDS = H. Hirt, *Geschichte der deutschen Sprache,* München 1919.

Idg = *Die Indogermanen,* Strassburg 1905-7.

Humboldt Versch = W. v. Humboldt, *Verschiedenheit des menschlichen Sprachbaues* (number of pages as in the original edition).

IF = *Indogermanische Forschungen.*

KZ = Kuhn's *Zeitschrift für vergleichende Sprachforschung.*

Lasch S = R. Lasch, *Sondersprachen u. ihre Entstehung,* Wien 1907.

LPh = O. Jespersen, *Lehrbuch der Phonetik,* 3te Aufl., Leipzig 1920.

Madvig 1857 = J. N. Madvig, *De grammatische Betegnelser,* Copenhagen 1857.

Kl = *Kleine philologische Schriften,* Leipzig 1875.

ME. = Middle English.

MEG = O. Jespersen, *Modern English Grammar,* Heidelberg 1909, 1914.

Meillet DI = A. Meillet, *Les Dialectes Indo-Européens,* Paris 1908.

Germ. = *Caractères généraux des Langues Germaniques,* Paris 1917.

Gr = *Aperçu d'une Histoire de la Langue Grecque,* Paris 1913.

LI = *Introduction à l'étude comp. des Langues Indo-Européennes,* 2e éd., Paris 1908.

Meinhof Ham = C. Meinhof, *Die hamitischen Sprachen,* Hamburg 1912.

MSA = *Die moderne Sprachforschung in Afrika,* Berlin 1910.

Meringer L = R. Meringer, *Aus dem Leben der Sprache,* Berlin 1908.

Misteli = F. Misteli, *Charakteristik der haupts. Typen des Sprachbaues,* Berlin 1893.

MSL = *Mémoires de la Société de Linguistique de Paris.*

Fr. Müller Gr = Friedrich Müller, *Grundriss der Sprachwissenschaft,* Wien 1876 ff.

Max Müller Ch = F. Max Müller, *Chips from a German Workshop,* vol. iv, London 1875.

NED = *A New English Dictionary,* by Murray, etc., Oxford 1884 ff.

Noreen UL = A. Noreen, *Abriss der urgermanischen Lautlehre,* Strassburg 1894.

VS = *Vårt Språk,* Lund 1903 ff.

Nyrop Gr = Kr. Nyrop, *Grammaire Historique de la Langue Française,* Copenhagen 1914 ff.

OE. = Old English (Anglo-Saxon).

Oertel = H. Oertel, *Lectures on the Study of Language,* New York 1901.

OFr. = Old French.

ON. = Old Norse.

Passy Ch = P. Passy, *Les Changements Phonétiques,* Paris 1890.

Paul P = H. Paul, *Prinzipien der Sprachgeschichte,* 4te Aufl., Halle 1909.

Gr = *Grundriss der germanischen Philologie.*

PBB = *Beitrage zur Geschichte der deutschen Sprache* (Paul u. Braune).

Pedersen GKS = H. Pedersen, *Vergl. Grammatik der keltischen Sprachen,* Göttingen 1909.

PhG = O. Jespersen, *Phonetische Grundfragen,* Leipzig 1904.

Porzezinski Spr = V. Porzezinski, *Einleitung in die Sprachwissenschaft,* Leipzig 1910.

Progr. = O. Jespersen, *Progress in Language,* London 1894.

Rask P = R. Rask [Prisskrift] *Undersögelse om det gamle Nordiske Sprogs Oprindelse*, Copenhagen 1818.

　　SA = *Samlede Afhandlinger*, Copenhagen 1834.

Raumer Gesch = R. v. Raumer, *Geschichte der germanischen Philologie*, München 1870.

Ronjat = J. Ronjat, *Le Développement du Langage chez un Enfant Bilingue*, Paris 1913.

Sandfeld Jensen S = Kr. Sandfeld Jensen, *Sprogvidenskaben*, Copenhagen 1913.

　　Sprw = *Die Sprachwissenschaft*, Leipzig 1915.

Saussure LG = F. de Saussure, *Cours de Linguistique Générale*, Lausanne 1916.

Sayce P = A. H. Sayce, *Principles of Comparative Philology*, 2nd ed., London 1875.

　　S = *Introduction to the Science of Language*, London 1880.

Scherer GDS = W. Scherer, *Zur Geschichte der deutschen Sprache*, Berlin 1878.

Schleicher I, II = A. Schleicher, *Sprachvergleichende Untersuchungen*, I–II, Bonn 1848, 1850.

　　Bed. = *Die Bedeutung der Sprache*, Weimar 1865.

　　C = *Compendium der vergl. Grammatik*, 4te Aufl., Weimar 1876.

　　D = *Die deutsche Sprache*, Stuttgart 1860.

　　Darw. = *Die Darwinische Theorie und die Sprachwissenschaft*, Weimar 1873.

　　NV = *Nomen und Verbum*, Leipzig 1865.

Schuchardt SlD = H. Schuchardt, *Slawo-Deutsches u. Slawo-Italienisches*, Graz 1885.

　　KS = *Kreolische Studien* (Wien, Akademie).

Simonyi US = S. Simonyi, *Die Ungarische Sprache*, Strassburg 1907.

Skt. = Sanskrit.

Sommer Lat. = F. Sommer, *Handbuch der latein. Laut- und Formenlehre*, Heidelberg 1902.

Stern = Clara and William Stern, *Die Kindersprache*, Leipzig 1907.

Stoffel Int. = C. Stoffel, *Intensives and Down-toners*, Heidelberg 1901.

Streitberg Gesch = W. Streitberg, *Geschichte der indogerm. Sprachwissenschaft*, Strassburg 1917.

　　Urg = *Urgermanische Grammatik*, Heidelberg 1896.

Sturtevant LCh = E. H. Sturtevant, *Linguistic Change*, Chicago 1917.

Sütterlin WSG = L. Sütterlin, *Das Wesen der sprachlichen Gebilde*, Heidelberg 1902.

　　WW = *Werden und Wesen der Sprache*, Leipzig 1913.

Sweet CP = H. Sweet, *Collected Papers*, Oxford 1913.

　　H = *The History of Language*, London 1900.

　　PS = *The Practical Study of Languages*, London 1899.

Tegnér SM = E. Tegnér, *Språkets makt öfver tanken*, Stockholm 1880.

Verner = K. Verner, *Afhandlinger og Breve*, Copenhagen 1903.

Wechssler L = E. Wechssler, *Giebt es Lautgesetze ?* Halle 1900.

Whitney G = W. D. Whitney, *Life and Growth of Language*, London 1875.

　　L = *Language and the Study of Language*, London 1868.

　　M = *Max Müller and the Science of Language*, New York 1892.

　　OLS = *Oriental and Linguistic Studies*, New York 1873–4.

Wundt S = W. Wundt, *Die Sprache*, Leipzig 1900.

PHONETIC SYMBOLS

ˈ stands before the stressed syllable.

· indicates length of the preceding sound.

[aˑ] as in *alms*.

[ai] as in *ice*.

[au] as in *house*.

[æ] as in *hat*.

[ei] as in *hate*.

[ɛ] as in *care* ; Fr. *tel*.

[ə] indistinct vowels.

[i] as in *fill* ; Fr. *qui*.

[iˑ] as in *feel* ; Fr. *fille*.

[o] as in Fr. *seau*.

[ou] as in *so*.

[ɔ] open *o*-sounds.

[u] as in *full* ; Fr. *fou*.

[uˑ] as in *fool* ; Fr. *épouse*.

[y] as in Fr. *vu*.

[ʌ] as in *cut*.

[ø] as in Fr. *feu*.

[œ] as in Fr. *sœur*.

[~] French nasalization.

[c] as in G. *ich*.

[x] as in G., Sc. *loch*.

[ð] as in *this*.

[j] as in *you*.

[þ] as in *thick*.

[ʃ] as in *she*.

[ʒ] as in *measure*.

['] in Russian palatalization, in Danish glottal stop.

BOOK I

HISTORY OF LINGUISTIC SCIENCE

CHAPTER I

BEFORE 1800

§ 1. Antiquity. § 2. Middle Ages and Renaissance. § 3. Eighteenth-century Speculation. Herder. § 4. Jenisch.

I.—§ 1. Antiquity.

THE science of language began, tentatively and approximately, when the minds of men first turned to problems like these : How is it that people do not speak everywhere the same language ? How were words first created ? What is the relation between a name and the thing it stands for ? Why is such and such a person, or such and such a thing, called *this* and not *that* ? The first answers to these questions, like primitive answers to other riddles of the universe, were largely theological : God, or one particular god, had created language, or God led all animals to the first man in order that he might give them names. Thus in the Old Testament the diversity of languages is explained as a punishment from God for man's crimes and presumption. These were great and general problems, but the minds of the early Jews were also occupied with smaller and more particular problems of language, as when etymological interpretations were given of such personal names as were not immediately self-explanatory.

The same predilection for etymology, and a similar primitive kind of etymology, based entirely on a more or less accidental similarity of sound and easily satisfied with any fanciful connexion in sense, is found abundantly in Greek writers and in their Latin imitators. But to the speculative minds of Greek thinkers the problem that proved most attractive was the general and abstract one, Are words natural and necessary expressions of the notions underlying them, or are they merely arbitrary and conventional signs for notions that might have been equally well expressed by any other sounds ? Endless discussions were carried on about this question, as we see particularly from Plato's *Kratylos*, and no very definite result was arrived at, nor could any be expected so long as one language only formed the basis of the discussion—even in our own days, after a century of comparative philology, the question still remains an open one. In Greece, the two catchwords *phúsei* (by nature) and *thései* (by convention) for centuries divided philosophers and grammarians into two camps, while some, like Sokrates in Plato's dialogue, though admitting that in language as actually existing there was no natural connexion between word and thing, still wished that an ideal language might be created in which words and things would be tied together in a perfectly rational way—thus paving the way for Bishop Wilkins and other modern constructors of philosophical languages.

Such abstract and *a priori* speculations, however stimulating and clever, hardly deserve the name of science, as this term is understood nowadays. Science presupposes careful observation and systematic classification of facts, and of that in the old Greek writers on language we find very little. The earliest masters in linguistic observation and classification were the old Indian grammarians. The language of the old sacred hymns had become in many points obsolete, but religion required that not one iota of these revered texts should be altered, and a scrupulous oral tradition kept them unchanged from generation to generation in every minute particular. This led to a wonderfully exact analysis of speech sounds, in which every detail of articulation was carefully described, and to a no less admirable analysis of grammatical forms, which were arranged systematically and described in a concise and highly ingenious, though artificial, terminology. The whole manner of treatment was entirely different from the methods of Western grammarians, and when the works of Panini and other Sanskrit grammarians were first made known to Europeans in the nineteenth century, they profoundly influenced our own linguistic science, as witnessed, among other things, by the fact that some of the Indian technical terms are still extensively used, for instance those describing various kinds of compound nouns.

In Europe grammatical science was slowly and laboriously developed in Greece and later in Rome. Aristotle laid the foundation of the division of words into " parts of speech " and introduced the notion of case (*ptôsis*). His work in this connexion was continued by the Stoics, many of whose grammatical distinctions and terms are still in use, the latter in their Latin dress, which embodies some curious mistakes, as when *geniké*, "the case of kind or species," was rendered *genitivus*, as if it meant "the case of origin," or, worse still, when *aitiatiké*, "the case of object," was rendered *accusativus*, as if from *aitiáomai*, 'I accuse.' In later times the philological school of Alexandria was particularly important, the object of research being the interpretation of the old poets, whose language was no longer instantly intelligible. Details of flexion and of the meaning of words were described and referred to the two categories of analogy or regularity and anomaly or irregularity. but real insight into the nature of language made very little progress either with the Alexandrians or with their Roman inheritors, and etymology still remained in the childlike stage.

I.—§ 2. Middle Ages and Renaissance.

Nor did linguistic science advance in the Middle Ages. The chief thing then was learning Latin as the common language of the Church and of what little there was of civilization generally ; but Latin was not studied in a scientific spirit, and the various vernacular languages, which one by one blossomed out into languages of literature, even less so.

The Renaissance in so far brought about a change in this, as it widened the horizon, especially by introducing the study of Greek. It also favoured grammatical studies through the stress it laid on correct Latin as represented in the best period of classical literature : it now became the ambition of humanists in all countries to write Latin like Cicero. In the following centuries we witness a constantly deepening interest in the various living languages of Europe, owing to the growing importance of native literatures and to increasing facilities of international traffic and communication in general. The most important factor here was, of course, the invention of printing, which rendered it incomparably more easy than formerly to obtain the means of studying foreign languages. It should be noted also that in those times the prevalent theological interest made it a much more common thing than nowadays for ordinary scholars to have some knowledge of Hebrew as the original language of the Old Testament. The acquaintance with a language so different in type from those spoken in Europe in many ways stimulated the interest in linguistic studies, though on the other hand it proved a fruitful source of error, because the position of the Semitic family of languages was not yet understood, and because Hebrew was thought to be the language spoken in Paradise, and therefore imagined to be the language from which all other languages were descended. All kinds of fanciful similarities between Hebrew and European languages were taken as proofs of the origin of the latter ; every imaginable permutation of sounds (or rather of letters) was looked upon as possible so long as there was a slight connexion in the sense of the two words compared, and however incredible it may seem nowadays, the fact that Hebrew was written from right to left, while we in our writing proceed from left to right, was considered justification enough for the most violent transposition of letters in etymological explanations. And yet all these flighty and whimsical comparisons served perhaps in some measure to pave the way for a more systematic treatment of etymology through collecting vast stores of words from which sober and critical minds might select those instances of indubitable connexion on which a sound science of etymology could eventually be constructed.

The discovery and publication of texts in the old Gothonic (Germanic) languages, especially Wulfila's Gothic translation of the Bible, compared with which Old English (Anglo-Saxon), Old German and Old Icelandic texts were of less, though by no means of despicable, account, paved the way for historical treatment of this important group of languages in the seventeenth and eighteenth centuries. But on the whole, the interest in the history of languages in those days was small, and linguistic thinkers thought it more urgent to establish vast treasuries of languages as actually spoken than to follow the development of any one language from century to century. Thus we see that the great philosopher Leibniz, who took much interest in linguistic pursuits and to whom we owe many judicious utterances on the possibility of a universal language, instigated Peter the Great to have vocabularies and specimens collected of all the various languages of his vast empire. To this initiative taken by Leibniz, and to the great personal interest that the Empress Catherine II took in these studies, we owe, directly or indirectly, the great repertories of all languages then known, first Pallas's *Linguarum totius orbis vocabularia comparativa* (1786–87), then Hervas's *Catálogo de las lenguas de las naziones conocidas* (1800–5), and finally Adelung's *Mithridates oder allgemeine Sprachenkunde* (1806–17). In spite of their inevitable shortcomings, their uncritical and unequal treatment of many languages, the preponderance of lexical over grammatical information, and the use of biblical texts as their sole connected illustrations, these great works exercised a mighty influence on the linguistic thought and research of the time, and contributed very much to the birth of the linguistic science of the nineteenth century. It should not be forgotten, moreover, that Hervas was one of the first to recognize the superior importance of grammar to vocabulary for deciding questions of relationship between languages.

It will be well here to consider the manner in which languages and the teaching of languages were generally viewed during the centuries preceding the rise of Comparative Linguistics. The chief language taught was Latin ; the first and in many cases the only grammar with which scholars came into contact was Latin grammar. No wonder therefore that grammar and Latin grammar came in the minds of most people to be synonyms. Latin grammar played an enormous rôle in the schools, to the exclusion of many subjects (the pupil's own native language, science, history, etc.)

which we are now beginning to think more essential for the education of the young. The traditional term for 'secondary school'
was in England 'grammar school' and in Denmark 'latinskole,'
and the reason for both expressions was obviously the same.
Here, however, we are concerned with this privileged position of
Latin grammar only in so far as it influenced the treatment of
languages in general. It did so in more ways than one.

Latin was a language with a wealth of flexional forms, and
in describing other languages the same categories as were found
in Latin were applied as a matter of course, even where there was
nothing in these other languages which really corresponded to what
was found in Latin. In English and Danish grammars paradigms
of noun declension were given with such cases as accusative, dative
and ablative, in spite of the fact that no separate forms for these
cases had existed for centuries. All languages were indiscriminately
saddled with the elaborate Latin system of tenses and moods in
the verbs, and by means of such Procrustean methods the actual
facts of many languages were distorted and misrepresented.
Discriminations which had no foundation in reality were nevertheless insisted on, while discriminations which happened to be
non-existent in Latin were apt to be overlooked. The mischief
consequent on this unfortunate method of measuring all grammar
after the pattern of Latin grammar has not even yet completely
disappeared, and it is even now difficult to find a single grammar
of any language that is not here and there influenced by the
Latin bias.

Latin was chiefly taught as a written language (witness the
totally different manner in which Latin was pronounced in
the different countries, the consequence being that as early as the
sixteenth century French and English scholars were unable to
understand each other's spoken Latin). This led to the almost
exclusive occupation with letters instead of sounds. The fact
that all language is primarily spoken and only secondarily written
down, that the real life of language is in the mouth and ear and
not in the pen and eye, was overlooked, to the detriment of a real
understanding of the essence of language and linguistic development; and very often where the spoken form of a language was
accessible scholars contented themselves with a reading knowledge.
In spite of many efforts, some of which go back to the sixteenth
century, but which did not become really powerful till the rise
of modern phonetics in the nineteenth century, the fundamental
significance of spoken as opposed to written language has not
yet been fully appreciated by all linguists. There are still too
many writers on philological questions who have evidently never
tried to think in sounds instead of thinking in letters and symbols,

and who would probably be sorely puzzled if they were to pronounce all the forms that come so glibly to their pens. What Sweet wrote in 1877 in the preface to his *Handbook of Phonetics* is perhaps less true now than it was then, but it still contains some elements of truth. "Many instances," he said, "might be quoted of the way in which important philological facts and laws have been passed over or misrepresented through the observer's want of phonetic training. Schleicher's failing to observe the Lithuanian accents, or even to comprehend them when pointed out by Kurschat, is a striking instance." But there can be no doubt that the way in which Latin has been for centuries made the basis of all linguistic instruction is largely responsible for the preponderance of eye-philology to ear-philology in the history of our science.

We next come to a point which to my mind is very important, because it concerns something which has had, and has justly had, enduring effects on the manner in which language, and especially grammar, is viewed and taught to this day. What was the object of teaching Latin in the Middle Ages and later ? Certainly not the purely scientific one of imparting knowledge for knowledge's own sake, apart from any practical use or advantage, simply in order to widen the spiritual horizon and to obtain the joy of pure intellectual understanding. For such a purpose some people with scientific leanings may here and there take up the study of some out-of-the-way African or American idiom. But the reasons for teaching and learning Latin were not so idealistic. Latin was not even taught and learnt solely with the purpose of opening the doors to the old classical or to the more recent religious literature in that language, but chiefly, and in the first instance, because Latin was a practical and highly important means of communication between educated people. One had to learn not only to read Latin, but also to write Latin, if one wanted to maintain no matter how humble a position in the republic of learning or in the hierarchy of the Church. Consequently, grammar was not (even primarily) the science of how words were inflected and how forms were used by the old Romans, but chiefly and essentially the art of inflecting words and of using the forms yourself, if you wanted to write correct Latin. This you must say, and these faults you must avoid—such were the lessons imparted in the schools. Grammar was not a set of facts observed but of rules to be observed, and of paradigms, i.e. of patterns, to be followed. Sometimes this character of grammatical instruction is expressly indicated in the form of the precepts given, as in such memorial verses as this: "Tolle *-me, -mi, -mu, -mis,* Si declinare *domus* vis ! " In other words, grammar was *prescriptive* rather than *descriptive*.

The current definition of grammar, therefore, was "ars bene dicendi et bene scribendi," "l'art de bien dire et de bien écrire," the art of speaking and writing correctly. J. C. Scaliger said, "Grammatici unus finis est recte loqui." To attain to correct diction ('good grammar') and to avoid faulty diction ('bad grammar'), such were the two objects of grammatical teaching. Now, the same point of view, in which the two elements of 'art' and of 'correctness' entered so largely, was applied not only to Latin, but to other languages as well, when the various vernaculars came to be treated grammatically.

The vocabulary, too, was treated from the same point of view. This is especially evident in the case of the dictionaries issued by the French and Italian Academies. They differ from dictionaries as now usually compiled in being not collections of all and any words their authors could get hold of within the limits of the language concerned, but in being selections of words deserving the recommendations of the best arbiters of taste and therefore fit to be used in the highest literature by even the most elegant or fastidious writers. Dictionaries thus understood were less descriptions of actual usage than prescriptions for the best usage of words.

The normative way of viewing language is fraught with some great dangers which can only be avoided through a comprehensive knowledge of the historic development of languages and of the general conditions of linguistic psychology. Otherwise, the tendency everywhere is to draw too narrow limits for what is allowable or correct. In many cases one form, or one construction, only is recognized, even where two or more are found in actual speech ; the question which is to be selected as the only good form comes to be decided too often by individual fancy or predilection, where no scientific tests can yet be applied, and thus a form may often be proscribed which from a less narrow point of view might have appeared just as good as, or even better than, the one preferred in the official grammar or dictionary. In other instances, where two forms were recognized, the grammarian wanted to give rules for their discrimination, and sometimes on the basis of a totally inadequate induction he would establish nice distinctions not really warranted by actual usage—distinctions which subsequent generations had to learn at school with the sweat of their brows and which were often considered most important in spite of their intrinsic insignificance. Such unreal or half-real subtle distinctions are the besetting sin of French grammarians from the 'grand siècle' onwards, while they have played a much less considerable part in England, where people have been on the whole more inclined to let things slide as best they may on the 'laissez faire' principle, and where no Academy was ever established to regulate language. But even in English rules are not unfrequently given in schools and in newspaper offices which are based on narrow views and hasty generalizations. Because a preposition at the end of a sentence may in some instances be clumsy or unwieldy, this is no reason why a final preposition should always and under all circumstances be considered a grave error. But it is of course easier for the schoolmaster to give an absolute and inviolable rule once and for all than to study carefully all the various considerations that might render a qualification desirable. If the ordinary books on *Common Faults in Writing and Speaking English* and similar works in other languages have not even now assimilated the teachings of Comparative and Historic Linguistics, it is no wonder that the grammarians of the seventeenth and eighteenth centuries, with whom we are here concerned, should be in many ways guided by narrow and insufficient views on what ought to determine correctness of speech.

Here also the importance given to the study of Latin was sometimes harmful ; too much was settled by a reference to Latin rules, even where the modern languages really followed rules of their own that were opposed to those of Latin. The learning of Latin grammar was supposed to be, and to some extent really was, a schooling in logic, as the strict observance of the rules of any foreign language is bound to be ; but the consequence of this was that when questions of grammatical correctness were to be settled, too much importance was often given to purely logical considerations, and scholars were sometimes apt to determine what was to be called ' logical ' in language according to whether it was or was not in conformity with Latin usage. This disposition, joined with the unavoidable conservatism of mankind, and more particularly of teachers, would in many ways prove a hindrance to natural developments in a living speech. But we must again take up the thread of the history of linguistic theory.

I.—§ 3. Eighteenth-century Speculation. Herder.

The problem of a natural origin of language exercised some of the best-known thinkers of the eighteenth century. Rousseau imagined the first men setting themselves more or less deliberately to frame a language by an agreement similar to (or forming part of) the *contrat social* which according to him was the basis of all social order. There is here the obvious difficulty of imagining how primitive men who had been previously without any speech came to feel the want of language, and how they could agree on what sound was to represent what idea without having already some means of communication. Rousseau's whole manner of putting and of viewing the problem is evidently too crude to be of any real importance in the history of linguistic science.

Condillac is much more sensible when he tries to imagine how a speechless man and a speechless woman might be led quite naturally to acquire something like language, starting with instinctive cries and violent gestures called forth by strong emotions. Such cries would come to be associated with elementary feelings, and new sounds might come to indicate various objects if produced repeatedly in connexion with gestures showing what objects the speaker wanted to call attention to. If these two first speaking beings had as yet very little power to vary their sounds, their child would have a more flexible tongue, and would therefore be able to, and be impelled to, produce some new sounds, the meaning of which his parents would guess at, and which they in their turn would imitate ; thus gradually a greater and greater number of words would come into existence, generation after generation working painfully to enrich and develop what had been already acquired, until it finally became a real language.

The profoundest thinker on these problems in the eighteenth century was Johann Gottfried Herder, who, though he did little or nothing in the way of scientific research, yet prepared the rise of linguistic science. In his prize essay on the *Origin of Language* (1772) Herder first vigorously and successfully attacks the orthodox view of his age—a view which had been recently upheld very emphatically by one Süssmilch—that language could not have been invented by man, but was a direct gift from God. One of Herder's strongest arguments is that if language had been framed by God and by Him instilled into the mind of man, we should expect it to be much more logical, much more imbued with pure reason than it is as an actual matter of fact. Much in all existing languages is so chaotic and ill-arranged that it could not be God's work, but must come from the hand of man. On the other hand, Herder does not think that language was really 'invented' by man—although this was the word used by the Berlin Academy when opening the competition in which Herder's essay gained the prize. Language was not deliberately framed by man, but sprang of necessity from his innermost nature ; the genesis of language according to him is due to an impulse similar to that of the mature embryo pressing to be born. Man, in the same way as all animals, gives vent to his feelings in tones, but this is not enough ; it is impossible to trace the origin of human language to these emotional cries alone. However much they may be refined and fixed, without understanding they can never become human, conscious language. Man differs from brute animals not in degree or in the addition of new powers, but in a totally different direction and development of all powers. Man's inferiority to animals in strength and sureness of instinct is compensated by his wider sphere of attention ; the whole disposition of his mind as an unanalysable entity constitutes the impassable barrier between him and the lower animals. Man, then, shows conscious reflexion when among the ocean of sensations that rush into his soul through all the senses he singles out one wave and arrests it, as when, seeing a lamb, he looks for a distinguishing mark and finds it in the bleating, so that next time when he recognizes the same animal he imitates the sound of bleating, and thereby creates a name for that animal. Thus the lamb to him is ' the bleater,' and nouns are created from verbs, whereas, according to Herder, if language had been the creation of God it would inversely have begun with nouns, as that would have been the logically ideal order of procedure. Another characteristic trait of primitive languages is the crossing of various shades of feeling and the necessity of expressing thoughts through strong, bold metaphors, presenting the most motley picture. " The genetic cause lies in the poverty of the human mind and in the flowing together of the emotions of a primitive human being." Another consequence is the wealth of synonyms in primitive language ; " alongside of real poverty it has the most unnecessary superfluity."

When Herder here speaks of primitive or ' original ' languages, he is thinking of Oriental languages, and especially of Hebrew. " We should never forget," says Edward Sapir,[1] " that Herder's time-perspective was necessarily very different from ours. While we unconcernedly take tens or even hundreds of thousands of years in which to allow the products of human civilization to develop, Herder was still compelled to operate with the less than six thousand years that orthodoxy stingily doled out. To us the two or three thousand years that separate our language from the Old Testament Hebrew seems a negligible quantity, when speculating on the origin of language in general ; to Herder, however, the Hebrew and the Greek of Homer seemed to be appreciably nearer the oldest conditions than our vernaculars—hence his exaggeration of their *ursprünglichkeit*."

Herder's chief influence on the science of speech, to my mind, is not derived directly from the ideas contained in his essay on the actual origin of speech, but rather indirectly through the whole of his life's work. He had a very strong sense of the value of everything that had grown naturally (das naturwüchsige) ; he prepared the minds of his countrymen for the manysided recep-

[1] See his essay on Herder's " Ursprung der sprache " in *Modern Philology*, 5. 117 (1907).

tiveness of the Romanticists, who translated and admired the popular poetry of a great many countries, which had hitherto been *terræ incognitæ* ; and he was one of the first to draw attention to the great national value of his own country's medieval literature and its folklore, and thus was one of the spiritual ancestors of Grimm. He sees the close connexion that exists between language and primitive poetry, or that kind of spontaneous singing that characterizes the childhood or youth of mankind, and which is totally distinct from the artificial poetry of later ages. But to him each language is not only the instrument of literature, but itself literature and poetry. A nation speaks its soul in the words it uses. Herder admires his own mother-tongue, which to him is perhaps inferior to Greek, but superior to its neighbours. The combinations of consonants give it a certain measured pace ; it does not rush forward, but walks with the firm carriage of a German. The nice gradation of vowels mitigates the force of the consonants, and the numerous spirants make the German speech pleasant and endearing. Its syllables are rich and firm, its phrases are stately, and its idiomatic expressions are emphatic and serious. Still in some ways the present German language is degenerate if compared with that of Luther, and still more with that of the Suabian Emperors, and much therefore remains to be done in the way of disinterring and revivifying the powerful expressions now lost. Through ideas like these Herder not only exercised a strong influence on Goethe and the Romanticists, but also gave impulses to the linguistic studies of the following generation, and caused many younger men to turn from the well-worn classics to fields of research previously neglected.

I.—§ 4. Jenisch.

Where questions of correct language or of the best usage are dealt with, or where different languages are compared with regard to their efficiency or beauty, as is done very often, though more often in dilettante conversation or in casual remarks in literary works than in scientific linguistic disquisitions, it is no far cry to the question, What would an ideal language be like ? But such is the matter-of-factness of modern scientific thought, that probably no scientific Academy in our own days would think of doing what the Berlin Academy did in 1794 when it offered a prize for the best essay on the ideal of a perfect language and a comparison of the best-known languages of Europe as tested by the standard of such an ideal. A Berlin pastor, D. Jenisch, won the prize, and in 1796 brought out his book under the title *Philosophisch-kritische vergleichung und würdigung von vierzehn ältern und neuern sprachen*

Europens—a book which is even now well worth reading, the more so because its subject has been all but completely neglected in the hundred and twenty years that have since intervened. In the Introduction the author has the following passage, which might be taken as the motto of Wilhelm v. Humboldt, Steinthal, Finck and Byrne, who do not, however, seem to have been inspired by Jenisch: "In language the whole intellectual and moral essence of a man is to some extent revealed. 'Speak, and you are' is rightly said by the Oriental. The language of the natural man is savage and rude, that of the cultured man is elegant and polished. As the Greek was subtle in thought and sensuously refined in feeling—as the Roman was serious and practical rather than speculative—as the Frenchman is popular and sociable—as the Briton is profound and the German philosophic—so are also the languages of each of these nations."

Jenisch then goes on to say that language as the organ for communicating our ideas and feelings accomplishes its end if it represents idea and feeling according to the actual want or need of the mind at the given moment. We have to examine in each case the following essential qualities of the languages compared, (1) richness, (2) energy or emphasis, (3) clearness, and (4) euphony. Under the head of richness we are concerned not only with the number of words, first for material objects, then for spiritual and abstract notions, but also with the ease with which new words can be formed (lexikalische bildsamkeit). The energy of a language is shown in its lexicon and in its grammar (simplicity of grammatical structure, absence of articles, etc.), but also in "the characteristic energy of the nation and its original writers." Clearness and definiteness in the same way are shown in vocabulary and grammar, especially in a regular and natural syntax. Euphony, finally, depends not only on the selection of consonants and vowels utilized in the language, but on their harmonious combination, the general impression of the language being more important than any details capable of being analysed.

These, then, are the criteria by which Greek and Latin and a number of living languages are compared and judged. The author displays great learning and a sound practical knowledge of many languages, and his remarks on the advantages and shortcomings of these are on the whole judicious, though often perhaps too much stress is laid on the literary merits of great writers, which have really no intrinsic connexion with the value of a language as such. It depends to a great extent on accidental circumstances whether a language has been or has not been used in elevated literature, and its merits should be estimated, so far as this is possible, independently of the perfection of its literature. Jenisch's prejudice in that respect is shown, for instance, when he says (p. 36) that the endeavours of Hickes are entirely futile, when he tries to make out regular declensions and conjugations in the barbarous language of Wulfila's translation of the Bible. But otherwise Jenisch is singularly free from prejudices, as shown by a great number of passages in which other languages are praised at the expense of his own. Thus, on p. 396, he declares German to be the most repellent contrast to that most supple modern language, French, on account of its unnatural word-order, its eternally trailing article, its want of participial constructions, and its interminable auxiliaries (as in ' ich werde geliebt werden, ich würde geliebt worden sein,' etc.), with the frequent separation of these auxiliaries from the main verb through extraneous intermediate words, all of which gives to German something incredibly awkward, which to the reader appears as lengthy and diffuse and to the writer as inconvenient and intractable. It is not often that we find an author appraising his own language with such severe impartiality, and I have given the passage also to show what kind of problems confront the man who wishes to compare the relative value of languages as wholes. Jenisch's view here forms a striking contrast to Herder's appreciation of their common mother-tongue.

Jenisch's book does not seem to have been widely read by nineteenth-century scholars, who took up totally different problems. Those few who read it were perhaps inclined to say with S. Lefmann (see his book on Franz Bopp, Nachtrag, 1897, p. xi) that it is difficult to decide which was the greater fool, the one who put this problem or the one who tried to answer it. This attitude, however, towards problems of valuation in the matter of languages is neither just nor wise, though it is perhaps easy to see how students of comparative grammar were by the very nature of their study led to look down upon those who compared languages from the point of view of æsthetic or literary merits. Anyhow, it seems to me no small merit to have been the first to treat such problems as these, which are generally answered in an off-hand way according to a loose general judgement, so as to put them on a scientific footing by examining in detail what it is that makes us more or less instinctively prefer one language, or one turn or expression in a language, and thus lay the foundation of that inductive æsthetic theory of language which has still to be developed in a truly scientific spirit.

CHAPTER II

BEGINNING OF NINETEENTH CENTURY

§ 1. Introduction. Sanskrit. § 2. Friedrich von Schlegel. § 3. Rasmus Rask. § 4. Jacob Grimm. § 5. The Sound Shift. § 6. Franz Bopp. § 7. Bopp continued. § 8. Wilhelm von Humboldt. § 9. Grimm once more.

II.—§ 1. Introduction. Sanskrit.

THE nineteenth century witnessed an enormous growth and development of the science of language, which in some respects came to present features totally unknown to previous centuries. The horizon was widened ; more and more languages were described, studied and examined, many of them for their own sake, as they had no important literature. Everywhere a deeper insight was gained into the structures even of such languages as had been for centuries objects of study ; a more comprehensive and more incisive classification of languages was obtained with a deeper understanding of their mutual relationships, and at the same time linguistic forms were not only described and analysed, but also explained, their genesis being traced as far back as historical evidence allowed, if not sometimes further. Instead of contenting itself with stating when and where a form existed and how it looked and was employed, linguistic science now also began to ask why it had taken that definite shape, and thus passed from a purely descriptive to an explanatory science.

The chief innovation of the beginning of the nineteenth century was the historical point of view. On the whole, it must be said that it was reserved for that century to apply the notion of history to other things than wars and the vicissitudes of dynasties, and thus to discover the idea of development or evolution as pervading the whole universe. This brought about a vast change in the science of language, as in other sciences. Instead of looking at such a language as Latin as one fixed point, and instead of aiming at fixing another language, such as French, in one classical form, the new science viewed both as being in constant flux, as growing, as moving, as continually changing. It cried aloud like Heraclitus

"Pánta reî," and like Galileo "Eppur si muove." And lo ! the
better this historical point of view was applied, the more secrets
languages seemed to unveil, and the more light seemed also to be
thrown on objects outside the proper sphere of language, such as
ethnology and the early history of mankind at large and of
particular countries.

It is often said that it was the discovery of Sanskrit that was
the real turning-point in the history of linguistics, and there is
some truth in this assertion, though we shall see on the one hand
that Sanskrit was not in itself enough to give to those who studied
it the true insight into the essence of language and linguistic science,
and on the other hand that real genius enabled at least one man
to grasp essential truths about the relationships and development
of languages even without a knowledge of Sanskrit. Still, it must
be said that the first acquaintance with this language gave a mighty
impulse to linguistic studies and exerted a lasting influence on
the way in which most European languages were viewed by scholars,
and it will therefore be necessary here briefly to sketch the history
of these studies. India was very little known in Europe till the
mighty struggle between the French and the English for the mastery
of its wealth excited a wide interest also in its ancient culture.
It was but natural that on this intellectual domain, too, the French
and the English should at first be rivals and that we should find
both nations represented in the pioneers of Sanskrit scholarship.
The French Jesuit missionary Cœurdoux as early as 1767 sent to
the French Institut a memoir in which he called attention to the
similarity of many Sanskrit words with Latin, and even compared
the flexion of the present indicative and subjunctive of Sanskrit
asmi, ' I am,' with the corresponding forms of Latin grammar.
Unfortunately, however, his work was not printed till forty years
later, when the same discovery had been announced independently
by others. The next scholar to be mentioned in this connexion
is Sir William Jones, who in 1786 uttered the following memorable
words, which have often been quoted in books on the history of
linguistics : " The Sanscrit language, whatever be its antiquity,
is of a wonderful structure ; more perfect than the Greek, more
copious than the Latin and more exquisitely refined than either ;
yet bearing to both of them a stronger affinity, both in the roots
of verbs and in the forms of grammar, than could possibly have
been produced by accident ; so strong, indeed, that no philologer
could examine them all three without believing them to have
sprung from some common source, which, perhaps, no longer
exists. There is a similar reason, though not quite so forcible, for
supposing that both the Gothic and the Celtic . . . had the same
origin with the Sanscrit ; and the old Persian might be added to

the same family." Sir W. Jones, however, did nothing to carry out in detail the comparison thus inaugurated, and it was reserved for younger men to follow up the clue he had given.

II.—§ 2. Friedrich von Schlegel.

One of the books that exercised a great influence on the development of linguistic science in the beginning of the nineteenth century was Friedrich von Schlegel's *Ueber die sprache und weisheit der Indier* (1808). Schlegel had studied Sanskrit for some years in Paris, and in his romantic enthusiasm he hoped that the study of the old Indian books would bring about a revolution in European thought similar to that produced in the Renaissance through the revival of the study of Greek. We are here concerned exclusively with his linguistic theories, but to his mind they were inseparable from Indian religion and philosophy, or rather religious and philosophic poetry. He is struck by the similarity between Sanskrit and the best-known European languages, and gives quite a number of words from Sanskrit found with scarcely any change in German, Greek and Latin. He repudiates the idea that these similarities might be accidental or due to borrowings on the side of the Indians, saying expressly that the proof of original relationship between these languages, as well as of the greater age of Sanskrit, lies in the far-reaching correspondences in the whole grammatical structure of these as opposed to many other languages. In this connexion it is noticeable that he is the first to speak of 'comparative grammar' (p. 28), but, like Moses, he only looks into this promised land without entering it. Indeed, his method of comparison precludes him from being the founder of the new science, for he says himself (p. 6) that he will refrain from stating any rules for change or substitution of letters (sounds), and require complete identity of the words used as proofs of the descent of languages. He adds that in other cases, "where intermediate stages are historically demonstrable, we may derive *giorno* from *dies*, and when Spanish so often has *h* for Latin *f*, or Latin *p* very often becomes *f* in the German form of the same word, and *c* not rarely becomes *h* [by the way, an interesting foreshadowing of one part of the discovery of the Germanic sound-shifting], then this may be the foundation of analogical conclusions with regard to other less evident instances." If he had followed up this idea by establishing similar 'sound-laws,' as we now say, between Sanskrit and other languages, he would have been many years ahead of his time; as it is, his comparisons are those of a dilettante, and he sometimes falls into the pitfalls of accidental similarities while overlooking the real correspondences. He is also led astray by the idea of a particularly close relationship between Persian and German, an idea which at that time was widely spread [1]—we find it in Jenisch and even in Bopp's first book.

Schlegel is not afraid of surveying the whole world of human languages ; he divides them into two classes, one comprising Sanskrit and its congeners, and the second all other languages. In the former he finds organic growth of the roots as shown by their capability of inner change or, as he terms it, ' flexion,' while in the latter class everything is effected by the addition of affixes (prefixes and suffixes). In Greek he admits that it would be possible to believe in the possibility of the grammatical endings (bildungssylben) having arisen from particles and auxiliary words amalgamated into the word itself, but in Sanskrit even the last semblance of this possibility disappears, and it becomes necessary to confess that the structure of the language is formed in a thoroughly organic way through flexion, i.e. inner changes and modifications of the radical sound, and not composed merely mechanically by the addition of words and particles. He admits, however, that affixes in some other languages have brought about something that resembles real flexion. On the whole he finds that the movement of grammatical art and perfection (der gang der bloss grammatischen kunst und ausbildung, p. 56) goes in opposite directions in the two species of languages. In the organic languages, which represent the highest state, the beauty and art of their structure is apt to be lost through indolence ; and German as well as Romanic and modern Indian languages show this degeneracy when compared with the earlier forms of the same languages. In the affix languages, on the other hand, we see that the beginnings are completely artless, but the ' art ' in them grows more and more perfect the more the affixes are fused with the main word.

As to the question of the ultimate origin of language, Schlegel thinks that the diversity of linguistic structure points to different beginnings. While some languages, such as Manchu, are so interwoven with onomatopœia that imitation of natural sounds must have played the greatest rôle in their formation, this is by no means the case in other languages, and the perfection of the oldest organic or flexional languages, such as Sanskrit, shows that they cannot be derived from merely animal sounds ; indeed, they form an additional proof, if any such were needed, that men did not everywhere start from a brutish state, but that the clearest and intensest reason existed from the very first beginning. On all these points Schlegel's ideas foreshadow views that are found in later works ; and it is probable that his fame as a writer outside the philological field gave to his linguistic speculations a notoriety which his often

[1] It dates back to Vulcanius, 1597 ; see Streitberg, IF 35. 182.

loose and superficial reasonings would not otherwise have acquired for them.

Schlegel's bipartition of the languages of the world carries in it the germ of a tripartition. On the .lowest stage of his second class he places Chinese, in which, as he acknowledges, the particles denoting secondary sense modifications consist in monosyllables that are completely independent of the actual word. It is clear that from Schlegel's own point of view we cannot here properly speak of ' affixes,' and thus Chinese really, though Schlegel himself does not say so, falls outside his affix languages and forms a class by itself. On the other hand, his arguments for reckoning Semitic languages among affix languages are very weak, and he seems also somewhat inclined to say that much in their structure resembles real flexion. If we introduce these two changes into his system, we arrive at the threefold division found in slightly different shapes in most subsequent works on general linguistics, the first to give it being perhaps Schlegel's brother, A. W. Schlegel, who speaks of (1) les langues sans aucune structure grammaticale— under which misleading term he understands Chinese with its unchangeable monosyllabic words ; (2) les langues qui emploient des affixes ; (3) les langues à inflexions.

Like his brother, A. W. Schlegel places the flexional languages highest and thinks them alone ' organic.' On the other hand, he subdivides flexional languages into two classes, synthetic and analytic, the latter using personal pronouns and auxiliaries in the conjugation of verbs, prepositions to supply the want of cases, and adverbs to express the degrees of comparison. While the origin of the synthetic languages loses itself in the darkness of ages, the analytic languages have been created in modern times ; all those that we know are due to the decomposition of synthetic languages. These remarks on the division of languages are found in the Introduction to the book *Observations sur la langue et la littérature provençale* (1818) and are thus primarily meant to account for the contrast between synthetic Latin and analytic Romanic.

II.—§ 3. Rasmus Rask.

We now come to the three greatest names among the initiators of linguistic science in the beginning of the nineteenth century. If we give them in their alphabetical order, Bopp, Grimm and Rask, we also give them in the order of merit in which most subsequent historians have placed them. The works that constitute their first claims to the title of founder of the new science came in close succession, Bopp's *Conjugationssystem* in 1816, Rask's *Undersøgelse* in 1818, and the first volume of Grimm's *Grammatik* in

1819. While Bopp is entirely independent of the two others, we shall see that Grimm was deeply influenced by Rask, and as the latter's contributions to our science began some years before his chief work just mentioned (which had also been finished in manuscript in 1814, thus two years before Bopp's *Conjugationssystem*), the best order in which to deal with the three men will perhaps be to take Rask first, then to mention Grimm, who in some ways was his pupil, and finally to treat of Bopp : in this way we shall also be enabled to see Bopp in close relation with the subsequent development of Comparative Grammar, on which he, and not Rask, exerted the strongest influence.

Born in a peasant's hut in the heart of Denmark in 1787, Rasmus Rask was a grammarian from his boyhood. When a copy of the *Heimskringla* was given him as a school prize, he at once, without any grammar or dictionary, set about establishing paradigms, and so, before he left school, acquired proficiency in Icelandic, as well as in many other languages. At the University of Copenhagen he continued in the same course, constantly widened his linguistic horizon and penetrated into the grammatical structure of the most diverse languages. Icelandic (Old Norse), however, remained his favourite study, and it filled him with enthusiasm and national pride that " our ancestors had such an excellent language," the excellency being measured chiefly by the full flexional system which Icelandic shared with the classical tongues, partly also by the pure, unmixed state of the Icelandic vocabulary. His first book (1811) was an Icelandic grammar, an admirable production when we consider the meagre work done previously in this field. With great lucidity he reduces the intricate forms of the language into a consistent system, and his penetrating insight into the essence of language is seen when he explains the vowel changes, which we now comprise under the name of mutation or umlaut, as due to the approximation of the vowel of the stem to that of the ending, at that time a totally new point of view. This we gather from Grimm's review, in which Rask's explanation is said to be " more astute than true " (" mehr scharfsinnig als wahr," *Kleinere schriften*, 7. 518). Rask even sees the reason of the change in the plural *blöð* as against the singular *blað* in the former having once ended in -*u*, which has since disappeared. This is, so far as I know, the first inference ever drawn to a prehistoric state of language.

In 1814, during a prolonged stay in Iceland, Rask sent down to Copenhagen his most important work, the prize essay on the origin of the Old Norse language (*Undersøgelse om det gamle nordiske eller islandske sprogs oprindelse*) which for various reasons was not printed till 1818. If it had been published when it was finished, and especially if it had been printed in a language

better known than Danish, Rask might well have been styled the
founder of the modern science of language, for his work contains
the best exposition of the true method of linguistic research
written in the first half of the nineteenth century and applies
this method to the solution of a long series of important questions.
Only one part of it was ever translated into another language,
and this was unfortunately buried in an appendix to Vater's
Vergleichungstafeln, 1822. Yet Rask's work even now repays
careful perusal, and I shall therefore give a brief résumé of its
principal contents.

Language according to Rask is our principal means of finding
out anything about the history of nations before the existence of
written documents, for though everything may change in religion,
customs, laws and institutions, language generally remains, if not
unchanged, yet recognizable even after thousands of years. But
in order to find out anything about the relationship of a language
we must proceed methodically and examine its whole structure
instead of comparing mere details ; what is here of prime importance
is the grammatical system, because words are very often taken
over from one language to another, but very rarely grammatical
forms. The capital error in most of what has been written on
this subject is that this important point has been overlooked.
That language which has the most complicated grammar is nearest
to the source ; however mixed a language may be, it belongs to
the same family as another if it has the most essential, most
material and indispensable words in common with it ; pronouns
and numerals are in this respect most decisive. If in such words
there are so many points of agreement between two languages that
it is possible to frame rules for the transitions of letters (in other
passages Rask more correctly says sounds) from the one language
to the other, there is a fundamental kinship between the two
languages, more particularly if there are corresponding similarities
in their structure and constitution. This is a most important
thesis, and Rask supplements it by saying that transitions of
sounds are naturally dependent on their organ and manner of
production.

Next Rask proceeds to apply these principles to his task of
finding out the origin of the Old Icelandic language. He describes
its position in the ' Gothic ' (Gothonic, Germanic) group and
then looks round to find congeners elsewhere. He rapidly discards
Greenlandic and Basque as being too remote in grammar and
vocabulary ; with regard to Keltic languages he hesitates, but
finally decides in favour of denying relationship. (He was soon
to see his error in this ; see below.) Next he deals at some length
with Finnic and Lapp, and comes to the conclusion that the simi-

larities are due to loans rather than to original kinship. But when he comes to the Slavonic languages his utterances have a different ring, for he is here able to disclose so many similarities in fundamentals that he ranges these languages within the same great family as Icelandic. The same is true with regard to Lithuanian and Lettic, which are here for the first time correctly placed as an independent sub-family, though closely akin to Slavonic. The comparisons with Latin, and especially with Greek, are even more detailed ; and Rask in these chapters really presents us with a succinct, but on the whole marvellously correct, comparative grammar of Gothonic, Slavonic, Lithuanian, Latin and Greek, besides examining numerous lexical correspondences. He does not yet know any of the related Asiatic languages, but throws out the hint that Persian and Indian may be the remote source of Icelandic through Greek. Greek he considers to be the ' source ' or ' root ' of the Gothonic languages, though he expresses himself with a degree of uncertainty which forestalls the correct notion that these languages have all of them sprung from the same extinct and unknown language. This view is very clearly expressed in a letter he wrote from St. Petersburg in the same year in which his *Undersøgelse* was published ; he here says : " I divide our family of languages in this way : the Indian (Dekanic, Hindostanic), Iranic (Persian, Armenian, Ossetic), Thracian (Greek and Latin), Sarmatian (Lettic and Slavonic), Gothic (Germanic and Skandinavian) and Keltic (Britannic and Gaellic) tribes " (SA 2. 281, dated June 11, 1818).

This is the fullest and clearest account of the relationships of our family of languages found for many years, and Rask showed true genius in the way in which he saw what languages belonged together and how they were related. About the same time he gave a classification of the Finno-Ugrian family of languages which is pronounced by such living authorities on these languages as Vilhelm Thomsen and Emil Setälä to be superior to most later attempts. When travelling in India he recognized the true position of Zend, about which previous scholars had held the most erroneous views, and his survey of the languages of India and Persia was thought valuable enough in 1863 to be printed from his manuscript, forty years after it was written. He was also the first to see that the Dravidian (by him called Malabaric) languages were totally different from Sanskrit. In his short essay on Zend (1826) he also incidentally gave the correct value of two letters in the first cuneiform writing, and thus made an important contribution towards the final deciphering of these inscriptions.

His long tour (1816–23) through Sweden, Finland, Russia, the Caucasus, Persia and India was spent in the most intense study of a great variety of languages, but unfortunately brought on the illness and disappointments which, together with economic anxieties, marred the rest of his short life.

When Rask died in 1832 he had written a great number of grammars of single languages, all of them remarkable for their accuracy in details and clear systematic treatment, more particularly of morphology, and some of them breaking new ground ; besides his Icelandic grammar already mentioned, his Anglo-Saxon, Frisian and Lapp grammars should be specially named. Historical grammar in the strict sense is perhaps not his forte, though in a remarkable essay of the year 1815 he explains historically a great many features of Danish grammar, and in his Spanish and Italian grammars he in some respects forestalls Diez's historical explanations. But in some points he stuck to erroneous views, a notable instance being his system of old Gothonic 'long vowels,' which was reared on the assumption that modern Icelandic pronunciation reflects the pronunciation of primitive times, while it is really a recent development, as Grimm saw from a comparison of all the old languages. With regard to consonants, however, Rask was the clearer-sighted of the two, and throughout he had this immense advantage over most of the comparative linguists of his age, that he had studied a great many languages at first hand with native speakers, while the others knew languages chiefly or exclusively through the medium of books and manuscripts. In no work of that period, or even of a much later time, are found so many first-hand observations of living speech as in Rask's *Retskrivningslære.* Handicapped though he was in many ways, by poverty and illness and by the fact that he wrote in a language so little known as Danish, Rasmus Rask, through his wide outlook, his critical sagacity and aversion to all fanciful theorizing, stands out as one of the foremost leaders of linguistic science.[1]

II.—§ 4. Jacob Grimm.

Jacob Grimm's career was totally different from Rask's. Born in 1785 as the son of a lawyer, he himself studied law and came under the influence of Savigny, whose view of legal institutions as the outcome of gradual development in intimate connexion with popular tradition and the whole intellectual and moral life of the

---

[1] I have given a life of Rask and an appraisement of his work in the small volume *Rasmus Rask* (Copenhagen, Gyldendal, 1918). See also Vilh. Thomsen, *Samlede afhandlinger*, 1. 47 ff. and 125 ff. A good and full account of Rask's work is found in Raumer, *Gesch.* ; cf. also Paul, *Gr.* Recent short appreciations of his genius may be read in Trombetti, *Come si fa la critica*, 1907, p. 41, Meillet, LI, p. 415, Hirt, Idg. pp. 74 and 578.

people appealed strongly to the young man's imagination. But
he was drawn even more to that study of old German popular
poetry which then began to be the fashion, thanks to Tieck and
other Romanticists ; and when he was in Paris to assist Savigny
with his historico-legal research, the old German manuscripts in
the Bibliothèque nationale nourished his enthusiasm for the
poetical treasures of the Middle Ages. He became a librarian
and brought out his first book, *Ueber den altdeutschen meistergesang*
(1811). At the same time, with his brother Wilhelm as constant
companion and fellow-worker, he began collecting popular traditions, of which he published a first instalment in his famous *Kinder-
und hausmärchen* (1812 ff.), a work whose learned notes and comparisons may be said to have laid the foundation of the science of
folklore. Language at first had only a subordinate interest to
him, and when he tried his hand at etymology, he indulged in the
wildest guesses, according to the method (or want of method) of
previous centuries. A. W. Schlegel's criticism of his early attempts
in this field, and still more Rask's example, opened Grimm's eyes
to the necessity of a stricter method, and he soon threw himself
with great energy into a painstaking and exact study of the oldest
stages of the German language and its congeners. In his review
(1812) of Rask's Icelandic grammar he writes : " Each individuality,
even in the world of languages, should be respected as sacred ;
it is desirable that even the smallest and most despised dialect
should be left only to itself and to its own nature and in nowise
subjected to violence, because it is sure to have some secret advantages over the greatest and most highly valued language." Here
we meet with that valuation of the hitherto overlooked popular
dialects which sprang from the Romanticists' interest in the
' people ' and everything it had produced. Much valuable
linguistic work was directly inspired by this feeling and by conscious opposition to the old philology, that occupied itself exclusively with the two classical languages and the upper-class
literature embodied in them. As Scherer expresses it (*Jacob
Grimm*, 2te ausg., Berlin, 1885, p. 152) : " The brothers Grimm
applied to the old national literature and to popular traditions
the old philological virtue of exactitude, which had up to then
been bestowed solely on Greek and Roman classics and on the Bible.
They extended the field of strict philology, as they extended the
field of recognized poetry. They discarded the aristocratic narrowmindedness with which philologists looked down on unwritten
tradition, on popular ballads, legends, fairy tales, superstition,
nursery rimes. . . . In the hands of the two Grimms philology
became national and popular ; and at the same time a pattern was
created for the scientific study of all the peoples of the earth and

for a comparative investigation of the entire mental life of mankind, of which written literature is nothing but a small epitome."

But though Grimm thus broke loose from the traditions of classical philology, he still carried with him one relic of it, namely the standard by which the merits of different languages were measured. "In reading carefully the old Gothonic (altdeutschen) sources, I was every day discovering forms and perfections which we generally envy the Greeks and Romans when we consider the present condition of our language.". . . "Six hundred years ago every rustic knew, that is to say practised daily, perfections and niceties in the German language of which the best grammarians nowadays do not even dream; in the poetry of Wolfram von Eschenbach and of Hartmann von Aue, who had never heard of declension and conjugation, nay who perhaps did not even know how to read and write, many differences in the flexion and use of nouns and verbs are still nicely and unerringly observed, which we have gradually to rediscover in learned guise, but dare not reintroduce, for language ever follows its inalterable course."

Grimm then sets about writing his great historical and comparative *Deutsche Grammatik*, taking the term 'deutsch' in its widest and hardly justifiable sense of what is now ordinarily called Germanic and which is in this work called Gothonic. The first volume appeared in 1819, and in the preface we see that he was quite clear that he was breaking new ground and introducing a new method of looking at grammar. He speaks of previous German grammars and says expressly that he does not want his to be ranged with them. He charges them with unspeakable pedantry; they wanted to dogmatize magisterially, while to Grimm language, like everything natural and moral, is an unconscious and unnoticed secret which is implanted in us in youth. Every German therefore who speaks his language naturally, i.e. untaught, may call himself his own living grammar and leave all schoolmasters' rules alone. Grimm accordingly has no wish to prescribe anything, but to observe what has grown naturally, and very appropriately he dedicates his work to Savigny, who has taught him how institutions grow in the life of a nation In the new preface to the second edition there are also some noteworthy indications of the changed attitude. "I am hostile to general logical notions in grammar; they conduce apparently to strictness and solidity of definition, but hamper observation, which I take to be the soul of linguistic science. . . . As my starting-point was to trace the never-resting (unstillstehende) element of our language which changes with time and place, it became necessary for me to admit one dialect after the other, and I could not even

forbear to glance at those foreign languages that are ultimately
related with ours."

Here we have the first clear programme of that historical
school which has since then been the dominating one in linguistics.
But as language according to this new point of view was constantly
changing and developing, so also, during these years, were Grimm's
own ideas. And the man who then exercised the greatest influence
on him was Rasmus Rask. When Grimm wrote the first edition
of his *Grammatik* (1819), he knew nothing of Rask but the Icelandic
grammar, but just before finishing his own volume Rask's prize
essay reached him, and in the preface he at once speaks of it in
the highest terms of praise, as he does also in several letters of
this period ; he is equally enthusiastic about Rask's Anglo-Saxon
grammar and the Swedish edition of his Icelandic grammar, neither
of which reached him till after his own first volume had been printed
off. The consequence was that instead of going on to the second
volume, Grimm entirely recast the first volume and brought it
out in a new shape in 1822. The chief innovation was the phonology or, as he calls it, " Erstes buch. Von den buchstaben," which
was entirely absent in 1819, but now ran to 595 pages.

II.—§ 5. The Sound Shift.

This first book in the 1822 volume contains much, perhaps
most, of what constitutes Grimm's fame as a grammarian, notably
his exposition of the ' sound shift ' (lautverschiebung), which it
has been customary in England since Max Müller to term ' Grimm's
Law.' If any one man is to give his name to this law, a better name
would be ' Rask's Law,' for all these transitions, Lat. Gr. $p = f$,
$t = p$ (*th*), $k = h$, etc., are enumerated in Rask's *Undersøgelse*,
p. 168, which Grimm knew before he wrote a single word about
the sound shift.

Now, it is interesting to compare the two scholars' treatment
of these transitions. The sober-minded, matter-of-fact Rask
contents himself with a bare statement of the facts, with just enough
well-chosen examples to establish the correspondence ; the way
in which he arranges the sounds shows that he saw their parallelism
clearly enough, though he did not attempt to bring everything
under one single formula, any more than he tried to explain why
these sounds had changed.[1] Grimm multiplies the examples and

---

[1] Only in one subordinate point did Rask make a mistake ($b = b$), which
is all the more venial as there are extremely few examples of this sound.
Bredsdorff (*Aarsagerne*, 1821, p. 21) evidently had the law from Rask, and
gives it in the comprehensive formula which Paul (Gr. 1. 86) misses in Rask
and gives as Grimm's meritorious improvement on Rask. " The Germanic

then systematizes the whole process in one formula so as to comprise also the 'second shift' found in High German alone—a shift well known to Rask, though treated by him in a different place (p. 68 f.). Grimm's formula looks thus :

Greek	p	b	f	t	d	th	k	g	ch
Gothic	f	p	b	th	t	d	h	k	g
High G.	b(v)f	p		d	z	t	g	ch	k,

which may be expressed generally thus, that tenuis (T) becomes aspirate (A) and then media (M), etc., or, tabulated :

Greek	T	M	A
Gothic	A	T	M
High G.	M	A	T.

For this Grimm would of course have deserved great credit, because a comprehensive formula is more scientific than a rough statement of facts—*if* the formula had been correct ; but unfortunately it is not so. In the first place, it breaks down in the very first instance, for there is no media in High German corresponding to Gr. *p* and Gothic *f* (cf. *poús, fotus, fuss,* etc.) ; secondly, High German has *h* just as Gothic has, corresponding to Greek *k* (cf. *kardía, hairto, herz,* etc.), and where it has *g,* Gothic has also *g* in accordance with rules unknown to Grimm and not explained till long afterwards (by Verner). But the worst thing is that the whole specious generalization produces the impression of regularity and uniformity only through the highly unscientific use of the word ' aspirate,' which is made to cover such phonetically disparate things as (1) combination of stop with following *h,* (2) combination of stop with following fricative, *pf, ts* written *z,* (3) voiceless fricative, *f, s* in G. *das,* (4) voiced fricative, *v,* ð written *th,* and (5) *h.* Grimm rejoiced in his formula, giving as it does three chronological stages in each of the three subdivisions (tenuis, media, aspirate) of each of the three classes of consonants (labial, dental,' guttural '). This evidently took hold of his fancy through the mystic power of the number three, which he elsewhere (Gesch 1. 191, cf. 241) finds pervading language generally : three original vowels, *a, i, u,* three genders, three numbers (singular, dual, plural), three persons, three ' voices ' (genera : active, middle, passive), three tenses (present, preterit, future), three declensions through *a, i, u.* As there is here an element of mysticism, so is there also in Grimm's highflown

family has most often aspirates where Greek has tenues, tenues where it has mediæ, and again mediæ where it has aspirates, e.g. *fod,* Gr. *pous* ; *horn,* Gr. *keras* ; Þrir, Gr. *treis* ; *padde,* Gr. *batrakhos* ; *kone,* Gr. *gunē* ; *ti,* Gr. *deka* ; *bœrer,* Gr. *pherō* ; *galde,* Gr. *kholē* ; *dœr,* Gr. *thura.*" To the word ' horn' was appended a foot-note to the effect that *h* without doubt here originally was the German *ch*-sound. This was one year before Grimm stated his law !

explanation of the whole process from pretended popular psychology, which is full of the cloudiest romanticism. "When once the language had made the first step and had rid itself of the organic basis of its sounds, it was hardly possible for it to escape the second step and not to arrive at the third stage,[1] through which this development was perfected. . . . It is impossible not to admire the instinct by which the linguistic spirit (sprachgeist) carried this out to the end. A great many sounds got out of joint, but they always knew how to arrange themselves in a different place and to find the new application of the old law. I am not saying that the shift happened without any detriment, nay from one point of view the sound shift appears to me as a barbarous aberration, from which other more quiet nations abstained, but which is connected with the violent progress and craving for freedom which was found in Germany in the beginning of the Middle Ages and which initiated the transformation of Europe. The Germans pressed forward even in the matter of the innermost sounds of their language," etc., with remarks on intellectual progress and on victorious and ruling races. Grimm further says that "die dritte stufe des verschobnen lauts den kreislauf abschliesse und nach ihr ein neuer ansatz zur abweichung wieder von vorn anheben müsse. Doch eben weil der sprachgeist seinen lauf vollbracht hat, scheint er nicht wieder neu beginnen zu wollen " (GDS 1. 292 f , 299). It would be difficult to attach any clear ideas to these words.

Grimm's idea of a ' kreislauf ' is caused by the notion that the two shifts, separated by several centuries, represent one continued movement, while the High German shift of the eighth century has really no more to do with the primitive Gothonic shift, which took place probably some time before Christ, than has, for instance, the Danish shift in words like *gribe*, *bide*, *bage*, from *gripœ*, *bitœ*, *bakœ* (about 1400), or the still more recent transition in Danish through which stressed *t* in *tid*, *tyve*, etc., sounds nearly like [ts], as in HG. *zeit*. There cannot possibly be any causal nexus between such transitions, separated chronologically by long periods, with just as little change in the pronunciation of these consonants as there has been in English.[2]

---

[1] The muddling of the negatives is Grimm's, not the translator's.

[2] I am therefore surprised to find that in a recent article (*Am. Journ. of Philol.* 39. 415, 1918) Collitz praises Grimm's view in preference to Rask's because he saw " an inherent connexion between the various processes of the shifting," which were " subdivisions of one great law in which the formula T : A : M may be used to illustrate the shifting (in a single language) of three different groups of consonants and the result of a double or threefold shifting (in three different languages) of a single group of consonants. This great law was unknown to Rask." Collitz recognizes that " Grimm's law will hold good only if we accept the term ' aspirate ' in the broad sense in which

Grimm was anything but a phonetician, and sometimes says things which nowadays cannot but produce a smile, as when he says (Gr 1. 3) " in our word *schrift*, for instance, we express eight sounds through seven signs, for *f* stands for *ph* " ; thus he earnestly believes that *sch* contains three sounds, *s* and the ' aspirate ' *ch*=*c*+*h* ! Yet through the irony of fate it was on the history of sounds that Grimm exercised the strongest influence. As in other parts of his grammar, so also in the " theory of letters " he gave fuller word lists than people had been accustomed to, and this opened the eyes of scholars to the great regularity reigning in this department of linguistic development. Though in his own etymological practice he was far from the strict idea of ' phonetic law ' that played such a prominent rôle in later times, he thus paved the way for it. He speaks of law at any rate in connexion with the consonant shift, and there recognizes that it serves to curb wild etymologies and becomes a test for them (Gesch 291). The consonant shift thus became *the* law in linguistics, and because it affected a great many words known to everybody, and in a new and surprising way associated well-known Latin or Greek words with words of one's own mother-tongue, it became popularly the keystone of a new wonderful science.

Grimm coined several of the terms now generally used in linguistics ; thus *umlaut* and *ablaut*, ' strong ' and ' weak ' declensions and conjugations. As to the first, we have seen that it was Rask who first understood and who taught Grimm the cause of this phenomenon, which in English has often been designated by the German term, while Sweet calls it ' mutation ' and others better ' infection.' With regard to ' ablaut ' (Sweet: gradation, best perhaps in English apophony), Rask termed it ' omlyd,' a word which he never applied to Grimm's ' umlaut,' thus keeping the two kinds of vowel change as strictly apart as Grimm does. Apophony was first discovered in that class of verbs which Grimm called ' strong ' ; he was fascinated by the commutation of the vowels in *springe, sprang, gesprungen*, and sees in it, as in *bimbambum*, something mystic and admirable, characteristic of the old German spirit. He was thus blind to the correspondences found in other languages, and his theory led him astray in the second volume, in which he constructed imaginary verbal roots to explain apophony wherever it was found outside the verbs.

it is employed by J. Grimm "—but ' broad ' here means ' wrong ' or ' unscientific.' There is no *kreislauf* in the case of initial $k = h$; only in a few of the nine series do we find three distinct stages (as in *tres, three, drei*) ; here we have in Danish three stages, of which the third is a reversal to the first (*tre*) ; in E. *mother* we have five stages : t, þ, ð, d, (OE. *modor*) and again ð. Is there an "inherent connexion between the various processes of this shifting " too ?

Though Grimm, as we have seen, was by his principles and whole tendency averse to prescribing laws for a language, he is sometimes carried away by his love for mediæval German, as when he gives as the correct nominative form *der boge*, though everybody for centuries had said *der bogen*. In the same way many of his followers would apply the historical method to questions of correctness of speech, and would discard the forms evolved in later times in favour of previously existing forms which were looked upon as more ' organic.'

It will not be necessary here to speak of the imposing work done by Grimm in the rest of his long life, chiefly spent as a professor in Berlin. But in contrast to the ordinary view I must say that what appears to me as most likely to endure is his work on syntax, contained in the fourth volume of his grammar and in monographs. Here his enormous learning, his close power of observation, and his historical method stand him in good stead, and there is much good sense and freedom from that kind of metaphysical systematism which was triumphant in contemporaneous work on classical syntax. His services in this field are the more interesting because he did not himself seem to set much store by these studies and even said that syntax was half outside the scope of grammar. This utterance belongs to a later period than that of the birth of historical and comparative linguistics, and we shall have to revert to it after sketching the work of the third great founder of this science, to whom we shall now turn.

II.—§ 6. Franz Bopp.

The third, by some accounted the greatest, among the founders of modern linguistic science was Franz Bopp. His life was uneventful. At the age of twenty-one (he was born in 1791) he went to Paris to study Oriental languages, and soon concentrated his attention on Sanskrit. His first book, from which it is customary in Germany to date the birth of Comparative Philology, appeared in 1816, while he was still in Paris, under the title *Ueber des conjugationssystem der sanskritsprache in vergleichung mit jenem der griechischen, lateinischen, persischen und germanischen sprache*, but the latter part of the small volume was taken up with translations from Sanskrit, and for a long time he was just as much a Sanskrit scholar, editing and translating Sanskrit texts, as a comparative grammarian. He showed himself in the latter character in several papers read before the Berlin Academy, after he had been made a professor there in 1822, and especially in his famous *Vergleichende grammatik des sanskrit, send, armenischen, griechischen, lateinischen, litauischen, altslawischen, gotischen und deutschen*, the first edition of which was published between 1833 and 1849, the second in 1857, and the third in 1868. Bopp died in 1867.

Of Bopp's *Conjugationssystem* a revised, rearranged and greatly improved English translation came out in 1820 under the title *Analytical Comparison of the Sanskrit, Greek, Latin and Teutonic Languages.* This was reprinted with a good introduction by F. Techmer in his *Internationale zeitschrift für allgem. sprachwissenschaft IV* (1888), and in the following remarks I shall quote this (abbreviated AC) instead of, or alongside of, the German original (abbreviated C).

Bopp's chief aim (and in this he was characteristically different from Rask) was to find out the ultimate origin of grammatical forms. He follows his quest by the aid of Sanskrit forms, though he does not consider these as the ultimate forms themselves : " I do not believe that the Greek, Latin, and other European languages are to be considered as derived from the Sanskrit in the state in which we find it in Indian books ; I feel rather inclined to consider them altogether as subsequent variations of one original tongue, which, however, the Sanskrit has preserved more perfect than its kindred dialects. But whilst therefore the language of the Brahmans more frequently enables us to conjecture the primitive form of the Greek and Latin languages than what we discover in the oldest authors and monuments, the latter on their side also may not unfrequently elucidate the Sanskrit grammar " (AC 3). Herein subsequent research has certainly borne out Bopp's view.

After finding out by a comparison of the grammatical forms of Sanskrit, Greek, etc., which of these forms were identical and what were their oldest shapes, he tries to investigate the ultimate origin of these forms. This he takes to be a comparatively easy consequence of the first task, but he was here too much under the influence of the philosophical grammar then in vogue. Gottfried Hermann (*De emendanda ratione Græcæ grammaticæ*, 1801), on purely logical grounds, distinguishes three things as necessary elements of each sentence, the subject, the predicate, and the copula joining the first two elements together ; as the power of the verb is to attribute the predicate to the subject, there is really only one verb, namely the verb *to be*. Bopp's teacher in Paris, Silvestre de Sacy, says the same thing, and Bopp repeats : " A verb, in the most restricted meaning of the term, is that part of speech by which a subject is connected with its attribute. According to this definition it would appear that there can exist only one verb, namely, the substantive verb, in Latin *esse* ; in English, *to be.* . . . Languages of a structure similar to that of the Greek, Latin etc., can express by one verb of this kind a whole logical proposition, in which, however, that part of speech which expresses the connexion of the subject with its attribute, which is the characteristic function of the verb, is generally entirely omitted or understood. The Latin verb *dat* expresses the proposition ' he gives,' or ' he is giving ' : the letter *t*, indicating the third person, is the subject, *da* expresses the attribute of giving, and the grammatical *copula* is understood. In the verb *potest*, the latter is expressed, and *potest* unites in itself the three essential parts of speech, *t* being the subject, *es* the copula, and *pot* the attribute."

Starting from this logical conception of grammar, Bopp is inclined to find everywhere the ' substantive verb ' *to be* in its two Sanskrit forms *as* and *bhu* as an integral part of verbal forms. He is not the first to think that terminations, which are now inseparable parts of a verb, were originally independent words; thus Horne Tooke (in *Epea pteroenta*, 1786, ii. 429) expressly says that " All those common terminations in any language . . . are themselves separate words with distinct meanings," and explains, for instance, Latin *ibo* from *i*, ' *go* ' + *b*, ' will,' from Greek *boúl-*(*omai*) + *o* ' *l*,' from *ego*. Bopp's explanations are similar to this, though they do not imply such violent shortenings as that of *boúl-*(*omai*) to *b*. He finds the root Sanskrit *as*, ' to be,' in Latin perfects like *scrip-s-i*, in Greek aorists like *e-tup-s-a* and in futures like *tup-s-o*. That the same addition thus indicates different tenses does not trouble Bopp greatly ; he explains Lat. *fueram* from *fu* + *es* + *am*, etc., and says that the root *fu* " contains, properly, nothing to indicate past time, but the usage of language having supplied the want of an adequate inflexion, *fui* received the sense of a perfect, and *fu-eram*, which would be nothing more than an imperfect, that of a pluperfect, and after the same manner *fu-ero* signifies ' I shall have been,' instead of ' I shall be ' " (AC 57). All Latin verbal endings containing *r* are thus explained as being ultimately formed with the substantive verb (*ama-rem*, etc.) ; thus among others the infinitives *fac-ere*, *ed-ere*, as well as *esse*, *posse* : " *E* is properly, in Latin, the termination of a simple infinitive active ; and the root *Es* produced anciently *ese*, by adding *e* ; the *s* having afterwards been doubled, we have *esse*. This termination *e* answers to the Greek infinitive in *ai*, *eînai* . . ." (AC 58).

If Bopp found a master-key to many of the verbal endings in the Sanskrit root *es*, he found a key to many others in the other root of the verb ' to be,' Sanskrit *bhu*. He finds it in the Latin imperfect *da-bam*, as well as in the future *da-bo*, the relation between which is the same as that between *er-am* and *er-o*. " *Bo, bis, bit* has a striking similarity with the Anglo-Saxon *beo, bys, byth*, the future tense of the verb substantive, a similarity which cannot be considered as merely accidental." [Here neither the form nor the function of the Anglo-Saxon is stated quite correctly.] But the ending in Latin *ama-vi* is also referred to the same root ; for the change of the *b* into *v* we are referred to Italian *amava*, from Lat. *amabam*; thus also *fui* is for *fuvi* and *potui* is for *pot-vi* : "languages manifest a constant effort to combine heterogeneous materials in such a manner as to offer to the ear or eye one perfect whole, like a statue executed by a skilful artist, that wears the appearance of a figure hewn out of one piece of marble " (AC 60).

The following may be taken as a fair specimen of the method followed in these first attempts to account for the origin of flexional forms : " The Latin passive forms *amat-ur*, *amant-ur*, would, in some measure, conform to this mode of joining the verb substantive, if the *r* was also the result of a permutation of an original *s* ; and this appears not quite incredible, if we compare the second person *ama-ris* with the third *amat-ur*. Either in one or the other there must be a transposition of letters, to which the Latin language is particularly addicted. If *ama-ris*, which might have been produced from *ama-sis*, has preserved the original order of letters, then *ama-tur* must be the transposition of *ama-rut* or *ama-sut*, and *ama-ntur* that of *ama-runt* or *ama-sunt*. If this be the case, the origin of the Latin passive can be accounted for, and although differing from that of the Sanskrit, Greek, and Gothic languages, it is not produced by the invention of a new grammatical form. It becomes clear, also, why many verbs, with a passive form, have an active signification ; because there is no reason why the addition of the verb substantive should necessarily produce a passive sense. There is another way of explaining *ama-ris*, if it really stands for *ama-sis* ; the *s* may be the radical consonant of the reflex pronoun *se*. The introduction of this pronoun would be particularly adapted to form the middle voice, which expresses the reflexion of the action upon the actor ; but the Greek language exemplifies the facility with which the peculiar signification of the middle voice passes into that of the passive." The reasoning in the beginning of this passage (the only one contained in C) carries us back to a pre-scientific atmosphere, of which there are few or no traces in Rask's writings ; the latter explanation (added in AC) was preferred by Bopp himself in later works, and was for many years accepted as the correct one, until scholars found a passive in *r* in Keltic, where the transition from *s* to *r* is not found as it is in Latin ; and as the closely corresponding forms in Keltic and Italic must obviously be explained in the same way, the hypothesis of a composition with *se* was generally abandoned. Bopp's partiality for the abstract verb is seen clearly when he explains the Icelandic passive in *-st* from *s* = *es* (C 132) ; here Rask and Grimm saw the correct and obvious explanation.

Among the other explanations given first by Bopp must be mentioned the Latin second person of the passive voice -*mini*, as in *ama-mini*, which he takes to be the nominative masculine plural of a participle corresponding to Greek -*menos* and found in a different form in Lat. *alumnus* (AC 51). This explanation is still widely accepted, though not by everybody.

With regard to the preterit of what Grimm was later to term the 'weak' verbs, Bopp vacillates between different explanations. In C 118 he thinks the *t* or *d* is identical with the ending of the participle, in which the case endings were omitted and supplanted by personal endings ; the syllable *ed* after *d* [in Gothic *sok-id-edum* ; 'Greek,' p. 119, must be a misprint for Gothic] is nothing but an accidental addition. But on p. 151 he sees in *sokidedun, sokidedi*, a connexion of *sok* with the preterit of the verb *Tun*, as if the Germans were to say *suchetaten, suchetäte* ; he compares the English use of *did* (*did seek*), and thinks the verb used is G. *tun*, Goth. *taujan*. The theory of composition is here restricted to those forms that contain two *d's*, i.e. the plural indicative and the subjunctive. In the English edition this twofold explanation is repeated with some additions : *d* or *t* as in Gothic *sok-i-da* and *oh-ta* originates from a participle found in Sanskr. *tyak-ta, likh-i-ta*, Lat. -*tus*, Gr. -*tós* ; this suffix generally has a passive sense, but in neuter verbs an active sense, and therefore would naturally serve to form a preterit tense with an active signification. He finds a proof of the connexion between this preterit and the participle in the fact that only such verbs as have this ending in the participle form their preterit by means of a dental, while the others (the 'strong' verbs, as Grimm afterwards termed them) have a participle in *an* and reduplication or a change of vowel in the preterit ; and Bopp compares the Greek aorist passive *etúphth-ēn, edóth-ēn*, which he conceives may proceed from the participle *tuphth-eís, doth-eís* (AC 37 ff.). This suggestion seems to have been commonly overlooked or abandoned, while the other explanation, from *dedi* as in English *did seek*, which Bopp gives p. 49 for the subjunctive and the indicative plural, was accepted by Grimm as the explanation of all the forms, even of those containing only one dental ; in later works Bopp agreed with Grimm and thus gave up the first part of his original explanation. The *did* explanation had been given already by D. von Stade (d. 1718, see Collitz, *Das schwache präteritum*, p. 1) ; Rask (P 270, not mentioned by Collitz) says : " Whence this *d* or *t* has come is not easy to tell, as it is not found in Latin and Greek, but as it is evident from the Icelandic grammar that it is closely connected with the past participle and is also found in the preterit subjunctive, it seems clear that it must have been an old characteristic of the past tense in every mood, but was lost in Greek when the above-mentioned participles in *tos* disappeared from the verbs " (cf. Ch. XIX § 12).

With regard to the vowels, Bopp in AC has the interesting theory that it is only through a defect in the alphabet that Sanskrit appears to have *a* in so many places ; he believes that the spoken language had often "the short Italian *e* and *o*," where *a* was written. "If this was the case, we can give a reason why, in words common to the Sanskrit and Greek, the Indian *akāra* [that is, short *a*] so often corresponds to ε and *o*, as, for instance, *asti*, he is, ἐστί ; *patis*, husband, πόσις ; *ambaras*, sky, ὄμβρος, rain, etc." Later, unfortunately, Bopp came under the influence of Grimm, who, as we saw, on speculative grounds admitted in the primitive language only the three vowels *a*, *i*, *u*, and Bopp and his followers went on believing that the Sanskrit *a* represented the original state of language, until the discovery of the ' palatal law ' (about 1880) showed (what Bopp's occasional remark might otherwise easily have led up to, if he had not himself discarded it) that the Greek tripartition into *a*, *e*, *o* represented really a more original state of things.

II.—§ 7. Bopp continued.

In a chapter on the roots in AC (not found in C), Bopp contrasts the structure of Semitic roots and of our own ; in Semitic languages roots must consist of three letters, neither more nor less, and thus generally contain two syllables, while in Sanskrit, Greek, etc., the character of the root " is not to be determined by the number of letters, but by that of the syllables, of which they contain only one " ; thus a root like *i*, ' to go,' would be unthinkable in Arabic. The consequence of this structure of the roots is that the inner changes which play such a large part in expressing grammatical modifications in Semitic languages must be much more restricted in our family of languages. These changes were what F. Schlegel termed flexions and what Bopp himself, two years before (C 7), had named "the truly organic way" of expressing relation and mentioned as a wonderful flexibility found in an extraordinary degree in Sanskrit, by the side of which composition with the verb ' to be ' is found only occasionally. Now, however, in 1820, Bopp repudiates Schlegel's and his own previous assumption that ' flexion ' was characteristic of Sanskrit in contradistinction to other languages in which grammatical modifications were expressed by the addition of suffixes. On the contrary, while holding that both methods are employed in all languages, Chinese perhaps alone excepted, he now thinks that it is the suffix method which is prevalent in Sanskrit, and that "the only real inflexions . . . possible

in a language, whose elements are monosyllables, are the change
of their vowels and the repetition of their radical consonants,
otherwise called reduplication." It will be seen that Bopp here
avoids both the onesidedness found in Schlegel's division of
languages and the other onesidedness which we shall encounter
in later theories, according to which *all* grammatical elements are
originally independent subordinate roots added to the main root.

In his *Vocalismus* (1827, reprinted 1836) Bopp opposes Grimm's
theory that the changes for which Grimm had introduced the term
ablaut were due to psychological causes; in other words, possessed
an inner meaning from the very outset. Bopp inclined to a
mechanical explanation [1] and thought them dependent on the
weight of the endings, as shown by the contrast between Sanskr.
vēda, Goth. *vait*, Gr. *oîda* and the plural, respectively *vidima, vitum,
ídmen*. In this instance Bopp is in closer agreement than Grimm
with the majority of younger scholars, who see in apophony
(ablaut) an originally non-significant change brought about
mechanically by phonetic conditions, though they do not find
these in the ' weight ' of the ending, but in the primeval accent :
the accentuation of Sanskrit was not known to Bopp when he
wrote his essay.

The personal endings of the verbs had already been identified
with the corresponding pronouns by Scheidius (1790) and Rask
(P 258) ; Bopp adopts the same view, only reproaching Scheidius
for thinking exclusively of the nominative forms of the pronouns.

It thus appears that in his early work Bopp deals with a great
many general problems, but his treatment is suggestive rather than
exhaustive or decisive, for there are too many errors in details
and his whole method is open to serious criticism. A modern
reader is astonished to see the facility with which violent changes
of sounds, omissions and transpositions of consonants, etc., are
gratuitously accepted. Bopp never reflected as deeply as Rask
did on what constitutes linguistic kinship, hence in C he accepts
the common belief that Persian was related more closely to German
than to Sanskrit, and in later life he tried to establish a relationship
between the Malayo-Polynesian and the Indo-European languages.
But in spite of all this it must be recognized that in his long laborious
life he accomplished an enormous amount of highly meritorious
work, not only in Sanskrit philology, but also in comparative
grammar, in which he gradually freed himself of his worst methodical errors. He was constantly widening his range of vision, taking
into consideration more and more cognate languages. The ingenious
way in which he explained the curious Keltic shiftings in initial

---

[1] Probably under the influence of Humboldt, who wrote to him (September 1826) : "Absichtlich grammatisch ist gewiss kein vokalwechsel."

consonants (which had so puzzled Rask as to make him doubt of a connexion of these languages with our family, but which Bopp showed to be dependent on a lost final sound of the preceding word) definitely and irrefutably established the position of those languages. Among other things that might be credited to his genius, I shall select his explanation of the various declensional classes as determined by the final sound of the stem. But it is not part of my plan to go into many details; suffice it to say that Bopp's great *Vergleichende grammatik* served for long years as the best, or really the only, exposition of the new science, and vastly contributed not only to elucidate obscure points, but also to make comparative grammar as popular as it is possible for such a necessarily abstruse science to be.

In Bopp's *Vergleichende grammatik* (%. § 108) he gives his classification of languages in general. He rejects Fr. Schlegel's bipartition, but his growing tendency to explain everything in Aryan grammar, even the inner changes of Sanskrit roots, by mechanical causes makes him modify A. W. Schlegel's tripartition and place our family of languages with the second instead of the third class. His three classes are therefore as follows: I. Languages without roots proper and without the power of composition, and thus without organism or grammar; to this class belongs Chinese, in which most grammatical relations are only to be recognized by the position of the words. II. Languages with monosyllabic roots, capable of composition and acquiring their organism, their grammar, nearly exclusively in this way; the main principle of word formation is the connexion of verbal and pronominal roots. To this class belong the Indo-European languages, but also all languages not comprised under the first or the third class. III. Languages with disyllabic roots and three necessary consonants as sole bearers of the signification of the word. This class includes only the Semitic languages. Grammatical forms are here created not only by means of composition, as in the second class, but also by inner modification of the roots.

It will be seen that Bopp here expressly avoids both expressions 'agglutination' and 'flexion,' the former because it had been used of languages contrasted with Aryan, while Bopp wanted to show the essential identity of the two classes; the latter because it had been invested with much obscurity on account of Fr. Schlegel's use of it to signify inner modification only. According to Schlegel, only such instances as English *drink / drank / drunk* are pure flexion, while German *trink-e / trank / ge-trunk-en*, and still more Greek *leip-ō / e-lip-on / le-loip-a*, besides an element of 'flexion' contain also affixed elements. It is clear that no language can use 'flexion' (in Schlegel's sense) exclusively, and consequently this cannot be made a principle on which to erect a classification of languages generally. Schlegel's use of the term ' flexion ' seems to have been dropped by all subsequent writers, who use it so as to include what is actually found in the grammar of such languages as Sanskrit and Greek, comprising under it inner and outer modifications, but of course not requiring both in the same form.

In view of the later development of our science, it is worthy of notice that neither in the brothers Schlegel nor in Bopp do we yet meet with the idea that the classes set up are not only a distribution of the languages found side by side in the world at this time, but also represent so many stages in historical development ; indeed, Bopp's definitions are framed so as positively to exclude any development from his Class II to Class III, as the character of the underlying roots is quite heterogeneous. On the other hand, Bopp's tendency to explain Aryan endings from originally independent roots paved the way for the theory of isolation, agglutination and flexion as three successive stages of the same language.

In his first work (C 56) Bopp had already hinted that in the earliest period known to us languages had already outlived their most perfect state and were in a process of decay ; and in his review of Grimm (1827) he repeats this : " We perceive them in a condition in which they may indeed be progressive syntactically but have, as far as grammar is concerned, lost more or less of what belonged to the perfect structure, in which the separate members stand in exact relation to each other and in which everything derived has still a visible and unimpaired connexion with its source " (Voc. 2). We shall see kindred ideas in Humboldt and Schleicher.

To sum up : Bopp set about discovering the ultimate origin of flexional elements, but instead of that he discovered Comparative Grammar—" à peu près comme Christophe Colomb a découvert l'Amérique en cherchant la route des Indes," as A. Meillet puts it (LI 413). A countryman of Rask may be forgiven for pushing the French scholar's brilliant comparison still further : in the same way as Norsemen from Iceland had discovered America before Columbus, without imagining that they were finding the way to India, just so Rasmus Rask through his Icelandic studies had discovered Comparative Grammar before Bopp, without needing to take the circuitous route through Sanskrit.

II.—§ 8. Wilhelm von Humboldt.

This will be the proper place to mention one of the profoundest thinkers in the domain of linguistics, Wilhelm von Humboldt (1767–1835), who, while playing an important part in the political world, found time to study a great many languages and to think deeply on many problems connected with philology and ethnography.[1]

In numerous works, the most important of which, *Ueber die Kawisprache auf der Insel Jawa*, with the famous introduction "Ueber die Verschiedenheit des menschlichen Sprachbaues und ihren Einfluss auf die geistige Entwickelung des Menschengeschlechts," was published posthumously in 1836–40, Humboldt developed his linguistic philosophy, of which it is not easy to give a succinct idea, as it is largely couched in a most abstruse style ; it is not surprising that his admirer and follower, Heymann Steinthal, in a series of books, gave as many different interpretations of Humboldt's thoughts, each purporting to be more correct than its predecessors. Still, I believe the following may be found to be a tolerably fair rendering of some of Humboldt's ideas.

He rightly insists on the importance of seeing in language a continued activity. Language is not a substance or a finished work, but action (Sie selbst ist kein werk, *ergon*, sondern eine tätigkeit, *energeia*). Language therefore cannot be defined except genetically. It is the ever-repeated labour of the mind to utilize articulated sounds to express thoughts. Strictly speaking, this is a definition of each separate act of speech ; but truly and essentially a language must be looked upon as the totality of such acts.

---

[1] Humboldt's relation to Bopp's general ideas is worth studying; see his letters to Bopp, printed as Nachtrag to S. Lefman's *Franz Bopp, sein leben und seine wissenschaft* (Berlin, 1897). He is (p. 5) on the whole of Bopp's opinion that flexions have arisen through agglutination of syllables, the independent meaning of which was lost ; still, he is not certain that all flexion can be explained in that way, and especially doubts it in the case of 'umlaut,' under which term he here certainly includes 'ablaut,' as seen by his reference (p. 12) to Greek future *stalô* from *stéllō* ; he adds that "some flexions are at the same time so significant and so widely spread in languages that I should be inclined to call them original ; for example, our *i* of the dative and *m* of the same case, both of which by their sharper sound seem intended to call attention to the peculiar nature of this case, which does not, like the other cases, denote a simple, but a double relation" (repeated p. 10). Humboldt doubts Bopp's identification of the temporal augment with the *a* privativum. He says (p. 14) that cases often originate from prepositions, as in American languages and in Basque, and that he has always explained our genitive, as in G. *manne-s*, as a remnant of *aus*. This is evidently wrong, as the *s* of *aus* is a special High German development from *t*, while the *s* of the genitive is also found in languages which do not share in this development of *t*. But the remark is interesting because, apart from the historical proof to the contrary which we happen to possess in this case, the derivation is no whit worse than many of the explanations resorted to by adherents of the agglutinative theory. But Humboldt goes on to say that in Greek and Latin he is not prepared to maintain that one single case is to be explained in this way. Humboldt probably had some influence on Bopp's view of the weak preterit, for he is skeptical with regard to the *did* explanation and inclines to connect the ending with the participle in *t*.

For the words and rules, which according to our ordinary notions make up a language, exist really only in the act of connected speech. The breaking up of language into words and rules is nothing but a dead product of our bungling scientific analysis (Versch 41). Nothing in language is static, everything is dynamic. Language has nowhere any abiding place, not even in writing; its dead part must continually be re-created in the mind; in order to exist it must be spoken or understood, and so pass in its entirety into the subject (ib. 63).

Humboldt speaks continually of languages as more perfect or less perfect. Yet "no language should be condemned or depreciated, not even that of the most savage tribe, for each language is a picture of the original aptitude for language" (Versch 304). In another place he speaks about special excellencies even of languages that cannot in themselves be recognized as superlatively good instruments of thought. Undoubtedly Chinese of the old style carries with it an impressive dignity through the immediate succession of nothing but momentous notions; it acquires a simple greatness because it throws away all unnecessary accessory elements and thus, as it were, takes flight to pure thinking. Malay is rightly praised for its ease and the great simplicity of its constructions. The Semitic languages retain an admirable art in the nice discrimination of sense assigned to many shades of vowels. Basque possesses a particular vigour, dependent on the briefness and boldness of expression imparted by the structure of its words and by their combination. Delaware and other American languages express in one word a number of ideas for which we should require many words. The human mind is always capable of producing something admirable, however one-sided it may be; such special points decide nothing with regard to the rank of languages (Versch 189 f.). We have here, as indeed continually in Humboldt, a valuation of languages with many brilliant remarks, but on the whole we miss the concrete details abounding in Jenisch's work. Humboldt, as it were, lifts us to a higher plane, where the air may be purer, but where it is also thinner and not seldom cloudier as well.

According to Humboldt, each separate language, even the most despised dialect, should be looked upon as an organic whole, different from all the rest and expressing the individuality of the people speaking it; it is characteristic of one nation's psyche, and indicates the peculiar way in which that nation attempts to realize the ideal of speech. As a language is thus symbolic of the national character of those who speak it, very much in each language had its origin in a symbolic representation of the notion it stands for; there is a natural nexus between certain sounds and certain general ideas, and consequently we often find similar sounds used for the same, or nearly the same, idea in languages not otherwise related to one another.

Humboldt is opposed to the idea of 'general' or 'universal' grammar as understood in his time ; instead of this purely deductive grammar he would found an inductive general grammar, based upon the comparison of the different ways in which the same grammatical notion was actually expressed in a variety of languages. He set the example in his paper on the Dual. His own studies covered a variety of languages ; but his works do not give us many actual concrete facts from the languages he had studied ; he was more interested in abstract reasonings on language in general than in details.

In an important paper, *Ueber das Entstehen der grammatischen Formen und ihren Einfluss auf die Ideenentwickelung* (1822), he says that language at first denotes only objects, leaving it to the hearer to understand or guess at (hinzudenken) their connexion. By and by the word-order becomes fixed, and some words lose their independent use and sound, so that in the second stage we see grammatical relations denoted through word-order and through words vacillating between material and formal significations. Gradually these become affixes, but the connexion is not yet firm, the joints are still visible, the result being an aggregate, not yet a unit. Thus in the third stage we have something analogous to form, but not real form. This is achieved in the fourth stage, where the word is *one*, only modified in its grammatical relations through the flexional sound ; each word belongs to one definite part of speech, and form-words have no longer any disturbing material signification, but are pure expressions of relation. Such words as Lat. *amavit* and Greek *epoiēsas* are truly grammatical forms in contradistinction to such combinations of words and syllables as are found in cruder languages, because we have here a fusion into one whole, which causes the signification of the parts to be forgotten and joins them firmly under one accent. Though Humboldt thus thinks flexion developed out of agglutination, he distinctly repudiates the idea of a gradual development and rather inclines to something like a sudden crystallization (see especially Steinthal's ed., p. 585).

Humboldt's position with regard to the classification of languages is interesting. In his works we continually meet with the terms agglutination [1] and flexion by the side of a new term, ' incorporation.' This he finds in full bloom in many American languages, such as Mexican, where the object may be inserted into the verbal form between the element indicating person and the

[1] Humboldt seems to be the inventor of this term (1821; see Streitberg, IF 35. 191).

root. Now, Humboldt says that besides Chinese, which has no grammatical form, there are three possible forms of languages, the flexional, the agglutinative and the incorporating, but he adds that all languages contain one or more of these forms (Versch 301). He tends to deny the existence of any exclusively agglutinative or exclusively flexional language, as the two principles are generally commingled (132). Flexion is the only method that gives to the word the true inner firmness and at the same time distributes the parts of the sentence according to the necessary interlacing of thoughts, and thus undoubtedly represents the pure principle of linguistic structure. Now, the question is, what language carries out this method in the most consistent way? True perfection may not be found in any one language : in the Semitic languages we find flexion in its most genuine shape, united with the most refined symbolism, only it is not pursued consistently in all parts of the language, but restricted by more or less accidental laws. On the other hand, in the Sanskritic languages the compact unity of every word saves flexion from any suspicion of agglutination ; it pervades all parts of the language and rules it in the highest freedom (Versch 188). Compared with incorporation and with the method of loose juxtaposition without any real word-unity, flexion appears as an intuitive principle born of true linguistic genius (ib.). Between Sanskrit and Chinese, as the two opposed poles of linguistic structure, each of them perfect in the consistent following one principle, we may place all the remaining languages (ib. 326). But the languages called agglutinative have nothing in common except just the negative trait that they are neither isolating nor flexional. The structural diversities of human languages are so great that they make one despair of a fully comprehensive classification (ib. 330).

According to Humboldt, language is in continued development under the influence of the changing mental power of its speakers. In this development there are naturally two definite periods, one in which the creative instinct of speech is still growing and active, and another in which a seeming stagnation begins and then an appreciable decline of that creative instinct. Still, the period of decline may initiate new principles of life and new successful changes in a language (Versch 184). In the form-creating period nations are occupied more with the language than with its purpose, i.e. with what it is meant to signify. They struggle to express thought, and this craving in connexion with the inspiring feeling of success produces and sustains the creative power of language (ib. 191). In the second period we witness a wearing-off of the flexional forms. This is found less in languages reputed crude or rough than in refined ones. Language is exposed to the most

violent changes when the human mind is most active, for then
it considers too careful an observation of the modifications of
sound as superfluous. To this may be added a want of perception
of the poetic charm inherent in the sound. Thus it is the transition from a more sensuous to a more intellectual mood that works
changes in a language. In other cases less noble causes are at
work. Rougher organs and less sensitive ears are productive
of indifference to the principle of harmony, and finally a prevalent
practical trend may bring about abbreviations and omissions of
all kinds in its contempt for everything that is not strictly necessary for the purpose of being understood. While in the first period
the elements still recall their origin to man's consciousness, there
is an æsthetic pleasure in developing the instrument of mental
activity ; but in the second period language serves only the practical needs of life. In this way such a language as English may
reduce its forms so as to resemble the structure of Chinese ; but
there will always remain traces of the old flexions ; and English
is no more incapable of high excellences than German (Versch
282–6). What these are Humboldt, however, does not tell us.

II.—§ 9. Grimm Once More.

Humboldt here foreshadowed and probably influenced ideas
to which Jacob Grimm gave expression in two essays written in
his old age and which it will be necessary here to touch upon.
In the essay on the pedantry of the German language (*Ueber das
pedantische in der deutschen sprache*, 1847), Grimm says that he
has so often praised his mother-tongue that he has acquired the
right once in a while to blame it. If pedantry had not existed
already, Germans would have invented it ; it is the shadowy side
of one of their virtues, painstaking accuracy and loyalty. Grimm's
essay is an attempt at estimating a language, but on the whole it
is less comprehensive and less deep than that of Jenisch. Grimm
finds fault with such things as the ceremoniousness with which
princes are spoken to and spoken of (*Durchlauchtigster, allerhöchst-
derselbe*), and the use of the pronoun *Sie* in the third person plural
in addressing a single person ; he speaks of the clumsiness of the
auxiliaries for the passive, the past and the future, and of the
word-order which makes the Frenchman cry impatiently "J'attends
le verbe." He blames the use of capitals for substantives and other
peculiarities of German spelling, but gives no general statement
of the principles on which the comparative valuation of different
languages should be based, though in many passages we see that
he places the old stages of the language very much higher than
the language of his own day.

The essay on the origin of language (1851) is much more important, and may be said to contain the mature expression of all Grimm's thoughts on the philosophy of language. Unfortunately, much of it is couched in that high-flown poetical style which may be partly a consequence of Grimm's having approached the exact study of language through the less exact studies of popular poetry and folklore ; this style is not conducive to clear ideas, and therefore renders the task of the reporter very difficult indeed. Grimm at some length argues against the possibility of language having been either created by God when he created man or having been revealed by God to man after his creation. The very imperfections and changeability of language speak against its divine origin. Language as gradually developed must be the work of man himself, and therein is different from the immutable cries and songs of the lower creation. Nature and natural instinct have no history, but mankind has. Man and woman were created as grown-up and marriageable beings, and there must have been created at once more than one couple, for if there had been only one couple, there would have been the possibility that the one mother had borne only sons or only daughters, further procreation being thus rendered impossible (!), not to mention the moral objections to marriages between brother and sister. How these once created beings, human in every respect except in language, were able to begin talking and to find themselves understood, Grimm does not really tell us ; he uses such expressions as ' inventors ' of words, but apart from the symbolical value of some sounds, such as *l* and *r*, he thinks that the connexion of word and sense was quite arbitrary. On the other hand, he can tell us a great deal about the first stage of human speech : it contained only the three vowels *a*, *i*, *u*, and only few consonant groups ; every word was a monosyllable, and abstract notions were at first absent. The existence in all (?) old languages of masculine and feminine flexions must be due to the influence of women on the formation of language. Through the distinction of genders Grimm says that regularity and clearness were suddenly brought about in everything concerning the noun as by a most happy stroke of fortune. Endings to indicate person, number, tense and mood originated in added pronouns and auxiliary words, which at first were loosely joined to the root, but later coalesced with it. Besides, reduplication was used to indicate the past ; and after the absorption of the reduplicational syllable the same effect was obtained in German through apophony. All nouns presuppose verbs, whose material sense was applied to the designation of things, as when G. *hahn* (' cock ') was thus called from an extinct verb *hanan,* corresponding to Lat. *canere,* ' to sing.'

In what Grimm says about the development of language it is easy to trace the influence of Humboldt's ideas, though they are worked out with great originality. He discerns three stages, the last two alone being accessible to us through historical documents. In the first period we have the creation and growing of roots and words, in the second the flourishing of a perfect flexion, and in the third a tendency to thoughts, which leads to the giving up of flexion as not yet (?) satisfactory. They may be compared to leaf, blossom and fruit, " the beauty of human speech did not bloom in its beginning, but in its middle period ; its ripest fruits will not be gathered till some time in the future." He thus sums up his theory of the three stages : " Language in its earliest form was melodious, but diffuse and straggling ; in its middle form it was full of intense poetical vigour ; in our own days it seeks to remedy the diminution of beauty by the harmony of the whole, and is more effective though it has inferior means." In most places Grimm still speaks of the downward course of linguistic development ; all the oldest languages of our family " show a rich, pleasant and admirable perfection of form, in which all material and spiritual elements have vividly interpenetrated each other," while in the later developments of the same languages the inner power and subtlety of flexion has generally been given up and destroyed, though partly replaced by external means and auxiliary words. On the whole, then, the history of language discloses a descent from a period of perfection to a less perfect condition. This is the point of view that we meet with in nearly all linguists ; but there is a new note when Grimm begins vaguely and dimly to see that the loss of flexional forms is sometimes compensated by other things that may be equally valuable or even more valuable ; and he even, without elaborate arguments, contradicts his own main contention when he says that " human language is retrogressive only apparently and in particular points, but looked upon as a whole it is progressive, and its intrinsic force is continually increasing." He instances the English language, which by sheer making havoc of all old phonetic laws and by the loss of all flexions has acquired a great force and power, such as is found perhaps in no other human language. Its wonderfully happy structure resulted from the marriage of the two noblest languages of Europe ; therefore it was a fit vehicle for the greatest poet of modern times, and may justly claim the right to be called a world's language ; like the English people, it seems destined to reign in future even more than now in all parts of the earth. This enthusiastic panegyric forms a striking contrast to what the next great German scholar with whom we have to deal, Schleicher, says about the same language, which to him shows only " how rapidly the language of a nation important both in history and literature can decline " (II. 231).

CHAPTER III

MIDDLE OF NINETEENTH CENTURY

§ 1. After Bopp and Grimm. § 2. K. M. Rapp. § 3. J. H. Bredsdorff.
§ 4. August Schleicher. § 5. Classification of Languages. § 6. Reconstruction. § 7. Curtius, Madvig and Specialists. § 8. Max Müller and Whitney.

III.—§ 1. After Bopp and Grimm.

BOPP and Grimm exercised an enormous influence on linguistic thought and linguistic research in Germany and other countries. Long even before their death we see a host of successors following in the main the lines laid down in their work, and thus directly and indirectly they determined the development of this science for a long time. Through their efforts so much new light had been shed on a number of linguistic phenomena that these took a quite different aspect from that which they had presented to the previous generation ; most of what had been written about etymology and kindred subjects in the eighteenth century seemed to the new school utterly antiquated, mere fanciful vagaries of incompetent blunderers, whereas now scholars had found firm ground on which to raise a magnificent structure of solid science. This feeling was especially due to the undoubted recognition of one great family of languages to which the vast majority of European languages, as well as some of the most important Asiatic languages, belonged : here we had one firmly established fact of the greatest magnitude, which at once put an end to all the earlier whimsical attempts to connect Latin and Greek words with Hebrew roots. As for the name of that family of languages, Rask hesitated between different names, ' European,' ' Sarmatic ' and finally ' Japhetic ' (as a counterpart of the Semitic and the Hamitic languages) ; Bopp at first had no comprehensive name, and on the title-page of his *Vergl. grammatik* contents himself with enumerating the chief languages described, but in the work itself he says that he prefers the name ' Indo-European,' which has also found wide acceptance, though more in France, England and Skandinavia than in Germany. Humboldt for a long while said ' Sanskritic,' but later he adopted ' Indo-Germanic,' and this has been the generally recognized name used in Germany, in spite of Bopp's protest- who said that ' Indo-klassisch ' would be more to the point ; ' Indo,

Keltic ' has also been proposed as designating the family through
its two extreme members to the East and West. But all these
compound names are clumsy without being completely pertinent,
and it seems therefore much better to use the short and convenient term 'the Aryan languages': Aryan being the oldest
name by which any members of the family designated themselves
(in India and Persia).[1]

Thanks to the labours of Bopp and Grimm and their co-workers
and followers, we see also a change in the status of the study of
languages. Formerly this was chiefly a handmaiden to philology
—but as this word is often in English used in a sense unknown
to other languages and really objectionable, namely as a synonym
of (comparative) study of languages, it will be necessary first to
say a few words about the terminology of our science. In this
book I shall use the word ' philology ' in its continental sense, which
is often rendered in English by the vague word 'scholarship,'
meaning thereby the study of the specific culture of one nation ;
thus we speak of Latin philology, Greek philology, Icelandic
philology, etc. The word 'linguist,' on the other hand, is not infrequently used in the sense of one who has merely a practical knowledge of some foreign language ; but I think I am in accordance
with a growing number of scholars in England and America if I
call such a man a 'practical linguist' and apply the word 'linguist'
by itself to the scientific student of language (or of languages) ;
'linguistics' then becomes a shorter and more convenient name
for what is also called the science of language (or of languages).

Now that the reader understands the sense in which I take
these two terms, I may go on to say that the beginning of the nineteenth century witnessed a growing differentiation between philology and linguistics in consequence of the new method introduced
by comparative and by historical grammar ; it was nothing less
than a completely new way of looking at the facts of language
and trying to trace their origin. While to the philologist the
Greek or Latin language, etc., was only a means to an end, to the
linguist it was an end in itself. The former saw in it a valuable,
and in fact an indispensable, means of gaining a first-hand knowledge of the literature which was his chief concern, but the linguist
cared not for the literature as such, but studied languages for their
own sake, and might even turn to languages destitute of literature
because they were able to throw some light on the life of language
in general or on forms in related languages. The philologist as
such would not think of studying the Gothic of Wulfila, as a know-

[1] It has been objected to the use of Aryan in this wide sense that the
name is also used in the restricted sense of Indian + Iranic ; but no separate
name is needed for that small group other than Indo-Iranic.

ledge of that language gives access only to a translation of parts
of the Bible, the ideas of which can be studied much better elsewhere ; but to the linguist Gothic was extremely valuable. The
differentiation, of course, is not an absolute one ; besides being
linguists in the new sense, Rask was an Icelandic philologist,
Bopp a Sanskrit philologist, and Grimm a German philologist ;
but the tendency towards the emancipation of linguistics was very
strong in them, and some of their pupils were pure linguists and
did no work in philology.

In breaking away from philology and claiming for linguistics
the rank of a new and independent science, the partisans of the
new doctrine were apt to think that not only had they discovered
a new method, but that the object of their study was different
from that of the philologists, even when they were both concerned
with language. While the philologist looked upon language as
part of the culture of some nation, the linguist looked upon it as
a natural object ; and when in the beginning of the nineteenth century philosophers began to divide all sciences into the two sharply
separated classes of mental and natural sciences (geistes- und
naturwissenschaften), linguists would often reckon their science
among the latter. There was in this a certain amount of pride
or boastfulness, for on account of the rapid rise and splendid
achievements of the natural sciences at that time, it began to be a
matter of common belief that they were superior to, and were possessed of a more scientific method than, the other class—the same
view that finds an expression in the ordinary English usage,
according to which ' science ' means natural science and the
other domains of human knowledge are termed the ' arts ' or the
' humanities.'

We see the new point of view in occasional utterances of the
pioneers of linguistic science.   Rask expressly says that " Language
is a natural object and its study resembles natural history "
(SA 2. 502) ; but when he repeats the same sentence (in *Retskrivningslære*, 8) it appears that he is thinking of language as opposed
to the more artificial writing, and the contrast is not between
mental and natural science, but between art and nature, between
what can and what cannot be consciously modified by man—it is
really a different question.

Bopp, in his review of Grimm (1827, reprinted *Vocalismus*,
1836, p. 1), says : " Languages are to be considered organic natural
bodies, which are formed according to fixed laws, develop as possessing an inner principle of life, and gradually die out because
they do not understand themselves any longer [!], and therefore
cast off or mutilate their members or forms, which were at first
significant, but gradually have become more of an extrinsic mass.

. . . It is not possible to determine how long languages may preserve their full vigour of life and of procreation," etc. This is highly figurative language which should not be taken at its face value ; but expressions like these, and the constant use of such words as 'organic' and 'inorganic' in speaking of formations in languages, and 'organism' of the whole language, would tend to widen the gulf between the philological and the linguistic point of view. Bopp himself never consistently followed the naturalistic way of looking at language, but in § 4 of this chapter we shall see that Schleicher was not afraid of going to extremes and building up a consistent natural science of language.

The cleavage between philology and linguistics did not take place without arousing warm feeling. Classical scholars disliked the intrusion of Sanskrit everywhere ; they did not know that language and did not see the use of it. They resented the way in which the new science wanted to reconstruct Latin and Greek grammar and to substitute new explanations for those which had always been accepted. Those Sanskritists chatted of guna and vrddhi and other barbaric terms, and even ventured to talk of a locative case in Latin, as if the number of cases had not been settled once for all long ago ! [1]

Classicists were no doubt perfectly right when they reproached comparativists for their neglect of syntax, which to them was the most important part of grammar ; they were also in some measure right when they maintained that linguists to a great extent contented themselves with a superficial knowledge of the languages compared, which they studied more in grammars and glossaries than in living texts, and sometimes they would even exult when they found proof of this in solecisms in Bopp's Latin translations from Sanskrit, and even on the title-page of *Glossarium Sanscritum a Franzisco Bopp*. Classical scholars also looked askance at the growing interest in the changes of sounds, or, as it was then usual to say, of letters. But when they were apt here to quote the scriptural phrase about the letter that killeth, while the spirit giveth life, they overlooked the fact that Nature has rendered it impossible for anyone to penetrate to the mind of anyone else except through its outer manifestations, and that it is consequently impossible to get at the spirit of a language except through its sounds : phonology must therefore form the necessary basis and prerequisite of the scientific study of any group of languages. Still, it cannot be denied that sometimes comparative phonology was treated in such a mechanical way as partly to dehumanize the study of language.

[1] In Lefmann's book on Bopp, pp. 292 and 299, there are some interesting quotations on this point.

When we look back at this period in the history of linguistics, there are certain tendencies and characteristics that cannot fail to catch our attention. First we must mention the prominence given to Sanskrit, which was thought to be the unavoidable requirement of every comparative linguist. In explaining anything in any of the cognate languages the etymologist always turned first to Sanskrit words and Sanskrit forms. This standpoint is found even much later, for instance in Max Müller's *Inaugural Address* (1868, Ch. 19) : " Sanskrit certainly forms the only sound foundation of Comparative Philology, and it will always remain the only safe guide through all its intricacies. A comparative philologist without a knowledge of Sanskrit is like an astronomer without a knowledge of mathematics." A linguist of a later generation may be excused for agreeing rather with Ellis, who says (*Transact. Philol. Soc.*, 1873–4, 21) : "Almost in our own days came the discovery of Sanskrit, and philology proper began—but, alas ! at the wrong end. Now, here I run great danger of being misunderstood. Although for a scientific sifting of the nature of language I presume to think that beginning at Sanskrit was unfortunate, yet I freely admit that, had that language not been brought into Europe . . . our knowledge of language would have been in a poor condition indeed. . . . We are under the greatest obligations to those distinguished men who have undertaken to unravel its secrets and to show its connexion with the languages of Europe. Yet I must repeat that for the pure science of language, to begin with Sanskrit was as much beginning at the wrong end as it would have been to commence zoology with palæontology—the relations of life with the bones of the dead."

Next, Bopp and his nearest successors were chiefly occupied with finding likenesses between the languages treated and discovering things that united them. This was quite natural in the first stage of the new science, but sometimes led to one-sidedness, the characteristic individuality of each language being lost sight of, while forms from many countries and many times were mixed up in a hotch-potch. Rask, on account of his whole mental equipment, was less liable to this danger than most of his contemporaries ; but Pott was evidently right when he warned his fellow-students that their comparative linguistics should be supplemented by separative linguistics (*Zählmethode*, 229), as it has been to a great extent in recent years.

Still another feature of the linguistic science of these days is the almost exclusive occupation of the student with dead languages. It was quite natural that the earliest comparativists should first give their attention to the oldest stages of the languages compared, since these alone enabled them to prove the essential kinship between the different members of the great Aryan family. In Grimm's grammar nearly all the space is taken up with Gothic, Old High German, Old Norse, etc., and comparatively little is said about recent developments of the same languages. In Bopp's comparative grammar classical Greek and Latin are, of course, treated carefully, but Modern Greek and the Romanic languages are not mentioned (thus also in Schleicher's *Compendium* and in Brugmann's *Grammar*), such later developments being left to specialists who were more or less considered to be outside the sphere of Comparative Linguistics and even of the science of language in general, though it would have been a much more correct view to include them in both, and though much more could really be learnt of the life of language from these studies than from comparisons made in the spirit of Bopp.

The earlier stages of different languages, which were compared by linguists, were, of course, accessible only through the medium of writing ; we have seen that the early linguists spoke constantly of letters and not of sounds. But this vitiated their whole outlook on languages. These were scarcely ever studied at first-hand, and neither in Bopp nor in Grimm nor in Pott or Benfey do we find such first-hand observations of living spoken languages as play a great rôle in the writings of Rask and impart an atmosphere of soundness to his whole manner of looking at languages. If languages were called natural objects, they were not yet studied as such or by truly naturalistic methods.

When living dialects were studied, the interest constantly centred round the archaic traits in them ; every survival of an old form, every trace of old sounds that had been dropped in the standard speech, was greeted with enthusiasm, and the significance of these old characteristics greatly exaggerated, the general impression being that popular dialects were always much more conservative than the speech of educated people. It was reserved for a much later time to prove that this view is completely erroneous, and that popular dialects, in spite of many archaic details, are on the whole further developed than the various standard languages with their stronger tradition and literary reminiscences.

III.—§ 2. K. M. Rapp.

It was from this archæological point of view only that Grimm encouraged the study of dialects, but he expressly advised students not to carry the research too far in the direction of discriminating minutiæ of sounds, because these had little bearing on the history of language as he understood it. In this connexion we may

mention an episode in the history of early linguistics that is sympto-
matic. K. M. Rapp brought out his *Versuch einer Physiologie
der Sprache nebst historischer Entwickelung der abendländischen
Idiome nach physiologischen Grundsätzen* in four volumes (1836,
1839, 1840, 1841). A physiological examination into the nature
and classification of speech sounds was to serve only as the basis
of the historical part, the grandiose plan of which was to find out
how Greek, Latin and Gothic sounded, and then to pursue the
destinies of these sound systems through the Middle Ages (Byzan-
tine Greek, Old Provençal, Old French, Old Norse, Anglo-Saxon, Old
High German) to the present time (Modern Greek, Italian, Spanish,
etc., down to Low and High German, with different dialects).
To carry out this plan Rapp was equipped with no small knowledge
of the earlier stages of these languages and a not contemptible
first-hand observation of living languages. He relates how from
his childhood he had a " morbidly sharpened ear for all acoustic
impressions " ; he had early observed the difference between
dialectal and educated speech and taken an interest in foreign
languages, such as French, Italian and English. He visited Denmark, and there made the acquaintance of and became the pupil
of Rask ; he often speaks of him and his works in terms of the
greatest admiration. After his return he took up the study of
Jacob Grimm ; but though he speaks always very warmly about
the other parts of Grimm's work, Grimm's phonology disappointed
him. " Grimm's theory of letters I devoured with a ravenous
appetite for all the new things I had to learn from it, but also with
heartburning on account of the equally numerous things that
warred against the whole of my previous research with regard to
the nature of speech sounds ; fascinated though I was by what
I read, it thus made me incredibly miserable." He set to his
great task with enthusiasm, led by the conviction that " the historical material gives here only one side of the truth, and that the
living language in all its branches that have never been committed
to writing forms the other and equally important side which is
still far from being satisfactorily investigated." It is easy to
understand that Rapp came into conflict with Grimm's *Buch-
stabenlehre*, that had been based exclusively on written forms,
and Rapp was not afraid of expressing his unorthodox views in
what he himself terms " a violent and arrogating tone." No
wonder, therefore, that his book fell into disgrace with the leaders
of linguistics in Germany, who noticed its errors and mistakes,
which were indeed numerous and conspicuous, rather than the new
and sane ideas it contained. Rapp's work is extraordinarily little
known ; in Raumer's *Geschichte der germanischen Philologie* and
similar works it is not even mentioned, and when I disinterred it

from undeserved oblivion in my *Fonetik* (1897, p. 35 ; cf. *Die neueren Sprachen*, vol. xiii, 1904) it was utterly unknown to the German phoneticians of my acquaintance. Yet not only are its phonetic observations [1] deserving of praise, but still more its whole plan, based as it is on a thorough comprehension of the mutual relations of sounds and writing, which led Rapp to use phonetic transcription throughout, even in connected specimens both of living and dead languages ; that this is really the only way in which it is possible to obtain a comprehensive and living understanding of the sound-system of any language (as well as to get a clear perception of the extent of one's own ignorance of it !) has not yet been generally recognized. The science of language would have made swifter and steadier progress if Grimm and his successors had been able to assimilate the main thoughts of Rapp.

III.—§ 3. J. H. Bredsdorff.

Another (and still earlier) work that was overlooked at the time was the little pamphlet *Om Aarsagerne til Sprogenes Forandringer* (1821) by the Dane J. H. Bredsdorff. Bopp and Grimm never really asked themselves the fundamental question, How is it that language changes : what are the driving forces that lead in course of time to such far-reaching differences as those we find between Sanskrit and Latin, or between Latin and French ? Now, this is exactly the question that Bredsdorff treats in his masterly pamphlet. Like Rapp, he was a very good phonetician; but in the pamphlet that concerns us here he speaks not only of phonetic but of other linguistic changes as well. These he refers to the following causes, which he illustrates with well-chosen examples : (1) Mishearing and misunderstanding ; (2) misrecollection ; (3) imperfection of organs ; (4) indolence : to this he inclines to refer nine-tenths of all those changes in the pronunciation of a language that are not due to foreign influences ; (5) tendency towards analogy : here he gives instances from the speech of children and explains by analogy such phenomena as the extension of *s* to all genitives, etc. ; (6) the desire to be distinct ; (7) the need of expressing new ideas. He recognizes that there are changes that cannot be brought under any of these explanations, e.g. the Gothonic sound shift (cf. above, p. 43 note), and he emphasizes the many ways in which foreign nations or foreign languages may influence a language. Bredsdorff's explanations may not always be correct;

---

[1] For example, the correct appreciation of Scandinavian *o* sounds and especially the recognition of syllables without any vowel, for instance, in G. *mittel, schmeicheln,* E. *heaven, little*; this important truth was unnoticed by linguists till Sievers in 1876 called attention to it and Brugmann in 1877 used it in a famous article.

but what constitutes the deep originality of his little book is the way in which linguistic changes are always regarded in terms of human activity, chiefly of a psychological character. Here he was head and shoulders above his contemporaries ; in fact, most of Bredsdorff's ideas, such as the power of analogy, were the same that sixty years later had to fight so hard to be recognized by the leading linguists of that time.[1]

III.—§ 4. August Schleicher.

In Rapp, and even more in Bredsdorff, we get a whiff of the scientific atmosphere of a much later time ; but most of the linguists of the twenties and following decades (among whom A. F. Pott deserves to be specially named) moved in essentially the same grooves as Bopp and Grimm, and it will not be necessary here to deal in detail with their work.

August Schleicher (1821–68) in many ways marks the culmination of the first period of Comparative Linguistics, as well as the transition to a new period with different aims and, partially at any rate, a new method. His intimate knowledge of many languages, his great power of combination, his clear-cut and always lucid exposition—all this made him a natural leader, and made his books for many years the standard handbooks of linguistic science. Unlike Bopp and Grimm, he was exclusively a linguist, or, as he called it himself, ' glottiker,' and never tired of claiming for the science of linguistics (' glottik '), as opposed to philology, the rank of a separate natural science. Schleicher specialized in Slavonic and Lithuanian ; he studied the latter language in its own home and took down a great many songs and tales from the mouths of the peasants ; he was for some years a professor in the University of Prague, and there acquired a conversational knowledge of Czech ; he spoke Russian, too, and thus in contradistinction to Bopp and Grimm had a first-hand knowledge of more than one foreign language ; his interest in living speech is also manifested in his specimens of the dialect of his native town, *Volkstümliches aus Sonneberg*. When he was a child his father very severely insisted on the constant and correct use of the educated language at home ; but the boy, perhaps all the more on account of the paternal prohibition, was deeply attracted to the

---

[1] A young German linguist, to whom I sent the pamphlet early in 1886, wrote to me : "Wenn man sich den spass machte und das ding übersetzte mit der bemerkung, es sei vor vier jahren erschienen, wer würde einem nicht trauen ? Merkwürdig, dass solche sachen so unbemerkt, ' dem kleinen veilchen gleich,' dahinschwinden können." A short time afterwards the pamphlet was reprinted with a short preface by Vilh. Thomsen (Copenhagen, 1886).

popular dialect he heard from his playfellows and to the fascinating folklore of the old townspeople, which he was later to take down and put into print. In the preface he says that the acquisition of foreign tongues is rendered considerably easier through the habit of speaking two dialects from childhood.

What makes Schleicher particularly important for the purposes of this volume is the fact that in a long series of publications he put forth not only details of his science, but original and comprehensive views on the fundamental questions of linguistic theory, and that these had great influence on the linguistic philosophy of the following decades. He was, perhaps, the most consistent as well as one of the clearest of linguistic thinkers, and his views therefore deserve to be examined in detail and with the greatest care.

Apart from languages, Schleicher was deeply interested both in philosophy and in natural science, especially botany. From these he fetched many of the weapons of his armoury, and they coloured the whole of his theory of language. In his student days at Tübingen he became an enthusiastic adherent of the philosophy of Hegel, and not even the Darwinian sympathies and views of which he became a champion towards the end of his career made him abandon the doctrines of his youth. As for science, he says that naturalists make us understand that in science nothing is of value except facts established through strictly objective observation and the conclusions based on such facts—this is a lesson that he thinks many of his colleagues would do well to take to heart. There can be no doubt that Schleicher in his practice followed a much more rigorous and sober method than his predecessors, and that his *Compendium* in that respect stands far above Bopp's *Grammar*. In his general reasonings on the nature of language, on the other hand, Schleicher did not always follow the strict principles of sober criticism, being, as we shall now see, too dependent on Hegelian philosophy, and also on certain dogmatic views that he had inherited from previous German linguists, from Schlegel downwards.

The Introductions to Schleicher's two first volumes are entirely Hegelian, though with a characteristic difference, for in the first he says that the changes to be seen in the realm of languages are decidedly historical and in no way resemble the changes that we may observe in nature, for " however manifold these may be, they never show anything but a circular course that repeats itself continually " (Hegel), while in language, as in everything mental, we may see new things that have never existed before. One generation of animals or plants is like another ; the skill of animals has no history, as human art has ; language is specifically human and mental : its development is therefore analogous to history, for in both we see a continual progress to new phases. In Schleicher's second volume, however, this view is expressly rejected in its main part, because Schleicher now wants to emphasize the natural character of language : it is true, he now says, that language shows a ' werden ' which may be termed history in the wider sense of this word, but which is found in its purest form in nature ; for instance, in the growing of a plant. Language belongs to the natural sphere, not to the sphere of free mental activity, and this must be our starting-point if we would discover the method of linguistic science (ii. 21).

It would, of course, be possible to say that the method of linguistic science is that of natural science, and yet to maintain that the object of linguistics is different from that of natural science, but Schleicher more and more tends to identify the two, and when he was attacked for saying, in his pamphlet on the Darwinian theory, that languages were material things, real natural objects, he wrote in defence *Ueber die bedeutung der sprache für die naturgeschichte des menschen*, which is highly characteristic as the culminating point of the materialistic way of looking at languages. The activity, he says, of any organ, e.g. one of the organs of digestion, or the brain or muscles, is dependent on the constitution of that organ. The different ways in which different species, nay even different individuals, walk are evidently conditioned by the structure of the limbs ; the activity or function of the organ is, as it were, nothing but an aspect of the organ itself, even if it is not always possible by means of the knife or microscope of the scientist to demonstrate the material cause of the phenomenon. What is true of the manner of walking is true of language as well ; for language is nothing but the result, perceptible through the ear, of the action of a complex of material substances in the structure of the brain and of the organs of speech, with their nerves, bones, muscles, etc. Anatomists, however, have not yet been able to demonstrate differences in the structures of these organs corresponding to differences of nationality—to discriminate, that is, the organs of a Frenchman (*quâ* Frenchman) from those of a German (*quâ* German). Accordingly, as the chemist can only arrive at the elements which compose the sun by examining the light which it emits, while the source of that light remains inaccessible to him, so must we be content to study the nature of languages, not in their material antecedents but in their audible manifestations. It makes no great difference, however, for " the two things stand to each other as cause and effect, as substance and phenomenon : a philosopher [i.e. a Hegelian] would say that they are identical."

Now I, for one, fail to understand how this can be what Schleicher believes it to be, " a refutation of the objection that language is nothing but a consequence of the activity of these organs." The sun exists independently of the human observer; but there could be no such thing as language if there was not besides the speaker a listener who might become a speaker in his turn. Schleicher speaks continually in his pamphlet as if structural differences in the brain and organs of speech were the real language, and as if it were only for want of an adequate method of examining this hidden structure that we had to content ourselves with studying language in its outward manifestation as audible speech. But this is certainly on the face of it preposterous, and scarcely needs any serious refutation. If the proof of the pudding is in the eating, the proof of a language must be in the hearing and understanding, but in order to be heard words must first be spoken, and in these two activities (that of producing and that of perceiving sounds) the real essence of language must consist, and these two activities are the primary (or why not the exclusive?) object of the science of language.

Schleicher goes on to meet another objection that may be made to his view of the 'substantiality of language,' namely, that drawn from the power of learning other languages. Schleicher doubts the possibility of learning another language to perfection; he would admit this only in the case of a man who exchanged his mother-tongue for another in his earliest youth; "but then he becomes by that very fact a different being from what he was: brain and organs of speech develop in another direction." If Mr. So-and-So is said to speak and write German, English and French equally well, Schleicher first inclines to doubt the fact; and then, granting that the same individual may "be at the same time a German, a Frenchman and an Englishman," he asks us to remember that all these three languages belong to the same family and may, from a broader point of view, be termed species of the same language; but he denies the possibility of anyone's being equally at home in Chinese and German, or in Arabic and Hottentot, etc., because these languages are totally different in their innermost essence. (But what of bilingual children in Finland, speaking Swedish and Finnish, or in Greenland, speaking Danish and Eskimo, or in Java, speaking Dutch and Malay?) Schleicher has to admit that our organs are to some extent flexible and capable of acquiring activities that they had not at first; but one definite function is and remains nevertheless the only natural one, and thus "the possibility of a man's acquiring foreign languages more or less perfectly is no objection to our seeing the material basis of language in the structure of the brain and organs of speech."

Even if we admit that Schleicher is so far right that in nearly all (or all?) cases of bilingualism one language comes more naturally than the other, he certainly exaggerates the difference, which is always one of degree ; and at any rate his final conclusion is wrong, for we might with the same amount of justice say that a man who has first learned to play the piano has acquired the structure of brain and fingers peculiar to a pianist, and that it is then unnatural for him also to learn to play the violin, because that would imply a different structure of these organs. In all these cases we have to do with a definite proficiency or skill, which can only be obtained by constant practice, though of course one man may be better predisposed by nature for it than another ; but then it is also the fact that people who speak no foreign language attain to very different degrees of proficiency in the use of their mother-tongue. It cannot be said too emphatically that we have here a fundamental question, and that Schleicher's view can never lead to a true conception of what language is, or to a real insight into its changes and historical development.

Schleicher goes on to say that the classification of mankind into races should not be based on the formation of the skull or on the character of the hair, or any such external criteria, as they are by no means constant, but rather on language, because this is a thoroughly constant criterion. This alone would give a perfectly natural system, one, for instance, in which all Turks would be classed together, while otherwise the Osmanli Turk belongs to the 'Caucasian' race and the so-called Tataric Turks to the 'Mongolian' race ; on the other hand, the Magyar and the Basque are not physically to be distinguished from the Indo-European, though their languages are widely dissimilar. According to Schleicher, therefore, the natural system of languages is also the natural system of mankind, for language is closely connected with the whole higher life of men, which is therefore taken into consideration in and with their language. In this book I am not concerned with the ethnographical division of mankind into races, and I therefore must content myself with saying that the very examples adduced by Schleicher seem to me to militate against his theory that a division of mankind based on language is the natural one : are we to reckon the Basque's son, who speaks nothing but French (or Spanish) as belonging to a different race from his father ? And does not Schleicher contradict himself when on p. 16 he writes that language is " ein völlig constantes merkmal," and p. 20 that it is " in fortwährender veränderung begriffen " ? So far as I see, Schleicher never expressly says that he thinks that the physical structure conditioning the structure of a man's language is hereditary, though some of his expressions point that way, and that may be what he means by the expression ' constant.' In other places (Darw. 25, Bed. 24) he allows external conditions of life to exercise some influence on the character of a language, as when languages of neighbouring peoples are similar (Aryans and Semites, for example, are the only nations possessing flexional languages). On such points, however, he gives only a few hints and suggestions.

III.—§ 5. Classification of Languages.

In the question of the classification of languages Schleicher introduces a deductive element from his strong preoccupation with Hegelian ideas. Hegel everywhere moves in trilogies ; Schleicher therefore must have three classes, and consequently has to tack together two of Pott's four classes (agglutinating and incorporating) ; then he is able philosophically to deduce the tripartition. For language consists in *meaning* (bedeutung ; matter, contents, root) and *relation* (beziehung ; form), tertium non datur. As it would be a sheer impossibility for a language to express form only, we obtain three classes :

I. Here meaning is the only thing indicated by sound ; relation is merely suggested by word-position : isolating languages.

II. Both meaning and relation are expressed by sound, but the formal elements are visibly tacked on to the root, which is itself invariable : agglutinating languages.

III. The elements of meaning and of relation are fused together or absorbed into a higher unity, the root being susceptible of inward modification as well as of affixes to denote form : flexional languages.

Schleicher employs quasi-mathematical formulas to illustrate these three classes : if we denote a root by R, a prefix by p and a suffix by s, and finally use a raised x to denote an inner modification, we see that in the isolated languages we have nothing but R (a sentence may be represented by $R\,R\,R\ldots$), a word in the second class has the formula $R\,s$ or $p\,R$ or $p\,R\,s$, but in the third class we may have $p\,R^x\,s$ (or $R^x\,s$).

Now, according to Schleicher the three classes of languages are not only found simultaneously in the tongues of our own day, but they represent three stages of linguistic development ; " to the *nebeneinander* of the system corresponds the *nacheinander* of history." Beyond the flexional stage no language can attain ; the symbolic denotation of relation by flexion is the highest accomplishment of language ; speech has here effectually realized its object, which is to give a faithful phonetic image of thought. But before a language can become flexional it must have passed through an isolating and an agglutinating period. Is this theory borne out by historical facts ? Can we trace back any of the existing flexional languages to agglutination and isolation ? Schleicher himself answers this question in the negative : the earliest Latin was of as good a flexional type as are the modern Romanic languages. This would seem a sort of contradiction in terms ; but the orthodox Hegelian is ready with an answer to any objection ; he has the word of his master that History cannot begin till the human spirit becomes " conscious of its own freedom," and this consciousness is only possible after the complete development of language. The formation of Language and History are accordingly successive stages of human activity. Moreover, as history and historiography, i.e. literature, come into existence simultaneously, Schleicher is enabled to express the same idea in a way that " is only seemingly paradoxical," namely, that the development of language is brought to a conclusion as soon as literature makes its appearance ; this is a crisis after which language remains fixed ; language has now become a means, instead of being the aim, of intellectual activity. We never meet with any language that is developing or that has become more perfect ; in historical times all languages move only downhill ; linguistic history means decay of languages as such, subjugated as they are through the gradual evolution of the mind to greater freedom.

The reader of the above survey of previous classifications will easily see that in the matter itself Schleicher adds very little of his own. Even the expressions, which are here given throughout in Schleicher's own words, are in some cases recognizable as identical with, or closely similar to, those of earlier scholars.

He made one coherent system out of ideas of classification and development already found in others. What is new is the philosophical substructure of Hegelian origin, and there can be no doubt that Schleicher imagined that by this addition he contributed very much towards giving stability and durability to the whole system. And yet this proved to be the least stable and durable part of the structure, and as a matter of fact the Hegelian reasoning is not repeated by a single one of those who give their adherence to the classification. Nor can it be said to carry conviction, and undoubtedly it has seemed to most linguists at the same time too rigid and too unreal to have any importance.

But apart from the philosophical argument the classification proved very successful in the particular shape it had found in Schleicher. Its adoption into two such widely read works as Max Müller's and Whitney's Lectures on the Science of Language contributed very much to the popularity of the system, though the former's attempt at ascribing to the tripartition a sociological importance by saying that juxtaposition (isolation) is characteristic of the 'family stage,' agglutination of 'the nomadic stage' and amalgamation (flexion) of the 'political stage' of human society was hardly taken seriously by anybody.

The chief reasons for the popularity of this classification are not far to seek. It is easy of handling and appeals to the natural fondness for clear-cut formulas through its specious appearance of regularity and rationality. Besides, it flatters widespread prejudices in so far as it places the two groups of languages highest that are spoken by those nations which have culturally and religiously exercised the deepest influence on the civilization of the world, Aryans and Semites. Therefore also Pott's view, according to which the incorporating or 'polysynthetic' American languages possess the same characteristics that distinguish flexion as against agglutination, only in a still higher degree, is generally tacitly discarded, for obviously it would not do to place some languages of American Indians higher than Sanskrit or Greek. But when these are looked upon as the very flower of linguistic development it is quite natural to regard the modern languages of Western Europe as degenerate corruptions of the ancient more highly flexional languages ; this is in perfect keeping with the prevalent admiration for classical antiquity and with the belief in a far past golden age. Arguments such as these may not have been consciously in the minds of the framers of the ordinary classification, but there can be no doubt that they have been unconsciously working in favour of the system, though very little thought seems to be required to show the fallacy of the assumption that high civilization has any intrinsic and necessary connexion with the *grammatical* construction of the language spoken by the race or nation concerned. No language of modern Europe presents the flexional type in a purer shape than Lithuanian, where we find preserved nearly the same grammatical system as in old Sanskrit, yet no one would assert that the culture of Lithuanian peasants is higher than that of Shakespeare, whose language has lost an enormous amount of the old flexions. Culture and language must be appraised separately, each on its own merits and independently of the other.

From a purely linguistic point of view there are many objections to the usual classification, and it will be well here to bring them together, though this will mean an interruption of the historical survey which is the main object of these chapters.

First let us look upon the tripartition as purporting a comprehensive classification of languages as existing side by side without any regard to historic development (the *nebeneinander* of Schleicher). Here it does not seem to be an ideal manner of classifying a great many objects to establish three classes of such different dimensions that the first comprises only Chinese and some other related languages of the Far East, and the third only two families of languages, while the second includes hundreds of unrelated languages of the most heterogeneous character. It seems certain that the languages of Class I represent one definite type of linguistic structure, and it may be that Aryan and Semitic should be classed together on account of the similarity of their structure, though this is by no means quite certain and has been denied (by Bopp, and in recent times by Porzezinski); but what is indubitable is that the ' agglutinating ' class is made to comprehend languages of the most diverse type, even if we follow Pott and exclude from this class all incorporating languages. Finnish is always mentioned as a typically agglutinative language, yet there we meet with such declensional forms as nominative *vesi* ' water,' *toinen* ' second,' partitive *vettä, toista,* genitive *veden, toisen,* and such verbal forms as *sido-n* ' I bind,' *sido-t* ' thou bindest,' *sito-o* ' he binds,' and the three corresponding persons in the plural, *sido-mme, sido-tte, sito-vat.* Here we are far from having one unchangeable root to which endings have been glued, for the root itself undergoes changes before the endings. In Kiyombe (Congo) the perfect of verbs is in many cases formed by means of a vowel change that is a complete parallel to the apophony in English *drink, drank,* thus *vanga* ' do,' perfect *venge, twala* ' bring,' perfect *twele* or *twede,* etc. (*Anthropos,* ii. p. 761). Examples like these show that flexion, in whatever way we may define this term, is not the prerogative of the Aryans and Semites, but may be found in other nations as well. ' Agglutination ' is either too vague a term to be used in classification, or else, if it is taken strictly according to the usual definition, it is too definite to comprise many of the languages which are ordinarily reckoned to belong to the second class.

It will be seen, also, that those writers who aim at giving descriptions of a variety of human tongues, or of them all, do not content themselves with the usual three classes, but have a greater number. This began with Steinthal, who in various works tried to classify languages partly from geographical, partly from structural points of view, without, however, arriving at any definite or consistent system. Friedrich Müller, in his great *Grundriss der Sprachwissenschaft,* really gives up the psychological or structural division of languages, distributing the more than hundred different languages that he describes among twelve races of mankind, characterized chiefly by external criteria that have nothing to do with language. Misteli establishes six main types : I. Incorporating. II. Root-isolating. III. Stem-isolating. IV. Affixing (Anreihende). V. Agglutinating. VI. Flexional. These he also distributes so as to form four classes : (1) languages with sentence-words : I ; (2) languages with no words : II, III and IV ; (3) languages with apparent words : V ; and (4) languages with real words : VI. But the latter division had better be left alone ; it turns on the intricate question "What constitutes a word ? " and ultimately depends on the usual depreciation of ' inferior races ' and corresponding exaltation of our own race, which is alone reputed capable of possessing ' real words.' I do not see why we should not recognize that the vocables of Greenlandic, Malay, Kafir or Finnish are just as ' real ' words as any in Hebrew or Latin.

Our final result, then, is that the tripartition is insufficient and inadequate to serve as a comprehensive classification of languages actually existing. Nor shall we wonder at this if we see the way in which the theory began historically in an *obiter dictum* of Fr. v. Schlegel at a time when the inner structure of only a few languages had been properly studied, and if we consider the lack of clearness and definiteness inherent in such notions as agglutination and flexion, which are nevertheless made the corner-stones of the whole system. We therefore must go back to the wise saying of Humboldt quoted on p. 59, that the structural diversities of languages are too great for us to classify them comprehensively.

In a subsequent part of this work I shall deal with the tripartition as representing three successive stages in the development of such languages as our own (the *nacheinander* of Schleicher), and try to show that Schleicher's view is not borne out by the facts of linguistic history, which give us a totally different picture of development.

From both points of view, then, I think that the classification here considered deserves to be shelved among the hasty generalizations in which the history of every branch of science is unfortunately so rich.

III.—§ 6. Reconstruction.

Probably Schleicher's most original and important contribution to linguistics was his reconstruction of the Proto-Aryan language, *die indogermanische ursprache.* The possibility of inferentially constructing this parent language, which to Sanskrit, Greek, Latin, Gothic, etc., was what Latin was to Italian, Spanish, French, etc., was early in his thoughts (see quotations illustrating the gradual growth of the idea in Oertel, p. 39 f.), but it was not till the first edition of his *Compendium* that he carried it out in detail, giving there for each separate chapter (vowels, consonants roots, stem-formation, declension, conjugation) first the Proto-Aryan forms and then those actually found in the different languages, from which the former were inferred. This arrangement has the advantage that the reader everywhere sees the historical evolution in the natural order, beginning with the oldest and then proceeding to the later stages, just as the Romanic scholar begins with Latin and then takes in successive stages Old French, Modern French, etc. But in the case of Proto-Aryan this procedure is apt to deceive the student and make him take these primitive forms as something certain, whose existence reposes on just as good evidence as the forms found in Sanskrit literature or in German or English as spoken in our own days. When he finds some forms given first and used to *explain* some others, there is some danger of his forgetting that the forms given first have a quite different status to the others, and that their only *raison d'être* is the desire of a modern linguist to explain existing forms in related languages which present certain similarities as originating from a common original form, which he does not find in his texts and has, therefore, to reconstruct. But apart from this there can be no doubt that the reconstruction of older forms (and the ingenious device, due to Schleicher, of denoting such forms by means of a preposed asterisk to distinguish them from forms actually found) has been in many ways beneficial to historical grammar. Only it may be questioned whether Schleicher did not go too far when he wished to base the whole grammar of all the Aryan languages on such reconstructions, instead of using them now and then to explain single facts.

Schleicher even ventured (and in this he seems to have had no follower) to construct an entire little fable in primitive Aryan: see "Eine fabel in indogermanischer ursprache," *Beiträge zur vergl. sprachforschung*, 5. 206 (1868). In the introductory remarks he complains of the difficulty of such attempts, chiefly because of the almost complete lack of particles capable of being inferred from the existing languages, but he seems to have entertained no doubt about the phonetic and grammatical forms of the words he employed. As the fable is not now commonly known, I give it here, with Schleicher's translation, as a document of this period of comparative linguistics.

AVIS AKVASAS KA

Avis, jasmin varna na ā ast, dadarka akvams, tam, **vāgham garum** vaghantam, tam, bhāram magham, tam, manum āku bharantam. Avis akvabhjams ā vavakat: kard **aghnutai mai vidanti manum** akvams agantam.

6

Akvāsas ā vavakant : krudhi avai, kard aghnutai vividvant-
svas : manus patis varnām avisāms karnanti svabhjam gharmam
vastram avibhjams ka varnā na asti.

Tat kukruvants avis agram ā bhugat.

[DAS] SCHAF UND [DIE] ROSSE

[Ein] schaf, [auf] welchem wolle nicht war (ein geschorenes
schaf) sah rosse, das [einen] schweren wagen fahrend, das [eine]
grosse last, das [einen] menschen schnell tragend. [Das] schaf
sprach [zu den] rossen : [Das] herz wird beengt [in] mir (es thut
mir herzlich leid), sehend [den] menschen [die] rosse treibend.

[Die] rosse sprachen : Höre schaf, [das] herz wird beengt [in
den] gesehen-habenden (es thut uns herzlich leid, da wir wissen) :
[der] mensch, [der] herr macht [die] wolle [der] schafe [zu einem]
warmen kleide [für] sich und [den] schafen ist nicht wolle (die
schafe aber haben keine wolle mehr, sie werden geschoren ; es
geht ihnen noch schlechter als den rossen).

Dies gehört habend bog (entwich) [das] schaf [auf das] feld
(es machte sich aus dem staube).

The question here naturally arises : Is it possible in the way
initiated by Schleicher to reconstruct extinct linguistic stages,
and what degree of probability can be attached to the forms thus
created by linguists ? The answer certainly must be that in some
instances the reconstruction may have a very strong degree of
probability, namely, if the data on which it is based are unambiguous and the form to be reconstructed is not far removed
from that or those actually found ; but that otherwise any reconstruction becomes doubtful, and naturally the more so according
to the extent of the reconstruction (as when a whole text is constructed) and to the distance in time that intervenes between the
known and the unknown stage. If we look at the genitives of
Lat. *genus* and Gr. *génos*, which are found as *generis* and *génous*,
it is easy to see that both presuppose a form with *s* between two
vowels, as we see a great many intervocalic *s*'s becoming *r* in Latin
and disappearing in Greek ; but when Schleicher gives as the
prototype of both (and of corresponding forms in the other languages) Aryan *ganasas*, he oversteps the limits of the permissible
in so far as he ascribes to the vowels definite sounds not really
warranted by the known forms. If we knew the modern Scandinavian languages and English only, we should not hesitate to
give to the Proto-Gothonic genitive of the word for ' mother '
the ending -*s*, cf. Dan. *moders*, E. *mother's* ; but G. *der mutter*
suffices to show that the conclusion is not safe, and as a matter
of fact, both in Old Norse and in Old English the genitive of this

word is without an *s*. An analogous case is presented when
Schleicher reconstructs the nom. of the word for ' father ' as
patars, because he presupposes *-s* as the invariable sign of every
nom. sg. masc., although in this particular word not a single one
of the old languages has *-s* in the nominative. All Schleicher's
reconstructions are based on the assumption that Primitive Aryan
had a very simple structure, only few consonant and fewer vowel
sounds, and great regularity in morphology ; but, as we shall see,
this assumption is completely gratuitous and was exploded only
a few years after his death. Gabelentz (Spr 182), therefore, was
right when he said, with a certain irony, that the Aryan *ursprache*
had changed beyond recognition in the short time between
Schleicher and Brugmann. The moral to be drawn from all
this seems to be that hypothetical and starred forms should be
used sparingly and with the extremest caution.

With regard to inferential forms denoted by a star, the following note may not be out of place here. Their purely theoretical
character is not always realized. An example will illustrate what
I mean. If etymological dictionaries give as the origin of F.
ménage (OF. *maisnage*) a Latin form **mansionaticum*, the etymology
may be correct although such a Latin word may never at any
time have been uttered. The word was framed at some date,
no one knows exactly when, from the word which at various
times had the forms (acc.) *mansionem*, **masione*, *maison*, by
means of the ending which at first had the form *-aticum* (as
in *viaticum*), and finally (through several intermediate stages)
became *-age*; but at what stage of each the two elements met to
make the word which eventually became *ménage*, no one can tell,
so that the only thing really asserted is that *if* the word had been
formed at a very early date (which is far from probable) it would
have been *mansionaticum*. It would, therefore, perhaps be more
correct to say that the word is from *mansione + -aticum*.

III.—§ 7. Curtius, Madvig, and Specialists.

Second only to Schleicher among the linguists of those days
was Georg Curtius (1820–85), at one time his colleague in the
University of Prague. Curtius's special study was Greek, and his
books on the Greek verb and on Greek etymology cleared up a
great many doubtful points ; he also contributed very much to
bridge the gulf between classical philology and Aryan linguistics.
His views on general questions were embodied in the book *Zur
Chronologie der indogermanischen Sprachforschung* (1873). While
Schleicher died when his fame was at its highest and his theories
were seemingly victorious in all the leading circles, Curtius had

the misfortune to see a generation of younger men, including some
of his own best disciples, such as Brugmann, advance theories that
seemed to him to be in conflict with the most essential principles
of his cherished science ; and though he himself, like Schleicher,
had always been in favour of a stricter observance of sound-
laws than his predecessors, his last book was a polemic against
those younger scholars who carried the same point to the excess
of admitting no exceptions at all, who believed in innumerable
analogical formations even in the old languages, and whose reconstructions of primitive forms appeared to the old man as
deprived of that classical beauty of the *ursprache* which was
represented in his own and Schleicher's works (*Zur Kritik der
neuesten Sprachforschung*, 1885). But this is anticipating.

If Curtius was a comparativist with a sound knowledge of
classical philology, Johan Nikolai Madvig was pre-eminently a
classical philologist who took a great interest in general linguistics
and brought his critical acumen and sober common sense to bear
on many of the problems that exercised the minds of his contemporaries. He was opposed to everything of a vague and mystical
nature in the current theories of language and disliked the tendency
of some scholars to find deep-lying mysterious powers at the root
of linguistic phenomena. But he probably went too far in his
rationalism, for example, when he entirely denied the existence
of the sound-symbolism on which Humboldt had expatiated.
He laid much stress on the identity of the linguistic faculty in
all ages : the first speakers had no more intention than people
to-day of creating anything systematic or that would be good
for all times and all occasions—they could have no other object
in view than that of making themselves understood at the moment ;
hence the want of system which we find everywhere in languages :
a different number of cases in singular and plural, different endings,
etc. Madvig did not escape some inconsistencies, as when he
himself would explain the use of the soft vowel *a* to denote the
feminine gender by a kind of sound-symbolism, or when he thought
it possible to determine in what order the different grammatical
ideas presented themselves to primitive man (tense relation first
in the verb, number before case in the noun). He attached too
little value to phonological and etymological research, but on
the whole his views were sounder than many which were set forth
on the same subjects at the time ; his papers, however, were very
little known, partly because they were written in Danish, partly
because his style was extremely heavy and difficult, and when
he finally brought out his *Kleine philologische schriften* in German
(1875), he expressed his regret in the preface at finding that
many of the theories he had put forward years before in Danish

had in the meantime been independently arrived at by Whitney, who had had the advantage of expressing them in a world-language.

One of the most important features of the period with which we are here dealing is the development of a number of special branches of historical linguistics on a comparative basis. Curtius's work on Greek might be cited as one example ; in the same way there were specialists in Sanskrit (Westergaard and Benfey among others), in Slavonic (Miklosich and Schleicher), in Keltic (Zeuss), etc. Grimm had numerous followers in the Gothonic or Germanic field, while in Romanic philology there was an active and flourishing school, headed by Friedrich Diez, whose *Grammatik der romanischen Sprachen* and *Etymologisches Wörterbuch der romanischen Sprachen* were perhaps the best introduction to the methodical study of linguistics that anyone could desire ; the writer of these lines looks back with the greatest gratitude to that period of his youth when he had the good fortune to make the acquaintance of these truly classical works. Everything was so well arranged, so carefully thought out and so lucidly explained, that one had everywhere the pleasant feeling that one was treading on firm ground, the more so as the basis of the whole was not an artificially constructed nebulous *ursprache*, but the familiar forms and words of an historical language. Here one witnessed the gradual differentiation of Latin into seven or eight distinct languages, whose development it was possible to follow century by century in well-authenticated texts. The picture thus displayed before one's eyes of actual linguistic growth in all domains—sounds, forms, word-formation, syntax—and (a very important corollary) of the interdependence of these domains, could not but leave a very strong impression—not merely enthusiasm for what had been achieved here, but also a salutary skepticism of theories in other fields which had not a similarly solid basis.

III.—§ 8. Max Müller and Whitney.

Working, as we have seen, in many fields, linguists had now brought to light a shoal of interesting facts affecting a great many languages and had put forth valuable theories to explain these facts ; but most of their work remained difficult of access except to the specialist, and very little was done by the experts to impart to educated people in general those results of the new science which might be enjoyed without deeper study. But in 1861 Max Müller gave the first series of those *Lectures on the Science of Language* which, in numerous editions, did more than anything else to popularize linguistics and served to initiate a great many students into our science. In many ways these lectures were excellently adapted for this purpose, for the author had a certain knack of selecting interesting illustrations and of presenting his subject in a way that tended to create the same enthusiasm for it that he felt himself. But his arguments do not bear a close inspection. Too often, after stating a problem, he is found to fly off at a tangent and to forget what he has set out to prove for the sake of an interesting etymology or a clever paradox. He gives an uncritical acceptance to many of Schleicher's leading ideas ; thus, the science of linguistics is to him a physical science and has nothing to do with philology, which is an historical science. If, however, we look at the book itself, we shall find that everything that he counts on to secure the interest of his reader, everything that made his lectures so popular, is really non-naturalistic : all those brilliant exposés of word-history are really like historical anecdotes in a book on social evolution ; they may have some bearing on the fundamental problems, but these are rarely or never treated as real problems of natural science. Nor does he, when taken to task, maintain his view very seriously, but partly retracts it and half-heartedly ensconces himself behind the dictum that everything depends on the definition you give of " physical science " (see especially Ch 234, 442, 497)—thus calling forth Whitney's retort that " the implication here is that our author has a right at his own good pleasure to lay down such a definition of a physical science as should make the name properly applicable to the study of this particular one among the products of human capacities. . . . So he may prove that a whale is a fish, if you only allow him to define what a fish is " (M 23 f.).

Though Schleicher and Max Müller in their own day had few followers in defining linguistics as a natural or physical science— the opposite view was taken, for instance, by Curtius (K 154), Madvig and Whitney—there can be no doubt that the naturalistic point of view practically, though perhaps chiefly unconsciously, had wide-reaching effects on the history of linguistic science. It was intimately connected with the problems chiefly investigated and with the way in which they were treated. From Grimm through Pott to Schleicher and his contemporaries we see a growing interest in phonological comparisons ; more and more " sound- laws " were discovered, and those found were more and more rigorously applied, with the result that etymological investigation was attended with a degree of exactness of which former genera- tions had no idea. But as these phonological studies were not, as a rule, based on a real, penetrating insight into the nature of speech-sounds, the work of the etymologist tended more and more to be purely mechanical, and the science of language was to a great extent deprived of those elements which are more intimately connected with the human 'soul.' Isolated vowels and consonants were compared, isolated flexional forms and isolated words were treated more and more in detail and explained by other isolated forms and words in other languages, all of them being like dead leaves shaken off a tree rather than parts of a living and moving whole. The speaking individual and the speaking community were too much lost sight of. Too often comparativists gained a considerable acquaintance with the sound-laws and the grammatical forms of various languages without knowing much about those languages themselves, or at any rate without possessing any degree of familiarity with them. Schleicher was not blind to the danger of this. A short time before his death he brought out an *Indogermanische Chrestomathie* (Weimar, 1869), and in the preface he justifies his book by saying that "it is of great value, besides learning the grammar, to be acquainted, however slightly, with the languages themselves. For a comparative grammar of related languages lays stress on what is common to a language and its sisters ; consequently, the languages may appear more alike than they are in reality, and their idiosyncrasies may be thrown into the shade. Linguistic specimens form, therefore, an indispensable supplement to comparative grammar." Other and even more weighty reasons might have been adduced, for grammar is after all only one side of a language, and it is certainly the best plan, if one wants to understand and appreciate the position of any language, to start with some connected texts of tolerable length, and only afterwards to see how its forms are related to and may be explained by those of other languages.

Though the mechanical school of linguists, with whom historical and comparative phonology was more and more an end in itself, prevailed to a great extent, the trend of a few linguists was different. Among these one must especially mention Heymann Steinthal, who drew his inspiration from Humboldt and devoted numerous works to the psychology of language. Unfortunately, Steinthal was greatly inferior to Schleicher in clearness and consistency of thought : "When I read a work of Steinthal's, and even many parts of Humboldt, I feel as if walking through shifting clouds," Max Müller remarks, with good reason, in a letter (*Life*, i. 256). This obscurity, in connexion with the remoteness of Steinthal's studies, which ranged from Chinese to the language of the Mande negroes, but paid little regard to European languages, prevented him from exerting any powerful influence on the linguistic thought of his generation, except perhaps through his emphatic assertion of the truth that language can only be understood and explained by means of psychology : his explanation of syntactic attraction paved the way for much in Paul's *Prinzipien*.

The leading exponent of general linguistics after the death of Schleicher was the American William Dwight Whitney, whose books, *Language and the Study of Language* (first ed. 1867) and its replica, *The Life and Growth of Language* (1875), were translated into several languages and were hardly less popular than those of his antagonist, Max Müller. Whitney's style is less brilliant than Max Müller's, and he scorns the cheap triumphs which the latter gains by the multiplication of interesting illustrations; he never wearies of running down Müller's paradoxes and inconsistencies,[1] from which he himself was spared by his greater general solidity and sobriety of thought. The chief point of divergence between them was, as already indicated, that Whitney looked upon language as a human institution that has grown slowly out of the necessity for mutual understanding; he was opposed to all kinds of mysticism, and words to him were conventional signs— not, of course, that he held that there ever was a gathering of people that settled the meaning of each word, but in the sense of " resting on a mutual understanding or a community of habit," no matter how brought about. But in spite of all differences between the two they are in many respects alike, when viewed from the coign of vantage of the twentieth century : both give expression to the best that had been attained by fifty or sixty years of painstaking activity to elucidate the mysteries of speech, and especially of Aryan words and forms, and neither of them was deeply original enough to see through many of the fallacies of the young science. Consequently, their views on the structure of Proto-Aryan, on roots and their rôle, on the building-up and decay of the form-system, are essentially the same as those of their contemporaries, and many of their theories have now crumbled away, including much of what they probably thought firmly rooted for all time.

[1] In numerous papers in *North Am. Review* and elsewhere, and finally in the pamphlet *Max Müller and the Science of Language, a Criticism* (New York, 1892). Müller's reply to the earlier attacks is found in *Chips from a German Workshop*, vol. iv.

CHAPTER IV

END OF NINETEENTH CENTURY

§ 1. Achievements about 1870.   § 2. New Discoveries.   § 3. Phonetic Laws
and Analogy.   § 4. General Tendencies.

IV.—§ 1. Achievements about 1870.

IN works of this period one frequently meets with expressions
of pride and joy in the wonderful results that had been achieved
in comparative linguistics in the course of a few decades. Thus
Max Müller writes : " All this becomes clear and intelligible by
the light of Comparative Grammar ; anomalies vanish, exceptions prove the rule, and we perceive more plainly every day
how in language, as elsewhere, the conflict between the freedom
claimed by each individual and the resistance offered by the
community at large establishes in the end a reign of law most
wonderful, yet perfectly rational and intelligible "; and again :
" There is nothing accidental, nothing irregular, nothing without
a purpose and meaning in any part of Greek or Latin grammar.
No one who has once discovered this hidden life of language,
no one who has once found out that what seemed to be merely
anomalous and whimsical in language is but, as it were, a
petrification of thought, of deep, curious, poetical, philosophical
thought, will ever rest again till he has descended as far as he
can descend into the ancient shafts of human speech," etc.
(Ch 41 f.). Whitney says : " The difference between the old
haphazard style of etymologizing and the modern scientific
method lies in this : that the latter, while allowing everything
to be theoretically possible, accepts nothing as actual which
is not proved by sufficient evidence ; it brings to bear upon
each individual case a wide circle of related facts ; it im-
poses upon the student the necessity of extended comparison
and cautious deduction ; it makes him careful to inform himself
as thoroughly as circumstances allow respecting the history of
every word he deals with " (L 386). And Benfey, in his
Geschichte der Sprachwissenschaft (1869, see pp. 562 f. and 596),
arrives at the conclusion that the investigation of Aryan languages
has already attained a very great degree of certainty, and that
the reconstruction of Primitive Aryan, both in grammar and

vocabulary, must be considered as in the main settled in such a way that only some details are still doubtful ; thus, it is certain that the first person singular ended in -*mi*, and that this is a phonetic reduction of the pronoun *ma*, and that the word for ' horse' was *akva*. This feeling of pride is certainly in a great measure justified if we compare the achievements of linguistic science at that date with the etymologies of the eighteenth century ; it must also be acknowledged that 90 per cent. of the etymologies in the best-known Aryan languages which must be recognized as established beyond any reasonable doubt had already been discovered before 1870, while later investigations have only added a small number that may be considered firmly established, together with a great many more or less doubtful collocations. But, on the other hand, in the light of later research, we can now see that much of what was then considered firm as a rock did not deserve the implicit trust then placed in it.

IV.—§ 2. New Discoveries.

This is true in the first place with regard to the phonetic structure ascribed to Proto-Aryan. A series of brilliant discoveries made about the year 1880 profoundly modified the views of scholars about the consonantal and still more about the vocalic system of our family of languages. This is particularly true of the so-called palatal law.[1] So long as it was taken for granted that Sanskrit had in all essential points preserved the ancient sound system, while Greek and the other languages represented younger stages, no one could explain why Sanskrit in some cases had the palatals *c* and *j* (sounds approximately like the initial sounds of E. *chicken* and *joy*) where the other languages have the velar sounds *k* and *g*. It was now recognized that so far from the distribution of the two classes of sounds in Sanskrit being arbitrary, it followed strict rules,

[1] Who was the discoverer of the palatal law ? This has been hotly discussed, and as the law was in so far anticipated by other discoveries of the 'seventies as to be " in the air," it is perhaps futile to try to fix the paternity on any single man. However, it seems now perfectly clear that Vilhelm Thomsen was the first to mention it in his lectures (1875), but unfortunately the full and able paper in which he intended to lay it before the world was delayed for a couple of years and then kept in his drawers when he heard that Johannes Schmidt was preparing a paper on the same subject : it was printed in 1920 in the second volume of his *Samlede Afhandlinger* (from the original manuscript). Esaias Tegnér had found the law independently and had printed five sheets of a book *De ariska språkens palataler*, which he withdrew when he found that Collitz and de Saussure had expressed similar views. Karl Verner, too, had independently arrived at the same results ; see his *Afhandlinger og Breve*, 109 ff., 305.

though these were not to be seen from Sanskrit itself. Where Sanskrit *a* following the consonant corresponded to Greek or Latin *o*, Sanskrit had velar *k* or *g*; where, on the other hand, it corresponded to Greek or Latin *e*, Sanskrit had palatal *c* or *j*. Thus we have, for instance, *c* in Sansk. *ca*, ' and ' = Greek *te*, Lat. *que*, but *k* in *kakša* = Lat. *coxa*; the difference between the two consonants in a perfect like *cakara*, ' have done,' is dependent on the same vowel alternation as that of Greek *léloipa*; *c* in the verb *pacati*, ' cooks,' as against *k* in the substantive *pakas*, ' cooking,' corresponds to the vowels in Greek *légei* as against *lógos*, etc. All this shows that Sanskrit itself must once have had the vowels *e* and *o* instead of *a*; before the front vowel *e* the consonant has then been fronted or palatalized, as *ch* in E. *chicken* is due to the following front vowel, while *k* has been preserved before *o* in *cock*. Sanskrit is thus shown to be in some important respects less conservative than Greek, a truth which was destined profoundly to modify many theories concerning the whole family of languages. As Curtius said, with some resentment of the change in view then taking place, "Sanskrit, once the oracle of the rising science and trusted blindly, is now put on one side; instead of the traditional *ex oriente lux* the saying is now *in oriente tenebræ* " (K 97).

The new views held in regard to Aryan vowels also resulted in a thorough revision of the theory of apophony (ablaut). The great mass of Aryan vowel alternations were shown to form a vast and singularly consistent system, the main features of which may be gathered from the following tabulation of a few select Greek examples, arranged into three columns, each representing one ' grade ':

	I	II	III
(1)	pétomai	pótē	eptómai
	(s)ékhō	(s)ókhos	éskhon
(2)	leípō	léloipa	élipon
(3)	peúthomai	—	eputhómēn
(4)	dérkomai	dédorka	édrakon
(5)	teínō (*tenjo)	tónos	tatós

It is outside our scope to show how this scheme gives us a natural clue to the vowels in such verbs as E. I *ride*, II *rode*, III *ridden* (2), G. I *werde*, II *ward*, III *geworden* (4), or I *binde*, II *band*, III *gebunden* (5). It will be seen from the Greek examples that grade I is throughout characterized by the vowel *e* and grade II by the vowel *o*; as for grade III, the vowel of I and II has entirely disappeared in (1), where there is no vowel between the two consonants, and in (2) and (3), where the element found after *e* and *o* and forming a diphthong with these has now become a full (syllabic) vowel *i* and *u* by itself. In (4) Sanskrit has in grade III a syllabic *r* (*adrçam* = Gr. *édrakon*), while Greek has *ra*, or in some instances *ar*, and Gothonic has *ur* or *or* according to the vowel of the following syllable. It was this fact that suggested to Brugmann his theory that in (5) Greek *a*, Lat. *in*, Goth. *un* in the third grade originated in syllabic *n̥*, and that *tatós* thus stood for **tn̥tós*; he similarly explained Gr. *déka*, Lat. *decem*, Gothic *taihun*, E. *ten* from **dekm̥* with syllabic *m*. I do not believe that his theory is entirely correct; but so much is certain, that in all instances grade III is characterized by a reduction of the vowel that appears in the two other grades as *e* and *o*, and there can be no doubt that this reduction is due to want of stress. This being so, it becomes impossible to consider *lip* the original root-form, which in *leip* and *loip* has been extended, and the new theory of apophony thus disposes of the old theory, based on the Indian grammarians' view that the shortest form was the root-form, which was then raised through 'guna' and 'vrddhi.' This now is reversed, and the fuller form is shown to be the oldest, which in some cases was shortened according to a process paralleled in many living languages. Bopp was right in his rejection of Grimm's theory of an inner, significatory reason for apophony, as apophony is now shown to have been due to a mechanical cause, though a different one from that suggested by Bopp (see above, p. 53); and Grimm was also wrong in another respect, because apophony is found from the first in noun-formations as well as in verbs, where Grimm believed it to have been instituted to indicate tense differences, with which it had originally nothing to do. Apophony even appears in other syllables than the root syllable; the new view thus quite naturally paved the way for skepticism with regard to the old doctrine that Aryan roots were necessarily monosyllabic; and scholars soon began to admit dissyllabic 'bases' in place of the old roots; instead of *lip*, the earliest accessible form thus came to be something like *leipo* or *leipe*. In this way the new vowel system had far-reaching consequences and made linguists look upon many problems in a new light. It should be noted, however, that the mechanical explanation of apophony from difference in accent applies only to grade III, in contradistinction to grades I and II; the reason of the alternation between the *e* of I and the *o* of II is by no means clear.

The investigations leading to the discovery of the palatal law and the new theory of apophony were only a part of the immense labour of a number of able linguists in the 'seventies and 'eighties, which cleared up many obscure points in Aryan phonology and morphology. One of the most famous discoveries was that of the Dane Karl Verner, that a whole series of consonant alternations in the old Gothonic languages was dependent on accent, and (more remarkable still) on the primeval accent, preserved in its oldest form in Sanskrit only, and differing from that of modern Gothonic languages in resting in some instances on the ending and in others on the root. When it was realized that the fact that German has *t* in *vater*, but *d* in *bruder*, was due to a different accentuation of the two words three or four thousand years ago, or that the difference between *s* and *r* in E. *was* and *were* was connected with the fact that perfect singulars in Sanskrit are stressed on the root, but plurals on the ending, this served not only to heighten respect for the linguistic science that was able to demonstrate such truths, but also to increase the feeling that the world of sounds was subject to strict laws comparable to those of natural science.

IV.—§ 3. Phonetic Laws and Analogy.

The ' blind ' operation of phonetic laws became the chief tenet of a new school of ' young-grammarians ' or ' junggrammatiker ' (Brugmann, Delbrück, Osthoff, Paul and others), who somewhat noisily flourished their advance upon earlier linguists and justly roused the anger not only of their own teachers, including Curtius, but also of fellow-students like Johannes Schmidt and Collitz. For some years a fierce discussion took place on the principles of linguistic science, in which young-grammarians tried to prove deductively the truth of their favourite thesis that " Sound-laws admit of no exceptions " (first, it seems, enounced by Leskien). Osthoff wrongly maintained that sound changes belonged to physiology and analogical change to psychology ; but though that distribution of the two kinds of change to two different domains was untenable, the distinction in itself was important and proved a valuable, though perhaps sometimes too easy instrument in the hands of the historical grammarian. It was quite natural that those who insisted on undeviating phonetic laws should turn their attention to those cases in which forms appeared that did not conform to these laws, and try to explain them ; and thus they inevitably were led to recognize the immense importance of analogical formations in the economy of all languages. Such formations had long been known, but little attention had been paid to them, and they were generally termed ' false analogies ' and looked upon as corruptions or inorganic formations found only or chiefly in a degenerate age, in which the true meaning and composition of the old forms was no longer understood. Men like Curtius were scandalized at the younger school explaining so many even of the noble forms of ancient Greek as due to this upstart force of analogy. His opponents contended that the name of 'false analogy' was wrong and misleading : the analogy in itself was perfect and was handled with unerring instinct in each case. They likewise pointed out that analogical formations, so far from being perversions of a late age, really represented one of the vital principles of language, without which it could never have come into existence.

One of the first to take the new point of view and to explain it clearly was Hermann Paul. I quote from an early article (as translated by Sweet, CP 112) the following passages, which really struck a new note in linguistic theory :

"There is one simple fact which should never be left out of sight, namely, that even in the parent Indogermanic language, long before its split-up, there were no longer any roots, stems, and suffixes, but only ready-made *words*, which were employed without the slightest thought of their composite nature. And it is only of such ready-made words that the store is composed from which everyone draws when he speaks. He has no stock of stems and terminations at his disposal from which he could construct the form required for each separate occasion. Not that he must necessarily have heard and learnt by heart every form he uses. This would, in fact, be impossible. He is, on the contrary, able of himself to form cases of nouns, tenses of verbs, etc., which he has either never heard or else not noticed specially ; but, as there is no combining of stem and suffix, this can only be done on the pattern of the other ready-made combinations which he has learnt from his fellows. These latter are first learnt one by one, and then gradually associated into groups which correspond to the grammatical categories, but are never clearly conceived as such without special training. This grouping not only greatly aids the memory, but also makes it possible to produce other combinations. And this is what we call *analogy*."

"It is, therefore, clear that, while speaking, everyone is incessantly producing analogical forms. *Reproduction by memory* and *new-formation by means of association* are its two indispensable factors. It is a mistake to assume a language as given in grammar and dictionary, that is, the whole body of possible words and forms, as something concrete, and to forget that it is nothing but an abstraction devoid of reality, and that *the actual language exists only in the individual*, from whom it cannot be separated even in scientific investigation, if we will understand its nature and development. To comprehend the existence of each separate spoken form, we must not ask ' Is it current in the language ? ' or ' Is it conformable to the laws of the language as deduced by the grammarians ? ' but ' Has he who has just employed it previously had it in his memory, or has he formed it himself for the first time, and, if so, according to what analogy ? ' When, for instance, anyone employs the plural *milben* in German, it may be that he has learnt it from others, or else that he has only heard the singular *milbe*, but knows that such words as *lerche, schwalbe*, etc., form their plural *lerchen*, etc., so that the association *milbe-milben* is unconsciously suggested to him. He may also have heard the plural *milben*, but remembers it so imperfectly that he would forget it entirely were it not associated in his mind with a series of similar forms which help him to recall it. It is, therefore, often difficult to determine the share memory and creative fancy have had in each separate case."

Linguists thus set about it seriously to think of language in terms of speaking individuals, who have learnt their mother-tongue in the ordinary way, and who now employ it in their daily intercourse with other men and women, without in each separate case knowing what they owe to others and what they have to create on the spur of the moment. Just as Sokrates fetched philosophy down from the skies, so also now linguists fetched words and forms down from vocabularies and grammars and placed them where their natural home is, in the minds and on the lips of ordinary men who are neither lexicographers nor grammarians, but who nevertheless master their language with sufficient ease and correctness for all ordinary purposes. Linguists now were confronted with some general problems which had not greatly troubled their predecessors (with the solitary exception of Bredsdorff, whose work was entirely overlooked), namely, What are the causes of changes in language ? How are they brought about, and how should they be classified ? Many articles on these questions appeared in linguistic periodicals about the year 1880, but the profoundest and fullest treatment was found in a masterly book by H. Paul, *Prinzipien der Sprach-geschichte*, the first edition of which (1880) exercised a very considerable influence on linguistic thought, while the subsequent editions were constantly enlarged and improved so as to contain a wealth of carefully sifted material to illustrate the various processes of linguistic change. It should also be noted that Paul paid more and more attention to syntax, and that this part of grammar, which had been neglected by Bopp and Schleicher and their contemporaries, was about this time taken up by some of the leading linguists, who showed that the comparative and historical method was capable of throwing a flood of light on syntax no less than on morphology (Delbrück, Ziemer).

IV.—§ 4. General Tendencies.

While linguists in the 'eighties were taking up, as we have seen, a great many questions of vast general importance that had not been treated by the older generation, on the other hand they were losing interest in some of the problems that had occupied their predecessors. This was the case with the question of the ultimate origin of grammatical endings. So late as 1869 Benfey included among Bopp's 'brilliant discoveries' his theory that the *s* of the aorist and of the future was derived from the verb *as*, 'to be,' and that the endings of the Latin imperfect *-bam* and future *-bo* were from the synonymous verb *fu* = Sanskrit *bhu* (Gesch 377), and the next year Raumer reckons the same theories among Bopp's 'most important discoveries.' But soon after this we see that speculations of this kind somehow go out of fashion. One of the last books to indulge in them to any extent is Scherer's once famous *Zur Geschichte der deutschen Sprache* (2nd ed., 1878), in the eighth chapter of which the writer disports himself among primitive roots, endings, prepositions and pronouns, which he identifies and differentiates with such extreme boldness and confidence in his own wild fancies that a sober-minded man of the twentieth century cannot but feel dazed and giddy. The ablest linguists of the new school simply left these theories aside: no new explanations of the same description were advanced, and the old ones were not substantiated by the ascertained phenomena of living languages. So much was found in these of the most absorbing interest that scholars ceased to care for what might lie behind Proto-Aryan; some even went so far as to deprecate in strong expressions any attempts at what they termed 'glottogonic' theories. To these matter-of-fact linguists all speculations as to the ultimate origin of language were futile and nebulous, a verdict which might be in no small degree justified by much of what had been written on the subject by quasi-philosophers and quasi-linguists. The aversion to these questions was shown as early as 1866, when La Société de Linguistique was founded in Paris. Section 2 of the statutes of the Society expressly states that "La Société n'admet aucune communication concernant, soit l'origine du langage, soit la création d'une langue universelle "—both of them questions which, as they *can* be treated in a scientific spirit, should not be left exclusively to dilettanti.

The last forty years have witnessed an extraordinary activity
on the part of scholars in investigating all domains of the Aryan
languages in the light of the new general views and by the aid
of the methods that have now become common property.
Phonological investigations have no doubt had the lion's share
and have to a great extent been signalized by that real insight
into physiological phonetics which had been wanting in earlier
linguists ; but very much excellent work has also been done in
morphology, syntax and semantics ; and in all these domains
much has been gained by considering words not as mere isolated
units, but as parts of sentences, or, better, of connected speech.
In phonetics more and more attention has been paid to sentence
phonetics and 'sandhi phenomena' ; the heightened interest in
everything concerning 'accent' (stress and pitch) has also led
to investigations of sentence-stress and sentence-melody ; the
intimate connexion between forms and their use or function in
the sentence, in other words their syntax, has been more and
more recognized ; and finally, if semantics (the study of the significations of words) has become a real science instead of being a
curiosity shop of isolated specimens, this has only been rendered
possible through seeing words as connected with other words to
form complete utterances. But this change of attitude could
not have been brought about unless linguists had studied texts
in the different languages to a far greater extent than had been
done in previous periods ; thus, naturally, the antagonism formerly
often felt between the linguistic and the purely philological study
of the same language has tended to disappear, and many scholars
have produced work both in their particular branch of linguistics
and in the corresponding philology. There can be no doubt that
this development has been profitable to both domains of scientific
activity.

Another beneficial change is the new attitude taken with
regard to the study of living speech. The science of linguistics
had long stood in the sign of Cancer and had been constantly
looking backwards—to its own great loss. Now, with the greater
stress laid on phonetics and on the psychology of language, the
necessity of observing the phenomena of actual everyday speech
was more clearly perceived. Among pioneers in this respect I
must specially mention Henry Sweet ; now there is a steadily
growing interest in living speech as the necessary foundation of
all general theorizing. And with interest comes knowledge.

It is outside the purpose of this volume to give the history
of linguistic study during the last forty years in the same way
as I have attempted to give it for the period before 1880, and I
must therefore content myself with a few brief remarks on

general tendencies. I even withstand the temptation to try and characterize the two greatest works on general linguistics that have appeared during this period, those by Georg v. d. Gabelentz and Wilhelm Wundt: important and in many ways excellent as they are, they have not exercised the same influence on contemporary linguistic research as some of their predecessors. Personally I owe incomparably much more to the former than to the latter, who is much less of a linguist than of a psychologist and whose pages seem to me often richer in words than in fertilizing ideas. As for the rest, I can give only a bare alphabetical list of some of the writers who during this period have dealt with the more general problems of linguistic change or linguistic theory, and must not attempt any appreciation of their works: Bally, Baudouin de Courtenay, Bloomfield, Bréal Delbrück, van Ginneken, Hale, Henry, Hirt, Axel Kock, Meillet Meringer, Noreen, Oertel, Pedersen, Sandfeld (Jensen), de Saussure, Schuchardt, Sechehaye, Streitberg, Sturtevant, Sütterlin, Sweet, Uhlenbeck, Vossler, Wechssler. In the following parts of my work there will be many opportunities of mentioning their views, especially when I disagree with them, for I am afraid it will be impossible always to indicate what I owe to their suggestions.

In the history of linguistic science we have seen in one period a tendency to certain large syntheses (the classification of languages into isolating, agglutinative and flexional, and the corresponding theory of three periods with its corollary touching the origin of flexional endings), and we have seen how these syntheses were later discredited, though never actually disproved, linguists contenting themselves with detailed comparisons and explanations of single words, forms or sounds without troubling about their ultimate origin or about the evolutionary tendencies of the whole system or structure of language. The question may therefore be raised, were Bopp and Schleicher wrong in attempting these large syntheses? It would appear from the expressions of some modern linguists that they thought that any such comprehensive generalization or any glottogonic theory were in itself of evil. But this can never be admitted. Science, of its very nature, aims at larger and larger generalizations, more and more comprehensive formulas, so as finally to bring about that " unification of knowledge " of which Herbert Spencer speaks. It was therefore quite right of the early linguists to propound those great questions; and their failure to solve them in a way that could satisfy the stricter demands of a later generation should not be charged too heavily against them. It was also quite right of the moderns to reject their premature solutions (though this was often done without any adequate examination), but

it was decidedly wrong to put the questions out of court altogether.[1] These great questions have to be put over and over
again, till a complete solution is found ; and the refusal to face
these difficulties has produced a certain barrenness in modern
linguistics, which must strike any impartial observer, however
much he admits the fertility of the science in detailed investigations. Breadth of vision is not conspicuous in modern
linguistics, and to my mind this lack is chiefly due to the fact
that linguists have neglected all problems connected with a
valuation of language. What is the criterion by which one word
or one form should be preferred to another ? (most linguists
refuse to deal with such questions of preference or of correctness
of speech). Are the changes that we see gradually taking place
in languages to be considered as on the whole beneficial or the
opposite ? (most linguists pooh-pooh such questions). Would it
be possible to construct an international language by which
persons in different countries could easily communicate with
one another ? (most linguists down to the present day have
looked upon all who favour such ideas as visionaries and Uto-
pians). It is my firm conviction that such questions as these
admit of really scientific treatment and should be submitted to
serious discussion. But before tackling those of them which
fall within the plan of this work, it will be well to deal with some
fundamental facts of what is popularly called the ' life ' of language,
and first of all with the manner in which a child acquires its
mother-tongue. For as language exists only in individuals and
means some specific activities of human beings which are not
inborn, but have to be learnt by each of them separately from
his fellow-beings, it is important to examine somewhat in detail
how this interaction of the individual and of the surrounding
society is brought about. This, then, will occupy us in Book II.

[1] " Es ist besser, bei solchen versuchen zu irren als gar nicht darüber
nachzudenken," Curtius, K 145.

BOOK *II*

THE CHILD

CHAPTER V

SOUNDS

§ 1. From Screaming to Talking. § 2. First Sounds. § 3. Sound-laws of the Next Stage. § 4. Groups of Sounds. § 5. Mutilations and Reduplications. § 6. Correction. § 7. Tone.

V.—§ 1. From Screaming to Talking.

A DANISH philosopher has said : " In his whole life man achieves nothing so great and so wonderful as what he achieved when he learnt to talk." When Darwin was asked in which three years of his life a man learnt most, he said : " The first three."

A child's linguistic development covers three periods—the screaming time, the crowing or babbling time, and the talking time. But the last is a long one, and must again be divided into two periods—that of the " little language," the child's own language, and that of the common language or language of the community. In the former the child is linguistically an individualist, in the latter he is more and more socialized.

Of the screaming time little need be said. A child's scream is not uttered primarily as a means of conveying anything to others, and so far is not properly to be called speech. But if from the child's side a scream is not a way of telling anything, its elders may still read something in it and hurry to relieve the trouble. And if the child comes to remark—as it soon will—that whenever it cries someone comes and brings it something pleasant, if only company, it will not be long till it makes use of this instrument whenever it is uneasy or wants something. The scream, which was at first a reflex action, is now a voluntary action. And many parents have discovered that the child has learnt to use its power of screaming to exercise a tyrannical power over them—so that they have had to walk up and down all night with a screaming child that prefers this way of spending the night to lying quietly in its cradle. The only course is brutally to let the baby scream till it is tired, and persist in never letting it get its desire *because* it screams for it, but only because what it desires is good for it. The child learns its lesson, and a scream is once more what it was at first, an involuntary, irresistible result of the fact that something is wrong.

Screaming has, however, another side. It is of physiological value as an exercise of all the muscles and appliances which are afterwards to be called into play for speech and song. Nurses say—and there may be something in it—that the child who screams loudest as a baby becomes the best singer later.

Babbling time produces pleasanter sounds which are more adapted for the purposes of speech. Cooing, crowing, babbling—i.e. uttering meaningless sounds and series of sounds—is a delightful exercise like sprawling with outstretched arms and legs or trying to move the tiny fingers. It has been well said that for a long time a child's dearest toy is its tongue—that is, of course, not the tongue only, but the other organs of speech as well, especially the lips and vocal chords. At first the movements of these organs are as uncontrolled as those of the arms, but gradually they become more systematic, and the boy knows what sound he wishes to utter and is in a position to produce it exactly.

First, then, come single vowels or vowels with a single consonant preceding them, as *la, ra, lö*, etc., though a baby's sounds cannot be identified with any of ours or written down with our letters. For, though the head and consequently the mouth capacity is disproportionally great in an infant and grows more rapidly than its limbs, there is still a great difference between its mouth capacity and that required to utter normal speech-sounds. I have elsewhere (PhG, p. 81 ff.) given the results of a series of measurings of the jaw in children and adults and discussed the importance of these figures for phonetic theory : while there is no growth of any importance during the talking period (for a child of five may have the same jaw-length as a man of thirty-seven), the growth is enormous during the first months of a child's life : in the case of my own child, from 45 mm. a few days after birth to 60 mm. at three months old and 75 mm. at eleven months, while the average of grown-up men is 99 mm. and of women 93 mm. The consequence is that the sounds of the baby are different from ours, and that even when they resemble ours the mechanism of production may be different from the normal one ; when my son during the first weeks said something like *la*, I was able to see distinctly that the tip of the tongue was not at all in the position required for our *l*. This want of congruence between the acoustic manners of operation in the infant and the adult no doubt gives us the key to many of the difficulties that have puzzled previous observers of small children.

Babbling or crowing begins not earlier than the third week ; it may be, not till the seventh or eighth week. The first sound exercises are to be regarded as muscular exercises pure and simple, as is clear from the fact that deaf-mutes amuse themselves with them, although they cannot themselves hear them. But the moment comes when the hearing child finds a pleasure in hearing its own sounds, and a most important step is taken when the little one begins to hear a resemblance between the sounds uttered by its mother or nurse and its own. The mother will naturally answer the baby's syllables by repeating the same, and when the baby recognizes the likeness, it secures an inexhaustible source of pleasure, and after some time reaches the next stage, when it tries itself to imitate what is said to it (generally towards the close of the first year). The value of this exercise cannot be over-estimated : the more that parents understand how to play this game with the baby—of saying something and letting the baby say it after, however meaningless the syllable-sequences that they make—the better will be the foundation for the child's later acquisition and command of language.

V.—§ 2. First Sounds.

It is generally said that the order in which the child learns to utter the different sounds depends on their difficulty : the easiest sounds are produced first. That is no doubt true in the main ; but when we go into details we find that different writers bring forward lists of sounds in different order. All are agreed, however, that among the consonants the labials, *p*, *b* and *m*, are early sounds, if not the earliest. The explanation has been given that the child can see the working of his mother's lips in these sounds and therefore imitates her movements. This implies far too much conscious thought on the part of the baby, who utters his ' ma ' or ' mo ' before he begins to imitate anything said to him by his surroundings. Moreover, it has been pointed out that the child's attention is hardly ever given to its mother's mouth, but is steadily fixed on her eyes. The real reason is probably that the labial muscles used to produce *b* or *m* are the same that the baby has exercised in sucking the breast or the bottle. It would be interesting to learn if blind children also produce the labial sounds first.

Along with the labial sounds the baby produces many other sounds—vowel and consonant—and in these cases one is certain that it has not been able to see how these sounds are produced by its mother. Even in the case of the labials we know that what distinguishes *m* from *b*, the lowering of the soft palate, and *b* from *p*, the vibrations of the vocal chords, is invisible. Some of the sounds produced by means of the tongue may be too hard to pronounce till the muscles of the tongue have been exercised in consequence of the child having begun to eat more solid things than milk.

By the end of the first year the number of sounds which the little babbler has mastered is already considerable, and he loves to combine long series of the same syllables, dadadada . . ., nenenene . . . , bygnbygnbygn . . . , etc. That is a game which need not even cease when the child is able to talk actual language. It is strange that among an infant's sounds one can often detect sounds—for instance k, g, h, and uvular r—which the child will find difficulty in producing afterwards when they occur in real words, or which may be unknown to the language which it will some day speak. The explanation lies probably in the difference between doing a thing in play or without a plan—when it is immaterial which movement (sound) is made—and doing the same thing of fixed intention when this sound, and this sound only, is required, at a definite point in the syllable, and with this or that particular sound before and after. Accordingly, great difficulties come to be encountered when the child begins more consciously and systematically to imitate his elders. Some sounds come without effort and may be used incessantly, to the detriment of others which the child may have been able previously to produce in play ; and a time even comes when the stock of sounds actually diminishes, while particular sounds acquire greater precision. Dancing masters, singing masters and gymnastic teachers have similar experiences. After some lessons the child may seem more awkward than it was before the lessons began.

The ' little language ' which the child makes for itself by imperfect imitation of the sounds of its elders seems so arbitrary that it may well be compared to the child's first rude drawings of men and animals. A Danish boy named *Gustav* (1.6)[1] called himself [dodado] and turned the name *Karoline* into [nnn]. Other Danish children made *skammel* into [gramn] or [gap], *elefant* into [vat], *Karen* into [gaja], etc. A few examples from English children : Hilary M. (1.6) called *Ireland* (her sister) [a·ni], Gordon M. (1.10) called *Millicent* (his sister) [dadu·]. Tony E. (1.11) called his playmate *Sheila* [dubabud].

V.—§ 3. Sound-laws of the Next Stage.

As the child gets away from the peculiarities of his individual ' little language,' his speech becomes more regular, and a linguist can in many cases see reasons for his distortions of normal words. When he replaces one sound by another there is always some common element in the formation of the two sounds, which causes

---

[1] In this book the age of a child is indicated by stating the number of years and months completed : 1.6 thus means " in the seventh month of the second year," etc.

a kindred impression on the ear, though *we* may have difficulty
in detecting it because we are so accustomed to noticing the
difference. There is generally a certain system in the sound
substitutions of children, and in many instances we are justified
in speaking of 'strictly observed sound-laws.' Let us now look
at some of these.

Children in all countries tend to substitute [t] for [k]: both
sounds are produced by a complete stoppage of the breath for the
moment by the tongue, the only difference being that it is the
back of the tongue which acts in one case, and the tip of
the tongue in the other. A child who substitutes *t* for *k* will
also substitute *d* for *g*; if he says 'tat' for 'cat' he will say
'do' for 'go.'

R is a difficult sound. Hilary M. (2.0) has no *r*'s in her speech.
Initially they become *w*, as in [wʌn] for 'run,' medially between
vowels they become *l*, as in [veli, beli] for 'very, berry,' in consonantal combinations they are lost, as in [kai, bʌʃ] for 'cry,
brush.' Tony E. (1.10 to 3.0) for medial *r* between vowels first
substituted *d*, as in [vedi] for 'very,' and later *g* [vegi]; similarly
in [muˑgi] for 'Muriel,' [tægi] for 'carry'; he often dropped
initial *r*, e.g. *oom* for 'room.' It is not unusual for children who
use *w* for *r* in most combinations to say [tʃ] for *tr* and [dʒ] for *dr*,
as in 'chee,' 'jawer' for 'tree,' 'drawer.' This illustrates the
fact that what to us is one sound, and therefore represented in
writing by *one* letter, appears to the child's ear as different sounds
—and generally the phonetician will agree with the child that
there are really differences in the articulation of the sound according
to position in the syllable and to surroundings, only the child
exaggerates the dissimilarities, just as we in writing one and the
same letter exaggerate the similarity.

The two *th* sounds offer some difficulties and are often imitated
as *f* and *v* respectively, as in 'frow' and 'muvver' for 'throw'
and 'mother'; others say 'ze' or 'de' for 'the.' Hilary M.
(2.0) has great difficulty with *th* and *s*; *th* usually becomes [ʃ],
[beʃ, tiˑʃ, friˑ] for 'Beth,' 'teeth,' 'three'; *s* becomes [ʃ],
e.g. [franʃiʃ, ʃtiˑm] for 'Francis,' 'steam'; in the same way
z becomes [ʒ] as in [lʌbʒ, bouʒ] for 'loves,' 'Bowes'; *sw* becomes
[fw] as in [fwiŋ, fwiˑt] for 'swing,' 'sweet.' She drops *l* in consonantal combinations, e.g. [kiˑn, kaim, kɔk, ʃiˑp] for 'clean,'
'climb,' 'clock,' 'sleep.'

Sometimes it requires a phonetician's knowledge to understand
the individual sound-laws of a child. Thus I pick out from some
specimens given by O'Shea, p. 135 f. (girl, 2.9), the following
words: *pell* (smell), *teeze* (sneeze), *poke* (smoke), *tow* (snow), and
formulate the rule: *s* + a nasal became the voiceless stop corre-

sponding to the nasal, a kind of assimilation, in which the place of articulation and the mouth-closure of the nasals were preserved, and the sound was made unvoiced and non-nasal as the *s*. In other combinations *m* and *n* were intact.

Some further faults are illustrated in Tony E.'s [tʃouz, pʌg, pus, tæm, pʌm, bæk, piˑz, nouʒ, ɔk, es, uˑ] for *clothes, plug, push, tram, plum, black, please, nose, clock, yes, you*.

V.—§ 4. Groups of Sounds.

Even when a sound by itself can be pronounced, the child often finds it hard to pronounce it when it forms part of a group of sounds. *S* is often dropped before another consonant, as in 'tummy' for 'stomach.' Other examples have already been given above. Hilary M. (2.0) had difficulty with *lp* and said [hæpl] for 'help.' She also said [ointən] for 'ointment'; C. M. L. (2.3) said 'sikkums' for 'sixpence.' Tony E. (2.0) turns *grannie* into [nægi]. When initial consonant groups are simplified, it is generally, though not always, the stop that remains : *b* instead of *bl-, br-, k* instead of *kr-, sk-, skr-, p* instead of *pl-, pr-, spr-*, etc. For the groups occurring medially and finally no general rule seems possible.

V.—§ 5. Mutilations and Reduplications.

To begin with, the child is unable to master long sequences of syllables ; he prefers monosyllables and often emits them singly and separated by pauses. Even in words that to us are inseparable wholes some children will make breaks between syllables, e.g. Shef-field, Ing-land. But more often they will give only part of the word, generally the last syllable or syllables ; hence we get pet-names like *Bet* or *Beth* for Elizabeth and forms like 'tatoes' for potatoes, 'chine' for machine, 'tina' for concertina, 'tash' for moustache, etc. Hilary M. (1.10) called an express-cart a *press-cart*, bananas and pyjamas *nanas* and *jamas*.

It is not, however, the production of long sequences of syllables in itself that is difficult to the child, for in its meaningless babbling it may begin very early to pronounce long strings of sounds without any break ; but the difficulty is to remember what sounds have to be put together to bring about exactly this or that word. We grown-up people may experience just the same sort of difficulty if after hearing once the long name of a Bulgarian minister or a Sanskrit book we are required to repeat it at once. Hence we should not wonder at such pronunciations as [pekəlout] for *petticoat* or [efelənt] for *elephant* (Beth M., 2.6) ; Hilary M. called a *caterpilla* a *pillarcat*. Other transpositions are *serreval* for *several* and *ocken* for *uncle*; cf. also *wops* for *wasp*.

To explain the frequent reduplications found in children's language it is not necessary, as some learned authors have done, to refer to the great number of reduplicated words in the languages of primitive tribes and to see in the same phenomenon in our own children an atavistic return to primitive conditions, on the Häckelian assumption that the development of each individual has to pass rapidly through the same ('phylogenetic') stages as the whole lineage of his ancestors. It is simpler and more natural to refer these reduplications to the pleasure always felt in repeating the same muscular action until one is tired. The child will repeat over and over again the same movements of legs and arms, and we do the same when we wave our hand or a handkerchief or when we nod our head several times to signify assent, etc. When we laugh we repeat the same syllable consisting of *h* and a more or less indistinct vowel, and when we sing a melody without words we are apt to 'reduplicate' indefinitely. Thus also with the little ones. Apart from such words as *papa* and *mamma*, to which we shall have to revert in another chapter (VIII, § 9), children will often form words from those of their elders by repeating one syllable; cf. *puff-puff*, *gee-gee*. Tracy (p. 132) records *pepe* for 'pencil,' *kaka* for 'Carrie.' For a few weeks (1.11) Hilary M. reduplicated whole words, e.g. *king-king*, *ring-ring* (i.e. bell), *water-water*. Tony F. (1.10) uses [toutó] for his own name. Hence pet-names like *Dodo*; they are extremely frequent in French —for instance, *Fifine*, *Lolotte*, *Lolo*, *Mimi*; the name *Daudet* has arisen in a similar way from *Claudet*, a diminutive of Claude.

It is a similar phenomenon (a kind of partial reduplication) when sounds at a distance affect one another, as when Hilary M. (2.0) said [gɔgi] for *doggie*, [bɔbin] for *Dobbin*, [dezmən di·n] for *Jesmond Dene*, [baikikl] for *bicycle*, [kekl] for *kettle*. Tracy (p. 133) mentions *bopoo* for 'bottle,' in which *oo* stands for the hollow sound of syllabic *l*. One correspondent mentions *whoofing-cough* for 'whooping-cough' (where the final sound has crept into the first word) and *chicken-pops* for 'chicken-pox.' Some children say 'aneneme' for *anemone;* and in S. L. (4.9) this caused a curious confusion during the recent war: "Mother, there must be two sorts of anenemies, flowers and Germans."

Dr. Henry Bradley once told me that his youngest child had a difficulty with the name *Connie*, which was made alternatingly [tɔni] and [kɔŋi], in both cases with two consonants articulated at the same point. Similar instances are mentioned in German books on children's language, thus *gigarr* for 'zigarre,' *baibift*

for ' bleistift,' *autobobil* (Meringer),[1] *fotofafieren* (Stern), *ambam*
for ' armband,' *dan* for ' dame,' *pap* for ' patte ' (Ronjat). I
have given many Danish examples in my Danish book. Gramm-
mont's child (see *Mélanges linguistiques offerts à A. Meillet*, 1902)
carried through these changes in a most systematic way.

V.—§ 6. Correction.

The time comes when the child corrects his mistakes—where
it said ' tat ' it now says ' cat.' Here there are two possibilities
which both seem to occur in actual life. One is that the child
hears the correct sound some time before he is able to imitate it
correctly ; he will thus still say *t* for *k*, though he may in some
way object to other people saying ' tum ' for ' come.' Passy
relates how a little French girl would say *tosson* both for *garçon*
and *cochon* ; but she protested when anybody else said " C'est
un petit cochon " in speaking about a boy, or vice versa. Such
a child, as soon as it can produce the new sound, puts it correctly
into all the places where it is required. This, I take it, is the
ordinary procedure. Frans (my own boy) could not pronounce
h and said *an, on* for the Danish pronouns *han, hun* ; but when
he began to pronounce this sound, he never misplaced it (2.4).

The other possibility is that the child learns how to pronounce
the new sound at a time when its own acoustic impression is not
yet quite settled ; in that case there will be a period during which
his use of the new sound is uncertain and fluctuating. When
parents are in too great a hurry to get a child out of some false
pronunciation, they may succeed in giving it a new sound, but
the child will tend to introduce it in places where it does not belong.
On the whole, it seems therefore the safest plan to leave it to the
child itself to discover that its sound is not the correct one.

Sometimes a child will acquire a sound or a sound combination
correctly and then lose it till it reappears a few months later.
In an English family where there was no question of the influence
of *h*-less servants, each child in succession passed through an *h*-less
period, and one of the children, after pronouncing *h* correctly,
lost the use of it altogether for two or three months. I have
had similar experiences with Danish children. S. L. (ab. 2) said
' bontin ' for *bonnet ;* but five months earlier she had said *bonnet*
correctly.

The path to perfection is not always a straight one. Tony E.
in order to arrive at the correct pronunciation of *please* passed
through the following stages : (1) [bi·], (2) [bli·], (3) [pi·z],

---

[1] An American child said *autonobile* [ɔtənobi·l] with partial assimilation
of *m* to the point-stop *t*.

(4) [pwiˑʒ], (5) [beisk, meis, mais] and several other impossible forms. Tracy (p. 139) gives the following forms through which the boy A. (1.5) had to pass before being able to say *pussy : pooheh, poofie, poopoohie, poofee.* A French child had four forms [mèni, pèti, mèti, mèsi] before being able to say *merci* correctly (Grammont). A Danish child passed through *bejab* and *vamb* before pronouncing *svamp* (' sponge '), etc.

It is certain that all this while the little brain is working, and even consciously working, though at first it has not sufficient command of speech to say anything about it. Meringer says that children do not practise, but that their new acquisitions of sounds happen at once without any visible preparation. He may be right in the main with regard to the learning of single sounds, though even there I incline to doubt the possibility of a universal rule ; but Ronjat (p. 55) is certainly right as against Meringer with regard to the way in which children learn new and difficult combinations. Here they certainly do practise, and are proudly conscious of the happy results of their efforts. When Frans (2.11) mastered the combination *fl*, he was very proud, and asked his mother : " Mother, can you say *flyve* ? " ; then he came to me and told me that he could say *bluse* and *flue*, and when asked whether he could say *blad*, he answered : " No, not yet ; Frans cannot say *b-lad* " (with a little interval between the *b* and the *l*). Five weeks later he said : " Mother, won't you play upon the *klaver* (piano) ? " and after a little while, " Frans can say *kla* so well." About the same time he first mispronounced the word *manchetter*, and then (when I asked what he was saying, without telling him that anything was wrong) he gave it the correct sound, and I heard him afterwards in the adjoining room repeat the word to himself in a whisper.

How well children observe sounds is again seen by the way in which they will correct their elders if they give a pronunciation to which they are not accustomed—for instance, in a verse they have learnt by heart. Beth M (2.6) was never satisfied with her parents' pronunciation of " What will you buy me when you get there ? " She always insisted on their gabbling the first words as quickly as they could and then coming out with an emphatic *there.*

V.—§ 7. Tone.

As to the differences in the tone of a voice, even a baby shows by his expression that he can distinguish clearly between what is said to him lovingly and what sharply, a long time before he understands a single word of what is said. Many children are

able at a very early age to hit off the exact note in which something is said or sung.   Here is a story of a boy of more advanced
age.   In Copenhagen he had had his hair cut by a Swedish lady
and did not like it.   When he travelled with his mother to Norway,
as soon as he entered the house, he broke out with a scream :
" Mother, I hope I'm not going to have my hair cut ? "   He had
noticed the Norwegian intonation, which is very like the Swedish,
and it brought an unpleasant association of ideas.

CHAPTER VI

WORDS

§ 1. Introductory. **§ 2.** First Period. **§ 3.** Father and Mother. **§ 4.** The Delimitation of Meaning. **§ 5.** Numerals. Time. **§ 6.** Various Difficulties. **§ 7.** Shifters. **§ 8.** Extent of Vocabulary. **§ 9.** Summary.

VI.—§ 1. Introductory.

IN the preceding chapter, in order to simplify matters, we have dealt with sounds only, as if they were learnt by themselves and independently of the meanings attached to them. But that, of course, is only an abstraction : to the child, as well as to the grown-up, the two elements, the outer, phonetic element, and the inner element, the meaning, of a word are indissolubly connected, and the child has no interest, or very little interest, in trying to imitate the sounds of its parents except just in so far as these mean something. That words have a meaning, the child will begin to perceive at a very early age. Parents may of course deceive themselves and attribute to the child a more complete and exact understanding of speech than the child is capable of. That the child looks at its father when it hears the word ' father,' may mean at first nothing more than that it follows its mother's glance ; but naturally in this way it is prepared for actually associating the idea of ' father ' with the sound. If the child learns the feat of lifting its arms when it is asked " How big is the boy ? " it is not to be supposed that the single words of the sentence are understood, or that the child has any conception of size ; he only knows that when this series of sounds is said he is admired if he lifts his arms up : and so the sentence as a whole has the effect of a word of command. A dog has the same degree of understanding. Hilary M. (1.0), when you said to her at any time the refrain " He greeted me so," from " Here come three knights from Spain," would bow and salute with her hand, as she had seen some children doing it when practising the song.

The understanding of what is said always precedes the power of saying the same thing oneself—often precedes it for an extraordinarily long time. One father notes that his little daughter of a year and seven months brings what is wanted and understands questions while she cannot say a word. It often happens that parents some fine day come to regret what they have said in the presence of a child without suspecting how much it understands. " Little pitchers have long ears."

One can, however, easily err in regard to the range and certainty of a child's understanding. The Swiss philologist Tappolet noticed that his child of six months, when he said " Where is the window ? " made vague movements towards the window. He made the experiment of repeating his question in French—with the same intonation as in German, and the child acted just as it had done before. It is, properly speaking, only when the child begins to talk that we can be at all sure what it has really understood, and even then it may at times be difficult to sound the depths of the child's conception.

The child's acquisition of the meaning of words is truly a highly complicated affair. How many things are comprehended under one word ? The answer is not easy in all cases. The single Danish word *tæppe* covers all that is expressed in English by carpet, rug, blanket, counterpane, curtain (theatrical). And there is still more complication when we come to abstract ideas. The child has somehow to find out for himself with regard to his own language what ideas are considered to hang together and so come under the same word. He hears the word ' chair ' applied to a particular chair, then to another chair that perhaps looks to him totally different, and again to a third : and it becomes his business to group these together.

What Stern tells about his own boy is certainly exceptional, perhaps unique. The boy ran to a door and said *das* ? (' That ? ' —his way of asking the name of a thing). They told him ' tür.' He then went to two other doors in the room, and each time the performance was repeated. He then did the same with the seven chairs in the room. Stern says, " As he thus makes sure that the objects that are alike to his eye and to his sense of touch have also the same name, he is on his way to general conceptions." We should, however, be wary of attributing general ideas to little children.

VI.—§ 2. First Period.

In the first period we meet the same phenomena in the child's acquisition of word-meanings that we found in his acquisition of sounds. A child develops conceptions of his own which are as unintelligible and strange to the uninitiated as his sounds.

Among the child's first passions are animals and pictures of animals, but for a certain time it is quite arbitrary what animals are classed together under a particular name. A child of nine months noticed that his grandfather's dog said 'bow-wow' and fancied that anything not human could say (and therefore should be called) *bow-wow*—pigs and horses included. A little girl of two called a horse *he* (Danish *hest*) and divided the animal kingdom into two groups, (1) horses, including all four-footed things, even a tortoise, and (2) fishes (pronounced *iz*), including all that moved without use of feet, for example, birds and flies. A boy of 1.8 saw a picture of a Danish priest in a ruff and was told that it was a *præst*, which he rendered as *bœp*. Afterwards seeing a picture of an aunt with a white collar which recalled the priest's ruff, he said again *bœp*, and this remained the name of the aunt, and even of another aunt, who was called 'other bæp.' These transferences are sometimes extraordinary. A boy who had had a pig drawn for him, the pig being called *öf*, at the age of 1.6 used *öf* (1) for a pig, (2) for drawing a pig, (3) for writing in general.

Such transferences may seem very absurd, but are not more so than some transferences occurring in the language of grown-up persons. The word *Tripos* passed from the sense of a three-legged stool to the man who sat on a three-legged stool to dispute with candidates for degrees at Cambridge. Then, as it was the duty of Mr. Tripos also to provide comic verses, these were called tripos verses, such verses being printed under that name till very near the end of the nineteenth century, though Mr. Tripos himself had disappeared long ago. And as the examination list was printed on the back of these verses, it was called the Tripos list, and it was no far cry to saying of a successful candidate, "he stands high on the Tripos," which now came to mean the examination itself.

But to return to the classifications in the minds of the children. Hilary M. (1.6 to 2.0) used the word *daisy* (1) of the flower itself, (2) of any flower, (3) of any conventional flower in a pattern, (4) of any pattern. One of the first words she said was *colour* (1.4), and she got into a way of saying it when anything striking attracted her attention. Originally she heard the word of a bright patch of colour in a picture. The word was still in use at the age of two. For some months anything that moved was a *fly*, every man was a *soldier*, everybody that was not a man was a *baby*. S. L. (1.8) used *bing* (1) for a door, (2) for bricks or building with bricks. The connexion is through the bang of a door or a tumbling castle of bricks, but the name was transferred to the objects. It is curious that at 1.3 she had the word *bang* for anything dropped, but not *bing*; at 1.8 she had both, *bing* being specialized as above. From books about children's language I quote two illustrations. Ronjat's son used the word *papement*, which stands for 'kaffemensch,' in speaking about the grocer's boy who brought coffee ; but as he had a kind of uniform with a flat cap, *papement* was also used of German and Russian officers in the illustrated papers. Hilde Stern (1.9) used *bichu* for drawer or chest of drawers ; it originated in the word *bücher* (books), which was said when her picture-books were taken out of the drawer.

A warning is, however, necessary. When a grown-up person says that a child uses the same word to denote various things, he is apt to assume that the child gives a word two or three definite meanings, as *he* does. The process is rather in this way. A child has got a new toy, a horse, and at the same time has heard its elders use the word 'horse,' which it has imitated as well as it can. It now associates the word with the delight of playing with its toy. If the next day it says the same sound, and its friends give it the horse, the child gains the experience that the sound brings the fulfilment of its wish : but if it sets its eye on a china cow and utters the same sound, the father takes note that the sound also denotes a cow, while for the child it is perhaps a mere experiment—" Could not I get my wish for that nice thing fulfilled in the same way ? " If it succeeds, the experiment may very well be repeated, and the more or less faulty imitation of the word ' horse ' thus by the co-operation of those around it may become also firmly attached to ' cow.'

When Elsa B. (1.10), on seeing the stopper of a bottle in the garden, came out with the word ' beer,' it would be rash to conclude (as her father did) that the word ' beer ' to her meant a ' stopper ' : all we know is that her thoughts had taken that direction, and that some time before, on seeing a stopper, she had heard the word ' beer.'

Parents sometimes unconsciously lead a child into error about the use of words. A little nephew of mine asked to taste his father's beer, and when refused made so much to-do that the father said, " Come, let us have peace in the house." Next day, under the same circumstances, the boy asked for ' peace in the house,' and this became the family name for beer. Not infrequently what is said on certain occasions is taken by the child to be the *name* of some object concerned ; thus a sniff or some sound imitating it may come to mean a flower, and ' hurrah ' a flag. S. L. from an early age was fond of flowers, and at 1.8 used ' pretty ' or ' pretty-pretty ' as a substantive instead of the word ' flower,' which she learnt at 1.10.

I may mention here that analogous mistakes may occur when missionaries or others write down words from foreign languages with which they are not familiar. In the oldest list of Greenlandic words (of 1587) there is thus a word *panygmah* given with the signification ' needle ' ; as a matter of fact it means ' my daughter's ' : the Englishman pointed at the needle, but the Eskimo thought he wanted to know whom it belonged to. In an old list of words in the now extinct Polabian language we find " *scumbe*, yesterday, *subuda*, to-day, *janidiglia*, to-morrow " : the questions were put on a Saturday, and the Slav answered accordingly, for *subuta* (the same word as Sabbath) means Saturday, *skumpe* ' fasting-day,' and *ja nedila* ' it is Sunday.'

According to O'Shea (p. 131) " a child was greatly impressed with the horns of a buck the first time he saw him. The father used the term ' sheep ' several times while the creature was being inspected, and it was discovered afterwards that the child had made the association between the word and the animal's horns, so now *sheep* signifies primarily horns, whether seen in pictures or in real life." It is clear that mistakes of that kind will happen more readily if the word is said singly than when it is embodied in whole connected sentences : the latter method is on the whole preferable for many reasons.

VI.—§ 3. Father and Mother.

A child is often faced by some linguistic usage which obliges him again and again to change his notions, widen them, narrow them, till he succeeds in giving words the same range of meaning that his elders give them.

Frequently, perhaps most frequently, a word is at first for the child a proper name. ' Wood ' means not a wood in general, but the particular picture which has been pointed out to the child in the dining-room. The little girl who calls her mother's black muff ' muff,' but refuses to transfer the word to her own white one, is at the same stage. Naturally, then, the word *father* when first heard is a proper name, the name of the child's own father. But soon it must be extended to other individuals who have something or other in common with the child's father. One child will use it of all *men*, another perhaps of all men with beards, while ' lady ' is applied to all pictures of faces without beards ; a third will apply the word to father, mother and grandfather. When the child itself applies the word to another man it is soon corrected, but at the same time it cannot avoid hearing another child call a strange man ' father ' or getting to know that the gardener is Jack's ' father,' etc. The word then comes to mean to the child ' a grown-up person who goes with or belongs to a little one,' and he will say, " See, there goes a dog with his father." Or, he comes to know that the cat is the kittens' father, and the dog the puppies' father, and next day asks, " Wasps, are they the flies' father, or are they perhaps their mother ? " (as Frans did, 4.10). Finally, by such guessing and drawing conclusions he gains full understanding of the word, and is ready to make acquaintance later with its more remote applications, as 'The King is the father of his people ; Father O'Flynn ; Boyle was the father of chemistry,' etc.

Difficulties are caused to the child when its father puts himself on the child's plane and calls his wife 'mother' just as he calls his own mother 'mother,' though at other moments the child hears him call her 'grandmother' or 'grannie.' Professor Sturtevant writes to me that a neighbour child, a girl of about five years, called out to him, "I saw your girl and your mother," meaning 'your daughter and your wife.' In many families the words 'sister' ('Sissie') or 'brother' are used constantly instead of his or her real name. Here we see the reason why so often such names of relations change their meaning in the history of languages ; G. *vetter* probably at first meant 'father's brother,' as it corresponds to Latin *patruus* ; G. *base*, from 'father's sister,' came to mean also 'mother's sister,' 'niece' and 'cousin.' The word that corresponds etymologically to our *mother* has come to mean 'wife' or 'woman' in Lithuanian and 'sister' in Albanian.

The same extension that we saw in the case of 'father' now may take place with real proper names. Tony E. (3.5), when a fresh charwoman came, told his mother not to have *this Mary* : the last charwoman's name was Mary.[1] In exactly the same way a Danish child applied the name of their servant, Ingeborg, as a general word for servant : "Auntie's Ingeborg is called Ann," etc., and a German girl said *viele Augusten* for 'many girls.' This, of course, is the way in which *doll* has come to mean a 'toy baby,' and we use the same extension when we say of a statesman that he is no *Bismarck*, etc.

VI.—§ 4. The Delimitation of Meaning.

The association of a word with its meaning is accomplished for the child by a series of single incidents, and as many words are understood only by the help of the situation, it is natural that the exact force of many of them is not seized at once. A boy of 4.10, hearing that his father had seen the King, inquired, "Has he a head at both ends ? "—his conception of a king being derived from playing-cards. Another child was born on what the Danes call Constitution Day, the consequence being that he confused birthday and Constitution Day, and would speak of " my Consti-

[1] Cf. Beach-la-Mar, below, Ch. XII § 1.

tution Day," and then his brother and sister also began to talk of their Constitution Day.

Hilary M. (2.0) and Murdoch D. (2.6) used *dinner, breakfast* and *tea* interchangeably—the words might be translated ' meal.' Other more or less similar confusions may be mentioned here. Tony F. (2.8) used the term *sing* for (1) reading, (2) singing, (3) any game in which his elders amused him.   Hilary said indifferently, ' Daddy, *sing* a story three bears,' and ' Daddy, *tell* a story three bears.'   She cannot remember which is *knife* and which is *fork*. Beth M. (2.6) always used *can't* when she meant *won't*.   It meant simply refusal to do what she did not want to.

VI.—§ 5. Numerals. Time.

It is interesting to watch the way in which arithmetical notions grow in extent and clearness.   Many children learn very early to say *one, two*, which is often said to them when they learn how to walk ; but no ideas are associated with these syllables.   In the same way many children are drilled to say *three* when the parents begin with *one, two*, etc.   The idea of plurality is gradually developed, but a child may very well answer *two* when asked how many fingers papa has ; Frans used the combinations *some-two* and *some-three* to express ' more than one ' (2.4).   At the age of 2.11 he was very fond of counting, but while he always got the first four numbers right, he would skip over 5 and 7 ; and when asked to count the apples in a bowl, he would say rapidly 1–2–3–4, even if there were only three, or stop at 3, even if there were five or more.   At 3.4 he counted objects as far as 10 correctly, but might easily pass from 11 to 13, and if the things to be counted were not placed in a row he was apt to bungle by moving his fingers irregularly from one to another.   When he was 3.8 he answered the question " What do 2 and 2 make ? " quite correctly, but next day to the same question he answered " Three," though in a doubtful tone of voice.   This was in the spring, and next month I noted : " His sense of number is evidently weaker than it was : the openair life makes him forget this as well as all the verses he knew by heart in the winter."   When the next winter came his counting exercises again amused him, but at first he was in a fix as before about anynumbers after 6, although he could repeat the numbers till 10 without a mistake.   He was fond of doing sums, and had initiated this game himself by asking : " Mother, if I have two apples and get one more, haven't I then three ?"   His sense of numbers was so abstract that he was caught by a tricky question : " If you have two eyes and one nose, how many ears have you ? " He answered at once, " Three ! "   A child thus seems to think in abstract numbers, and as he learns his numbers as 1, 2, 3, 4, etc., not as one pear, two pears, three pears, one may well be skeptical about the justification for the recommendation made by many pedagogues that at an early stage of the school-life a child should learn to reckon with concrete things rather than with abstract numbers.

A child will usually be familiar with the sound of higher numerals long before it has any clear notion of what they mean. Frans (3.6) said, " They are coming by a train that is called four thirty-four," and (4.4) he asked, " How much is twice hundred ? Is that a thousand ? "

A child's ideas of time are necessarily extremely vague to begin with ; it cannot connect very clear or very definite notions with the expressions it constantly hears others employ, such as ' last Sunday,' ' a week ago,' or ' next year.' The other day I heard a little girl say : " This is where we sat *next time*," evidently meaning ' last time.' All observers of children mention the frequent confusion of words like *to-morrow* and *yesterday*, and the linguist remembers that Gothic *gistradagis* means ' to-morrow,' though it corresponds formally with E. *yesterday* and G. *gestern*.

VI.—§ 6. Various Difficulties.

Very small children will often say *up* both when they want to be taken up and when they want to be put down on the floor. This generally means nothing else than that they have not yet learnt the word *down*, and *up* to them simply is a means to obtain a change of position. In the same way a German child used *hut auf* for having the hat taken off as well as put on, but Meumann rightly interprets this as an undifferentiated desire to have something happen with the hat. But even with somewhat more advanced children there are curious confusions.

Hilary M. (2.0) is completely baffled by words of opposite meaning. She will say, " Daddy, my pinny is too *hot* ; I must warm it at the fire." She goes to the fire and comes back, saying, " That's better ; it's quite *cool* now." (The same confusion of *hot* and *cold* was also reported in the case of one Danish and one German child ; cf. also Tracy, p. 134.) One morning while dressing she said, " What a *nice* windy day," and an hour or two later, before she had been out, " What a *nasty* windy day." She confuses *good* and *naughty* completely Tony F. (2.5) says, " Turn the *dark* out."

Sometimes a mere accidental likeness may prove too much for the child. When Hilary M. had a new doll (2.0) her mother said to her : " And is that your *son* ?" Hilary was puzzled. and

looking out of the window at the sun, said : "No, that's my sun."
It was very difficult to set her out of this confusion.[1] Her sister
Beth (3.8), looking at a sunset, said : "That's what you call a *sun-
set* ; where Ireland (her sister) is (at school) it's a *summerset*."
About the same time, when staying at *Longwood Farm*, she said :
"I suppose if the trees were cut down it would be *Shortwood
Farm* ?"

An English friend writes to me : "I misunderstood the text,
'And there fell from his eyes as it were scales,' as I knew the word
scales only in the sense 'balances.' The phenomenon seemed to
me a strange one, but I did not question that it occurred, any
more than I questioned other strange phenomena recounted in
the Bible. In the lines of the hymn—

> Teach me to live that I may dread
> The grave as little as my bed—

I supposed that the words 'as little as my bed' were descriptive
of my future grave, and that it was my duty according to the
hymn to fear the grave."

Words with several meanings may cause children much difficulty. A Somerset child said, "Moses was not a good boy, and
his mother smacked 'un and smacked 'un and smacked 'un till
she couldn't do it no more, and then she put 'un in the ark of
bulrushes." This puzzled the teacher till he looked at the passage
in Exodus : "And when she could *hide* him no longer, she laid
him in an ark of bulrushes." Here, of course, we have technically
two different words *hide* ; but to the child the difficulty is
practically as great where we have what is called one and the
same word with two distinct meanings, or when a word is used
figuratively.

The word 'child' means two different things, which in some
languages are expressed by two distinct words. I remember my
own astonishment at the age of nine when I heard my godmother
talk of her children. "But you have no children." "Yes, Clara
and Eliza." I knew them, of course, but they were grown up.

Take again the word *old*. A boy knew that he was three years,
but could not be induced to say 'three years old'; no, he is three
years new, and his father too is new, as distinct from his grandmother, who he knows is old. A child asked, "Why have
grand dukes and *grand* pianos got the same name ?" (Glenconner, p. 21).

When Frans was told (4.4) "Your eyes are running," he was
much astonished, and asked, "Are they running away ?"

[1] Cf. below on the disappearance of the word *son* because it sounds like
sun (Ch. XV. § 7).

Sometimes a child knows a word first in some secondary sense. When a country child first came to Copenhagen and saw a soldier, he said, " There is a tin-soldier " (2.0). Stern has a story about his daughter who was taken to the country and wished to pat the backs of the pigs, but was checked with the words, " Pigs always lie in dirt," when she was suddenly struck with a new idea ; " Ah, that is why they are called pigs, because they are so dirty : but what would people call them if they didn't lie in the dirt ? " History repeats itself : only the other day a teacher wrote to me that one of his pupils had begun his essay with the words : " Pigs are rightly called thus, for they are such swine."

Words of similar sound are apt to be confused. Some children have had trouble till mature years with *soldier* and *shoulder*, *hassock* and *cassock*, *diary* and *dairy*. Lady Glenconner writes : " They almost invariably say ' lemon ' [for melon], and if they make an effort to be more correct they still mispronounce it. ' Don't say melling.' ' Very well, then, mellum.' " Among other confusions mentioned in her book I may quote *Portugal* for ' purgatory,' King Solomon's three hundred *Columbines*, David and his great friend *Johnson*, Cain and *Mabel*—all of them showing how words from spheres beyond the ordinary ken of children are assimilated to more familiar ones.

Schuchardt has a story of a little coloured boy in the West Indies who said, " It's *three* hot in this room " : he had heard *too*=*two* and literally wanted to ' go one better.' According to Mr. James Payne, a boy for years substituted for the words ' *Hallowed* be Thy name ' ' *Harold* be Thy name.' Many children imagine that there is a *pole* to mark where the North Pole is, and even (like Helen Keller) that polar bears climb the Pole.

This leads us naturally to what linguists call ' popular etymology '—which is very frequent with children in all countries. I give a few examples from books. A four-year-old boy had heard several times about his nurse's *neuralgia*, and finally said : " I don't think it's *new* ralgia, I call it old ralgia." In this way *anchovies* are made into *hamchovies*, *whirlwind* into *worldwind*, and *holiday* into *hollorday*, a day to holloa. Professor Sturtevant writes : A boy of six or seven had frequently had his ear irrigated ; when similar treatment was applied to his nose, he said that he had been ' nosigated '—he had evidently given his own interpretation to the first syllable of *irrigate*.

There is an element of ' popular etymology ' in the following joke which was made by one of the Glenconner children when four years old : " I suppose you wag along in the *wagonette*, the *landau* lands you at the door, and you sweep off in the *brougham* " (pronounced broom).

VI.—§ 7. Shifters.

A class of words which presents grave difficulty to children are those whose meaning differs according to the situation, so that the child hears them now applied to one thing and now to another. That was the case with words like 'father,' and 'mother.' Another such word is 'enemy.' When Frans (4.5) played a war-game with Eggert, he could not get it into his head that he was Eggert's enemy : no, it was only Eggert who was the enemy. A stronger case still is 'home.' When a child was asked if his grandmother had been at home, and answered : "No, grandmother was at grandfather's," it is clear that for him 'at home ' meant merely 'at my home.' Such words may be called shifters. When Frans (3.6) heard it said that 'the one' (glove) was as good as 'the other,' he asked, "Which is the one and which is the other ? "—a question not easy to answer.

The most important class of shifters are the personal pronouns. The child hears the word 'I' meaning 'Father,' then again meaning 'Mother,' then again 'Uncle Peter,' and so on unendingly in the most confusing manner. Many people realize the difficulty thus presented to the child, and to obviate it will speak of themselves in the third person as 'Father' or 'Grannie' or 'Mary,' and instead of saying 'you' to the child, speak of it by its name. The child's understanding of what is said is thus facilitated for the moment : but on the other hand the child in this way hears these little words less frequently and is slower in mastering them.

If some children soon learn to say 'I' while others speak of themselves by their name, the difference is not entirely due to the different mental powers of the children, but must be largely attributed to their elders' habit of addressing them by their name or by the pronouns. But Germans would not be Germans, and philosophers would not be philosophers, if they did not make the most of the child's use of 'I,' in which they see the first sign of self-consciousness. The elder Fichte, we are told, used to celebrate not his son's birthday, but the day on which he first spoke of himself as 'I.' The sober truth is, I take it, that a boy who speaks of himself as 'Jack' can have just as full and strong a perception of himself as opposed to the rest of the world as one who has learnt the little linguistic trick of saying 'I.' But this does not suit some of the great psychologists, as seen from the following quotation : "The child uses no pronouns ; it speaks of itself in the third person, because it has no idea of its 'I' (Ego) nor of its 'Not-I,' because it knows nothing of itself nor of others."

It is not an uncommon case of confusion for a child to use 'you' and 'your' instead of 'I,' 'me,' and 'mine.' The child has noticed that 'will you have?' means 'will Jack have?' so that he looks on 'you' as synonymous with his own name. In some children this confusion may last for some months. It is in some cases connected with an inverted word-order, 'do you' meaning 'I do'—an instance of 'echoism' (see below). Some times he will introduce a further complication by using the personal pronoun of the third person, as though he had started the sentence with 'Jack'—then 'you have his coat' means 'I have my coat.' He may even speak of the person addressed as 'I.' 'Will I tell a story?' = 'Will you tell a story?' Frans was liable to use these confused forms between the ages of two and two and a-half, and I had to quicken his acquaintance with the right usage by refusing to understand him when he used the wrong. Beth M. (2.6) was very jealous about her elder sister touching any of her property, and if the latter sat on her chair, she would shriek out: "That's *your* chair; that's *your* chair."

The forms *I* and *me* are a common source of difficulty to English children. Both Tony E. (2.7 to 3.0) and Hilary M. (2.0) use *my* for *me*; it is apparently a kind of blending of *me* and *I*; e.g. "Give Hilary medicine, make *my* better," "Maggy is looking at *my*," "Give it *my*." See also O'Shea, p. 81: '*my* want to do this or that; *my* feel bad; that is *my* pencil; take *my* to bed.'

His and *her* are difficult to distinguish: "An ill lady, *his* legs were bad" (Tony E., 3.3).

C. M. L. (about the end of her second year) constantly used *wour* and *wours* for *our* and *ours*, the connexion being with *we*, as 'your' with *you*. In exactly the same way many Danish children say *vos* for *os* on account of *vi*. But all this really falls under our next chapter.

VI.—§ 8. Extent of Vocabulary.

The number of words which the child has at command is constantly increasing, but not uniformly, as the increase is affected by the child's health and the new experiences which life presents to him. In the beginning it is tolerably easy to count the words the child uses; later it becomes more difficult, as there are times when his command of speech grows with astonishing rapidity. There is great difference between individual children. Statistics have often been given of the extent of a child's vocabulary at different ages, or of the results of comparing the vocabularies of a number of children.

An American child who was closely observed by his mother, Mrs. Winfield S. Hall, had in the tenth month 3 words, in the eleventh 12, in the twelfth 24, in the thirteenth 38, in the fourteenth 48, in the fifteenth 106, in the sixteenth 199, and in the seventeenth 232 words (*Child Study Monthly*, March 1897). During the first month after the same boy was six years old, slips of paper and pencils were distributed over the house and practically everything which the child said was written down. After two or three days these were collected and the words were put under their respective letters in a book kept for that purpose. New sets of papers were put in their places and other lists made. In addition to this, the record of his life during the past year was examined and all of his words not already listed were added. In this way his summer vocabulary was obtained; conversations on certain topics were also introduced to give him an opportunity to use words relating to such topics. The list is printed in the *Journal of Childhood and Adolescence*, January 1902, and is well worth looking through. It contains 2,688 words, apart from proper names and numerals. No doubt the child was really in command of words beyond that total.

This list perhaps is exceptional on account of the care with which it was compiled, but as a rule I am afraid that it is not wise to attach much importance to these tables of statistics. One is generally left in the dark whether the words counted are those that the child has understood, or those that it has actually used —two entirely different things. The passive or receptive knowledge of a language always goes far beyond the active or productive.

One also gets the impression that the observers have often counted up words without realizing the difficulties involved. What is to be counted as a word ? Are *I, me, we, us* one word or four ? Is *teacup* a new word for a child who already knows *tea* and *cup* ? And so for all compounds. Is *box* (= a place at a theatre) the same word as *box* (= workbox) ? Are the two *thats* in 'that man that you see' two words or one ? It is clear that the process of counting involves so much that is arbitrary and uncertain that very little can be built on the statistics arrived at.

It is more interesting perhaps to determine what words at a given age a child does *not* know, or rather does not understand when he hears them or when they occur in his reading. I have myself collected such lists, and others have been given me by teachers, who have been astonished at words which their classes did not understand. A teacher can never be too cautious about assuming linguistic knowledge in his pupils—and this applies not only to foreign words, about which all teachers are on the alert, but also to what seem to be quite everyday words of the language of the country.

In connexion with the growth of vocabulary one may ask how many words are possessed by the average grown-up man ? Max Müller in his *Lectures* stated on the authority of an English clergyman that an English farm labourer has only about three hundred words at command. This is the most utter balderdash, but nevertheless it has often been repeated, even by such an authority on psychology as Wundt. A Danish boy can easily learn seven hundred English words in the first year of his study of the language—and are we to believe that a grown Englishman, even of the lowest class, has no greater stock than such a beginner ? If you go through the list of 2,000 to 3,000 words used by the American boy of six referred to above, you will easily convince yourself that they would far from suffice for the rudest labourer. A Swedish dialectologist, after a minute investigation, found that the vocabulary of Swedish peasants amounted to at least 26,000 words, and his view has been confirmed by other investigators. This conclusion is not invalidated by the fact that Shakespeare in his works uses only about 20,000 words and Milton in his poems only about 8,000. It is easy to see what a vast number of words of daily life are seldom or never required by a poet, especially a poet like Milton, whose works are on elevated subjects. The words used by Zola or Kipling or Jack London would no doubt far exceed those used by Shakespeare and Milton.[1]

VI.—§ 9. Summary.

To sum up, then. There are only very few words that are explained to the child, and so long as it is quite small it will not even understand the explanations that might be given. Some it learns because, when the word is used, the object is at the same time pointed at, but most words it can only learn by drawing conclusions about their meaning from the situation in which they arise or from the context in which they are used. These conclusions, however, are very uncertain, or they may be correct for the particular occasion and not hold good on some other, to the child's mind quite similar, occasion. Grown-up people are in the same position with regard to words they do not know, but which they come across in a book or newspaper, e.g. *demise*. The meanings of many words are at the same time extraordinarily vague and yet so strictly limited (at least in some respects) that the least deviation is felt as a mistake. Moreover, the child often learns a secondary or figurative meaning of a word before its simple

[1] Cf. the fuller treatment of this question in GS ch. ix.

meaning. But gradually a high degree of accuracy is obtained, the fittest meanings surviving—that is (in this connexion) those that agree best with those of the surrounding society. And thus the individual is merged in society, and the social character of language asserts itself through the elimination of everything that is the exclusive property of one person only.

CHAPTER VII

GRAMMAR

§ 1. Introductory. § 2. Substantives and Adjectives. § 3. Verbs. § 4. Degrees of Consciousness. § 5. Word-formation. § 6. Word-division. § 7. Sentences. § 8. Negation and Question. § 9. Prepositions and Idioms.

VII.—§ 1. Introductory.

To learn a language it is not enough to know so many words. They must be connected according to the particular laws of the particular language. No one tells the child that the plural of ' hand ' is *hands*, of ' foot ' *feet*, of ' man ' *men*, or that the past of ' am ' is *was*, of ' love ' *loved* ; it is not informed when to say *he* and when *him*, or in what order words must stand. How can the little fellow learn all this, which when set forth in a grammar fills many pages and can only be explained by help of many learned words ?

Many people will say it comes by ' instinct,' as if ' instinct ' were not one of those fine words which are chiefly used to cover over what is not understood, because it says so precious little and seems to say so precious much. But when other people, using a more everyday expression, say that it all ' comes quite of itself,' I must strongly demur : so far is it from ' coming of itself ' that it demands extraordinary labour on the child's part. The countless grammatical mistakes made by a child in its early years are a tell-tale proof of the difficulty which this side of language presents to him—especially, of course, on account of the unsystematic character of our flexions and the irregularity of its so-called ' rules ' of syntax.

At first each word has only one form for the child, but he soon discovers that grown-up people use many forms which resemble one another in different connexions, and he gets a sense of the purport of these forms, so as to be able to imitate them himself or even develop similar forms of his own. These latter forms are what linguists call analogy-formations : by analogy with ' Jack's hat ' and ' father's hat ' the child invents such as ' uncle's hat ' and ' Charlie's hat '—and inasmuch as these forms are ' correct,' no one can say on hearing them whether the child

has really invented them or has first heard them used by others.
It is just on account of the fact that the forms developed on the
spur of the moment by each individual are in the vast majority
of instances perfectly identical with those used already by other
people, that the principle of analogy comes to have such paramount
importance in the life of language, for we are all thereby driven
to apply it unhesitatingly to all those instances in which we have
no ready-made form handy : without being conscious of it, each
of us thus now and then really creates something never heard
before by us or anybody else.

VII.—§ 2. Substantives and Adjectives.

The -*s* of the possessive is so regular in English that it is not
difficult for the child to attach it to all words as soon as the
character of the termination has dawned upon him. But at first
there is a time with many children in which words are put together
without change, so that ' Mother hat ' stands for ' Mother's hat ' ;
cf. also sentences like " Baby want baby milk."

After the *s*-form has been learnt, it is occasionally attached to
pronouns, as *you's* for ' your,' or more rarely *I's* or *me's* for ' my.'

The -*s* is now in English added freely to whole groups of words,
as in *the King of England's power*, where the old construction was
the King's power of England, and in *Beaumont and Fletcher's plays*
(see on the historical development of this group genitive my
ChE iii.). In Danish we have exactly the same construction,
and Danish children will very frequently extend it, placing the
-*s* at the end of a whole interrogative sentence, e.g., ' Hvem er
det da's ? ' (as if in English, ' Who is it then's,' instead of ' Whose
is it then ? '). Dr. H. Bradley once wrote to me : " One of your
samples of children's Danish is an exact parallel to a bit of child's
English that I noted long ago. My son, when a little boy, used
to say ' Who is that-'s ' (with a pause before the *s*) for ' Whom
does that belong to ? ' "

Irregular plurals are often regularized, *gooses* for ' geese,'
tooths, knifes, etc O'Shea mentions one child who inversely
formed the plural *chieves* for *chiefs* on the analogy of *thieves*.

Sometimes the child becomes acquainted with the plural form
first, and from it forms a singular. I have noticed this several
times with Danish children, who had heard the irregular plural
kœr, ' cows,' and then would say *en kœ* instead of *en ko* (while
others from the singular *ko* form a regular plural *koer*). French
children will say *un chevau* instead of *un cheval*.

In the comparison of adjectives analogy-formations are
frequent with all children, e.g. *the littlest, littler, goodest, baddest,*

splendider, etc. **One** child is reported as saying *quicklier,* another as saying *quickerly,* instead of the received *more quickly.* A curious formation is " P'raps it was John, but *p'rapser* it was Mary."

O'Shea **(p. 108)** notices a period of transition when the child may use the analogical form at one moment and the traditional one the next. Thus S. (4.0) will say *better* perhaps five times where he says *gooder* once, but in times of excitement he will revert to the latter form.

VII.—§ 3. Verbs.

The child at first tends to treat all verbs on the analogy of *love, loved, loved,* or *kiss, kissed, kissed,* thus *catched, buyed, frowed* for ' caught, bought, threw or thrown,' etc., but gradually it learns the irregular forms, though in the beginning with a good deal of hesitation and confusion, as *done* for ' did,' *hunged* for ' hung,' etc. O'Shea gives among other sentences (p. 94) : " I *drunked* my milk." " Budd *swunged* on the rings." " Grandpa *boughted* me a ring." " I *caughted* him." " Aunt Net *camed* to-day." " He *gaved* it to me "—in all of which the irregular form has been supplemented with the regular ending.

A little Danish incident may be thus rendered in English. The child (4.6) : " I have seed a chestnut." " Where have you seen it ? " He : " I seen it in the garden." This shows the influence of the form last heard.

I once heard a French child say " Il a pleuvy " for ' plu ' from ' pleuvoir.' Other analogical forms are *prendu* for ' pris ' ; *assire* for ' asseoir ' (from the participle *assis*), *se taiser* for ' se taire ' (from the frequent injunction *taisez-vous*). Similar formations are frequent in all countries.

VII.—§ 4. Degrees of Consciousness.

Do the little brains *think* about these different forms and their uses ? Or is the learning of language performed as unconsciously as the circulation of the blood or the process of digestion ? Clearly they do not think about grammatical forms in the way pursued in grammar-lessons, with all the forms of the same word arranged side by side of one another, with rules and exceptions. Still there is much to lead us to believe that the thing does not go of itself without some thinking over. The fact that in later years we speak our language without knowing how we do it, the right words and phrases coming to us no one knows how or whence, is no proof that it was always so. We ride a bicycle without giving a thought to the machine, look around us, talk with a friend, etc., and yet there was a time when every movement had to be mastered by slow and painful efforts. There would be nothing strange in supposing that it is the same with the acquisition of language.

Of course, it would be idle to ask children straight out if they think about these things, and what they think. But now and then one notices something which shows that at an early age they think about points of grammar a good deal. When Frans was 2.9, he lay in bed not knowing that anyone was in the next room, and he was heard to say quite plainly: "Små hænder hedder det—lille hånd—små hænder—lille hænder, næ små hænder." ("They are called small hands—little hand—small hands—little hands, no, small hands": in Danish *lille* is not used with a plural noun.) Similar things have been related to me by other parents, one child, for instance, practising plural forms while turning over the leaves of a picture-book, and another one, who was corrected for saying *nak* instead of *nikkede* ('nodded'), immediately retorted "*Stikker stak, nikker nak,*" thus showing on what analogy he had formed the new preterit. Frequently children, after giving a form which their own ears tell them is wrong, at once correct it: 'I sticked it in—I stuck it in.'

A German child, not yet two, said: "Papa, hast du mir was mitgebringt—gebrungen—gebracht?" almost at a breath (Gabelontz), and another (2.5) said *hausin,* but then hesitated and added: "Man kann auch häuser sagen" (Meringer).

VII.—§ 5. Word-formation.

In the forming of words the child's brain is just as active. In many cases, again, it will be impossible to distinguish between what the child has heard and merely copied and what it has itself fashioned to a given pattern. If a child, for example, uses the word 'kindness,' it is probable that he has heard it before, but it is not certain, because he might equally well have formed the word himself. If, however, we hear him say 'kindhood,' or 'kindship,' or 'wideness,' 'broadness,' 'stupidness,' we know for certain that he has made the word up himself, because the resultant differs from the form used in the language he hears around him. A child who does not know the word 'spade' may call the tool a *digger*; he may speak of a lamp as a *shine*. He may say *it suns* when the sun is shining (cf. it rains), or ask his mother to *sauce* his pudding. It is quite natural that the enormous number of nouns and verbs of exactly the same form in English (*blossom, care, drink, end, fight, fish, ape, hand, dress,* etc.) should induce children to make new verbs according to the same pattern;

I quote a few of the examples given by O'Shea : " I am going to
basket these apples." " I *pailed* him out " (took a turtle out of
a washtub with a pail). " 1 *needled* him " (put a needle through
a fly).

Other words are formed by means of derivative endings, as
sorrified, lessoner (O'Shea 32), *flyable* (able to fly, Glenconner 3);
" This tooth ought to come out, because it is *crookening* the others "
(a ten-year-old, told me by Professor Ayres). Compound nouns,
too, may be freely formed, such as *wind-ship, eye-curtain* (O'Shea),
a *fun-copy* of Romeo and Juliet (travesty, Glenconner 19).
Bryan L. (ab. 5) said *springklers* for chrysalises (' because they
wake up in the spring ').

Sometimes a child will make up a new word through ' blend-
ing ' two, as when Hilary M. (1 8 to 2) spoke of *rubbish* = the
*rub*ber to pol*ish* the boots, or of the *backet*, from *bat* and ra*cquet*.
Beth M. (2.0) used *breakolate*, from *break*fast and cho*colate*, and
Chally as a child's name, a compound of two sisters, *Ch*arity and
S*ally*.

VII.—§ 6. Word-division.

We are so accustomed to see sentences in writing or print
with a little space left after each word, that we have got altogether wrong conceptions of language as it is spoken. Here words
follow one another without the least pause till the speaker
hesitates for a word or has come to the end of what he has to
say. ' Not at all ' sounds like ' not a tall.' It therefore requires
in many cases a great deal of comparison and analysis on the
part of the child to find out what is one and what two or three
words. We have seen before that the question ' How big is the
boy ? ' is to the child a single expression, beyond his powers of
analysis, and to a much later age it is the same with other phrases.
The child, then, may make false divisions, and either treat a group
of words as one word or one word as a group of words. A girl
(2.6) used the term ' Tanobijeu ' whenever she wished her
younger brother to get out of her way. Her parents finally discovered that she had caught up and shortened a phrase that
some older children had used—' 'Tend to your own business '
(O'Shea).

A child, addressing her cousin as ' Aunt Katie,' was told " I
am not Aunt Katie, I am merely Katie." Next day she said :
" Good-morning, Aunt merely-Katie " (translated). A child who
had been praised with the words, ' You are a good boy,' said to
his mother, " You're a good boy, mother " (2.8).

Cecil H. (4.0) came back from a party and said that she had
been given something very nice to eat. " What was it ? "

"Rats." "No, no." "Well, it was mice then." She had been asked if she would have 'some-ice,' and had taken it to be 'some mice.' S. L. (2.6) constantly used 'ababana' for 'banana'; the form seems to have come from the question "Will you have a banana?" but was used in such a sentence as "May I have an ababana?" Children will often say *napple* for *apple* through a misdivision of *an-apple*, and *normous* for *enormous*; cf. Ch. X § 2.

A few examples may be added from children's speech in other countries. Ronjat's child said *nésey* for 'échelle,' starting from u'ne échelle; Grammont's child said *un tarbre*, starting from *cet arbre*, and *ce nos* for 'cet os,' from *un os*; a German child said *motel* for 'hotel,' starting from the combination 'im (h) otel' (Stern). Many German children say *arrhöe*, because they take the first syllable of 'diarrhöe' as the feminine article. A Dutch child heard the phrase ''k weet 't niet' ('I don't know'), and said "Papa, hij kweet 't niet" (Van Ginneken). A Danish child heard his father say, "Jeg skal op i *ministeriet*" ("I'm going to the Government office"), and took the first syllable as *min* (my); consequently he asked, "Skal du i dinisteriet?" A French child was told that they expected Munkácsy (the celebrated painter, in French pronounced as Mon-), and asked his aunt: "Est-ce que *ton Kácsy* ne viendra pas?" Antoinette K. (7.), in reply to "C'est bien, je te félicite," said, "Eh bien, moi je ne te *fais* pas *livile.*"

The German 'Ich habe *antgewortet*' is obviously on the analogy of *angenommen*, etc. (Meringer). Danish children not unfrequently take the verb *telefonere* as two words, and in the interrogative form will place the personal pronoun in the middle of it, 'Tele hun fonerer?' ('Does she telephone?') A girl asked to see *ele mer fant* (as if in English she had said 'ele more phant'). Cf. 'Give me *more handier-cap*' for 'Give me a greater handicap' —in a foot-race (O'Shea 108).

VII.—§ 7. Sentences.

In the first period the child knows nothing of grammar: it does not connect words together, far less form sentences, but each word stands by itself. 'Up' means what we should express by a whole sentence, 'I want to get up,' or 'Lift me up'; 'Hat' means 'Put on my hat,' or 'I want to put my hat on,' or 'I have my hat on,' or 'Mamma has a new hat on'; 'Father' can be either 'Here comes Father,' or 'This is Father,' or 'He is called Father,' or 'I want Father to come to me,' or 'I want this or that from Father.' This particular group of sounds is vaguely associated with the mental picture of the person in question, and is uttered at the sight of him or at the mere wish to see him or something else in connexion with him.

When we say that such a word means what we should express by a whole sentence, this does not amount to saying that the child's ' Up ' *is* a sentence, or a sentence-word, as many of those who have written about these questions have said. We might just as well assert that clapping our hands is a sentence, because it expresses the same idea (or the same frame of mind) that is otherwise expressed by the whole sentence ' This is splendid.' The word ' sentence ' presupposes a certain grammatical structure, which is wanting in the child's utterance.

Many investigators have asserted that the child's first utterances are not means of imparting information, but always an expression of the child's wishes and requirements. This is certainly somewhat of an exaggeration, since the child quite clearly can make known its joy at seeing a hat or a plaything, or at merely being able to recognize it and remember the word for it ; but the statement still contains a great deal of truth, for without strong feelings a child would not say much, and it is a great stimulus to talk that he very soon discovers that he gets his wishes fulfilled more easily when he makes them known by means of certain sounds.

Frans (1.7) was accustomed to express his longings in general by help of a long *m* with rising tone, while at the same time stretching out his hand towards the particular thing that he longed for. This he did, for example, at dinner, when he wanted water. One day his mother said, " Now see if you can say *vand* (water)," and at once he said what was an approach to the word, and was delighted at getting something to drink by that means. A moment later he repeated what he had said, and was inexpressibly delighted to have found the password which at once brought him something to drink. This was repeated several times. Next day, when his father was pouring out water for himself, the boy again said ' van,' ' van,' and was duly rewarded. He had not heard the word during the intervening twenty-four hours, and nothing had been done to remind him of it. After some repetitions (for he only got a few drops at a time) he pronounced the word for the first time quite correctly. The day after, the same thing occurred ; the word was never heard but at dinner. When he became rather a nuisance with his constant cries for water, his mother said : " Say please "—and immediately came his " Bebe vand " (" Water, please ")—his first attempt to put two words together.

Later—in this formless period—the child puts more and more words together, often in quite haphazard order : ' My go snow '

('I want to go out into the snow'), etc. A Danish child of 2.1 said the Danish words (imperfectly pronounced, of course) corresponding to "Oh papa lamp mother boom," when his mother had struck his father's lamp with a bang. Another child said "Papa hen corn cap" when he saw his father give corn to the hens out of his cap.

When Frans was 1.10, passing a post-office (which Danes call 'posthouse'), he said of his own accord the Danish words for 'post, house, bring, letter' (a pause between the successive words) —I suppose that the day before he had heard a sentence in which these words occurred. In the same month, when he had thrown a ball a long way, he said what would be in English 'dat was good.' This was not a sentence which he had put together for himself, but a mere repetition of what had been said to him, clearly conceived as a whole, and equivalent to 'bravo.' Sentences of this kind, however, though taken as units, prepare the way for the understanding of the words 'that' and 'was' when they turn up in other connexions.

One thing which plays a great rôle in children's acquisition of language, and especially in their early attempts to form sentences, is Echoism : the fact that children echo what is said to them. When one is learning a foreign language, it is an excellent method to try to imitate to oneself in silence every sentence which one hears spoken by a native. By that means the turns of phrases, the order of words, the intonation of the sentence are firmly fixed in the memory—so that they can be recalled when required, or rather recur to one quite spontaneously without an effort. What the grown man does of conscious purpose our children to a large extent do without a thought—that is, they repeat aloud what they have just heard, either the whole, if it is a very short sentence, or more commonly the conclusion, as much of it as they can retain in their short memories. The result is a matter of chance—it need not always have a meaning or consist of entire words. Much, clearly, is repeated without being understood, much, again, without being more than half understood. Take, for example (translated) :

Shall I carry you ?—Frans (1.9) : Carry you.
Shall Mother carry Frans ?—Carry Frans.
The sky is so blue.—So boo.
I shall take an umbrella.—Take rella.

Though this feature in a child's mental history has been often noticed, no one seems to have seen its full significance. One of the acutest observers (Meumann, p. 28) even says that it has no importance in the development of the child's speech. On the contrary, I think that Echoism explains very much indeed. First let us bear in mind the mutilated forms of words which a child

uses : *'chine* for machine, *'gar* for cigar, *Trix* for Beatrix, etc.
Then a child's frequent use of an indirect form of question rather
than direct, ' Why you smoke, Father ? ' which can hardly be
explained except as an echo of sentences like ' Tell me why you
smoke.' This plays a greater rôle in Danish than in English,
and the corresponding form of the sentence has been frequently
remarked by Danish parents. Another feature which is nearly
constant with Danish children at the age when echoing is habitual
is the inverted word order : this is used after an initial adverb
(*nu kommer hun*, etc.), but the child will use it in all cases (*kommer
hun*, etc.). Further, the extremely frequent use of the infinitive,
because the child hears it towards the end of a sentence, where
it is dependent on a preceding *can*, or *may*, or *must*. ' Not eat
that ' is a child's echo of ' You mustn't eat that.' In German
this has become the ordinary form of official order : " Nicht
hinauslehnen " (" Do not lean out of the window ").

VII.—§ 8. Negation and Question.

Most children learn to say ' no ' before they can say ' yes '
—simply because negation is a stronger expression of feeling than
affirmation. Many little children use *nenenene* (short *ĕ*) as a
natural expression of fretfulness and discomfort. It is perhaps
so natural that it need not be learnt : there is good reason for
the fact that in so many languages words of negation begin with
n (or *m*). Sometimes the *n* is heard without a vowel : it is only
the gesture of ' turning up one's nose ' made audible.

At first the child does not express what it is that it does
not want—it merely puts it away with its hand, pushes away,
for example, what is too hot for it. But when it begins to express
in words what it is that it will not have, it does so often in the
form ' Bread no,' often with a pause between the words, as two
separate utterances, as when we might say, in our fuller forms of
expression : ' Do you offer me bread ? I won't hear of it.' So
with verbs : ' I sleep no.' Thus with many Danish children,
and I find the same phenomenon mentioned with regard to children
of different nations. Tracy says (p. 136): " Negation was expressed
by an affirmative sentence, with an emphatic *no* tacked on at
the end, exactly as the deaf-mutes do." The blind-deaf Helen
Keller, when she felt her little sister's mouth and her mother
spelt ' teeth ' to her, answered : " Baby teeth—no, baby eat—
no," i.e., baby cannot eat because she has no teeth. In the same
way, in German, ' Stul nei nei—schossel,' i.e., I won't sit on the
chair, but in your lap, and in French, ' Papa abeié ato non, iaian
abeié non,' i.e., Papa n'est pas encore habillé, Suzanne n'est pas

habillée (Stern, 189, 203). It seems thus that this mode of expression will crop up everywhere as an emphatic negation.

Interrogative sentences come generally rather early—it would be better to say questions, because at first they do not take the form of interrogative sentences, the interrogation being expressed by bearing, look or gesture : when it begins to be expressed by intonation we are on the way to question expressed in speech. Some of the earliest questions have to do with place : ' Where is . . . ? ' The child very often hears such sentences as ' Where is its little nose ? ' which are not really meant as questions ; we may also remark that questions of this type are of great practical importance for the little thing, who soon uses them to beg for something which has been taken away from him or is out of his reach. Other early questions are ' What's that ? ' and ' Who ? '

Later—generally, it would seem, at the close of the third year —questions with ' why ' crop up : these are of the utmost importance for the child's understanding of the whole world and its manifold occurrences, and, however tiresome they may be when they come in long strings, no one who wishes well to his child will venture to discourage them. Questions about time, such as ' When ? How long ? ' appear much later, owing to the child's difficulty in acquiring exact ideas about time.

Children often find a difficulty in double questions, and when asked ' Will you have brown bread or white ? ' merely answer the last word with ' Yes.' So in reply to ' Is that red or yellow ? ' ' Yes ' means ' yellow ' (taken from a child of 4.11). I think this is an instance of the short memories of children, who have already at the end of the question forgotten the beginning, but Professor Mawer thinks that the real difficulty here is in making a choice : they cannot decide between alternatives : usually they are silent, and if they say ' Yes ' it only means that they do not want to go without both or feel that they must say something.

VII.—§ 9. Prepositions and Idioms.

Prepositions are of very late growth in a child's languag Much attention has been given to the point, and Stern has collected statistics of the ages at which various children have first used prepositions : the earliest age is 1.10, the average age is 2.3. It does not, however, seem to me to be a matter of much interest how early an individual word of some particular grammatical class is first used ; it is much more interesting to follow up the gradual growth of the child's command of this class and to see how the first inevitable mistakes and confusions arise in the little brain. Stern makes the interesting remark that when the tendency to use prepositions first appears, it grows far more rapidly than the power to discriminate one preposition from another; with his own children there came a time when they employed the same word as a sort of universal preposition in all relations. Hilda used *von*, Eva *auf*. I have never observed anything corresponding to this among Danish children.

All children start by putting the words for the most important concepts together without connective words, so ' Leave go bedroom ' (' May I have leave to go into the bedroom ? '), ' Out road ' (' I am going out on the road '). The first use of prepositions is always in set phrases learnt as wholes, like ' go to school,' ' go to pieces,' ' lie in bed,' ' at dinner.' Not till later comes the power of using prepositions in free combinations, and it is then that mistakes appear. Nor is this surprising, since in all languages prepositional usage contains much that is peculiar and arbitrary, chiefly because when we once pass beyond a few quite clear applications of time and place, the relations to be expressed become so vague and indefinite, that logically one preposition might often seem just as right as another, although usage has laid down a fast law that this preposition must be used in this case and that in another. I noted down a great number of mistakes my own boy made in these words, but in all cases I was able to find some synonymous or antonymous expression in which the preposition used would have been the correct one, and which may have been vaguely before his mind.

The multiple meanings of prepositions sometimes have strange results. A little girl was in her bath, and hearing her mother say : " I will wash you in a moment," answered : " No, you must wash me in the bath " ! She was led astray by the two uses of *in*. We know of the child at school who was asked " What is an average ? " and said : " What the hen lays eggs on." Even men of science are similarly led astray by prepositions. It is perfectly natural to say that something has passed over the threshold of consciousness : the metaphor is from the way in which you enter a house by stepping over the threshold. If the metaphor were kept, the opposite situation would be expressed by the statement that such and such a thing is outside the threshold of consciousness. But psychologists, in the thoughtless way of little children, take *under* to be always the opposite of *over*, and so speak of things ' lying under (or below) the threshold of our consciousness,' and have even invented a Latin word for the unconscious, viz. *subliminal*.[1]

H. G. Wells writes (*Soul of a Bishop*, 94) : " He was lugging things now into speech that so far had been *scarcely above the threshold* of his conscious thought." Here we see the wrong interpretation of the preposition *over* dragging with it the synonym *above*.

Children may use verbs with an object which require a preposition (' Will you *wait* me ? '), or which are only used intransitively (' Will you *jump* me ? '), or they may mix up an infinitival with a direct construction (' Could you hear me sneezed ? '). But it is surely needless to multiply examples.

When many years ago, in my *Progress in Language*, I spoke of the advantages, even to natives, of simplicity in linguistic structure, Professor Herman Möller, in a learned review, objected to me that to the adult learning a foreign tongue the chief difficulty consists in " the countless chicaneries due to the tyrannical and capricious usage, whose tricks there is no calculating ; but these offer to the native child no such difficulty as morphology may," and again, in speaking of the choice of various prepositions, which is far from easy to the foreigner, he says : " But any considerable mental exertion on the part of the native child learning its mother-tongue is here, of course, out of the question." Such assertions as these cannot be founded on actual observation ; at any rate, it is my experience in listening to children's talk that long after they have reached the point where they make hardly any mistake in pronunciation and verbal forms, etc., they are still capable of using many turns of speech which are utterly opposed to the spirit of the language, and which are in the main of the same kind as those which foreigners are apt to fall into. Many of the child's mistakes are due to mixtures or blendings of two turns of expression, and not a few of them may be logically justified. But learning a language implies among other things learning what you may *not* say in the language, even though no reasonable ground can be given for the prohibition.

CHAPTER VIII

SOME FUNDAMENTAL PROBLEMS

§ 1. Why is the Native Language learnt so well ? § 2. Natural Ability and Sex. § 3. Mother-tongue and Other Tongue. § 4. Playing at Language. § 5. Secret Languages. § 6. Onomatopœia. § 7. Word-inventions. § 8. ‘Mamma’ and ‘Papa.’

VIII.—§ 1. Why is the Native Language learnt so well ?

How does it happen that children in general learn their mother-tongue so well ? That this is a problem becomes clear when we contrast a child's first acquisition of its mother-tongue with the later acquisition of any foreign tongue. The contrast is indeed striking and manifold : *here* we have a quite little child, without experience or prepossessions ; *there* a bigger child, or it may be a grown-up person with all sorts of knowledge and powers : *here* a haphazard method of procedure ; *there* the whole task laid out in a system (for even in the schoolbooks that do not follow the old grammatical system there is a certain definite order of progress from more elementary to more difficult matters) : *here* no professional teachers, but chance parents, brothers and sisters, nursery-maids and playmates ; *there* teachers trained for many years specially to teach languages : *here* only oral instruction ; *there* not only that, but reading-books, dictionaries and other assistance. And yet this is the result : *here* complete and exact command of the language as a native speaks it, however stupid the children ; *there*, in most cases, even with people otherwise highly gifted, a defective and inexact command of the language. On what does this difference depend ?

The problem has never been elucidated or canvassed from all sides, but here and there one finds a partial answer, often given out to be a complete answer. Often one side of the question only is considered, that which relates to sounds, as if the whole problem had been solved when one had found a reason for children acquiring a better pronunciation of their mother-tongue than one generally gets in later life of a foreign speech.

Many people accordingly tell us that children's organs of speech are especially flexible, but that this suppleness of the tongue and lips is lost in later life. This explanation. however, does not hold water, as is shown sufficiently by the countless mistakes in sound made by children. If their organs were as flexible as is pretended, they could learn sounds correctly at once, while as a matter of fact it takes a long time before all the sounds and groups of sounds are imitated with tolerable accuracy. Suppleness is not something which is original, but something acquired later, and acquired with no small difficulty, and then only with regard to the sounds of one's own language, and not universally.

The same applies to the second answer (given by Bremer, *Deutsche Phonetik*, 2), namely, that the child's ear is especially sensitive to impressions. The ear also requires development, since at first it can scarcely detect a number of *nuances* which we grown-up people hear most distinctly.

Some people say that the reason why a child learns its native language so well is that it has no established habits to contend against. But that is not right either : as any good observer can see, the process by which the child acquires sounds is pursued through a continuous struggle against bad habits which it has acquired at an earlier stage and which may often have rooted themselves remarkably firmly.

Sweet (H 19) says among other things that the conditions of learning vernacular sounds are so favourable because the child has nothing else to do at the time. On the contrary, one may say that the child has an enormous deal to do while it is learning the language ; it is at that time active beyond all belief : in a short time it subdues wider tracts than it ever does later in a much longer time. The more wonderful is it that along with those tasks it finds strength to learn its mother-tongue and its many refinements and crooked turns.

Some point to heredity and say that a child learns that language most easily which it is disposed beforehand to learn by its ancestry, or in other words that there are inherited convolutions of the brain which take in this language better than any other. Perhaps there is something in this, but we have no definite, carefully ascertained facts. Against the theory stands the fact that the children of immigrants acquire the language of their foster-country to all appearance just as surely and quickly as children of the same age whose forefathers have been in the country for ages. This may be observed in England, in Denmark, and still more in North America. Environment clearly has greater influence than descent.

The real answer in my opinion (which is not claimed to be absolutely new in every respect) lies partly in the child itself, partly in the behaviour towards it of the people around it. In the first place, the time of learning the mother-tongue is the most favourable of all, namely, the first years of life. If one assumes that mental endowment means the capacity for development, without doubt all children are best endowed in their first years : from birth onwards there is a steady decline in the power of grasping what is new and of accommodating oneself to it. With some this decline is a very rapid one—they quickly become fossilized and unable to make a change in their habits ; with others one can notice a happy power of development even in old age ; but no one keeps very long in its full range the adaptability of his first years.

Further, we must remember that the child has far more abundant opportunities of hearing his mother-tongue than one gets, as a rule, with any language one learns later. He hears it from morning to night, and, be it noted, in its genuine shape, with the right pronunciation, right intonation, right use of words and right syntax : the language comes to him as a fresh, ever-bubbling spring. Even before he begins to say anything himself, his first understanding of the language is made easier by the habit that mothers and nurses have of repeating the same phrases with slight alterations, and at the same time doing the thing which they are talking about. " Now we must wash the little face, now we must wash the little forehead, now we must wash the little nose, now we must wash the little chin, now we must wash the little ear," etc. If *men* had to attend to their children, they would never use so many words—but in that case the child would scarcely learn to understand and talk as soon as it does when it is cared for by women.[1]

Then the child has, as it were, private lessons in its mother-tongue all the year round. There is nothing of the kind in the learning of a language later, when at most one has six hours a week and generally shares them with others. The child has another priceless advantage : he hears the language in all possible situations and under such conditions that language and situation ever correspond exactly to one another and mutually illustrate one another. Gesture and facial expression harmonize with the words

[1] Women know
The way to rear up children, (to be just)
They know a simple, merry, tender knack
Of stringing pretty words that make no sense,
And kissing full sense into empty words,
Which things are corals to cut life upon,
Although such trifles : children learn by such
Love's holy earnest in a pretty play
And get not over-early solemnized . . .
Such good do mothers. Fathers love as well
—Mine did, I know—but still with heavier brains,
And wills more consciously responsible,
And not as wisely, since less foolishly.
ELIZABETH BROWNING : *Aurora Leigh*, 10.

uttered and keep the child to a right understanding. Here there
is nothing unnatural, such as is often the case in a language-lesson
in later years, when one talks about ice and snow in June or
excessive heat in January. And what the child hears is just what
immediately concerns him and interests him, and again and again
his own attempts at speech lead to the fulfilment of his dearest
wishes, so that his command of language has great practical
advantages for him.

Along with what he himself sees the use of, he hears a great
deal which does not directly concern him, but goes into the little
brain and is stored up there to turn up again later. Nothing is
heard but leaves its traces, and at times one is astonished to
discover what has been preserved, and with what exactness. One
day, when Frans was 4.11 old, he suddenly said : " Yesterday—
isn't there some who say yesterday ? " (giving *yesterday* with the
correct English pronunciation), and when I said that it was an
English word, he went on : " Yes, it is Mrs. B. : she often says
like that, yesterday." Now, it was three weeks since that lady
had called at the house and talked English. It is a well-known
fact that hypnotized persons can sometimes say whole sentences
in a language which they do not know, but have merely heard in
childhood. In books about children's language there are many
remarkable accounts of such linguistic memories which had lain
buried for long stretches of time. A child who had spent the
first eighteen months of its life in Silesia and then came to Berlin,
where it had no opportunity of hearing the Silesian pronunciation,
at the age of five suddenly came out with a number of Silesian
expressions, which could not after the most careful investigation
be traced to any other source than to the time before it could talk
(Stern, 257 ff.). Grammont has a story of a little French girl,
whose nurse had talked French with a strong Italian accent ; the
child did not begin to speak till a month after this nurse had left,
but pronounced many words with Italian sounds, and some of
these peculiarities stuck to the child till the age of three.

We may also remark that the baby's teachers, though, regarded
as teachers of language, they may not be absolutely ideal, still
have some advantages over those one encounters as a rule later in
life. The relation between them and the child is far more cordial
and personal, just because they are not teachers first and foremost.
They are immensely interested in every little advance the child
makes. The most awkward attempt meets with sympathy, often
with admiration, while its defects and imperfections never expose
it to a breath of unkind criticism. There is a Slavonic proverb,
" If you wish to talk well, you must murder the language first."
But this is very often overlooked by teachers of language, who

demand faultless accuracy from the beginning, and often keep
their pupils grinding so long at some little part of the subject that
their desire to learn the language is weakened or gone for good.
There is nothing of this sort in the child's first learning of his
language.

It is here that our distinction between the two periods comes
in, that of the child's own separate 'little language' and that
of the common or social language. In the first period the little
one is the centre of a narrow circle of his own, which waits for
each little syllable that falls from his lips as though it were a
grain of gold. What teachers of languages in later years would
rejoice at hearing such forms as we saw before used in the time
of the child's 'little language,' *fant* or *vat* or *ham* for 'elephant'?
But the mother really does rejoice: she laughs and exults when
he can use these syllables about his toy-elephant, she throws the
cloak of her love over the defects and mistakes in the little one's
imitations of words, she remembers again and again what his
strange sounds stand for, and her eager sympathy transforms
the first and most difficult steps on the path of language to the
merriest game.

It would not do, however, for the child's 'little language' and
its dreadful mistakes to become fixed. This might easily happen,
if the child were never out of the narrow circle of its own family,
which knows and recognizes its 'little language.' But this is
stopped because it comes more and more into contact with others—
uncles and aunts, and especially little cousins and playmates:
more and more often it happens that the mutilated words are not
understood, and are corrected and made fun of, and the child
is incited in this way to steady improvement: the 'little language'
gradually gives place to the 'common language,' as the child
becomes a member of a social group larger than that of his own
little home.

We have now probably found the chief reasons why a child
learns his mother-tongue better than even a grown-up person
who has been for a long time in a foreign country learns the
language of his environment. But it is also a contributory reason
that the child's linguistic needs, to begin with, are far more limited
than those of the man who wishes to be able to talk about anything, or at any rate about something. Much more is also linguistically required of the latter, and he must have recourse to
language to get all his needs satisfied, while the baby is well looked
after even if it says nothing but *wawawawa*. So the baby has
longer time to store up his impressions and continue his experiments, until by trying again and again he at length gets his lesson
learnt in all its tiny details, while the man in the foreign country,

who *must* make himself understood, as a rule goes on trying only till he has acquired a form of speech which he finds natives understand : at this point he will generally stop, at any rate as far as pronunciation and the construction of sentences are concerned (while his vocabulary may be largely increased). But this 'just recognizable' language is incorrect in thousands of small details, and, inasmuch as bad little habits quickly become fixed, the kind of language is produced which we know so well in the case of resident foreigners—who need hardly open their lips before everyone knows they are not natives, and before a practised ear can detect the country they hail from.[1]

VIII.—§ 2. Natural Ability and Sex.

An important factor in the acquisition of language which we have not considered is naturally the individuality of the child. Parents are apt to draw conclusions as to the abilities of their young hopeful from the rapidity with which he learns to talk ; but those who are in despair because their Tommy cannot say a single word when their neighbours' Harry can say a great deal may take comfort. Slowness in talking *may* of course mean deficiency of ability, or even idiocy, but not necessarily. A child who chatters early may remain a chatterer all his life, and children whose motto is 'Slow and sure' may turn out the deepest, most independent and most trustworthy characters in the end. There are some children who cannot be made to say a single word for a long time, and then suddenly come out with a whole sentence, which shows how much has been quietly fructifying in their brain. Carlyle was one of these : after eleven months of taciturnity he heard a child cry, and astonished all by saying, " What ails wee Jock ? " Edmund Gosse has a similar story of his own childhood, and other examples have been recorded elsewhere (Meringer, 194 ; Stern, 257).

[1] This is not the place to speak of the way in which prevalent methods of teaching foreign languages can be improved. A slavish copying of the manner in which English children learn English is impracticable, and if it were practicable it would demand more time than anyone can devote to the purpose. One has to make the most of the advantages which the pupils possess over babies, thus, their being able to read, their power of more sustained attention, etc. Phonetic explanation of the new sounds and phonetic transcription have done wonders to overcome difficulties of pronunciation. But in other respects it is possible to some extent to assimilate the teaching of a foreign language to the method pursued by the child in its first years : one should not merely sprinkle the pupil, but plunge him right down into the sea of language and enable him to swim by himself as soon as possible, relying on the fact that a great deal will arrange itself in the brain without the inculcation of too many special rules and explanations. For details I may refer to my book, *How to Teach a Foreign Language* (London, George Allen and Unwin).

The linguistic development of an individual child is not always in a steady rising line, but in a series of waves. A child who seems to have a boundless power of acquiring language suddenly stands still or even goes back for a short time. The cause may be sickness, cutting teeth, learning to walk, or often a removal to new surroundings or an open-air life in summer. Under such circumstances even the word 'I' may be lost for a time.

Some children develop very rapidly for some years until they have reached a certain point, where they stop altogether, while others retain the power to develop steadily to a much later age. It is the same with some races : negro children in American schools may, while they are little, be up to the standard of their white schoolfellows, whom they cannot cope with in later life.

The two sexes differ very greatly in regard to speech—as in regard to most other things. Little girls, on the average, learn to talk earlier and more quickly than boys ; they outstrip them in talking correctly ; their pronunciation is not spoilt by the many bad habits and awkwardnesses so often found in boys. It has been proved by statistics in many countries that there are far more stammerers and bad speakers among boys and men than among girls and women. The general receptivity of women, their great power of, and pleasure in, imitation, their histrionic talent, if one may so say—all this is a help to them at an early age, so that they can get into other people's way of talking with greater agility than boys of the same age.

Everything that is conventional in language, everything in which the only thing of importance is to be in agreement with those around you, is the girls' strong point. Boys may often show a certain reluctance to do exactly as others do : the peculiarities of their 'little language' are retained by them longer than by girls, and they will sometimes steadily refuse to correct their own abnormalities, which is very seldom the case with girls. Gaucherie and originality thus are two points between which the speech of boys is constantly oscillating. Cf. below, Ch. XIII.

VIII.—§ 3. Mother-tongue and Other Tongue.

The expression "mother-tongue" should not be understood too literally : the language which the child acquires naturally is not, or not always, his mother's language. When a mother speaks with a foreign accent or in a pronounced dialect, her children as a rule speak their language as correctly as other children, or keep only the slightest tinge of their mother's peculiarities. I have seen this very distinctly in many Danish families, in which the mother has kept up her Norwegian language all her life, and in which the children have spoken pure Danish. Thus also in two families I know, in which a strong Swedish accent in one mother, and an unmistakable American pronunciation in the other, have not prevented the children from speaking Danish exactly as if their mothers had been born and bred in Denmark. I cannot, therefore, agree with Passy, who says that the child learns his mother's sound system (Ch § 32), or with Dauzat's dictum to the same effect (V 20). The father, as a rule, has still less influence ; but what is decisive is the speech of those with whom the child comes in closest contact from the age of three or so, thus frequently servants, but even more effectually playfellows of his own age or rather slightly older than himself, with whom he is constantly thrown together for hours at a time and whose prattle is constantly in his ears at the most impressionable age, while he may not see and hear his father and mother except for a short time every day, at meals and on such occasions. It is also a well-known fact that the children of Danish parents in Greenland often learn the Eskimo language before Danish ; and Meinhof says that German children in the African colonies will often learn the language of the natives earlier than German (MSA 139).

This is by no means depreciating the mother's influence, which is strong indeed, but chiefly in the first period, that of the child's ' little language.' But that is the time when the child's imitative power is weakest. His exact attention to the minutiæ of language dates from the time when he is thrown into a wider circle and has to make himself understood by many, so that his language becomes really identical with that of the community, where formerly he and his mother would rest contented with what *they*, but hardly anyone else, could understand.

The influence of children on children cannot be overestimated.[1] Boys at school make fun of any peculiarities of speech noticed in schoolfellows who come from some other part of the country. Kipling tells us in *Stalky and Co.* how Stalky and Beetle carefully *kicked* McTurk out of his Irish dialect. When I read this, I was vividly reminded of the identical method my new friends applied to me when at the age of ten I was transplanted from Jutland to a school in Seeland and excited their merriment through some Jutlandish expressions and intonations. And so we may say that the most important factor in spreading the common or standard language is children themselves.

It often happens that children who are compelled at home to talk without any admixture of dialect talk pure dialect when playing with their schoolfellows out of doors. They can keep the

---

[1] Hence, also, the second or third child in a family will, as a rule, learn to speak more rapidly than the eldest.

two forms of speech distinct. In the same way they can learn two languages less closely connected. At times this results in very strange blendings. at least for a time ; but many children will easily pass from one language to the other without mixing them up, especially if they come in contact with the two languages in different surroundings or on the lips of different people.

It is, of course, an advantage for a child to be familiar with two languages : but without doubt the advantage may be, and generally is, purchased too dear. First of all the child in question hardly learns either of the two languages as perfectly as he would have done if he had limited himself to one. It may seem, on the surface, as if he talked just like a native, but he does not really command the fine points of the language. Has any bilingual child ever developed into a great artist in speech, a poet or orator ?

Secondly, the brain effort required to master two languages instead of one certainly diminishes the child's power of learning other things which might and ought to be learnt. Schuchardt rightly remarks that if a bilingual man has two strings to his bow, both are rather slack, and that the three souls which the ancient Roman said he possessed, owing to his being able to talk three different languages, were probably very indifferent souls after all. A native of Luxemburg, where it is usual for children to talk both French and German, says that few Luxemburgers talk both languages perfectly. "Germans often say to us : ' You speak German remarkably well for a Frenchman,' and French people will say, ' They are Germans who speak our language excellently.' Nevertheless, we never speak either language as fluently as the natives. The worst of the system is, that instead of learning things necessary to us we must spend our time and energy in learning to express the same thought in two or three languages at the same time." [1]

VIII.—§ 4. Playing at Language.

The child takes delight in making meaningless sounds long after it has learnt to talk the language of its elders. At 2.2 Frans amused himself with long series of such sounds, uttered with the most confiding look and proper intonation, and it was a joy to him when I replied with similar sounds. He kept up this game for years. Once (4.11) after such a performance he asked me : " Is that English ? "—" No."—" Why not ? "—" Because I under-stand English, but I do not understand what you say." An hour later he came back and asked : "Father, do you know all languages ? "—" No, there are many I don't know."—" Do you

[1] I translate this from Ido, see *The International Language*, May 1912.

know German ? "—" Yes." (Frans looked rather crestfallen :
the servants had often said of his invented language that he
was talking · German. So he went on) " Do you know
Japanese ?"—" No."—(Delighted) "So remember when I say
something you don't understand, it's Japanese."

It is the same everywhere. Hawthorne writes : " Pearl mumbled
something into his ear, that sounded, indeed, like human language,
but was only such gibberish as children may be heard amusing
themselves with, by the hour together " (*The Scarlet Letter*, 173).
And R. L. Stevenson : " Children prefer the shadow to the substance.
When they might be speaking intelligibly together, they chatter
senseless gibberish by the hour, and are quite happy because they
are making believe to speak French " (*Virginibus P.*, 236 ; cf.
Glenconner, p. 40 ; Stern, pp. 76, 91, 103). Meringer's boy (2.1)
took the music-book and sang a tune of his own making with
incomprehensible words.

Children also take delight in varying the sounds of real words,
introducing, for instance, alliterations, as " Sing a song of sixpence,
A socket full of sye," etc. Frans at 2.3 amused himself by rounding
all his vowels (o for a, y for i), and at 3.1 by making all words of
a verse line he had learnt begin with d, then the same words begin
with t. O'Shea (p. 32) says that " most children find pleasure
in the production of variations upon some of their familiar words.
Their purpose seems to be to test their ability to be original. The
performance of an unusual act affords pleasure in linguistics as in
other matters. II., learning the word *dessert*, to illustrate, plays
with it for a time and exhibits it in a dozen or more variations—
dissert, dishert, dĕsot, des'sert, and so on."

Rhythm and rime appeal strongly to the children's minds.
One English observer says that " a child in its third year will
copy the rhythm of songs and verses it has heard in nonsense
words." The same thing is noted by Meringer (p. 116) and
Stern (p. 103). Tony E. (2.10) suddenly made up the rime
" My mover, I lov-er," and Gordon M. (2.6) never tired of repeating
a phrase of his own composition, " Custard over mustard." A
Danish girl of 3.1 is reported as having a "curious knack of
twisting all words into rimes : bestemor hestemor prestemor,
Gudrun sludrun pludrun, etc."

VIII.—§ 5. Secret Languages.

Children, as we have seen, at first employ play-language for
its own sake, with no *arrière-pensée*, but as they get older they
may see that such language has the advantage of not being understood by their elders, and so they may develop a ' secret language '

consciously. Some such languages are confined to one school, others may be in common use among children of a certain age all over a country. 'M-gibberish' and 'S-gibberish' consist in inserting *m* and *s*, as in *goming mout tomdaym* or *gosings outs tosdays* for 'going out to-day'; 'Marrowskying' or 'Hospital Greek' transfers the initial letters of words, as *renty of plain* for 'plenty of rain,' *flutterby* for 'butterfly'; 'Ziph' or 'Hypernese' (at Winchester) substitutes *wa* for the first of two initial consonants and inserts *p* or *g*, making 'breeches' into *wareechepes* and 'penny' into *pegennepy*. From my own boyhood in Denmark I remember two languages of this sort, in which a sentence like 'du er et lille asen' became *dupu erper etpet lilpillepe apasenpen* and *durbe erbe erbe lirbelerbe arbeserbe* respectively. Closely corresponding languages, with insertion of *p* and addition of *-erbse*, are found in Germany; in Holland we find 'de schoone Mei' made into *depé schoopóonepé Meipéi*, besides an *-erwi-taal* with a variation in which the ending is *-erf*. In France such a language is called *javanais;* 'je vais bien' is made into *je-de-que vais-dai-qai bien-den-qen*. In Savoy the cowherds put *deg* after each syllable and thus make 'a-te kogneu se vaçhi' ('as-tu connu ce vacher ?' in the local dialect) into *a-degá te-dege ko-dego gnu-degu sé-degé va-dega chi-degi?* Nay, even among the Maoris of New Zealand there is a similar secret language, in which instead of 'kei te, haere au ki reira' is said *te-kei te-i-te te-haere-te-re te-a te-u te-ki te-re-te-i-te-ra*. Human nature is pretty much the same everywhere.[1]

VIII.—§ 6. Onomatopœia.

Do children really create new words ? This question has been much discussed, but even those who are most skeptical in that respect incline to allow them this power in the case of words which imitate sounds. Nevertheless, it should be remembered that the majority of onomatopœic words heard from children are not their own invention, but are acquired by them in the same way as other words. Hence it is that such words have different forms in different languages. Thus to English *cockadoodledoo* corresponds French *coquerico*, German *kikeriki* and Danish *kykeliky*, to E. *quack-quack*, F. *cancan*, Dan. *raprap*, etc. These words are an imperfect representation of the birds' natural cry, but from their likeness to it they are easier for the child to seize than an entirely arbitrary name such as *duck*.

But, side by side with these, children do invent forms of their own, though the latter generally disappear quickly in favour of the

---

[1] I have collected a bibliographical list of such 'secret languages' in *Nord. Tidsskrift f. Filologi*, 4r. vol. 5.

traditional forms. Thus Frans (2.3) had coined the word *vakvak*, which his mother had heard sometimes without understanding what he meant, when one day he pointed at some crows while repeating the same word ; but when his mother told him that these birds were called *krager*, he took hold of this word with eagerness and repeated it several times, evidently recognizing it as a better name than his own. A little boy of 2.1 called soda-water *ft*, another boy said *ging* or *gingging* for a clock, also for the railway train, while his brother said *dann* for a bell or clock ; a little girl (1.9) said *pooh* (whispered) for ' match, cigar, pipe,' and *gagag* for ' hen,' etc.

When once formed, such words may be transferred to other things, where the sound plays no longer any rôle. This may be illustrated through two extensions of the same word *bŏom* or *bom*, used by two children first to express the sound of something falling on the floor ; then Ellen K. (1.9) used it for a ' blow,' and finally for anything disagreeable, e.g. soap in the eyes, while Kaare G. (1.8), after seeing a plate smashed, used the word for a broken plate and afterwards for anything broken, a hole in a dress, etc., also when a button had come off or when anything else was defective in any way.

VIII.—§ 7. Word-inventions.

Do children themselves create words—apart from onomatopœic words ? To me there is no doubt that they do. Frans invented many words at his games that had no connexion, or very little connexion, with existing words. He was playing with a little twig when I suddenly heard him exclaim : " This is called *lampetine*," but a little while afterwards he said *lanketine*, and then again *lampetine*, and then he said, varying the play, " Now it is *kluatine* and *traniklualalilua* " (3.6). A month later I write : " He is never at a loss for a self-invented word ; for instance, when he has made a figure with his bricks which resembles nothing whatever, he will say, ' That shall be *lindam*.' " When he played at trains in the garden, there were many stations with fanciful names, and at one time he and two cousins had a word *kukukounen* which they repeated constantly and thought great fun, but whose inner meaning I never succeeded in discovering. An English friend writes about his daughter : " When she was about two and a quarter she would often use some nonsense word in the middle of a perfectly intelligible sentence. When you asked her its meaning she would explain it by another equally unintelligible, and so on through a series as long as you cared to make it." At 2.10 she pretended she had lost her bricks, and when you showed her that they were just by her, she insisted that they were not ' bricks ' at all, but *mums*.

In all accounts of children's talk you find words which cannot
be referred back to the normal language, but which have cropped
up from some unsounded depth of the child's soul. I give a few
from notes sent to me by Danish friends : *goi* ' comb,' *putpui*
' stocking, or any other piece of garment,' *i-a-a* ' chocolate,'
gön ' water to drink, milk ' (kept apart from the usual word *vand*
for water, which she used only for water to wash in), *hesh* ' newspaper, book.' Some such words have become famous in psychological literature because they were observed by Darwin and
Taine. Among less famous instances from other books I may
mention *tibu* ' bird ' (Strümpel), *adi* ' cake ' (Ament), *be'lum-be'lum*
' toy with two men turning about,' *wakaka* ' soldier,' *nda* ' jar,'
pamma ' pencil,' *bium* ' stocking ' (Meringer).

An American correspondent writes that his boy was fond of
pushing a stick over the carpet after the manner of a carpet-
sweeper and called the operation *jazing*. He coined the word
borkens as a name for a particular sort of blocks with which he
was accustomed to play. He was a nervous child and his imagination created objects of terror that haunted him in the dark, and to
these he gave the name of *Boons*. This name may, however, be
derived from *baboons*. Mr. Harold Palmer tells me that his
daughter (whose native language was French) at an early age
used [ˈfuˈwɛ] for ' soap ' and [dɛˈdɛtʃ] for ' horse, wooden horse,
merry-go-round.'

Dr. F. Poulsen, in his book *Rejser og rids* (Copenhagen, 1920),
says about his two-year-old daughter that when she gets hold
of her mother's fur-collar she will pet it and lavish on it all kinds
of tender self-invented names, such as *apu* or *a-fo-me-me*. The latter
word, " which has all the melodious euphony and vague signification
of primitive language," is applied to anything that is rare and
funny and worth rejoicing at. On a summer day's excursion there
was one new *a-fo-me-me* after the other.

In spite of all this, a point on which all the most distinguished
investigators of children's language of late years are agreed is
that children never invent words. Wundt goes so far as to say
that " the child's language is the result of the child's environment,
the child being essentially a passive instrument in the matter "
(S 1. 296)—one of the most wrong-headed sentences I have ever
read in the works of a great scientist. Meumann says : " Preyer
and after him almost every careful observer among child-psycholo-
gists have strongly held the view that it is impossible to speak
of a child inventing a word." Similarly Meringer, L 220, Stern,
126, 273, 337 ff., Bloomfield, SL 12.

These investigators seem to have been led astray by expressions
such as ' shape out of nothing,' ' invent,' ' original creation '

(Urschöpfung), and to have taken this doctrinaire attitude in partial defiance of the facts they have themselves advanced. Expressions like those adduced occur over and over again in their discussions, and Meumann says openly : " Invention demands a methodical proceeding with intention, a conception of an end to be realized." Of course, if that is necessary it is clear that we can speak of invention of words in the case of a chemist seeking a word for a new substance, and not in the case of a tiny child. But are there not many inventions in the technical world, which we do not hesitate to call inventions, which have come about more or less by chance ? Wasn't it so probably with gunpowder ? According to the story it certainly was so with blotting-paper : the foreman who had forgotten to add size to a portion of writing-paper was dismissed, but the manufacturer who saw that the paper thus spoilt could be turned to account instead of the sand hitherto used made a fortune. So according to Meumann blotting-paper has never been ' invented.' If in order to acknowledge a child's creation of a word we are to postulate that it has been produced out of nothing, what about bicycles, fountain-pens, typewriters— each of which was something existing before, carried just a little further ? Are they on that account not inventions ? One would think not, when one reads these writers on children's language, for as soon as the least approximation to a word in the normal language is discovered, the child is denied both ' invention ' and ' the speech-forming faculty ' ! Thus Stern (p. 338) says that his daughter in her second year used some words which might be taken as proof of the power to create words, but for the fact that it was here possible to show how these ' new ' words had grown out of normal words. *Eischei*, for instance, was used as a verb meaning ' go, walk,' but it originated in the words *eins, zwei* (one, two) which were said when the child was taught to walk. Other examples are given comparable to those mentioned above (106, 115) as mutilations of the first period. Now, even if all those words given by myself and others as original inventions of children could be proved to be similar perversions of ' real ' words (which is not likely), I should not hesitate to speak of a word-creating faculty, for *eischei*, ' to walk,' is both in form and still more in meaning far enough from *eins, zwei* to be reckoned a totally new word.

We can divide words ' invented ' by children into three classes :

A. The child gives both sound and meaning.
B. The grown-up people give the sound, and the child the meaning.
C. The child gives the sound, grown-up people the meaning.

But the three classes cannot always be kept apart, especially when the child imitates the grown-up person's sound so badly or seizes the meaning so imperfectly that very little is left of what the grown-up person gives. As a rule, the self-created words will be very short-lived; still, there are exceptions.

O'Shea's account of one of these words is very instructive. "She had also a few words of her own coining which were attached spontaneously to objects, and these her elders took up, and they became fixed in her vocabulary for a considerable period. A word resembling *Ndobbin* was employed for every sort of thing which she used for food. The word came originally from an accidental combination of sounds made while she was eating. By the aid of the people about her in responding to this term and repeating it, she 'selected' it and for a time used it purposefully. She employed it at the outset for a specific article of food; then her elders extended it to other articles, and this aided her in making the extension herself. Once started in this process, she extended the term to many objects associated with her food, even objects as remote from her original experience as dining-room, high-chair, kitchen, and even apple and plum trees" (O'Shea, 27).

To Class A I assign most of the words already given as the child's creations, whether the child be great or small.

Class B is that which is most sparsely represented. A child in Finland often heard the well-known line about King Karl (Charles XII), "Han stod i rök och damm" ("He stood in smoke and dust"), and taking *rö* to be the adjective meaning 'red,' imagined the remaining syllables, which he heard as *kordamm*, to be the name of some piece of garment. This amused his parents so much that *kordamm* became the name of a dressing-gown in that family.

To Class C, where the child contributes only the sound and the older people give a meaning to what on the child's side was meaningless—a process that reminds one of the invention of blotting-paper—belong some of the best-known words, which require a separate section.

VIII.—§ 8. 'Mamma' and 'Papa.'

In the nurseries of all countries a little comedy has in all ages been played—the baby lies and babbles his 'mamama' or 'amama' or 'papapa' or 'apapa' or 'bababa' or 'ababab' without associating the slightest meaning with his mouth-games, and his grown-up friends, in their joy over the precocious child, assign to these syllables a rational sense, accustomed as they are themselves to the fact of an uttered sound having a content, a thought, an idea, corresponding to it. So we get a whole class of words, distinguished by a simplicity of sound-formation—never two consonants together, generally the same consonant repeated with an *a* between, frequently also with an *a* at the end—words found in many languages, often in different forms, but with essentially the same meaning.

First we have words for 'mother.' It is very natural that the mother who is greeted by her happy child with the sound 'mama' should take it as though the child were *calling* her 'mama,' and since she frequently comes to the cradle when she hears the sound, the child himself does learn to use these syllables when he wants to call her. In this way they become a recognized word for the idea 'mother'—now with the stress on the first syllable, now on the second. In French we get a nasal vowel either in the last syllable only or in both syllables. At times we have only one syllable, *ma*. When once these syllables have become a regular word they follow the speech laws which govern other words; thus among other forms we get the German *muhme*, the meaning of which ('aunt') is explained as in the words mentioned, p. 118. In very early times *ma* in our group of languages was supplied with a termination, so that we get the form underlying Greek *mētēr*, Lat. *mater* (whence Fr. *mère*, etc.), our own *mother*, G. *mutter*, etc. These words became the recognized grown-up words, while *mama* itself was only used in the intimacy of the family. It depends on fashion, however, how 'high up' *mama* can be used: in some countries and in some periods children are allowed to use it longer than in others.

The forms *mama* and *ma* are not the only ones for 'mother.' The child's *am* has also been seized and maintained by the grown-ups. The Albanian word for 'mother' is *ama*, the Old Norse word for 'grandmother' is *amma*. The Latin *am-ita*, formed from *am* with a termination added, came to mean 'aunt' and became in OFr. *ante*, whence E. *aunt* and Modern Fr. *tante*. In Semitic languages the words for 'mother' also have a vowel before *m*: Assyrian *ummu*, Hebrew *'ēm*, etc.

Baba, too, is found in the sense 'mother,' especially in Slavonic languages, though it has here developed various derivative meanings, 'old woman,' 'grandmother,' or 'midwife.' In Tonga we have *bama* 'mother.'

Forms with *n* are also found for 'mother'; so Sanskrit *nanā*, Albanian *nane*. Here we have also Gr. *nannē* 'aunt' and Lat. *nonna*; the latter ceased in the early Middle Ages to mean 'grandmother' and became a respectful way of addressing women of a certain age, whence we know it as *nun*, the feminine counterpart of 'monk.' From less known languages I may mention Greenlandic *a'na·na* 'mother,' *'a·na* 'grandmother.'

Now we come to words meaning ' father,' and quite naturally, where the sound-groups containing *m* have already been interpreted in the sense 'mother,' a word for ' father ' will be sought in the syllables with *p*. It is no doubt frequently noticed in the nursery that the baby says *mama* where one expected *papa*, and vice versa ; but at last he learns to deal out the syllables ' rightly,' as we say. The history of the forms *papa, pappa* and *pa* is analogous to the history of the *m* syllables already traced. We have the same extension of the sound by *tr* in the word *pater*, which according to recognized laws of sound-change is found in the French *père*, the English *father*, the Danish *fader*, the German *vater*, etc. Philologists no longer, fortunately, derive these words from a root *pa* ' to protect,' and see therein a proof of the ' highly moral spirit ' of our aboriginal ancestors, as Fick and others did. *Papa*, as we know, also became an honourable title for a reverend ecclesiastic, and hence comes the name which we have in the form *Pope*.

Side by side with the *p* forms we have forms in *b*—Italian *babbo*, Bulgarian *babá*, Serbian *bába*, Turkish *baba*. Beginning with the vowel we have the Semitic forms *ab, abu* and finally *abba*, which is well known, since through Greek *abbas* it has become the name for a spiritual father in all European languages, our form being *Abbot*.

Again, we have some names for ' father ' with dental sounds : Sanskrit *tatá*, Russian *tata, tyatya*, Welsh *tat*, etc. The English *dad*, now so universal, is sometimes considered to have been borrowed from this Welsh word, which in certain connexions has an initial *d*, but no doubt it had an independent origin. In Slavonic languages *déd* is extensively used for ' grandfather ' or ' old man.' Thus also *deite, teite* in German dialects. *Tata* ' father ' is found in Congo and other African languages, also (*tatta*) in Negro-English (Surinam). And just as words for ' mother ' change their meaning from ' mother ' to ' aunt,' so these forms in some languages come to mean ' uncle ': Gr. *theios* (whence Italian *zio*), Lithuanian *dede*, Russian *dyadya*.

With an initial vowel we get the form *atta*, in Greek used in addressing old people, in Gothic the ordinary word for ' father,' which with a termination added gives the proper name *Attila*, originally ' little father '; with another ending we have Russian *otec*. Outside our own family of languages we find, for instance, Magyar *atya*, Turkish *ata*, Basque *aita*, Greenlandic *a'ta·ta* ' father,' while in the last-mentioned language *a·ta* means ' grandfather.' [1]

---

[1] I subjoin a few additional examples. Basque *aita* 'father,' *ama* 'mother,' *anaya* 'brother' (*Zeitsch. f. rom. Phil.* 17, 146). Manchu *ama* 'father,' *eme* 'mother ' (the vowel relation as in *haha* ' man,' *hehe* ' woman,'

The nurse, too, comes in for her share in these names, as she too is greeted by the child's babbling and is tempted to take it as the child's name for her; thus we get the German and Scandinavian *amme*, Polish *niania*, Russian *nyanya*, cf. our *Nanny*. These words cannot be kept distinct from names for 'aunt,' cf. *amita* above, and in Sanskrit we find *mama* for 'uncle.'

It is perhaps more doubtful if we can find a name for the child itself which has arisen in the same way; the nearest example is the Engl. *babe*, *baby*, German *bube* (with *u* as in *muhme* above); but *babe* has also been explained as a word derived normally from OFr. *baube*, from Lat. *balbus* 'stammering.' When the name *Bab* or *Babs* (*Babbe* in a Danish family) becomes the pet-name for a little girl, this has no doubt come from an interpretation put on her own meaningless sounds. Ital. *bambo* (*bambino*) certainly belongs here. We may here mention also some terms for 'doll,' Lat. *pupa* or *puppa*, G. *puppe*; with a derivative ending we have Fr. *poupée*, E. *puppet* (Chaucer, A 3254, *popelote*). These words have a rich semantic development, cf. *pupa* (Dan. *puppe*, etc.) 'chrysalis,' and the diminutive Lat. *pupillus*, *pupilla*, which was used for 'a little child, minor,' whence E. *pupil* 'disciple,' but also for the little child seen in the eye, whence E. (and other languages) *pupil*, 'central opening of the eye.'

A child has another main interest—that is, in its food, the breast, the bottle, etc. In many countries it has been observed that very early a child uses a long *m* (without a vowel) as a sign that it wants something, but we can hardly be right in supposing that the sound is originally meant by children in this sense. They do not use it consciously till they see that grown-up people on hearing the sound come up and find out what the child wants. And it is the same with the developed forms which are uttered by the child in its joy at getting something to eat, and which are therefore interpreted as the child's expression for food: *am*, *mam*, *mammam*, or the same words with a final *a*—that is, really the same groups of sounds which came to stand for 'mother.' The determination of a particular form to a particular meaning is always due to the adults, who, however, can subsequently *teach* it to the child. Under this heading comes the sound *ham*, which Taine observed to be one child's expression for hunger or thirst (*h* mute?), and similarly the word *mum*, meaning 'something to eat,' invented,

Gabelentz, S 389). Kutenai *pa* 'brother's daughter,' *papa* 'grandmother (said by male), grandfather, grandson,' *pat!* 'nephew,' *ma* 'mother,' *nana* 'younger sister' (of girl), *alnana* 'sisters,' *tite* 'mother-in-law,' *titu* 'father' (of male)—(Boas, *Kutenai Tales*, Bureau of Am. Ethnol. 59, 1918). Cf. also Sapir, "Kinship Terms of the Kootenay Indians" (*Amer. Anthropologist*, vol. 20). In the same writer's *Yana Terms of Relationship* (Univ. of California, 1918) there seems to be very little from this source.

as we are told, by Darwin's son and often uttered with a rising intonation, as in a question, 'Will you give me something to eat ?' Lindner's child (1.5) is said to have used *papp* for everything eatable and *mem* or *mŏm* for anything drinkable. In normal language we have forms like Sanskrit *māmsa* (Gothic *mimz*) and *mās* 'flesh,' our own *meat* (which formerly, like Dan. *mad*, meant any kind of food), German *mus* 'jam' (whence also *gemüse*), and finally Lat. *mandere* and *manducare* 'to chew' (whence Fr. *manger*) —all developments of this childish *ma(m)*.

As the child's first nourishment is its mother's breast, its joyous *mamama* can also be taken to mean the breast. So we have the Latin *mamma* (with a diminutive ending *mammilla*, whence Fr. *mamelle*), and with the other labial sound Engl. *pap*, Norwegian and Swed. dial. *pappe*, Lat. *papilla*; with a different vowel, It. *poppa*, Fr. *poupe*, 'teat of an animal, formerly also of a woman'; with *b*, G. *bübbi*, obsolete E. *bubby*; with a dental, E. *teat* (G. *zitze*), Ital. *tetta*, Dan. *titte*, Swed. dial. *tatte*. Further we have words like E. *pap* 'soft food,' Latin *papare* 'to eat,' orig. 'to suck,' and some G. forms for the same, *pappen, pampen, pampfen*. Perhaps the beginning of the word *milk* goes back to the baby's *ma* applied to the mother's breast or milk ; the latter half may then be connected with Lat. *lac*. In Greenlandic we have *ama·ma* 'suckle.'

Inseparable from these words is the sound, a long *m* or *am*, which expresses the child's delight over something that tastes good ; it has by-forms in the Scotch *nyam* or *nyamnyam*, the English seaman's term *yam* 'to eat,' and with two dentals the French *nanan* 'sweetmeats.' Some linguists will have it that the Latin *amo* 'I love' is derived from this *am*, which expresses pleasurable satisfaction. When a father tells me that his son (1.10) uses the wonderful words *nanancei* for 'chocolate' and *jajajaja* for picture-book, we have no doubt here also a case of a grown person's interpretation of the originally meaningless sounds of a child.

Another meaning that grown-up people may attach to syllables uttered by the child is that of 'good-bye,' as in English *tata*, which has now been incorporated in the ordinary language.[1] Stern probably is right when he thinks that the French *adieu* would not have been accepted so commonly in Germany and other countries if it had not accommodated itself so easily, especially in the form commonly used in German, *ade*, to the child's natural word.

---

[1] *Tata* is also used for 'a walk' (to go out for a ta-ta, or to go out ta-tas) and for 'a hat'—meanings that may very well have developed from the child's saying these syllables when going out or preparing to go out.

There are some words for 'bed, sleep' which clearly belong to this class : Tuscan *nanna* 'cradle,' Sp. *hacer la nana* 'go to sleep,' E. *bye-bye* (possibly associated with *good-bye*, instead of which is also said *byebye*) ; Stern mentions *baba* (Berlin), *beibei* (Russian), *bobo* (Malay), but *bischbisch*, which he also gives here, is evidently (like the Danish *visse*) imitative of the sound used for hushing.

Words of this class stand in a way outside the common words of a language, owing to their origin and their being continually new-created. One cannot therefore deduce laws of sound-change from them in their original shape ; and it is equally wrong to use them as evidence for an original kinship between different families of language and to count them as loan-words, as is frequently done (for example, when the Slavonic *baba* is said to be borrowed from Turkish). The English *papa* and *mam(m)a*, and the same words in German and Danish, Italian, etc., are almost always regarded as borrowed from French ; but Cauer rightly points out that Nausikaa (*Odyssey* 6. 57) addresses her father as *pappa fil*, and Homer cannot be suspected of borrowing from French. Still, it is true that fashion may play a part in deciding how long children may be permitted to say *papa* and *mamma*, and a French fashion may in this respect have spread to other European countries, especially in the seventeenth century. We may not find these words in early use in the *literatures* of the different countries, but this is no proof that the words were not used in the nursery. As soon as a word of this class has somewhere got a special application, this can very well pass as a loan-word from land to land—as we saw in the case of the words *abbot* and *pope*. And it may be granted with respect to the primary use of the words that there are certain national or quasi-national customs which determine what grown people expect to hear from babies, so that one nation expects and recognizes *papa*, another *dad*, a third *atta*, for the meaning 'father.'

When the child hands something to somebody or reaches out for something he will generally say something, and if, as often happens, this is *ta* or *da*, it will be taken by its parents and others as a real word, different according to the language they speak ; in England as *there* or *thanks*, in Denmark as *tak* 'thanks'[1] or *tag* 'take,' in Germany as *da* 'there,' in France as *tiens* 'hold,' in Russia as *day* 'give,' in Italy as *to*, (= *togli*) 'take.' The form *tē* in Homer is interpreted by some as an imperative of *teinō* 'stretch.' These instances, however, are slightly different

---

[1] The Swede Bolin says that his child said *tatt-tatt*, which he interprets as *tack*, even when handing something to others.

in character from those discussed in the main part of this chapter.[1]

[1] The views advanced in § 8 have some points in contact with the remarks found in Stern's ch. xix, p. 300, only that I lay more stress on the arbitrary interpretation of the child's meaningless syllables on the part of the grown-ups, and that I cannot approve his theory of the *m* syllables as ' centripetal ' and the *p* syllables as ' centrifugal affective-volitional natural sounds.' Paul (P § 127) says that the nursery-language with its *bowwow, papa, mama,* etc., " is not the invention of the children ; it is handed over to them just as any other language " ; he overlooks the share children have themselves in these words, or in some of them ; nor are they, as he says, formed by the grown-ups with a purely pedagogical purpose. Nor can I find that Wundt's chapter " Angebliche worterfindung des kindes " (S 1. 273-287) contains decisive arguments. Curtius (K 88) thinks that Gr. *patēr* was first shortened into *pā* and this then extended into *páppa*—but certainly it is rather the other way round.

CHAPTER IX

THE INFLUENCE OF THE CHILD ON LINGUISTIC DEVELOPMENT

§ 1. Conflicting Views.   § 2. Meringer.   Analogy.   § 3. Herzog's Theory of Sound Changes.   § 4. Gradual Shiftings.   § 5. Leaps.   § 6. Assimilations, etc.   § 7. Stump-words.

IX.—§ 1. Conflicting Views.

WE all know that in historical times languages have been constantly changing, and we have much indirect evidence that in prehistoric times they did the same thing. But when it is asked if these changes, unavoidable as they seem to be, are to be ascribed primarily to children and their defective imitation of the speech of their elders, or if children's language in general plays no part at all in the history of language, we find linguists expressing quite contrary views, without the question having ever been really thoroughly investigated.

Some hold that the child acquires its language with such perfection that it cannot be held responsible for the changes recorded in the history of languages : others, on the contrary, hold that the most important source of these changes is to be found in the transmission of the language to new generations. How undecided the attitude even of the foremost linguists may be towards the question is perhaps best seen in the views expressed at different times by Sweet. In 1882 he reproaches Paul with paying attention only to the shiftings going on in the pronunciation of the same individual, and not acknowledging "the much more potent cause of change which exists in the fact that one generation can learn the sounds of the preceding one by imitation only. It is an open question whether the modifications made by the individual in a sound he has once learnt, independently of imitation of those around him, are not too infinitesimal to have any appreciable effect " (CP 153). In the same spirit he asserted in 1899 that the process of learning our own language in childhood is a very slow one, " and the results are always imperfect. . . . If languages were learnt perfectly by the children of each generation, then languages would not change : English children would still speak a language as old at least as ' Anglo-Saxon,' and there would be

11

no such languages as French and Italian. The changes in languages are simply slight mistakes, which in the course of generations completely alter the character of the language " (PS 75). But only one year later, in 1900, he maintains that the child's imitation " is in most cases practically perfect "—" the main cause of sound-change must therefore be sought elsewhere. The real cause of sound-change seems to be organic shifting—failure to hit the mark, the result either of carelessness or sloth . . . a slight deviation from the pronunciation learnt in infancy may easily pass unheeded, especially by those who make the same change in their own pronunciation " (H 19 f.). By the term " organic shifting " Sweet evidently, as seen from his preface, meant shifting in the pronunciation of the adult, thus a modification of the sound learnt ' perfectly ' in childhood. Paul, who in the first edition (1880) of his *Prinzipien der Sprachgeschichte* did not mention the influence of children, in all the following editions (2nd, 1886, p. 58 ; 3rd, 1898, p. 58 ; 4th, 1909, p. 63) expressly says that " die hauptveranlassung zum lautwandel in der übertragung der laute auf neue individuen liegt," while the shiftings within the same generation are very slight. Paul thus modified his view in the opposite direction of Sweet [1]—and did so under the influence of Sweet's criticism of his own first view !

When one finds scholars expressing themselves in this manner and giving hardly any reasons for their views, one is tempted to believe that the question is perhaps insoluble, that it is a mere toss-up, or that in the sentence " children's imitation is nearly perfect " the stress may be laid, according to taste, now on the word *nearly*, and now on the word *perfect*. I am, however, convinced that we can get a little farther, though only by breaking up the question, instead of treating it as one vague and indeterminate whole.

IX.—§ 2. Meringer. Analogy.

Among recent writers Meringer has gone furthest into the question, adhering in the main to the general view that, just as in other fields, social, economic, etc., it is grown-up men who take the lead in new developments, so it is grown-up men, and not women or children, who carry things forward in the field of

[1] The same inconsistency is found in Dauzat, who in 1910 thought that nothing, and in 1912 that nearly everything, was due to imperfect imitation by the child (V 22 ff., Ph 53, cf. 3). Wechssler (L p. 86) quotes passages from Bremer, Passy, Rousselot and Wallensköld, in which the chief cause of sound changes is attributed to the child ; to these might be added Storm (*Phonetische Studien*, 5. 200) and A. Thomson (IF 24, 1909, p. 9), probably also Grammont (*Mél. linguist.* 61). Many writers seem to imagine that the question is settled when they are able to adduce a certain number of *parallel* changes in the pronunciation of some child and in the historical evolution of languages.

language. In one place he justifies his standpoint by a reference
to a special case, and I will take this as the starting-point of my
own consideration of the question. He says : " It can be shown
by various examples that they [changes in language] are decidedly
not due to children. In Ionic, Attic and Lesbian Greek the
words for ' hundreds ' are formed in *-kosioi* (*diakósioi*, etc.), while
elsewhere (in Doric and Bœotian) they appear as *-kátioi*. How
does the *o* arise in *-kósioi* ? It is generally said that it comes
from *o* in the ' tens ' in the termination *-konta*. Can it be children
who have formed the words for hundreds on the model of the
words for tens, children under six years old, who are just learning
to talk ? Such children generally have other things to attend
to than to practise themselves in numerals above a hundred."
Similar formations are adduced from Latin, and it is stated that
the personal pronouns are especially subject to change, but children
do not use the personal pronouns till an age when they are already
in firm possession of the language. Meringer then draws the
conclusion that the share which children take in bringing about
linguistic change is a very small one.

Now, I should like first to remark that even if it is possible to
point to certain changes in language which cannot be ascribed
to little children, this proves nothing with regard to the very
numerous changes which lie outside these limits. And next,
that all the cases here mentioned are examples of formation by
analogy. But from the very nature of the case, the conditions
requisite for the occurrence of such formations are exactly the
same in the case of adults and in that of the children. For what
are the conditions ? Some one feels an impulse to express something, and at the moment has not got the traditional form at
command, and so is driven to evolve a form of his own from the
rest of the linguistic material. It makes no difference whether
he has never heard a form used by other people which expresses
what he wants, or whether he has heard the traditional form,
but has not got it ready at hand at the moment. The method of
procedure is exactly the same whether it takes place in a three-
year-old or in an eighty-three-year-old brain : it is therefore
senseless to put the question whether formations by analogy are
or are not due to children. A formation by analogy is by
definition a non-traditional form. It is therefore idle to ask if
it is due to the fact that the language is transmitted from generation
to generation and to the child's imperfect repetition of what has
been transmitted to it, and Meringer's argument thus breaks
down in every respect.

It must not, of course, be overlooked that children naturally
come to invent more formations by analogy than grown-up people,

because the latter in many cases have heard the older forms so often that they find a place in their speech without any effort being required to recall them. But that does not touch the problem under discussion ; besides, formations by analogy are unavoidable and indispensable, in the talk of all, even of the most 'grown-up': one cannot, indeed, move in language without having recourse to forms and constructions that are not directly and fully transmitted to us : speech is not alone reproduction, but just as much new-production, because no situation and no impulse to communication is in every detail exactly the same as what has occurred on earlier occasions.

IX.—§ 3. Herzog's Theory of Sound Changes.

If, leaving the field of analogical changes, we begin to inquire whether the purely phonetic changes can or must be ascribed to the fact that a new generation has to learn the mother-tongue by imitation, we shall first have to examine an interesting theory in which the question is answered in the affirmative, at least with regard to those phonetic changes which are gradual and not brought about all at once; thus, when in one particular language one vowel, say [e·], is pronounced more and more closely till finally it becomes [i·], as has happened in E. *see* formerly pronounced [se·] with the same vowel as in G. *see*, now [si·]. E. Herzog maintains that such changes happen through transference to new generations, even granted that the children imitate the sound of the grown-up people perfectly. For, it is said, children with their little mouths cannot produce acoustically the same sound as adults, except by a different position of the speech-organs ; this position they keep for the rest of their lives, so that when they are grown-up and their mouth is of full size they produce a rather different sound from that previously heard—which altered sound is again imitated by the next generation with yet another position of the organs, and so on. This continuous play of generation *v.* generation may be illustrated in this way :

ARTICULATION *corresponding to* SOUND.

1st generation	{ young	A1	..	..	..	.. S1
	{ old	A1	..	..	..	.. S2
2nd generation	{ young	A2	..	..	..	.. S2
	{ old	A2	..	..	..	.. S3
3rd generation	{ young	A3	..	..	..	.. S3
	{ old	A3	..	..	..	.. S4, etc.[1]

[1] See E. Herzog, *Streitfragen der roman. philologie*, i. (1904), p. 57—I modify his symbols a little.

It is, however, easy to prove that this theory cannot be correct.
(1) It is quite certain that the increase in size of the mouth is
far less important than is generally supposed (see my *Fonetik*,
p. 379 ff., PhG, p. 80 ff. ; cf. above, V § 1).   (2) It cannot be proved
that people, after once learning one definite way of producing a
sound, go on producing it in exactly the same way, even if the
acoustic result is a different one.   It is much more probable that
each individual is constantly adapting himself to the sounds heard
from those around him, even if this adaptation is neither as
quick nor perhaps as perfect as that of children, who can very
rapidly accommodate their speech to the dialect of new surroundings : if very far-reaching changes are rare in the case of grown-up
people, this proves nothing against such small adaptations as
are here presupposed.   In favour of the continual regulation of
the sound through the ear may be adduced the fact that adults
who become perfectly deaf and thus lose the control of sounds
through hearing may come to speak in such a way that their
words can hardly be understood by others.   (3) The theory in
question also views the relations between successive generations
in a way that is far removed from the realities of life : from the
wording one might easily imagine that there were living together
at any given time only individuals of ages separated by, say,
thirty years' distance, while the truth of the matter is that a
child is normally surrounded by people of all ages and learns its
language more or less from all of them, from Grannie down to
little Dick from over the way, and that (as has already been
remarked) its chief teachers are its own brothers and sisters and
other playmates of about the same age as itself.   If the theory
were correct, there would at any rate be a marked difference
in vowel-sounds between anyone and his grandfather, or, still
more, great-grandfather : but nothing of the kind has ever been
described.   (4) The chief argument, however, against the theory
is this, that were it true, then all shiftings of sounds at all times
and in all languages would proceed in exactly the same direction.
But this is emphatically contradicted by the history of language.
The long *a* in English in one period was rounded and raised into
o, as in OE. *stan, na, ham*, which have become *stone, no, home ;*
but when a few centuries later new long *a*'s had entered the
language, they followed the opposite direction towards *e*, now
[ei], as in *name, male, take*.   Similarly in Danish, where an old
stratum of long *a*'s have become *å*, as in *ål, gås*, while a later stratum
tends rather towards [æ], as in the present pronunciation of *gade*,
hale, etc.   At the same time the long *a* in Swedish tends towards
the rounded pronunciation (cf. Fr. *âme, pas*) : in one sister language
we thus witness a repetition of the old shifting, in the other a

tendency in the opposite direction. And it is the same with all those languages which we can pursue far enough back : they all present the same picture of varying vowel shiftings in different directions, which is totally incompatible with Herzog's view.

IX.—§ 4. Gradual Shiftings.

We shall do well to put aside such artificial theories and look soberly at the facts. When some sounds in one century go one way, and in another, another, while at times they remain long unchanged, it all rests on this, that for human habits of this sort there is no standard measure. Set a man to saw a hundred logs, measuring No. 2 by No. 1, No. 3 by No. 2, and so on, and you will see considerable deviations from the original measure—perhaps all going in the same direction, so that No. 100 is very much longer than No. 1 as the result of the sum of a great many small deviations—perhaps all going in the opposite direction ; but it is also possible that in a certain series he was inclined to make the logs too long, and in the next series too short, the two sets of deviations about balancing one another.

It is much the same with the formation of speech sounds : at one moment, for some reason or other, in a particular mood, in order to lend authority or distinction to our words, we may happen to lower the jaw a little more, or to thrust the tongue a little more forward than usual, or inversely, under the influence of fatigue or laziness, or to sneer at someone else, or because we have a cigar or potato in our mouth, the movements of the jaw or of the tongue may fall short of what they usually are. We have all the while a sort of conception of an average pronunciation, of a normal degree of opening or of protrusion, which we aim at, but it is nothing very fixed, and the only measure at our disposal is that we are or are not understood. What is understood is all right : what does not meet this requirement must be repeated with greater correctness as an answer to ' I beg your pardon ? '

Everyone thinks that he talks to-day just as he did yesterday, and, of course, he does so in nearly every point. But no one knows if he pronounces his mother-tongue in every respect in the same manner as he did twenty years ago. May we not suppose that what happens with faces happens here also ? One lives with a friend day in and day out, and he appears to be just what he was years ago, but someone who returns home after a long absence is at once struck by the changes which have gradually accumulated in the interval.

Changes in the sounds of a language are not, indeed, so rapid as those in the appearance of an individual, for the simple reason that it is not enough for one man to alter his pronunciation, many must co-operate : the social nature and social aim of language has the natural consequence that all must combine in the same movement, or else one neutralizes the changes introduced by the other ; each individual also is continually under the influence of his fellows, and involuntarily fashions his pronunciation according to the impression he is constantly receiving of other people's sounds. But as regards those little gradual shiftings of sounds which take place in spite of all this control and its conservative influence, changes in which the sound and the articulation alter simultaneously, I cannot see that the transmission of the language to a new generation need exert any essential influence : we may imagine them being brought about equally well in a society which for hundreds of years consisted of the same adults who never died and had no issue.

IX.—§ 5. Leaps.

While in the shiftings mentioned in the last paragraphs articulation and acoustic impression went side by side, it is different with some shiftings in which the old sound and the new resemble one another to the ear, but differ in the position of the organs and the articulations. For instance when [þ] as in E. *thick* becomes [f] and [ð] as in E. *mother* becomes [v], one can hardly conceive the change taking place in the pronunciation of people who have learnt the right sound as children. It is very natural, on the other hand, that children should imitate the harder sound by giving the easier, which is very like it, and which they have to use in many other words : forms like *fru* for *through*, *wiv*, *muvver* for *with*, *mother*, are frequent in the mouths of children long before they begin to make their appearance in the speech of adults, where they are now beginning to be very frequent in the Cockney dialect. (Cf. MEG i. 13. 9.) The same transition is met with in Old Fr., where we have *muef* from *modu*, *nif* from *nidu*, *fief* from *feodu*, *seif*, now *soif*, from *site*, *estrif* (E. *strife*) from *stridh*, *glaive* from *gladiu*, *parvis* from *paradis*, and possibly *avoutre* from *adulteru*, *poveir*, now *pouvoir*, from *potere*. In Old Gothonic we have the transition from þ to f before *l*, as in Goth. *plaqus* = MHG. *vlach*, Goth. *plaihan*=OHG. *flêhan*, *pliuhan*=OHG. *fliohan* ; cf. also E. *file*, G. *feile*=ON. *þēl*, OE. *þengel* and *fengel* ' prince,' and probably G. *finster*, cf. OHG. *dinstar* (with *d* from þ), OE. *þeostre*. In Latin we have the same transition, e.g. in *fumus*, corresponding to Sansk. *dhumás*, Gr. *thumós*.[1]

---

[1] In Russian *Marfa*, *Fyodor*, etc., we also have *f* corresponding to original þ, but in this case it is not a transition within one and the same language, but an imperfect imitation on the part of the (adult !) Russians of a sound in a foreign language (Greek *th*) which was not found in their own language

The change from the back-open consonant [x]—the sound in G. *buch* and Scotch *loch*—to *f*, which has taken place in *enough*, *cough*, etc., is of the same kind. Here clearly we have no gradual passage, but a jump, which could hardly take place in the case of those who had already learnt how to pronounce the back sound, but is easily conceivable as a case of defective imitation on the part of a new generation. I suppose that the same remark holds good with regard to the change from *kw* to *p*, which is found in some languages, for instance, Gr. *hippos*, corresponding to Lat. *equus*, Gr. *hepomai*=Lat. *sequor*, *hêpar*=Lat. *jecur*; Rumanian *apa* from Lat. *aqua*, Welsh *map*, ' son '=Gaelic *mac*, *pedwar*=Ir. *cathir*, ' four,' etc. In France I have heard children say [pizin] and [pidin] for *cuisine*.

IX.—§ 6. Assimilations, etc.

There is an important class of sound changes which have this in common with the class just treated, that the changes take place suddenly, without an intermediate stage being possible, as in the changes considered in IX § 4. I refer to those cases of assimilation, loss of consonants in heavy groups and transposition (metathesis), with which students of language are familiar in all languages. Instances abound in the speech of all children ; see above, V § 4.

If now we dared to assert that such pronunciations are never heard from people who have passed their babyhood, we should here have found a field in which children have exercised a great influence on the development of language : but of course we cannot say anything of the sort. Any attentive observer can testify to the frequency of such mispronunciations in the speech of grown-up people. In many cases they are noticed neither by the speaker nor by the hearer, in many they may be noticed, but are considered too unimportant to be corrected, and finally, in some cases the speaker stops to repeat what he wanted to say in a corrected form. Now it would not obviously do, from their frequency in adult speech, to draw the inference : '' These changes are not to be ascribed to children,'' because from their frequent appearance on the lips of the children one could equally well infer : ''They are not to be ascribed to grown-up people '' When we find in Latin *impotens* and *immeritus* with *m* side by side with *indignus* and *insolitus* with *n*, or when English *handkerchief* is pronounced with [ŋk] instead of the original [ndk], the change is not to be charged against children or grown-up people exclusively, but against both parties together : and so when *t* is lost in *waistcoat* [weskət], or *postman* or *castle*, or *k* in *asked*. There is certainly this difference, that when the change is made by older people, we get in the speech of the same individual first the heavier and then the easier form, while the child may take up the easier pronunciation first, because it hears the [n] before a lip consonant as [m], and before a back consonant as [ŋ], or because it fails altogether to hear the middle consonant in *waistcoat, postman, castle* and *asked*. But all this is clearly of purely theoretical interest, and the result remains that the influence of the two classes, adults and children, cannot possibly be separated in this domain.[1]

IX.—§ 7. Stump-words.

Next we come to those changes which result in what one may call 'stump-words.' There is no doubt that words may undergo violent shortenings both by children and adults, but here I believe we can more or less definitely distinguish between their respective contributions to the development of language. If it is the end of the word that is kept, while the beginning is dropped, it is probable that the mutilation is due to children, who, as we have seen (VII § 7), echo the conclusion of what is said to them and forget the beginning or fail altogether to apprehend it. So we get a number of mutilated Christian names, which can then be used by grown-up people as pet-names. Examples are *Bert* for Herbert or Albert, *Bella* for Arabella, *Sander* for Alexander, *Lottie* for Charlotte, *Trix* for Beatrix, and with childlike sound-substitution *Bess* (and *Bet, Betty*) for Elizabeth. Similarly in other languages, from Danish I may mention *Bine* for Jakobine, *Line* for Karoline, *Stine* for Kristine, *Dres* for Andres: there are many others.

If this way of shortening a word is natural to a child who hears the word for the first time and is not able to remember the beginning when he comes to the end of it, it is quite different when others clip words which they know perfectly well: they will naturally keep the beginning and stop before they are half through the word, as soon as they are sure that their hearers understand what is alluded to. Dr. Johnson was not the only one who " had a way of contracting the names of his friends, as Beauclerc, *Beau*; Boswell, *Bozzy*; Langton, *Lanky*; Murphy, *Mur*; Sheridan, *Sherry*; and Goldsmith, *Goldy*, which Gold-

---

[1] Reduplications and assimilations at a distance, as in Fr. *tante* from the older *ante* (whence E. *aunt*, from Lat. *amita*) and *porpentine* (frequent in this and analogous forms in Elizabethan writers) for *porcupine* (*porkepine, porkespine*) are different from the ordinary assimilations of neighbouring sounds in occurring much less frequently in the speech of adults than in children; cf., however, below, Ch. XV 4.

smith resented " (Boswell, *Life*, ed. P. Fitzgerald, 1900, i. 486).
Thackeray constantly says *Pen* for Arthur Pendennis, *Cos* for
Costigan, *Fo* for Foker, *Pop* for Popjoy, *old Col* for Colchicum.
In the beginning of the last century Napoleon Bonaparte was
generally called *Nap* or *Boney* ; later we have such shortened
names of public characters as *Dizzy* for Disraeli, *Pam* for Palmerston,
Labby for Labouchere, etc. These evidently are due to adults,
and so are a great many other clippings, some of which have
completely ousted the original long words, such as *mob* for mobile,
brig for brigantine, *fad* for fadaise, *cab* for cabriolet, *navvy* for
navigator, while others are still felt as abbreviations, such as
photo for photograph, *pub* for public-house, *caps* for capital letters,
spec for speculation, *sov* for sovereign, *zep* for Zeppelin, *divvy*
for dividend, *hip* for hypochondria, *the Cri* and *the Pav* for the
Criterion and the Pavilion, and many other clippings of words
which are evidently far above the level of very small children.
The same is true of the abbreviations in which school and college
slang abounds, words like *Gym*(nastics), *undergrad*(uate), *trig*-
(onometry), *lab*(oratory), *matric*(ulation), *prep*(aration), *the Guv*
for the governor, etc. The same remark is true of similar
clippings in other languages, such as *kilo* for kilogram, G. *ober*
for oberkellner, French *aristo*(crate), *reac*(tionnaire), college terms
like *desse* for descriptive (géométrie d.), *philo* for philosophie,
preu for premier, *seu* for second ; Danish numerals like *tres*
for tresindstyve (60), *halvfjerds*(indstyve), *firs*(indstyve). We are
certainly justified in extending the principle that abbreviation
through throwing away the end of the word is due to those who
have previously mastered the full form, to the numerous instances
of shortened Christian names like *Fred* for Frederick, *Em* for
Emily, *Alec* for Alexander, *Di* for Diana, *Vic* for Victoria, etc.
In other languages we find similar clippings of names more or less
carried through systematically, e.g. Greek *Zeuxis* for Zeuxippos,
Old High German *Wolfo* for Wolfbrand, Wolfgang, etc., Icelandic
Sigga for Sigríðr, *Siggi* for Sigurðr, etc.

I see a corroboration of my theory in the fact that there are
hardly any *family* names shortened by throwing away the beginning : children as a rule have no use for family names.[1] The
rule, however, is not laid down as absolute, but only as holding
in the main. Some of the exceptions are easily accounted for.
'*Cello* for violoncello undoubtedly is an adults' word, originating

[1] Karl Sundén, in his diligent and painstaking book on *Elliptical Words
in Modern English* (Upsala, 1904) [i.e. clipped proper names, for common
names are not treated in the long lists given], mentions only two examples
of surnames in which the final part is kept (*Bart* for Islebart, *Piggy* for
Guineapig, from obscure novels), though he has scores of examples in which
the beginning is preserved.

in France or Italy : but here evidently it would not do to take
the beginning, for then there would be confusion with violin
(violon). *Phone* for telephone : the beginning might just as well
stand for telegraph. *Van* for caravan : here the beginning would
be identical with *car*. *Bus*, which made its appearance immediately
after the first omnibus was started in the streets of London
(1829), probably was thought expressive of the sound of these
vehicles and suggested *bustle*. But *bacco* (*baccer, baccy*) for tobacco
and *taters* for potatoes belong to a different sphere altogether :
they are not clippings of the usual sort, but purely phonetic
developments, in which the first vowel has been dropped in rapid
pronunciation (as in *I s'pose*), and the initial voiceless stop has
then become inaudible ; Dickens similarly writes *'tickerlerly* as
a vulgar pronunciation of particularly.[1]

---

[1] It is often said that stress is decisive of what part is left out in word-
clippings, and from an a priori point of view this is what we should expect.
But as a matter of fact we find in many instances that syllables with weak
stress are preserved, e.g. in *Mac*(donald), *Pen*(dennis), the *Cri, Vic, Nap,
Nat* for Nathaniel (orig. pronounced with [t], not [þ]), *Val* for Percival,
Trix, etc. The middle is never kept as such with omission of the beginning
and the ending ; *Liz* (whence *Lizzy*) has not arisen at one stroke from Elizabeth, but mediately through *Eliz*. Some of the adults' clippings originate
through abbreviations in *writing*, thus probably most of the college terms
(*exam, trig*, etc.), thus also journalists' clippings like *ad* for advertisement,
par for paragraph ; cf. also *caps* for capitals. On stump-words see also
below, Ch. XIV, §§ 8 and 9.

CHAPTER X

THE INFLUENCE OF THE CHILD—*continued*

§ 1. Confusion of Words. § 2. Metanalysis. § 3. Shiftings of Meanings.
§ 4. Differentiations. § 5. Summary. § 6. Indirect Influence. § 7.
New Languages.

X.—§ 1. Confusion of Words.

SOME of the most typical childish sound-substitutions can hardly
be supposed to leave any traces in language as permanently
spoken, because they are always thoroughly corrected by the
children themselves at an early age; among these I reckon the almost
universal pronunciation of *t* instead of *k*. When, therefore, we
do find that in some words a *t* has taken the place of an earlier
k, we must look for some more specific cause of the change : but
this may, in some cases at any rate, be found in a tendency of
children's speech which is totally independent of the inability
to pronounce the sound of *k* at an early age, and is, indeed, in
no way to be reckoned among phonetic tendencies, namely, the
confusion resulting from an association of two words of similar
sound (cf. above, p. 122). This, I take it, is the explanation of
the word *mate* in the sense ' husband or wife,' which has replaced
the earlier *make* : a confusion was here natural, because the word
mate, ' companion,' was similar not only in sound, but also in
signification. The older name for the ' soft roe ' of fishes was
milk (as Dan. *mælk*, G. *milch*), but from the fifteenth century
milt has been substituted for it, as if it were the same organ as
the *milt*, ' the spleen.' Children will associate words of similar
sound even in cases where there is no connecting link in their
significations ; thus we have *bat* for earlier *bak*, *bakke* (the animal,
vespertilio), though the other word *bat*, ' a stick,' is far removed
in sense.

I think we must explain the following cases of isolated sound-
substitution as due to the same confusion with unconnected words
in the minds of children hearing the new words for the first time :
trunk in the sense of ' proboscis of an elephant,' formerly *trump*,
from Fr. *trompe*, confused with *trunk*, ' stem of a tree '; *stark-
naked*, formerly *start-naked*, from *start*, ' tail,' confused with *stark*,
' stiff '; *vent*, ' air-hole,' from Fr. *fente*, confused with *vent*,

' breath ' (for this *v* cannot be due to the Southern dialectal transition from *f*, as in *vat* from *fat*, for that transition does not, as a rule, take place in French loans) ; *cocoa* for *cacao*, confused with *coconut ; match*, from Fr. *mèche*, by confusion with the other *match* ; *chine*, ' rim of cask,' from *chime*, cf. G. *kimme*, ' border,' confused with *chine*, ' backbone.' I give some of these examples with a little diffidence, though I have no doubt of the general principle of childish confusion of unrelated words as one of the sources of irregularities in the development of sounds.

These substitutions cannot of course be separated from instances of ' popular etymology,' as when the phrase *to curry favour* was substituted for the former *to curry favel*, where *favel* means ' a fallow horse,' as the type of fraud or duplicity (cf. G. *den fahlen hengst reiten*, ' to act deceitfully,' *einen auf einem fahlen pferde ertappen*, ' to catch someone lying ').

X.—§ 2. Metanalysis.

We now come to the phenomenon for which I have ventured to coin the term ' metanalysis,' by which I mean that words or word-groups are by a new generation analyzed differently from the analysis of a former age. Each child has to find out for himself, in hearing the connected speech of other people, where one word ends and the next one begins, or what belongs to the kernel and what to the ending of a word, etc. (VII § 6). In most cases he will arrive at the same analysis as the former generation, but now and then he will put the boundaries in another place than formerly, and the new analysis may become general. *A naddre* (the ME. form for OE. *an nædre*) thus became *an adder, a napron* became *an apron, an nauger : an auger, a numpire : an umpire* ; and in psychologically the same way *an ewte* (older form *evete*, OE. *efete*) became *a newt* : metanalysis accordingly sometimes shortens and sometimes lengthens a word. *Riding* as a name of one of the three districts of Yorkshire is due to a metanalysis of *North Thriding* (ON. *þriðjungr*, ' third part '), as well as of *East Thriding, West Thriding*, after the sound of *th* had been assimilated to the preceding *t*.

One of the most frequent forms of metanalysis consists in the subtraction of an *s*, which originally belonged to the kernel of a word, but is mistaken for the plural ending ; in this way we have *pea* instead of the earlier *peas, pease, cherry* for ME. *cherris*, Fr. *cerise, asset* from *assets*, Fr. *assez*, etc. Cf. also the vulgar *Chinee, Portuguee*, etc.[1]

[1] See my MEG ii. 5. 6, and my paper on ' Subtraktionsdannelser," in *Festskrift til Vilh. Thomsen*, 1894, p. 1 ff.

The influence of a new generation is also seen in those cases in which formerly separate words coalesce into one, as when *he breakfasts, he breakfasted*, is said instead of *he breaks fast, he broke fast* ; cf. *vouchsafe, don* (third person, *vouchsafes, dons*), instead of *vouch safe, do on* (third person, *vouches safe, does on*). Here, too, it is not probable that a person who has once learnt the real form of a word, and thus knows where it begins and where it ends, should have subsequently changed it : it is much more likely that all such changes originate with children who have once made a wrong analysis of what they have heard and then go on repeating the new forms all their lives.

X.—§ 3. Shiftings of Meanings.

Changes in the meaning of words are often so gradual that one cannot detect the different steps of the process, and changes of this sort, like the corresponding changes in the sounds of words, are to be ascribed quite as much to people already acquainted with the language as to the new generation. As examples we may mention the laxity that has changed the meaning of *soon*, which in OE. meant ' at once,' and in the same way of *presently*, originally ' at present, now,' and of the old *anon. Dinner* comes from OF. *disner*, which is the infinitive of the verb which in other forms was *desjeun*, whence modern French *déjeune* (Lat. *desjejunare) ; it thus meant ' breakfast,' but the hour of the meal thus termed was gradually shifted in the course of centuries, so that now we may have dinner twelve hours after breakfast. When *picture*, which originally meant ' painting,' came to be applied to drawings, photographs and other images ; when *hard* came to be used as an epithet not only of nuts and stones, etc., but of words and labour ; when *fair*, besides the old sense of ' beautiful,' acquired those of ' blond ' and ' morally just ' ; when *meat*, from meaning all kinds of food (as in *sweetmeats, meat and drink*), came to be restricted practically to one kind of food (butcher's meat) ; when the verb *grow*, which at first was used only of plants, came to be used of animals, hairs, nails, feelings, etc., and, instead of implying always increase, might even be combined with such a predicative as *smaller and smaller* ; when *pretty*, from the meaning ' skilful, ingenious,' came to be a general epithet of approval (cf. the modern American, *a cunning child*=' sweet '), and, besides meaning good-looking, became an adverb of degree, as in *pretty bad* : neither these nor countless similar shiftings need be ascribed to any influence on the part of the learners of English ; they can easily be accounted for as the product of innumerable small extensions and restrictions on the part of the users of the language after they have once acquired it.

But along with changes of this sort we have others that have come about with a leap, and in which it is impossible to find intermediate stages between two seemingly heterogeneous meanings, as when *bead*, from meaning a 'prayer,' comes to mean 'a perforated ball of glass or amber.' In these cases the change is occasioned by certain connexions, where the whole sense can only be taken in one way, but the syntactical construction admits of various interpretations, so that an ambiguity at one point gives occasion for a new conception of the meaning of the word. The phrase *to count your beads* originally meant 'to count your prayers,' but because the prayers were reckoned by little balls, the word *beads* came to be transferred to these objects, and lost its original sense.[1] It seems clear that this misapprehension could not take place in the brains of those who had already associated the word with the original signification, while it was quite natural on the part of children who heard and understood the phrase as a whole, but unconsciously analyzed it differently from the previous generation.

There is another word which also meant 'prayer' originally, but has lost that meaning, viz. *boon* ; through such phrases as 'ask a boon' and 'grant a boon' it came to be taken as meaning 'a favour' or 'a good thing received.'

Orient was frequently used in such connexions as 'orient pearl' and 'orient gem,' and as these were lustrous, *orient* became an adjective meaning 'shining,' without any connexion with the geographical orient, as in Shakespeare, *Venus* 981, "an orient drop" (a tear), and Milton, PL i. 546, "Ten thousand banners rise into the air, With orient colours waving."

There are no connecting links between the meanings of 'glad' and 'obliged,' 'forced,' but when *fain* came to be chiefly used in combinations like 'he was fain to leave the country,' it was natural for the younger generation to interpret the whole phrase as implying necessity instead of gladness.

We have similar phenomena in certain syntactical changes. When *me thinks* and *me likes* gave place to *I think* and *I like*, the chief cause of the change was that the child heard combinations like *Mother thinks* or *Father likes*, where *mother* and *father* can be either nominative or accusative-dative, and the construction is thus syntactically ambiguous. This leads to a 'shunting' of the meaning as well as of the construction of the verbs, which must

---

[1] Semantic changes through ambiguous syntactic combinations have recently been studied especially by Carl Collin ; see his *Semasiologiska studier*, 1906, and *Le Développement de Sens du Suffixe -ATA*, Lund, 1918, ch. iii and iv. Collin there treats especially of the transition from abstract to concrete nouns ; he does not, as I have done above, speak of the rôle of the younger generation in such changes.

have come about in a new brain which was not originally acquainted with the old construction.

As one of the factors bringing about changes in meaning many scholars mention forgetfulness ; but it is important to keep in view that what happens is not real forgetting, that is, snapping of threads of thought that had already existed within the same consciousness, but the fact that the new individual never develops the threads of thought which in the elder generation bound one word to another. Sometimes there is no connexion of ideas in the child's brain : a word is viewed quite singly as a whole and isolated, till later perhaps it is seen in its etymological relation. A little girl of six asked when she was born. " You were born on the 2nd of October." "Why, then, I was born on my birthday ! " she cried, her eyes beaming with joy at this wonderfully happy coincidence. Originally *Fare well* was only said to some one going away. If now the departing guest says *Farewell* to his friend who is staying at home, it can only be because the word *Farewell* has been conceived as a fixed formula, without any consciousness of the meaning of its parts.

Sometimes, on the other hand, new connexions of thought arise, as when we associate the word *bound* with *bind* in the phrase ' he is bound for America.' Our ancestors meant ' he is ready to go ' (ON. *búinn*, ' ready '), not ' he is under an obligation to go.' The establishment of new associations of this kind seems naturally to take place at the moment when the young mind makes acquaintance with the word : the phenomenon is, of course, closely related to " popular etymology " (see Ch. VI § 6).

X.—§ 4. Differentiations.

Linguistic ' splittings ' or differentiations, whereby one word becomes two, may also be largely due to the transmission of the language to a new generation. The child may hear two pronunciations of the same word from different people, and then associate these with different ideas. Thus Paul Passy learnt the word *meule* in the sense of ' grindstone ' from his father, and in the sense of ' haycock ' from his mother ; now the former in both senses pronounced [mœl], and the latter in both [mø·l], and the child thus came to distinguish [mœl] ' grindstone ' and [mø·l] ' haycock ' (Ch 23).

Or the child may have learnt the word at two different periods of its life, associated with different spheres. This, I take it, may be the reason why some speakers make a distinction between two pronunciations of the word *medicine*, in two and in three syllables : they take [medsin], but study [medisin].

Finally, the child can itself split words. A friend writes : " I remember that when a schoolboy said that it was a good thing that the new Headmaster was Dr. Wood, because he would then know when boys were ' shamming,' a schoolfellow remarked, ' Wasn't it funny ? He did not know the difference between Doct*or* and Doct*er*.' " In Danish the Japanese are indiscriminately called either *Japanerne* or *Japaneserne* ; now, I once overheard my boy (6.10) lecturing his playfellows : " *Japaneserne*, that is the soldiers of Japan, but *Japanerne*, that is students and children and such-like." It is, of course, possible that he may have heard one form originally when shown some pictures of Japanese soldiers, and the other on another occasion, and that this may have been the reason for his distinction. However this may be, I do not doubt that a number of differentiations of words are to be ascribed to the transmission of the language to a new generation. Others may have arisen in the speech of adults, such as the distinction between *off* and *of* (at first the stressed and unstressed form of the same preposition), or between *thorough* and *through* (the former is still used as a preposition in Shakespeare : " thorough bush, thorough brier "). But complete differentiation is not established till some individuals from the very first conceive the forms as two independent words.

X.—§ 5. Summary.

Instead of saying, as previous writers on these questions have done, either that children have no influence or that they have the chief influence on the development of language, it will be seen that I have divided the question into many, going through various fields of linguistic change and asking in each what may have been the influence of the child. The result of this investigation has been that there are certain fields in which it is both impossible and really also irrelevant to separate the share of the child and of the adult, because both will be apt to introduce changes of that kind ; such are assimilations of neighbouring sounds and droppings of consonants in groups. Also, with regard to those very gradual shiftings either of sound or of meaning in which it is natural to assume many intermediate stages through which the sound or signification must have passed before arriving at the final result, children and adults must share the responsibility for the change. Clippings of words occur in the speech of both classes, but as a rule adults will keep the beginning of a word, while very small children will perceive or remember only the end of a word and use that for the whole. But finally there are some kinds of changes which must wholly or chiefly be charged to the account of children : such are those leaps in sound or signification in which intermediate stages are out of the question, as well as confusions of similar words and misdivisions of words, and the most violent differentiations of words.

I wish, however, here to insist on one point which has, I think, become more and more clear in the course of our disquisition, namely, that we ought not really to put the question like this : Are linguistic changes due to children or to grown-up people ? The important distinction is not really one of age, which is evidently one of degree only, but that between the first learners of the sound or word in question and those who use it after having once learnt it. In the latter case we have mainly to do with infinitesimal glidings, the results of which, when summed up in the course of long periods of time, may be very considerable indeed, but in which it will always be possible to detect intermediate links connecting the extreme points. In contrast to these changes occurring *after* the correct (or original) form has been acquired by the individual, we have changes occurring *simultaneously* with the first acquisition of the word or form in question, and thus due to the fact of its transmission to a new generation, or, to speak more generally, and, indeed, more correctly, to new individuals. The exact age of the learner here is of little avail, as will be seen if we take some examples of metanalysis. It is highly probable that the first users of forms like *a pea* or *a cherry*, instead of *a pease* and *a cherries*, were little children ; but *a Chinee* and *a Portuguee* are not necessarily, or not pre-eminently, children's words : on the other hand, it is to me indubitable that these forms do not spring into existence in the mind of someone who has previously used the forms *Chinese* and *Portuguese* in the singular number, but must be due to the fact that the forms *the Chinese* and *the Portuguese* (used as plurals) have been at once apprehended as made up of *Chinee, Portuguee* + the plural ending -*s* by a person hearing them for the first time ; similarly in all the other cases. We shall see in a later chapter that the adoption (on the part of children and adults alike) of sounds and words from a foreign tongue presents certain interesting points of resemblance with these instances of change : in both cases the innovation begins when some individual is first made acquainted with linguistic elements that are new to him.

X.—§ 6. Indirect Influence.

We have hitherto considered what elements of the language may be referred to a child's first acquisition of language. But we have not yet done with the part which children play in linguistic development. There are two things which must be sharply distinguished from the phenomena discussed in the preceding chapter—the first, that grown-up people in many cases catch up the words and forms used by children and thereby give them a power of survival which they would not have otherwise ; the second, that grown-up people alter their own language so as to meet children half-way.

As for the first point, we have already seen examples in which mothers and nurses have found the baby's forms so pretty that they have adopted them themselves. Generally these forms are confined to the family circle, but they may under favourable circumstances be propagated further. A special case of the highest interest has been fully discussed in the section about words of the *mamma*-class.

As for the second point, grown-up people often adapt their speech to the more or less imaginary needs of their children by pronouncing words as they do, saying *dood* and *tum* for ' good ' and ' come,' etc. This notion clearly depends on a misunderstanding, and can only retard the acquisition of the right pronunciation ; the child understands *good* and *come* at least as well, if not better, and the consequence may be that when he is able himself to pronounce [g] and [k] he may consider it immaterial, because one can just as well say [d] and [t] as [g] and [k], or may be bewildered as to which words have the one sound and which the other. It can only be a benefit to the child if all who come in contact with it speak from the first as correctly, elegantly and clearly as possible—not, of course, in long, stilted sentences and with many learned book-words, but naturally and easily. When the child makes a mistake, the most effectual way of correcting it is certainly the indirect one of seeing that the child, soon after it has made the mistake, hears the correct form. If he says ' A waps stinged me ' : answer, ' It stung you : did it hurt much when the wasp stung you ? ' etc. No special emphasis even is needed ; next time he will probably use the correct form.

But many parents are not so wise ; they will say *stinged* themselves when once they have heard the child say so. And nurses and others have even developed a kind of artificial nursery language which they imagine makes matters easier for the little ones, but which is in many respects due to erroneous ideas of how children ought to talk rather than to real observation of the way children do talk. Many forms are handed over traditionally from one nurse to another, such as *totties*, *tootems* or *tootsies* for ' feet ' (from *trotters ?*), *toothy-peg* for ' tooth,' *tummy* or *tumtum* for ' stomach,' *tootleums* for ' babies,' *shooshoo* for ' a fly.' I give a connected specimen of this nursery language (from Egerton,

Keynotes, 85): " Didsum was denn ? Oo did ! Was ums de prettiest itta sweetums denn ? Oo was. An' did um put 'em in a nasty shawl an' joggle 'em in an ole puff-puff, um did, was a shame ' Hitchy cum, hitchy cum, hitchy cum hi, Chinaman no likey me." This reminds one of pidgin-English, and in a later chapter we shall see that that and similar bastard languages are partly due to the same mistaken notion that it is necessary to corrupt one's language to be easily understood by children and inferior races.

Very frequently mothers and nurses talk to children in diminutives. When many of these have become established in ordinary speech, losing their force as diminutives and displacing the proper words, this is another result of nursery language. The phenomenon is widely seen in Romance languages, where *auricula*, Fr. *oreille*, It. *orecchio*, displaces *auris*, and *avicellus*, Fr. *oiseau*, It. *uccello*, displaces *avis* ; we may remember that classical Latin had already *oculus*, for ' eye.' [1] It is the same in Modern Greek. An example of the same tendency, though not of the same formal means of a diminutive ending, is seen in the English *bird* (originally = ' young bird ') and *rabbit* (originally = ' young rabbit '), which have displaced *fowl* and *coney*.

A very remarkable case of the influence of nursery language on normal speech is seen in many countries, viz. in the displacing of the old word for ' right ' (as opposed to left). The distinction of right and left is not easy for small children : some children in the upper classes at school only know which is which by looking at some wart, or something of the sort, on one of their hands, and have to think every time. Meanwhile mothers and nurses will frequently insist on the use of the right (dextera) hand, and when they are not understood, will think they make it easier for the child by saying ' No, the *right* hand,' and so it comes about that in many languages the word that originally means ' correct ' is used with the meaning ' dexter.' So we have in English *right*, in German *recht*, which displaces *zeso*, Fr. *droit*, which displaces *destre* ; in Spanish also *la derecha* has begun to be used instead of *la diestra* ; similarly in Swedish *den vackra handen* instead of *högra*, and in Jutlandish dialects *den kjön hånd* instead of *höjre*.

X.—§ 7. New Languages.

In a subsequent chapter (XIV § 5) we shall consider the theory that epochs in which the changes of some language proceed at a

---

[1] I know perfectly well that in these and in other similar words there were reasons for the original word disappearing as unfit (shortness, possibility of mistakes through similarity with other words, etc.). What interests me here is the fact that the substitute is a word of the nursery.

more rapid pace than at others are due to the fact that in times
of fierce, widely extended wars many men leave home and remain
abroad, either as settlers or as corpses, while the women left behind
have to do the field-work, etc., and neglect their homes, the consequence being that the children are left more to themselves, and
therefore do not get their mistakes in speech corrected as much
as usual.

A somewhat related idea is at the bottom of a theory advanced
as early as 1886 by the American ethnologist Horatio Hale (see
"The Origin of Languages," in the American Association for the
Advancement of Science, XXXV, 1886, and "The Development of
Language," the Canadian Institute, Toronto, 1888). As these
papers seem to have been entirely unnoticed by leading philologists, I shall give a short abstract of them, leaving out what appears
to me to be erroneous in the light of recent linguistic thought and
research, namely, his application of the theory to explain the
supposed three stages of linguistic development, the monosyllabic,
the agglutinative and the flexional.

Hale was struck with the fact that in Oregon, in a region not
much larger than France, we find at least thirty different families
of languages living together. It is impossible to believe that
thirty separate communities of speechless precursors of man should
have begun to talk independently of one another in thirty distinct
languages in this district. Hae therefore concludes that the
origin of linguistic stocks is to be found in the language-making
instinct of very young children. When two children who are
just beginning to speak are thrown much together, they sometimes
invent a complete language, sufficient for all purposes of mutual
intercourse, and yet totally unintelligible to their parents. In
an ordinary household, the conditions under which such a language
would be formed are most likely to occur in the case of twins,
and Hale now proceeds to mention those instances—five in all—
that he has come across of languages framed in this manner by
young children. He concludes : "It becomes evident that, to
ensure the creation of a speech which shall be a parent of a new
language stock, all that is needed is that two or more young children
should be placed by themselves in a condition where they will be
entirely, or in a large degree, free from the presence and influence
of their elders. They must, of course, continue in this condition
long enough to grow up, to form a household, and to have
descendants to whom they can communicate their new speech."

These conditions he finds among the hunting tribes of America,
in which it is common for single families to wander off from the
main band. "In modern times, when the whole country is occupied, their flight would merely carry them into the territory of

another tribe, among whom, if well received, they would quickly be absorbed.   But in the primitive period, when a vast uninhabited region stretched before them, it would be easy for them to find some sheltered nook or fruitful valley. . . . If under such circumstances disease or the casualties of a hunter's life should carry off the parents, the survival of the children would, it is evident, depend mainly upon the nature of the climate and the ease with which food could be procured at all seasons of the year.   In ancient Europe, after the present climatal conditions were established, it is doubtful if a family of children under ten years of age could have lived through a single winter.   We are not, therefore, surprised to find that no more than four or five language stocks are represented in Europe. . . . Of Northern America, east of the Rocky Mountains and north of the tropics, the same may be said. . . . But there is one region where Nature seems to offer herself as the willing nurse and bountiful stepmother of the feeble and unprotected . . . California.   Its wonderful climate (follows a long description). . . . Need we wonder that, in such a mild and fruitful region, a great number of separate tribes were found, speaking languages which a careful investigation has classed in nineteen distinct linguistic stocks ? "   In Oregon, and in the interior of Brazil, Hale finds similar climatic conditions with the same result, a great number of totally dissimilar languages, while in Australia, whose climate is as mild as that of any of these regions, we find hundreds, perhaps thousands, of petty tribes, as completely isolated as those of South America, but all speaking languages of the same stock—because "the other conditions are such as would make it impossible for an isolated group of young children to survive.   The whole of Australia is subject to severe droughts, and is so scantily provided with edible products that the aborigines are often reduced to the greatest straits."

This, then, is Hale's theory.   Let us now look a little closer into the proofs adduced.   They are, as it will be seen, of a twofold order.   He invokes the language-creating tendencies of young children on the one hand, and on the other the geographical distribution of linguistic stocks or genera.

As to the first, it is true that so competent a psychologist as Wundt denies the possibility in very strong terms.[1]   But facts certainly do not justify this foregone conclusion.   I must first refer the reader to Hale's own report of the five instances known

---

[1] " Einige namentlich in der ältern litteratur vorkommende angaben über kinder, die sich zusammen aufwachsend eine eigene sprache gebildet haben sollen, sind wohl ein für allemal in das gebiet der fabel zu verweisen " (S 1. 286).

to him. Unfortunately, the linguistic material collected by him is so scanty that we can form only a very imperfect idea of the languages which he says children have developed and of the relation between them and the language of the parents. But otherwise his report is very instructive, and I shall call special attention to the fact that in most cases the children seem to have been ' spoilt ' by their parents ; this is also the case with regard to one of the families, though it does not appear from Hale's own extracts from the book in which he found his facts (G. Watson, *Universe of Language*, N.Y., 1878).

The only word recorded in this case is *ni-si-boo-a* for ' carriage ' ; how that came into existence, I dare not conjecture ; but when it is said that the syllables of it were sometimes so repeated that they made a much longer word, this agrees very well with what I have myself observed with regard to ordinary children's playful word-coinages. In the next case, described by E. R. Hun, M.D., of Albany, more words are given. Some of these bear a strong resemblance to French, although neither the parents nor servants spoke that language ; and Hale thinks that some person may have " amused herself, innocently enough, by teaching the child a few words of that tongue." This, however, does not seem necessary to explain the words recorded. *Feu*, pronounced, we are told, like the French word, signified ' fire, light, cigar, sun ' : it may be either E. *fire* or else an imitation of the sound *fff* without a vowel, or [fəˑ] used in blowing out a candle or a match or in smoking, so as to amuse the child, exactly as in the case of one of my little Danish friends, who used *fff* as the name for ' smoke, steam,' and later for ' funnel, chimney,' and finally anything standing upright against the sky, for instance, a flagstaff. *Petee-petee*, the name which the Albany girl gave to her brother, and which Dr. Hun derived from F. *petit*, may be just as well from E. *pet* or *petty* ; and to explain her word for ' I,' *ma*, we need not go to F. *moi*, as E. *me* or *my* may obviously be thus distorted by any child Her word for ' not ' is said to have been *ne-pas*, though the exact pronunciation is not given. This cannot have been taken from the French, at any rate not from real French, as *ne* and *pas* are here separated, and *ne* is more often than not prouounced without the vowel or omitted altogether ; the girl's word, if pronounced something like [ˈnepaˑ] may be nothing else than an imperfect childish pronunciation of *never*, cf. the negroes' form *nebber*. *Too*, ' all, everything,' of course resembles Fr. *tout*, but how should anyone have been able to teach this girl, who did not speak any intelligible language, a French word of this abstract character ? Some of the other words admit of a natural explanation from English : *go-go*, ' delicacy, as sugar, candy or dessert,' is probably *goody-goody*, or a reduplicated form of *good*; *deer*, 'money,' may be from *dear*, 'expensive'; *odo*, 'to send for, to go out, to take away,' is evidently *out*, as in *ma odo*, 'I want to go out'; *gaän*, 'God,' must be the English word, in spite of the difference in pronunication, for the child would never think of inventing this idea on its own accord; *pa-ma*, 'to go to sleep, pillow, bed,' is from *by-bye* or an independent word of the *mamma*-class; *mea*, 'cat, fur,' of course is imitative of the sound of the cat. For the rest of the words I have no conjectures to offer. Some of the derived meanings are curious, though perhaps not more startling than many found in the speech of ordinary children; *papa* and *mamma* separately had their usual signification, but *papa-mamma* meant 'church, prayer-book, cross, priest': the parents were punctual in church observances; *gar odo*, 'horse out, to send for the horse,' came to mean 'pencil and paper,' as the father used, when the carriage was wanted, to write an order and send it to the stable. In the remaining three cases of 'invented' languages no specimens are given, except *shindikik*, 'cat.' In all cases the children seem to have talked together fluently when by themselves in their own gibberish.

But there exists on record a case better elucidated than Hale's five cases, namely that of the Icelandic girl Sæunn. (See Jonasson and Eschricht in *Dansk Maanedsskrift*, Copenhagen, 1858.) She was born in the beginning of the last century on a farm in Húnavatns-syssel in the northern part of Iceland, and began early to converse with her twin brother in a language that was entirely unintelligible to their surroundings. Her parents were disquieted, and therefore resolved to send away the brother, who died soon afterwards. They now tried to teach the girl Icelandic, but soon (too soon, evidently!) came to the conclusion that she could not learn it, and then they were foolish enough to learn *her* language, as did also her brothers and sisters and even some of their friends. In order that she might be confirmed, her elder brother translated the catechism and acted as interpreter between the parson and the girl. She is described as intelligent—she even composed poetry in her own language—but shy and distrustful. Jonasson gives a few specimens of her language, some of which Eschricht succeeds in interpreting as based on Icelandic words, though strangely disfigured. The language to Jonasson, who had heard it, seemed totally dissimilar to Icelandic in sounds and construction; it had no flexions, and lacked pronouns. The vocabulary was so limited that she very often had to supplement a phrase by means of nods or gestures; and it was difficult to carry on a conversation with her in the dark. The ingenuity of some of the compounds and metaphors is greatly admired by

Jonasson, though to the more sober mind of Eschricht they appear rather childish or primitive, as when a ' wether ' is called *mepok-ill* from *me* (imitation of the sound) + *pok*, ' a little bag ' (Icel. *poki*) + *ill*, ' to cut.' The only complete sentence recorded is ' Dirfa offo nonona uhuh,' which means : ' Sigurdur gets up extremely late.' In his analysis of the whole case Eschricht succeeds in stripping it of the mystical glamour in which it evidently appeared to Jonasson as well as to the girl's relatives ; he is undoubtedly right in maintaining that if the parents had persisted in only talking Icelandic to her, she would soon have forgotten her own language ; he compares her words with some strange disfigurements of Danish which he had observed among children in his own family and acquaintanceship.

I read this report a good many years ago, and afterwards I tried on two occasions to obtain precise information about similar cases I had seen mentioned, one in Halland (Sweden) and the other in Finland, but without success. But in 1903, when I was lecturing on the language of children in the University of Copenhagen, I had the good fortune to hear of a case not far from Copenhagen of two children speaking a language of their own. I investigated the case as well as I could, by seeing and hearing them several times and thus checking the words and sentences which their teacher, who was constantly with them, kindly took down in accordance with my directions. I am thus enabled to give a fairly full account of their language, though unfortunately my investigation was interrupted by a long voyage in 1904.

The boys were twins, about five and a half years old when I saw them, and so alike that even the people who were about them every day had difficulty in distinguishing them from each other. Their mother (a single woman) neglected them shamefully when they were quite small, and they were left very much to shift for themselves. For a long time, while their mother was ill in a hospital, they lived in an out-of-the-way place with an old woman, who is said to have been very deaf, and who at any rate troubled herself very little about them. When they were four years old, the parish authorities discovered how sadly neglected they were and that they spoke quite unintelligibly, and therefore sent them to a ' children's home ' in Seeland, where they were properly taken care of. At first they were extremely shy and reticent, and it was a long time before they felt at home with the other children. When I first saw them, they had in so far learnt the ordinary language that they were able to understand many everyday sentences spoken to them, and could do what they were told (e.g. ' Take the footstool and put it in my room near the stove '), but they could not speak Danish and said very little

in the presence of anybody else. When they were by themselves
they conversed pretty freely and in a completely unintelligible
gibberish, as I had the opportunity to convince myself when
standing behind a door one day when they thought they were
not observed. Afterwards I got to be in a way good friends with
them—they called me *py-ma*, *py* being their word for 'smoke,
smoking, pipe, cigar,' so that I got my name from the chocolate
cigars which I used to ingratiate myself with them—and then I
got them to repeat words and phrases which their teacher had
written out for me, and thus was enabled to write down everything
phonetically.

An analysis of the sounds occurring in their words showed
me that their vocal organs were perfectly normal. Most of the
words were evidently Danish words, however much distorted and
shortened ; a voiceless *l*, which does not occur in Danish, and
which I write here *lh*, was a very frequent sound. This, combined
with an inclination to make many words end in *-p*, was enough
to disguise words very effectually, as when *sort* (black) was made
lhop. I shall give the children's pronunciations of the names of
some of their new playfellows, adding in brackets the Danish
substratum : *lhep* (Svend), *lhip* (Vilhelm), *lip* (Elisabeth), *lop*
(Charlotte), *bap* (Mandse) ; similarly the doctor was called *dop*.
In many cases there was phonetic assimilation at a distance, as
when milk (mælk) was called *bep*, flower (blomst) *bop*, light (lys)
lhylh, sugar (sukker) *lholh*, cold (kulde) *lhulh*, sometimes also *ulh*.
bed (seng) *sœjs*, fish (fisk) *se-is*.

I subjoin a few complete sentences : *nina enaj una enaj hœna
mad enaj*, 'we shall not fetch food for the young rabbits ' : *nina*
rabbit (kanin), *enaj* negation (nej, no), repeated several times in
each negative sentence, as in Old English and in Bantu languages,
una young (unge). *Bap ep dop*, 'Mandse has broken the hobby-
horse,' literally 'Mandse horse piece.' *Hos ia bov lhalh*, ' brother's
trousers are wet, Maria,' literally ' trousers Maria brother water.'
The words are put together without any flexions, and the word-
order is totally different from that of Danish.

Only in one case was I unable to identify words that I understood either as ' little language ' forms of Danish words or else
as sound-imitations ; but then it must be remembered that they
spoke a good deal that neither I nor any of the people about them
could make anything of. And then, unfortunately, when I began
to study it, their language was already to a great extent ' human-
ized ' in comparison to what it was when they first came to the
children's home. In fact, I noticed a constant progress during
the short time I observed the boys, and in some of the last
sentences I have noted I even find the genitive case employed.

§ 7]   NEW LANGUAGES   187

The idiom of these twins cannot, of course, be called an independent, still less a complete or fully developed language; but if they were able to produce something so different from the language spoken around them at the beginning of the twentieth century and in a civilized country, there can to my mind be no doubt that Hale is right in his contention that children left to themselves even more than these were, in an uninhabited region where they were still not liable to die from hunger or cold, would be able to develop a language for their mutual understanding that might become so different from that of their parents as really to constitute a new stock of language. So that we can now pass to the other—geographical—side of what Hale advances in favour of his theory.

So far as I can see, the facts here tally very well with the theory. Take, on the one hand, the Eskimo languages, spoken with astonishingly little variation from the east coast of Greenland to Alaska, an immense stretch of territory in which small children if left to themselves would be sure to die very soon indeed. Or take the Finnish-Ugrian languages in the other hemisphere, exhibiting a similar close relationship, though spread over wide areas. And then, on the other hand, the American languages already adduced by Hale. I do not pretend to any deeper knowledge of these languages; but from the most recent works of very able specialists I gather an impression of the utmost variety in phonetics, in grammatical structure and in vocabulary; see especially Roland B. Dixon and Alfred L. Kroeber, "The Native Languages of California," in the *American Anthropologist*, 1903. Even where recent research seems to establish some kind of kinship between families hitherto considered as distinguished stocks (as in Dixon's interesting paper, "Linguistic Relationships within the Shasta-Achomawi Stock," XV Congrès des Américanistes, 1906) the similarities are still so incomplete, so capricious and generally so remote that they seem to support Hale's explanation rather than a gradual splitting of the usual kind.

As for Brazil, I shall quote some interesting remarks from C. F. P. v. Martius, *Beiträge zur Ethnographie u. Sprachenkunde Amerika's*, 1867, i. p. 46 : "In Brazil we see a scant and unevenly distributed native population, uniform in bodily structure, temperament, customs and manner of living generally, but presenting a really astonishing diversity in language. A language is often confined to a few mutually related individuals; it is in truth a family heirloom and isolates its speakers from all other people so as to render any attempt at understanding impossible. On the vessel in which we travelled up the rivers in the interior of Brazil, we often, among twenty Indian rowers, could count only three or four that were at all able to speak together . . . they sat there side by side dumb and stupid."

Hale's theory is worthy, then, of consideration, and now, at the close of our voyage round the world of children's language, we have gained a post of vantage from which we can overlook the whole globe and see that the peculiar word-forms which children use in their ' little language ' period can actually throw light on the distribution of languages and groups of languages over the great continents. Yes,

> Scorn not the little ones ! You oft will find
> They reach the goal, when great ones lag behind.

BOOK III

THE INDIVIDUAL AND THE WORLD

CHAPTER XI

THE FOREIGNER

§ 1. The Substratum Theory. § 2. French *u* and Spanish *h*. § 3. Gothonic and Keltic. § 4. Etruscan and Indian Consonants. § 5. Gothonic Sound-shift. § 6. Natural and Specific Changes. § 7. Power of Substratum. § 8. Types of Race-mixture. § 9. Summary. § 10. General Theory of Loan-words. § 11. Classes of Loan-words. § 12. Influence on Grammar. § 13. Translation-loans.

XI.—§ 1. The Substratum Theory.

It seems evident that if we wish to find out the causes of linguistic change, a fundamental division must be into—

(1) Changes that are due to the transference of the language to new individuals, and

(2) Changes that are independent of such transference.

It may not be easy in practice to distinguish the two classes, as the very essence of the linguistic life of each individual is a continual give-and-take between him and those around him; still, the division is in the main clear, and will consequently be followed in the present work.

The first class falls again naturally into two heads, according as the new individual does not, or does already, possess a language. With the former, i.e. with the native child learning his 'mother-tongue,' we have dealt at length in Book II, and we now proceed to an examination of the influence exercised on a language through its transference to individuals who are already in possession of another language—let us, for the sake of shortness, call them foreigners.

While some earlier scholars denied categorically the existence of mixed languages, recent investigators have attached a very great importance to mixtures of languages, and have studied actually occurring mixtures of various degrees and characters with the greatest accuracy : I mention here only one name, that of Hugo Schuchardt, who combines profundity and width of knowledge with a truly philosophical spirit, though the form of his numerous scattered writings makes it difficult to gather a just idea of his views on many questions.

Many scholars have recently attached great importance to the subtler and more hidden influence exerted by one language on another in those cases in which a population abandons its original language and adopts that of another race, generally in consequence of military conquest. In these cases the theory is that people keep many of their speech-habits, especially with regard to articulation and accent, even while using the vocabulary, etc., of the new language, which thus to a large extent is tinged by the old language. There is thus created what is now generally termed a *substratum* underlying the new language. As the original substratum modifying a language which gradually spreads over a large area varies according to the character of the tribes subjugated in different districts, this would account for many of those splittings-up of languages which we witness everywhere.

Hirt goes so far as to think it possible by the help of existing dialect boundaries to determine the extensions of aboriginal languages (Idg 19).

There is certainly something very plausible in this manner of viewing linguistic changes, for we all know from practical everyday experience that the average foreigner is apt to betray his nationality as soon as he opens his mouth : the Italian's or the German's English is just as different from the 'real thing' as, inversely, the Englishman's Italian or German is different from the Italian or German of a native : the place of articulation, especially that of the tongue-tip consonants, the aspiration or want of aspiration of *p, t, k*, the voicing or non-voicing of *b, d, g*, the diphthongization or monophthongization of long vowels, the syllabification, various peculiarities in quantity and in tone-movements—all such things are apt to colour the whole acoustic impression of a foreigner's speech in an acquired language, and it is, of course, a natural supposition that the aboriginal inhabitants of Europe and Asia were just as liable to transfer their speech habits to new languages as their descendants are nowadays. There is thus a priori a strong probability that linguistic substrata have exercised some influence on the development of conquering languages. But when we proceed to apply this natural inference to concrete examples of linguistic history, we shall see that the theory does not perhaps suffice to explain everything that its advocates would have it explain, and that there are certain difficulties which have not always been faced or appraised according to their real value. A consideration of these concrete examples will naturally lead up to a discussion of the general principles involved in the substratum theory.

XI.—§ 2. French *u* and Spanish *h*.

First I shall mention Ascoli's famous theory that French [y·] for Latin *u*, as in *dur*, etc., is due to Gallic influence, cf. Welsh *i* in *din* from *dun*, which presupposes a transition from *u* to [y].

Ascoli found a proof in the fact that Dutch also has the pronunciation [y·], e.g. in *duur*, on the old Keltic soil of the Belgæ, to which
Schuchardt (SlD 126) added his observation of [y] in dialectal
South German (Breisgau), in a district in which there had formerly
been a strong Keltic element. This looks very convincing at
first blush. On closer inspection, doubts arise on many points.
The French transition cannot with certainty be dated very early,
for then *c* in *cure* would have been palatalized and changed as
c before *i* (Lenz, KZ 39. 46); also the treatment of the vowel
in French words taken over into English, where it is not identified
with the native [y], but becomes [iu], is best explained on the assumption that about 1200 A.D. the sound had not advanced farther
on its march towards the front position than, say, the Swedish
'mixed-round' sound in *hus*. The district in which [y] is found
for *u* is not coextensive with the Keltic possessions; there were
very few Kelts in what is now Holland, and inversely South German
[y] for *u* does not cover the whole Keltic domain; [y] is found
outside the French territory proper, namely, in Franco-Provençal
(where the substratum was Ligurian) and in Provençal (where there
were very few Galli; cf. Wechssler, L 113). Thus the province
of [y] is here too small and there too large to make the argument
conclusive. Even more fatal is the objection that the Gallic
transition from *u* to *y* is very uncertain (Pedersen, GKS 1. § 353).
So much is certain, that the fronting of *u* was not a *common* Keltic
transition, for it is not found in the Gaelic (Goidelic) branch.[1]
On the other hand, the transition from [u] to [y] occurs elsewhere,
independent of Keltic influence, as in Old Greek (cf. also the Swedish
sound in *hus*): why cannot it, then, be independent in French ?

Another case adduced by Ascoli is initial *h* instead of Latin
f in the country anciently occupied by the Iberians. Now, Basque
has no *f* sound at all in any connexion; if the same aversion to
f had been the cause of the Spanish substitution of *h* for *f*, we should
expect the substitution to have been made from the moment when
Latin was first spoken in Hispania, and we should expect it to be
found in all positions and connexions. But what do we find
instead ? First, that Old Spanish had *f* in many cases where modern
Spanish has *h* (i e. really no sound at all), and this cannot be

---

[1] Cf. against the assumption of Keltic influence in this instance Meyer-
Lübke, *Die Romanischen Sprachen*, *Kultur der Gegenwart*, p. 457, and Ett-
mayer in Streitberg's *Gesch.* 2. 265. H. Mutschmann, *Phonology of the North-
Eastern Scotch Dialect*, 1909, p. 53, thinks that the fronting of *u* in Scotch
is similar to that of Latin *ū* on Gallic territory, and like it is ascribable to
the Keltic inhabitants : he forgets, however, that the corresponding fronting
is not found in the Keltic spoken in Scotland. Moreover, the complicated
Scotch phenomena cannot be compared with the French transition, for
the sound of [u] remains in many cases, and [i] generally corresponds to
earlier [o], whatever the explanation may be.

altogether ascribed to 'Latinizing scribes.' On the contrary, the transition $f > h$ seems to have taken place many centuries after the Roman invasion, since the Spanish-speaking Jews of Salonika, who emigrated from Spain about 1500, have to this day preserved the f sound among other archaic traits (see F. Hanssen, *Span. Gramm.* 45; Wiener, *Modern Philology*, June 1903, p. 205). And secondly, that f has been kept in certain connexions; thus, before [w], as in *fui, fuiste, fué*, etc., before r and l, as in *fruto, flor*, etc. This certainly is inexplicable if the cause of $f > h$ had been the want of power on the part of the aborigines to produce the f sound at all, while it is simple enough if we assume a later transition, taking place possibly at first between two vowels, with a subsequent generalization of the f-less forms. Diez is here, as not infrequently, more sensible than some of his successors (see *Gramm. d. roman. spr.*, 4th ed., 1. 283 f., 373 f.).

XI.—§ 3. Gothonic and Keltic.

Feist (KI 480 ff.; cf. PBB 36. 307 ff., 37. 112 ff.) applies the substratum theory to the Gothonic (Germanic) languages. The Gothons are autochthonous in northern Europe, and very little mixed with other races; they must have immigrated just after the close of the glacial period. But the arrival of Aryan (Indogermanic) tribes cannot be placed earlier than about 2000 B.C.; they made the original inhabitants give up their own language. The nation that thus Aryanized the Gothons cannot have been other than the Kelts; their supremacy over the Gothons is proved by several loan-words for cultural ideas or state offices, such as Gothic *reiks* 'king,' *andbahts* 'servant.' The Aryan language which the Kelts taught the Gothons was subjected in the process to considerable changes, the old North Europeans pronouncing the new language in accordance with their previous speech habits; instead of taking over the free Aryan accent, they invariably stressed the initial syllable, and they made sad havoc of the Aryan flexion.

The theory does not bear close inspection. The number of Keltic loan-words is not great enough for us to infer such an overpowering ascendancy on the part of the Kelts as would force the subjected population to make a complete surrender of their own tongue. Neither in number nor in intrinsic significance can these loans be compared with the French loans in English: and yet the Normans did not succeed in substituting their own language for English. Besides, if the theory were true, we should not merely see a certain number of Keltic loan-words, but the whole speech, the complete vocabulary as well as the entire grammar, would be Keltic; yet as a matter of fact there is a wide gulf between Keltic and Gothonic, and many details, lexical and grammatical, in the latter group resemble other Aryan languages rather than Keltic. The stressing of the first syllable is said to be due to the aboriginal language. If that were so, it would mean that this population, in adopting the new speech, had at once transferred its own habit of stressing the first syllable to all the new words, very much as Icelanders are apt to do nowadays. But this is not in accordance with well established facts in the Gothonic languages : we know that when the consonant shift took place, it found the stress on the same syllables as in Sanskrit, and that it was this stress on many middle or final syllables that afterwards changed many of the shifted consonants from voiceless to voiced (Verner's law).[1] This fact in itself suffices to prove that the consonant shift and the stress shift cannot have taken place simultaneously, and thus cannot be due to one and the same cause, as supposed by Feist. Nor can the havoc wrought in the old flexions be due to the inability of a new people to grasp the minute *nuances* and intricate system of another language than its own ; for in that case too we should have something like the formless ' Pidgin English ' from the very beginning, whereas the oldest Gothonic languages still preserve a great many old flexions and subtle syntactical rules which have since disappeared. As a matter of fact, many of the flexions of primitive Aryan were much better preserved in Gothonic languages than in Keltic.

XI.—§ 4. Etruscan and Indian Consonants.

In another place in the same work (KI 373) Feist speaks of the Etruscan language, and says that this had only one kind of stop consonants, represented by the letters *k* (*c*), *t*, *p*, besides the aspirated stops *kh*, *th*, *ph*, which in some instances correspond to Latin and Greek tenues. This, he says, reminds one very strongly of the sound system of High German (oberdeutschen) dialects, and more particularly of those spoken in the Alps. Feist here (and in PBB 36. 340 ff.) maintains that these sounds go back to a Pre-Gothonic Alpine population, which he identifies with the ancient Rhætians ; and he sees in this a strong support of a linguistic connexion between the Rhætians and Etruscans. He finds further striking analogies between the Gothonic and the Armenian sound systems ; the predilection for voiceless stops and aspirated sounds in Etruscan, in the domain of the ancient Rhætians and in Asia Minor is accordingly ascribed to the speech habits of one and the same aboriginal race.

---

[1] Curiously enough, Feist uses this argument himself against Hirt in his earlier paper, PBB 37. 121.

Here, too, there are many points to which I must take exception. It is not quite certain that the usual interpretation of Etruscan letters is correct; in fact, much may be said in favour of the hypothesis that the letters rendered *p, t, k* stand really for the sounds of *b, d, g,* and that those transcribed *ph, th, kh* (or Greek φ, ϑ, χ) represent ordinary *p, t, k*. However this may be, Feist seems to be speaking here almost in the same breath of the first (or common Gothonic) shift and of the second (or specially High German) shift, although they are separated from each other by several centuries and neither cover the same geographical ground nor lead to the same phonetic result. Neither Armenian nor primitive Gothonic can be said to be averse to voiced stops, for in both we find voiced *b, d, g* for the old ' mediæ aspiratæ.' And in both languages the old voiceless stops became at first probably not aspirates, but simply voiceless spirants, as in English *father, thing,* and Scotch loc*h*. Further, it should be noted that we do not find the tendency to unvoice stops and to pronounce affricates either in Rhæto-Romanic (Ladin) or in Tuscan Italian ; both languages have unaspirated *p, t, k* and voiced *b, d, g,* and the Tuscan pronunciation of *c* between two vowels as [x], thus in *la casa* [la xa·sa], but not in *a casa* = [akka·sa], could not be termed ' aspiration' except by a non-phonetician; this pronunciation can hardly have anything to do with the old Etruscan language.

According to a theory which is very widely accepted, the Dravidian languages exerted a different influence on the Aryan languages when the Aryans first set foot on Indian soil, in making them adopt the 'cacuminal' (or 'inverted') sounds *ḍ, ṭ, ṇ* with *ḍh* and *ṭh,* which were not found in primitive Aryan. But even this theory does not seem to be quite proof against objections. It is easy to admit that natives accustomed to one place of articulation of their *d, t, n* will unconsciously produce the *d, t, n* of a new language they are learning in the same place ; but then they will do it everywhere Here, however, both Dravidian and Sanskrit possess pure dental *d, t, n,* pronounced with the tip of the tongue touching the upper teeth, besides cacuminal *ḍ, ṭ, ṇ,* in which it touches the gum or front part of the hard palate. In Sanskrit we find that the cacuminal articulation occurs only under very definite conditions, chiefly under the influence of *r*. Now, a trilled tongue-point *r* in most languages, for purely physiological reasons which are easily accounted for, tends to be pronounced further back than ordinary dentals ; and it is therefore quite natural that it should spontaneously exercise an influence on neighbouring dentals by drawing them back to its own point of articulation. This may have happened in India quite independently of the occurrence of the same sounds in other vernaculars, just as we find the same influence very pronouncedly in Swedish and in East Norwegian, where *d, t, n, s* are cacuminal (supradental) in such words as *bord, kort, barn, först*, etc. According to Grandgent (*Neuere Sprachen*, 2. 447), *d* in his own American English is pronounced further back than elsewhere before and after *r*, as in *dry, hard*; but in none of these cases need we conjure up an extinct native population to account for a perfectly natural development.

XI.—§ 5. Gothonic Sound-shift.

Since the time of Grimm the Gothonic consonant changes have harassed the minds of linguists; they became *the* sound-shift and were considered as something *sui generis*, something out of the common, which required a different explanation from all other sound-shifts. Several explanations have been offered, to some of which we shall have to revert later; none, however, has been so popular as that which attributes the shift to an ethnic substratum. This explanation is accepted by Hirt, Feist, Meillet and others, though their agreement ceases when the question is asked: What nationality and what language can have been the cause of the change? While some cautiously content themselves with saying that there must have been an original population, others guess at Kelts, Finns, Rhætians or Etrurians—all fascinating names to minds of a speculative turn.

The latest treatment of the question that I have seen is by K. Wessely (in *Anthropos*, XII–XIII 540 ff., 1917). He assumes the following different substrata, beginning with the most recent: a Rhæto-Romanic for the Upper-German shift, a Keltic for the common High-German shift, and a Finnic for the first Germanic shift with the Vernerian law. This certainly has the merit of neatly separating sound-shifts that are chronologically apart, except with regard to the last-mentioned shift, for here the Finns are made responsible for two changes that were probably separated by centuries and had really no traits in common. It is curious to see the transition from *p* to *f* and from *t* to *þ*—both important elements of the first shift—here ascribed to Finnic, for as a matter of fact the two sounds *f* and *þ* are not found in present-day Finnish, and were not found in primitive Ugro-Finnic.[1]

---

[1] Feist, on the other hand (PBB 36. 329), makes the Kelts responsible for the shift from *p* to *f*, because initial *p* disappears in Keltic: but disappearance is not the same thing as being changed into a spirant, and there is no necessity for assuming that the sound before disappearing had been changed into *f*. Besides, it is characteristic of the Gothonic shift that it affects all stops equally, without regard to the place of articulation, while the Keltic change affects only the one sound *p*.

When Wessely thinks that the change discovered by Verner is also due to Finnic influence, his reasons are two : an alleged parallelism with the Finnic consonant change which he terms ' Setälä's law,' and then the assumption that such a shift, conditioned by the place of the accent, is foreign to the Aryan race (p. 543). When, however, we find a closely analogous case only four hundred years ago in English, where a number of consonants were voiced according to the place of the stress,[1] are we also to say that it is foreign to the Anglo-Saxon race and therefore presupposes some non-Aryan substratum ? As a matter of fact, the parallelism between the English and the old Gothonic shift is much closer than that between the latter and the Finnic consonant-gradation : in English and in old Gothonic the stress place is decisive, while in the Finnic shift it is very doubtful whether stress goes for anything; in both English and old Gothonic the same consonants are affected (spirants, in English also the combinations [tʃ, ks], but otherwise no stops), while in Finnic it is the stops that are primarily affected. In old Gothonic, as in English, the change is simply voicing, and we have nothing corresponding to the reduction of double consonants and of consonant groups in Finnic *pappi / papin*, *ottaa / otat*, *kukka / kukan*, *parempi / paremman*, *jalka / jalan*, etc. On the whole, Wessely's paper shows how much easier it is to advance hypotheses than to find truths.

XI.—§ 6. Natural and Specific Changes.

Meillet (MSL 19. 164 and 172 ; cf. *Bulletin* 19. 50 and *Germ.* 18) thinks that we must distinguish between such phonetic changes as are natural, i.e. due to universal tendencies, and such as are peculiar to certain languages. In the former class he includes the opening and the voicing of intervocalic consonants ; there is also a natural and universal tendency to shorten long words and to slur the pronunciation towards the end of a word. In the latter class (changes which are peculiar to and characteristic of a particular language) he reckons the consonant shifts in Gothonic and Armenian, the weakening of consonants in Greek and in Iranian, the tendency to unround back vowels in English and Slav. Such changes can only be accounted for on the supposition of a change of language : they must be due to people whose own language had habits foreign to Aryan. Unfortunately, Meillet cannot tell us how to measure the difference between natural and

---

[1] ME. *knowleche, stonēs* [stoˑnes], *off, with* [wiþ] become MnE. *knowledge, stones* [stounz], *of* [ɔv, əv], *with* [wið], etc. ; cf. also *possess, discern* with [z], *exert* with [gz], but *exercise* with [ks]. See my *Studier over eng. kasus*, 1891, 178 ff., now **MEG** i. 6. 5 ff., and (for the phonetic explanation) **LPh** p. 121.

peculiar shifts ; he admits that they cannot always be clearly separated ; and when he says that there are some extreme cases ' relativement nets,' such as those named above, I must confess that I do not see why the change from the sharp tenuis, as in Fr. *p, t, k,* to a slightly aspirated sound, as in English (*Bulletin* 19. 50),[1] or the relaxing of the closure which finally led to the sounds of [f, þ, x], should be less ' natural ' than a hundred other changes and should require the calling in of a *deus ex machina* in the shape of an aboriginal population. The unrounding of E. *u* in *hut*, etc., to which he alludes, began about 1600—what ethnic substratum does that postulate, and is any such required, more than for, say, the diphthongizing of long *a* and *o* ?

Meillet (MSL 19. 172) also says that there are certain speech sounds which are, as it were, natural and are found in nearly all languages, thus *p, t, k, n, m,* and among the vowels *a, i, u,* while other sounds are found only in some languages, such as the two English *th* sounds or, among the vowels, Fr. *u* and Russian *y*. But when he infers that sounds of the former class are stable and remain unchanged for many centuries, whereas those of the latter are apt to change and disappear, the conclusion is not borne out by actual facts. The consonants *p, t, k, n, m* are said to have remained unchanged in many Aryan languages from the oldest times till the present day—that is, only initially before vowels, which is a very important reservation and really amounts to an admission that in the vast majority of cases these sounds are just as unstable as most other things on this planet, especially if we remember that nothing could well be more unstable than *k* before front vowels, as seen in It. [tʃ] and Sp. [þ] in *cielo*, Fr. [s] in *ciel*, and [ʃ] in *chien*, Eng. and Swedish [tʃ] in *chin, kind*, Norwegian [c] in *kind*, Russian [tʃ] in *četyre* ' four ' and [s] in *sto* ' hundred,' etc.   As an example of a typically unstable sound Meillet gives bilabial *f*, and it is true that this sound is so rare that it is difficult to find it represented in any language ; the reason is simply that the upper teeth normally protrude above the lower jaw, and that consequently the lower lip articulates easily against the upper teeth, with the natural result that where we should theoretically expect the bilabial *f* the labiodental *f* takes its place.   And *s*, which is found almost universally, and should therefore on Meillet's theory be very stable, is often seen to change into *h* or [x] or to disappear.   On the whole, then, we see that it is not the ' naturalness ' or universality of a

---

[1] Sharp tenues and aspirated tenues may alternate even in the life of one individual, as I have observed in the case of my own son, who at the age of 1.9 used the sharp French sounds, but five months later substituted strongly aspirated *p, t, k*, with even stronger aspiration than the usual Danish sounds, which it took him ten or eleven months to learn with perfect certainty.

consonant so much as its position in the syllable and word that
decides the question ' change or no change.' The relation between
stability and naturalness is seen, perhaps, most clearly in such an
instance as long [aˑ] : this sound is so natural that English, from
the oldest Aryan to present-day speech, has never been without
it ; yet at no time has it been stable, but as soon as one class of
words with long [aˑ] is changed, a new class steps into its shoes :
(1) Aryan *māter*, now *mother* ; (2) lengthening of a short *a* before
n : *gās*, *brāhta*, now *goose*, *brought* ; (3) levelling of *ai* : *stān*, now
stone ; (4) lengthening of short *a* : *cāld*, now *cold* ; (5) later lengthening of *a* in open syllable : *nāme*, now [neim] ; (6) mod. *carve*, *calm*,
path and others from various sources ; and (7) vulgar speech is now
developing new levellings of diphthongs in [maˑl, paˑ(ə)] for *mile*,
power.

XI.—§ 7. Power of Substratum.

V. Bröndal has made the attempt to infuse new blood into
the substratum theory through his book, *Substrater og Laan i
Romansk og Germansk* (Copenhagen, 1917). The effect of a substratum, according to him, is the establishment of a ' constant
idiom,' working "without regard to place and time " (p. 76) and
changing, for instance, Latin into Old French, Old French into
Classical French, and Classical French into Modern French. His
task, then, is to find out certain tendencies operating at these
various periods ; these are ascribed to the Keltic substratum,
and Bröndal then passes in review a great many languages spoken
in districts where Kelts are known to have lived in former times,
in order to find the same tendencies there. If he succeeds in this
to his own satisfaction, it is only because the ' tendencies ' established are partly so vague that they will fit into any language,
partly so ill-defined phonetically that it becomes possible to press
different, nay, in some cases even directly contrary movements
into the same class. But considerations of space forbid me to
enter on a detailed criticism here. I must content myself with
taking exception to the principle that the effect of the ethnic
substratum may show itself several generations after the speech
substitution took place. If Keltic ever had ' a finger in the pie,'
it must have been immediately on the taking over of the new
language. An influence exerted in such a time of transition may
have far-reaching after-effects, like anything else in history, but
this is not the same thing as asserting that a similar modification
of the language may take place after the lapse of some centuries
as an effect of the same cause. Suppose we have a series of manuscripts, A, B, C, D, etc., of which B is copied from A, C from B,

etc., and that B has an error which is repeated in all the following copies ; now, if M suddenly agrees with A (which the copyist has never seen), we infer that this reading is independent of A. In the same way with a language : each individual learns it from his contemporaries, but has no opportunity of hearing those who have died before his own time. It is possible that the transition from *a* to *œ* in Old English (as in *fœder*) is due to Keltic influence, but when we find, many centuries later, that *a* is changed into [æ] (the present sound) in words which had not *œ* in OE., e.g. *crab, hallow, act*, it is impossible to ascribe this, as Bröndal does, to a ' constant Keltic idiom ' working through many generations who had never spoken or heard any Keltic. ' Atavism,' which skips over one or more generations, is unthinkable here, for words and sounds are nothing but habits acquired by imitation.

So far, then, our discussion of the substratum theory has brought us no very positive results. One of the reasons why the theories put forward of late years havebeen on the whole so unsatisfactory is that they deal with speech substitutions that have taken place so far back that absolutely nothing, or practically nothing, is known of those displaced languages which are supposed to have coloured languages now existing. What do we know beyond the mere name of Ligurians or Veneti or Iberians ? Of the Pre-Germanic and Pre-Keltic peoples we know not even the names. As to the old Kelts who play such an eminent rôle in all these speculations, we know extremely little about their language at this distant date, and it is possible that in some cases, at any rate, the Kelts may have been only comparatively small armies conquering this or that country for a time, but leaving as few linguistic traces behind them as, say, the armies of Napoleon in Russia or the Cimbri and Teutoni in Italy. Linguists have turned from the ' glottogonic ' speculations of Bopp and his disciples, only to indulge in dialectogonic speculations of exactly the same visionary type.

XI.—§ 8. Types of Race-mixture.

It would be a great mistake to suppose that the conditions, and consequently the linguistic results, are always the same, whenever two different races meet and assimilate. The chief classes of race-mixture have been thus described in a valuable paper by George Hempl (*Transactions of the American Philological Association*, XXIX, p. 31 ff., 1898).

(1) The conquerors are a comparatively small body, who become the ruling class, but are not numerous enough to impose their language on the country. They are forced to learn the language of their subjects, and their grandchildren may come to know that

language better than they know the language of their ancestors. The language of the conquerors dies out, but bequeaths to the native language its terms pertaining to government, the army, and those other spheres of life that the conquerors had specially under their control. Historic examples are the cases of the Goths in Italy and Spain, the Franks in Gaul, the Normans in France and the Norman-French in England. Of course, the greater the number of the conquerors and the longer they had been close neighbours of the people they conquered, or maintained the bonds that united them to their mother-country, the greater was their influence. Thus the influence of the Franks on the language of France was greater than that of the Goths on the language of Spain, and the influence of the Norman-French in England was greater still. Yet in each case the minority ultimately succumbed.

(2a) The conquest is made by many bodies of invaders, who bring with them their whole households and are followed for a long period of time by similar hordes of their kinsmen. The conquerors constitute the upper and middle classes and a part of the lower classes of the new community. The natives recede before the conquerors or become their slaves : their speech is regarded as servile and is soon laid aside, except for a few terms pertaining to the humbler callings, the names of things peculiar to the country and place-names. Examples : Angles and Saxons in Britain and Europeans in America and Australia, though in the last case we can hardly speak of race-mixture between the natives and the immigrants.

(2b) A more powerful nation conquers the people and annexes its territory, which is made a province, to which not only governors and soldiers, but also merchants and even colonists are sent. These become the upper class and the influential part of the middle class. If centuries pass and the province is still subjected to the direct influence of the ruling country, it will more and more imitate the speech and the habits and customs of that country. Such was the history of Italy, Spain and Gaul under the Romans ; similar, also, is the story of the Slavs of Eastern Germany and of the Dutch in New York State ; such is the process going on to-day among the French in Louisiana and among the Germans in their original settlements in Pennsylvania.

(3) Immigrants come in scattered bands and at different times ; they become servants or follow other humble callings. It is usually not to their advantage to associate with their fellow-countrymen, but rather to mingle with the native population. The better they learn to speak the native tongue, the faster they get on in the world. If their children in their dress or speech betray their foreign origin, they are ridiculed as 'Dutch' or Irish,

or whatever it may be.   They therefore take pains to rid themselves
of all traces of their alien origin and avoid using the speech of their
parents.   In this way vast numbers of newcomers may be assimilated year by year till they constitute a large part of the new race,
while their language makes practically no impression on the language of the country.   This is the story of what is going on in all
parts of the United States to-day.

It will be seen that in classes 1 and 3 the speech of the natives
prevails, while in the two classes comprised under 2 it is that of
the conqueror which eventually triumphs.   Further, that, in all
cases except type 2b, that language prevails which is spoken by
what is at the time the majority.

Sound substitution is found in class 3 in the case of foreigners
who come to America after they have learnt to speak, and of the
children of foreigners who keep up their original language at home.
If, however, while they are still young, they are chiefly thrown
with English-speaking people, they usually gain a thorough mastery
of the English language ; thus most of the children, and practically
all of the grandchildren, of immigrants, by the time they are grown-
up, speak English without foreign taint.   Their origin has thus
no permanent influence on their adopted language.   The same
thing is true when a small ruling minority drops its foreign speech
and learns that of the majority (class 1), and practically also
(class 2a) when a native minority succumbs to a foreign majority,
though here the ultimate language may be slightly influenced
by the native dialect.

It is different with class 2b : when a whole population comes
in the course of centuries to surrender its natural speech for that
of a ruling minority, sound substitution plays an important part,
and to a great extent determines the character and future of the
language.   Hempl here agrees with Hirt in seeing in this fact
the explanation of much (N.B. not all !) of the difference between
the Romanic languages and of the difference between natural
High German and High German spoken in Low German territory,
and he is therefore not surprised when he is told by Nissen that
the dialects of modern Italy correspond geographically pretty
closely to the non-Latin languages once spoken in the Peninsula.
But he severely criticizes Hirt for going so far as to explain the
differentiation of Aryan speech by the theory of sound substitution.
Hirt assumes conditions like those in class 1, and yet thinks that
the results would be like those of class 2a   " It is essential to Hirt's
theory that the conquering bodies of Indo-Europeans should be
small compared with the number of the people they conquered. . . .
If we wish to prove that the differentiation of Indo-European
speech was like the differentiation of Romance speech, we must

be able to show that the conditions under which the differentiations took place were alike or equivalent. But even a cursory examination of the manner in which the Romance countries were Romanized . . . will make it clear that no parallel could possibly be drawn between the conditions under which the Romance languages arose and those that we can suppose to have existed while the Indo-European languages took shape." Hempl also criticizes the way in which the Germanic consonant-shift is supposed by Hirt to be due to sound-substitution : when instead of the original

$$t \qquad th \qquad d \qquad dh$$

Germanic has

$$\text{þ} \qquad \text{þ} \qquad t \qquad ð,$$

these latter sounds, on Hirt's theory, must be either the native sounds that the conquered people substituted for the original sounds, or else they have developed out of such sounds as the natives substituted. If the first be true, we ask ourselves why the conquered people did not use their *t* for the Indo-European *t*, instead of substituting it for *d*, and then substituting þ for the Indo-European *t*. If the second supposition be true, the native population introduced into the language sounds very similar to the original *t*, *th*, *d*, *dh*, and all the change from that slightly variant form to the one that we find in Germanic was of subsequent development —and must be explained by the usual methods after all.

I have dwelt so long on Hempl's paper because, in spite of its (to my mind) fundamental importance, it has been generally overlooked by supporters of the substratum theory. To construct a true theory, it will be necessary to examine the largest possible number of facts with regard to race-mixture capable of being tested by scientific methods. In this connexion the observations of Lenz in South America and of Puşcariu in Rumania are especially valuable. The former found that the Spanish spoken in Chile was greatly influenced in its sounds by the speech of the native Araucanians (see *Zeitschr. f. roman. Philologie*, 17. 188 ff., 1893). Now, what were the facts in regard to the population speaking this language ? The immigrants were chiefly men, who in many cases necessarily married native women and left the care of their children to a great extent in the hands of Indian servants. As the natives were more warlike than in many other parts of South America, there was for a very long time a continuous influx of Spanish soldiers, many of whom, after a short time, settled down peacefully in the country. More Spanish soldiers, indeed, arrived in Chile in the course of the sixteenth and seventeenth centuries than in the whole of the rest of

South America. Accordingly, by the beginning of the eighteenth century the Indians had been either driven back or else assimilated, and at the beginning of the War of Liberation early in the nineteenth century Chile was the only State in which there was a uniform Spanish-speaking population. In the greater part of Chile the population is denser than anywhere else in South America, and this population speaks nothing but Spanish, while in Peru and Bolivia nearly the whole rural population still speaks more or less exclusively Keshua or Aimará, and these languages are also used occasionally, or at any rate understood, by the whites. Chile is thus the only country in which a real Spanish people's dialect could develop. (In Hempl's classification this would be a typical case of class 2*a*.) In the other Spanish-American countries the Spanish-speakers are confined to the upper ruling class, there being practically no lower class with Spanish as its mothertongue, except in a couple of big cities. Thus we understand that the Peruvian who has learnt his Spanish at school has a purer Castilian pronunciation than the Chilean ; yet, apart from pronunciation, the educated Chilean's Spanish is much more correct and fluent than that of the other South Americans, whose language is stiff and vocabulary scanty, because they have first learnt some Indian language in childhood. Lenz's Chileans, who have often been invoked by the adherents of the unlimited substratum theory, thus really serve to show that sound substitution takes place only under certain well-defined conditions.

Puşcariu (in *Prinzipienfragen der romanischen Sprachwissenschaft, Beihefte zur Zschr. f. rom. Phil.*, 1010) says that in a Saxon village which had been almost completely Rumanianized he had once talked for hours with a peasant without noticing that he was not a native Rumanian : he was, however, a Saxon, who spoke Saxon with his wife, but Rumanian with his son, because the latter language was easier to him, as he had acquired the Rumanian basis of articulation. Here, then, there was no sound substitution, and in general we may say that the less related two languages are, the fewer will be the traces of the original language left on the new language (p. 49). The reason must be that people who naturally speak a closely related language are easily understood even when their acquired speech has a tinge of dialect : there is thus no inducement for them to give up their pronunciation. Puşcariu also found that it was much more difficult for him to rid himself of his dialectal traits in Rumanian than to acquire a correct pronunciation of German or French. He therefore disbelieves in a direct influence exerted by the indigenous languages on the formation of the Romanic languages (and thus goes much further than Hempl). All these languages, and particularly Rumanian, during the first centuries of the Middle Ages underwent radical transformations not paralleled in the thousand years ensuing. This may have been partly due to an influence exerted by ethnic mixture on the whole character of the young nations and through that also on their language. But other factors have certainly also played an important rôle, especially the grouping round new centres with other political aims than those of ancient Rome, and consequent isolation from the rest of the Romanic peoples. Add to this the very important emancipation of the ordinary conversational language from the yoke of Latin. In the first Christian centuries the influence of Latin was so overpowering in official life and in the schools that it obstructed a natural development. But soon after the third century the educational level rapidly sank, and political events broke the power not only of Rome, but also of its language. The speech of the masses, which had been held in fetters for so long, now asserted itself in full freedom and with elemental violence, the result being those far-reaching changes by which the Romanic languages are marked off from Latin. Language and nation or race must not be confounded : witness Rumania, whose language shows very few dialectal variations, though the populations of its different provinces are ethnically quite distinct (ib. p. 51).

XI.—§ 9. Summary.

The general impression gathered from the preceding investigation must be that it is impossible to ascribe to an ethnic substratum all the changes and dialectal differentiations which some linguists explain as due to this sole cause. Many other influences must have been at work, among which an interruption of intercourse created by natural obstacles or social conditions of various kinds would be of prime importance. If we take ethnic substrata as the main or sole source of dialectal differentiation, it will be hard to account for the differences between Icelandic and Norwegian, for Iceland was very sparsely inhabited when the ' land-taking ' took place, and still harder to account for the very great divergences that we witness between the dialects spoken in the Faroe Islands. A mere turning over the leaves of Bennike and Kristensen's maps of Danish dialects (or the corresponding maps of France) will show the impossibility of explaining the crisscross of boundaries of various phonetic phenomena as entirely due to ethnical differences in the aborigines. On the other hand, the speech of Russian peasants is said to be remarkably free from dialectal divergences, in spite of the fact that it has spread in comparatively recent times over districts inhabited by populations with languages of totally different types (Finnic, Turkish, Tataric). I thus incline to think that sound substitution cannot have produced radical changes, but has only played a minor part in the development of languages. There are, perhaps, also interesting things to be learnt from conditions in Finland. Here Swedish has for many centuries been the language of the ruling minority, and it was only in the course of the nineteenth century that Finnish attained to the dignity of a literary language. The sound systems of Swedish and Finnish are extremely unlike : Finnish lacks many of the Swedish sounds, such as *b, d* (what is written *d* is either mute or else a kind of weak *r*), *g* and *f*. No word can begin with more than one consonant, consequently Swedish *strand* and *skräddare,* ' tailor,' are represented in the form of the loan-words *ranta* and *räätäli.* Now, in spite of the fact that most Swedish-speaking people have probably spoken Finnish as children and have had Finnish servants and playfellows to teach them the language, none of these peculiarities have influenced their Swedish : what makes them recognizable as hailing from Finland (' finska brytningen ') is not simplification of consonant groups or substitution of *p* for *b*, etc., but such small things as the omission of the ' compound tone,' the tendency to lengthen the second consonant in groups like *ns*, and European (' back ') *u* instead of the Swedish mixed vowel.

But if sound substitution as a result of race-mixture and of conquest cannot have played any very considerable part in the differentiation of languages as wholes, there is another domain in which sound substitution is very important, that is, in the shape which loan-words take in the languages into which they are introduced. However good the pronunciation of the first introducer of a word may have been, it is clear that when a word is extensively used by people with no intimate and first-hand knowledge of the language from which it was taken, most of them will tend to pronounce it with the only sounds with which they are familiar, those of their own language. Thus we see that the English and Russians, who have no [y] in their own speech, substitute for it the combination [ju, iu] in recent loans from French Scandinavians have no voiced [z] and [ʒ] and therefore, in such loans from French or English as *kusine, budget, jockey*, etc., substitute the voiceless [s] and [ʃj], or [sj]. The English will make a diphthong of the final vowels of such words as *bouquet, beau* [buˑkei, bou], and will slur the *r* of such French words as *boulevard*, etc. The same transference of speech habits from one's native language also affects such important things as quantity, stress and tone : the English have no final short stressed vowels, such as are found in *bouquet, beau ;* hence their tendency to lengthen as well as diphthongize these sounds, while the French will stress the final syllable of recent loans, such as *jury*, *reporter*. These phenomena are so universal and so well known that they need no further illustration.

The more familiar such loan-words are, the more unnatural it would be to pronounce them with foreign sounds or according to foreign rules of quantity and stress ; for this means in each case a shunting of the whole speech-apparatus on to a different track for one or two words and then shifting back to the original ' basis of articulation '—an effort that many speakers are quite incapable of and one that in any case interferes with the natural and easy flow of speech.

XI.—§ 10. General Theory of Loan-words.

In the last paragraphs we have already broached a very important subject, that of loan-words.[1] No language is entirely free from borrowed words, because no nation has ever been completely isolated. Contact with other nations inevitably leads to borrowings, though their number may vary very considerably. Here we meet with a fundamental principle, first formulated by E. Windisch (in his paper " Zur Theorie der Mischsprachen und Lehnwörter," *Verh. d. sächsischen Gesellsch. d. Wissensch.*, XLIX, 1897, p. 107 ff.) : " It is not the foreign language a nation learns that turns into a mixed language, but its own native language becomes mixed under the influence of a foreign language." When we try to learn and talk a foreign tongue we do not introduce into it words taken from our own language ; our endeavour will always be to speak the other language as purely as possible, and generally we are painfully conscious of every native word that we intrude into phrases framed in the other tongue. But what we thus avoid in speaking a foreign language we very often do in our own. Frederick the Great prided himself on his good French, and in his French writings we do not find a single German word, but whenever he wrote German his sentences were full of French words and phrases. This being the general practice, we now understand why so few Keltic words were taken over into French and English. There was nothing to induce the ruling classes to learn

[1] I use the terms *loan-words* and *borrowed words* because they are convenient and firmly established, not because they are exact. There are two essential respects in which linguistic borrowing differs from the borrowing of, say, a knife or money : the lender does not deprive himself of the use of the word any more than if it had not been borrowed by the other party, and the borrower is under no obligation to return the word at any future time. Linguistic ' borrowing ' is really nothing but imitation, and the only way in which it differs from a child's imitation of its parents' speech is that here something is imitated which forms a part of a speech that is not imitated as a whole.

the language of the inferior natives : it could never be fashionable
for them to show an acquaintance with a despised tongue by using
now and then a Keltic word.   On the other hand, the Kelt would
have to learn the language of his masters, and learn it well ; and
he would even among his comrades like to show off his knowledge
by interlarding his speech with words and turns from the language
of his betters.   Loan-words always show a superiority of the nation
from whose language they are borrowed, though this superiority
may be of many different kinds.

In the first place, it need not be extensive : indeed, in some
of the most typical cases it is of a very partial character and
touches only on one very special point.   I refer to those instances
in which a district or a people is in possession of some special
thing or product wanted by some other nation and not produced
in that country.   Here quite naturally the name used by the natives
is taken over along with the thing.   Obvious examples are the
names of various drinks : *wine* is a loan from Latin, *tea* from Chinese,
coffee from Arabic, *chocolate* from Mexican, and *punch* from Hindustani.   A certain type of carriage was introduced about 1500
from Hungary and is known in most European languages by its
Magyar name : E. *coach*, G. *kutsche*, etc.   *Moccasin* is from
Algonquin, *bamboo* from Malay, *tulip* and *turban* (ultimately the
same word) from Persian.   A slightly different case is when some
previously unknown plant or animal is made known through some
foreign nation, as when we have taken the name of *jasmine* from
Persian, *chimpanzee* from some African, and *tapir* from some
Brazilian language.   It is characteristic of all words of this kind
that only a few of them are taken from each foreign language,
and that they have nearly all of them gone the round of all
civilized languages, so that they are now known practically all
over the world.

Other loan-words form larger groups and bear witness to the
cultural superiority of some nation in some one specified sphere
of activity or branch of knowledge : such are the Arabic words
relating to mathematics and astronomy (*algebra, zero, cipher,
azimuth, zenith,* in related fields *tariff, alkali, alcohol*), the Italian
words relating to music (*piano, allegro, andante, solo, soprano,*
etc.) and commerce (*bank, bankrupt, balance, traffic, ducat, florin*)
—one need not accumulate examples, as everybody interested in
the subject of this book will be able to supply a great many from
his own reading.   The most comprehensive groups of this kind
are those French, Latin and Greek words that have flooded the
whole world of Western civilization from the Middle Ages and
the Renaissance and have given a family-character to all those
parts of the vocabularies of otherwise different languages which

are concerned with the highest intellectual and technical activities. See the detailed discussion of these strata of loan-words in English in GS ch. v and vi.

When one nation has imbibed for centuries the cultural influence of another, its language may have become so infiltrated with words from the other language that these are found in most sentences, at any rate in nearly every sentence dealing with things above the simplest material necessities. The best-known examples are English since the influx of French and classical words, and Turkish with its wholesale importations from Arabic. Another example is Basque, in which nearly all expressions for religious and spiritual ideas are Romanic. Basque is naturally very poor in words for general ideas; it has names for special kinds of trees, but 'tree' is *arbolia*, from Spanish *árbol*, 'animal' is *animale*, 'colour' *colore*, 'plant' *planta* or *landare*, 'flower' *lore* or *lili*, 'thing' *gauza*, 'time' *dembora*. Thus also many of its names for utensils and garments, weights and measures, arms, etc., are borrowed; 'king' is *errege*, 'law' *lege, laqe*, 'master' *maisu*, etc. (See *Zs. f. roman. Phil.*, 17. 140 ff.)

In a great many cases linguistic borrowing must be considered a necessity, but this is not always so. When a nation has once got into the habit of borrowing words, people will very often use foreign words where it would have been perfectly possible to express their ideas by means of native speech-material, the reason for going out of one's own language being in some cases the desire to be thought fashionable or refined through interlarding one's speech with foreign words, in others simply laziness, as is very often the case when people are rendering thoughts they have heard or read in a foreign tongue. Translators are responsible for the great majority of these intrusive words, which might have been avoided by a resort to native composition or derivation, or very often by turning the sentence a little differently from the foreign text. The most thoroughgoing speech mixtures are due much less to real race-mixture than to continued cultural contact, especially of a literary character, as is seen very clearly in English, where the Romanic element is only to a very small extent referable to the Norman conquerors, and far more to the peaceful relations of the following centuries. That Greek and Latin words have come in through the medium of literature hardly needs saying. Many of these words are superfluous: "The native words *cold, cool, chilly, icy, frosty*, might have seemed sufficient for all purposes, without any necessity for importing *frigid, gelid* and *algid*, which, as a matter of fact, are found neither in Shakespeare nor in the Authorized Version of the Bible nor in the poetical works of Milton, Pope, Cowper and Shelley" (GS § 136). But on the other hand it cannot be denied that the imported words have in many instances enriched the language through enabling its users to obtain greater variety and to find expressions for many subtle shades of thought. The question of the value of loan-words cannot be dismissed offhand, as the 'purists' in many countries are inclined to imagine, with the dictum that foreign words should be shunned like the plague, but requires for its solution a careful consideration of the merits and demerits of each separate foreign term viewed in connexion with the native resources for expressing that particular idea.

XI.—§ 11. Classes of Loan-words.

It is quite natural that there should be a much greater inclination everywhere to borrow 'full' words (substantives, adjectives, notional verbs) than 'empty' words (pronouns, prepositions, conjunctions, auxiliary verbs), to which class most of the 'grammatical' words belong   But there is no hard-and-fast limit between the two classes. It is rare for a language to take such words as numerals from another language ; yet examples are found here and there—thus, in connexion with special games, etc. Until comparatively recently, dicers and backgammon-players counted in England by means of the French words *ace, deuce, tray, cater, cinque, size,* and with the English game of lawn tennis the English way of counting (fifteen love, etc.) has been lately adopted in Russia and to some extent also in Denmark. In some parts of England Welsh numerals were until comparatively recent times used in the counting of sheep. Cattle-drivers in Jutland used to count from 20 to 90 in Low German learnt in Hamburg and Holstein, where they sold their cattle. In this case the clumsiness and want of perspicuity of the Danish expressions (*halvtredsindstyve* for Low German *föfdix*, etc.) may have been one of the reasons for preferring the German words ; in the same way the clumsiness of the Eskimo way of counting ("third toe on the second foot of the fourth man," etc.) has favoured the introduction into Greenlandic of the Danish words for 100 and 1,000 : with an Eskimo ending, *untritigdlit* and *tusintigdlit.* Most Japanese numerals are Chinese. And of course *million* and *milliard* are used in most civilized countries.

Prepositions, too, are rarely borrowed by one language from another. Yet the Latin (Ital.) *per* is used in English, German and Danish, and the French *à* in the two latter languages, and both are extending their domain beyond the commercial language in which they were first used. The Greek *kata,* at first also commercial, has in Spanish found admission into the ordinary language and has become the pronoun *cada* 'each.'

Personal and demonstrative pronouns, articles and the like are scarcely ever taken over from one language to another. They are so definitely woven into the innermost texture of a language that no one would think of giving them up, however much he might like to adorn his speech with words from a foreign source. If, therefore, in one instance we find a case of a language borrowing words of this kind, we are justified in thinking that exceptional causes must have been at work, and such really proves to be the case in English, which has adopted the Scandinavian forms *they*, *them*, *their*. It is usual to speak of English as being a mixture of native Old English ('Anglo-Saxon') and French, but as a matter of fact the French influence, powerful as it is in the vocabulary and patent as it is to the eyes of everybody, is superficial in comparison with the influence exercised in a much subtler way by the Scandinavian settlers in the North of England. The French influence is different in extent, but not in kind, from the French influence on German or the old Gothonic influence on Finnic ; it is perhaps best compared with the German influence on Danish in the Middle Ages. But the Scandinavian influence on English is of a different kind. The number of Danish and Norwegian settlers in England must have been very large, as is shown by the number of Scandinavian place-names ; yet that does not account for everything. A most important factor was the great similarity of the two languages, in spite of numerous points of difference. Accordingly, when their fighting was over, the invaders and the original population would to some extent be able to make themselves understood by one another, like people talking two dialects of the same language, or like students from Copenhagen and from Lund nowadays. Many of the most common words were absolutely identical, and others differed only slightly Hence it comes that in the Middle English texts we find a great many double forms of the same word, one English and the other Scandinavian, used side by side, some of these doublets even surviving till the present day, though now differentiated in sense (e.g. *whole*, *hale* ; *no*, *nay* ; *from*, *fro* ; *shirt*, *skirt*), while in other cases one only of the two forms, either the native or the Scandinavian, has survived ; thus the Scandinavian *sister* and *egg* have ousted the English *sweostor* and *ey*. We find, therefore, a great many words adopted of a kind not usually borrowed ; thus, everyday verbs and adjectives like *take*, *call*, *hit*, *die*, *ill*, *ugly*, *wrong*, and among substantives such non-technical ones as *fellow*, *sky*, *skin*, *wing*, etc. (For details see my GS ch. iv.) All this indicates an intimate fusion of the two races and of the two languages, such as is not provided for in any of the classes described by Hempl (above, § 8). In most speech-mixtures the various elements remain distinct and can be separated, just as after shuffling a pack of cards you can pick out the hearts, spades, etc. ; but in the case of English and Scandinavian we have a subtler and more intimate fusion, very much as when you put a lump of sugar into a cup of tea and a few minutes afterwards are quite unable to say which is tea and which is sugar.

XI.—§ 12. Influence on Grammar.

The question has often been raised whether speech-mixture affects the grammar of a language which has borrowed largely from some other language. The older view is expressed pointedly by Whitney (L 199) : " Such a thing as a language with a mixed grammatical apparatus has never come under the cognizance of linguistic students : it would be to them a monstrosity ; it seems an impossibility." This is an exaggeration, and cannot be justified, for the simple reason that the vocabulary of a language and its ' grammatical apparatus ' cannot be nicely separated in the way presupposed : indeed, much of the borrowed material mentioned in our last paragraphs does belong to the grammatical apparatus. But there is, of course, some truth in Whitney's dictum. When a word is borrowed it is not as a rule taken over with all the elaborate flexion which may belong to it in its original home ; as a rule, one form only is adopted, it may be the nominative or some other case of a noun, the infinitive or the present or the naked stem of a verb. This form is then either used unchanged or with the endings of the adopting language, generally those of the most ' regular ' declension or conjugation. It is an exceptional case when more than one flexional form is taken over, and this case does not occur in really popular loans. In learned usage we find in older Danish such case-flexion as gen. *Christi*, dat. *Christo*, by the side of nom. *Christus*, also, e.g., *i theatro*, and still sometimes in German we have the same usage : e.g. *mit den pronominibus*. In a somewhat greater number of instances the plural form is adopted as well as the singular form, as in English *fungi, formulæ, phenomena, seraphim*, etc., but the natural tendency is always towards using the native endings, *funguses, formulas*, etc., and this has prevailed in all popular words, e.g. *ideas, circuses, museums*. As the formation of cases, tenses, etc., in different languages is often very irregular, and the distinctive marks are often so intimately connected with the kernel of the word and so unsubstantial as not to be easily distinguished, it is quite natural that no one should think of borrowing such endings, etc., and applying them to native words. Schuchardt once thought that the English genitive ending *s* had been adopted into Indo-Portuguese (in the East Indies), where *gobernadors casa* stands for ' governor's house,' but he now explains the form more correctly as originating in the possessive pronoun *su*: *gobernador su casa* (dem g. sein haus, *Sitzungsber. der preuss. Akademie*, 1917, 524).

It was at one time commonly held that the English plural ending *s*, which in Old English was restricted in its application, owes its extension to the influence of French. This theory, I believe, was finally disposed of by the six decisive arguments I brought forward against it in 1891 (reprinted in ChE § 39). But after what has been said above on the Scandinavian influence, I incline to think that E. Classen is right in thinking that the Danes count for something in bringing about the final victory of -*s* over its competitor -*n*, for the Danes had no plural in -*n*, and -*s* reminded them of their own -*r* (*Mod. Language Rev.* 14. 94 ; cf. also -*s* in the third person of verbs, Scand. -*r*). Apart from this particular point, it is quite natural that the Scandinavians should have exercised a general levelling influence on the English language, as many niceties of grammar would easily be sacrificed where mutual intelligibility was so largely brought about by the common vocabulary. Accordingly, we find that in the regions in which the Danish settlements were thickest the wearing away of grammatical forms was a couple of centuries in advance of the same process in the southern parts of the country.

Derivative endings certainly belong to the 'grammatical apparatus' of a language ; yet many such endings have been taken over into another language as parts of borrowed words and have then been freely combined with native speech-material. The phenomenon is extremely frequent in English, where we have, for instance, the Romanic endings -*ess* (*shepherdess, seeress*), -*ment* (*endearment, bewilderment*), -*age* (*mileage, cleavage, shortage*), -*ance* (*hindrance, forbearance*) and many more. In Danish and German the number of similar instances is much more restricted, yet we have, for instance, recent words in -*isme*, -*ismus* and -*ianer* ; cf. also older words like *bageri, bäckerei*, etc. It is the same with prefixes : English has formed many words with *de-, co-, inter-, pre-, anti-* and other classical prefixes : *de-anglicize, co-godfather, intermarriage, at pre-war prices, anti-slavery*, etc. (quotations in my GS § 124 ; cf. MEG ii. 14. 66). *Ex-* has established itself in many languages: *ex-king, ex-roi, ex-konge, ex-könig*, etc. In Danish the prefix *be-*, borrowed from German, is used very extensively with native words : *bebrejde, bebo, bebygge*, and this is not the only German prefix that is productive in the Scandinavian languages.

With regard to syntax, very little can be said except in a general way : languages certainly do influence each other syntactically, and those who know a foreign language only imperfectly are apt to transfer to it methods of construction from their own tongue. Many instances of this have been collected by Schuchardt, SID. But it is doubtful whether these syntactical influences have the same *permanent* effects on any language as those exerted on one's own language by the habit of translating foreign works into it : in this purely literary way a great many idioms and turns of phrases have been introduced into English, German and the Scandinavian languages from French and Latin, and into Danish and Swedish from German. The accusative and infinitive construction, which had only a very restricted use in Old English, has very considerably extended its domain through Latin influence, and the so-called 'absolute construction' (in my own grammatical terminology called 'nexus subjunct') seems to be entirely due to imitation of Latin syntax. In the Balkan tongues there are some interesting instances of syntactical agreement between various languages, which must be due to oral influence through the necessity imposed on border peoples of passing continually from one language to another : the infinitive has disappeared from Greek, Rumanian and Albanian, and the definite article is placed after the substantive in Rumanian, Albanian and Bulgarian.

XI.—§ 13. Translation-loans.

Besides direct borrowings we have also indirect borrowings or ' translation loan-words,' words modelled more or less closely on foreign ones, though consisting of native speech-material. I take some examples from the very full and able paper " Notes sur les Calques Linguistiques " contributed by Kr. Sandfeld to the *Festschrift Vilh. Thomsen*, 1912 : *ædificatio* : G. erbauung, Dan. opbyggelse ; *æquilibrium* : G. gleichgewicht, Dan. ligevægt ; *beneficium* : G. wohltat, Dan. velgerning ; *conscientia* : Goth. miþwissi, G. gewissen, Dan. samvittighed, Swed. samvete, Russ. soznanie ; *omnipotens* : E. almighty, G. allmächtig, Dan. almægtig ; *arrière-pensée* : hintergedanke, bagtanke ; *bien-être* : wohlsein, velvære ; *exposition* : austellung, udstilling ; etc. Sandfeld gives many more examples, and as he has in most instances been able to give also corresponding words from various Slavonic languages as well as from Magyar, Finnic, etc., he rightly concludes that his collections serve to throw light on that community in thought and expression which Bally has well termed " la mentalité européenne." (But it will be seen that English differs from most European languages in having a much greater propensity to swallowing foreign words raw, as it were, than to translating them.)

CHAPTER XII
PIDGIN AND CONGENERS

§ 1. Beach-la-Mar. § 2. Grammar. § 3. Sounds. § 4. Pidgin. § 5. Grammar, etc. § 6. General Theory. § 7. Mauritius Creole. § 8. Chinook Jargon. § 9. Chinook continued. § 10. Makeshift Languages. § 11. Romanic Languages.

XII.—§ 1. Beach-la-Mar.

As a first typical example of a whole class of languages now found in many parts of the world where people of European civilization have come into contact with men of other races, we may take the so-called *Beach-la-mar* (or Beche-le-mar, or Beche de mer English);[1] it is also sometimes called Sandalwood English. It is spoken and understood all over the Western Pacific, its spread being largely due to the fact that the practice of 'blackbirding' often brought together on the same plantation many natives from different islands with mutually incomprehensible languages, whose only means of communication was the broken English they had picked up from the whites. And now the natives learn this language from each other, while in many places the few Europeans have to learn it from the islanders. "Thus the native use of Pidgin-English lays down the rules by which the Europeans let themselves be guided when learning it. Even Englishmen do not find it quite easy at the beginning to understand Pidgin-English, and have to learn it before they are able to speak it properly " (Landtman).

[1] The etymology of this name is rather curious: Portuguese *bicho de mar*, from *bicho* 'worm,' the name of the sea slug or trepang, which is eaten as a luxury by the Chinese, was in French modified into *bêche de mer*, 'seaspade'; this by a second popular etymology was made into English *beach-la-mar* as if a compound of *beach*.
My sources are H. Schuchardt, KS v. (Wiener Academie, 1883) ; id. in ESt xiii. 158 ff., 1889; W. Churchill, *Beach-la-Mar, the Jargon or Trade Speech of the Western Pacific* (Carnegie Institution of Washington, 1911); Jack London, *The Cruise of the Snark* (Mills & Boon, London, 1911 ?), G. Landtman in *Neuphilologische Mittleilungen* (Helsingfors, 1918, p. 62 ff. Landtman calls it " the Pidgin-English of British New Guinea," where he learnt it, though it really differs from Pidgin-English proper ; see below) ; " The Jargon English of Torres Straits" in *Reports of the Cambridge Anthropological Expedition to Torres Straits*, vol. iii. p. 25 1 ff., Cambridge, 1907.

I shall now try to give some idea of the structure of this lingo.

The vocabulary is nearly all English. Even most of the words which ultimately go back to other languages have been admitted only because the English with whom the islanders were thrown into contact had previously adopted them into their own speech, so that the islanders were justified in believing that they were really English. This is true of the Spanish or Portuguese *savvy*, 'to know,' and *pickaninny*, 'child' or 'little one' (a favourite in many languages on account of its symbolic sound; see Ch. XX § 8), as well as the Amerindian *tomahawk*, which in the whole of Australia is the usual word for a small axe. And if we find in Beach-la-mar the two Maori words *tapu* or *taboo* and *kai*, or more often *kaikai*, 'to eat' or 'food,' they have probably got into the language through English—we know that both are very extensively used in Australia, while the former is known all over the civilized world. *Likkilik* or *liklik*, 'small, almost,' is said to be from a Polynesian word *liki*, but may be really a perversion of Engl. *little*. Landtman gives a few words from unknown languages used by the Kiwais, though not derived from their own language. The rest of the words found in my sources are English, though not always pure English, in so far as their signification is often curiously distorted.

Nusipepa means 'a letter, any written or printed document,' *mary* is the general term for 'woman' (cf. above, p. 118), *pisupo* (peasoup) for all foreign foods which are preserved in tins; *squareface*, the sailor's name for a square gin-bottle, is extended to all forms of glassware, no matter what the shape. One of the earliest seafarers is said to have left a bull and a cow on one of the islands and to have mentioned these two words together; the natives took them as one word, and now *bullamacow* or *pulumakau* means 'cattle, beef, also tinned beef'; *pulomokau* is now given as a native word in a dictionary of the Fijian language.[1] *Bulopenn*, which means 'ornament,' is said to be nothing but the English *blue paint*. All this shows the purely accidental character of many of the linguistic acquisitions of the Polynesians.

As the vocabulary is extremely limited, composite expressions are sometimes resorted to in order to express ideas for which we have simple words, and not unfrequently the devices used appear to us very clumsy or even comical. A piano is called 'big fellow bokus (box) you fight him he cry,' and a

---

[1] Similarly the missionary G. Brown thought that *tobi* was a native word of the Duke of York Islands for 'wash,' till one day he accidentally discovered that it was their pronunciation of English *soap*.

concertina 'little fellow bokus you shove him he cry, you pull him he cry.' *Woman he got faminil* ('family') *inside* means 'she is with child.' *Inside* is also used extensively about mental states : *jump inside* 'be startled,' *inside tell himself* 'to consider,' *inside bad* 'grieved or sorry,' *feel inside* 'to know,' *feel another kind inside* 'to change one's mind.' *My throat he fast* 'I was dumb.' *He took daylight a long time* 'lay awake.' *Bring fellow belong make open bottle* 'bring me a corkscrew.' *Water belong stink* 'perfumery.' The idea of being bald is thus expressed : *grass belong head belong him all he die finish*, or with another variant, *coconut belong him grass no stop*, for *coconut* is taken from English slang in the sense 'head' (Schuchardt has the sentence : *You no savvy that fellow white man coconut belong him no grass ?*). For 'feather' the combination *grass belong pigeon* is used, *pigeon* being a general term for any bird.

A man who wanted to borrow a saw, the word for which he had forgotten, said : 'You give me brother belong tomahawk, he come he go.' A servant who had been to Queensland, where he saw a train, on his return called it 'steamer he walk about along bush.' Natives who watched Landtman when he enclosed letters in envelopes named the latter 'house belong letter.' Many of these expressions are thus picturesque descriptions made on the spur of the moment if the proper word is not known.

XII.—§ 2. Grammar.

These phrases have already illustrated some points of the very simple grammar of this lingo. Words have only one form, and what is in our language expressed by flexional forms is either left unexpressed or else indicated by auxiliary words. The plural of nouns is like the singular (though the form *men* is found in my texts alongside of *man*) ; when necessary, the plural is indicated by means of a prefixed *all* : *all he talk* 'they say' (also *him fellow all* 'they') ; *all man* 'everybody' ; a more indefinite plural is *plenty man* or *full up man*. For 'we' is said *me two fella* or *me three fellow*, as the case may be ; *me two fellow Lagia* means 'I and Lagia.' If there are more, *me altogether man* or *me plenty man* may be said, though *we* is also in use. *Fellow* (*fella*) is a much-vexed word ; it is required, or at any rate often used, after most pronouns, thus, *that fellow hat, this fellow knife, me fellow, you fellow, him fellow* (not *he fellow*) ; it is foun very often after an adjective and seems to be required to prop up the adjective before the substantive : *big fellow name, big fellow tobacco, another fellow man*. In other cases no *fellow* is used, and it seems difficult to give definite rules ; after a numeral it is frequent : *two fellow men* (*man ?*), *three fellow bottle*. There is a curious employment in *ten fellow ten one fellow*, which means 101. It is used adverbially in *that man he cry big fellow* ' he cries loudly.'

The genitive is expressed by means of *belong* (or *belong-a*, *long*, *along*), which also serves for other prepositional relations. Examples : *tail belong him*, *pappa belong me*, *wife belong you*, *belly belong me walk about too much* (I was seasick), *me savvee talk along white man* ; *rope along bush* means liana. *Missis ! man belong bullamacow him stop* (the butcher has come). *What for you wipe hands belong-a you on clothes belong esseppoon ?* (spoon, i.e. napkin). Cf. above the expressions for ' bald.' *Piccaninny belong banana* ' a young b. plant.' *Belong* also naturally means ' to live in, be a native of ' ; *boy belong island, he belong Burri-burrigan*. The preposition *along* is used about many local relations (in, at, on, into, on board). From such combinations as *laugh along* (l. at) and *he speak along this fella* the transition is easy to cases in which *along* serves to indicate the indirect object : *he give'm this fella Eve along Adam*, and also a kind of direct object, as in *fight alonga him, you gammon along me* (deceive, lie to me), and with the form *belong* : *he puss-puss belong this fellow* (*puss-puss* orig. a cat, then as a verb to caress, make love to).

There is no distinction of gender : *that woman he brother belong me* = ' she is my sister ' ; *he* (before the verb) and *him* (in all other positions) serve both for he, she and it. There is a curious use of *'m*, *um* or *em*, in our texts often written *him*, after a verb as a ' vocal sign of warning that an object of the verb is to follow,' no matter what that object is.

Churchill says that " in the adjective comparison is unknown ; the islanders do not know how to think comparatively—at least, they lack the form of words by which comparison may be indicated ; *this big, that small* is the nearest they can come to the expression of the idea that one thing is greater than another." But Landtman recognizes *more big* and also *more better* : ' no good make him that fashion, more better make him all same.' The same double comparative I find in another place, used as a kind of verb meaning ' ought to, had better ' : *more better you come out*. *Too* simply means ' much ' : *he savvy too much* ' he knows much ' (praise, no blame), *he too much talk*. A synonym is *plenty too much*. Schuchardt gives the explanation of this trait : " The white man was the teacher of the black man, who imitated his manner of speaking. But the former would constantly use the strongest expressions and exaggerate in a manner that he would only occasionally resort to in speaking to his own countrymen. He did not say, 'You are very lazy,' but 'You are too lazy,' and this will account for the fact that 'very' is called *too much* in Beach-la-mar as well as *tumussi* in the Negro-English of Surinam " (*Spr. der Saramakkaneger*, p. iv).

Verbs have no tense-forms; when required, a future may be indicated by means of *by and by*: *brother belong-a-me by and by he dead* (my br. is dying), *bymby all men laugh along that boy; he small now, bymbye he big.* It may be qualified by additions like *bymby one time, bymby little bit, bymby big bit,* and may be used also of the 'postpreterit' (of futurity relative to a past time): *by and by boy belong island he speak.* Another way of expressing the future is seen in *that woman he close up born* (!) *him piccaninny* 'that woman will shortly give birth to a child.' The usual sign of the perfect is *been*, the only idiomatic form of the verb to be: *you been take me along three year; I been look round before.* But *finish* may also be used: *me look him finish* (I have seen him), *he kaikai all finish* (he has eaten it all up).

Where we should expect forms of the verb 'to be,' there is either no verb or else *stop* is used: *no water stop* (there is no water), *rain he stop* (it rains), *two white men stop Matupi* (live in), *other day plenty money he stop* (. . . I had . . .). For 'have' they say *got*. *My belly no got kaikai* (I am hungry), *he got good hand* (is skilful).

XII.—§ 3. Sounds.

About the phonetic structure of Beach-la-mar I have very little information; as a rule the words in my sources are spelt in the usual English way. Churchill speaks in rather vague terms about difficulties which the islanders experience in imitating the English sounds, and especially groups of consonants: " Any English word which on experiment proved impracticable to the islanders has undergone alteration to bring it within the scope of their familiar range of sounds or has been rejected for some facile synonym." Thus, according to him, the conjunction *if* could not be used on account of the *f*, and that is the reason for the constant use of *suppose* (*s'pose, pose, posum* = s'pose him)—but it may be allowable to doubt this, for as a matter of fact *f* occurs very frequently in the language—for instance, in the well-worn words *fellow* and *finish*. *Suppose* probably is preferred to *if* because it is fuller in form and less abstract, and therefore easier to handle, while the islanders have many occasions to hear it in other combinations than those in which it is an equivalent of the conjunction.

Landtman says that with the exception of a few sounds
(*j, ch*, and *th* as in *nothing*) the Kiwai Papuans have little difficulty in pronouncing English words.

Schuchardt gives a little more information about pronunciation, and instances *esterrong = strong, esseppoon = spoon, essauce-
pen = saucepan, pellate = plate, coverra = cover, millit = milk,
bock-kiss = box* (in Churchill *bokus, bokkis*) as mutilations due
to the native speech habits. He also gives the following letter
from a native of the New Hebrides, communicated to him by
R. H. Codrington; it shows many sound substitutions :

*Misi Kamesi Arelu Jou no kamu ruki mi Mi no ruki iou Jou
ruku Mai Poti i ko Mae tete Vakaromala mi raiki i tiripi Ausi
parogi iou i rukauti Mai Poti mi nomoa kaikai mi angikele nau
Poti mani Mae i kivi iou Jamu Vari koti iou kivi tamu te pako
paraogi mi i penesi nomoa te Pako.*

Oloraiti Ta, MATASO.

This means as much as :

Mr. Comins, (How) are you ? You no come look me ; me
no look you ; you look my boat he go Mae to-day. Vakaromala
me like he sleep house belong you, he look out my boat, me no
more kaikai, me hungry now, boat man Mae he give you yam
very good, you give some tobacco belong (here = to) me, he
finish, no more tobacco.

All right Ta, MATASO.

There are evidently many degrees of approximation to the
true English sounds.

This letter also shows the characteristic tendency to add a
vowel, generally a short *i*, to words ending in consonants. This
is old, for I find in Defoe's *Farther Adventures of Robinson Crusoe*
(1719, p. 211) : " All those natives, as also those of Africa, when
they learn English, they always add two E's at the end of the
words where we use one, and make the accent upon them, as
makee, takee and the like." (Note the un-phonetic expressions !)
Landtman, besides this addition, as in *belongey*, also mentions
a more enigmatic one of *lo* to words ending in vowels, as *clylo* for
' cry ' (cf. below on Pidgin).

XII.—§ 4. Pidgin.

I now turn to Pidgin-English. As is well known, this is the
name of the jargon which is very extensively used in China, and
to some extent also in Japan and California, as a means of communication between English-speaking people and the yellow

population. The name is derived from the Chinese distortion of the Engl. word *business*. Unfortunately, the sources available for Pidgin-English as actually spoken in the East nowadays are neither so full nor so exact as those for Beach-la-mar, and the following sketch, therefore, is not quite satisfactory.[1]

Pidgin-English must have developed pretty soon after the first beginning of commercial relations between the English and Chinese. In *Engl. Studien*, 44. 298, Prick van Wely has printed some passages of C. F. Noble's *Voyage to the East Indies in 1747 and 1748*, in which the Chinese are represented as talking to the writer in a " broken and mixed dialect of English and Portuguese," the specimens given corresponding pretty closely to the Pidgin of our own days. Thus, *he no cari Chinaman's Joss, hap oter Joss*, which is rendered, ' that man does not worship our god, but has another god ' ; the Chinese are said to be unable to pronounce *r* and to use the word *chin-chin* for compliments and *pickenini* for ' small.'

The latter word seems now extinct in Pidgin proper, though we have met it in Beach-la-mar, but *Joss* is still very frequent in Pidgin : it is from Portuguese *Deus, Deos* (or Span. *Dios*) : *Joss-house* is a temple or church, *Joss-pidgin* religion, *Joss-pidgin man* a clergyman, *topside Joss-pidgin man* a bishop. *Chin-chin*, according to the same source, is from Chinese *ts'ing-ts'ing*, Pekingese *ch'ing-ch'ing*, a term of salutation answering to ' thank you, adieu,' but the English have extended its sphere of application very considerably, using it as a noun meaning ' salutation, compliment,' and as a verb meaning " to worship (by bowing and striking the chin), to reverence, adore, implore, to deprecate anger, to wish one something, invite, ask " (Leland). The explanation given here within parentheses shows how the Chinese word has been interpreted by popular etymology, and no doubt it owes its extensive use partly to its sound, which has taken the popular fancy. *Chin-chin joss* means religious worship of any kind.

Simpson says : " Many of the words in use are of unknown origin. In a number of cases the English suppose them to be

---

[1] There are many specimens in Charles G. Leland, *Pidgin-English Sing-Song, or Songs and Stories in the China-English Dialect, with a Vocabulary* (5th ed., London, 1900), but they make the impression of being artificially made-up to amuse the readers, and contain a much larger proportion of Chinese words than the rest of my sources would warrant. Besides various articles in newspapers I have used W. Simpson, " China's Future Place in Philology " (*Macmillan's Magazine*, November 1873) and Dr. Legge's article " Pigeon English " in *Chambers's Encyclopædia*, 1901 (s.v. China). The chapters devoted to Pidgin in Karl Lentzner's *Dictionary of the Slang-English of Australia and of some Mixed Languages* (Halle, 1892) give little else but wholesale reprints of passages from some of the sources mentioned above.

Chinese, while the Chinese, on the other hand, take them to be English." Some of these, however, admit now of explanation, and not a few of them point to India, where the English have learnt them and brought them further East. Thus *chit*, *chitty*, 'a letter, an account,' is Hindustani *chiṭṭhī*; *godown* 'warehouse' is an English popular interpretation of Malay *gadong*, from Tamil *gidangi*. *Chowchow* seems to be real Chinese and to mean 'mixed preserves,' but in Pidgin it has acquired the wider signification of 'food, meal, to eat,' besides having various other applications : a chowchow cargo is an assorted cargo, a 'general shop' is a chowchow shop. *Cumshaw* 'a present' is Chinese. But *tiffin*, which is used all over the East for 'lunch,' is really an English word, properly *tiffing*, from the slang verb *to tiff*, to drink, esp. to drink out of meal-times. In India it was applied to the meal, and then reintroduced into England and believed to be a native Indian word.

XII.—§ 5. Grammar, etc.

Among points not found in Beach-la-mar I shall mention the extensive use of *piecee*, which in accordance with Chinese grammar is required between a numeral and the noun indicating what is counted; thus in a Chinaman's description of a three-masted screw steamer with two funnels; "Thlee piecee bamboo, two piecee puff-puff, walk-along inside, no can see " (walk-along = the engine). *Side* means any locality : *he belongey China-side now* (he is in China), *topside* above, or high, *bottom-side* below, *farside* beyond, *this-side* here, *allo-side* around. In a similar way *time* (pronounced *tim* or *teem*) is used in *that-tim* then, when, *what-tim* when ? *one-tim* once, only, *two-tim* twice, again, *nother-tim* again.

In one respect the Chinese sound system is accountable for a deviation from Beach-la-mar, namely in the substitution of *l* for *r* : *loom, all light* for 'room, all right,' etc., while the islanders often made the inverse change. But the tendency to add a vowel after a final consonant is the same : *makee, too muchee*, etc. The enigmatic termination *lo*, which Landtman found in some words in New Guinea, is also added to some words ending in vowel sounds in Pidgin, according to Leland, who instances *die-lo*, die; in his texts I find the additional examples *buy-lo, say-lo, pay-lo, hear-lo*, besides *wailo*, or *wylo*, which is probably from *away*; it means 'go away, away with you ! go, depart, gone.' Can it be the Chinese sign of the past tense *la*, *lao*, generalized ?

Among usual expressions must be mentioned *number one* (*numpa one*) 'first-class, excellent,' *catchee* 'get, possess, hold, bring,' etc., *ploper* (*plopa*) 'proper, good, nice, correct'*: you belong ploper ?* 'are you well ? '

Another word which was not in use among the South Sea islanders, namely *have*, in the form *hab* or *hap* is often used in Pidgin, even to form the perfect. *Belong* (*belongy*) is nearly as frequent as in Beach-la-mar, but is used in a different way : 'My belongy Consoo boy,' 'I am the Consul's servant.' 'You belong clever inside,' 'you are intelligent.' The usual way of asking the price of something is 'how much belong ? '

XII.—§ 6. General Theory.

Lingos of the same type as Beach-la-mar and Pidgin-English are found in other parts of the world where whites and natives meet and have to find some medium of communication. Thus a Danish doctor living in Belgian Congo sends me a few specimens of the ' Pidgin' spoken there : to indicate that his master has received many letters from home, the ' boy ' will say, " Massa catch plenty mammy-book " *mammy* meaning ' woman, wife '). *Breeze* stands for air in general ; if the boy wants to say that he has pumped up the bicycle tyres, he will say, " Plenty breeze live for inside," *live* being here the general term for ' to be ' (Beach-l. *tock*) ; 'is your master in ? ' becomes ' Massa live ? ' and the answer is ' he no live ' or ' he live for hup ' (i.e. he is upstairs). If a man has a stomach-ache he will say ' he hurt me for belly plenty too much '—*too much* is thus used exactly as in Beach-la-mar and Chinese Pidgin. The similarity of all these jargons, in spite of unavoidable smaller differences, is in fact very striking indeed.

It may be time now to draw the moral of all this. And first I want to point out that these languages are not ' mixed languages ' in the proper sense of that term. Churchill is not right when he says that Beach-la-mar " gathered material from every source, it fused them all." As a matter of fact, it is English, and nothing but English, with very few admixtures, and all of these are such words as had previously been adopted into the English speech of those classes of the population, sailors, etc., with whom the natives came into contact : they were therefore justified in their belief that these words formed part of the English tongue and that what they learned themselves was real English. The natives really adhere to Windisch's rule about the adoption of loan-words (above, XI § 10). If there are more Chinese words in Pidgin than there are Polynesian ones in Beach-la-mar, this is a natural consequence of the fact that the Chinese civilization ranked incomparably

much higher than the Polynesian, and that therefore the
English living in China would adopt these words into their own
speech. Still, their number is not very large. And we have
seen that there are some words which the Easterners must
naturally suppose to be English, while the English think that
they belong to the vernacular, and in using them each party
is thus under the delusion that he is rendering a service to the
other.

This leads me to my second point : those deviations from
correct English, those corruptions of pronunciation and those
simplifications of grammar, which have formed the object of
this short sketch, are due just as much to the English as to the
Easterners, and in many points they began with the former
rather than with the latter (cf. Schuchardt, *Auf anlass des
Volapüks*, 1888, 8 ; KS 4. 35, SID 36 ; ESt 15. 292). From
Schuchardt I take the following quotation : " The usual question
on reaching the portico of an Indian bungalow is, *Can missus see ?*
—it being a popular superstition amongst the Europeans that
to enable a native to understand English he must be addressed
as if he were deaf, and in the most infantile language." This
tendency to meet the ' inferior races ' half-way in order to facilitate matters for them is by Churchill called " the one supreme
axiom of international philology : the proper way to make a
foreigner understand what you would say is to use broken
English. He speaks it himself, therefore give him what he uses."
We recognize here the same mistaken notion that we have seen
above in the language of the nursery, where mothers and others
will talk a curious sort of mangled English which is believed to
represent real babytalk, though it has many traits which are
purely conventional. In both cases these more or less artificial
perversions are thought to be an aid to those who have not yet
mastered the intricacies of the language in question, though the
ultimate result is at best a retardation of the perfect acquisition
of correct speech.

My view, then, is that Beach-la-mar as well as Pidgin is
English, only English learnt imperfectly, in consequence partly
of the difficulties always inherent in learning a totally different
language, partly of the obstacles put in the way of learning by
the linguistic behaviour of the English-speaking people themselves. The analogy of its imperfections with those of a baby's
speech in the first period is striking, and includes errors of pronunciation, extreme simplification of grammar, scantiness of
vocabulary, even to such peculiarities as that the word *too* is
apprehended in the sense of ' very much,' and such phrases as
you better go, etc.

15

XII.—§ 7. Mauritius Creole.

The view here advanced on the character of these 'Pidgin' languages is corroborated when we see that other languages under similar circumstances have been treated in exactly the same way as English. With regard to French in the island of Mauritius, formerly Ile de France, we are fortunate in possessing an excellent treatment of the subject by M. C. Baissac (*Étude sur le Patois Créole Mauricien*, Nancy, 1880 ; cf. the same writer's *Le Folk-lore de l'Ile-Maurice*, Paris, 1888, Les littératures populaires, tome xxvii). The island was uninhabited when the French occupied it in 1715 ; a great many slaves were imported from Madagascar, and as a means of intercourse between them and their French masters a French Creole language sprang up, which has survived the English conquest (1810) and the subsequent wholesale introduction of coolies from India and elsewhere. The paramount element in the vocabulary is French ; one may read many pages in Baissac's texts without coming across any foreign words, apart from the names of some indigenous animals and plants. In the phonetic structure there are a few all-pervading traits : the front-round vowels are replaced by the corresponding unrounded vowels or in a few cases by [u], and instead of [ʃ, ʒ] we find [s, z] ; thus *éré* heureux, *éne plime* une plume, *sakéne* chacun(e), *zize* juge, *zunu* genou, *suval* cheval : I replace Baissac's notation, which is modelled on the French spelling, by a more phonetic one according to his own indications ; but I keep his final *e muet*.

The grammar of this language is as simple as possible. Substantives have the same form for the two numbers : *dé suval* deux chevaux. There is no definite article. The adjective is invariable, thus also *sa* for ce, cet, cette, ces, ceci, cela, celui, celle, ceux, celles. *Mo* before a verb is 'I,' before a substantive it is possessive : *mo koné* I know, *mo lakaze* my house ; in the same way *to* is you and your, but in the third person a distinction is made, for *li* is he or she, but his or her is *so*, and here we have even a plural, *zaute* from 'les autres,' which form is also used as a plural of the second person : *mo va alle av zaut*, I shall go with you.

The genitive is expressed by word-order without any preposition : *lakase so papa* his father's house ; also with *so* before the nominative : *so piti ppa Azor* old Azor's child.

The form in which the French words have been taken over presents some curious features, and in some cases illustrates the difficulty the blacks felt in separating the words which they heard in the French utterance as one continuous stream of

sounds. There is evidently a disinclination to begin a word with
a vowel, and sometimes an initial vowel is left out, as *bitation*
habitation, *tranzé* étranger, but in other cases *z* is taken from
the French plural article : *zozo* oiseau, *zistoire*, *zenfan*, *zimaze*
image, *zalfan* éléphant, *zanimo* animal, or *n* from the French
indefinite article : *name* ghost, *nabi* (or *zabi*) habit. In many
cases the whole French article is taken as an integral part of the
word, as *lérat* rat, *léroi*, *licien* chien, *latabe* table, *lére* heure (often
as a conjunction ' when ') ; thus also with the plural article
lizié from *les yeux*, but without the plural signification : *éne*
lizié an eye. Similarly *éne lazoie* a goose. Words that are often
used in French with the so-called partitive article keep this ; thus
disel salt, *divin* wine, *duri* rice, *éne dipin* a loaf ; here also we
meet with one word from the French plural : *éne dizéf* an egg,
from *des œufs*. The French mass-word with the partitive article
du monde has become *dimunde* or *dumune*, and as it means
' people ' and no distinction is made between plural and singular,
it is used also for ' person ' : *éne vié dimunde* an old man.

Verbs have only one form, generally from the French infinitive or past participle, which in most cases would fall together
(*manzé* = manger, mangé ; *kuri* = courir, couru) ; this serves
for all persons in both numbers and all moods. But tenses are
indicated by means of auxiliary words : *va* for the future, *té*
(from *été*) for the ordinary past, and *fine* for the perfect : *mo*
manzé I eat, *mo va manzé* I shall eat, *mo té manzé* I ate, *mo*
fine manzé I have eaten, *mo fine fini* I have finished. Further,
there is a curious use of *aprè* to express what in English are called
the progressive or expanded tenses : *mo aprè manzé* I am eating,
mo té aprè manzé I was eating, and of *pour* to express the immediate future : *mo pour manzé* I am going to eat, and finally an
immediate past may be expressed by *fék* : *mo fék manzé* I have
just been eating (je ne fais que de manger). As these may be
combined in various ways (*mo va fine manzé* I shall have eaten,
even *mo té va fék manzé* I should have eaten a moment ago, etc.),
the language has really succeeded in building up a very fine and
rich verbal system with the simplest possible means and with
perfect regularity.

The French separate negatives have been combined into one word
each : *napa* not (there is not), *narien* nothing, and similarly *nék* only.

In many cases the same form is used for a substantive or
adjective and for a verb : *mo soif, mo faim* I am thirsty and
hungry ; *li content so madame* he is fond of his wife.

Côte (or *à côte*) is a preposition ' by the side of, near,' but
also means ' where ' : *la case àcote li resté* ' the house in which he
lives ' ; cf. Pidgin *side*.

In all this, as will easily be seen, there is very little French grammar ; this will be especially evident when we compare the French verbal system with its many intricacies : difference according to person, number, tense and mood with their endings, changes of root-vowels and stress-place, etc., with the unchanged verbal root and the invariable auxiliary syllables of the Creole. But there is really as little in the Creole dialect of Malagasy grammar, as I have ascertained by looking through G. W. Parker's *Grammar* (London, 1883) : both nations in forming this means of communication have, as it were, stripped themselves of all their previous grammatical habits and have spoken as if their minds were just as innocent of grammar as those of very small babies, whether French or Malagasy. Thus, and thus only, can it be explained that the grammar of this variety of French is for all practical purposes identical with the grammar of those two varieties of English which we have previously examined in this chapter

No one can read Baissac's collection of folk-tales from Mauritius without being often struck with the felicity and even force of this language, in spite of its inevitable *naïveté* and of the childlike simplicity of its constructions. If it were left to itself it might develop into a really fine idiom without abandoning any of its characteristic traits. But as it is, it seems to be constantly changing through the influence of real French, which is more and more taught to and imitated by the islanders, and the day may come when most of the features described in this rapid sketch will have given place to something which is less original, but will be more readily understood by Parisian globe-trotters who may happen to visit the distant island.

XII.—§ 8. Chinook Jargon.

The view here advanced may be further put to the test if we examine a totally different language developed in another part of the world, viz. in Oregon. I give its history in an abridged form from Hale.[1] When the first British and American trading ships appeared on the north-west coast of America, towards the end of the eighteenth century, they found a great number of distinct languages, the Nootka, Nisqually, Chinook. Chihailish and

[1] See *An International Idiom. A Manual of the Oregon Trade Language, or Chinook Jargon,* by Horatio Hale (London, 1890). Besides this I have used a *Vocabulary of the Jargon or Trade Language of Oregon* [by Lionnet] published by the Smithsonian Institution (1853), and George Gibbs, *A Dictionary of the Chinook Jargon* (Smithsonian Inst., 1863). Lionnet spells the words according to the French fashion, while Gibbs and Hale spell them in the English way. I have given them with the continental values of the vowels in accordance with the indications in Hale's glossary.

others, all of them harsh in pronunciation, complex in structure, and each spoken over a very limited space. The traders learnt a few Nootka words and the Indians a few English words. Afterwards the traders began to frequent the Columbia River, and naturally attempted to communicate with the natives there by means of the words which they had found intelligible at Nootka. The Chinooks soon acquired these words, both Nootka and English. When later the white traders made permanent establishments in Oregon, a real language was required ; and it was formed by drawing upon the Chinook for such words as were requisite, numerals, pronouns, and some adverbs and other words. Thus enriched, 'the Jargon,' as it now began to be styled, became of great service as a means of general intercourse. Now, French Canadians in the service of the fur companies were brought more closely into contact with the Indians, hunted with them, and lived with them on terms of familiarity. The consequence was that several French words were added to the slender stock of the Jargon, including the names of various articles of food and clothing, implements, several names of the parts of the body, and the verbs to run, sing and dance, also one conjunction, *puis*, reduced to *pi*.

" The origin of some of the words is rather whimsical. The Americans, British and French are distinguished by the terms *Boston*, *Kinchotsh* (King George), and *pasaiuks*, which is presumed to be the word *Français* (as neither *f*, *r* nor the nasal *n* can be pronounced by the Indians) with the Chinook plural termination *uks* added. . . . ' Foolish ' is expressed by *pelton* or *pilton*, derived from the name of a deranged person, one Archibald Pelton, whom the Indians saw at Astoria ; his strange appearance and actions made such an impression upon them, that thenceforward anyone behaving in an absurd or irrational manner " was termed *pelton*.

The phonetic structure is very simple, and contains no sound or combination that is not easy to Englishmen and Frenchmen as well as to Indians of at least a dozen tribes. The numerous harsh Indian velars either disappear entirely or are softened to *h* and *k*. On the other hand, the *d*, *f*, *r*, *v*, *z* of the English and French become in the mouth of a Chinook *t*, *p*, *l*, *w*, *s*. Examples :

Chinook :		
thliakso	*yakso*	hair
etsghot	*itshut*	black bear
tkalaitanam	*kalaitan*	arrow, shot, bullet
ntshaika	*nesaika*	we
mshaika	*mesaika*	we
thlaitshka	*klaska (tlaska)*	they
tkhlon	*klon (tlun)*	three

English :	handkerchief	hakatshum (kenkeshim)	handkerchief
	cry	klai, kalai (kai)	cry, mourn
	fire	paia	fire, cook, ripe
	dry	tlai, delai	dry
French :	courir	kuli	run
	la bouche	labus (labush)	mouth
	le mouton	lemuto	sheep

The forms in parentheses are those of the French glossary (1853).

It will be noticed that many of the French words have the definite article affixed (a trait noticed in many words in the French Creole dialect of Mauritius). More than half of the words in Hale's glossary beginning with *l* have this origin, thus *labutai* bottle, *lakloa* cross, *lamie* an old woman (la vieille), *lapushet* fork (la fourchette), *latlá* noise (faire du train), *lidú* finger, *lejaub* (or *diaub, yaub*) devil (le diable), *léma* hand, *liplét* missionary (le prêtre), *litá* tooth. The plural article is found in *lisáp* egg (les œufs)—the same word in which Mauritius French has also adopted the plural form.

Some of the meanings of English words are rather curious ; thus, *kol* besides ' cold ' means ' winter,' and as the years, as with the old Scandinavians, are reckoned by winters, also ' year.' *Sun* (*son*) besides ' sun ' also means ' day.' *Spos* (often pronounced *pos*), as in Beach-la-mar, is a common conjunction, ' if, when.'

The grammar is extremely simple. Nouns are invariable ; the plural generally is not distinguished from the singular ; sometimes *haiu* (*ayo*) ' much, many ' is added by way of emphasis. The genitive is shown by position only : *kahta nem maika papa ?* (lit., what name thou father) what is the name of your father ? The adjective precedes the noun, and comparison is indicated by periphrasis. ' I am stronger than thou ' would be *weke maika skukum kahkwa naika*, lit. ' not thou strong as I.' The superlative is indicated by the adverb *haiás* ' great, very ': *haiás oliman okuk kanim*, that canoe is the oldest, lit., very old that canoe, or (according to Gibbs) by *elip* ' first, before ': *elip klosh* ' best.'

The numerals and pronouns are from the Chinook, but the latter, at any rate, are very much simplified. Thus the pronoun for ' we ' is *nesaika*, from Chinook *ntshaika*, which is the exclusive form, meaning ' we here,' not including the person or persons addressed.

Like the nouns, the verbs have only one form, the tense being left to be inferred from the context, or, if strictly necessary, being indicated by an adverb. The future, in the sense of 'about to, ready to,' may be expressed by *tike*, which means properly 'wish,' as *naika papa tike mimalus* (*mimelust*) my father is about to die. The verb 'to be' is not expressed: *maika pelton*, thou art foolish.

There is a much-used verb *mámuk*, which means 'make, do, work' and forms causatives, as *mamuk chako* 'make to come, bring,' *mamuk mimalus* 'kill.' With a noun: *mamuk lalam* (Fr. la rame) 'make oar,' i.e. 'to row,' *mamuk pepe* (make paper) 'write,' *mamuk po* (make blow) 'fire a gun.'

There is only one true preposition, *kopa*, which is used in various senses—to, for, at, in, among, about, etc.; but even this may generally be omitted and the sentence remain intelligible. The two conjunctions *spos* and *pi* have already been mentioned.

XII.—§ 9. Chinook continued.

In this way something is formed that may be used as a language in spite of the scantiness of its vocabulary. But a good deal has to be expressed by the tone of the voice, the look and the gesture of the speaker. "The Indians in general," says Hale (p. 18), "are very sparing of their gesticulations. No languages, probably, require less assistance from this source than theirs. . . . We frequently had occasion to observe the sudden change produced when a party of the natives, who had been conversing in their own tongue, were joined by a foreigner, with whom it was necessary to speak in the Jargon. The countenances, which had before been grave, stolid and inexpressive, were instantly lighted up with animation; the low, monotonous tone became lively and modulated; every feature was active; the head, the arms and the whole body were in motion, and every look and gesture became instinct with meaning."

In British Columbia and in parts of Alaska this language is the prevailing medium of intercourse between the whites and the natives, and there Hale thinks that it is likely to live "for hundreds, and perhaps thousands, of years to come." The language has already the beginning of a literature: songs, mostly composed by women, who sing them to plaintive native tunes. Hale gives some lyrics and a sermon preached by Mr. Eells, who has been accustomed for many years to preach to the Indians in the Jargon and who says that he sometimes even thinks in this idiom.

Hale counted the words in this sermon, and found that to express the whole of its "historic and descriptive details, its arguments and its appeals," only 97 different words were required, and not a single grammatical inflexion. Of these words, 65 were from Amerindian languages (46 Chinook, 17 Nootka, 2 Salish), 23 English and 7 French.

It is very instructive to go through the texts given by Hale and to compare them with the real Chinook text analysed in Boas's *Handbook of American Indian Languages* (Washington, 1911, p. 666 ff.): the contrast could not be stronger between simplicity carried to the extreme point, on the one hand, and an infinite complexity and intricacy on the other. But though it must be admitted that astonishingly much can be expressed in the Jargon by its very simple and few means, a European mind, while bewildered in the entangled jumble of the Chinook language, cannot help missing a great many *nuances* in the Jargon, where thoughts are reduced to their simplest formula and where everything is left out that is not strictly necessary to the least exacting minds.

XII.—§ 10. Makeshift Languages.

To sum up, this Oregon trade language is to be classed together with Beach-la-mar and Pidgin-English, not perhaps as ' bastard ' or ' mongrel ' languages—such expressions taken from biology always convey the wrong impression that a language is an ' organism ' and had therefore better be avoided— but rather as makeshift languages or minimum languages, means of expression which do not serve all the purposes of ordinary languages, but may be used as substitutes where fuller and better ones are not available.

The analogy between this Jargon and the makeshift languages of the East is closer than might perhaps appear at first blush, only we must make it clear to ourselves that English is in the two cases placed in exactly the inverse position. Pidgin and Beach-la-mar are essentially English learnt imperfectly by the Easterners, the Oregon Jargon is essentially Chinook learnt imperfectly by the English. Just as in the East the English not only suffered but also abetted the yellows in their corruption of the English language, so also the Amerindians met the English half-way through simplifying their own speech. If in Polynesia and China the makeshift language came to contain some Polynesian and Chinese words, they were those which the English themselves had borrowed into their own language and which the yellows therefore must think formed a legitimate part of the language they wanted to speak ; and in the same way the American Jargon contains such words from the European languages as had been previously adopted by the reds. If the Jargon embraces so many French terms for the various parts of the body, one concomitant reason probably is that these names in the original Chinook language presented special difficulties through being specialized and determined by possessive affixes (my foot, for instance, is *lekxeps*, thy foot *tāmēps*, its foot *lelaps*, our (dual inclusive) feet *tetxaps*, your (dual) feet *temtaps* ; I simplify the notation in Boas s *Handbook*, p. 586), so that it was incomparably easier to take the French *lepi* and use it unchanged in all cases, no matter what the number, and no matter who the possessor was. The natives, who had learnt such words from the French, evidently used them to other whites under the impression that thereby they could make themselves more readily understood, and the British and American traders probably imagined them to be real Chinook ; anyhow, their use meant a substantial economy of mental exertion.

The chief point I want to make, however, is with regard to grammar. In all these languages, both in the makeshift English and French of the East and in the makeshift Amerindian of the North-West, the grammatical structure has been simplified very much beyond what we find in any of the languages involved in their making, and simplified to such an extent that it may be expressed in very few words, and those nearly the same in all these languages, the chief rule being common to them all, that substantives, adjectives and verbs remain always unchanged. The vocabularies are as the poles asunder—in the East English and French, in America Chinook, etc.—but the morphology of all these languages is practically identical, because in all of them it has reached the vanishing-point. This shows conclusively that the reason of this simplicity is not the Chinese substratum or the influence of Chinese grammar, as is so often believed. Pidgin-English cannot be described, as is often done, as English with Chinese pronunciation and Chinese grammar, because in that case we should expect Beach-la-mar to be quite different from it, as the substratum there would be Melanesian, which in many ways differs from Chinese, and further we should expect the Mauritius Creole to be French with Malagasy pronunciation and Malagasy grammar, and on the other hand the Oregon trade language to be Chinook with English pronunciation and English grammar—but in none of these cases would this description tally with the obvious facts. We might just as well say that the speech of a two-year-old child in England is English with Chinese grammar, and that of the two-year-old French child is French modelled on Chinese grammar : the truth on the contrary, is that in all these seemingly so different cases the same mental factor is at work, namely, imperfect mastery of a language, which in its initial stage, in the child with its first language and in the grown-up with a second language learnt by imperfect methods, leads to a superficial knowledge of the most indispensable words, with total disregard of grammar. Often, here and there, this is combined with a wish to express more than is possible with the means at hand, and thus generates the attempts to express the inexpressible by means of those more or less ingenious and more or less comical devices, with paraphrases and figurative or circuitous designations, which we have seen first in the chapters on children's language and now again in Beach-la-mar and its congeners.

Exactly the same characteristics are found again in the *lingua geral Brazilica*, which in large parts of Brazil serves as the means of communication between the whites and Indians or negroes and also between Indians of different tribes. It "possesses neither declension nor conjugation" and "places words after one another without grammatical flexion, with disregard of *nuances* in sentence structure, but in energetic brevity," it is "easy of pronunciation," with many vowels and no hard consonant groups—in all these respects it differs considerably from the original Tupí, from which it has been evolved by the Europeans.[1]

Finally, I would point the contrast between these makeshift languages and slang: the former are an outcome of linguistic poverty; they are born of the necessity and the desire to make oneself understood where the ordinary idiom of the individual is of no use, while slang expressions are due to a linguistic exuberance: the individual creating them knows perfectly well the ordinary words for the idea he wants to express, but in youthful playfulness he is not content with what is everybody's property, and thus consciously steps outside the routine of everyday language to produce something that is calculated to excite merriment or even admiration on the part of his hearers. The results in both cases may sometimes show related features, for some of the figurative expressions of Beach-la-mar recall certain slang words by their bold metaphors, but the motive force in the two kinds is totally different, and where a comic effect is produced, in one case it is intentional and in the other unintentional.

XII.—§ 11. Romanic Languages.

When Schuchardt began his studies of the various Creole languages formed in many parts of the world where Europeans

[1] See Martius, *Beitr. zur Ethnogr. und Sprachenkunde Amerikas* (Leipzig, 1867), i. 364 ff. and ii. 23 ff.

speaking various Romanic and other languages had come into contact with negroes, Polynesians and other races, it was with the avowed intention of throwing light on the origin of the Romanic languages from a contact between Latin and the languages previously spoken in the countries colonized by the Romans. We may now raise the question whether Beach-la-mar—to take that as a typical example of the kind of languages dealt with in this chapter—is likely to develop into a language which to the English of Great Britain will stand in the same relation as French or Portuguese to Latin. The answer cannot be doubtful if we adhere tenaciously to the points of view already advanced. Development into a separate language would be imaginable only on condition of a complete, or a nearly complete, isolation from the language of England (and America)—and how should that be effected nowadays, with our present means of transport and communication ? If such isolation were indeed possible, it would also result in the breaking off of communication between the various islands in which Beach-la-mar is now spoken, and that would probably entail the speedy extinction of the language itself in favour of the Polynesian language of each separate island. On the contrary, what will probably happen is a development in the opposite direction, by which the English of the islanders will go on constantly improving so as to approach correct usage more and more in every respect : better pronunciation and syntax, more flexional forms and a less scanty vocabulary—in short, the same development that has already to a large extent taken place in the English of the coloured population in the United States. But this means a gradual extinction of Beach-la-mar as a separate idiom through its complete absorption in ordinary English (cf. above, p. 228, on conditions at Mauritius).

Do these ' makeshift languages,' then, throw any light on the development of the Romanic languages ? They may be compared to the very first initial stage of the Latin language as spoken by the barbarians, many of whom may be supposed to have mutilated Latin in very much the same way as the Pacific islanders do English. But by and by they learnt Latin much better, and if now the Romanic languages have simplified the grammatical structure of Latin, this simplification is not to be placed on the same footing as the formlessness of Beach-la-mar, for that is complete and has been achieved at one blow : the islanders have never (i.e. have not yet) learnt the English form-system. But the inhabitants of France, Spain, etc., did learn the Latin form system as well as the syntactic use of the forms. This is seen by the fact that when French and the other languages began to be written down, there remained in them a large quantity of forms and syntactic applications that agree with Latin but have since then become extinct : in its oldest written form, therefore, French is very far from the amorphous condition of Beach-la-mar : in its nouns it had many survivals of the Latin case system (gen. pl. corresponding to -orum ; an oblique case different from the nominative and formed in various ways according to the rules of Latin declensions), in the verbs we find an intricate system of tenses, moods and persons, based on the Latin flexions. It is true that these had been already to some degree simplified, but this must have happened in the same gradual way as the further simplification that goes on before our very eyes in the written documents of the following centuries : the distance from the first to the tenth century must have been bridged over in very much the same way as the distance between the tenth and the twentieth century. No cataclysm such as that through which English has become Beach-la-mar need on any account be invoked to explain the perfectly natural change from Latin to Old French and from Old French to Modern French.

CHAPTER XIII

THE WOMAN

§ 1. Women's Languages. § 2. Tabu. § 3. Competing Languages. § 4. Sanskrit Drama. § 5. Conservatism. § 6. Phonetics and Grammar § 7. Choice of Words. § 8. Vocabulary. § 9. Adverbs. § 10. Periods. § 11. General Characteristics.

XIII.—§ 1. Women's Languages.

THERE are tribes in which men and women are said to speak totally different languages, or at any rate distinct dialects. It will be worth our while to look at the classical example of this, which is mentioned in a great many ethnographical and linguistic works, viz. the Caribs or Caribbeans of the Small Antilles. The first to mention their distinct sex dialects was the Dominican Breton, who, in his *Dictionnaire Caraïbe-français* (1664), says that the Caribbean chief had exterminated all the natives except the women, who had retained part of their ancient language. This is repeated in many subsequent accounts, the fullest and, as it seems, most reliable of which is that by Rochefort, who spent a long time among the Caribbeans in the middle of the seventeenth century : see his *Histoire naturelle et morale des Iles Antilles* (2e éd., Rotterdam, 1665, p. 449 ff.). Here he says that "the men have a great many expressions peculiar to them, which the women understand but never pronounce themselves. On the other hand, the women have words and phrases which the men never use, or they would be laughed to scorn. Thus it happens that in their conversations it often seems as if the women had another language than the men. . . The savage natives of Dominica say that the reason for this is that when the Caribs came to occupy the islands these were inhabited by an Arawak tribe which they exterminated completely, with the exception of the women, whom they married in order to populate the country. Now, these women kept their own language and taught it to their daughters. . . . But though the boys understand the speech of their mothers and sisters, they nevertheless follow their fathers and brothers and conform to their speech from the age of five or six. . . . It is asserted that there is some similarity between the speech of the continental Arawaks and that of the Carib women. But the Carib men and women on the continent speak the same language, as they have never corrupted their natural speech by marriage with strange women."

This evidently is the account which forms the basis of everything that has since been written on the subject. But it will be noticed that Rochefort does not really speak of the speech of the two sexes as totally distinct languages or dialects, as has often been maintained, but only of certain differences within the same language. If we go through the comparatively full and evidently careful glossary attached to his book, in which he denotes the words peculiar to the men by the letter H and those of the women by F, we shall see that it is only for about one-tenth of the vocabulary that such special words have been indicated to him, though the matter evidently interested him very much, so that he would make all possible efforts to elicit them from the natives. In his lists, words special to one or the other sex are found most frequently in the names of the various degrees of kinship; thus, 'my father' in the speech of the men in *youmáan,* in that of the women *noukóuchili,* though both in addressing him say *bába;* 'my grandfather' is *itámoulou* and *nárgouti* respectively, and thus also for maternal uncle, son (elder son, younger son), brother-in-law, wife, mother, grandmother, daughter, cousin—all of these are different according as a man or a woman is speaking. It is the same with the names of some, though far from all, of the different parts of the body, and with some more or less isolated words, as friend, enemy, joy, work, war, house, garden, bed, poison, tree, sun, moon, sea, earth. This list comprises nearly every notion for which Rochefort indicates separate words, and it will be seen that there are innumerable ideas for which men and women use the same word. Further, we see that where there are differences these do not consist in small deviations, such as different prefixes or suffixes added to the same root, but in totally distinct roots. Another point is very important to my mind : judging by the instances in which plural forms are given in the lists, the words of the two sexes are inflected in exactly the same way ; thus the grammar is common to both, from which we may infer that we have not really to do with two distinct languages in the proper sense of the word.

Now, some light may probably be thrown on the problem of this women's language from a custom mentioned in some of the old books written by travellers who have visited these islands. Rochefort himself (p. 497) very briefly says that " the women do not eat till their husbands have finished their meal," and Lafitau (1724) says that women never eat in the company of their husbands and never mention them by name, but must wait upon them as their slaves ; with this Labat agrees.

XIII.—§ 2. Tabu.

The fact that a wife is not allowed to mention the name of her husband makes one think that we have here simply an instance of a custom found in various forms and in varying degrees throughout the world—what is called verbal tabu : under certain circumstances, at certain times, in certain places, the use of one or more definite words is interdicted, because it is superstitiously believed to entail certain evil consequences, such as exasperate demons and the like. In place of the forbidden words it is therefore necessary to use some kind of figurative paraphrase, to dig up an otherwise obsolete term, or to disguise the real word so as to render it more innocent.

Now as a matter of fact we find that verbal tabu was a common practice with the old Caribs : when they were on the war-path they had a great number of mysterious words which women were never allowed to learn and which even the young men might not pronounce before passing certain tests of bravery and patriotism ; these war-words are described as extraordinarily difficult (" un baragoin fort difficile," Rochefort, p. 450). It is easy to see that when once a tribe has acquired the habit of using a whole set of terms under certain frequently recurring circumstances, while others are at the same time strictly interdicted, this may naturally lead to so many words being reserved exclusively for one of the sexes that an observer may be tempted to speak of separate ' languages ' for the two sexes. There is thus no occasion to believe in the story of a wholesale extermination of all male inhabitants by another tribe, though on the other hand it is easy to understand how such a myth may arise as an explanation of the linguistic difference between men and women, when it has become strong enough to attract attention and therefore has to be accounted for.

In some parts of the world the connexion between a separate women's language and tabu is indubitable. Thus among the Bantu people of Africa. With the Zulus a wife is not allowed to mention the name of her father-in-law and of his brothers, and if a similar word or even a similar syllable occurs in the ordinary language, she must substitute something else of a similar meaning. In the royal family the difficulty of understanding the women's language is further increased by the woman's being forbidden to mention the names of her husband, his father and grandfather as well as his brothers. If one of these names means something like " the son of the bull," each of these words has to be avoided, and all kinds of paraphrases have to be used. According to Kranz the interdiction holds good not only for meaning elements ·of the name, but even for certain sounds entering into them ; thus, if the name contains the sound z, *amanzi* ' water ' has to be altered into *amandabi*. If a woman were to contravene this rule she would be indicted for sorcery and put to death. The substitutes thus introduced tend to be adopted by others and to constitute a real women's language.

With the Chiquitos in Bolivia the difference between the grammars of the two sexes is rather curious (see V. Henry, " Sur le parler des hommes et le parler des femmes dans la langue chiquita," *Revue de linguistique*, xii. 305, 1879). Some of Henry's examples may be thus summarized : men indicate by the addition of *-tii* that a male person is spoken about, while the women do not use this suffix and thus make no distinction between ' he ' and ' she,' ' his ' and ' her.' Thus in the men's speech the following distinctions would be made :

> He went to his house : *yebotii ti n-ipoostii.*
> He went to her house : *yebotii ti n-ipoos.*
> She went to his house : *yebo ti n-ipoostii.*

But to express all these different meanings the women would have only one form, viz.

> *yebo ti n-ipoos,*

which in the men's speech would mean only ' She went to her house.'

To many substantives the men prefix a vowel which the women do not employ, thus *o-petas* ' turtle,' *u-tamokos* ' dog,' *i-pis* ' wood.' For some very important notions the sexes use distinct words ; thus, for the names of kinship, ' my father ' is *iyai* and *išupu*, ' my mother ' *ipaki* and *ipapa*, ' my brother ' *tsaruki* and *ičibausi* respectively.

Among the languages of California, Yana, according to Dixon and Kroeber (*The American Anthropologist*, n.s. 5. 15), is the only language that shows a difference in the words used by men and women—apart from terms of relationship, where a distinction according to the sex of the speaker is made among many Californian tribes as well as in other parts of the world, evidently " because the relationship itself is to them different, as the sex is different." But in Yana the distinction is a linguistic one, and curiously enough, the few specimens given all present a trait found already in the Chiquito forms, namely, that the forms spoken by women are shorter than those of the men, which appear as extensions, generally by suffixed *-(n)a*, of the former.

It is surely needless to multiply instances of these customs, which are found among many wild tribes ; the curious reader may be referred to Lasch, S. pp. 7–13, and H. Ploss and M. Bartels, *Das Weib in der Natur und Völkerkunde* (9th ed., Leipzig, 1908). The latter says that the Suaheli system is not carried through so as to replace the ordinary language, but the Suaheli have for every object which they do not care to mention by its real name a symbolic word understood by everybody concerned. In especial such symbols are used by women in their mysteries to denote obscene things. The words chosen are either ordinary names for innocent things or else taken from the old language or other Bantu languages, mostly Kiziguha, for among the Waziguha secret rites play an enormous rôle. Bartels finally says that with us, too, women have separate names for everything connected with sexual life, and he thinks that it is the same feeling of shame that underlies this custom and the interdiction of pronouncing the names of male relatives. This, however, does not explain everything, and, as already indicated, superstition certainly has a large share in this as in other forms of verbal tabu. See on this the very full account in the third volume of Frazer's *The Golden Bough.*

XIII.—§ 3. Competing Languages.

A difference between the language spoken by men and that spoken by women is seen in many countries where two languages are struggling for supremacy in a peaceful way—thus without any question of one nation exterminating the other or the male part of it. Among German and Scandinavian immigrants in America the men mix much more with the English-speaking population, and therefore have better opportunities, and also more occasion, to learn English than their wives, who remain more within doors. It is exactly the same among the Basques, where the school, the military service and daily business relations contribute to the extinction of Basque in favour of French, and where these factors operate much more strongly on the male than on the female population : there are families in which the wife talks Basque, while the husband does not even understand Basque and does not allow his children to learn it (Bornecque et Mühlen, *Les Provinces fran-çaises*, 53). Vilhelm Thomsen informs me that the old Livonian language, which is now nearly extinct, is kept up with the greatest fidelity by the women, while the men are abandoning it for Lettish. Albanian women, too, generally know only Albanian, while the men are more often bilingual.

XIII.—§ 4. Sanskrit Drama.

There are very few traces of real sex dialects in our Aryan languages, though we have the very curious rule in the old Indian drama that women talk Prakrit (*prākrta*, the natural or vulgar language) while men have the privilege of talking Sanskrit (*sam-*

skrta, the adorned language). The distinction, however, is not one of sex really, but of rank, for Sanskrit is the language of gods, kings, princes, brahmans, ministers, chamberlains, dancing-masters and other men in superior positions and of a very few women of special religious importance, while Prakrit is spoken by men of an inferior class, like shopkeepers, law officers, aldermen, bathmen, fishermen and policemen, and by nearly all women. The difference between the two 'languages' is one of degree only : they are two strata of the same language, one higher, more solemn, stiff and archaic, and another lower, more natural and familiar, and this easy, or perhaps we should say slipshod, style is the only one recognized for ordinary women. The difference may not be greater than that between the language of a judge and that of a costermonger in a modern novel, or between Juliet's and her nurse's expressions in Shakespeare, and if all women, even those we should call the 'heroines' of the plays, use only the lower stratum of speech, the reason certainly is that the social position of women was so inferior that they ranked only with men of the lower orders and had no share in the higher culture which, with the refined language, was the privilege of a small class of selected men.

XIII.—§ 5. Conservatism.

As Prakrit is a 'younger' and 'worn-out' form of Sanskrit, the question here naturally arises : What is the general attitude of the two sexes to those changes that are constantly going on in languages ? Can they be ascribed exclusively or predominantly to one of the sexes ? Or do both equally participate in them ? An answer that is very often given is that as a rule women are more conservative than men, and that they do nothing more than keep to the traditional language which they have learnt from their parents and hand on to their children, while innovations are due to the initiative of men. Thus Cicero in an often-quoted passage says that when he hears his mother-in-law Lælia, it is to him as if he heard Plautus or Nævius, for it is more natural for women to keep the old language uncorrupted, as they do not hear many people's way of speaking and thus retain what they have first learnt (*De oratore*, III. 45). This, however, does not hold good in every respect and in every people. The French engineer, Victor Renault, who lived for a long time among the Botocudos (in South America) and compiled vocabularies for two of their tribes, speaks of the ease with which he could make the savages who accompanied him invent new words for anything. " One of them called out the word in a loud voice, as if seized by a sudden idea, and the others would repeat it amid laughter and excited shouts, and then it was universally adopted. But the curious thing is that it was nearly always the women who busied themselves in inventing new words as well as in composing songs, dirges and rhetorical essays. The word-formations here alluded to are probably names of objects that the Botocudos had not known previously . . . as for horse, *krainejoune*, ' head-teeth '; for ox, *po-kekri*, ' foot-cloven '; for donkey, *mgo-jonne-orône*, ' beast with long ears.' But well-known objects which have already got a name have often similar new denominations invented for them, which are then soon accepted by the family and community and spread more and more " (*v* Martius, *Beitr. zur Ethnogr. u. Sprachenkunde Amerikas*, 1867, i. 330).

I may also quote what E. R. Edwards says in his *Étude phonétique de la langue japonaise* (Leipzig, 1903, p. 79) : " In France and in England it might be said that women avoid neologisms and are careful not to go too far away from the written forms : in Southern England the sound written *wh* [ʍ] is scarcely ever pronounced except in girls' schools. In Japan, on the contrary, women are less conservative than men, whether in pronunciation or in the selection of words and expressions. One of the chief reasons is that women have not to the same degree as men undergone the influence of the written language. As an example of the liberties which the women take may be mentioned that there is in the actual pronunciation of Tokyo a strong tendency to get rid of the sound (*w*), but the women go further in the word *atashi*, which men pronounce *watashi* or *watakshi*, ' I.' Another tendency noticed in the language of Japanese women is pretty widely spread among French and English women, namely, the excessive use of intensive words and the exaggeration of stress and tone-accent to mark emphasis. Japanese women also make a much more frequent use than men of the prefixes of politeness *o-*, *go-* and *mi-*."

XIII.—§ 6. Phonetics and Grammar.

In connexion with some of the phonetic changes which have profoundly modified the English sound system we have express statements by old grammarians that women had a more advanced pronunciation than men, and characteristically enough these statements refer to the raising of the vowels in the direction of [i]; thus in Sir Thomas Smith (1567), who uses expressions like " mulierculæ quædam delicatiores, et nonnulli qui volunt isto modo .. videri loqui urbanius," and in another place " fœminæ quædam delicatiores," further in Mulcaster (1582)[1] and in Milton's

---

[1] " *Ai* is the man's diphthong, and soundeth full : *ei*, the woman's, and soundeth finish [i.e. fineish] in the same both sense, and vse, *a woman is deintie, and feinteth soon, the man fainteth not bycause he is nothing daintie.*" Thus what is now distinctive of refined as opposed to vulgar pronunciation was then characteristic of the fair sex

teacher, Alexander Gill (1621), who speaks about "nostræ Mopsæ, quæ quidem ita omnia attenuant."

In France, about 1700, women were inclined to pronounce *e* instead of *a*; thus Alemand (1688) mentions *Barnabé* as "façon de prononcer mâle" and *Bernabé* as the pronunciation of "les gens polis et délicats . . . les dames surtout"; and Grimarest (1712) speaks of "ces marchandes du Palais, qui au lieu de *madame, boulevart*, etc., prononcent *medeme, boulevert*" (Thurot i. 12 and 9).

There is one change characteristic of many languages in which it seems as if women have played an important part even if they are not solely responsible for it : I refer to the weakening of the old fully trilled tongue-point *r*. I have elsewhere (*Fonetik*, p. 417 ff.) tried to show that this weakening, which results in various sounds and sometimes in a complete omission of the sound in some positions, is in the main a consequence of, or at any rate favoured by, a change in social life : the old loud trilled point sound is natural and justified when life is chiefly carried on out-of-doors, but indoor life prefers, on the whole, less noisy speech habits, and the more refined this domestic life is, the more all kinds of noises and even speech sounds will be toned down. One of the results is that this original *r* sound, the rubadub in the orchestra of language, is no longer allowed to bombard the ears, but is softened down in various ways, as we see chiefly in the great cities and among the educated classes, while the rustic population in many countries keeps up the old sound with much greater conservatism. Now we find that women are not unfrequently mentioned in connexion with this reduction of the trilled *r* ; thus in the sixteenth century in France there was a tendency to leave off the trilling and even to go further than to the present English untrilled point *r* by pronouncing [z] instead, but some of the old grammarians mention this pronunciation as characteristic of women and a few men who imitate women (Erasmus : mulierculæ Parisinæ ; Sylvius : mulierculæ . . . Parrhisinæ, et earum modo quidam parum viri ; Pillot : Parisinæ mulierculæ . . . adeo delicatulæ sunt, ut pro *pere* dicant *pese*). In the ordinary language there are a few remnants of this tendency; thus, when by the side of the original *chaire* we now have also the form *chaise*, and it is worthy of note that the latter form is reserved for the everyday signification (Engl. chair, seat) as belonging more naturally to the speech of women, while *chaire* has the more special signification of 'pulpit, professorial chair.' Now the same tendency to substitute [z]—or after a voiceless sound [s]—for *r* is found in our own days among the ladies of Christiania, who will say *gzuelig* for *gruelig* and *fsygtelig* for *frygtelig* (Brekke, *Bidrag til dansknorskens lydlære*, 1881, p. 17 ; I have often heard the sound myself). And even in far-off Siberia we find that the Chuckchi women will say *nidzak* or *nizak* for the male *nirak* ' two,' *zërka* for *rërka* ' walrus,' etc. (Nordqvist ; see fuller quotations in my *Fonetik*, p. 431).

In present-day English there are said to be a few differences in pronunciation between the two sexes ; thus, according to Daniel Jones, *soft* is pronounced with a long vowel [so·ft] by men and with a short vowel [soft] by women ; similarly [ɡɛəl] is said to be a special ladies' pronunciation of *girl*, which men usually pronounce [ɡə·l] ; cf. also on *wh* above, p. 243. So far as I have been able to ascertain, the pronunciation [tʃuldrən] for [tʃildrən] *children* is much more frequent in women than in men. It may also be that women are more inclined to give to the word *waistcoat* the full long sound in both syllables, while men, who have occasion to use the word more frequently, tend to give it the historical form [weskət] (for the shortening compare *breakfast*). But even if such observations were multiplied—as probably they might easily be by an attentive observer—they would be only more or less isolated instances, without any deeper significance, and on the whole we must say that from the phonetic point of view there is scarcely any difference between the speech of men and that of women : the two sexes speak for all intents and purposes the same language.

XIII.—§ 7. Choice of Words.

But when from the field of phonetics we come to that of vocabulary and style, we shall find a much greater number of differences, though they have received very little attention in linguistic works. A few have been mentioned by Greenough and Kittredge : " The use of *common* in the sense of ' vulgar ' is distinctly a feminine peculiarity. It would sound effeminate in the speech of a man. So, in a less degree, with *person* for ' woman,' in contrast to ' lady.' *Nice* for ' fine ' must have originated in the same way " (W, p. 54).

Others have told me that men will generally say ' It's very *good* of you,' where women will say ' It's very *kind* of you.' But such small details can hardly be said to be really characteristic of the two sexes. There is no doubt, however, that women in all countries are shy of mentioning certain parts of the human body and certain natural functions by the direct and often rude denominations which men, and especially young men, prefer when among themselves. Women will therefore invent innocent and euphemistic words and paraphrases, which sometimes may in the long run come to be looked upon as the plain or blunt names, and therefore in their turn have to be avoided and replaced by more decent words.

In Pinero's *The Gay Lord Quex* (p. 116) a lady discovers some French novels on the table of another lady, and says : " This is a little—h'm—isn't it ? "—she does not even dare to say the word 'indecent,' and has to express the idea in inarticulate language. The word 'naked' is paraphrased in the following description by a woman of the work of girls in ammunition works : " They have to take off every stitch from their bodies in one room, and run *in their innocence and nothing else* to another room where the special clothing is " (Bennett, *The Pretty Lady*, 176).

On the other hand, the old-fashioned prudery which prevented ladies from using such words as *legs* and *trousers* (" those manly garments which are rarely mentioned by name," says Dickens, *Dombey*, 335) is now rightly looked upon as exaggerated and more or less comical (cf. my GS § 247).

There can be no doubt that women exercise a great and universal influence on linguistic development through their instinctive shrinking from coarse and gross expressions and their preference for refined and (in certain spheres) veiled and indirect expressions. In most cases that influence will be exercised privately and in the bosom of the family ; but there is one historical instance in which a group of women worked in that direction publicly and collectively ; I refer to those French ladies who in the seventeenth century gathered in the Hôtel de Rambouillet and are generally known under the name of *Précieuses*. They discussed questions of spelling and of purity of pronunciation and diction, and favoured all kinds of elegant paraphrases by which coarse and vulgar words might be avoided. In many ways this movement was the counterpart of the literary wave which about that time was inundating Europe under various names—Gongorism in Spain, Marinism in Italy, Euphuism in England ; but the Précieuses went further than their male confrères in desiring to influence everyday language. When, however, they used such expressions as, for ' nose,' ' the door of the brain,' for ' broom ' ' the instrument of cleanness,' and for ' shirt ' ' the constant companion of the dead and the living ' (la compagne perpétuelle des morts et des vivants), and many others, their affectation called down on their heads a ripple of laughter, and their endeavours would now have been forgotten but for the immortal satire of Molière in *Les Précieuses ridicules* and *Les Femmes savantes*. But apart from such exaggerations the feminine point of view is unassailable, and there is reason to congratulate those nations, the English among them, in which the social position of women has been high enough to secure greater purity and freedom from coarseness in language than would have been the case if men had been the sole arbiters of speech.

Among the things women object to in language must be specially mentioned anything that smacks of swearing[1]; where a man will

---

[1] There are great differences with regard to swearing between different nations; but I think that in those countries and in those circles in which

say " He told an infernal lie," a women will rather say, " He told a most dreadful fib." Such euphemistic substitutes for the simple word ' hell ' as ' the other place,' ' a very hot ' or ' a very uncomfortable place ' probably originated with women. They will also use *ever* to add emphasis to an interrogative pronoun, as in " Whoever told you that ? " or " Whatever do you mean ? " and avoid the stronger ' who the devil ' or ' what the dickens.' For surprise we have the feminine exclamations ' Good gracious,' ' Gracious me,' ' Goodness gracious,' ' Dear me ' by the side of the more masculine ' Good heavens,' ' Great Scott.' ' To be sure ' is said to be more frequent with women than with men. Such instances might be multiplied, but these may suffice here. It will easily be seen that we have here civilized counterparts of what was above mentioned as sexual tabu ; but it is worth noting that the interdiction in these cases is ordained by the women themselves, or perhaps rather by the older among them, while the young do not always willingly comply.

Men will certainly with great justice object that there is a danger of the language becoming languid and insipid if we are always to content ourselves with women's expressions, and that vigour and vividness count for something. Most boys and many men have a dislike to some words merely because they feel that they are used by everybody and on every occasion : they want to avoid what is commonplace and banal and to replace it by new and fresh expressions, whose very newness imparts to them a flavour of their own. Men thus become the chief renovators of language, and to them are due those changes by which we sometimes see one term replace an older one, to give way in turn to a still newer one, and so on. Thus we see in English that the old verb *weorpan*, corresponding to G. *werfen*, was felt as too weak and therefore supplanted by *cast*, which was taken from Scandinavian ; after some centuries *cast* was replaced by the stronger *throw*, and this now, in the parlance of boys especially, is giving way to stronger expressions like *chuck* and *fling*. The old verbs, or at any rate *cast*, may be retained in certain applications, more particularly in some fixed combinations and in figurative significations, but it is now hardly possible to say, as Shakespeare does, " They cast their caps up." Many such innovations on their first appearance are counted as slang, and some never make their way into received speech ; but I am not in this connexion concerned with the distinction between slang

swearing is common it is found much more extensively among men than among women : this at any rate is true of Denmark. There is, however, a general social movement against swearing, and now there are many men who never swear. A friend writes to me : "The best English men hardly swear at all. . . . I imagine some of our fashionable women now swear as much as the men they consort with."

and recognized language, except in so far as the inclination or disinclination to invent and to use slang is undoubtedly one of the "human secondary sexual characters." This is not invalidated by the fact that quite recently, with the rise of the feminist movement, many young ladies have begun to imitate their brothers in that as well as in other respects.

XIII.—§ 8. Vocabulary.

This trait is indissolubly connected with another : the vocabulary of a woman as a rule is much less extensive than that of a man. Women move preferably in the central field of language, avoiding everything that is out of the way or bizarre, while men will often either coin new words or expressions or take up old-fashioned ones, if by that means they are enabled, or think they are enabled, to find a more adequate or precise expression for their thoughts. Woman as a rule follows the main road of language, where man is often inclined to turn aside into a narrow footpath or even to strike out a new path for himself. Most of those who are in the habit of reading books in foreign languages will have experienced a much greater average difficulty in books written by male than by female authors, because they contain many more rare words, dialect words, technical terms, etc. Those who want to learn a foreign language will therefore always do well at the first stage to read many ladies' novels, because they will there continually meet with just those everyday words and combinations which the foreigner is above all in need of, what may be termed the indispensable small-change of a language.

This may be partly explicable from the education of women, which has up to quite recent times been less comprehensive and technical than that of men. But this does not account for everything, and certain experiments made by the American professor Jastrow would tend to show that we have here a trait that is independent of education. He asked twenty-five university students of each sex, belonging to the same class and thus in possession of the same preliminary training, to write down as rapidly as possible a hundred words, and to record the time. Words in sentences were not allowed. There were thus obtained 5,000 words, and of these many were of course the same. But the community of thought was greater in the women ; while the men used 1,375 different words, their female class-mates used only 1,123. Of 1,266 unique words used, 29·8 per cent. were male, only 20·8 per cent. female. The group into which the largest number of the men's words fell was the animal kingdom ; the group into which the largest number of the women's words fell was wearing apparel and fabrics ; while the men used only 53 words belonging to the class of foods, the women used 179. "In general the feminine traits revealed by this study are an attention to the immediate surroundings, to the finished product, to the ornamental, the individual, and the concrete; while the masculine preference is for the more remote, the constructive, the useful, the general and the abstract." (See Havelock Ellis, *Man and Woman*, 4th ed., London, 1904, p. 189.)

Another point mentioned by Jastrow is the tendency to select words that rime and alliterative words; both these tendencies were decidedly more marked in men than in women. This shows what we may also notice in other ways, that men take greater interest in words as such and in their acoustic properties, while women pay less attention to that side of words and merely take them as they are, as something given once for all. Thus it comes that some men are confirmed punsters, while women are generally slow to see any point in a pun and scarcely ever perpetrate one themselves. Or, to get to something of greater value : the science of language has very few votaries among women, in spite of the fact that foreign languages, long before the reform of female education, belonged to those things which women learnt best in and out of schools, because, like music and embroidery, they were reckoned among the specially feminine 'accomplishments.'

Woman is linguistically quicker than man : quicker to learn, quicker to hear, and quicker to answer. A man is slower : he hesitates, he chews the cud to make sure of the taste of words, and thereby comes to discover similarities with and differences from other words, both in sound and in sense, thus preparing himself for the appropriate use of the fittest noun or adjective.

XIII.—§ 9. Adverbs.

While there are a few adjectives, such as *pretty* and *nice*, that might be mentioned as used more extensively by women than by men, there are greater differences with regard to adverbs. Lord Chesterfield wrote (*The World*, December 5, 1754) : " Not contented with enriching our language by words absolutely new, my fair countrywomen have gone still farther, and improved it by the application and extension of old ones to various and very different significations. They take a word and change it, like a guinea into shillings for pocket-money, to be employed in the several occasional purposes of the day. For instance, the adjective *vast* and its adverb *vastly* mean anything, and are the fashionable words of the most fashionable people. A fine woman . . . is *vastly* obliged, or *vastly* offended, *vastly* glad, or *vastly* sorry. Large objects are

vastly great, small ones are *vastly* little ; and I had lately the
pleasure to hear a fine woman pronounce, by a happy metonymy,
a very small gold snuff-box, that was produced in company,
to be *vastly* pretty, because it was so *vastly* little." Even if
that particular adverb to which Lord Chesterfield objected has
now to a great extent gone out of fashion, there is no doubt
that he has here touched on a distinctive trait : the fondness of
women for hyperbole will very often lead the fashion with regard
to adverbs of intensity, and these are very often used with disregard
of their proper meaning, as in German *riesig klein*, English *awfully
pretty*, *terribly nice*, French *rudement joli*, *affreusement délicieux*,
Danish *rædsom morsom* (horribly amusing), Russian *strast' kakoy
lovkiy* (terribly able), etc.   *Quite*, also, in the sense of ' very,' as
in ' she was quite charming ; it makes me quite angry,' is, according to Fitzedward Hall, due to the ladies.   And I suspect that *just
sweet* (as in Barrie : " Grizel thought it was just sweet of him ")
is equally characteristic of the usage of the fair sex.

There is another intensive which has also something of the
eternally feminine about it, namely *so*.   I am indebted to Stoffel
(Int. 101) for the following quotation from *Punch* (January 4,
1896) : " This little adverb is a great favourite with ladies, in conjunction with an adjective.   For instance, they are very fond of
using such expressions as ' He is *so* charming ! '   ' It is *so* lovely ! '
etc."   Stoffel adds the following instances of strongly intensive
so as highly characteristic of ladies' usage : ' Thank you *so* much ! '
' It was *so* kind of you to think of it ! '   ' That's *so* like you ! '
' I'm *so* glad you've come ! '   ' The bonnet is *so* lovely ! '

The explanation of this characteristic feminine usage is, I think,
that women much more often than men break off without finishing
their sentences, because they start talking without having thought
out what they are going to say ; the sentence ' I'm so glad you've
come ' really requires some complement in the shape of a clause
with *that*, ' so glad that I really must kiss you,' or, ' so glad that I
must treat you to something extra,' or whatever the consequence
may be.   But very often it is difficult in a hurry to hit upon something adequate to say, and ' so glad that I cannot express it '
frequently results in the inexpressible remaining unexpressed, and
when that experiment has been repeated time after time, the linguistic consequence is that a strongly stressed *so* acquires the force
of ' very much indeed.'   It is the same with *such*, as in the
following two extracts from a modern novel (in both it is a lady
who is speaking) : " Poor Kitty ! she has been in *such* a state of
mind," and " Do you know that you look *such* a duck this afternoon.
. . . This hat suits you *so*—you are *such* a *grande dame* in it."
Exactly the same thing has happened with Danish *så* and *sådan*,

G. *so* and *such* ; also with French *tellement*, though there perhaps not to the same extent as in English.

We have the same phenomenon with *to a degree*, which properly requires to be supplemented with something that tells us what the degree is, but is frequently left by itself, as in ' His second marriage was irregular to a degree.'

XIII.—§ 10. Periods.

The frequency with which women thus leave their exclamatory sentences half-finished might be exemplified from many passages in our novelists and dramatists.   I select a few quotations. The first is from the beginning of *Vanity Fair* : " This almost caused Jemima to faint with terror. ' Well, I never,' said she. ' What an audacious '—emotion prevented her from completing either sentence." Next from one of Hankin's plays. " Mrs. Eversleigh : I must say ! (but words fail her)."   And finally from Compton Mackenzie's *Poor Relations* : " ' The trouble you must have taken,' Hilda exclaimed."   These quotations illustrate types of sentences which are becoming so frequent that they would seem soon to deserve a separate chapter in modern grammars, ' Did you ever ? ' ' Well, I never ! ' being perhaps the most important of these ' stop-short ' or ' pull-up ' sentences, as I think they might be termed.

These sentences are the linguistic symptoms of a peculiarity of feminine psychology which has not escaped observation. Meredith says of one of his heroines : " She thought in blanks, as girls do, and some women," and Hardy singularizes one of his by calling her " that novelty among women—one who finished a thought before beginning the sentence which was to convey it."

The same point is seen in the typical way in which the two sexes build up their sentences and periods ; but here, as so often in this chapter, we cannot establish absolute differences, but only preferences that may be broken in a great many instances and yet are characteristic of the sexes as such. If we compare long periods as constructed by men and by women, we shall in the former find many more instances of intricate or involute structures with clause within clause, a relative clause in the middle of a conditional clause or vice versa, with subordination and sub-subordination, while the typical form of long feminine periods is that of co-ordination, one sentence or clause being added to another on the same plane and the gradation between the respective ideas being marked not grammatically, but emotionally, by stress and intonation, and in writing by underlining. In learned terminology we may say that men are fond of hypotaxis and women of parataxis.

Or we may use the simile that a male period is often like a set of
Chinese boxes, one within another, while a feminine period is like
a set of pearls joined together on a string of *ands* and similar words.
In a Danish comedy a young girl is relating what has happened
to her at a ball, when she is suddenly interrupted by her brother,
who has slyly taken out his watch and now exclaims : " I declare !
you have said *and then* fifteen times in less than two and a half
minutes."

XIII.—§ 11. General Characteristics.

The greater rapidity of female thought is shown linguistically,
among other things, by the frequency with which a woman will use
a pronoun like *he* or *she*, not of the person last mentioned, but
of somebody else to whom her thoughts have already wandered,
while a man with his slower intellect will think that she is still
moving on the same path.   The difference in rapidity of perception
has been tested experimentally by Romanes : the same paragraph
was presented to various well-educated persons, who were asked
to read it as rapidly as they could, ten seconds being allowed for
twenty lines.   As soon as the time was up the paragraph was
removed, and the reader immediately wrote down all that he or
she could remember of it.   It was found that women were usually
more successful than men in this test.   Not only were they able
to read more quickly than the men, but they were able to give a
better account of the paragraph as a whole.   One lady, for instance,
could read exactly four times as fast as her husband, and even
then give a better account than he of that small portion of the
paragraph he had alone been able to read.   But it was found that
this rapidity was no proof of intellectual power, and some of the
slowest readers were highly distinguished men.   Ellis (*Man and W.*
195) explains this in this way : with the quick reader it is as though
every statement were admitted immediately and without inspection
to fill the vacant chambers of the mind, while with the slow reader
every statement undergoes an instinctive process of cross-examination ; every new fact seems to stir up the accumulated stores of
facts among which it intrudes, and so impedes rapidity of mental
action.

This reminds me of one of Swift's " Thoughts on Various Subjects " : " The common fluency of speech in many men, and most
women, is owing to the scarcity of matter, and scarcity of words ; for
whoever is a master of language, and hath a mind full of ideas, will
be apt in speaking to hesitate upon the choice of both : whereas
common speakers have only one set of ideas, and one set of words
to clothe them in ; and these are always ready at the mouth.   So

people come faster out of a church when it is almost empty, than when a crowd is at the door " (*Works*, Dublin, 1735, i. 305).

The volubility of women has been the subject of innumerable jests : it has given rise to popular proverbs in many countries,[1] as well as to Aurora Leigh's resigned " A woman's function plainly is—to talk " and Oscar Wilde's sneer, " Women are a decorative sex. They never have anything to say, but they say it charmingly." A woman's thought is no sooner formed than uttered. Says Rosalind, " Do you not know I am a woman ? when I think, I must speak " (*As You Like It*, III. 2. 264). And in a modern novel a young girl says : " I talk so as to find out what I think. Don't you ? Some things one can't judge of till one hears them spoken " (Housman, *John of Jingalo*, 346).

The superior readiness of speech of women is a concomitant of the fact that their vocabulary is smaller and more central than that of men. But this again is connected with another indubitable fact, that women do not reach the same extreme points as men, but are nearer the average in most respects. Havelock Ellis, who establishes this in various fields, rightly remarks that the statement that genius is undeniably of more frequent occurrence among men than among women has sometimes been regarded by women as a slur upon their sex, but that it does not appear that women have been equally anxious to find fallacies in the statement that idiocy is more common among men. Yet the two statements must be taken together. Genius is more common among men by virtue of the same general tendency by which idiocy is more common among men. The two facts are but two aspects of a larger zoological fact—the greater variability of the male (*Man and W.* 420).

In language we see this very clearly : the highest linguistic genius and the lowest degree of linguistic imbecility are very rarely found among women. The greatest orators, the most famous literary artists, have been men ; but it may serve as a sort of consolation to the other sex that there are a much greater number of men than of women who cannot put two words together intelligibly, who stutter and stammer and hesitate, and are unable to find suitable expressions for the simplest thought. Between these two extremes the woman moves with a sure and supple tongue which is ever ready to find words and to pronounce them in a clear and intelligible manner.

---

[1] " Où femme y a, silence n'y a." " Deux femmes font un plaid, trois un grand caquet, quatre un plein marché." " Due donne e un' oca fanno una fiera " (Venice). " The tongue is the sword of a woman, and she never lets it become rusty " (China). " The North Sea will sooner be found wanting in water than a woman at a loss for a word " (Jutland).

Nor are the reasons far to seek why such differences should have developed. They are mainly dependent on the division of labour enjoined in primitive tribes and to a great extent also among more civilized peoples. For thousands of years the work that especially fell to men was such as demanded an intense display of energy for a comparatively short period, mainly in war and in hunting. Here, however, there was not much occasion to talk, nay, in many circumstances talk might even be fraught with danger. And when that rough work was over, the man would either sleep or idle his time away, inert and torpid, more or less in silence. Woman on the other hand, had a number of domestic occupations which did not claim such an enormous output of spasmodic energy. To her was at first left not only agriculture, and a great deal of other work which in more peaceful times was taken over by men ; but also much that has been till quite recently her almost exclusive concern—the care of the children, cooking, brewing, baking, sewing, washing, etc.,—things which for the most part demanded no deep thought, which were performed in company and could well be accompanied with a lively chatter. Lingering effects of this state of things are seen still, though great social changes are going on in our times which may eventually modify even the linguistic relations of the two sexes.

CHAPTER XIV

CAUSES OF CHANGE

XIV.—§ 1. Anatomy.

In accordance with the programme laid down in the opening paragraph of Book III, we shall now deal in detail with those linguistic changes which are not due to transference to new individuals. The chapter on woman's language has served as a kind of bridge between the two main divisions, in so far as the first sections treated of those women's dialects which were, or were supposed to be, due to the influence of foreigners.

Many theories have been advanced to explain the indubitable fact that languages change in course of time. Some scholars have thought that there ought to be one fundamental cause working in all instances, while others, more sensibly, have maintained that a variety of causes have been and are at work, and that it is not easy to determine which of them has been decisive in each observed case of change. The greatest attention has been given to phonetic change, and in reading some theorists one might almost fancy that sounds were the only thing changeable, or at any rate that phonetic changes were the only ones in language which had to be accounted for. Let us now examine some of the theories advanced.

Sometimes it is asserted that sound changes must have their cause in changes in the anatomical structure of the articulating organs. This theory, however, need not detain us long (see the able discussion in Oertel, p. 194 ff.), for no facts have been alleged to support it, and one does not see why small anatomical variations should cause changes so long as any teacher of languages on the phonetic method is able to teach his pupils practically every speech sound, even those that their own native language has been without for centuries. Besides, many phonetic changes do not at all lead to new sounds being developed or old ones lost, but simply to the old sounds being used in new places or disused in some of the places where they were formerly found. Some tribes have a custom of mutilating their lips or teeth, and that of course must have caused changes in their pronunciation, which are said to have persisted even after the custom was given up. Thus, according to Meinhof (MSA 60) the Yao women insert a big wooden disk within the upper lip, which makes it impossible for them to pronounce [f], and as it is the women that teach their children to speak, the sound of [f] has disappeared from the language, though now it is beginning to reappear in loan-words. It is clear, however, that such customs can have exercised only the very slightest influence on language in general.

XIV.—§ 2. Geography.

Some scholars have believed in an influence exercised by climatic or geographical conditions on the character of the sound system, instancing as evidence the harsh consonants found in the languages of the Caucasus as contrasted with the pleasanter sounds heard in regions more favoured by nature. But this influence cannot be established as a general rule. "The aboriginal inhabitants of the north-west coast of America found subsistence relatively easy in a country abounding in many forms of edible marine life; nor can they be said to have been subjected to rigorous climatic conditions; yet in phonetic harshness their languages rival those of the Caucasus. On the other hand, perhaps no people has ever been subjected to a more forbidding physical environment than the Eskimos, yet the Eskimo language not only impresses one as possessed of a relatively agreeable phonetic system when compared with the languages of the north-west coast, but may even be thought to compare favourably with American Indian languages generally " (Sapir, *American Anthropologist*, XIV (1912), 234). It would also on this theory be difficult to account for the very considerable linguistic changes which have taken place in historical times in many countries whose climate, etc., cannot during the same period have changed correspondingly.

A geographical theory of sound-shifting was advanced by Heinrich Meyer-Benfey in *Zeitschr. f. deutsches Altert.* 45 (1901), and has recently been taken up by H. Collitz in *Amer. Journal of Philol.* 39 (1918), p. 413. Consonant shifting is chiefly found in mountain regions; this is most obvious in the High German shift, which started from the Alpine district of Southern Germany. After leaving the region of the high mountains it gradually decreases in strength; yet it keeps on extending, with steadily diminishing energy, over part of the area of the Franconian dialects. But having reached the plains of Northern Germany, the movement stops. The same theory applies to languages in which a similar shifting is found, e.g. Old and Modern Armenian, the Soho language in South Africa, etc. " However strange it may appear at the first glance," says Collitz, " that certain consonant changes should depend on geographical surroundings, the connexion is easily understood. The change of media to tenuis and that of tenuis to affricate or aspirate are linked together by a common feature, viz. an increase in the intensity of expiration. As the common cause of both these shiftings we may therefore regard a change in the manner in which breath is used for pronunciation. The habitual use of a larger volume of breath means an increased activity of the lungs. Here we have reached the point where the connexion with geographical or climatic conditions is clear, because nobody will deny that residence in the mountains, especially in the high mountains, stimulates the lungs."

When this theory was first brought to my notice, I wrote a short footnote on it (PhG 176), in which I treated it with perhaps too little respect, merely mentioning the fact that my countrymen, the Danes, in their flat country were developing exactly the same shift as the High Germans (making *p*, *t*, *k* into strongly aspirated or affricated sounds and unvoicing *b*, *d*, *g*) ; I then asked ironically whether that might be a consequence of the indubitable fact that an increasing number of Danes every summer go to Switzerland and Norway for their holidays. And even now, after the theory has been endorsed by so able an advocate as Collitz, I fail to see how it can hold water. The induction seems faulty on both sides, for the shift is found among peoples living in plains, and on the other hand it is not shared by all mountain peoples—for example, not by the Italian and Ladin speaking neighbours of the High Germans in the Alps. Besides, the physiological explanation is not impeccable, for walking in the mountains affects the way in which we breathe, that is, it primarily affects the lungs, but the change in the consonants is primarily one not in the lungs, but in the glottis ; as the connexion between these two things is not necessary, the whole reasoning is far from being cogent. At any rate, the theory can only with great difficulty be applied to the first Gothonic shift, for how do we know that that started in mountainous regions ? and who knows whether the sounds actually found as *f*, *þ* and *h* for original *p*, *t*, *k*, had first been aspirated and affricated stops ? It seems much more probable that the transition was a direct one, through slackening and opening of the stoppage, but in that case it has nothing to do with the lungs or way of breathing.

XIV.—§ 3. National Psychology.

We are much more likely to ' burn,' as the children say, when, instead of looking for the cause in such outward circumstances, we try to find it in the psychology of those who initiate the change. But this does not amount to endorsing all the explanations of this kind which have found favour with linguists. Thus, since the times of Grimm it has been usual to ascribe the well-known consonant shift to psychological traits believed to be characteristic of the Germans. Grimm says that the sound shift is a consequence of the progressive tendency and desire of liberty found in the Germans (GDS 292) ; it is due to their courage and pride in the period of the great migration of tribes (ib. 306) : " When quiet and morality returned, the sounds remained, and it may be reckoned as evidence of the superior gentleness and moderation of the Gothic, Saxon and Scandinavian tribes that they contented themselves with the first shift, while the wilder force of the High Germans was impelled to the second shift." (Thus also Westphal.) Curtius finds energy and juvenile vigour in the Germanic sound shift (KZ 2. 331, 1852). Müllenhof saw in the transition from *p, t, k* to *f, þ, h* a sign of weakening, the Germans having apparently lost the power of pronouncing the hard stops ; while further, the giving up of the aspirated *ph, th, kh, bh, dh, gh* was due to enervation or indolence. But the succeeding transition from the old *b, d, g* to *p, t, k* showed that they had afterwards pulled themselves together to new exertions, and the regularity with which all these changes were carried through evidenced a great steadiness and persevering force (*Deutsche Altertumsk*. 3. 197). His disciple Wilhelm Scherer saw in the whole history of the German language alternating periods of rise and decline in popular taste ; he looked upon sound changes from the æsthetic point of view and ascribed the (second) consonant shift to a feminine period in which consonants were neglected because the nation took pleasure in vocalic sounds.

XIV.—§ 4. Speed of Utterance.

Wundt gives a different though somewhat related explanation of the Germanic shift as due to a " revolution in culture, as the subjugation of a native population through warlike immigrants, with resulting new organization of the State " (S 1. 424) : this increased the speed of utterance, and he tries in detail to show that increased speed leads naturally to just those changes in consonants which are found in the Gothonic shift (1. 420 ff.). But even if we admit that the average speed of talking (tempo der rede) is now probably greater than formerly, the whole theory is built up on so many doubtful or even manifestly incorrect details both in linguistic history and in general phonetic theory that it cannot be accepted. It does not account for the actual facts of the consonant shifts ; moreover, it is difficult to see why such phenomena as this shift, if they were dependent on the speed of utterance, should occur only at these particular historical times and within comparatively narrow geographical limits, for there is much to be said for the view that in all periods the speech of the Western nations has been constantly gaining in rapidity as life in general has become accelerated, and in no period probably more than during the last century, which has witnessed no radical consonant shift in any of the leading civilized nations.

XIV.—§ 5. Periods of Rapid Change.

All these theories, different though they are in detail, have this in common, that they endeavour to explain one particular change, or set of changes, from one particular psychological trait supposed to be prevalent at the time when the change took place, but they fail because we are not able scientifically to demonstrate any intimate connexion between the pronunciation of particular sounds and a certain state of mind, and also because our knowledge of the fluctuations of collective psychology is still so very imperfect. But it is interesting to contrast these theories with the explanation of the very same sound shifts mentioned in a previous chapter (XI), and there shown to be equally unsatisfactory, the explanation, namely, that the fundamental cause of the consonant shift is to be found in the peculiar pronunciation of an aboriginal population. In both cases the Gothonic shifts are singled out, because since the time of Grimm the attention of scholars has been focused on these changes more than on any others—they are looked upon as changes *sui generis*, and therefore requiring a special explanation, such as is not thought necessary in the case of the innumerable minor changes that fill most of the pages of the phonological section of any historical grammar. But the sober truth seems to be that these shifts are not different in kind from those that have made, say, Fr. *sève, frère, chien, ciel, faire, changer* out of Lat. *sapa, fratrem, canem, kœlum, fakere, cambiare*, etc., or those that have changed the English vowels in *fate, feet, fight, foot, out* from what they were when the letters which denote them still had their 'continental' values. Our main endeavour, therefore, must be to find out general reasons why sounds should not always remain unchanged. This seems more important, at any rate as a preliminary investigation, than attempting offhand to assign particular reasons why in such and such a century this or that sound was changed in some particular way.

If, however, we find a particular period especially fertile in linguistic changes (phonetic, morphological, semantic, or all at once), it is quite natural that we should turn our attention to the social state of the community at that time in order, if possible, to discover some specially favouring circumstances. I am thinking especially of two kinds of condition which may operate. In the first place, the influence of parents, and grown-up people generally, may be less than usual, because an unusual number of parents may be away from home, as in great wars of long duration, or may have been killed off, as in the great plagues ; cf. also what was said above of children left to shift for themselves in certain favoured regions of North America (Ch. X § 7). Secondly, there may be periods in which the ordinary restraints on linguistic change make themselves less felt than usual, because the whole community is animated by a strong feeling of independence and wants to break loose from social ties of many kinds, including those of a powerful school organization or literary tradition. This probably was the case with North America in the latter half of the eighteenth century, when the new nation wished to manifest its independence of old England and therefore, among other things, was inclined to throw overboard that respect for linguistic authority which under normal conditions makes for conservatism. If the divergence between American and British English is not greater than it actually is, this is probably due partly to the continual influx of immigrants from the old country, and partly to that increased facility of communication between the two countries in recent times which has made mutual lin-guistic influence possible to an extent formerly undreamt-of. But in the case of the Romanic languages both of the conditions mentioned were operating : during the centuries in which they were framed and underwent the strongest differentiation, wars with the intruding ' barbarians ' and a series of destructive plagues kept away or killed a great many grown-up people, and at the same time each country released itself from the centralizing in-fluence of Rome, which in the first centuries of the Christian era had been very powerful in keeping up a fairly uniform and con-servative pronunciation and phraseology throughout the whole Empire.[1] There were thus at that time various forces at work which, taken together, are quite sufficient to explain the wide

---

[1] The uniformity in the speech of the whole Roman Empire during the first centuries of our Christian era was kept up, among other things, through the habit of removing soldiers and officials from one country to the other. This ceased later, each district being left to shift more or less for itself.

divergence in linguistic structure that separated French, Provençal, Spanish, etc., from classical Latin (cf. above, XI § 8, p. 206).

In the history of English, one of the periods most fertile in change is the fourteenth and fifteenth centuries : the wars with France, the Black Death (which is said to have killed off about one-third of the population) and similar pestilences, insurrections like those of Wat Tyler and Jack Cade, civil wars like those of the Roses, decimated the men and made home-life difficult and unsettled. In the Scandinavian languages the Viking age is probably the period that witnessed the greatest linguistic changes —if I am right, not, as has sometimes been said, on account of the heroic character of the period and the violent rise in self-respect or self-assertion, but for the more prosaic reason that the men were absent and the women had other things to attend to than their children's linguistic education. I am also inclined to think that the unparalleled rapidity with which, during the last hundred years, the vulgar speech of English cities has been differentiated from the language of the educated classes (nearly all long vowels being shifted, etc.) finds its natural explanation in the unexampled misery of child-life among industrial workers in the first half of the last century—one of the most disgraceful blots on our overpraised civilization.

XIV.—§ 6. The Ease Theory.

If we now turn to the actuating principles that determine the general changeability of human speech habits, we shall find that the moving power everywhere is an impetus starting from the individual, and that there is a curbing power in the mere fact that language exists not for the individual alone, but for the whole community. The whole history of language is, as it were, a tug-of-war between these two principles, each of which gains victories in turn.

First of all we must make up our minds with regard to the disputed question whether the changes of language go in the direction of greater ease, in other words, whether they manifest a tendency towards economy of effort. The prevalent opinion among the older school was that the chief tendency was, in Whitney's words, " to make things easy to our organs of speech, to economize time and effort in the work of expression " (L 28). Curtius very emphatically states that " Bequemlichkeit ist und bleibt der hauptanlass des lautwandels unter allen umständen " (*Griech. etym.* 23 ; cf. C 7). But Leskien, Sievers, and since them other recent writers, hold the opposite view (see quotations and summaries in Oertel 204 f., Wechssler L 88 f.), and their view has prevailed to the extent that Sütterlin (WW 33) characterizes the old view as " empty talk," " a wrong scent," and " worthless subterfuges now rejected by our science."

Such strong words may, however, be out of place, for is it so very foolish to think that men in this, as in all other respects, tend to follow ' the line of least resistance ' and to get off with as little exertion as possible ? The question is only whether this universal tendency can be shown to prevail in those phonetic changes which are dealt with in linguistic history.

Sütterlin thinks it enough to mention some sound changes in which the new sound is more difficult than the old ; these being admitted, he concludes (and others have said the same thing) that those other instances in which the new sound is evidently easier than the old one cannot be explained by the principle of ease. But it seems clear that this conclusion is not valid : the correct inference can only be that the tendency towards ease may be at work in some cases, though not in all, because there are other forces which may at times neutralize it or prove stronger than it. We shall meet a similar all-or-nothing fallacy in the chapter on Sound Symbolism.

Now, it is sometimes said that natives do not feel any difficulty in the sounds of their own language, however difficult these may be to foreigners. This is quite true if we speak of a *conscious* perception of this or that sound being difficult to produce ; but it is no less true that the act of speaking always requires some exertion, muscular as well as psychical, on the part of the speaker, and that he is therefore apt on many occasions to speak with as little effort as possible, often with the result that his voice is not loud enough, or that his words become indistinct if he does not move his tongue, lips, etc., with the required precision or force. You may as well say that when once one has learnt the art of writing, it is no longer any effort to form one's letters properly ; and yet how many written communications do we not receive in which many of the letters are formed so badly that we can do little but guess from the context what each form is meant for ! There can be no doubt that the main direction of change in the development of our written alphabet has been towards forms requiring less and less exertion—and similar causes have led to analogous results in the development of spoken sounds.

It is not always easy to decide which of two articulations is the easier one, and opinions may in some instances differ—we may also find in two neighbouring nations opposite phonetic developments, each of which may perhaps be asserted by speakers of the language to be in the direction of greater ease. " To judge of the difficulty of muscular activity, the muscular quantity at play cannot serve as an absolute measure. Is [d] absolutely more awkward to produce than [ð] ?   When a man is running full tilt, it is under certain circumstances easier for him to rush against the wall than to stop suddenly at some distance from it : when the tongue is in motion, it may be easier for it to thrust itself against the roof of the mouth or the teeth, i.e. to form a stop (a plosive), than to halt at a millimetre's distance, i.e. to form a fricative " (Verner 78).   In the same sense I wrote in 1904 : " Many an articulation which obviously requires greater muscular movements is yet easier of execution than another in which the movement is less, but has to be carried out with greater precision : it requires less effort to chip wood than to operate for cataract " (PhG 181).

In other cases, however, no such doubt is possible : [s], [f] or [x] require more muscular exertion than [h], and a replacement of one of them by [h] therefore necessarily means a lessening of effort.   Now, I am firmly convinced that whenever a phonologist finds one of these oral fricatives standing regularly in one language against [h] in another, he will at once take the former sound to be the original and [h] to be the derived sound : an indisputable indication that the instinctive feeling of all linguists is still in favour of the view that a movement towards the easier sound is the rule, and not the exception.

In thus taking up the cudgels for the ease theory I am not afraid of hearing the objection that I ascribe too great power to human laziness, indolence, inertia, shirking, easygoingness, sloth, sluggishness, lack of energy, or whatever other beautiful synonyms have been invented for 'economy of effort' or 'following the line of least resistance.'   The fact remains that there *is* such a 'tendency' in all human beings, and by taking it into account in explaining changes of sound we are doing nothing else than applying here the same principle that attributes many simplifications of form to 'analogy' : we see the same psychological force at work in the two different domains of phonetics and morphology.

It is, of course, no serious objection to this view that if this had been always the direction of change, speaking must have been uncommonly troublesome to our earliest ancestors [1]—who says it wasn't ?—or that " if certain combinations were really irksome in themselves, why should they have been attempted at all ; why should they often have been maintained so long ? " (Oertel 204)—as if people at a remote age had been able to compare consciously two articulations and to choose the easier one !

[1] " Dass unsere ältesten vorfahren sich das sprechen erstaunlich unbequem gemacht haben," Delbrück, E 155.

Neither in language nor in any other activity has mankind at once hit upon the best or easiest expedients.

XIV.—§ 7. Sounds in Connected Speech.

In the great majority of linguistic changes we have to consider the ease or difficulty, not of the isolated sound, but of the sound in that particular conjunction with other sounds in which it occurs in words.[1] Thus in the numerous phenomena comprised under the name of assimilation. There is an interesting account in the *Proceedings of the Philological Society* (December 17, 1886) of a discussion of these problems, in which Sweet, while maintaining that " cases of saving of effort were very rare or non-existent " and that " all the ordinary sounds of language were about on a par as to difficulty of production," said that assimilation " sprang from the desire to save space in articulation and secure ease of transition. Thus *pn* became *pm*, or else *mn*." But in both these changes there is saving of effort, for in the former the movement of the tip of the tongue required for [n], and in the latter the movement of the soft palate required for [p], is done away with [2]: the term " saving of space " can have no other meaning than economy of muscular energy. And the same is true of what Sweet terms " saving of time," which he finds effected by dropping superfluous sounds, especially at the end of words, e.g. [g] after [ ] in E. *sing*. Here, of course, one articulation (of the velum) is saved—and this need not even be accompanied by the saving of any time, for in such cases the remaining sound is often lengthened so as to make up for the loss.[3]

If, then, all assimilations are to be counted as instances of saving of effort, it is worth noting that a great many phonetic

[1] Sometimes appearances may be deceptive : when [nr, mr] become [ndr, mbr], it looks on the paper as if something had been added and as if the transition therefore militated against the principle of ease : in reality, the old and the new combinations require exactly the same amount of muscular activity, and the change simply consists in want of precision in the movement of the velum palati, which comes a fraction of a second too soon. If anything, the new group is a trifle easier than the old. See LPh 5. 6 for explanation and examples (E. *thunder* from þunor sb., þunrian vb. ; *timber*, cf. Goth. *timrian*, G. *zimmer*, etc.).

[2] This is rendered most clear by my ' analphabetic ' notation (α means lips, β tip of tongue, δ soft palate, velum palati, and ε glottis ; 0 stands for closed position, 1 for approximation, 3 for open position) ; the three sound combinations are thus analysed (cf. my *Lehrbuch der Phonetik*) :

	p	n	p	m	m	n
α	0	3	0	0	0	3
β	3	0	3	3	3	0
δ	0	3	0	3	3	3
ε	3	1	3	1	1	1

[3] The only clear cases of saving of time are those in which long sounds are shortened, and even they must be looked upon as a saving of effort.

changes which are not always given under the heading of assimilation should really be looked upon as such.   If Lat. *saponem* yields Fr. *savon*, this is the result of a whole series of assimilations : first [p] becomes [b], because the vocal vibrations continue from the vowel before to the vowel after the consonant, the opening of the glottis being thus saved ; then the transition of [b] to [v] between vowels may be considered a partial assimilation to the open lip position of the vowels ; the vowel [o] is nasalized in consequence of an assimilation to the nasal [n] (anticipation of the low position of the velum), and the subsequent dropping of the consonant [n] is a clear case of a different kind of assimilation (saving of a tip movement) ; at an early stage the two final sounds of *saponem* had disappeared, first [m] and later the indistinct vowel resulting from *e* : whether we reckon these disappearances as assimilations or not, at any rate they constitute a saving of effort. All droppings of sounds, whether consonants (as *t* in E. *castle*, *postman*, etc.) or vowels (as in E. *p'rhaps*, *bus'ness*, etc.), are to be viewed in the same light, and thus by their enormous number in the history of all languages form a strong argument in favour of the ease theory.

There is one more thing to be considered which is generally overlooked.   In such assimilations as It. *otto*, *sette*, from *octo*, *septem*, a greater ease is effected not only by the assimilation as such, by which one of the consonants is dropped—for that would have been obtained just as well if the result had been *occo*, *seppe*— but also by the fact that it is the tip action which has been retained in both cases, for the tip of the tongue is much more flexible and more easily moved than either the lips or the back of the tongue. On the whole, many sound changes show how the tip is favoured at the cost of other organs, thus in the frequent transition of final -*m* to -*n*, found, for instance, in old Gothonic, in Middle English, in ancient Greek, in Balto-Slavic, in Finnish and in Chinese.

In the discussion referred to above Sweet was seconded by Lecky, who said that " assimilations vastly multiplied the number of elementary sounds in a language, and therefore could not be described as facilitating pronunciation." This is a great exaggeration, for in the vast majority of instances assimilation introduces no new sounds at all (see, for instance, the lists in my LPh ch. xi.). Lecky was probably thinking of such instances as when [k, g] before front vowels become [tʃ, dʒ] or similar combinations, or when mutation caused by [i] changes [u, o] into [y, ø], which sounds were not previously found in the language.   Here we might perhaps say that those individuals who for the sake of their own ease introduced new sounds made things more difficult for coming generatioms (though even that is not quite certain), and the case would then be analogous to that of a man who has learnt a foreign expression for a new idea and then introduces it into his own language, thus burdening his countrymen with a new word instead of thinking how the same idea might have been rendered by means of native speech-material—in both cases a momentary alleviation is obtained at the cost of a permanent disadvantage, but neither case can be alleged against the view that the prevalent tendency among human beings is to prefer the easiest and shortest cut.

XIV.—§ 8. Extreme Weakenings.

When this lazy tendency is indulged to the full, the result is an indistinct protracted vocal murmur, with here and there possibly one or other sound (most often an *s*) rising to the surface : think, for instance, of the way in which we often hear grace said, prayers mumbled and other similar formulas muttered inarticulately, with half-closed lips and the least possible movement of the rest of the vocal organs. This is tolerated more or less in cases in which the utterance is hardly meant as a communication to any human being ; otherwise it will generally be met with a request to repeat what has been said, the social curb being thus applied to the easygoing tendencies of the individual. Now, as a matter of fact, there are in every language a certain number of word-forms that can only be explained by this very laziness in pronouncing, which in extreme cases leads to complete unintelligibility.

Russian *sudar'* (*gosudar'*), ' sir,' is colloquially shortened into a mere *s*, which may in subservient speech be added to almost any word as a meaningless enclitic. And curiously enough the same sound is used in exactly the same way in conversational Spanish, as *buenos* for *bueno* ' good,' only here it is a weakening of *señor* (Hanssen, *Span. gramm.* 60) : thus two entirely different words, from identical psychological motives, yield the same result in two distant countries. Fr. *monsieur*, instead of [mõsjœ·r], a might be expected, sounds [mosjø] and extremely frequently [msjø] and even [psjø], with a transition not otherwise found in French. *Madame* before a name is very often shortened into [mam] ; in English the same word becomes a single sound in *yes'm*. The weakening of *mistress* into *miss* and the old-fashioned *mas* for *master* also belong here, as do It. forms for *signore*, *signora* : *gnor si*, *gnor no*, *gnora si*, *sor Luigi*, *la sora sposa*, and Sp. *usted* ' you ' for *vuestra merced*. Formulas of greeting and of politeness are liable to similar truncations, e.g. E. *how d(e) do*, Dan. [gda'] or even [da'] for *goddag*, G. [gmõin, gmõ] for *guten morgen*, [na·mt] for *guten abend* ; Fr. *s'il vous plaît* often becomes [siuplɛ, splɛ], and the synonymous Dan. *vær så god* is shortened into *værsgo*, of which often only [sgo'] remains. In Russian popular speech some small words are frequently inserted as a vague indication that the utterance or idea belongs to some one else : *griu, grit, grim, gril*, various mutilated forms of the verb *govorit'* ' say,' *mol* from *molvit'* ' speak,' *de* from *dejati* (Boyer et Speranski, *Manuel* 293 ff.) ; cp. the obsolete E. *co, quo*, for *quoth*. In all the Balkan languages a particle *vre* is extensively used, which Hatzidakis has explained from the vocative of OGr. *mōrós*. Modern Gr. *thà* is now a particle of futurity, but originates in *thená*, from *thélei*, ' he will ' + *nà* from *hína*, ' that.' These examples must suffice to show that we have here to do with a universal tendency in all languages.

XIV.—§ 9. The Principle of Value.

To explain such deviations from normal phonetic development some scholars have assumed that a word or form in frequent use is liable to suffer exceptional treatment. Thus Vilhelm Thomsen, in his brilliant paper (1879) on the Romanic verb *andare, andar, anar, aller*, which he explains convincingly from Lat. *ambulare*, says that this verb " belongs to a group of words which in all languages stand as it were without the pale of the laws, that is, words which from their frequent employment are exposed to far more violent changes than other words, and therefore to some extent follow paths of their own." [1] Schuchardt (*Ueber die lautgesetze*, 1885) turned upon the ' young grammarians,' Paul among the rest, who did not recognize this principle, and said that one word (or one sound) may need 10,000 repetitions in order to be changed into another one, and that consequently another word, which in the same time is used only 8,000 times, must be behindhand in its phonetic development. Quite apart from the fact that this number is evidently too small (for a moderately loquacious woman will easily pronounce such a word as *he* half a dozen times as often as these figures every year), it is obvious that the reasoning must be wrong, for were frequency the only decisive factor, G. *morgen* would have been treated in every other connexion exactly as it is in *guten morgen*, and that is just what has not happened. Frequency of repetition would in itself tend to render the habitude firmly rooted, thus really capable of resisting change, rather than the opposite ; and instead of the purely mechanical explanation from the number of times a word is repeated, we must look for

[1] In the reprint in *Samlede Afhandlinger*, ii. 417 (1920), a few lines are added in which Thomsen fully accepts the explanation which I gave as far back as 1886.

a more psychological explanation. This naturally must be found in the ease with which a word is understood in the given connexion or situation, and especially in its worthlessness for the purpose of communication. Worthlessness, however, is not the moving power, but merely the reason why less restraint than usual is imposed on the ever-present inclination of speakers to minimize effort. A parallel from another, though cognate, sphere of human activity may perhaps bring out my point of view more clearly. The taking off of one's hat, combined with a low bow, served from the first to mark a more or less servile submissiveness to a prince or conqueror ; then the gesture was gradually weakened, and a slight raising of the hat came to be a polite greeting even between equals ; this is reduced to a mere touching of the hat or cap, and among friends the slightest movement of the hand in the direction of the hat is thought a sufficient greeting. When, however, it is important to indicate deference, the full ceremonial gesture is still used (though not to the same extent by all nations) ; otherwise no value is attached to it, and the inclination to spare oneself all unnecessary exertion has caused it to dwindle down to the slightest muscular action possible.

The above instances of the truncation of everyday formulas, etc., illustrate the length to which the ease principle can be carried when a word has little significatory value and the intention of the speaker can therefore be vaguely, but sufficiently, understood if the proper sound is merely suggested or hinted at. But in most words, and even in the words mentioned above, when they are to bear their full meaning, the pronunciation cannot be slurred to the same extent, if the speaker is to make himself understood. It is consequently his interest to pronounce more carefully, and this means greater conservatism and slower phonetic development on the whole.

There are naturally many degrees of relative value or worthlessness, and words may vary accordingly. An illustration may be taken from my own mother-tongue : the two words *rigtig nok*, literally ' correct enough,' are pronounced ['recti 'nɔk] or ['regdi 'nɔk] when keeping their full signification, but when they are reduced to an adverb with the same import as the weakened English *certainly* or (*it is*) *true* (*that*), there are various shortened pronunciations in frequent use : ['rectnɔg, 'regdnɔg, 'regnɔg, 'renɔg, 'renəg]. The worthlessness may affect a whole phrase, a word, or merely one syllable or sound.

XIV.—§ 10. Application to Case System, etc.

Our principle is important in many domains of linguistic history. If it is asked why the elaborate Old English system of cases and genders has gradually disappeared, an answer that will meet with the approval of most linguists of the ordinary school is (in the words of J. A. H. Murray) : " The total loss of grammatical gender in English, and the almost complete disappearance of cases, are purely phonetic phenomena "—supplemented, of course, by the recognition of the action of analogy, to which is due, for instance, the levelling of the nom. and dative plural OE. *stanas* and *stanum* under the single form *stones*. The main explanation thus is the following : a phonetic law, operating without regard to the signification, caused the OE. unstressed vowels *-a, -e, -u* to become merged in an obscure *-e* in Middle English ; as these endings were very often distinctive of cases, the Old English cases were consequently lost. Another phonetic law was operating similarly by causing the loss of final *-n*, which also played an important rôle in the old case system. And in this way phonetic laws and analogy have between them made a clean sweep of it, and we need look nowhere else for an explanation of the decay of the old declensions.

Here I beg to differ : a ' phonetic law ' is not an explanation, but something to be explained ; it is nothing else but a mere statement of facts, a formula of correspondence, which says nothing about the cause of change, and we are therefore justified if we try to dig deeper and penetrate to the real psychology of speech. Now, let us for a moment suppose that each of the terminations *-a, -e, -u* bore in Old English its own distinctive and sharply defined meaning, which was necessary to the right understanding of the sentences in which the terminations occurred (something like the endings found in artificial languages like Ido). Would there in that case be any probability that a phonetic law tending to their levelling could ever have succeeded in establishing itself ? Most certainly not ; the all-important regard for intelligibility would have been sure to counteract any inclination towards a slurred pronunciation of the endings. Nor would there have been any occasion for new formations by analogy, as the formations were already sufficiently analogous. But such a regularity was very far from prevailing in Old English, as will be particularly clear from the tabulation of the declensions as printed in my *Chapters on English*, p. 10 ff. : it makes the whole question of causality appear in a much clearer light than would be possible by any other arrangement of the grammatical facts : the cause of the decay of the Old English apparatus of declensions lay in its manifold incongruities. The same termination did not always denote the same thing : *-u* might be the nom. sg. masc. (*sunu*) or fem. (*duru*), or the acc. or the dat., or the nom. or acc. pl. neuter (*hofu*) ; *-a* might be the nom. sg. masc. (*guma*), or the dat. sg. masc. (*suna*), or the gen. sg. fem. (*dura*), or the nom. pl. masc. or fem., or finally the gen. pl. ; -*an* might be the acc. or dat. or gen. sg. or the nom. or acc. pl., etc. If we look at it from the point of view of function, we get the same picture ; the nom. pl., for instance, might be denoted by the endings -*as*, -*an*, -*a*, -*e*, -*u*, or by mutation without ending, or by the unchanged kernel ; the dat. sg. by -*e*, -*an*, -*re*, -*um*, by mutation, or the unchanged kernel. The whole is one jumble of inconsistency, for many relations plainly distinguished from each other in one class of words were but imperfectly, if at all, distinguishable in another class. Add to this that the names used above, dative, accusative, etc., have no clear and definite meaning in the case of Old English, any more than in the case of kindred tongues ; sometimes it did not matter which of two or more cases the speaker chose to employ : some verbs took indifferently now one, now another case, and the same is to some extent true with regard to prepositions. No wonder, therefore, that speakers would often hesitate which of two vowels to use in the ending, and would tend to indulge in the universal inclination to pronounce weak syllables indistinctly and thus confuse the formerly distinct vowels *a*, *i*, *e*, *u* into the one neutral vowel [ə], which might even be left out without detriment to the clear understanding of each sentence.[1] The only endings that were capable of withstanding this general rout were the two in *s*, -*as* for the plural and -*es* for the gen. sg. ; here the consonant was in itself more solid, as it were, than the other consonants used in case endings (*n*, *m*), and, which is more decisive, each of these terminations was confined to a more sharply limited sphere of use than the other endings, and the functions for which they served, that of the plural and that of the genitive, are among the most indispensable ones for clearness of thought. Hence we see that these endings from the earliest period of the English language tend to be applied to other classes of nouns than those to which they were at first confined (-*as* to masc. *o* stems . . .), so as to be at last used with practically all nouns.

If explanations like Murray's of the simplification of the English case system are widely accepted, while views like those attempted here will strike most readers of linguistic works as unfamiliar, the reason may, partly at any rate, be the usual arrangement of historical and other grammars. Here we first have chapters on phonology, in which the facts are tabulated,

---

[1] The above remarks are condensed from the argument in ChE 38 ff. Note also what is said below (Ch. XIX § 13) on the loss of Lat. final -*s* in the Romanic languages after it had ceased to be necessary for the grammatical understanding of sentences.

each vowel being dealt with separately, no matter what its function is in the flexional system ; then, after all the sounds have been treated in this way, we come to morphology (accidence, formenlehre), in which it is natural to take the phonological facts as granted or already known : these therefore come to be looked upon as primary and morphology as secondary, and no attention is paid to the *value* of the sounds for the purposes of mutual understanding.

But everyday observations show that sounds have not always the same value. In ordinary conversation one may frequently notice how a proper name or technical term, when first introduced, is pronounced with particular care, while no such pains is taken when it recurs afterwards : the stress becomes weaker, the unstressed vowels more indistinct, and this or that consonant may be dropped. The same principle is shown in all the abbreviations of proper names and of long words in general which have been treated above (Ch IX § 7) : here the speaker has felt assured that his hearer has understood what or who he is talking about, as soon as he has pronounced the initial syllable or syllables, and therefore does not take the trouble to pronounce the rest of the word. It has often been pointed out (see, e.g., Curtius K 72) that stem or root syllables are generally better preserved than the rest of the word : the reason can only be that they have greater importance for the understanding of the idea as a whole than other syllables.[1] But it is especially when we come to examine stress phenomena that we discover the full extent of this principle of value.

XIV.—§ 11. Stress Phenomena.

Stress is generally believed to be dependent exclusively on the force with which the air-current is expelled from the lungs, hence the name of ' expiratory accent ' ; but various observations and considerations have led me to give another definition (LPh 7. 32, 1913) : stress is energy, intensive muscular activity not

---

[1] Against this it has been urged that Fr. *oncle* has not preserved the stem syllable of Lat. *avunculus* particularly well. But this objection is a little misleading. It is quite true that at the time when the word was first framed the syllable *av-* contained the main idea and *-unculus* was only added to impart an endearing modification to that idea (' dear little uncle ') ; but after some time the semantic relation was altered ; *avus* itself passed out of use, while *avunculus* was handed down from generation to generation as a ready-made whole, in which the ordinary speaker was totally unable to suspect that *av-* was the really significative stem. He consequently treated it exactly as any other polysyllable of the same structure, and *avun-* (phonetically [awuŋ, auuŋ]) was naturally made into one syllable. Nothing, of course, can be protected by a sense of its significance unless it is still felt as significant. That hardly needs saying.

of one organ, but of *all the speech organs at once.* To pronounce a ' stressed ' syllable all organs are exerted to the utmost. The muscles of the lungs are strongly innervated ; the movements of the vocal chords are stronger, leading on the one hand in voiced sounds to a greater approximation of the vocal chords, with less air escaping, but greater amplitude of vibrations and also greater risings or fallings of the tone. In voiceless sounds, on the other hand, the vocal chords are kept at greater distance (than in unstressed syllables) and accordingly allow more air to escape. In the upper organs stress is characterized by marked articulations of the velum palati, of the tongue and of the lips. As a result of all this, stressed syllables are loud, i.e. can be heard at great distance, and distinct, i.e. easy to perceive in all their components. Unstressed syllables, on the contrary, are produced with less exertion in every way : in voiced sounds the distance between the vocal chords is greater, which leads to the peculiar ' voice of murmur ' ; but in voiceless sounds the glottis is not opened very wide. In the upper organs we see corresponding slack movements ; thus the velum does not shut off the nasal cavity very closely, and the tongue tends towards a neutral position, in which it moves very little either up and down or backwards and forwards. The lips also are moved with less energy, and the final result is dull and indistinct sounds. Now, all this is of the greatest importance in the history of languages.

The psychological importance of various elements is the chief, though not the only, factor that determines sentence stress (see, for instance, the chapters on stress in my LPh xiv. and MEG v.). Now, it is well known that sentence stress plays a most important rôle in the historical development of any language ; it has determined not only the difference in vowel between [woz] and [wəz], both written *was*, or between the demonstrative [ðæt] and the relative [ðət], both written *that*, but also that between *one* and *an* or *a*, originally the same word, and between Fr. *moi* and *me, toi* and *te* —one might give innumerable other instances. Value also plays a not unimportant rôle in determining which syllable among several in long words is stressed most, and in some languages it has revolutionized the whole stress system. This happened with old Gothonic, whence in modern German, Scandinavian, and in the native elements of English we have the prevalent stressing of the root syllable, i.e. of that syllable which has the greatest psychological value, as in ǀ*wishes,* beǀ*speak,* etc.

Now, it is generally said that if double forms arise like *one* and *an, moi* and *me,* the reason is that the sounds were found under ' different phonetic conditions ' and therefore developed differently, exactly as the difference between *an* and *a* or between Fr. *fol* and *fou* is due to the same word being placed in one instance before a word beginning with a vowel and in the other before a consonant, that is to say, in different external conditions. But it won't do to identify the two things : in the latter case we really have something external or mechanical, and here we may rightly use the expression ' phonetic condition,' but the difference between a strongly and a weakly stressed form of the same word depends on something internal, on the very soul of the word. Stress is not what the usual way of marking it in writing and printing might lead us to think—something that hangs outside or above the word—but is at least as important an element of the word as the ' speech sounds ' which go to make it up. Stress alternation in a sentence cannot consequently be reckoned a ' phonetic condition ' of the same order as the initial sound of the next word. If we say that the different treatment of the vowel seen in *one* and *an* or *moi* and *me* is occasioned by varying degrees of stress, we have ' explained ' the secondary sound change only, but not the primary change, which is that of stress itself, and that change is due to the different significance of the word under varying circumstances, i.e. to its varying value for the purposes of the exchange of ideas. Over and above mechanical principles we have here and elsewhere psychological principles, which no one can disregard with impunity.

XIV.—§ 12. Non-phonetic Changes.

Considerations of ease play an important part in all departments of language development. It is impossible to draw a sharp line between phonetic and syntactic phenomena. We have what might be termed prosiopesis when the speaker begins, or thinks he begins, to articulate, but produces no audible sound till one or two syllables after the beginning of what he intended to say. This phonetically is ' aphesis,' but in many cases leads to the omission of whole words ; this may become a regular speech habit, more particularly in the case of certain set phrases, e.g. (Good) *morning* | (Do you) *see* ? | (Will) *that do?* | (I shall) *see you again this afternoon* ; Fr. (na)*turellement* | (Je ne me) *rappelle plus*, etc.

On the other hand, we have aposiopesis if the speaker does not finish his sentence, either because he hesitates which word to employ or because he notices that the hearer has already caught his meaning. Hence such syntactic shortenings as *at Brown's* (house, or shop, or whatever it may be), which may then be extended to other places in the sentence ; the *grocer's* was closed | *St. Paul's* is very grand, etc. Similar abbreviations due to the natural disinclination to use more circumstantial expressions than are necessary to convey one's meaning are seen when, instead of *my straw hat*, one says simply *my straw*, if it is clear to one's hearers that one is talking of a hat ; thus *clay* comes to be used for *clay pipe*, *return* for *return ticket* ('We'd better take returns') *the Haymarket* for *the Haymarket Theatre*, etc Sometimes these shortenings become so common as to be scarcely any longer felt as such, e.g. *rifle, landau, bugle*, for *rifle gun, landau carriage, bugle horn* (further examples MEG ii. 8. 9). In Maupassant (*Bel Ami* 81) I find the following scrap of conversation which illustrates the same principle in another domain : " Voilà six mois que je suis *employé aux bureaux du chemin de fer du Nord.*" " Mais comment diable n'as-tu pas trouvé mieux qu'une place *d'employé au Nord ?* " [1]

The tendency to economize effort also manifests itself when the general ending *-er* is used instead of a more specific expression : *sleeper* for *sleeping-car* ; *bedder* at college for *bedmaker ; speecher, footer, brekker* (Harrow) for *speech-day, football, breakfast*, etc. Thus also when some noun or verb of a vague or general meaning is used because one will not take the trouble to think of the exact expression required, very often *thing* (sometimes extended *thingumbob*, cf. Dan. *tingest*, G. *dingsda*), Fr. *chose, machin* (even in place of a personal name); further, the verb *do* or *fix* (this especially in America). In some cases this tendency may permanently affect the meaning of a common noun which has to serve so often instead of a specific name that at last it acquires a special signification; thus, *corn* in England = 'wheat,' in Ireland = ' oats,' in America = ' maize,' *deer*, orig. ' animal,' Fr. *herbe*, now ' grass,' etc. As many people, either from ignorance or from carelessness, are far from being precise in thought and expression—they " Mean not, but blunder round about a meaning "—words come to be applied in senses unknown to former generations, and some of these senses may gradually become fixed and established. In some cases the final result of such want of precision may even be beneficial ; thus English at first had no means of expressing futurity in verbs. Then it became more and more customary to say ' he will come,' which at first meant ' he has the will to come,' to express his future coming apart from his volition —thus, also, 'it will rain,' etc. Similarly ' I shall go,' which

---

[1] Compare also the results of the same principle seen in writing. In a letter a proper name or technical term when first introduced is probably written in full and very distinctly, while afterwards it is either written carelessly or indicated by a mere initial. Any shorthand-writer knows how to utilize this principle systematically.

originally meant 'I am obliged to go,' was used in a less accurate way, where no obligation was thought of, and thus the language acquired something which is at any rate a make-shift for a future tense of the verb. But considerations of space prevent me from diving too deeply into questions of semantic change.

CHAPTER XV

CAUSES OF CHANGE—*continued*

§ 1 Emotional Exaggerations. § 2. Euphony. § 3. Organic Influences. § 4. Lapses and Blendings. § 5. Latitude of Correctness. § 6. Equidistant and Convergent Changes. § 7. Homophones. § 8. Significative Sounds preserved. § 9. Divergent Changes and Analogy. § 10. Extension of Sound Laws. § 11. Spreading of Sound Change. § 12. Reaction. § 13. Sound Laws and Etymological Science. § 14. Conclusion.

XV.—§ 1. Emotional Exaggerations.

In the preceding chapter we have dwelt at great length on those changes which tend to render articulations easier and more convenient. But, important as they are, these are not the only changes that speech sounds undergo : there are other moods than that of ordinary listless everyday conversation, and they may lead to modifications of pronunciation which are different from and may even be in direct opposition to those mentioned or hinted at above. Thus, anger or other violent emotions may cause emphatic utterance, in which, e.g., stops may be much more strongly aspirated than they are in usual quiet parlance ; even French, which has normally unaspirated ('sharp') [t] and [k], under such circumstances may aspirate them strongly—'*Mais taisez-vous donc !*' Military commands are characterized by peculiar emphasizings, even in some cases distortions of sounds and words. Pomposity and consequential airs are manifested in the treatment of speech sounds as well as in other gestures. Irony, scoffing, banter, amiable chaffing—each different mood or temper leaves its traces on enunciation. Actors and orators will often use stronger articulations than are strictly necessary to avoid those misunderstandings or that unintelligibility which may ensue from slipshod or indistinct pronunciation.[1] In short, anyone who will take careful note of the way in which people do really talk will find in the most everyday conversation as well as on more solemn occasions the greatest variety of such modifications and deviations from what might be termed 'normal' pronunciation ; these, however, pass

---

[1] " His pronunciation of some words is so distinct that an idea crossed me once that he might be an actor " (Shaw, *Cashel Byron's Profession*, 66).

unnoticed under ordinary circumstances, when the attention is directed exclusively to the contents and general purport of the spoken words. A vowel or a consonant will be made a trifle shorter or longer than usual, the lips will open a little too much, an [e] will approach [æ] or [i], the off-glide after a final [t] will sound nearly as [s], the closure of a [d] will be made so loosely that a little air will escape and the sound therefore will be approximately a [ð] or a weak fricative point [r], etc. Most of these modifications are so small that they cannot be represented by letters, even by those of a very exact phonetic alphabet, but they exist all the same, and are by no means insignificant to those who want to understand the real essence of speech and of linguistic change, for life is built up of such minutiæ. The great majority of such alterations are of course made quite unconsciously, but by the side of these we must recognize that there are some individuals who more or less consciously affect a certain mode of enunciation, either from artistic motives, because they think it beautiful, or simply to 'show off'—and sometimes such pronunciations may set the fashion and be widely imitated (cf. below, p. 292).

Tender emotions may lead to certain lengthenings of sounds. The intensifying effect of lengthening was noticed by A. Gill, Milton's teacher, in 1621, see Jiriczek's reprint, p. 48 : "Atque vt Hebræi, ad amphorem vocis aliculus significationem, syllabas adaugent [cf. here below, Ch. XX § 9] ; sic nos syllabarum tempora : vt, *grĕt* [the diæresis denotes vowel-length] magnus, *grēet* ingens ; *monstrus* prodigiosum, *mŏnstrus* valde prodigiosum, *mŏŏnstrus* prodigiosum adeo vt hominem stupidet." Cf. also the lengthening in the exclamation *God!*, by novelists sometimes written *Gawd* or *Gord*. But it is curious that the same emotional lengthening will sometimes affect a consonant (or first part of a diphthong) in a position in which otherwise we always have a short quantity ; thus, Danish clergymen, when speaking with unction, will lengthen the [l] of *glæde* 'joy,' which is ridiculed by comic writers through the unphonetic spelling *ge-læde* ; and in the same way I find in Kipling (*Stalky* 119) : "We'll make it a *be-autiful* house," and in O. Henry (*Roads of Destiny* 133) : "A regular Paradise Lost for elegance of scenery and *be-yooty* of geography." I suppose that the spellings *ber-luddy* and *bee-luddy*, which I find in recent novels, are meant to indicate the pronunciation [blˑ-ʌdi], thus the exact counterpart of the Danish example. An unstressed vowel before the stressed syllable is similarly lengthened in "Dee-lightful couple!" (Shaw, *Doctor's Dilemma* 41) ; American girl students will often say ['diˑliʃ] for *delicious*.

XV.—§ 2. Euphony.

It was not uncommon in the seventeenth and eighteenth centuries to ascribe phonetic changes to a desire for euphony, a view which is represented in Bopp's earliest works. But as early as 1821 Bredsdorff says that " people will always find that euphonious which they are accustomed to hear : considerations of euphony consequently will not cause changes in a language, but rather make for keeping it unchanged. Those changes which are generally supposed to be based on euphony are due chiefly to convenience, in some instances to care of distinctness." This is quite true, but scarcely the whole truth. Euphony depends not only on custom, but even more on ease of articulation and on ease of perception : what requires intricate or difficult movements of the organs of speech will always be felt as cacophonous, and so will anything that is indistinct or blurred. But nations, as well as individuals, have an artistic feeling for these things in different degrees, and that may influence the phonetic character of a language, though perhaps chiefly in its broad features, while it may be difficult to point out any particular details in phonological history which have been thus worked upon. There can be no doubt that the artistic feeling is much more developed in the French than in the English nation, and we find in French fewer obscure vowels and more clearly articulated consonants than in English (cf. also my remarks on French accent, GS § 28).

XV.—§ 3. Organic Influences.

Some modifications of speech sounds are due to the fact that the organs of speech are used for other purposes than that of speaking. We all know the effect of someone trying to speak with his mouth full of food, or with a cigar or a pipe hanging between his lips and to some extent impeding their action. Various emotions are expressed by facial movements which may interfere with the production of ordinary speech sounds. A child that is crying speaks differently from one that is smiling or laughing. A smile requires a retraction of the corners of the mouth and a partial opening of the lips, and thus impedes the formation of that lip-closure which is an essential part of the ordinary [m] ; hence most people when smiling will substitute the labiodental *m*, which to the ear greatly resembles the bilabial [m]. A smile will also often modify the front-round vowel [y] so as to make it approach [i]. Sweet may be right in supposing that " the habit of speaking with a constant smile or grin " is the reason for the Cockney unrounding of the vowel in [nau] for *no*. Schuchardt

(*Zs. f. rom. Phil.* 5. 314) says that in Andalusian *quia !* instead of *ca !* the lips, under the influence of a certain emotion, are drawn scoffingly aside. Inversely, the rounding in *Josu !* instead of *Jesu !* is due to wonder (ib.); and exactly in the same way we have the surprised or pitying exclamation *jøses !* from *Jesus* in Danish. Compare also the rounding in Dan. and G. [nø·] for [ne·, nɛ·] (*nej, nein*). Lundell mentions that in Swedish a caressing *lilla vän* often becomes *lylla vön*, and I have often observed the same rounding in Dan. *min lille ven.* Schuchardt also mentions an Italian [ʃ] instead of [s] under the influence of pain or anger (*mi duole la teſta* ; *ti do uno ſchiaffo*) ; a Danish parallel is the frequent [ʃluð'ər] for *sludder* 'nonsense.' We are here verging on the subject of the symbolic value of speech sounds, which will occupy us in a later chapter (XX).

Observe, too, how people will pronounce under the influence of alcohol : the tongue is not under control and is incapable of accurately forming the closure necessary for [t], which therefore becomes [r], and the thin rill necessary for [s], which therefore comes to resemble [ʃ] ; there is also a general tendency to run sounds and syllables together.[1]

XV.—§ 4. Lapses and Blendings.

All these deviations are due to influences from what is outside the sphere of language as such. But we now come to something of the greatest importance in the life of language, the fact, namely, that deviations from the usual or normal pronunciation are very often due to causes inside the language itself, either by lingering reminiscences of what has just been spoken or by anticipation of something that the speaker is just on the point of pronouncing. The process of speech is a very complicated one, and while one thing is being said, the mind is continually active in preparing what has to be said next, arranging the ideas and fashioning the linguistic expression in all its details. Each word is a succession of sounds, and for each of these a complicated set of orders has to be issued from the brain to the various speech organs. Sometimes these get mixed up, and a command is sent down to one organ a moment too early or too late. The inclination to make mistakes naturally increases with the number of identical or

[1] Dickens, *D. Cop.* 2. 149 never*berrer,* 150 I'm*afraid* you're*norwell* (ib. also *r* for *n* : Amigoarawaysoo, Goori = Good night). | *Our Mut. Fr.* 602 le*rrers.* | Thackeray, *Newc.* 163 *Whas* that ? | Anstey, *Vice V.* 328 *shupper,* I *sh*pose, wharriplease, say tharragain. | Meredith, *R. Feverel* 272 Nor a bi*r* of it. | Walpole, *Duch. of Wrex.* 323–4 non*shensh,* Wa*sh* the matter ? | Galsworthy, *In Chanc.* 17 cur*sh,* un*sh*tood'm. Cf. also Fijn van Draat, ESt 34. 363 ff.

similar sounds in close proximity. This is well known from those
'jaw-breaking' tongue-tests with which people amuse themselves in all countries and of which I need give only one typical
specimen :

> She sells seashells on the seashore ;
> The shells she sells are seashells, I'm sure,
> For if she sells seashells on the seashore,
> Then I'm sure she sells seashore shells.

If the mind is occupied with one sound while another is being
pronounced, and thus either runs in advance of or lags behind
what should be its immediate business, the linguistic result may
be of various kinds. The simplest case of influencing is assimilation of two contiguous sounds, which we have already considered
from a different point of view. Next we have assimilative influence on a sound at a distance, as when we lapse into *she shells*
instead of *sea shells* or *she sells* ; such is Fr. *chercher* for older
sercher (whence E. *search*) from Lat. *circare*, Dan. and G. vulgar
ſerſant for *sergeant* ; a curious mixed case is the pronunciation of
transition as [træn'siʒən]: the normal development is [træn'ziʃən],
but the voice-articulation of the two hissing sounds is reversed
(possibly under accessory influence from the numerous words in
which we have [træns] with [s], and from words ending in [iʒən],
such as *vision, division*). Further examples of such assimilation
at a distance or consonant-harmonization (*malmsey* from *malvesie*,
etc.) may be found in my LPh 11. 7, where there are also examples
of the corresponding harmonizings of vowels : Fr. *camarade*, It.
uguale, Braganza, from *camerade, eguale, Brigantia*, etc. In Ugro-
Finnic and Turkish this harmony of vowels has been raised to
a principle pervading the whole structure of the language, as
seen, e.g., most clearly in the varying plural endings in Yakut
agalar, äsälär, ogolor, dörölör, ' fathers, bears, children, muzzles.'

What escapes at the wrong place and causes confusion may
be a part of the same word or of a following word · as examples
of the latter case may be given a few of the lapses recorded in
Meringer and Mayer's *Versprechen und Verlesen* (Stuttgart, 1895):
instead of saying *Lateinisches lehnwort* Meringer said *Laten-
isches* . . . and then corrected himself ; *paster noster* instead of
pater noster ; *wenn das wesser* . . . *wetter wieder besser ist*. This
phenomenon is termed in Danish *at bakke snagvendt* (for *snakke
bagvendt*) and in English *Spoonerism*, from an Oxford don, W. A.
Spooner, about whom many comic lapses are related (" Don't
you ever feel a half-warmed fish " instead of " half-formed
wish ").

The simplest and most frequently occurring cases in which
the order for a sound is issued too early or too late are those trans-

positions of two sounds which the linguists term 'metatheses.' They occur most frequently with *s* in connexion with a stop (*wasp, waps*; *ask, ax*) and with *r* (chiefly, perhaps exclusively, the trilled form of the sound) and a vowel (*third*, OE. *þridda*). A more complicated instance is seen in Fr. *trésor* for *tésor, thesaurum*. If the mind does not realize how far the vocal organs have got, the result may be the skipping of some sound or sounds; this is particularly likely to happen when the same sound has to be repeated at some little distance, and we then have the phenomenon termed 'haplology,' as in *eighteen*, OE. *eahtatiene*, and in the frequent pronunciation *probly* for *probably*, Fr. *contrôle, idolatrie* for *contrerôle, idololatrie*, Lat. *stipendium* for *stipipendium*, and numerous similar instances in every language (LPh 11. 9). Sometimes a sound may be skipped because the mind is confused through the fact that the same sound has to be pronounced a little later; thus the old Gothonic word for 'bird' (G. *vogel*, OE. *fugol*; E. *fowl* with a modified meaning) is derived from the verb *fly*, OE. *fleogan*, and originally had some form like *fluglo (OE. had an adj. *flugol*); in recent times *flugelman* (G. flügelmann) has become *fugleman*. It. has *Federigo* for *Frederigo*—thus the exactly opposite result of what has been brought about in *trésor* from the same kind of mental confusion.

When words are often repeated in succession, sounds from one of them will often creep into another, as is seen very often in numerals: the nasal which was found in the old forms for 7, 9 and 10 and is still seen in E. *seven, nine, ten*, has no place in the word for 8, and accordingly we have in the ordinal ON. *sjaundi, átti, níundi, tíundi*, but already in ON. we find *áttandi* by the side of *átti*, and in Dan. the present-day forms are *syvende, ottende, niende, tiende*; in the same way OFr. had *sedme, uidme, noefme, disme* (which have all now disappeared with the exception of *dime* as a substantive). In the names of the months we had the same formation of a series in OFr.: *septembre, octembre, novembre, decembre*, but learned influence has reinstated *octobre*. G. *elf* for older *eilf* owes its vowel to the following *zwelf*; and as now the latter has given way to *zwölf* (the vowel being rounded in consequence of the *w*) many dialects count *zehn, ölf, zwölf*. Similarly, it seems to be due to their frequent occurrence in close contact with the verbal forms in *-no* that the Italian plural pronouns *egli, elle* are extended with that ending: *eglino amano, elleno dicono*. Diez compares the curious Bavarian *wo-st bist, dem-st gehörst*, etc., in which the personal ending of the verb is transferred to some other word with which it has nothing to do (on this phenomenon see Herzog, *Streitfragen d. roman. phil.* 48, Buergel Goodwin, *Umgangsspr. in Südbayern* 99).

In speaking, the mind is occupied not only with the words one is already pronouncing or knows that one is going to pronounce, but also with the ideas which one has to express but for which one has not yet chosen the linguistic form. In many cases two synonyms will rise to the consciousness at the same time, and the hesitation between them will often result in a compromise which contains the head of one and the tail of another word. It is evident that this process of blending is intimately related to those we have just been considering; see the detailed treatment in Ch. XVI § 6.

Syntactical blends are very frequent. Hesitation between *different from* and *other than* will result in *different than* or *another from*, and similarly we occasionally find *another to, different to, contrary than, contrary from, opposite from, anywhere than*. After a clause introduced by *hardly* or *scarcely* the normal conjunction is *when*, but sometimes we find *than*, because that is regular after the synonymous *no sooner*.

XV.—§ 5. Latitude of Correctness.

It is a natural consequence of the essence of human speech and the way in which it is transmitted from generation to generation that we have everywhere to recognize a certain latitude of correctness, alike in the significations in which the words may be used, in syntax and in pronunciation. The nearer a speaker keeps to the centre of what is established or usual, the easier will it be to understand him. If he is 'eccentric' on one point or another, the result may not always be that he conveys no idea at all, or that he is misunderstood, but often merely that he is understood with some little difficulty, or that his hearers have a momentary feeling of something odd in his choice of words, or expressions or pronunciation. In many cases, when someone has overstepped the boundaries of what is established, his hearers do not at once catch his meaning and have to gather it from the whole context of what follows: not unfrequently the meaning of something you have heard as an incomprehensible string of syllables will suddenly flash upon you without your knowing how it has happened. Misunderstandings are, of course, most liable to occur if words of different meaning, which in themselves would give sense in the same collocation, are similar in sound: in that case a trifling alteration of one sound, which in other words would create no difficulty at all, may prove pernicious. Now, what is the bearing of these considerations on the question of sound changes?

The latitude of correctness is very far from being the same in different languages. Some sounds in each language move within narrow boundaries, while others have a much larger field assigned to them ; each language is punctilious in some, but not in all points. Deviations which in one language would be considered trifling, in another would be intolerable perversions. In German, for instance, a wide margin is allowed for the (local and individual) pronunciation of the diphthong written *eu* or *äu* (in *eule, träume*) : it may begin with [ɔ] or [œ] or even [æ, a], and it may end in [i], or the corresponding rounded vowel [y], or one of the mid front vowels, rounded or not, it does not matter much ; the diphthong is recognized or acknowledged in many shapes, while the similar diphthong in English, as in *toy, voice*, allows a far less range of variation (for other examples see LPh 16. 22).

Now, it is very important to keep in mind that there is an intimate connexion between phonetic latitude and the significations of words. If there are in a language a great many pairs of words which are identical in sound except for, say, the difference between [e·] and [i·] (or between long and short [i], or between voiced [b] and voiceless [p], or between a high and a low tone, etc.), then the speakers of that language necessarily will make that distinction with great precision, as otherwise too many misunderstandings would result. If, on the other hand, no mistakes worth speaking of would ensue, there is not the same inducement to be careful. In English, and to a somewhat lesser degree in French, it is easy to make up long lists of pairs of words where the sole difference is between voice and voicelessness in the final consonant (*cab cap, bad bat, frog frock,* etc.) ; hence final [b] and [p], [d] and [t], [g] and [k] are kept apart conscientiously, while German possesses very few such pairs of words ; in German, consequently, the natural tendency to make final consonants voiceless has not been checked, and all final stopped consonants have now become voiceless. In initial and medial position, too, there are very few examples in German of the same distinction (see the lists, LPh 6. 78), and this circumstance makes us understand why Germans are so apt to efface the difference between [b, d, g] and [p, t, k]. On the other hand, the distinction between a long and a short vowel is kept much more effectively in German than in French, because in German ten or twenty times as many words would be liable to confusion through pronouncing a long instead of a short vowel or vice versa. In French no two words are kept apart by means of stress, as in English or German ; so the rule laid down in grammars that the stress falls on the final syllable of the word is very frequently broken through for rhythmic and other reasons. Other similar instances might easily be advanced.

XV.—§ 6. Equidistant and Convergent Changes.

Phonetic shifts are of two kinds : the shifted sound may be identical with one already found in the language, or it may be a new sound. In the former, but not in the latter kind, fresh possibilities of confusions and misunderstandings may arise. Now, in some cases one sound (or series of sounds) marches into a position which has just been abandoned by another sound (or series of sounds), which has in its turn shifted into some other place. A notable instance is the old Gothonic consonant shift : Aryan *b*, *d*, *g* cannot have become Gothonic *p*, *t*, *k* till after primitive *p*, *t*, *k* had already become fricatives [f, þ, x (h)], for had the shift taken place before, intolerable confusion would have reigned in all parts of the vocabulary. Another instructive example is seen in the history of English long vowels. Not till OE. long *a* had been rounded into something like [ɔ·] (OE. *stan*, ME. *stoon*, *stone*) could a new long *a* develop, chiefly through lengthening of an old short *a* in certain positions. Somewhat later we witness the great vowel-raising through which the phonetic value of the long vowels (written all the time in essentially the same way) has been constantly on the move and yet the distance between them has been kept, so that no confusions worth speaking of have ever occurred. If we here leave out of account the rounded back vowels and speak only of front vowels, the shift may be thus represented through typical examples (the first and the last columns show the spelling, the others the sounds) :

Middle English.		Elizabethan.	Present English.	
(1) *bite*	bi·tə	beit	bait	*bite*
(2) *bete*	be·tə	bi·t	bi·t	*beet*
(3) *bete*	bɛ·tə	be·t	bi·t	*beat*
(4) *abate*	a·¹ba·tə	ə¹bæ·t	ə¹beit	*abate*

When the sound of (2) was raised into [i·], the sound of (1) had already left that position and had been diphthongized, and when the sound of (3) was raised from an open into a close *e*, (2) had already become [i·] ; (4) could not become (æ·] or [ɛ·] till (3) had become a comparatively close *e* sound. The four vowels, as it were, climbed the ladder without ever reaching each other— a climbing which took centuries and in each case implied intermediate steps not indicated in our survey. No clashings could occur so long as each category kept its distance from the sounds above and below, and thus we find that the Elizabethans as scrupulously as Chaucer kept the four classes of words apart in their rimes. But in the seventeenth century class (3) was raised, and as no corresponding change had taken place with (2), the two classes have now fallen together with the single sound [i·]. This entails a certain number of homophones such as had not been created through the preceding equidistant changes.

XV.—§ 7. Homophones.

The reader here will naturally object that the fact of new homophones arising through this vowel change goes against the theory that the necessity of certain distinctions can keep in check the tendency to phonetic changes. But homophones do not always imply frequent misunderstandings : some homophones are more harmless than others. Now, if we look at the list of the homophones created by this raising of the close *e* (MEG i. 11. 74), we shall soon discover that very few mistakes of any consequence could arise through the obliteration of the distinction between this vowel and the previously existing [i·]. For substantives and verbal forms (like *bean* and *been, beet beat, flea flee, heel heal, leek leak, meat meet, reed read, sea see, seam seem, steel steal*), or substantives and adjectives (like *deer dear, leaf lief, shear sheer, week weak*) will generally be easily distinguished by their position in the sentence ; nor will a plural such as *feet* be often mistaken for the singular *feat*. Actual misunderstandings of any importance are only imaginable when the two words belong to the same ' part of speech,' but of such pairs we meet only few : *beach beech, breach breech, mead meed, peace piece, peal peel, quean queen, seal ceil, wean ween, wheal wheel*. I think the judicious reader will agree with me that confusions due to these words being pronounced in the same way will be few and far between, and one understands that they cannot have been powerful enough to prevent hundreds of other words from having their sound changed. An effective prevention can only be expected when the falling together in sound would seriously impair the understanding of many sentences.

It is, moreover, interesting to note how many of the words which were made identical with others through this change were already rare at the time or have at any rate become obsolete since : this is true of *breech, lief, meed, mete* (adj.), *quean, weal, wheal, ween* and perhaps a few others. Now, obsolescence of some words is always found in connexion with such convergent sound changes. In some cases the word had already become rare before the change in sound took place, and then it is obvious that it cannot have offered serious resistance to the change that was setting in. In other cases the dying out of a word must be looked upon as a consequence of the sound change which had actually taken place. Many scholars are now inclined to see in phonetic coalescence one of the chief reasons why words fall into disuse, see, e.g., Liebisch (PBB XXIII, 228, many German examples in O. Weise, *Unsere Mutterspr.*, 3d ed., 206) and Gilliéron, *La faillite de l'étymologie phonétique* (Neuveville, 1919—a book whose sensational title is hardly justified by its contents).

The drawbacks of homophones [1] are counteracted in various ways. Very often a synonym steps forward, as when *lad* or *boy* is used in nearly all English dialects to supplant *son*, which has become identical in sound with *sun* (cf. above p. 120, a childish instance). Very often it becomes usual to avoid misunderstandings through some addition, as when we say *the sole of her foot*, because *her sole* might be taken to mean *her soul*, or when the French say *un dé à coudre* or *un dé à jouer* (cf. E. *minister of religion* and *cabinet minister*, the *right-hand* corner, the *subject-matter*, where the same expedient is used to obviate ambiguities arisen from other causes). Chinese, of course, is the classical example of a language abounding in homophones caused by convergent sound changes, and it is highly interesting to study the various ways in which that language has remedied the resulting drawbacks, see, e.g., B. Karlgren, *Ordet och pennan i Mittens rike* (Stockholm, 1918), p. 49 ff. But on the whole we must say that the ways in which these phonetic inconveniences are counteracted are the same as those in which speakers react against misunderstandings arising from semantic or syntactic causes : as soon as they perceive that their meaning is not apprehended they turn their phrases in a different way, choosing some other expression for their thought, and by this means language is gradually freed from ambiguity.

---

[1] The inconveniences arising from having many homophones in a language are eloquently set forth by Robert Bridges, *On English Homophones* (S.P.E., Oxford, 1919)—but I would not subscribe to all the Laureate's views, least of all to his practical suggestions and to his unjustifiable attacks on some very meritorious English phoneticians. He seems also to exaggerate the dangers, e.g. of the two words *know* and *no* having the same sound, when he says (p. 22) that unless a vowel like that in *law* be restored to the negative *no*, " I should judge that the verb *to know* is doomed. The third person singular of its present tense is *nose*, and its past tense is *new*, and the whole inconvenience is too radical and perpetual to be received all over the world." But surely the rôle of these words in connected speech is so different, and is nearly always made so clear by the context, that it is very difficult to imagine real sentences in which there would be any serious change of mistaking *know* for *no*, or *knows* for *nose*, or *knew* for *new*. I repeat : it is not homophony as such—the phenomenon shown in the long lists lexicographers can draw up of words of the same sound—that is decisive, but the chances of mistakes in connected speech. It has been disputed whether the loss of Gr. *humeis*, ' ye,' was due to its identity in sound with *hemeis*, ' we '; Hatzidakis says that the new formation *eseis* is earlier than the falling together of *e* and *u* [y] in the sound [i]. But according to Dieterich and C. D. Buck (*Classical Philology*, 9. 90, 1914) the confusion of *u* and *i* or *e* dates back to the second century. Anyhow, all confusion is now obviated, for both the first and the second persons pl. have new forms which are unambiguous : *emeis* and *eseis* or *seis*.

XV.—§ 8. Significative Sounds preserved.

My contention that the significative side of language has in so far exercised an influence on phonetic development that the possibility of many misunderstandings may effectually check the coalescence of two hitherto distinct sounds should not be identified with one of the tenets of the older school (Curtius included) against which the ' young grammarians ' raised an emphatic protest, namely, that a tendency to preserve significative sounds and syllables might produce exceptions to the normal course of phonetic change.   Delbrück and his friends may be right in much of what they said against Curtius—for instance, when he explained the retention of *i* in some Greek optative forms through a consciousness of the *original* meaning of this suffix ; but their denial was in its way just as exaggerated as his affirmation. It cannot justly be urged against the influence of signification that a preservation of a sound on that account would only be imaginable on the supposition that the speaker was conscious of a threatened sound change and wanted to avoid it.   One need not suppose a speaker to be on his guard against a ' sound law ' : the only thing required is that he should feel, or be made to feel, that he is not understood when he speaks indistinctly ; if on that account he has to repeat his words he will naturally be careful to pronounce the sound he has skipped or slurred, and may even be tempted to exaggerate it a little.

There do not seem to be many quite unimpeachable examples of words which have received exceptional phonetic treatment to obviate misunderstandings arising from homophony ; other explanations (analogy from other forms of the same word, etc.) can generally be alleged more or less plausibly.   But this does seem to be the easiest explanation of the fact that the E. preposition *on* has always the full vowel [ɔ], though in nine cases out of ten it is weakly stressed and though all the other analogous prepositions (*to, for, of, at*) in the corresponding weak positions in sentences are generally pronounced with the ' neutral ' vowel [ə].   But if *on* were similarly pronounced, ambiguity would very often result from its phonetic identity with the weak forms of the extremely frequent little words *an* (the indefinite article) and *and* (possibly also *in*), not to mention the great number of [ən]s in words like *drunken, shaken, deepen,* etc., where the forms without *-en* also exist.   With the preposition *upon* the same considerations do not hold good, hence the frequency of the pronunciation [əpən] in weak position. Considerations of clearness have also led to the disuse of the formerly frequent form *o* (*o'*) which was the ' natural ' development of each of the two prepositions *on* and *of*.   The form written *a* survives only in some fossilized combinations like *ashore*; in several others it has now disappeared (*set the clock going*, formerly *a-going*, etc.).

Sometimes, when all ordinary words are affected by a certain sound change, some words prove refractory because in their case the old sound is found to be more expressive than the new one. When the long E. [i·] was diphthongized into [ai], the words *pipe* and *whine* ceased to be good echoisms, but some dialects have *peep* ' complain,' which keeps the old sound of the former, and the Irish say *wheen* (Joyce, *English as we speak it in Ireland*, 103). In *squeeze* the [i·] sound has been retained as more expressive— the earlier form was *squize*; and the same is the case with some words meaning ' to look narrowly ' : *peer, peek, keek*, earlier *pire, pike, kike* (cf. Dan. *pippe, kikke, kige*, G. *kieken*).[1] In the same way, when the old [a·] was changed into [ɛ·, ei], the word *gape* ceased to be expressive (as it is still in Dan. *gabe*), but in popular speech the tendency to raise the vowel was resisted, and the old sound [ga·p] persisted, spelt *garp* as a London form in 1817 (Ellis, EEP v. 228) and still common in many dialects (see *gaup, garp* in EDD); Professor Hempl told me that [ga·p] was also a common pronunciation in America. In the chapter on Sound Symbolism (XX) we shall see some other instances of exceptional phonetic treatment of symbolic words (especially *tiny, teeny, little, cuckoo*).

XV.—§ 9. Divergent Changes and Analogy.

Besides equidistant and convergent sound changes we have divergent changes, through which sounds at one time identical have separated themselves later. This is a mere consequence of the fact that it is rare for a sound to be changed equally in all positions in which it occurs. On the contrary, one must admit that the vast majority of sound changes are conditioned by some such circumstance as influence of neighbouring sounds, position as initial, medial or final (often with subdivisions, as position between vowels, etc.), place in a strongly or weakly stressed syllable, and so forth. One may take as examples some familiar instances from French : Latin *c* (pronounced [k]), is variously treated before *o* (*corpus*> *corps*), *a* (*canem*> *chien*), and *e* (*centum* > *cent*) ; in *amicum*> *ami* it has totally disappeared. Lat. *a*

[1] The NED has not arrived at this explanation; it says : "*Peer* is not a phonetic development of *pire*, and cannot, so far as is at present known, be formally identified with that word " ; " the verbs *keek, peek*, and *peep* are app. closely allied to each other. *Kike* and *pike*, as earlier forms of *keek* and *peek*, occur in Chaucer ; *pepe, peep* is of later appearance. . . . The phonetic relations between the forms *pike, peek, peak*, are as yet unexplained."

becomes *e* in a stressed open syllable (*natum* > *né*), except before a nasal (*amat* > *aime*) ; but after *c* we have a different treatment (*canem* > *chien*), and in a close syllable it is kept (*arborem* > *arbre*) ; in weak syllables it is kept initially (*amorem* > *amour*), but becomes [ə] (spelt *e*) finally (*bona* > *bonne*). This enumeration of the chief rules will serve to show the far-reaching differentiation which in this way may take place among words closely related as parts of the same paradigm or family of words ; thus, for Lat. *amo, amas, amat, amamus, amatis, amant* we get OFr. *aim, aimes, aime, amons, amez, aiment,* until the discrepancy is removed through analogy, and we get the regular modern forms *aime, aimes, aime, aimons, aimez, aiment.* The levelling tendency, however, is not strong enough to affect the initial *a* in *amour* and *amant,* which are felt as less closely connected with the verbal forms. What were at first only small differences may in course of time become greater through subsequent changes, as when the difference between *feel* and *felt, keep* and *kept,* etc., which was originally one of length only, became one of vowel quality as well, through the raising of long [e·] to [i·], while short [e] was not raised. And thus in many other cases. Different nations differ greatly in the degree in which they permit differentiation of cognate words ; most nations resent any differentiation in initial sounds, while the Kelts have no objection to ' the same word ' having as many as four different beginnings (for instance *t-, d-, n-, nh-*) according to circumstances. In Icelandic the word for ' other, second ' has for centuries in different cases assumed such different forms as *annarr, önnur, öðrum, aðrir,* forms which in the other Scandinavian languages have been levelled down.

It is a natural consequence of the manner in which phonology is usually investigated and represented in manuals of historical grammar—which start with some old stage and follow the various changes of each sound in later stages—that these divergent changes have attracted nearly the sole attention of scholars ; this has led to the prevalent idea that sound laws and analogy are the two opposed principles in the life of languages, the former tending always to destroy regularity and harmony, and the latter reconstructing what would without it be chaos and confusion.[1]

---

[1] See, for instance, the following strong expressions : " Une langue est sans cesse rongée et menacée de ruine par l'action des lois phonétiques, qui, livrées à elles-mêmes, opéreraient avec une régularité fatale et désagréeraient le système grammatical. . . . Heureusement l'analogie (c'est ainsi qu'on désigne la tendance inconsciente à conserver ou recréer ce que les lois phonétiques menacent ou détruisent) a peu à peu effacé ces différences . . . il s'agit d'une perpétuelle dégradation due aux changements phonétiques aveugles, et qui est toujours ou prévenue ou réparée par une réorganisation parallèle du système " (Bally, LV 44 f.).

This view, however, is too rigorous and does not take into account the manysidedness of linguistic life. It is not every irregularity that is due to the operation of phonetic laws, as we have in all languages many survivals of the confused manner in which ideas were arranged and expressed in the mind of primitive man. On the other hand, there are many phonetic changes which do not increase the number of existing irregularities, but make for regularity and a simpler system through abolishing phonetic distinctions which had no semantic or functional value ; such are, for instance, those convergent changes of unstressed vowels which have simplified the English flexional system (Ch. XIV § 10 above). And if we were in the habit of looking at linguistic change from the other end, tracing present sounds back to former sounds instead of beginning with antiquity, we should see that convergent changes are just as frequent as divergent ones. Indeed, many changes may be counted under both heads ; an *a*, which is dissociated from other *a*'s through becoming *e*, is identified with and from henceforth shares the destiny of other *e*'s, etc.

XV.—§ 10. Extension of Sound Laws.

If a phonetic change has given to some words two forms without any difference in signification, the same alternation may be extended to other cases in which the sound in question has a different origin (' phonetic analogy '). An undoubted instance is the unhistoric *r* in recent English. When the consonantal [r] was dropped finally and before a consonant while it was retained before a vowel, and words like *better, here* thus came to have two forms [betə, hiə] and [betər (ɔf), hiər (ən ðɛ·ə)] *better off, here and there*, the same alternation was transferred to words like *idea, drama* [ai'diə, dra·mə], so that the sound [r] is now very frequently inserted before a word beginning with a vowel : *I'd no idea-r-of this, a drama-r-of Ibsen* (many references MEG i. 13. 42). In French final *t* and *s* have become mute, but are retained before a vowel : *il est* [ɛ] *venu, il est* [ɛt] *arrivé* ; *les* [le] *femmes, les* [lez] *hommes* ; and now vulgar speakers will insert [t] or [z] in the wrong place between vowels : *pa-t assez, j'allai-t écrire, avant-z-hier, moi-z-aussi* ; this is called ' cuir ' or ' velours.'

In course of time a ' phonetic law ' may undergo a kind of metamorphosis, being extended to a greater and greater number of combinations. As regards recent times we are sometimes able to trace such a gradual development. A case in point is the dropping of [j] in [ju·] after certain consonants in English [see MEG i. 13, 7). It began with *r* as in *true, rude* ; next came *l* when preceded by a consonant, as in *blue, clue* ; in these cases

[j] is never heard. But after *l* not preceded by another consonant there is a good deal of vacillation, thus in *Lucy, absolute*; after [s, z] as in *Susan, resume* there is a strong tendency to suppress [j], though this pronunciation has not yet prevailed,[1] and after [t, d, n], as in *tune, due, new*, the suppression is in Britain only found in vulgar speakers, while in some parts of the United States it is heard from educated speakers as well. In the speech of these the sound law may be said to attack any [juˑ] after any point consonant, while it will have to be formulated in various less comprehensive terms for British speakers belonging to older or younger generations. It is extremely difficult, not to say impossible, to reconcile such occurrences with the orthodox 'young grammarian' theory of sound changes being due to a shifting of the organic feeling or motor sensation (verschiebung des bewegungsgefühls) which is supposed to have necessarily taken place wherever the same sound was under the same phonetic conditions. For what are here the same phonetic conditions? The position after *r*, after *l* combinations, after *l* even when standing alone, after all point consonants? Each generation of English speakers will give a different answer to this question. Now, it is highly probable that many of the comprehensive prehistoric sound changes, of which we see only the final result, while possible intermediate stages evade our inquiry, have begun in the same modest way as the transition from [juˑ] to [uˑ] in English : with regard to them we are in exactly the same position as a man who had heard only such speakers as say consistently [truˑ, ruˑd, bluˑ, luˑsi, suˑzn, riˑzuˑm, tuˑn, duˑ, nuˑ] and who would then naturally suppose that [j] in the combination [juˑ] had been dropped all at once after any point consonant.

XV.—§ 11. Spreading of Sound Change.

Sound laws (to retain provisionally that firmly established term) have by some linguists, who rightly reject the comparison with natural laws (e.g. Meringer), been compared rather with the 'laws' of fashion in dress. But I think it is important to make a distinction here : the comparison with fashions throws no light whatever on the question how sound changes *originate*—it can tell us nothing about the first impulse to drop [j] in certain positions before [uˑ]; but the comparison is valid when we come to consider the question how such a change when first begun in one individual *spreads to other individuals*. While the former question has been

---

[1] Some speakers will say [suˑ] in *Susan, supreme, superstition*, but will take care to pronounce [sjuˑ] in *suit, sue*. Others are more consistent one way or the other.

dealt with at some length in the preceding investigation, it now remains for us to say something about the latter. The spreading of phonetic change, as of any other linguistic change, is due to imitation, conscious and unconscious, of the speech habits of other people. We have already met with imitation in the chapters dealing with the child and with the influence exerted by foreign languages. But man is apt to imitate throughout the whole of his life, and this statement applies to his language as much as to his other habits. What he imitates, in this as in other fields, is not always the best ; a real valuation of what would be linguistically good or preferable does not of course enter the head of the ' man in the street.' But he may imitate what he thinks pretty, or funny, and especially what he thinks characteristic of those people whom for some reason or other he looks up to. Imitation is essentially a social phenomenon, and if people do not always imitate the best (the best thing, the best pronunciation), they will generally imitate ' their betters,' i.e. those that are superior to them—in rank, in social position, in wealth, in everything that is thought enviable. What constitutes this superiority cannot be stated once for all ; it varies according to surroundings, age, etc. A schoolboy may feel tempted to imitate a rough, swaggering boy a year or two older than himself rather than his teachers or parents, and in later life he may find other people worthy of imitation, according to his occupation or profession or individual taste. But when he does imitate he is apt to imitate everything, even sometimes things that are not worth imitating. In this way Percy, in *Henry IV, Second Part*, II. 3. 24—

> was indeed the glasse
> Wherein the noble youth did dresse themselues.
> He had no legges, that practic'd not his gate,
> And *speaking thicke* [1] (*which Nature made his blemish*)
> *Became the accents of the valiant.*
> *For those that could speake low and tardily,*
> *Would turne their owne perfection to abuse,*
> *To seeme like him. So that in speech,* in gate . . .
> He was the marke, and glasse, coppy, and booke,
> That fashion'd others.

The spreading of a new pronunciation through imitation must necessarily take some time, though the process may in some instances be fairly rapid. In some historical instances we are able to see how a new sound, taking its rise in some particular part of a country, spreads gradually like a wave, until finally it has pervaded the whole of a linguistic area. It cannot become universal all at once ; but it is evident that the more natural a new

[1] I.e. " With confused and indistinct articulation ; also, with a husky or hoarse voice "—NED.

mode of pronunciation seems to members of a particular speech community, the more readily will it be accepted and the more rapid will be its diffusion. Very often, both when the new pronunciation is easier and when there are special psychological inducements operating in one definite direction, the new form may originate independently in different individuals, and that of course will facilitate its acceptation by others. But as a rule a new pronunciation does not become general except after many attempts : it may have arisen many times and have died out again, until finally it finds a fertile soil in which to take firm root. It may not be superfluous to utter a warning against a fallacy which is found now and then in linguistic works : when some Danish or English document, say, of the fifteenth century contains a spelling indicative of a pronunciation which we should call ' modern,' it is hastily concluded that people in those days spoke in that respect exactly as they do now, whatever the usual spelling and the testimony of much later grammarians may indicate to the contrary. But this is far from certain. The more isolated such a spelling is, the greater is the probability that it shows nothing but an individual or even momentary deviation from what was then the common pronunciation—the first swallow ' who found with horror that he'd not brought spring.'

XV.—§ 12. Reaction.

Even those who have no linguistic training will have some apperception of sounds as such, and will notice regular correspondences, and even occasionally exaggerate them, thereby producing those ' hypercorrect ' forms which are of specially frequent occurrence when dialect speakers try to use the ' received standard ' of their country. The psychology of this process is well brought out by B. I. Wheeler, who relates (*Transact. Am. Philol. Ass.* 32. 14, 1901 ; I change his symbols into my own phonetic notation) : " In my own native dialect I pronounced *new* as [nu·]. I have found myself in later years inclined to say [nju·], especially when speaking carefully and particularly in public ; so also [tju·zdi] *Tuesday*. There has developed itself in connexion with these and other words a dual sound-image [u· : ju·] of such validity that whenever [u·] is to be formed after a dental [alveolar] explosive or nasal, the alternative [ju·] is likely to present itself and create the effect of momentary uncertainty. Less frequently than in *new*, *Tuesday*, the [j] intrudes itself in *tune, duty, due, dew, tumour, tube, tutor*, etc. ; but under special provocation I am liable to use it in any of these, and have even caught myself, when in a mood of uttermost precision, passing beyond the bounds of the imitative adoption of the new sound into self-annexed territory, and creating [dju·] *do* and [tju·] *two*." One more instance from America may be given : " In the dialect of Missouri and the neighbouring States, final *a* in such words as *America, Arizona, Nevada* becomes *y—Americy, Arizony, Nevady.* All educated people in that region carefully correct this vulgarism out of their speech ; and many of them carry the correction too far and say *Missoura, praira,* etc." (Sturtevant, LCH 79). Similarly, many Irish people, noticing that refined English has [i·] in many cases where they have [e·] (*tea, sea, please,* etc.) adopt [i·] in these words, and transfer it erroneously to words like *great, pear, bear,* etc. (MEG i. 11. 73) ; they may also, when correcting their own *ar* into *er*, in such words as *learn*, go too far and speak of *derning* a stocking (Joyce, *English as we speak it in Ireland*, 93). Cf. from England such forms as *ruing, certing,* for *ruin, certain.*

From Germany I may mention that Low German speakers desiring to talk High German are apt to say *zeller* instead of *teller*, because High German in many words has *z* for their *t* (*zahl, zahm*, etc.), and that those who in their native speech have *j* for *g* (Berlin, etc., *eine jute jebratene jans ist eine jute jabe jottes*) will sometimes, when trying to talk correctly, say *getzt, gahr* for *jetzt, jahr*.[1]

It will be easily seen that such hypercorrect forms are closely related to those ' spelling pronunciations ' which become frequent when there is much reading of a language whose spelling is not accurately phonetic ; the nineteenth century saw a great number of them, and their number is likely to increase in this century— especially among social upstarts, who are always fond of showing off their new-gained superiority in this and similar ways. But they need not detain us here, as being really foreign to our subject, the natural development of speech sounds. I only wish to point out that many forms which are apparently due to influence from spelling may not have their origin *exclusively* from that source, but may be genuine archaic forms that have been preserved through purely oral tradition by the side of more worn-down forms of the same word. For it must be admitted that two or three forms of the same word may coexist and be used according to the more or less solemn style of utterance employed. Even

---

[1] Even in speaking a foreign language one may unconsciously apply phonetic correspondences ; a countryman of mine thus told me that he once, in his anger at being charged an exorbitant price for something, exclaimed : " Das sind doch *unblaue* preise ! "—coining in the hurry the word *unblaue* for the Danish *ublu* (shameless), because the negative prefix *un-* corresponds to Dan. *u-*, and *au* very often stands in German where Dan. has *u* (*haus = hus*, etc.). On hearing his own words, however, he immediately saw his mistake and burst out laughing

among savages, who are unacquainted with the art of writing,
we are told that archaic forms of speech are often kept up and
remembered as parts of old songs only, or as belonging to solemn
rites, cults, etc.

XV.—§ 13. Sound Laws and Etymological Science.

In this and the preceding chapter I have tried to pass in review
the various circumstances which make for changes in the phonetic
structure of languages. My treatment is far from exhaustive and
may have other defects ; but I want to point out the fact that
nowhere have I found any reason to accept the theory that sound
changes always take place according to rigorous or ' blind ' laws
admitting no exceptions. On the contrary, I have found many
indications that complete consistency is no more to be expected
from human beings in pronunciation than in any other sphere.

It is very often said that if sound laws admitted of exceptions
there would be no possibility of a science of etymology. Thus
Curtius wrote as early as 1858 (as quoted by Oertel 259) : " If
the history of language really showed such sporadic aberrations,
such pathological, wholly irrational phonetic malformations, we
should have to give up all etymologizing. For only that which
is governed by law and reducible to a coherent system can form
the object of scientific investigation ·, whatever is due to chance
may at best be guessed at, but will never yield to scientific inference." In his practice, however, Curtius was not so strict as his
followers. Leskien, one of the recognized leaders of the ' young
grammarians,' says (Deklination, xxvii) : " If exceptions are
admitted at will (abweichungen), it amounts to declaring that
the object of examination, language, is inaccessible to scientific
comprehension." Since then, it has been repeated over and over
again that without strict adherence to phonetic laws etymological
science is a sheer impossibility, and sometimes those who have
doubted the existence of strict laws in phonology have been looked
upon as obscurantists adverse to a scientific treatment of language in general, although, of course, they did not believe that
everything is left to chance or that they were free to put forward
purely arbitrary exceptions.

There are, however, many instances in which it is hardly
possible to deny etymological connexion, though ' the phonetic
laws are not observed.' Is not Gothic azgo with its voiced consonants evidently ' the same word ' as E. ash, G. asche, Dan. aske,
with their voiceless consonants ? G. neffe with short vowel must
nevertheless be identical with MHG. neve, OHG. nevo ; E. pebble
with OE. papol ; rescue with ME. rescowe ; flagon with Fr. flacon,

though each of these words contains deviations from what we find in other cases. It is hard to keep apart two similar forms for 'heart,' one with initial *gh* in Skt. *hrd* and Av. *zered-*, and another with initial *k* in Gr. *kardía, kēr*, Lat. *cor*, Goth. *haírto*, etc. The Greek ordinals *hébdomos, ógdoos* have voiced consonants over against the voiceless combinations in *heptá, oktṓ*, and yet cannot be separated from them. All this goes to show (and many more cases might be instanced) that there are in every language words so similar in sound and signification that they cannot be separated, though they break the 'sound laws': in such cases, where etymologies are too palpable, even the strictest scholars momentarily forget their strictness, maybe with great reluctance and in the secret hope that some day the reason for the deviation may be discovered and the principle thus be maintained.

Instead of exacting strict adherence to sound laws everywhere as the basis of any etymologizing, it seems therefore to be in better agreement with common sense to say: whenever an etymology is not palpably evident, whenever there is some difficulty because the compared words are either too remote in sound or in sense or belong to distant periods of the same language or to remotely related languages, your etymology cannot be reckoned as *proved* unless you have shown by other strictly parallel cases that the sound in question has been treated in exactly the same way in the same language. This, of course, applies more to old than to modern periods, and we thus see that while in living languages accessible to direct observation we do not find sound laws observed without exceptions, and though we must suppose that, on account of the essential similarity of human psychology, conditions have been the same at all periods, it is not unreasonable, in giving etymologies for words from old periods, to act as if sound changes followed strict laws admitting no exceptions; this is simply a matter of proof, and really amounts to this: where the matter is doubtful, we must require a great degree of probability in that field which allows of the simplest and most easily controllable formulas, namely the phonetic field. For here we have comparatively definite phenomena and are consequently able with relative ease to compute the possibilities of change, while this is infinitely more difficult in the field of significations. The possibilities of semantic change are so manifold that the only thing generally required when the change is not obvious is to show some kind of parallel change, which need not even have taken place in the same language or group of languages, while with regard to sounds the corresponding changes must have occurred in the same language and at the same period in order for the evidence to be sufficient to establish the etymology in question.

It would perhaps be best if linguists entirely gave up the habit of speaking about phonetic 'laws,' and instead used some such expression as phonetic formulas or rules. But if we are to keep the word 'law,' we may with some justice think of the use of that word in juridical parlance. When we read such phrases as : this assumption is against phonetic laws, or, phonetic laws do not allow us this or that etymology, or, the writer of some book under review is guilty of many transgressions of established phonetic laws, etc., such expressions cannot help suggesting the idea that phonetic laws resemble paragraphs of some criminal law. We may formulate the principle in something like the following way : If in the etymologies you propose you do not observe these rules, if, for instance, you venture to make Gr. *kaléo* = E. *call* in spite of the fact that Gr. *k* in other words corresponds to E. *h*, then you incur the severest punishment of science, your etymology is rejected, and you yourself are put outside the pale of serious students.

In another respect phonetic laws may be compared with what we might call a Darwinian law in zoology, such as this : the fore-limbs of the common ancestor of mammals have developed into flippers in whales and into hands in apes and men. The similarity between both kinds of laws is not inconsiderable. A microscopic examination of whales, even an exact investigation by means of the eye alone, will reveal innumerable little deviations : no two flippers are exactly alike. And in the same way no two persons speak in exactly the same way. But the fact that we cannot in detail account for each of these *nuances* should not make us doubt that they are developed in a perfectly natural way, in accordance with the great law of causality, nor should we despair of the possibility of scientific treatment, even if some of the flippers and some of the sounds are not exactly what we should expect. A law of fore-limb development can only be deduced through such observation of many flippers as will single out what is typical of whales' flippers, and then a comparison with the typical fore-limbs of their ancestors or of their congeners among existing mammals And in the same way we do not find laws of phonetic development until, after leaving what can be examined as it were microscopically, we go on telescopically to examine languages which are far removed from each other in space or time : then small differences disappear, and we discover nothing but the great lines of a regular evolution which is the outcome of an infinite number of small movements in many different directions.

XV.—§ 14. Conclusion.

It has been one of the leading thoughts in the two chapters devoted to the causes of linguistic change that phonetic changes, to be fully understood, should not be isolated from other changes, for in actual linguistic life we witness a constant interplay of sound and sense. Not only should each sound change be always as far as possible seen in connexion with other sound changes going on in the same period in the same language (as in the great vowel-raising in English), but the effects on the speech material as a whole should in each case be investigated, so as to show what homophones (if any) were produced, and what danger they entailed to the understanding of natural sentences. Sounds should never be isolated from the words in which they occur, nor words from sentences. No hard-and-fast boundary can be drawn between phonetic and non-phonetic changes. The psychological motives for both kinds of changes are the same in many cases, and the way in which both kinds spread through imitation is absolutely identical : what was said on this subject above (§ 11) applies without the least qualification to any linguistic change, whether in sounds, in grammatical forms, in syntax, in the signi- fication of words, or in the adoption of new words and dropping of old ones.

We shall here finally very briefly consider something which plays a certain part in the development of language, but which has not been adequately dealt with in what precedes, namely, the desire to play with language. We have already met with the effects of playfulness in one of the chapters devoted to children (p. 148) : here we shall see that the same tendency is also powerful in the language of grown-up people, though most among young people. There is a certain exuberance which will not rest con- tented with traditional expressions, but finds amusement in the creation and propagation of new words and in attaching new meanings to old words : this is the exact opposite of that linguistic poverty which we found was at the bottom of such minimum languages as Pidgin-English. We find it in the wealth of pet- names which lovers have for each other and mothers for their children, in the nicknames of schoolboys and of ' pals ' of later life, as well as in the perversions of ordinary words which at times become the fashion among small sets of people who are constantly thrown together and have plenty of spare time ; cf. also the ' little language ' of Swift and Stella. Most of these forms of speech have a narrow range and have only an ephemeral existence, but in the world of *slang* the same tendencies are constantly at work.

Slang words are often confused with vulgarisms, though the

two things are really different. The vulgar tongue is a class dialect, and a vulgarism is an element of the normal speech of low-class people, just as ordinary dialect words are elements of the natural speech of peasants in one particular district; slang words, on the other hand, are words used in conscious contrast to the natural or normal speech: they can be found in all classes of society in certain moods, and on certain occasions when a speaker wants to avoid the natural or normal word because he thinks it too flat or uninteresting and wants to achieve a different effect by breaking loose from the ordinary expression. A vulgarism is what will present itself at once to the mind of a person belonging to one particular class; a slang word is something that is wilfully substituted for the first word that will present itself. The distinction will perhaps appear most clearly in the case of grammar : if a man says *them boys* instead of *those boys*, or *knowed* instead of *knew*, these are the normal forms of his language, and he knows no better, but the educated man looks down upon these forms as vulgar. Inversely, an educated man may amuse himself now and then by using forms which he perfectly well knows are not the received forms, thus *wunk* from *wink, collode* from *collide, praught* from *preach* (on the analogy of *taught*) ; " We handshook and *candlestuck*, as somebody said, and went to bed " (H. James). But, of course, slang is more productive in the lexical than in the grammatical portion of language. And there is something that makes it difficult in practice always to keep slang and vulgar speech apart, namely, that when a person wants to leave the beaten path of normal language he is not always particular as to the source whence he takes his unusual words, and he may therefore sometimes take a vulgar word and raise it to the dignity of a slang word.

A slang word is at first individual, but may through imitation become fashionable in certain sets ; after some time it may either be accepted by everybody as part of the normal language, or else, more frequently, be so hackneyed that no one finds pleasure in using it any longer.

Slang words may first be words from the ordinary language used in a different sense, generally metaphorically. Sometimes we meet with the same figurative expression in the slang of various countries, as when the ' head ' is termed *the upper story* (*upper loft, upper works*) in English, *everste etage* in Danish, and *oberstübchen* in German ; more often different images are chosen in different languages, as when for the same idea we have *nut* or *chump* in English and *pære* (' pear ') in Danish, *coco* or *ciboule* (or *boule*) in French. Slang words of this character may in some instances give rise to expressions the origin of which is totally forgotten. In old slang there is an expression for the tongue, *the red rag* ; this is shortened into *the rag*, and I suspect that the verb *to rag*, ' to scold, rate, talk severely to ' ("of obscure origin," NED), is simply from this substantive (cf. *to jaw*).

Secondly, slang words may be words of the normal language used in their ordinary signification, but more or less modified in regard to form. Thus we have many shortened forms, *exam, quad, pub*, for *examination, quadrangle, public-house*, etc. Not unfrequently the shortening process is combined with an extension, some ending being more or less arbitrarily substituted for the latter part of the word, as when *football* becomes *footer*, and *Rugby football* and *Association football* become *Rugger* and *Socker*, or when at Cambridge a freshman is called a *fresher* and a bedmaker a *bedder*.

In schoolboys' slang (Harrow) there is an ending *-agger* which may be added instead of the latter part of any word ; about 1885 Prince Albert Victor when at Cambridge was nicknamed *the Pragger* ; an Agnostic was called a *Nogger*, etc. I strongly suspect that the word *swagger* is formed in the same way from *swashbuckler*. Another schoolboys' ending is *-g* : *fog, seg, lag*, for ' first, second, last,' *gag* at Winchester for ' gathering ' (a special kind of Latin exercise). Charles Lamb mentions from Christ's Hospital *crug* for ' a quarter of a loaf,' evidently from *crust* ; *sog* = sovereign, *snag* = snail (old), *swig* = swill ; words like *fag, peg away*, and others are perhaps to be explained from the same tendency. Arnold Bennett in one of his books says of a schoolboy that his vocabulary comprised an extraordinary number of words ending in *gs* : *foggs, seggs*, for first, second, etc. It is interesting to note that in French argot there are similar endings added to more or less mutilated words : *-aque, -èque, -oque* (Sainéan, *L'Argot ancien*, 1907, 50 and especially 57).

There is also a peculiar class of roundabout expressions in which the speaker avoids the regular word, but hints at it in a covert way by using some other word, generally a proper name, which bears a resemblance to it or is derived from it, really or seemingly. Instead of saying ' I want to go to bed,' he will say, ' I am for Bedfordshire,' or in German ' Ich gehe nach Bethlehem ' or ' nach Bettingen,' in Danish ' gå til Slumstrup, Sovstrup, Hvilsted.' Thus also ' send a person to Birching-lane,' i.e. to whip him, ' he has been at Hammersmith,' i.e. has been beaten, thrashed ; ' you are on the highway to Needham,' i.e. on the high-road to poverty, etc. (Cf. my paper on " Punning or Allusive Phrases " in *Nord. Tidsskr. f. Fil.* 3 r. 9. 66.)

The language of poetry is closely related to slang, in so far as both strive to avoid commonplace and everyday expressions. The difference is that where slang looks only for the striking or unexpected expression, and therefore often is merely eccentric or funny (sometimes only would-be comic), poetry looks higher and craves abiding beauty—beauty in thought as well as beauty in form, the latter obtained, among other things, by rhythm, alliteration, rime, and harmonious variety of vowel sounds.

In some countries these forms tend to become stereotyped, and then may to some extent kill the poetic spirit, poetry becoming artificiality instead of art; the later Skaldic poetry may serve as an illustration. Where there is a strong literary tradition—and that may be found even where there is no written literature—veneration for the old literature handed down from one's ancestors will often lead to a certain fossilization of the literary language, which becomes a shrine of archaic expressions that no one uses naturally or can master without great labour. If this state of things persists for centuries, it results in a cleavage between the spoken and the written language which cannot but have the most disastrous effects on all higher education: the conditions prevailing nowadays in Greece and in Southern India may serve as a warning. Space forbids me more than a bare mention of this topic, which would deserve a much fuller treatment; for details I may refer to K. Krumbacher, *Das Problem der neugriechischen Schriftsprache*, Munich, 1902 (for the other side of the case see G. N. Hatzidakis, *Die Sprachfrage in Griechenland*, Athens, 1905) and G. V. Ramamurti, *A Memorandum on Modern Telugu*, Madras, 1913.

BOOK IV

THE DEVELOPMENT OF LANGUAGE

CHAPTER XVI

ETYMOLOGY

XVI.—§ 1. Achievements.

FEW things have been more often quoted in works on linguistics
than Voltaire's *mot* that in etymology vowels count for nothing
and consonants for very little. But it is now said just as often
that the satire might be justly levelled at the pseudo-scientific
etymology of the eighteenth century, but has no application to our
own times, in which etymology knows how to deal with both
vowels and consonants, and—it should be added, though it is
often forgotten—with the meanings of words. One often comes
across outbursts of joy and pride in the achievements of modern
etymological science, like the following, which is quoted here *instar
omnium* : " Nowadays etymology has got past the period of more
or less ' happy thoughts ' (glücklichen einfälle) and has developed
into a science in which, exactly as in any other science, serious
persevering work must lead to reliable results " (H. Schröder,
Ablautstudien, 1910, X ; cf. above, Max Müller and Whitney, p. 89).

There is no denying that much has been achieved, but it is
equally true that a skeptical mind cannot fail to be struck with
the uncertainty of many proposed explanations : very often
scholars have not got beyond ' happy thoughts,' many of which
have not even been happy enough to have been accepted by
anybody except their first perpetrators. From English alone,
which for twelve hundred years has had an abundant written
literature, and which has been studied by many eminent linguists,
who have had many sister-languages with which to compare it, it would be an easy matter to compile a long list of
words, well-known words of everyday occurrence, which etymologists have had to give up as beyond their powers of solution
(*fit, put, pull, cut, rouse, pun, fun, job*). And equally perplexing
are many words now current all over Europe, some of them
comparatively recent and yet completely enigmatic : *race, baron,
baroque, rococo, zinc.*

XVI.—§ 2. Doubtful Cases.

Or let us take a word of that class which forms the staple subject of etymological disquisitions, one in which the semantic side is literally as clear as sunshine, namely the word for 'sun. Here we have, among others, the following forms : (1) *sun*, OE. *sunne*, Goth. *sunno*; (2) Dan., Lat. *sol*, Goth. *sauil*, Gr. *hélios*; (3) OE. *sigel*, *sœgl*, Goth. *sugil*; (4) OSlav. *slŭnĭce*, Russ. *solnce* (now with mute *l*). That these forms are related cannot be doubted, but their mutual relation, and their relation to Gr. *seléné*, which means 'moon,' and to OE. *swegel* 'sky,' have never been cleared up. Holthausen derives *sunno* from the verb *sinnan* 'go' and OE. *sigel* from the verb *sigan* 'descend, go down'—but is it really probable that our ancestors should have thought of the sun primarily as the one that goes, or that sets ? The word *south* (orig. **sunþ*; the *n* as in OHG. *sund* is still kept in Dan. *sønden*) is generally explained as connected with *sun*, and the meaning 'sunny side' is perfectly natural; but now H. Schröder thinks that it is derived from a word meaning 'right' (OE. *swiðre*, orig. 'stronger,' a comparative of the adj. found in G. *geschwind*), and he says that the south is to the right when you look at the sun at sunrise—which is perfectly true, but why should people have thought of the south as being to the right when they wanted to speak of it in the afternoon or evening ?

Let me take one more example to show that our present methods, or perhaps our present data, sometimes leave us completely in the lurch with regard to the most ordinary words. We have a series of words which may all, without any formal difficulties, be referred to a root-form *seqw-*. Their significations are, respectively—

(1) 'say,' E. *say*, OE. *secgan*, ON. *segja*, G. *sagen*, Lith. *sakýti*. To this is referred Gr. *énnepe*, *enispein*, Lat. *inseque* and possibly *inquam*.

(2) 'show, point out,' OSlav. *sočiti*, Lat. *signum*.

(3) 'see,' E. *see*, OE. *seon*, Goth. *saihwan*, G. *sehen*, etc.

(4) 'follow,' Lat. *sequor*, Gr. *hépomai*, Skr. *sácate*. Here belongs Lat. *socius*, OE. *secg* 'man,' orig. 'follower.'

Now, are these four groups 'etymologically identical' ? Opinions differ widely, as may be seen from C. D. Buck, "Words of Speaking and Saying" (*Am. Journ. of Philol.* 36. 128, 1915). They may be thus tabulated, a comma meaning supposed identity and a dash the opposite :

1, 2–3, 4 Kluge, Falk, **Torp**.

1, 2, 3–4 Brugmann.

1, 2, 3, 4 Wood, Buck.[1]

---

[1] With regard to Lat. *signum* it should be noted that it is by others explained as coming from Lat. *secare* and as meaning a notch.

For the transition in meaning from ' see ' to ' say　we are referred to such words as *observe, notice,* G. *bemerkung,* while in G. *anweisen,* and still more in Lat. *dico,* there is a similar transition from ' show ' to ' say.' Wood derives the signification ' follow ' from ' point out,' through ' show, guide, attend.' With regard to the relation between 3 and 4, it has often been said that to see is to follow with the eyes. In short, it is possible, if you take some little pains, to discover notional ties between all four groups which may not be so very much looser than those between other words which everybody thinks related. And yet ? I cannot see that the knowledge we have at present enables us, or can enable us, to do more than leave the mutual relation of these groups an open question. One man's guess is just as good as another's, or one man's yes as another man's no—if the connexion of these words is ' science,' it is, if I may borrow an expression from the old archæologist Samuel Pegge, *scientia ad libitum.* Personal predilection and individual taste have not been ousted from etymological research to the extent many scholars would have us believe.

Or we may perhaps say that among the etymologies found in dictionaries and linguistic journals some are solid and firm as rocks, but others are liquid and fluctuate like the sea ; and finally not a few are in a gaseous state and blow here and there as the wind listeth. Some of them are no better than poisonous gases, from which may Heaven preserve us ![1]

XVI.—§ 3. Facts, not Fancies.

As early as 1867 Michel Bréal, in an excellent article (reprinted in M 267 ff.), called attention to the dangers resulting from the general tendency of comparative linguists to " jump intermediate steps in order at once to mount to the earliest stages of the language," but his warning has not taken effect, so that etymologists in dealing with a word found only in comparatively recent times will often try to reconstruct what might have been its Proto-Aryan form and compare that with some word found in some other language. Thus, Falk and Torp refer G. *krieg* to an Aryan primitive form **grêigho-, *grîgho-,* which is compared with Irish

---

[1] It is, of course, impossible to say how great a proportion of the etymologies given in dictionaries should strictly be classed under each of the following heads : (1) certain, (2) probable, (3) possible, (4) improbable, (5) impossible—but I am afraid the first two classes would be the least numerous. Meillet (Gr 59) has some excellent remarks to the same effect ; according to him, " pour une étymologie sûre, les dictionnaires en offrent plus de dix qui sont douteuses et dont, en appliquant une méthode rigoureuse, on ne saurait faire la preuve."

brig ' force.' But the German word is not found in use till the middle period ; it is peculiar to German and unknown in related languages (for the Scandinavian and probably also the Dutch words are later loans from Germany). These writers do not take into account how improbable it is that such a word, if it were really an old traditional word for this fundamental idea, should never once have been recorded in any of the old documents of the whole of our family of languages. What should we think of the man who would refer *boche*, the French nickname for ' German ' which became current in 1914, and before that time had only been used for a few years and known to a few people only, to a Proto-Aryan root-form ? Yet the method in both cases is identical ; it presupposes what no one can guarantee, that the words in question are of those which trot along the royal road of language for century after century without a single side-jump, semantic or phonetic. Such words are the favourites of linguists because they have always behaved themselves since the days of Noah ; but others are full of the most unexpected pranks, which no scientific ingenuity can discover if we do not happen to know the historical facts. Think of *grog*, for example. Admiral Vernon, known to sailors by the nickname of " Old Grog " because he wore a cloak of grogram (this, by the way, from Fr. *gros grain*), in 1740 ordered a mixture of rum and water to be served out instead of pure rum, and the name was transferred from the person to the drink. If it be objected that such leaps are found only in slang, the answer is that slang words very often become recognized after some time, and who knows but that may have been the case with *krieg* just as well as with many a recent word ?

At any rate, facts weigh more than fancies, and whoever wants to establish the etymology of a word must first ascertain all the historical facts available with regard to the place and time of its rise, its earliest signification and syntactic construction, its diffusion, the synonyms it has ousted, etc. Thus, and thus only, can he hope to rise above loose conjectures. Here the great historical dictionaries, above all the Oxford *New English Dictionary*, render invaluable service. And let me mention one model article outside these dictionaries, in which Hermann Möller has in my opinion given a satisfactory solution of the riddle of G. *ganz* : he explains it as a loan from Slav *konici* ' end,' used especially adverbially (perhaps with a preposition in the form *v-konec* or *v-konc*) ' to the end, completely ' ; Slav *c* = G. *z*, Slav *k* pronounced essentially as South G. *g* ; the gradual spreading and various significations and derived forms are accounted for with very great learning (*Zs. f. D. Alt.* 36. 326 ff.). It is curious that this article should have been generally overlooked or neglected, though the writer seems to have met all the legitimate requirements of a scientific etymology.

XVI.—§ 4. Hope.

I have endeavoured to fulfil these requirements in the new explanation I have given of the word *hope* (Dan. *hâbe*, Swed. *hoppas*, G. *hoffen*), now used in all Gothonic tongues in exactly the same signification. Etymologists are at variance about this word. Kluge connects it with the OE. noun *hyht*, and from that form infers that Gothonic **hopôn* stands for **huqôn*, from an Aryan root *kug*; he says that a connexion with Lat. *cupio* is scarcely possible. Walde likewise rejects connexion between *cupio* and either *hope* or Goth. *hugjan*. To Falk and Torp *hope* has probably nothing to do with *hyht*, but probably with *cupio*, which is derived from a root **kup = kvap*, found in Lat. *vapor* ' steam,' and with a secondary form **kub*, in *hope*, and **kvab* in Goth. *af-hwapjan* ' choke '—a wonderful medley of significations. H. Möller (*Indoeur.-Semit. sammenlignende Glossar* 63), in accordance with his usual method, establishes an Aryo-Semitic root **k̂-u̯-*, meaning ' ardere ' and transferred to ' ardere amore, cupiditate, desiderio,' the root being extended with *b-* : *p-* in *hope* and *cupio*, with *gh-* in Goth. *hugs*, and with *ĝ-* in OE. *hyht*. Surely a typical example of the perplexity of our etymologists, who disagree in everything except just in the one thing which seems to me extremely doubtful, that *hope* with the present spiritual signification goes back to common Aryan. Now, what are the real facts of the matter ? Simply these, that the word *hope* turns up at a comparatively late date in historical times at one particular spot, and from there it gradually spreads to the neighbouring countries. In Denmark (*hâb, hâbe*) and in Sweden (*hopp, hoppas*) it is first found late in the Middle Ages as a religious loan from Low German *hope, hopen*. High German *hoffen* is found very rarely about 1150, but does not become common till a hundred years later ; it is undoubtedly taken (with sound substitution) from Low German and moves in Germany from north to south. Old Saxon has the subst. *tō-hopa*, which has probably come from OE., where we have the same form for the subst., *tō-hopa*. This is pretty common in religious prose, but in poetry it is found only once (Boet.)—a certain indication that the word is recent. The subst. without *tō* is comparatively late (Ælfric, ab. 1000). The verb is found in rare instances about a hundred years earlier, but does not become common till later. Now, it is important to notice that the verb in the old period never takes a direct object, but is always connected with the preposition *tō* (compare the subst.), even in modern usage we have *to hope to, for, in.* Similarly in G., where the phrase was *auf etwas hoffen* ; later the verb took a genitive, then a pronoun in the accusative, and finally an ordinary object ; in biblical language we find also *zu gott hoffen.* Now, I would connect our word with the form *hopu,* found twice as part of a compound in *Beowulf* (450 and 764), where ' refuge ' gives good sense : *hopan to,* then, is to ' take one's refuge to,' and *to-hopa* ' refuge.' This verb I take to be at first identical with *hop* (the only OE. instance I know of this is Ælfric, *Hom.* 1. 202 : *hoppode ongean his drihten*). We have also one instance of a verb *onhupian* (*Cura Past.* 441) ' draw back, recoil,' which agrees with ON. *hopa* ' move backwards' (to the quotations in Fritzner may be added Laxd. 49, 15, þeir Osvígssynir hopudu undan).[1] The original meaning seems to have been ' bend, curb, bow, stoop,' either in order to leap, or to flee, from something bad, or towards something good ; cf. the subst. *hip,* OE. *hype,* Goth. *hups,* Dan. *hofte,* G. *hüfte,* Lat. *cubitus,* etc. (Holthausen, *Anglia Beibl.,* 1904, 350, deals with these words, but does not connect them with *hop, -hopu,* or *hope.*) The transition from bodily movement to the spiritual ' hope ' may have been favoured by the existence of the verb OE. *hogian* ' think,' but is not in itself more difficult than with, e.g., Lat. *ex(s)ultare* ' leap up, rejoice,' or Dan. *lide på* ' lean to, confide in, trust,' *tillid* ' confidence, reliance ' ; and a new word for ' hope ' was required because the old *wen* (Goth. *wens*), vb. *wenan,* had at an early age acquired a more general meaning ' opinion, probability,' vb. ' suppose, imagine.' The difficulty that the word for ' hope ' has single or short *p* (in Swed., however, *pp*), while *hop,* OE. *hoppian,* has double or long *p,* is no serious hindrance to our etymology, because the gemination may easily be accounted for on the principle mentioned below (Ch. XX § 9), that is, as giving a more vivid expression of the rapid action.

XVI.—§ 5. Requirements.

It is, of course, impossible to determine once for all by hard-and-fast rules how great the correspondence must be for us to recognize two words as ' etymologically identical,' nor to say to which of the two sides, the phonetic and the semantic, we should attach the greater importance. With the rise of historical phonology the tendency has been to require exact correspondence in the former respect, and in semantics to be content with more or less easily found parallels. One example will show how

---

[1] **Westphalian also has** *hoppen* ' zurückweichen.' ESt. 54. 88

particular many scholars are in matters of sound. The word *nut*
(OE. *hnutu*, G. *nuss*, ON. *hnot*, Dan. *nød*) is by Paul declared " not
related to Lat. *nux* " and by Kluge " neither originally akin with
nor borrowed from Lat. *nux*," while the NED does not even mention
nux and thus must think it quite impossible to connect it with
the English word. We have here in two related languages two
words resembling each other not only in sound, but in stem-
formation and gender, and possessing exactly the same signification,
which is as concrete and definite as possible. And yet we are
bidden to keep them asunder ! Fortunately I am not the first
to protest against such barbarity : H. Pedersen (KZ n.f. 12. 251)
explains both words from **dnuk-*, which by metathesis has
become **knud-*, while Falk and Torp as well as Walde thin'
the latter form the original one, which in Latin has been
shifted into **dnuk-*. Which of these views is correct (both may
be wrong) is of less importance than the victory of common
sense over phonological pedantry.

There are two explanations which have had very often to do
duty where the phonological correspondence is not exact, namely
root-variation (root-expansion with determinatives) and apophony
(ablaut). Of the former Uhlenbeck (PBB 30. 252) says : " The
theory of root determinatives no doubt contains a kernel of truth,
but it has only been fatal to etymological science, as it has drawn
the attention from real correspondences between well-substantiated
words to delusive similarities between hypothetical abstractions."
Apophony inspires more confidence, and in many cases offers fully
reliable explanations ; but this principle, too, has been often
abused, and it is difficult to find its true limitations. Many special
applications of it appear questionable ; thus, when G. *stumm*, Dan.
stum, is explained as an apophonic form of the adj. *stam*, Goth.
stamms, from which we have the verb *stammer*, G. *stammeln*, Dan.
stamme : is it really probable that the designation of muteness
should be taken from the word for stammering ? This appears
especially improbable when we consider that at the time when
the new word *stumm* made its appearance there was already another
word for ' mute,' namely *dumm*, *dumb*, the word which has been
preserved in English. I therefore propose a new etymology :
stumm is a blending of the two synonyms *still(e)* and *dum(b)*, made
up of the beginning of the one and the ending of the other word ;
through adopting the initial *st-* the word was also associated with
stump, and we get an exact correspondence between *dumm*, *dum*,
stumm, *stum*, applied to persons, and *dumpf*, *stumpf*, Dan. *dump*,
stump, applied to things. Note that in those languages (G., Dan.)
in which the new word *stum(m)* was used, the unchanged *dum(m)*
was free to develop the new sense ' stupid ' (or was the creation

of *stum* occasioned by the old word tending already to acquire this secondary meaning ?), while *dumb* in English stuck to the old signification.

XVI.—§ 6. Blendings.

Blendings of synonyms play a much greater rôle in the development of language than is generally recognized. Many instances may be heard in everyday life, most of them being immediately corrected by the speaker (see above, XV § 4), but these momentary lapses cannot be separated from other instances which are of more permanent value because they are so natural that they will occur over and over again until speakers will hardly feel the blend as anything else than an ordinary word. M. Bloomfield (IF 4. 71) says that he has been many years conscious of an irrepressible desire to assimilate the two verbs *quench* and *squelch* in both directions by forming *squench* and *quelch*, and he has found the former word in a negro story by Page. The expression ' irrepressible desire ' struck me on reading this, for I have myself in my Danish speech the same feeling whenever I am to speak of tending a patient, for I nearly always say *plasse* as a result of wavering between *pleje* [*plaiə*] and *passe*. Many examples may be found in G. A. Bergström, *On Blendings of Synonymous or Cognate Expressions in English*, Lund, 1906, and Louise Pound, *Blends, Their Relation to English Word Formation*, Heidelberg, 1914. But neither of these two writers has seen the full extent of this principle of formation, which explains many words of greater importance than those nonce words which are found so plentifully in Miss Pound's paper. Let me give some examples, some of them new, some already found by others :

> *blot* = *bl*emish, *black* + *spot*, p*lot*, do*t* ; there is also an obsolete sp*lot*.
> *blunt* = *bl*ind + st*unt*.
> *crouch* = *cr*inge, *crook*, *crawl*, †*crouk* + *couch*.
> *flush* = *fl*ash + *blush*.
> *frush* = *fr*og + th*rush* (all three names of the same disease in a horse's foot).
> *glaze* (Shakespeare) = *gl*are + *gaze*.
> *good-bye* = *good*-night, *good*-morning + *godbye* (God be with ye).
> *knoll* = *kn*ell + *toll*.
> *scroll* = *scr*ow + *roll*.
> *slash* = *sl*ay, *sl*ing, *sl*at + *gash*, da*sh.*
> *slender* = *sl*ight (*sl*im) + *tender*.

Such blends **are** especially frequent in words expressive of sounds or in some other way symbolical, as, for instance :

flurry = *fl*ing, *fl*ow and many other *fl*-words + *hurry* (note also sc*urry*).

gruff = *gru*m, *gri*m + *rough.*

slide = *sl*ip + *glide.*

troll = *tri*ll + *roll* (in some senses perhaps rather from *t*read, *tr*undle + *roll*).

twirl = *tw*ist + *whirl.*

In slang blends abound, e.g. :

tosh (Harrow) = *t*ub + wa*sh.* (Sometimes explained as *toe-wash.*)

blarmed = *bl*amed, *bl*essed **and** other *bl*-words + d*arned* (damned).

be danged = *da*mned + *h*anged.

I swow = *sw*ear + v*ow.*

brunch = *br*eakfast + l*unch* (so also, though more rarely *brupper* (. . . + s*upper*), *tunch* (tea + l*unch*), *tupper* = *t*ea + s*upper*).[1]

XVI.—§ 7. Echo-words.

Most etymologists are very reluctant to admit echoism : thus Diez rejects onomatopœic origin of It. *pisciare*, Fr. *pisser*—an echo-word if ever there was one—and says, " One can easily go too far in supposing onomatopœia : as a rule it is more advisable to build on existing words " ; this he does by deriving this verb from a non-existing **pipisare*, *pipsare*, from *pipa* 'pipe, tube.' Falk and Torp refer *dump* (Dan. *dumpe*) to Swed. *dimpa*, a Gothonic root *demp*, supposed to be an extension of an Aryan root *dhen* : thus they are too deaf to hear the sound of the heavy fall expressed by *um(p)*, cf. Dan. *bumpe, bums, plumpe, skumpe, jumpe*, and similar words in other languages.

It may be fancy, but I think I hear the same sound in Lat. *plumbum*, which I take to mean at first not the metal, but the plummet that was dumped or plumped into the water and was denominated from the sound ; as this was generally made of lead, the word came to be used for the metal. Most etymologists take it for granted that *plumbum* is a loan-word, some being honest enough to confess that they do not know from what language, while others without the least scruple or hesitation say that it was taken from Iberian : our ignorance of that language is so

[1] Lewis Carrol's 'portmanteau words' are of course, famous,

deep that no one can enter an expert's protest against such a supposition.[1] But if my hypothesis is right, the words *plummet* (from OFr. *plommet*, a diminutive of *plomb*) as well as the verb Fr. *plonger*, whence E. *plunge*, from Lat. **plumbicare*, are not only derivatives from *plumbum* (the only thing mentioned by other scholars), but also echo-words, and they, or at any rate the verb, must to a great extent owe their diffusion to their felicitously symbolic sound. In a novel I find : " Plump went the lead "— showing how this sound is still found adequate to express the falling of the lead in sounding. The NED says under the verb *plump* : " Some have compared L. *plumbare* . . . to throw the lead-line . . . but the approach of form between *plombar* and the LG. *plump-plomp* group seems merely fortuitous " (!). I see sound symbolism in *all* the words *plump*, while the NED will only allow it in the most obvious cases. From the sound of a body plumping into the water we have interesting developments in the adverb, as in the following quotations : I said, *plump* out, that I couldn't stand any more of it (Bernard Shaw) | The famous diatribe against Jesuitism points *plumb* in the same direction (Morley) | fall *plum* into the jaws of certain critics (Swift) | Nollie was a *plumb* little idiot (Galsworthy). In the last sense ' entirely ' it is especially frequent in America, e.g. They lost their senses, *plumb* lost their senses (Churchill) | she's *plum* crazy, it's *plum* bad, etc. Related words for fall, etc., are *plop, plout, plunk, plounce*. Much might also be said in this connexion of various *pop* and *bob* words, but I shall refrain.

XVI.—§ 8. Some Conjunctions.

Sometimes obviously correct etymologies yet leave some psychological points unexplained. One of my pet theories concerns some adversative conjunctions. Lat. *sed* has been supplanted by *magis* : It. *ma*, Sp. *mas*, Fr. *mais*. The transition is easily accounted for ; from ' more ' it is no far cry to ' rather ' (cf. G. *vielmehr*), which can readily be employed to correct or gainsay what has just been said. The Scandinavian word for ' but ' is *men*, which came into use in the fifteenth century and is explained as a blending

---

[1] Speculation has been rife, but without any generally accepted results, as to the relation between *plumbum* and words for the same metal in cognate languages : Gr. *molibos, molubdos* and similar forms, Ir. *luaide*, E. *lead* (G. *lot*, ' plummet, half an ounce '), Scand. *bly*, OSlav. *olovo*, OPruss. *alwis* ; see Curtius, Prellwitz, Boisacq, Hirt Idg. 686, Schrader *Sprachvergl. u. Urgesch.*, 3d. ed., ii. 1. 95 ; Herm. Möller, *Sml. Glossar* 87, says that *molibos* and *plumbum* are extensions of the root *m-l* ' mollis esse ' and explains the difference between the initial sounds by referring to *multum* : comp. *plus*—certainly most ingenious, but not convincing. Some of these words may originally have been echo-words for the plumping plummet.

of *meden* in its shortened form *men* (now *mens*) ' while ' and Low
German *men* ' but,' which stands for older *niwan*, from the negative
ni and *wan* ' wanting ' ; the meaning has developed through that
of ' except ' and the sound is easily understood as an instance of
assimilation. The same phonetic development is found in Dutch
maar, OFris. *mar*, from *en ware* ' were not,' the same combination
which has yielded G. *nur*. Thus we have four different ways of
getting to expressions for ' but,' none of which presents the least
difficulty to those familiar with the semantic ways of words. But
why did these various nations seize on new words ? Weren't the
old ones good enough ?

Here I must call attention to two features that are common
to these new conjunctions, first their syntactic position, which
is invariably in the beginning of the sentence, while such synonymous words as Lat. *autem* and G. *aber* may be placed after one
or more words ; then their phonetic agreement in one point : *magis*,
men, *maar* all begin with *m*. Now, both these features are found
in two words for ' but,' about whose etymological origin I can
find no information, Finnic *mutta* and Santal *menkhan*, as well as
in *me*, which is used in the *Ancrene Riwle* and a few other early
Middle English texts and has been dubiously connected with the
Scandinavian (and French ?) word. How are we to explain these
curious coincidences ? I think by the nature of the sound [m],
which is produced when the lips are closed while the tongue rests
passively and the soft palate is lowered so as to allow air to escape
through the nostrils—in short, the position which is typical of
anybody who is quietly thinking over matters without as yet
saying anything, with the sole difference that in his case the vocal
chords are passive, while they are made to vibrate to bring forth
an *m*.

Now, it very often happens that a man wants to say something,
but has not yet made up his mind as to *what* to say ; and in this
moment of hesitation, while thoughts are in the process of conception, the lungs and vocal chords will often be prematurely
set going, and the result is [m] (sometimes preceded by the corresponding voiceless sound), often written *hm* or *h'm*, which thus
becomes the interjection of an unshaped contradiction. Not
infrequently this [m] precedes a real word ; thus *M'yes* (written
in this way by Shaw, *Misalliance* 154, and Merrick, *Conrad* 179)
and Dan. *mja*, to mark a hesitating consent.

This will make it clear why words beginning with *m* are so
often chosen as adversative conjunctions : people begin with this
sound and go on with some word that gives good sense and which
happens to begin with *m* : *mais*, *maar*. The Dan. *men* in the
mouth of some early speakers is probably this [m], sliding into

the old conjunction *en*, just as *myes* is *m* + *yes* ; while other original users of *men* may have been thinking of *men* = *meden*, and others again of Low German *men* : these three etymologies are not mutually destructive, for all three origins may have concurrently contributed to the popularity of *men*. Modern Greek and Serbian *ma* are generally explained as direct loans from Italian, but may be indigenous, as may also dialectal Rumanian *ma* in the same sense, for in the hesitating [m] as the initial sound of objections we have one of those touches of nature which make the whole world kin.[1]

XVI.—§ 9. Object of Etymology.

What is the object of etymological science ? " To determine the true signification of a word," answers one of the masters of etymological research (Walde, *Lat. et. Wörterb.* xi). But surely in most cases that can be achieved without the help of etymology. We know the true sense of hundreds of words about the etymology of which we are in complete ignorance, and we should know exactly what the word *grog* means, even if the tradition of its origin had been accidentally lost. Many people still believe that an account of the origin of a name throws some light on the essence of the thing it stands for ; when they want to define say ' religion ' or ' civilization,' they start by stating the (real or supposed) origin of the name—but surely that is superstition, though the first framers of the name ' etymology ' (from Gr. *etumon* ' true ') must have had the same idea in their heads. Etymology tells us nothing about the things, nor even about the present meaning of a word, but only about the way in which a word has come into existence. At best, it tells us not what *is* true, but what *has been* true.

The overestimation of etymology is largely attributable to the " conviction that there can be nothing in language that had not an intelligible purpose, that there is nothing that is now irregular that was not at first regular, nothing irrational that was not originally rational " (Max Müller)—a conviction which is still found to underlie many utterances about linguistic matters, but which readers of the present volume will have seen is erroneous in many ways. On the whole, Max Müller naïvely gives expression to what is unconsciously at the back of much that is said and believed about language ; thus, when he says (L 1. 44) : " I must ask you at present to take it for granted that everything in language had originally a meaning. As language can have no other object but to express our meaning, it might seem to follow almost by

[1] I have discussed this more in detail and added other *m*-words of a somewhat related character in *Studier tillegnade E. Tegnér*, 1918, p. 49 ff.

necessity that language should contain neither more nor less than what is required for that purpose." Yes, so it would if language had been constructed by an omniscient and omnipotent being, but as it was developed by imperfect human beings, there is every possibility of their having failed to achieve their purpose and having done either more or less than was required to express their meaning. It would be wrong to say that language (i.e. speaking man) created first what was strictly necessary, and afterwards what might be considered superfluous ; but it would be equally wrong to say that linguistic luxuries were always created before necessaries ; yet that view would probably be nearer the truth than the former. Much of what in former ages was felt to be necessary to express thoughts was afterwards felt as pedantic crisscross and gradually eliminated ; but at all times many things have been found in language that can never have been anything else but superfluous, exactly as many people use a great many superfluous gestures which are not in the least significant and in no way assist the comprehension of their intentions, but which they somehow feel an impulse to perform. In language, as in life generally, we have too little in some respects, and too much in others.

XVI.—§ 10. Reconstruction.

Kluge somewhere (PBB 37. 479, 1911) says that the establishment of the common Aryan language is the chief task of our modern science of linguistics (to my mind it can never be more than a fragment of that task, which must be to understand the nature of language), and he thinks optimistically that " reconstructions with their reliable methods have taken so firm root that we are convinced that we know the common Aryan *grundsprache* just as thoroughly as any language that is more or less authenticated through literature." This is a palpable exaggeration, for no one nowadays has the courage of Schleicher to print even the smallest fable in Proto-Aryan, and if by some miraculous accident we were to find a text written in that language we may be sure it would puzzle us just as much as Tokharian does.

Reconstruction has two sides, an outer and an inner. With regard to sounds, it seems to me that very often the masters of linguistics treat us to reconstructed forms that are little short of impossible. This is not the place to give a detailed criticism of the famous theory of ' nasalis sonans,' but I hope elsewhere to be able to state why I think this theory a disfiguring excrescence on linguistic science : no one has ever been able to find in any existing language such forms as *mnto* with stressed syllabic

[n], given as the old form of our word *mouth* (Falk and Torp even give *stmnto* in order to connect the word with Gr. *stóma*), or as *dkmtóm* (whence Lat. *centum*, etc.) or *bhrghntįes* or *gumskete* (Brugmann). Not only are these forms phonetically impossible, but the theory fails to explain the transitions to the forms actually existing in real languages, and everything is much easier if we assume forms like [ʌm, ʌn] with some vowel like that of E *un-*. The use in Proto-Aryan reconstructions of non-syllabic *i* and *u* also in some respects invites criticism, but it will be better to treat these questions in a special paper.

Semantic reconstruction calls for little comment here. It is evident from the nature of the subject that no such strict rules can be given in this domain as in the domain of sound ; but nowadays scholars are more realistic than formerly. Most of them will feel satisfied when *moon* and *month* are associated with words having the same two significations in related languages, without indulging in explanations of both from a root *me* ' to measure ' ; and when our *daughter* has been connected with Gr. *thugáter*, Skt. *duhitár* and corresponding words in other languages, no attempt is made to go beyond the meaning common to these words ' daughter ' and to speculate what had induced our ancestors to bestow that word on that particular relation, as when Lassen derived it from the root *duh* ' to milk ' and pictured an idyllic family life, in which it was the business of the young girls to milk the cows, or when Fick derived the same word from the root *dheugh* ' to be useful ' (G. *taugen* : ' wie die *magd, maid* von *mögen* '), as if the daughters were the only, or the most, efficient members of the family. Unfortunately, such speculations are still found lingering in many recent handbooks of high standing : Kluge hesitates whether to assign the word *mutter, mother*, to the root *ma* in the sense ' mete out ' or in the sense found in Sanskrit ' to form,' used of the fœtus in the womb. A resigned acquiescence in inevitable ignorance and a sense of reality should certainly be characteristics of future etymologists.

CHAPTER XVII

PROGRESS OR DECAY?

§ 1. Linguistic Estimation. § 2. Degeneration ? § 3. Appreciation of Modern Tongues. § 4. The Scientific Attitude. § 5. Final Answer. § 6. Sounds. § 7. Shortenings. § 8. Objections. Result. § 9. Verbal Forms. § 10. Synthesis and Analysis. § 11. Verbal Concord.

XVII.—§ 1. Linguistic Estimation.

THE common belief of linguists that one form or one expression is just as good as another, provided they are both found in actual use, and that each language is to be considered a perfect vehicle for the thoughts of the nation speaking it, is in some ways the exact counterpart of the conviction of the Manchester school of economics that everything is for the best in the best of all possible worlds if only no artificial hindrances are put in the way of free exchange, for demand and supply will regulate everything better than any Government would be able to. Just as economists were blind to the numerous cases in which actual wants, even crying wants, were not satisfied, so also linguists were deaf to those instances which are, however, obvious to whoever has once turned his attention to them, in which the very structure of a language calls forth misunderstandings in everyday conversation, and in which, consequently, a word has to be repeated or modified or expanded or defined in order to call forth the idea intended by the speaker : he took his stick—no, not John's, but *his own* ; or : I mean *you* in the plural) or, you all, or you girls) ; no, a *box on the ear ; un dé à jouer, non pas un dé à coudre ;* nein, ich meine *Sie persönlich* (with very strong stress on *Sie*), etc. Every careful writer in any language has had the experience that on re-reading his manuscript he has discovered that a sentence which he thought perfectly clear when he wrote it lends itself to misunderstanding and has to be put in a different way ; sometimes he has to add a clarifying parenthesis, because his language is defective in some respect, as when Edward Carpenter {*Art of Creation* 171), in speaking of the deification of the Babe, writes : " It is not likely that Man—the human male—left to himself would have done this ; but to woman it was natural," thus avoiding the misunderstanding that he was speaking of the whole species, comprising both sexes. Herbert Spencer writes : " Charles had recently obtained—a post in the Post Office I was about to say, but the cacophony stopped me ; and then I was about to say, an office in the Post Office, which is nearly as bad ; let me say— a place in the Post Office " (*Autobiogr.* 2. 73—but of course the defect is not really one of sound, as implied by the expression ' cacophony,' but one of signification, as both words *post* and *office* are ambiguous, and the attempted collocation would therefore puzzle the reader or hearer, because the same word would have to be apprehended in two different senses in close succession). Similar instances might be alleged from any language.

No language is perfect, but if we admit this truth (or truism), we must also admit by implication that it is not unreasonable to investigate the relative value of different languages or of different details in languages. When comparative linguists set themselves against the narrowmindedness of classical scholars who thought Latin and Greek the only worthy objects of study, and emphasized the value of all, even the least literary languages and dialects, they were primarily thinking of their value to the scientist, who finds something of interest in each of them, but they had no idea of comparing the relative value of languages from the point of view of their users—and yet the latter comparison is of much greater importance than the former.

XVII.—§ 2. Degeneration?

People will often use the expressions ' evolution ' and ' development ' in connexion with language, but most linguists, when taken to task, will maintain that these expressions as applied to languages should be used without the implication which is commonly attached to them when used of other objects, namely, that there is a progressive tendency towards something better or nearer perfection. They will say that ' evolution ' means here simply changes going on in languages, without any judgment as to the value of these changes.

But those who do pronounce such a judgment nearly always take the changes as a retrogressive rather than a progressive development : " Tongues, like governments, have a natural tendency to degeneration," said Dr. Samuel Johnson in the Preface to his Dictionary, and the same lament has been often repeated since his time. This is quite natural : people have always had a tendency to believe in a golden age, that is, in a remote past gloriously different to the miserable present. Why not, then, have the same belief with regard to language, the more so because one cannot fail to notice things in contemporary speech which (superficially at any rate) look like corruptions of the ' good old ' forms ? Everything ' old ' thus comes to be considered ' good.' Lowell and others think they have justified many of the commonly reviled Americanisms if they are able to show them to have existed in England in the sixteenth century, and similar considerations are met with everywhere. The same frame of mind finds support in the usual grammar-school admiration for the two classical languages and their literatures. People were taught to look down upon modern languages as mere dialects or *patois* and to worship Greek and Latin ; the richness and fullness of forms found in those languages came naturally to be considered the very *beau idéal* of linguistic structure. Bacon gives a classical expression to this view when he declares " ingenia priorum seculorum nostris fuisse multo acutiora et subtiliora " (*De augm. scient.*[1]). To men fresh from the ordinary grammar-school training, no language would seem really respectable that had not four or five distinct cases and three genders, or that had less than five tenses and as many moods in its verbs. Accordingly, such poor languages as had either lost much of their original richness in grammatical forms (*e.g.* French, English, or Danish), or had never had any, so far as one knew (*e.g.* Chinese), were naturally looked upon with something of the pity bestowed on relatives in reduced circum-stances, or the contempt felt for foreign paupers. It is well known how in West-European languages, in English, German, Danish, Swedish, Dutch, French, etc., obsolete forms were artificially kept alive and preferred to younger forms by most grammarians ; but we see exactly the same point of view in such a language as Magyar, where, under the influence of the historical studies of the grammarian Révai, the belief in the excellence of the ' veneranda antiquitas ' as compared with the corruption of the modern language has been prevalent in schools and in literature. (See Simonyi US 259 ; cf. on Modern Greek and Telugu above, p. 301.)

Comparative linguists had one more reason for adopting this manner of estimating languages. To what had the great victories won by their science been due ? Whence had they got the material for that magnificent edifice which had proved spacious enough to hold Hindus and Persians, Lithuanians and Slavs, Greeks, Romans, Germans and Kelts ? Surely it was neither from Modern English nor Modern Danish, but from the oldest stages of each linguistic group. The older a linguistic document was, the

---

[1] Quoted here from John Wilkins, *An Essay towards a Real Character and a Philosophical Language*, 1668, p. 448 : Wilkins there subjects Bacon's saying to a crushing criticism, laying bare a great many radical deficiencies in Latin to bring out the logical advantages of his own artificial ' philo-sophical ' language.

more valuable it was to the first generation of comparative linguists. An English form like *had* was of no great use, but Gothic *habaide-deima* was easily picked to pieces, and each of its several elements lent itself capitally to comparison with Sanskrit, Lithuanian and Greek. The linguist was chiefly dependent for his material on the old and archaic languages ; his interest centred round their fuller forms : what wonder, then, if in his opinion those languages were superior to all others ? What wonder if by comparing *had* and *habaidedeima* he came to regard the English form as a mutilated and worn-out relic of a splendid original ? or if, noting the change from the old to the modern form, he used strong language and spoke of degeneration, corruption, depravation, decline, phonetic decay, etc. ?

The view that the modern languages of Europe, Persia and India are far inferior to the old languages, or the one old language, from which they descend, we have already encountered in the historical part of this work, in Bopp, Humboldt, Grimm and their followers. It looms very large in Schleicher, according to whom the history of language is all a Decline and Fall, and in Max Müller, who says that " on the whole, the history of all the Aryan languages is nothing but a gradual process of decay." Nor is it yet quite extinct.

XVII.—§ 3. Appreciation of Modern Tongues.

Some scholars, however, had an indistinct feeling that this unconditional and wholesale depreciation of modern languages could not contain the whole truth, and I have collected various passages, nearly always of a perfunctory or incidental character, in which these languages are partly rehabilitated. Humboldt (Versch 284) speaks of the modern use of auxiliary verbs and prepositions as a convenience of the intellect which may even in some isolated instances lead to greater definiteness. On Grimm see above, p. 62. Rask (SA 1. 191) says that it is possible that the advantages of simplicity may be greater than those of an elaborate linguistic structure. Madvig turns against the uncritical admiration of the classical languages, but does not go further than saying that the modern analytical languages are just as good as the old synthetic ones, for thoughts can be expressed in both with equal clearness. Kräuter (*Archiv f. neu. spr.* 57. 204) says: "That decay is consistent with clearness and precision is shown by French ; that it is not fatal to poetry is seen in the language of Shakespeare." Osthoff (*Schriftspr. u. Volksmundart*, 1883, 13) protests against a one-sided depreciation of the language of Lessing and Goethe in favour of the language of Wulfila or

Otfried, or vice versa : a language possesses an inestimable charm
if its phonetic system remains unimpaired and its etymologies
are transparent ; but pliancy of the material of language and
flexibility to express ideas is really no less an advantage ; everything depends on the point of view : the student of architecture
has one point of view, the people who are to live in the house
another.

Among those who thus half-heartedly refused to accept the
downhill theory to its full extent must be mentioned Whitney,
many passages in whose writings show a certain hesitation to
make up his mind on this question. When speaking of the loss
of old forms he says that "some of these could well be spared,
but others were valuable, and their relinquishment has impaired
the power of expression of the language." To phonetic corruption
we owe true grammatical forms, which make the wealth of every
inflective language ; but it is also destructive of the very edifice
which it has helped to build. He speaks of "the legitimate
tendency to neglect and eliminate distinctions which are practically
unnecessary," and will not admit "that we can speak our minds
any less distinctly than our ancestors could, with all their apparatus
of inflexions " ; gender is a luxury which any language can well
afford to dispense with, but language is impoverished by the
obliteration of the subjunctive mood. The giving up of grammatical
endings is akin to wastefulness, and the excessive loss in English
makes truly for decay (L 31, 73, 74, 76, 77, 84, 85 ; G 51, 105, 104).

XVII.—§ 4. The Scientific Attitude.

Why are all such expressions either of depreciation or of partial
appreciation of the modern languages so utterly unsatisfactory ?
One reason is that they are so vague and dependent on a general
feeling of inferiority or the reverse, instead of being based on a
detailed comparative estimation of real facts in linguistic structure.
If, therefore, we want to arrive at a scientific answer to the question
" Decay or progress ? " we must examine actual instances of changes,
but must take particular care that these instances are not chosen
at random, but are typical and characteristic of the total structure
of the languages concerned. What is wanted is not a comparison
of isolated facts, but the establishment of general laws and tendencies, for only through such can we hope to decide whether
or no we are justified in using terms like 'development' and
'evolution' in linguistic history.

The second reason why the earlier pronouncements quoted
above do not satisfy us is that their authors nowhere raise the
question of the method by which linguistic value is to be measured

by what standard and what tests the comparative merits of languages or of forms are to be ascertained. Those linguists who looked upon language as a product of nature were by that very fact precluded from establishing a rational basis for determining linguistic values ; nor is it possible to find one if we look at things from the one-sided point of view of the linguistic historian. An almost comical instance of this is found when Curtius (*Sprachwiss. u. class. phil.* 39) says that the Greek accusative *póda* is better than Sanskrit *padam*, because it is possible at once to see that it belongs to the third declension. What is to be taken into account is of course the interests of the speaking community, and if we consistently consider language as a set of human actions with a definite end in view, namely, the communication of thoughts and feelings, then it becomes easy to find tests by which to measure linguistic values, for from that point of view it is evident that THAT LANGUAGE RANKS HIGHEST WHICH GOES FARTHEST IN THE ART OF ACCOMPLISHING MUCH WITH LITTLE MEANS, OR, IN OTHER WORDS, WHICH IS ABLE TO EXPRESS THE GREATEST AMOUNT OF MEANING WITH THE SIMPLEST MECHANISM.

The estimation has to be thoroughly and frankly *anthropocentric*. This may be a defect in other sciences, in which it is a merit on the part of the investigator to be able to abstract himself from human considerations ; in linguistics, on the contrary, on account of the very nature of the object of study, one must constantly look to the human interest, and judge everything from that, and from no other, point of view. Otherwise we run the risk of going astray in all directions.

It will be noticed that my formula contains two requirements : it demands a maximum of efficiency and a minimum of effort. Efficiency means expressiveness, and effort means bodily and mental labour, and thus the formula is simply one of modern energetics. But unfortunately we are in possession of no method by which to measure either expressiveness or effort exactly, and in cases of conflict it may be difficult to decide to which of the two sides we are to attach the greater importance, how great a surplus of efficiency is required to counterbalance a surplus of exertion, or inversely. Still, in many cases no doubt can arise, and we are often able to state progress, because there is either a clear gain in efficiency or a diminution of exertion, or both.

There is one objection which is likely to present itself to many of my readers, namely, that natives handle their language without the least exertion or effort (cf. XIV § 6, p. 262). Madvig (1857, 73 ff. = Kl 260 ff.) admits that a simplification in linguistic structure will make the language easier to learn for foreigners, but denies that it means increased ease for the native. Similarly Wechssier (L 149) says that " der begriff der schwierigkeit und unbequemlichkeit für die einheimischen nicht existiert." I might quote against him his countryman Gabelentz, who expressly says that the difficulties of the German languages are felt by natives, a view that is endorsed by Schuchardt in various places.[1] To my mind there is not the slightest doubt that different languages differ very much in easiness even to native speakers. In the chapters devoted to children we have already seen that the numerous mistakes made by them in every possible way testify to the labour involved in learning one's own language. This labour must naturally be greater in the case of a highly complicated linguistic structure with many rules and still more exceptions to the rules, than in languages constructed simply and regularly.

Nor is the difficulty of correct speech confined to the first mastering of the language. Even to the native who has spoken the same language from a child, its daily use involves no small amount of exertion. Under ordinary circumstances he is not conscious of any exertion in speaking; but such a want of conscious feeling is no proof that the exertion is absent. And it is a strong argument to the contrary that it is next to impossible for you to speak correctly if you are suffering from excessive mental work; you will constantly make slips in grammar and idiom as well as in pronunciation; you have not the same command of language as under normal conditions. If you have to speak on a difficult and unfamiliar subject, on which you would not like to say anything but what is to the point or strictly justifiable, you will sometimes find that the thoughts themselves claim so much mental energy that there is none left for speaking with elegance, or even with complete regard to grammar: to your own vexation you will have a feeling that your phrases are confused and your language incorrect. A pianist may practise a difficult piece of music so as to have it " at his fingers' ends "; under ordinary circumstances he will be able to play it quite mechanically, without ever being conscious of effort; but, nevertheless, the effort is there. How great the effort is appears when some day or other the musician is ' out of humour,' that is, when his brain is at work on other subjects or is not in its usual working order. At once his execution will be stumbling and faulty.

[1] Cf. also what Paul says (P 144) about one point in German grammar (strong and weak forms of adjectives): " But the difficulty of the correct maintenance of the distinction is shown in numerous offences made by writers against the rules of grammar "—of course, not only by writers, but by ordinary speakers as well.

XVII.—§ 5. Final Answer.

I may here anticipate the results of the following investigation and say that in all those instances in which we are able to examine the history of any language for a sufficient length of time, we find that languages have a progressive tendency. But if languages progress towards greater perfection, it is not in a bee-line, nor are all the changes we witness to be considered steps in the right direction. The only thing I maintain is that *the sum total of these changes, when we compare a remote period with the present time, shows a surplus of progressive over retrogressive or indifferent changes,* so that the structure of modern languages is nearer perfection than that of ancient languages, if we take them as wholes instead of picking out at random some one or other more or less significant detail. And of course it must not be imagined that progress has been achieved through deliberate acts of men conscious that they were improving their mother-tongue. On the contrary, many a step in advance has at first been a slip or even a blunder, and, as in other fields of human activity, good results have only been won after a good deal of bungling and ' muddling along.' [1] My attitude towards this question is the same as that of Leslie Stephen, who writes in a letter (*Life* 454): " I have a perhaps unreasonable amount of belief, not in a millennium, but in the world on the whole blundering rather forwards than backwards."

Schleicher on one occasion used the fine simile : " Our words, as contrasted with Gothic words, are like a statue that has been rolling for a long time in the bed of a river till its beautiful limbs have been worn off, so that now scarcely anything remains but a polished stone cylinder with faint indications of what it once was " (D 34). Let us turn the tables by asking : Suppose, however, that it would be quite out of the question to place the statue on a pedestal to be admired ; what if, on the one hand, it was not ornamental enough as a work of art, and if, on the other hand, human well-being was at stake if it was not serviceable in a rolling-mill : which would then be the better—a rugged and unwieldy statue, making difficulties at every rotation, or an even, smooth, easygoing and well-oiled roller ?

After these preliminary considerations we may now proceed to a comparative examination of the chief differences between ancient and modern stages of our Western European languages.

---

[1] It has often been pointed out how Great Britain has ' blundered ' into creating her world-wide Empire, and Gretton, in *The King's Government* (1914), applies the same view to the development of governmental institutions.

XVII.—§ 6. Sounds.

The student who goes through the chapters devoted to sound changes in historical and comparative grammars will have great difficulty in getting at any great lines of development or general tendencies : everything seems just haphazard and fortuitous ; a long *i* is here shortened and there diphthongized or lowered into *e*, etc. The history of sounds is dependent on surroundings in many, though not in all circumstances, but surroundings do not always act in the same way ; in short, there seem to be so many conflicting tendencies that no universal or even general rules can be evolved from all these 'sound laws.' Still less would it seem possible to state anything about the comparative value of the forms before and after the change, for it does not seem to matter a bit for the speaking community whether it says *stān* as in Old English or *stone* as now, and thus in innumerable cases. Nay, from one point of view it may seem that any change militates against the object of language (cf. Wechssler L 28), but this is true only of the very moment when the change sets in while people are accustomed to the old sound (or the old signification), and even then the change is only injurious provided it impedes understanding or renders understanding less easy, which is far from always being the case.

There is one scholar who has asserted the existence of a universal progressive tendency in languages, or, as he calls it, a humanization of language, namely Baudouin de Courtenay (*Vormenschlichung der Sprache*, 1893). He is chiefly thinking of the sound system,[1] and he maintains that there is a tendency towards eliminating the innermost articulations and using instead sounds that are formed nearer to the teeth and lips. Thus some back (postpalatal, velar) consonants become *p*, *b*, while others develop into *s* sounds ; cf. Slav *slovo* ' word ' with Lat. *cluo*, etc. Baudouin also mentions the frequent palatalization of back consonants, as in French and Italian *ce, ci, ge, gi*, but as this is due to the influence of the following front vowel, it should not perhaps be mentioned as a universal tendency of human language. It is further said that throat sounds, which play such a great rôle in Semitic languages, have been discarded in most modern languages. But it may be objected that sometimes throat sounds do develop in modern periods, as in the Danish ' stød ' and in English dialectal *bu'er* for

---

[1] In the realm of significations he sees the ' humanization ' of language exclusively in the development of abstract terms. An important point of disagreement between Baudouin and myself is in regard to morphology, where he sees only ' oscillations ' in historical times, in which he is unable to discover a continuous movement in any definite direction, while I maintain that languages here manifest a definite progressive tendency.

butter, etc. A universal tendency of sounds to move away from
the throat cannot be said to be firmly established ; but for our
purpose it is more important to say that even were it true, the
value of such a tendency for the speaking community would not
be great enough to justify us in speaking of progress towards a
truly 'human' language as opposed to the more beastlike language
of our primeval ancestors. It is true that Baudouin (p. 25) says
that it is possible to articulate in the front and upper part with
less effort and with greater precision than in the interior and
lower parts of the speaking apparatus, but if this is true with regard
to the mouth proper, it cannot be maintained with regard to the
vocal chords, where very important effects may be produced in the
most precise way by infinitely little exertion. Thus in no single
point can I see that Baudouin de Courtenay has made out a strong
case for *his* conception of 'humanization of language.'

XVII.—§ 7. Shortenings.

But there is another phonetic tendency which is much more
universal and infinitely more valuable than the one asserted by
Baudouin de Courtenay, namely, the tendency to shorten words.
Words get shorter and shorter in consequence of a great many
of those changes that we see constantly going on in all languages :
vowels in weak syllables are pronounced more and more indistinctly and finally disappear altogether, as when OE. *lufu, stānas,
sende*, through ME. *luve, stanes, sende* with pronounced *e*'s, have
become our modern monosyllables *love, stones, send*, or when
Latin *bonum, homo, viginti* have become Fr. *bon, on, vingt*, and
Lat. *bona, hominem*, Fr. *bonne, homme*, where the vowel was kept,
because it was *a* or protected by the consonant group, but has
now also disappeared in normal pronunciation. Final vowels
have been dropped extensively in Danish and German dialects,
and so have the *u*'s and *i*'s in Russian, which are now kept in the
spelling merely as signs of the quality of the preceding consonant.
It would be easy to multiply instances. Nor are the consonants
more stable ; the dropping of final ones is seen most easily in
Modern French, because they are retained in spelling, as in *tout,
vers, champ, chant*, etc. In the two last examples two consonants have disappeared, the *m* and *n*, however, leaving a trace
in the nasalized pronunciation of the vowel, as also in *bon, nom*,
etc. Final *r* and *l* often disappear in Fr. words like *quatre, simple*,
and medial consonants have been dropped in such cases as *côte*
from *coste*, *bête* from *beste*, *sauf* [so·f] from *salvo*, etc. We have
corresponding omissions in English, where in very old times *n*
was dropped in such cases as *us, five, other*, while the German

forms *uns, fünf, ander* have kept the old consonants ; in more recent times *l* was dropped in *half, calm*, etc., *gh* [x] in *light, bought*, etc., and *r* in the prevalent pronunciation of *warm, part*, etc. Initial consonants are more firmly fixed in many languages, yet we see them lost in the E. combinations *kn, gn, wr*, where *k, g, w* used to be sounded, e.g. in *know, gnaw, wrong*. Consonant assimilation means in most cases the same thing as dropping of one consonant, for no trace of the consonant is left, at any rate after the compensating lengthening has been given up, as is often the case, e.g. in E. *cupboard, blackguard* [kʌbəd, blægaˑd].

So far we have given instances of what might be called the most regular or constant types of phonetic change leading to shorter forms ; but the same result is the natural outcome of a process which occurs more sporadically. This is haplology, by which one sound or one group of sounds is pronounced once only instead of twice, the hearer taking it through a kind of acoustic delusion as belonging both to what precedes and to what follows. Examples are *a goo(d) deal, wha(t) to do, nex(t) time, simp(le)ly, England* from *Englaland, eighteen* from OE. *eahtatiene, honesty* from *honestete, Glou(ce)ster, Worcester* [wustə], familiarly *pro(ba)bly*, vulgarly *lib(ra)ry, Febr(uar)y*. From other languages may be quoted Fr. *cont(re)rôle, ido(lo)lâtre, Neu(ve)ville*, Lat. *nu(tri)trix, sti(pi)pendium*, It. *qual(che)cosa, cosa* for *che cosa*, etc. (Cf. my LPh 11. 9.)

The accumulation through centuries of such influences results in those instances of seemingly violent contractions with which every student of historical linguistics is familiar. One classical example has already been mentioned above, E. *had*, corresponding to Gothic *habaidedeima* ; other examples are *lord*, with its three or four sounds, which was formerly *laverd*, and in Old English *hlāford ;* the old Gothonic form of the same word contained indubitably as many as twelve sounds ; Latin *augustum* has in French through *aoust* become *août*, pronounced [au] or even [u] ; Latin *oculum* has shrunk into four sounds in Italian *occhio*, three in Spanish *ojo*, and two in Fr. *œil ;* It. *medesimo*, Sp. *mismo*, and Fr. *même* represent various stages of the shrinking of Lat. *metipsimum ;* cf. also Fr. *ménage* from *mansion-* + *-aticum*. Primitive Norse *ne veit ek hvat* 'not know I what' has become Dan. *noget* 'something,' often pronounced [noˑð] or [nɔˑð].

In all these cases the shortening process has taken centuries, but we have other instances in which it has come about quite suddenly, without any intermediate stages, namely, in those stump-words which we have already considered (Ch. IX § 7 ; cf. XIV § 12 on corresponding syntactical shortenings).

XVII.—§ 8. Objections. Result.

There cannot therefore be the slightest doubt that the general tendency of all languages is towards shorter and shorter forms : the ancient languages of our family, Sanskrit, Zend, etc., abound in very long words ; the further back we go, the greater the number of *sesquipedalia*. It cannot justly be objected that we see sometimes examples of phonetic lengthenings, as in E. *sound* from ME. *soun*, Fr. *son*, E. *whilst, amongst* from ME. *whiles, amonges* ; a similar excrescence of *t* after *s* is seen in G. *obst, pabst*, Swed. *eljest* and others ; after *n, t* is added in G. *jemand, niemand* (two syllables, while there is nothing added to the trisyllabic *jedermann*)—for even if such instances might be multiplied, their number and importance is infinitely smaller than those in the opposite direction. (On the seeming insertion of *d* in *ndr*, see p. 264, note). In some cases we witness a certain reaction against word forms that are felt to be too short and therefore too indistinct (see Ch. XV § 1, XX § 9), but on the whole such instances are few and far between : the prevailing tendency is towards shorter forms.

Another objection must be dealt with here. It is said that it is only the purely phonetic development that tends to make words shorter, but that in languages as wholes words do not become shorter, because non-phonetic forces counteract the tendency. In modern languages we thus have some analogical formations which are longer than the forms they have supplanted, as when *books* has one sound more than OE. *bēc*, or when G. *bewegte* takes the place of *bewog*. Further, we have in modern languages many auxiliary words (prepositions, modal verbs) in places where they were formerly not required. That this objection is not valid if we take the whole of the language into consideration may perhaps be proved statistically if we compute the length of the same long text in various languages : the Gospel of St. Matthew contains in Greek about 39,000 syllables, in Swedish about 35,000, in German 33,000, in Danish 32,500, in English 29,000, and in Chinese only 17,000 (the figures for the Authorized English Version and for Danish are my own calculation ; the other figures I take from Tegnér SM 51, Hoops in *Anglia, Beiblatt* 1896, 293, and Sturtevant LCh 175). In comparing these figures it should even be taken into consideration that translations naturally tend to be more long-winded and verbose than the original, so that the real gain in shortness may be greater than indicated.[1]

---

[1] On the other hand, it is not, perhaps, fair to count the number of *syllables*, as these may vary very considerably, and some languages favour syllables with heavy consonant groups unknown in other tongues. The most rational measure of length would be to count the numbers of distinct (not sounds, but) articulations of separate speech organs—but that task is at any rate beyond *my* powers.

Next, we come to consider the question whether the tendency towards shorter forms is a valuable asset in the development of languages or the reverse. The answer cannot be doubtful. Take the old example, English *had* and Gothic *habaidedeima* : the English form is preferable, on the principle that anyone who has to choose between walking one mile and four miles will, other things being equal, prefer the shorter cut. It is true that if we take words to be self-existing natural objects, *habaidedeima* has the air of a giant and *had* of a mere pigmy : this valuation lies at the bottom of many utterances even by recent linguistic thinkers, as when Sweet (H 10) speaks of the vanishing of sounds as "a purely destructive change." But if we adopt the anthropocentric standard which has been explained above, and realize that what we call a word is really and primarily the combined action of human muscles to produce an audible effect, we see that the shortening of a form means a diminution of effort and a saving of time in the communication of our thoughts. If, as it is said, *had* has suffered from wear and tear in the long course of time, this means that the wear and tear of people now using this form in their speech is less than if they were still encumbered with the old giant *habaidedeima*. Voltaire was certainly very wide of the mark when he wrote : " C'est le propre des barbares d'abréger les mots "— long and clumsy words are rather to be considered as signs of barbarism, and short and nimble ones as signs of advanced culture.

Though I thus hold that the development towards shorter forms of expression is *on the whole* progressive, i.e. beneficial, I should not like to be too dogmatic on this point and assert that it is *always* beneficial : shortness may be carried to excess and thus cause obscurity or difficulty of understanding. This may be seen in the telegraphic style as well as in the literary style of some writers too anxious to avoid prolixity (some of Pope's lines might be quoted in illustration of the classical : brevis esse laboro, obscurus fio). But in the case of the language of a whole community the danger certainly is very small indeed, for there will always be a natural and wholesome reaction against such excessive shortness. There is another misunderstanding I want to guard against when saying that the shortening makes on the whole for progress. It must not be thought that I lay undue stress on this point, which is after all chiefly concerned with a greater or smaller amount of physical or muscular exertion · this should neither be underrated nor overrated ; but it will be seen that neither in my former work nor in this does the consideration of this point of mere shortness or length take up more than a fraction of the space allotted to the more psychical sides of the question, to which we shall now turn our attention and to which I attach much more importance.

XVII.—§ 9. Verbal Forms.

We may here recur to Schleicher's example, E. *had* and Gothic *habaidedeima*. It is not only in regard to economy of muscular exertion that the former carries the day over the latter. *Had* corresponds not only to *habaidedeima*, but it unites in one short form everything expressed by the Gothic *habaida, habaides, habaidedu, habaideduts, habaidedum, habaideduþ, habaidedun, habaidedjau, habaidedeis, habaidedi, habaidedeiwa, habaidedeits, habaidedeima, habaidedeiþ, habaidedeina*—separate forms for two or three persons in three numbers in two distinct moods! It is clear, therefore, that the English form saves a considerable amount of brainwork to all English-speaking people—not only to children, who have fewer forms to learn, but also to adults, who have fewer forms to choose between and to keep distinct whenever they open their mouths to speak. Someone might, perhaps, say that on the other hand English people are obliged always to join personal pronouns to their verbal forms to indicate the person, and that this is a drawback counterbalancing the advantage, so that the net result is six of one and half a dozen of the other. This, however, would be a very superficial objection. For, in the first place, the personal pronouns are the same for all tenses and moods, but the endings are not. Secondly, the possession of endings does not exempt the Goths from having separate personal pronouns ; and whenever these are used, as is very often the case in the first and second persons, those parts of the verbal endings which indicate persons are superfluous. They are no less superfluous in those extremely numerous cases in which the subject is either separately expressed by a noun or is understood from the preceding proposition, thus in the vast majority of the cases of the third person. If we compare a few pages of Old English prose with a modern rendering we shall see that in spite of the reduction in the latter of the person-indicating endings, personal pronouns are not required in any great number of sentences in which they were dispensed with in Old English. So that, altogether, the numerous endings of the older languages must be considered uneconomical.

If Gothic, Latin and Greek, etc., burden the memory by the number of their flexional endings, they do so even more by the many irregularities in the formation of these endings. In all the languages of this type, anomaly and flexion invariably go together. The intricacies of verbal flexion in Latin and Greek are well known, and it requires no small amount of mental energy to master the

various modes of forming the present stems in Sanskrit—to take
only one instance. Many of these irregularities disappear in
course of time, chiefly, but not exclusively, through analogical
formations, and though it is true that a certain number of new
irregularities may come into existence, their number is relatively
small when compared with those that have been removed. Now,
it is not only the forms themselves that are irregular in the early
languages, but also their uses : logical simplicity prevails much
more in Modern English syntax than in either Old English or
Latin or Greek. But it is hardly necessary to point out that
growing regularity in a language means a considerable gain to all
those who learn it or speak it.

It has been said, however, by one of the foremost authorities
on the history of English, that "in spite of the many changes
which this system [i.e. the complicated system of strong verbs]
has undergone in detail, it remains just as intricate as it was in
Old English " (Bradley, *The Making of English* 51). It is true
that the way in which vowel change is utilized to form tenses
is rather complicated in Modern English (*drink drank, give gave,
hold held*, etc.), but otherwise an enormous simplification has taken
place. The personal endings have been discarded with the exception of *-s* in the third person singular of the present (and the
obsolete ending *-est* in the second person, and then this has been
regularized, *thou sangest* having taken the place of *þu sunge*) ; the
change of vowel in *ic sang, þu sunge, we sungon* in the indicative
and *ic sunge, we sungen* in the subjunctive has been given up,
and so has the accompanying change of consonant in many cases.
Thus, instead of the following forms, *cēosan, cēose, cēoseþ, cēosaþ,
cēosen, cēas, curon, cure, curen, coren*, we have the following modern
ones, which are both fewer in number and less irregular : *choose,
chooses, chose, chosen*—certainly an advance from a more to a less
intricate system (cf. GS § 178).

An extreme, but by no means unique example of the simplification found in modern languages is the English *cut*, which can
serve both as present and past tense, both as singular and plural,
both in the first, second and third persons, both in the infinitive,
in the imperative, in the indicative, in the subjunctive, and as a
past (or passive) participle ; compare with this the old languages
with their separate forms for different tenses, moods, numbers
and persons ; and remember, moreover, that the identical form,
without any inconvenience being occasioned, is also used as a
noun (*a cut*), and you will admire the economy of the living tongue.
A characteristic feature of the structure of languages in their
early stages is that each form contains in itself several minor
modifications which are often in the later stages expressed separately

by means of auxiliary words. Such a word as Latin *cantavisset* unites into one inseparable whole the equivalents of six ideas : (1) ' sing,' (2) pluperfect, (3) that indefinite modification of the verbal idea which we term subjunctive, (4) active, (5) third person, and (6) singular.

XVII.—§ 10. Synthesis and Analysis.

Such a form, therefore, is much more concrete than the forms found in modern languages, of which sometimes two or more have to be combined to express the composite notion which was rendered formerly by one. Now, it is one of the consequences of this change that it has become easier to express certain minute, but by no means unimportant, shades of thought by laying extra stress on some particular element in the speech-group. Latin *cantaveram* amalgamates into one indissoluble whole what in E. *I had sung* is analysed into three components, so that you can at will accentuate the personal element, the time element or the action. Now, it is possible (who can affirm and who can deny it ?) that the Romans could, if necessary, make some difference in speech between *cántaveram* (non saltaveram) ' I had *sung*,' and *cantaverám* (non cantabam), ' I *had* sung '; but even then, if it was the personal element which was to be emphasized, an *ego* had to be added. Even the possibility of laying stress on the temporal element broke down in forms like *scripsi, minui, sum, audiam*, and innumerable others. It seems obvious that the freedom of Latin in this respect must have been inferior to that of English. Moreover, in English, the three elements, ' I,' ' had,' and ' sung,' can in certain cases be arranged in a different order, and other words can be inserted between them in order to modify and qualify the meaning of the sentence. Note also the conciseness of such answers as " Who had sung ? " " I had." " What had you done ? " " Sung." " I believe he has enjoyed himself." " I know he has." And contrast the Latin " Cantaveram et saltaveram et luseram et riseram " with the English " I had sung and danced and played and laughed." What would be the Latin equivalent of " Tom never *did* and never *will* beat me " ?

In such cases, analysis means suppleness, and synthesis means rigidity ; in analytic languages you have the power of kaleidoscopically arranging and rearranging the elements that in synthetic forms like *cantaveram* are in rigid connexion and lead a Siamese-twin sort of existence. The synthetic forms of Latin verbs remind one of those languages all over the world (North America, South America, Hottentot, etc.) in which such ideas as ' father ' or ' mother ' or ' head ' or ' eye ' cannot be expressed separately but only in connexion with an indication of *whose* father, etc., one is speaking about : in one language the verbal idea (in the finite moods), in the other the nominal idea, is necessarily fused with the personal idea.

XVII.—§ 11. Verbal Concord.

This formal inseparability of subordinate elements is at the root of those rules of concord which play such a large rôle in the older languages of our Aryan family, but which tend to disappear in the more recent stages. By concord we mean the fact that a secondary word (adjective or verb) is made to agree with the primary word (substantive or subject) to which it belongs. Verbal concord, by which a verb is governed in number and person by the subject, has disappeared from spoken Danish, where, for instance, the present tense of the verb meaning ' to travel ' is uniformly *rejser* in all persons of both numbers ; while the written language till towards the end of the nineteenth century kept up artificially the plural *rejse*, although it had been dead in the spoken language for some three hundred years. The old flexion is an article of luxury, as a modification of the idea belonging properly to the subject is here transferred to the predicate, where it has no business ; for when we say ' mændene rejse ' (die männer reisen), we do not mean to imply that they undertake several journeys (cf. Madvig Kl 28, *Nord. tsk. f. filol.*, n.r. 8. 134).

By getting rid of this superfluity, Danish has got the start of the more archaic of its Aryan sister-tongues. Even English, which has in most respects gone farthest in simplifying its flexional system, lags here behind Danish, in that in the present tense of most verbs the third person singular deviates from the other persons by ending in -*s*, and the verb *be* preserves some other traces of the old concord system, not to speak of the form in -*st* used with *thou* in the language of religion and poetry. Small and unimportant as these survivals may seem, still they are in some instances impediments to the free and easy expression of thought. In Danish, for instance, there is not the slightest difficulty in saying ' enten du eller jeg har uret,' as *har* is used both in the first and second persons singular and plural. But when an Englishman tries to render the same simple sentiment he is baffled ; either you or I *are* wrong ' is felt to be incorrect, and so is ' either you or I *am* wrong ' ; he might say ' either you are wrong, or I,' but then this manner of putting it, if grammatically admissible (with or without the addition of *am*), is somewhat stiff and awkward ; and there is no perfectly natural way out of the difficulty, for Dean Alford's proposal to say ' either you or I *is* wrong ' (*The Queen's Engl.* 155) is not to be recommended. The advantage of having verbal forms that are no respecters of persons is seen directly in such perfectly natural expressions as ' either you or I must be wrong,' or ' either you or I may be wrong,' or ' either you or I began it '—and indirectly from the more or less artificial rules of Latin and Greek grammars on this point ; in the following passages the Gordian knot is cut in different ways :

Shakespeare *LLL* v. 2. 346 Nor God, nor I, *delights* in perjur'd men | id. *As* I. 3. 99 Thou and I *am* one | Tennyson *Poet. W.* 369 For whatsoever knight against us came Or I or he *have* easily overthrown | Galsworthy *D* 30 *Am* I and all women really what they think us ? | Shakespeare *H4B* IV. 2. 121 Heauen, and not wee, *haue* safely fought to day (Folio, where the Quarto has : God, and not wee, *hath*. . . .)

The same difficulty often appears in relative clauses ; Alford (l.c. 152) calls attention to the fact of the Prayer Book reading " Thou art the God that *doeth* wonders," whereas the Bible version runs " Thou art the God that *doest* wonders." Compare also :

Shakespeare *As* III. 5. 55 'Tis not her glasse, but you that *flatters* her | id. *Meas.* II. 2. 80 It is the law, not I, *condemne* your brother | Carlyle *Fr. Rev.* 38, There is none but you and I that *has* the people's interest at heart (translated from : Il n'y a que vous et moi qui *aimions* le peuple).

In all such cases the construction in Danish is as easy and natural as it generally is in the English preterit : " It was not her glass, but you that flattered her." The disadvantage of having verbal forms which enforce the indication of person and number is perhaps seen most strikingly in a French sentence like this from Romain Rolland's *Jean Christophe* (7. 221) : " Ce mot, naturellement, ce n'est ni toi, ni moi, qui *pouvons* le dire "—the verb agrees with that which *cannot* be the subject (we) ! For what is meant is really : ' celui qui peut le dire, ce n'est ni moi ni toi.'

CHAPTER XVIII
PROGRESS

XVIII.—§ 1. Nominal Forms.

In the flexion of substantives and adjectives we see phenomena corresponding to those we have just been considering in the verbs. The ancient languages of our family have several forms where modern languages content themselves with fewer ; forms originally kept distinct are in course of time confused, either through a phonetic obliteration of differences in the endings or through analogical extension of the functions of one form. The single form *good* is now used where OE. used the forms *god, godne, gode, godum, godes, godre, godra, godu, godum, godena* ; Ital. *uomo* or French *homme* is used for Lat. *homo, hominem, homini, homine* —nay, if we take the spoken form into consideration, Fr. [om] corresponds not only to these Latin forms, but also to *homines, hominibus*. Where the modern language has one or two cases, in an earlier stage it had three or four, and still earlier seven or eight. The difficulties inherent in the older system cannot, however, be measured adequately by the number of forms each word is susceptible of, but are multiplied by the numerous differences in the formation of the same case in different classes of declension : sometimes we even find anomalies which affect one word only.

Those who would be inclined to maintain that new irregularities may and do arise in modern languages which make up for whatever earlier irregularities have been discarded in the course of the historical development will do well to compile a systematic list of *all* the flexional forms of two different stages of the same languages, arranged exactly according to the same principles : this is the only way in which it is possible really to balance losses and profits in a language. This is what I have done in my *Progress in Language* § 111 ff. (reprinted in ChE § 9 ff.), where I have contrasted the case systems of Old and Modern English :

the result is that the former system takes 7 (+ 3) pages, and the latter only 2 pages. Those pages, with their abbreviations and tabulations, do not, perhaps, offer very entertaining reading, but I think they are more illustrative of the real tendencies of language than either isolated examples or abstract reasonings, and they cannot fail to convince any impartial reader of the enormous gain achieved through the changes of the intervening nine hundred years in the general structure of the English language.

For our general purposes it will be worth our while here to quote what Friedrich Müller (Gr i. 2. 7) says about a totally different language : " Even if the Hottentot distinguishes ' he,' ' she ' and ' it,' and strictly separates the singular from the plural number, yet by his expressing ' he ' and ' she ' by one sound in the third person, and by another in the second, he manifests that he has no perception at all of our two grammatical categories of gender and number, and consequently those elements of his language that run parallel to our signs of gender and number must be of an entirely different nature." Fr. Müller should not perhaps throw too many stones at the poor Hottentots, for his own native tongue is no better than a glass house, and we might with equal justice say, for instance : " As the Germans express the plural number in different manners in words like *gott—götter, hand—hände, vater—väter, frau—frauen*, etc., they must be entirely lacking in the sense of the category of number." Or let us take such a language as Latin ; there is nothing to show that *dominus* bears the same relation to *domini* as *verbum* to *verba, urbs* to *urbes, mensis* to *menses, cornu* to *cornua, fructus* to *fructūs*, etc. ; even in the same word the idea of plurality is not expressed by the same method for all the cases, as is shown by a comparison of *dominus—domini, dominum—dominos, domino—dominis, domini—dominorum*. Fr. Müller is no doubt wrong in saying that such anomalies preclude the speakers of the language from conceiving the notion of plurality ; but, on the other hand, it seems evident that a language in which a difference so simple even to the understanding of very young children as that between one and more than one can only be expressed by a complicated apparatus must rank lower than another language in which this difference has a single expression for all cases in which it occurs. In this respect, too, Modern English stands higher than the oldest English, Latin or Hottentot.

XVIII.—§ 2. Irregularities Original.

It was the belief of the older school of comparativists that each case had originally one single ending, which was added to all nouns indifferently (e.g. *-as* for the genitive sg.), and that the irregularities found in the existing oldest languages were of later growth ; the actually existing forms were then derived from the supposed unity form by all kinds of phonetic tricks and dodges. Now people have begun to see that the primeval language cannot have been quite uniform and regular (see, for instance, Walde in Streitberg's *Gesch.*, 2. 194 ff.). If we look at facts, and not at imagined or reconstructed forms, we are forced to acknowledge that in the oldest stages of our family of languages not only did the endings present the spectacle of a motley variety, but the kernel of the word was also often subject to violent changes in different cases, as when it had in different forms different accentuation and (or) different apophony, or as when in some of the most frequently occurring words some cases were formed from one ' stem ' and others from another, for instance, the nominative from an *r* stem and the oblique cases from an *n* stem. In the common word for ' water ' Greek has preserved both stems, nom. *hudōr*, gen. *hudatos*, where *a* stands for original [ən]. Whatever the origin of this change of stems, it is a phenomenon belonging to the earlier stages of our languages, in which we also sometimes find an alteration between the *r* stem in the nominative and a combination of the *n* and the *r* stems in the other cases, as in Lat. *jecur* ' liver,' *jecinoris* ; *iter* ' voyage,' *itineris*, which is supposed to have supplanted *itinis*, formed like *feminis* from *femur*. In the later stages we always find a simplification, one single form running through all cases , this is either the nominative stem, as in E. *water*, G. *wasser* (corresponding to Gr. *hudōr*), or the oblique case-stem, as in the Scandinavian forms, Old Norse *vatn*, Swed. *vatten*, Dan. *vand* (corresponding to Gr. *hudat-*), or finally a contaminated form, as in the name of the Swedish lake *Vättern* (Noreen's explanation), or in Old Norse and Dan. *skarn* ' dirt,' which has its *r* from a form like the Gr. *skōr*, and its *n* from a form like the Gr. genitive *skatos* (older [skəntos]). The simplification is carried furthest in English, where the identical form *water* is not only used unchanged where in the older languages different case forms would have been used (' the water is cold,' ' the surface of the water,' ' he fell into the water,' ' he swims in the water '), but also serves as a verb (' did you water the flowers ? '), and as an adjunct as a quasi-adjective (' a water melon,' ' water plants ').

In most cases irregularities have been done away with in the way here indicated, one of the forms (or stems) being generalized ; but in other cases it may have happened, as Kretschmer supposes (in Gercke and Norden, *Einleit. in die Altertumswiss*, I, 501) that irregular flexion caused a word to go out of use entirely ; thus in Modern G⁻eek *hêpar* was supplanted by *sukōti*,[1] *phréar* by *pēgadi*, *húdōr* by *neró*, *oûs* by *aphtí* (= *ōtíon*), *kúōn* by *skullí* ; this possibly also accounts for *commando* taking the place of Lat. *jubeo*.

Some scholars maintain that the medieval languages were more regular than their modern representatives ; but if we look more closely into what they mean, we shall see that they are not speaking of any regularity in the sense in which the word has here been used—the only regularity which is of importance to the speakers of the language—but of the regular correspondence of a language with some earlier language from which it is derived. This is particularly the case with E. Littré, who, in his essays on *L'Histoire de la Langue Française*, was full of enthusiasm for Old French, but chiefly for the fidelity with which it had preserved some features of Latin. There was thus the old distinction of two cases : nom. sg. *murs*, acc. sg. *mur*, and in the plural inversely nom. *mur* and acc. *murs*, with its exact correspondence with Latin *murus*, *murum*, pl. *muri*, *muros*. When this ' règle de *l*'s ' was discovered, and the use or omission of *s*, which had hitherto been looked upon as completely arbitrary in Old French, was thus accounted for, scholars were apt to consider this as an admirable trait in the old language which had been lost in modern French, and the same view obtained with regard to the case distinction found in other words, such as OFr. nom. *maire*, acc. *majeur*, or nom. *emperere*, acc. *emperëur*, corresponding to the Latin forms with changing stress, *májor*, *majórem*, *imperátor*, *imperatórem*, etc. But, however interesting such things may be to the historical linguist, there is no denying that to the users of French the modern simpler flexion is a gain as compared with this more complex system. " Des sprachhistorikers freud ist des sprachbrauchers leid," as Schuchardt somewhere shrewdly remarks.

XVIII.—§ 3. Syntax.

There were also in the old languages many irregularities in the syntactic use of the cases, as when some verbs governed the genitive and others the dative, etc. Even if it may be possible in many instances to account historically for these uses, to the speakers of the languages they must have appeared to be mere caprices which had to be learned separately for each verb, and it is therefore a great advantage when they have been gradually done away with, as has been the case, to a great extent, even in a language like German, which has retained many old case forms. Thus verbs like *entbehren, vergessen, bedürfen, wahrnehmen*, which formerly took the genitive, are now used more and more with the

---

[1] Thus also the corresponding Lat. *jecur* by *ficatum*, Fr. *foie*.

simple accusative—a simplification which, among other things,
makes the construction of sentences in the passive voice easier
and more regular.

The advantage of discarding the old case distinctions is seen
in the ease with which English and French speakers can say,
e.g., 'with or without my hat,' or 'in and round the church,'
while the correct German is 'mit meinem hut oder ohne denselben'
and 'in der kirche und um dieselbe'; Wackernagel writes:
"Was in ihm und um ihn und über ihm ist." When the prepositions are followed by a single substantive without case distinction,
German, of course, has the same simple construction as English,
e.g. 'mit oder ohne geld,' and sometimes even good writers will
let themselves go and write 'um und neben dem hochaltare'
(Goethe), or 'Ihre tochter wird meine frau mit oder gegen ihren
willen' (these examples from Curme, *German Grammar* 191).
Cf. also: 'Ich kann deinem bruder nicht helfen und ihn unter-
stützen.'

Many extremely convenient idioms unknown in the older
synthetic languages have been rendered possible in English through
the doing away with the old case distinctions, such as : Genius,
demanding bread, is given a stone after its possessor's death (Shaw)
(cf. my ChE § 79) | he was offered, and declined, the office of
poet-laureate (Gosse) | the lad was spoken highly of | I love, and
am loved by, my wife | these laws my readers, whom I consider
as my subjects, are bound to believe in and to obey (Fielding) |
he was heathenishly inclined to believe in, or to worship, the
goddess Nemesis (id.) | he rather rejoiced in, than regretted, his
bruise (id.) | many a dun had she talked to, and turned away
from her father's door (Thackeray) | their earthly abode, which
has seen, and seemed almost to sympathize in, all their honour
(Ruskin).

XVIII.—§ 4. Objections.

Against my view of the superiority of languages with few
case distinctions, Arwid Johannson, in a very able article (in
IF I, see especially p. 247 f.), has adduced a certain number of
ambiguous sentences from German :

> Soweit die deutsche zunge klingt und *gott* im himmel
> lieder singt (is *gott* nominative or dative ?) | Seinem landsmann,
> dem er in seiner ganzen bildung ebensoviel verdankte, wie
> *Goethe* (nominative or dative ?) | Doch würde die gesellschaft
> *der Indierin* (genitive or dative ?) lästig gewesen sein | Dar-
> in hat Caballero wohl nur einen konkurrenten, die Eliot,
> *welche* freilich *die spanische dichterin* nicht ganz erreicht | Nur

Diopeitbes feindet insgeheim dich an und *die schwester* des Kimon und *dein weib* Telesippa. (In the last two sentences what is the subject, and what the object ?)

According to Johannson, these passages show the disadvantages of doing away with formal distinctions, for the sentences would have been clear if each separate case had had its distinctive sign ; " the greater the wealth of forms, the more intelligible the speech." And they show, he says, that such ambiguities will occur, even where the strictest rules of word order are observed. I shall not urge that this is not exactly the case in the last sentence if *die schwester* and *dein weib* are to be taken as accusatives, for then *an* should have been placed at the very end of the sentence ; nor that, in the last sentence but one, the mention of George Eliot as the ' konkurrent ' of Fernan Caballero seems to show a partiality to the Spanish authoress on the part of the writer of the sentence, so that the reader is prepared to take *welche* as the nominative case ; *freilich* would seem to point in the same direction. But these, of course, are only trifling objections ; the essential point is that we must grant the truth of Johannson's contention that we have here a flaw in the German language ; the defects of its grammatical system may and do cause a certain number of ambiguities. Neither is it difficult to find the reasons of these defects by considering the structure of the language in its entirety, and by translating the sentences in question into a few other languages and comparing the results.

First, with regard to the formal distinctions between cases, the really weak point cannot be the fewness of these endings, for in that case we should expect the same sort of ambiguities to be very common in English and Danish, where the formal case distinctions are considerably fewer than in German ; but as a matter of fact such ambiguities are more frequent in German than in the other two languages. And, however paradoxical it may seem at first sight, one of the causes of this is the greater wealth of grammatical forms in German. Let us substitute other words for the ambiguous ones, and we shall see that the amphibology will nearly always disappear, because most other words will have different forms in the two cases, e.g.

Soweit die deutsche zunge klingt und *dem allmächtigen* (or, *der allmächtige*) lieder singt | Seinem landsmann, dem er ebensoviel verdankte, wie *dem grossen dichter* (or, *der grosse dichter*) | Doch würde die gesellschaft *des Indiers* (or, *dem Indier*) lästig gewesen sein | Darin hat Calderon wohl nur einen konkurrenten, Shakespeare, *welcher* freilich *den span-*

ischen dichter nicht erreicht (or, *den . . . der spanische dich-ter . . .*) | Nur Diopeithes feindet dich insgeheim an, und *der bruder* des Kimon und *sein freund* T. (or, *den bruder . . . seinen freund*).

It is this very fact that countless sentences of this sort are perfectly clear which leads to the employment of similar constructions even where the resulting sentence is by no means clear ; but if all, or most, words were identical in the nominative and the dative, like *gott*, or in the dative and genitive, like *der Indierin*, constructions like those used would be impossible to imagine in a language meant to be an intelligible vehicle of thought. And so the ultimate cause of the ambiguities is the inconsistency in the formation of the several cases. But this inconsistency is found in all the old languages of the Aryan family : cases which in one gender or with one class of stems are kept perfectly distinct, are in others identical. I take some examples from Latin, because this is perhaps the best known language of this type, but Gothic or Old Slavonic would show inconsistencies of the same kind. *Domini* is genitive singular and nominative plural (corresponding to, e.g., *verbi* and *verba*) ; *verba* is nominative and accusative pl. (corresponding to *domini* and *dominos*) ; *domino* is dative and ablative ; *dominæ* gen. and dative singular and nominative plural ; *te* is accusative and ablative ; *qui* is singular and plural ; *quæ* singular fem. and plural fem. and neuter, etc. Hence, while *patres filios amant* or *patres filii amant* are perfectly clear, *patres consules amant* allows of two interpretations ; and in how many ways cannot such a proposition as *Horatius et Virgilius poetæ Varii amici erant* be construed ? *Menenii patris munus* may mean ' the gift of father Menenius,' or ' the gift of Menenius's father ' ; *expers illius periculi* either ' free from that danger ' or ' free from (sharing) that person's danger ' ; in an infinitive construction with two accusatives, the only way to know which is the subject and which the object is to consider the context, and that is not always decisive, as in the oracular response given to the Æacide Pyrrhus, as quoted by Cicero from Ennius : " Aio *te*, Æacida, *Romanos* vincere posse." Such drawbacks seem to be inseparable from the structure of the highly flexional Aryan languages ; although they are not logical consequences of a wealth of forms, yet historically they cling to those languages which have the greatest number of grammatical endings. And as we are here concerned not with the question how to construct an artificial language (and even there I should not advise the adoption of many case distinctions), but with the valuation of natural languages as actually existing in their earlier and modern stages, we cannot accept Johannson's verdict : " The greater the wealth of forms, the more intelligible the speech."

XVIII.—§ 5. Word Order.

If the German sentences quoted above are **ambiguous, it is** not only on account of the want of clearness in the forms employed, but also on account of the German rules of word order. One rule places the verb last in subordinate sentences, and in two of the sentences there would be no ambiguity in principal sentences : Die deutsche zunge klingt und *singt gott* im himmel lieder ; or, Die deutsche zunge klingt, und *gott im himmel singt* lieder | *Sie erreicht* freilich nicht die spanische dichterin ; or, Die spanische dichterin *erreicht sie* freilich nicht. In one of the remaining sentences the ambiguity is caused by the rule that the verb must be placed immediately after an introductory subjunct : if we omit *doch* the sentence becomes clear : Die *gesellschaft der Indierin würde* lästig gewesen sein, or, *Die gesellschaft würde der Indierin* lästig gewesen sein. Here, again we see the ill consequences of inconsistency of linguistic structure ; some of the rules for word position serve to show grammatical relations, but in certain cases they have to give way to other rules, which counteract this useful purpose. If you change the order of words in a German sentence, you will often find that the meaning is not changed, but the result will be an unidiomatic construction (bad grammar) ; while in English a transposition will often result in perfectly good grammar, only the meaning will be an entirely different one from the original sentence. This does not amount to saying that the German rules of position are useless and the English ones all useful, but only to saying that in English word order is utilized to express difference of meaning to a far greater extent than in German.

One critic cites against me " one example, which figures in almost every Rhetoric as a violation of clearness : *And thus the son the fervid sire address'd*," and he adds : " The use of a separate form for nominative and accusative would clear up the ambiguity immediately." The retort is obvious : no doubt it would, but so would the use of a natural word order. Word order is just as much a part of English grammar as case-endings are in other languages ; a violation of the rules of word order may cause the same want of intelligibility as the use of *dominum* instead of *dominus* would in Latin. And if the example is found in almost every English Rhetoric, I am glad to say that equally ambiguous sentences are very rare indeed in other English books. Even in poetry, where there is such a thing as poetic licence, and where the exigencies of rhythm and rime, as well as the fondness for archaic and out-of-the-way expressions, will often induce deviations from the word order of prose, real ambiguity will very seldom arise on that account. It is true that it has been disputed which is the subject in Gray's line:

And all the air a solemn stillness holds,

but then it does not matter much, for the ultimate understanding of the line must be exactly the same whether the air holds stillness or stillness holds the air. In ordinary language we may find similar collocations, but it is worth saying with some emphasis that there can never be any doubt as to which is the subject and which the object. The ordinary word order is, Subject-Verb-Object, and where there is a deviation there must always be some special reason for it. This may be the wish, especially for the sake of some contrast, to throw into relief some member of the sentence. If this is the subject, the purpose is achieved by stressing it, but the word order is not affected. But if it is the object, this may be placed in the very beginning of the sentence, but in that case English does not, like German and Danish, require inversion of the verb, and the order consequently is, Object-Subject-Verb, which is perfectly clear and unambiguous. See, for instance, Dickens's sentence: "*Talent, Mr. Micawber* has; *capital, Mr. Micawber* has not*," and the following passage from a recent novel: "Even Royalty had not quite their glow and glitter; *Royalty you* might see any day, driving, bowing, smiling. The Queen had a smile for every one; but *the Duchess no one, not even Lizzie,* ever saw." Thus, also, in Shakespeare's:

Things base and vilde, holding no quantity,
Loue can transpose to forme and dignity (*Mids.* I. 1. 233),

and in Longfellow's translation from Logau:

A blind man is a poor man, and blind a poor man is;
For the former seeth no man, and *the latter no man* sees.

The reason for deviating from the order, Subject-Verb-Object, may again be purely grammatical: a relative or an interrogative pronoun must be placed first; but here, too, English grammar precludes ambiguity, as witness the following sentences: This picture, which surpasses Mona Lisa | This picture, which Mona Lisa surpasses | What picture surpasses Mona Lisa? | What picture does Mona Lisa surpass? In German (dieses bild, welches die M. L. übertrifft, etc.) all four sentences would be ambiguous, in Danish the two last would be indistinguishable; but English shows that a small number of case forms is not incompatible with perfect clearness and perspicuity. If the famous oracular answer (*Henry VI, 2nd Part,* I. 4. 33), "The Duke yet liues, that Henry shall depose," is ambiguous, it is only because it is in verse, where you expect inversions : in ordinary prose it could be understood only in one way, as the word order would be reversed if *Henry* was meant as the object.

XVIII.—§ 6. Gender.

Besides case distinctions the older Aryan languages have a rather complicated system of gender distinctions, which in many instances agrees with, but in many others is totally independent of, and even may be completely at war with, the natural distinction between male beings, female beings and things without sex. This grammatical gender is sometimes looked upon as something valuable for a language to possess ; thus Schroeder (*Die formale Unterscheidung* 87) says : "The formal distinction of genders is decidedly an enormous advantage which the Aryan, Semitic and Egyptian languages have before all other languages." Aasen (*Norsk Grammatik* 123) finds that the preservation of the old genders gives vividness and variety to a language ; he therefore, in constructing his artificial Norwegian 'landsmaal,' based it on those dialects which made a formal distinction between the masculine and feminine article. But other scholars have recognized the disadvantages accruing from such distinctions ; thus Tegnér (SM 50) regrets the fact that in Swedish it is impossible to give such a form to the sentence ' sin make må man ej svika ' as to make it clear that the admonition is applicable to both husband and wife, because *make,* ' mate,' is masculine, and *maka* feminine. In Danish, where *mage* is common to both sexes, no such difficulty arises. Gabelentz (Spr 234) says : "Das grammatische geschlecht bringt es weiter mit sich dass wir deutschen nie eine frauensperson als einen menschen und nicht leicht einen mann als eine person bezeichnen."

As a matter of fact, German gender is responsible for many difficulties, not only when it is in conflict with natural sex, as when one may hesitate whether to use the pronoun *es* or *sie* in reference to a person just mentioned as *das mädchen* or *das weib,* or *er* or *sie* in reference to *die schildwache,* but also when sexless things are concerned, and *er* might be taken as either referring to the man or to *der stuhl* or to *der wald* just mentioned, etc. In France, grammarians have disputed without end as to the propriety or not of referring to the (feminine) word *personnes* by means of the pronoun *ils* (see Nyrop, *Kongruens* 24, and Gr. iii. § 712) : "Les personnes que vous attendiez sont *tous logés* ici." As a negative pronoun *personne* is now frankly masculine : ' personne n'est mal·

heureux.' With *gens* the old feminine gender is still kept up when an adjective precedes, as in *les bonnes gens*, thus also *toutes les bonnes gens*, but when the adjective has no separate feminine form, schoolmasters prefer to say *tous les honnêtes gens*, and the masculine generally prevails when the adjective is at some distance from *gens*, as in the old school-example, *Instruits par l'expérience, toutes les vieilles gens sont soupçonneux.* There is a good deal of artificiality in the strict rules of grammarians on this point, and it is therefore good that the Arrêté ministériel of 1901 tolerates greater liberty; but conflicts are unavoidable, and will rise quite naturally, in any language that has not arrived at the perfect stage of complete genderlessness (which, of course, is not identical with inability to express sex-differences).

Most English pronouns make no distinction of sex: *I, you, we, they, who, each, somebody,* etc. Yet, when we hear that Finnic and Magyar, and indeed the vast majority of languages outside the Aryan and Semitic world, have no separate forms for *he* and *she*, our first thought is one of astonishment; we fail to see how it is possible to do without this distinction. But if we look more closely we shall see that it is at times an inconvenience to have to specify the sex of the person spoken about. Coleridge (*Anima Poetæ* 190) regretted the lack of a pronoun to refer to the word *person*, as it necessitated some stiff and strange construction like 'not letting the person be aware wherein offence had been given,' instead of 'wherein he or she has offended.' It has been said that if a genderless pronoun could be substituted for *he* in such a proposition as this: 'It would be interesting if each of the leading poets would tell us what he considers his best work,' ladies would be spared the disparaging implication that the leading poets were all men. Similarly there is something incongruous in the following sentence found in a German review of a book: "Was Maria und Fritz so zueinander zog, war, dass *jeder* von ihnen *am anderen* sah, wie *er* unglücklich war." Anyone who has written much in Ido will have often felt how convenient it is to have the common-sex pronouns *lu* (he or she), *singlu, altru,* etc. It is interesting to see the different ways out of the difficulty resorted to in actual language. First the cumbrous use of *he or she*, as in Fielding *TJ* 1. 174, the reader's heart (if he or she have any) | Miss Muloch *H.* 2. 128, each one made his or her comment.[1] Secondly, the use of *he* alone: If anybody behaves in such and such a manner, he will be punished (cf. the wholly

[1] This ungainly repetition is frequent in the Latin of Roman law, e.g. *Digest.* IV. 5. 2, *Qui quæve . . .* capite *diminuti diminutæ* esse dicentur, in *eos easve . . .* iudicium dabo. | XLIII. 30, *Qui quæve* in potestate Lucii Titii est, si *is eave* apud te est, dolove malo tuo factum est quominus apud

unobjectionable, but not always applicable, formula : Whoever behaves in such and such a manner will be punished). This use of *he* has been legalized by the Act 13 and 14 Vict., cap. 21. 4 : "That in all acts words importing the masculine gender shall be deemed and taken to include females." Third, the sexless but plural form *they* may be used. If you try to put the phrase, ' Does anybody prevent you ? ' in another way, beginning with ' Nobody prevents you,' and then adding the interrogatory formula, you will perceive that ' does he ' is too definite, and ' does he or she ' too clumsy ; and you will therefore naturally say (as Thackeray does, *P* 2. 260), " Nobody prevents you, do they ? " In the same manner Shakespeare writes (*Lucr.* 125) : " Everybody to rest themselves betake." The substitution of the plural for the singular is not wholly illogical ; for *everybody* is much the same thing as ' all men,' and *nobody* is the negation of ' all men ' ; but the phenomenon is extended to cases where this explanation will not hold good, as in G. Eliot, *M.* 2. 304, I shouldn't like to punish any one, even if *they'd* done me wrong. (For many examples from good writers see my MEG. ii. 5, 56.)

The English interrogative *who* is not, like the *quis* or *quæ* of the Romans, limited to one sex and one number, so that our question ' Who did it ? ' to be rendered exactly in Latin, would require a combination of the four : *Quis hoc fecit ? Quæ hoc fecit ? Qui hoc fecerunt ? Quæ hoc fecerunt ?* or rather, the abstract nature of *who* (and of *did*) makes it possible to express such a question much more indefinitely in English than in any highly flexional language ; and indefiniteness in many cases means greater precision, or a closer correspondence between thought and expression.

XVIII.—§ 7. Nominal Concord.

We have seen in the case of the verbs how widely diffused in all the old Aryan languages is the phenomenon of Concord. It is the same with the nouns. Here, as there, it consists in secondary words (here chiefly adjectives) being made to agree with principal words, but while with the verbs the agreement was in number and person, here it is in number, case and gender. This is well known in Greek and Latin ; as examples from Gothic may here be given Luk. 1. 72, *gamunan triggwos weihaizos seinaizos,* ' to remember

te esset, ita *eum eamve* exhibeas. | XI. 3, Qui *servum servam* alienum *alienam* recepisse persuasisseve quid ei dicitur dolo malo, quo *eum eam* deteriorem faceret, in eum, quanti ea res erit, in duplum iudicium dabo. I owe these and some other Latin examples to my late teacher, Dr. O. Siesbye. From French, Nyrop (*Kongruens,* p. 12) gives some corresponding examples : *tous ceux et toutes celles* qui, ayant été orphelins, avaient eu une enfance malheureuse (Philippe), and from Old French : Lors donna congié à *ceus et à celes* que il avoit rescous (Villehardouin).

His holy covenant,' and 1. 75, *allans dagans unsarans,* 'all our days.' The English translation shows how English has discarded this trait, for there is nothing in the forms of (*his*), *holy, all* and *our,* as in the Gothic forms, to indicate what substantive they belong to.

Wherever the same adjectival idea is to be joined to two substantives, the concordless junction is an obvious advantage, as seen from a comparison of the English ' my wife and children ' with the French ' ma femme et mes enfants,' or of ' the *local* press and committees' with ' *la* presse *locale* et *les* comités *locaux.*' Try to translate exactly into French or Latin such a sentence as this : " What are the present state and wants of mankind ? " (Ruskin). Cf. also the expression ' a verdict of wilful murder against *some* person or persons *unknown,*' where *some* and *unknown* belong to the singular as well as to the plural forms ; Fielding writes (*TJ* 3. 65) : " *Some particular* chapter, or perhaps chapters, *may be obnoxious.*" Where an English editor of a text will write : " Some (indifferently singular and plural) word or words wanting here," a Dane will write : " Et (sg.) eller flere (pl.) ord (indifferent) mangler her." These last examples may be taken as proof that it might even in some cases be advantageous to have forms in the substantives that did not show number ; still, it must be recognized that the distinction between one and more than one rightly belongs to substantival notions, but logically it has as little to do with adjectival as with verbal notions (cf. above, Ch. XVII § 11). In ' black spots ' it is the spots, but not the qualities of black, that we count. And in ' two black spots ' it is of course quite superfluous to add a dual or plural ending (as in Latin *duo, duæ*) in order to indicate once more what the word *two* denotes sufficiently, namely, that we have not to do with a singular. Compare, finally, E. *to the father and mother,* Fr. *au père et à la mère,* G. *zu dem vater und der mutter* (*zum vater und zur mutter*).

If it is admitted that it is an inconvenience whenever you want to use an adjective to have to put it in the form corresponding in case, number and gender to its substantive, it may be thought a redeeming feature of the language which makes this demand that, on the other hand, it allows you to place the adjective at some distance from the substantive, and yet the hearer or reader will at once connect the two together. But here, as elsewhere in ' energetics,' the question is whether the advantage counterbalances the disadvantage ; in other words, whether the fact that you are free to place your adjective where you will is worth the price you pay for it in being always saddled with the heavy apparatus of adjectival flexions. Why should you want to remove the adjective from the substantive, which naturally must be in your thought when you are thinking of the adjective There is one natural employment of the adjective in which it has very often to stand at some distance from the substantive, namely, when it is predicative ; but then the example of German shows the needlessness of concord in that case, for while the adjunct adjective is inflected (ein *guter* mensch, eine *gute* frau, ein *gutes* buch, *gute* bücher) the predicative is invariable like the adverb (der mensch ist *gut*, die frau ist *gut*, das buch ist *gut*, die bücher sind *gut*). It is chiefly in poetry that a Latin adjective is placed far from its substantive, as in Vergil : " Et bene apud memores veteris stat gratia facti " (*Æn.* IV. 539), where the form shows that *veteris* is to be taken with *facti* (but then, where does *bene* belong ? it might be taken with *memores, stat* or *facti*). In Horace's well-known aphorism : " Æquam memento rebus in arduis servare mentem," the flexional form of *æquam* allows him to place it first, far from *mentem*, and thus facilitates for him the task of building up a perfect metrical line ; but for the reader it would certainly be preferable to have had *æquam mentem* together at once, instead of having to hold his attention in suspense for five words, till finally he comes upon a word with which to connect the adjective. There is therefore no economizing of the energy of reader or hearer. Extreme examples may be found in Icelandic skaldic poetry, in which the poets, to fulfil the requirements of a highly complicated metrical system, entailing initial and medial rimes, very often place the words in what logically must be considered the worst disorder, thereby making their poem as difficult to understand as an intricate chess-problem is to solve—and certainly coming short of the highest poetical form.

XVIII.—§ 8. The English Genitive.

If we compare a group of Latin words, such as *opera virorum omnium bonorum veterum*, with a corresponding group in a few other languages of a less flexional type : OE. *ealra godra ealdra manna weorc* ; Danish *alle gode gamle mænds værker* ; Modern English *all good old men's works*, we perceive by analyzing the ideas expressed by the several words that the Romans said really : ' work,' plural, nominative or accusative + ' man,' plural, masculine, genitive + ' all,' plural, genitive + ' good,' plural, masculine, genitive + ' old,' plural, masculine, genitive. Leaving *opera* out of consideration, we find that plural number is expressed four times, genitive case also four times, and masculine gender twice ; [1]

[1] If instead of *omnium veterum* I had chosen, for instance, *multorum antiquorum*, the meaning of masculine gender would have been rendered four times : for languages, especially the older ones, are not distinguished by consistency.

in Old English the signs of number and case are found four times each, while there is no indication of gender ; in Danish the plural number is marked four times and the case once. And finally, in Modern English, we find each idea expressed once only ; and as nothing is lost in clearness, this method as being the easiest and shortest, must be considered the best. Mathematically the different ways of rendering the same thing might be represented by the formulas : anx + bnx + cnx = (an + bn + cn)x = (a+b+c)nx.

This unusual faculty of 'parenthesizing' causes Danish, and to a still greater degree English, to stand outside the definition of the Aryan family of languages given by the earlier school of linguists, according to which the Aryan substantive and adjective can never be without a sign indicating case. Schleicher (NV 526) says : " The radical difference between Magyar and Indo-Germanic (Aryan) words is brought out distinctly by the fact that the post-positions belonging to co-ordinated nouns can be dispensed with in all the nouns except the last of the series, e.g. *a jó embernek*, ' dem guten menschen ' (*a* for *az*, demonstrative pronoun, article ; *jó*, good ; *ember*, man, *-nek*, *-nak*, postposition with pretty much the same meaning as the dative case), for *az-nak* (annak) *jó-nak ember-nek*, as if in Greek you should say το ἀγαϑο ἀνϑρώπῳ. An attributive adjective preceding its noun always has the form of the pure stem, the sign of plurality and the postposition indicating case not being added to it. Magyars say, for instance, *Hunyady Mátyás magyar király-nak* (to the Hungarian king Mathew Hun-yady), *-nak* belonging here to all the preceding words. Nearly the same thing takes place where several words are joined together by means of ' and.' "

Now, this is an exact parallel to the English group genitive in cases like ' all good old men's works,' ' the King of England's power,' ' Beaumont and Fletcher's plays,' ' somebody else's turn,' etc. The way in which this group genitive has developed in comparatively recent times may be summed up as follows (see the detailed exposition in my ChE ch. iii.) : In the oldest English *-s* is a case-ending, like all others found in flexional lan-guages ; it forms together with the body of the noun one indivi-sible whole, in which it is sometimes impossible to tell where the kernel of the word ends and the ending begins (compare *endes* from *ende* and *heriges* from *here*) ; only some words have this ending, and in others the genitive is indicated in other ways. As to syntax, the meaning or function of the genitive is complicated and rather vague, and there are no fixed rules for the position of the genitive in the sentence.

In course of time we witness a gradual development towards greater regularity and precision. The partitive, objective, descriptive and some other functions of the genitive become obsolete; the genitive is invariably put immediately before the word it belongs to ; irregular forms disappear, the *s* ending alone surviving as the fittest, so that at last we have one definite ending with one definite function and one definite position.

In Old English, when several words belonging together were to be put in the genitive, each of them had to take the genitive mark, though this was often different in different words, and thus we had combinations like *anes reades mannes*, ' a red man's ' | *þære godlican lufe*, ' the godlike love's ' | *ealra godra ealdra manna weorc*, etc. Now the *s* used everywhere is much more independent, and may be separated from the principal word by an adverb like *else* or by a prepositional group like *of England*, and one *s* is sufficient at the end even of a long group of words. Here, then, we see in the full light of comparatively recent history a giving up of the old flexion with its inseparability of the constituent elements of the word and with its strictness of concord ; an easier and more regular system is developed, in which the ending leads a more independent existence and may be compared with the ' agglutinated ' elements of such a language as Magyar or even with the ' empty words ' of Chinese grammar. The direction of this development is the direct opposite of that assumed by most linguists for the development of languages in prehistoric times.

XVIII.—§ 9. Bantu Concord.

One of the most characteristic traits of the history of English is thus seen to be the gradual getting rid of concord as of something superfluous. Where concord is found in our family of languages, it certainly is an heirloom from a primitive age, and strikes us now as an outcome of a tendency to be more explicit than to more advanced people seems strictly necessary. It is on a par with the ' concord of negatives,' as we might term the emphasizing of the negative idea by seemingly redundant repetitions. In Old English it was the regular idiom to say : *nan man nyste nan þing*, ' no man not-knew nothing '; so it was in Chaucer's time : he *neuere* yet *no* vileynye *ne* sayde In all his lyf unto *no* manner wight ; and it survives in the vulgar speech of our own days : there was *niver nobody* else gen (gave) me *nothin* ' (George Eliot) ; whereas standard Modern English is content with one negation : no man knew anything, etc. That concord is really a primitive trait (though not, of course, found equally distributed among all ' primitive peoples ') will be seen also by a rapid glance at the structure of t1e South African group of languages called Bantu, for here we find not only repetition of negatives, but also other phenomena of concord in specially luxuriant growth.

I take the following examples chiefly from W. H. I. Bleek's excellent, though unfortunately unfinished, *Comparative Grammar*, though I am well aware that expressions like *si-m-tanda* (we love him) "are never used by natives with this meaning without being determined by some other expression" (Torrend, p. 7). The Zulu word for 'man' is *umuntu*; every word in the same or a following sentence having any reference to that word must begin with something to remind you of the beginning of *umuntu*. This will be, according to fixed rules, either *mu* or *u*, or *w* or *m*. In the following sentence, the meaning of which is 'our handsome man (or woman) appears, we love him (or her),' these reminders (as I shall term them) are printed in italics:

*umu*ntu	*we*tu	*omu*chle *u*yabonakala,	si*m*tanda (1)
man	ours	handsome appears,	we love.

If, instead of the singular, we take the corresponding plural *abantu*, 'men, people' (whence the generic name of Bantu), the sentence looks quite different:

*aba*ntu *b*etu *aba*chle *ba*yabonakala, si*ba*tanda (2).

In the same way, if we successively take as our starting-point *ilizwe*, 'country,' the corresponding plural *amazwe*, 'countries,' *isizwe*, 'nation,' *izizwe*, 'nations,' *intombi*, 'girl,' *izintombi*, 'girls,' we get:

*ili*zwe	*l*etu	*eli*chle	*li*yabonakala,	si*li*tanda (5)
*ama*zwe	*e*tu	*ama*chle	*a*yabonakala,	si*wa*tanda (6)
*isi*zwe	*s*etu	*esi*chle	*si*yabonakala,	si*si*tanda (7)
*izi*zwe	*z*etu	*ezi*chle	*zi*yabonakala,	si*zi*tanda (8)
*into*mbi	*y*etu	*en*chle	*i*yabonakala,	si*yi*tanda (9)
*izin*tombi	*z*etu	*ezin*chle	*zi*yabonakala,	si*zi*tanda (10)
(girls)	our	handsome	appear,	we love.[1]

In other words, every substantive belongs to one of several classes, of which some have a singular and others a plural meaning; each of these classes has its own prefix, by means of which the concord of the parts of a sentence is indicated. (An inhabitant

---

[1] The change of the initial sound of the reminder belonging to the adjective is explained through composition with a 'relative particle' *a*; *au* becoming *o*, and *ai*, *e*. The numbers within parentheses refer to the numbers of Bleek's classes. Similar sentences from Tonga are found in Torrend's *Compar. Gr.* p. 6 f.

of the country of Uganda is called *muganda*, pl. *baganda* or *waganda* ; the language spoken there is *luganda*.)

It will be noticed that adjectives such as 'handsome' or 'ours' take different shapes according to the word to which they refer ; in the Zulu Lord's Prayer 'thy' is found in the following forms : *lako* (referring to *igama*, 'name,' for *iligama*, 5), *bako*, (*ubu*kumkani, 'kingdom,' 14), *yako* (*intando*, 'will,' 9). So also the genitive case of the same noun has a great many different forms, for the genitive relation is expressed by the reminder of the governing word + the 'relative particle' *a* (which is combined with the following sound) ; take, for instance, *inkosi*, 'chief, king' :

> *umu*ntu *w*enkosi, 'the king's man' (1 ; *we* for *w + a + i*).
> *aba*ntu *b*enkosi, 'the king's men' (2).
> *ili*zwe *l*enkosi, 'the king's country' (5).
> *ama*zwe enkosi, 'the king's countries' (6).
> *isi*zwe *s*enkosi, 'the king's nation' (7).
> *uku*tanda *kw*enkosi, 'the king's love' (15).

Livingstone says that these apparently redundant repetitions "impart energy and perspicuity to each member of a proposition, and prevent the possibility of a mistake as to the antecedent." These prefixes are necessary to the Bantu languages ; still, Bleek is right as against Livingstone in speaking of the repetitions as cumbersome, just as the endings of Latin *multorum virorum antiquorum* are cumbersome, however indispensable they may have been to the contemporaries of Cicero.

These African phenomena have been mentioned here chiefly to show to what lengths concord may go in the speech of some primitive peoples. The prevalent opinion is that each of these prefixes (*umu, aba, ili*, etc.) was originally an independent word, and that thus words like *umuntu, ilizwe*, were at first compounds like E. *steamship*, where it would evidently be possible to imagine a reference to this word by means of a repeated *ship* (our ship, which ship is a great ship, the ship appears, we love the ship) ; but at any rate the Zulus extend this principle to cases that would be parallel to an imagined repetition of *friendship* by means of the same *ship*, or to referring to *steamer* by means of the ending *er* (Bleek 107). Bleek and others have tried to find out by an analysis of the words making up the different classes what may have been the original meaning of the class-prefix, but very often the connecting tie is extremely loose, and in many cases it seems that a word might with equal right have belonged to another class than the one to which it actually belongs. The connexion also frequently seems to be a derived rather than an original one, and much in this class-division is just as arbitrary as the reference of Aryan nouns to each of the three genders. In several of the classes the words have a definite numerical value, so that they go together in pairs as corresponding singular and plural nouns ; but the existence of a certain number of exceptions shows that these numerical values cannot originally have been associated with the class prefixes, but must be due to an extension by analogy (Bleek 140 ff.). The starting-point may have been substantives standing to each other in the relation of ' person ' to ' people,' ' soldier ' to ' army,' ' tree ' to ' forest,' etc. The prefixes of such words as the latter of each of these pairs will easily acquire a certain sense of plurality, no matter what they may have meant originally, and then they will lend themselves to forming a kind of plural in other nouns, being either put instead of the prefix belonging properly to the noun (*amazwe*, ' countries,' 6 ; *ilizwe*, ' country,' 5), or placed before it (*ma-luto*, ' spoons,' 6, *luto*, ' spoon,' 11).

In some of the languages " the forms of some of the prefixes have been so strongly contracted as almost to defy identification." (Bleek 234). All the prefixes probably at first had fuller forms than appear now. Bleek noticed that the *ma-* prefix never, except in some degraded languages, had a corresponding *ma-* as particle, but, on the contrary, is followed in the sentence by *ga-, ya-,* or *u-,* and *mu-* (3) generally has a corresponding particle *gu-*. Now, Sir Harry Johnston (*The Uganda Protectorate*, 1902, 2. 891) has found that on Mount Eldon and in Kavirondo there are some very archaic forms of Bantu languages, in which *gumu-* and *gama-* are the commonly used forms of the *mu-* and *ma-* prefixes, as well as *baba-* and *bubu-* for ordinary *ba-, bu-* ; he infers that the original forms of *mu-, ma-* were *ngumu-, ngama-*. I am not so sure that he is right when he says that these prefixes were originally " words which had a separate meaning of their own, either as directives or demonstrative pronouns, as indications of sex, weakness, little-ness or greatness, and so on "—for, as we shall see in a subsequent chapter, such grammatical instruments may have been at first inseparable parts of long words—parts which had no meaning of their own—and have acquired some more or less vague gram-matical meaning through being extended gradually to other words with which they had originally nothing to do. The actual irregularity in their distribution certainly seems to point in that direction.

XVIII.—§ 10. Word Order Again.

Mention has already been made here and there of word order and its relation to the great question of simplification of grammatical structure ; but it will be well in this place to return to the subject in a more comprehensive way. The theory of word order has long been the Cinderella of linguistic science : how many even of the best and fullest grammars are wholly, or almost wholly, silent about it ! And yet it presents a great many problems of high importance and of the greatest interest, not only in those languages in which word order has been extensively utilized for grammatical purposes, such as English and Chinese, but in other languages as well.

In historical times we see a gradual evolution of strict rules for word order, while our general impression of the older stages of our languages is that words were often placed more or less at random. This is what we should naturally expect from primitive man, whose thoughts and words are most likely to have come to him rushing helter-skelter, in wild confusion. One cannot, of course, apply so strong an expression to languages such as Sanskrit, Greek or Gothic ; still, compared with our modern languages, it cannot be denied that there is in them much more of what from one point of view is disorder, and from another freedom.

This is especially the case with regard to the mutual position of the subject of a sentence and its verb. In the earliest times, sometimes one of them comes first, and sometimes the other. Then there is a growing tendency to place the subject first, and as this position is found not only in most European languages but also in Chinese and other languages of far-away, the phenomenon must be founded in the very nature of human thought, though its non-prevalence in most of the older Aryan languages goes far to show that this particular order is only natural to *developed* human thought.

Survivals of the earlier state of things are found here and there ; thus, in German ballad style : " Kam ein schlanker bursch gegangen." But it is well worth noticing that such an arrangement is generally avoided, in German as well as in the other modern languages of Western Europe, and in those cases where there is some reason for placing the verb before the subject, the speaker still, as it were, satisfies his grammatical instinct by putting a kind of sham subject before the verb, as in E. *there* comes a time when . . ., Dan. *der* kommer en tid da . . ., G. *es* kommt eine zeit wo . . ., Fr. *il* arrive un temps où . . .

In Keltic the habitual word order placed the verb first, but little by little the tendency prevailed to introduce most sentences by a periphrasis, as in ' (it) is the man that comes,' and as that came to mean merely ' the man comes,' the word order Subject-Verb was thus brought about circuitously.

Before this particular word order, Subject-Verb, was firmly established in modern Gothonic languages, an exception obtained wherever the sentence began with some other word than the subject; this might be some important member of the proposition that was placed first for the sake of emphasis, or it might be some unimportant little adverb, but the rule was that the verb should at any rate have the second place, as being felt to be in some way the middle or central part of the whole, and the subject had then to be content to be placed after the verb. This was the rule in Middle English and in Old French, and it is still strictly followed in German and Danish : Gestern *kam das schiff* | Pigen *gav jeg kagen, ikke drengen.* Traces of the practice are still found in English in parenthetic sentences to indicate who is the speaker (' Oh, yes,' said he), and after a somewhat long subjunct, if there is no object (' About this time died the gentle Queen Elizabeth '), where this word order is little more than a stylistic trick to avoid the abrupt effect of ending the sentence with an isolated verb like *died.* Otherwise the order Subject-Verb is almost universal in English.

XVIII.—§ 11. Compromises.

The inverted order, Verb-Subject, is used extensively in many languages to express questions, wishes and invitations. But, as already stated, this order was not originally peculiar to such sentences. A question was expressed, no matter how the words were arranged, by pronouncing the whole sentence, or the most important part of it, in a peculiar rising tone. This manner of indicating questions is, of course, still kept up in modern speech, and is often the only thing to show that a question is meant (' John ? ' | ' John is here ? '). But although there was thus a natural manner of expressing questions, and although the inverted word order was used in other sorts of sentences as well, yet in course of time there came to be a connexion between the two things, so that putting the verb before the subject was felt as implying a question. The rising tone then came to be less necessary, and is much less marked in inverted sentences like ' Is John here ? ' than in sentences with the usual word order : ' John is here ? '

Now, after this method of indicating questions had become comparatively fixed, and after the habit of thinking of the subject first had become all but universal, these two principles entered into conflict, the result of which has been, in English, Danish and French, the establishment in some cases of various kinds of compromise, in which the interrogatory word order has formally carried the day, while really the verb, that is to say the verb which means something, is placed after its subject. In English, this is attained by means of the auxiliary *do* : instead of Shakespeare's "Came he not home to-night ? " (*Ro.* II. 4. 2) we now say, " Did he not (or, Didn't he) come home to-night ? " and so in all cases where a similar arrangement is not already brought about by the presence of some other auxiliary, ' Will he come ? ', ' Can he come ? ', etc. Where we have an interrogatory pronoun as a subject, no auxiliary is required, because the natural front position of the pronoun maintains the order Subject-Verb (Who came ? | What happened ?). But if the pronoun is not the subject, *do* is required to establish the balance between the two principles (Who(m) did you see ? | What does he say ?).

In Danish, the verb *mon*, used in the old language to indicate a weak necessity or a vague futurity, fulfils to a certain extent the same office as the English *do* ; up to the eighteenth century *mon* was really an auxiliary verb, followed by the infinitive : ' Mon han komme ? ' ; but now the construction has changed, the indicative is used with *mon* : ' Mon han kommer ? ', and *mon* is no longer a verb, but an interrogatory adverb, which serves the purpose of placing the subject before the verb, besides making the question more indefinite and vague : ' Kommer han ? ' means ' Does he come ? ' or ' Will he come ? ' but ' Mon han kommer ? ' means ' Does he come (Will he come), do you think ? '

French, finally, has developed two distinct forms of compromise between the conflicting principles, for in ' Est-ce que Pierre bat Jean ? ' *est-ce* represents the interrogatory and *Pierre bat* the usual word order, and in ' Pierre bat-il Jean ? ' the real subject is placed before and the sham subject after the verb. Here also, as in Danish, the ultimate result is the creation of ' empty words,' or interrogatory adverbs : *est-ce-que* in every respect except in spelling is one word (note that it does not change with the tense of the main verb), and thus is a sentence prefix to introduce questions ; and in popular speech we find another empty word, namely *ti* (see, among other scholars, G. Paris, *Mélanges ling.* 276). The origin of this *ti* is very curious. While the *t* of Latin *amat*, etc., coming after a vowel, disappeared at a very early period of the French language, and so produced *il aime*, etc., the same *t* was kept in Old French wherever a consonant protected it,[1] and so gave the forms *est*, *sont*, *fait* (from *fact*, for *facit*), *font*, *chantent*, etc. From *est-il*, *fait-il*, etc., the *t* was then by analogy reintroduced in *aime-t-il*, instead of the earlier *aime il*. Now, towards the end of the Middle Ages, French final consonants were as a rule

[1] This protecting consonant was dropped in pronunciation at a later period.

dropped in speech, except when followed immediately by a word beginning with a vowel. Consequently, while *t* is mute in sentences like ' Ton frère *dit* | Tes frères *disent*,' it is sounded in the corresponding questions, ' Ton frère *dit-il* ? Tes frères *disent-ils* ? As the final consonants of *il* and *ils* are also generally dropped, even by educated speakers, the difference between interrogatory and declarative sentences in the spoken language depends solely on the addition of *ti* to the verb : written phonetically, the pairs will be :

[tɔ̃ frɛ·r di — tɔ̃ frɛ·r di ti]
[te frɛ·r di·z — te frɛ·r di·z ti].

Now, popular instinct seizes upon this *ti* as a convenient sign of interrogative sentences, and, forgetting its origin, uses it even with a feminine subject, turning ' Ta sœur di(t) ' into the question ' Ta sœur di ti ? ', and in the first person : ' Je di ti ? ' ' Nous dison ti ? ' ' Je vous fais-ti tort ? ' (Maupassant). In novels this is often written as if it were the adverb *y* : C'est-y pas vrai ? | Je suis t'y bête ! | C'est-y vous le monsieur de l'Académie qui va avoir cent ans ? (Daudet). I have dwelt on this point because, besides showing the interest of many problems of word order, it also throws some light on the sometimes unexpected ways by which languages must often travel to arrive at new expressions for grammatical categories.

It was mentioned above that the inverted order, Verb-Subject, is used extensively, not only in questions, but also to express wishes and invitations. Here, too, we find in English compromises with the usual order, Subject-Verb. For, apart from such formulas as ' Long live the King ! ' a wish is generally expressed by means of *may*, which is placed first, while the real verb comes after the subject : ' May she be happy ! ', and instead of the old ' Go we ! ' we have now ' Let us go ! ' with *us*, the virtual subject, placed before the real verb. When a pronoun is wanted with an imperative, it used to be placed after the verb, as in Shakespeare : ' *Stand thou* forth ' and ' *Fear* not *thou*,' or in the Bible : ' *Turn ye* unto him,' but now the usual order has prevailed : ' *You try !* ' ' *You take* that seat, and *somebody fetch* a few more chairs ! ' But if the auxiliary *do* is used, we have the compromise order : ' *Don't you stir !* '

XVIII.—§ 12. Order Beneficial ?

I have here selected one point, the place of the subject, to illustrate the growing regularity in word order ; but the same tendency is manifested in other fields as well : the place of the object (or of two objects, if we have an indirect besides a direct object), the place of the adjunct adjective, the place of a sub-ordinate adverb, which by coming regularly before a certain case may become a preposition 'governing' that case, etc. It cannot be denied that the tendency towards a more regular word order is universal, and in accordance with the general trend of this inquiry we must next ask the question : Is this tendency a beneficial one ? Does the more regular word order found in recent stages of our languages constitute a progress in linguistic structure ? Or should it be deplored because it hinders freedom of movement ?

In answering this question we must first of all beware of letting our judgment be run away with by the word 'freedom.' Because freedom is desirable elsewhere, it does not follow that it should be the best thing in this domain ; just as above we did not allow ourselves to be imposed on by the phrase 'wealth of forms,' so here we must be on our guard against the word 'free' : what if we turned the question in another way : Which is preferable, order or disorder ? It may be true that, viewed exclusively from the standpoint of the speaker, freedom would seem to be a great advantage, as it is a restraint to him to be obliged to follow strict rules ; but an orderly arrangement is decidedly in the interest of the hearer, as it very considerably facilitates his understanding of what is said ; it is therefore, though indirectly, in the interest of the speaker too, because he naturally speaks for the purpose of being understood. Besides, he is soon in his turn to become the hearer : as no one is exclusively hearer or speaker, there can be no real conflict of interest between the two.

If it be urged in favour of a free word order that we owe a certain regard to the interests of poets, it must be taken into consideration, first, that we cannot all of us be poets, and that a regard to all those of us who resemble Molière's M. Jourdain in speaking prose without being aware of it is perhaps, after all, more important than a regard for those very few who are in the enviable position of writing readable verse ; secondly, that a statistical investigation would, no doubt, give as its result that those poets who make the most extensive use of inversions are not among the greatest of their craft ; and, finally, that so many methods are found of neutralizing the restraint of word order, in the shape of particles, passive voice, different constructions of sentences, etc., that no artist in language need despair.

So far, we have scarcely done than clear the ground before answering our question. And now we must recognize that there are some rules of word order which cannot be called beneficial in any way ; they are like certain rules of etiquette, in so far as one can see no reason for their existence, and yet one is obliged to

bow to them. Historians may, in some cases, be able to account
for their origin and show that they had a *raison d'être* at some
remote period ; but the circumstances that called them into existence then have passed away, and they are now felt to be restraints
with no concurrent advantage to reconcile us to their observance
Among rules of this class we may reckon those for placing the
French pronouns now before, and now after, the verb, now with
the dative and now with the accusative first, ' elle *me le* donne | elle
le lui donne | donnez-*le moi* | ne *me le* donnez pas.' And, again,
the rules for placing the verb, object, etc., in German subordinate
clauses otherwise than in main sentences. That the latter rules
are defective and are inferior to the English rules, which are the
same for the two kinds of sentences, was pointed out before, when
we examined Johannson's German sentences (p. 341), but here
we may state that the real, innermost reason for condemning them
is their inconsistency : the same rule does not apply in all cases.
It seems possible to establish the important principle that the
more consistent a rule for word order is, the more useful it is in
the economy of speech, not only as facilitating the understanding
of what is said, but also as rendering possible certain thoroughgoing changes in linguistic structure.

XVIII.—§ 13. Word Order and Simplification.

This, then, is the conclusion I arrive at, that as simplification
of grammatical structure, abolition of case distinctions, and so
forth, always go hand in hand with the development of a fixed
word order, this cannot be accidental, but there must exist a
relation of cause and effect between the two phenomena. Which,
then, is the *prius* or cause ? To my mind undoubtedly the fixed
word order, so that the grammatical simplification is the *posterius*
or effect. It is, however, by no means uncommon to find a half-
latent conception in people's minds that the flexional endings were
first lost ' by phonetic decay,' or ' through the blind operation
of sound laws,' and that then a fixed word order had to step in
to make up for the loss of the previous forms of expression. But
if this were true we should have to imagine an intervening period
in which the mutual relations of words were indicated in neither
way ; a period, in fact, in which speech was unintelligible and
consequently practically useless. The theory is therefore untenable.
It follows that a fixed word order must have come in first : it
would come quite gradually as a natural consequence of greater
mental development and general maturity, when the speaker's
ideas no longer came into his mind helter-skelter, but in orderly
sequence If before the establishment of some sort of fixed

word order any tendency to slur certain final consonants or vowels
of grammatical importance had manifested itself, it could not
have become universal, as it would have been constantly checked
by the necessity that speech should be intelligible, and that therefore those marks which showed the relation of different words
should not be obliterated. But when once each word was placed
at the exact spot where it properly belonged, then there was no
longer anything to forbid the endings being weakened by assimilation, etc., or being finally dropped altogether.

To bring out my view I have been obliged in the preceding
paragraph to use expressions that should not be taken too literally ;
I have spoken as if the changes referred to were made ' in the
lump,' that is, as if the word order was first settled in every
respect, and after that the endings began to be dropped. The
real facts are, of course, much more complicated, changes of one
kind being interwoven with changes of the other in such a way as
to render it difficult, if not impossible, in any particular case to
discover which was the *prius* and which the *posterius*. We are
not able to lay our finger on one spot and say : Here final *m* or
n was dropped, because it was now rendered superfluous as a case-
sign on account of the accusative being invariably placed after
the verb, or for some other such reason. Nevertheless, the essential
truth of my hypothesis seems to me unimpeachable. Look at
Latin final *s*. Cicero (*Orat.* 48. 161) expressly tells us, what is
corroborated by a good many inscriptions, that there existed a
strong tendency to drop final *s* ; but the tendency did not prevail.
The reason seems obvious ; take a page of Latin prose and try
the effect of striking out all final *s*'s, and you will find that it will
be extremely difficult to determine the meaning of many passages ;
a consonant playing so important a part in the endings of nouns
and verbs could not be left out without loss in a language possessing
so much freedom in regard to word position as Latin. Consequently it was kept, but in course of time word position became
more and more subject to laws ; and when, centuries later, after
the splitting up of Latin into the Romanic languages, the tendency
to slur over final *s* knocked once more at the door, it met no longer
with the same resistance : final *s* disappeared, first in Italian and
Rumanian, then in French, where it was kept till about the end
of the Middle Ages, and it is now beginning to sound a retreat in
Spanish ; see on Andalusian Fr. Wulff, *Un Chapitre de Phonétique
Andalouse*, 1889.

The main line of development in historical times has, I take
it, been the following : first, a period in which words were placed
somewhere or other according to the fancy of the moment, but
many of them provided with signs that would show their mutual

relations ; next, a period with retention of these signs, combined
with a growing regularity in word order, and at the same time in
many connexions a more copious employment of prepositions ;
then an increasing indistinctness and finally complete dropping
of the endings, word order (and prepositions) being now sufficient
to indicate the relations at first shown by endings and similar
means.

Viewed in this light, the transition from freedom in word
position to greater strictness must be considered a beneficial
change, since it has enabled the speakers to do away with more
circumstantial and clumsy linguistic means. Schiller says :

Jeden anderen meister erkennt man an dem, was er ausspricht ;
Was er weise verschweigt, zeigt mir den meister des stils.

(Every other master is known by what he says, but the master
of style by what he is wisely silent on.) What style is to the
individual, the general laws of language are to the nation, and we
must award the palm to that language which makes it possible
" to be wisely silent " about things which in other languages have
to be expressed in a troublesome way, and which have often to
be expressed over and over again (vir*orum* omni*um* bon*orum*
veter*um*, eal*ra* god*ra* eald*ra* mann*a*). Could any linguistic expedient
be more worthy of the genus *homo sapiens* than using for different
purposes, with different significations, two sentences like ' John
beats Henry ' and ' Henry beats John,' or the four Danish ones,
' Jens slaar Henrik—Henrik slaar Jens—slaar Jens Henrik ?—
slaar Henrik Jens ? ' (John beats Henry—H. beats J.—does J.
beat H. ?—does H. beat J. ?), or the Chinese use of *či* in different
places (Ch. XIX § 3) ? Cannot this be compared with the ingenious
Arabic system of numeration, in which 234 means something
entirely different from 324, or 423, or 432, and the ideas of " tens "
and " hundreds " are elegantly suggested by the order of the
characters, not, as in the Roman system, ponderously expressed ?

Now, it should not be forgotten that this system, " where more
is meant than meets the ear," is not only more convenient, but
also clearer than flexions, as actually found in existing languages,
for word order in those languages which utilize it grammatically
is used much more consistently than any endings have ever been
in the old Aryan languages. It is not true, as Johannson would
have us believe, that the dispensing with old flexional endings was
too dearly bought, as it brought about increasing possibilities of
misunderstandings ; for in the evolution of languages the discarding of old flexions goes hand in hand with the development
of simpler and more regular expedients that are rather less liable
than the old ones to produce misunderstandings. Johannson

writes : "In contrast to Jespersen I do not consider that the masterly expression is the one which is 'wisely silent,' and consequently leaves the meaning to be partly guessed at, but the one which is able to impart the meaning of the speaker or writer clearly and perfectly "—but here he seems rather wide of the mark. For, just as in reading the arithmetical symbol 234 we are perfectly sure that two hundred and thirty-four is meant, and not three hundred and forty-two, so in reading and hearing ' The boy hates the girl ' we cannot have the least doubt who hates whom. After all, there is less guesswork in the grammatical understanding of English than of Latin ; cf. the examples given above, Ch. XVIII § 4, p. 343.

The tendency towards a fixed word order is therefore a progressive one, directly as well as indirectly. The substitution of word order for flexions means a victory of spiritual over material agencies.

XVIII.—§ 14. Summary.

We may here sum up the results of our comparison of the main features of the grammatical structures of ancient and modern languages belonging to our family of speech. We have found certain traits common to the old stages and certain others characteristic of recent ones, and have thus been enabled to establish some definite tendencies of development and to find out the general direction of change ; and we have shown reasons for the conviction that this development has on the whole and in the main been a beneficial one, thus justifying us in speaking about ' progress in language.' The points in which the superiority of the modern languages manifested itself were the following :

(1) The forms are generally shorter, thus involving less muscular exertion and requiring less time for their enunciation.

(2) There are not so many of them to burden the memory.

(3) Their formation is much more regular.

(4) Their syntactic use also presents fewer irregularities.

(5) Their more analytic and abstract character facilitates expression by rendering possible a great many combinations and constructions which were formerly impossible or unidiomatic.

(6) The clumsy repetitions known under the name of concord have become superfluous.

(7) A clear and unambiguous understanding is secured through a regular word order.

These several advantages have not been won all at once, and languages differ very much in the velocity with which they have been moving in the direction indicated ; thus High German is in many respects behindhand as compared with Low German ;

European Dutch as compared with African Dutch ; Swedish as
compared with Danish ; and all of them as compared with English ;
further, among the Romanic languages we see considerable variations in this respect. What is maintained is chiefly that there
is a general tendency for languages to develop along the lines here
indicated, and that this development may truly, from the anthropocentric point of view, which is the only justifiable one, be termed
a progressive evolution.

But is this tendency really general, or even universal, in the
world of languages ? It will easily be seen that my examples
have in the main been taken from comparatively few languages,
those with which I myself and presumably most of my readers
are most familiar, all of them belonging to the Gothonic and
Romanic branches of the Aryan family. Would the same theory
hold good with regard to other languages ? Without pretending
to an intimate knowledge of the history of many languages, I
yet dare assert that my conclusions are confirmed by all those
languages whose history is accessible to us. Colloquial Irish and
Gaelic have in many ways a simpler grammatical structure than
the Oldest Irish. Russian has got rid of some of the complications
of Old Slavonic, and the same is true, even in a much higher degree,
of some of the other Slavonic languages ; thus, Bulgarian has
greatly simplified its nominal and Serbian its verbal flexions. The
grammar of spoken Modern Greek is much less complicated than
that of the language of Homer or of Demosthenes. The structure
of Modern Persian is nearly as simple as English, though that of
Old Persian was highly complicated. In India we witness a
constant simplification of grammar from Sanskrit through Prakrit
and Pali to the modern languages, Hindi, Hindostani (Urdu),
Bengali, etc. Outside the Aryan world we see the same movement :
Hebrew is simpler and more regular than Assyrian, and spoken
Arabic than the old classical language, Koptic than Old Egyptian.
Of most of the other languages we are not in possession of written
records from very early times ; still, we may affirm that in Turkish
there has been an evolution, though rather a slow one, of a similar
kind ; and, as we shall see in a later chapter, Chinese seems to
have moved in the same direction, though the nature of its writing
makes the task of penetrating into its history a matter of extreme
difficulty. A comparative study of the numerous Bantu languages
spoken all over South Africa justifies us in thinking that their
evolution has been along the same lines : in some of them the
prefixes characterizing various classes of nouns have been reduced
in number and in extent (cf. above, § 9). Of one of them we have
a grammar two hundred years old, by Brusciotto à Vetralla
(re-edited by H. Grattan Guinness, London, 1882). A comparison

of his description with the language now spoken in the same region (Mpongwe) shows that the class signs have dwindled down considerably and the number of the classes has been reduced from 16 to 10. In short, though we can only prove it with regard to a minority of the multitudinous languages spoken on the globe, this minority embraces *all* the languages known to us for so long a period that we can talk of their history, and we may, therefore, confidently maintain that what may be briefly termed the tendency towards grammatical simplification is a universal fact of linguistic history.

That this simplification is progressive, i.e. beneficial, was overlooked by the older generation of linguistic thinkers, because they saw a kosmos, a beautiful and well-arranged world, in the old languages, and missed in the modern ones several things that they had been accustomed to regard with veneration. To some extent they were right : every language, when studied in the right spirit, presents so many beautiful points in its systematic structure that it may be called a 'kosmos.' But it is not in every way a kosmos ; like everything human, it presents fine and less fine features, and a comparative valuation, such as the one here attempted, should take both into consideration. There is undoubtedly an exquisite beauty in the old Greek language, and the ancient Hellenes, with their artistic temperament, knew how to turn that beauty to the best account in their literary productions ; but there is no less beauty in many modern languages —though its appraisement is a matter of taste, and as such evades scientific inquiry. But the æsthetic point of view is not the decisive one : language is of the utmost importance to the whole practical and spiritual life of mankind, and therefore has to be estimated by such tests as those applied above ; if that is done, we cannot be blind to the fact that modern languages as wholes are more practical than ancient ones, and that the latter present so many more anomalies and irregularities than our present-day languages that we may feel inclined, if not to apply to them Shakespeare's line, " Misshapen chaos of well-seeming forms," yet to think that the development has been from something nearer chaos to something nearer kosmos.

CHAPTER XIX

ORIGIN OF GRAMMATICAL ELEMENTS

XIX.—§ 1. The Old Theory.

WHAT has been given in the last two chapters to clear up the problem "Decay or progress?" has been based, as will readily be noticed, exclusively on easily controllable facts of linguistic history. So far, then, it has been very smooth sailing. But now we must venture out into the open sea of prehistoric speculations. Our voyage will be the safer if we never lose sight of land and have a reliable compass tested in known waters.

In our historical survey of linguistic science we have already seen that the prevalent theory concerning the prehistoric development of our speech is this: an originally isolating language, consisting of nothing but formless roots, passed through an agglutinating stage, in which formal elements had been developed, although these and the roots were mutually independent, to the third and highest stage found in flexional languages, in which formal elements penetrated the roots and made inseparable unities with them. We shall now examine the basis of this theory.

In the beginning was the root. This is "the result of strict and careful induction from the facts recorded in the dialects of the different members of the family" (Whitney L 260). "The firm foundation of the theory of roots lies in its logical necessity as an inference from the doctrine of the historical growth of grammatical apparatus" (Whitney G 200). "An instrumentality cannot but have had rude and simple beginnings, such as, in language, the so-called roots . . . such imperfect hints of expression as we call roots" (Whitney, *Views of L.* 338). These are really three different statements : induction from the facts, a logical inference from the doctrine about grammatical apparatus (i.e. the usually accepted doctrine, but on what is that built up except on the root theory ?), and the *a priori* argument that an ' instrumentality' must have simple beginnings. Even granted that these three arguments given at different times, each of them in turn as the sole argument, must be taken as supplementing each other, the three-legged stool on which the root theory is thus made to sit is a very shaky one, for none of the three legs is very solid, as we shall soon have occasion to see.

XIX.—§ 2. Roots.

In the beginning was the root—but what was it like ? Bopp took over the conception of root from the Indian grammarians, and like them was convinced that roots were all monosyllabic, and that view was accepted by his followers. These latter at times attributed other phonetic qualities to these roots, e.g. that they always had a short vowel (Curtius C 22). I quote from a very recent treatise (Wood, "Indo-European Root-formation," *Journal of Germ. Philol.* 1. 291) : " I range myself with those who believe that IE. roots were monosyllabic . . . these roots began, for the most part, with a vowel. The vowels certainly were the first utterances,[1] and though we cannot make the beginning of IE. speech coeval with that of human speech, we may at least assume that language, at that time, was in a very primitive state."

The number of these roots was not very great (Curtius, l.c. ; Wood 294). This seems a natural enough conclusion when we picture the earliest speech as the most meagre thing possible.

These few short monosyllabic roots were real words—this is a necessary assumption if we are to imagine a root stage as a real language, and it is often expressly stated ; Curtius, for instance, insists that roots are real and independent words (C 22, K 132) ; cf. also Whitney, who says that the root *VAK* "had also once an independent status, that it was a word " (L 255). We shall see afterwards that there is another possible conception of what a ' root ' is ; but let us here grant that it is a real word. The question whether a language is possible which contains nothing but such root words was always answered affirmatively by a reference to Chinese—and it will therefore be well here to give a short sketch of the chief structural features of that language.

[1] Why so ? Did sheep and cows also begin with vowels only, adding *b* and *m* afterwards to make up their *bah* and *moo* ?

XIX.—§ 3. Structure of Chinese.

Each word consists of one syllable, neither more nor less. Each of these monosyllables has one of four or five distinct musical tones (not indicated here). The parts of speech are not distinguished: *ta* means, according to circumstances, great, much, magnitude, enlarge. Grammatical relations, such as number, person, tense, case, etc., are not expressed by endings and similar expedients ; the word in itself is invariable. If a substantive is to be taken as plural, this as a rule must be gathered from the context ; and it is only when there is any danger of misunderstanding, or when the notion of plurality is to be emphasized, that separate words are added, e.g. *ki* ' some,' *šu* ' number.' The most important part of Chinese grammar is that dealing with word order : *ta kuok* means ' great state(s),' but *kuok ta* ' the state is great,' or, if placed before some other word which can serve as a verb, ' the greatness (size) of the state ' ; *tsï niu* ' boys and girls,' but *niu tsï* ' girl (female child),' etc. Besides words properly so called, or as Chinese grammarians call them ' full words,' there are several ' empty words ' serving for grammatical purposes, often in a wonderfully clever and ingenious way. Thus *či* has besides other functions that of indicating a genitive relation more distinctly than would be indicated by the mere position of the words ; *min* (people) *lik* (power) is of itself sufficient to signify ' the power of the people,' but the same notion is expressed more explicitly by *min či lik*. The same expedient is used to indicate different sorts of connexion : if *či* is placed after the subject of a sentence it makes it a genitive, thereby changing the sentence into a kind of subordinate clause : *wang pao min* = ' the king protects the people ' ; but if you say *wang či pao min yeu* (is like) *fu* (father) *či pao tsï*, the whole may be rendered, by means of the English verbal noun, ' the king's protecting the people is like the father's protecting his child.' Further, it is possible to change a whole sentence into a genitive ; for instance, *wang pao min či tao* (manner) *k'o* (can) *kien* (see, be seen), ' the manner in which the king protects (the manner of the king's protecting) his people is to be seen ' ; and in yet other positions *či* can be used to join a word-group consisting of a subject and verb, or of verb and object, as an adjunct (attribute) to a noun ;. we have participles to express the same modification of the idea : *wang pao či min* ' the people protected by the king ' ; *pao min či wang* ' a king protecting the people.' Observe here the ingenious method of distinguishing the active and passive voices by strictly adhering to the natural order and placing the subject before and the object after the verb. If we put *i* before, and *ku* after, a single word, it means ' on account of, because of ' (cf. E. for . . . 's sake) ; if we place a whole sentence between these ' brackets,' as we might term them, they are a sort of conjunction, and must be translated ' because.' [1]

XIX.—§ 4. History of Chinese.

These few examples will give some faint idea of the Chinese language, and—if the whole older generation of scholars is to be trusted—at the same time of the primeval structure of our own language in the root-stage. But is it absolutely certain that Chinese has retained its structure unchanged from the very first period ? By no means. As early as 1861, R. Lepsius, from a comparison of Chinese and Tibetan, had derived the conviction that " the monosyllabic character of Chinese is not original, but is a lapse (!) from an earlier polysyllabic structure." J. Edkins, while still believing that the structure of Chinese represents " the speech first used in the world's grey morning " (*The Evolution of the Chinese Language*, 1888), was one of the foremost to examine the evidence offered by the language itself for the determination of its earlier pronunciation. This, of course, is a much more complicated problem in Chinese than in our alphabetically written languages ; for a Chinese character, standing for a complete word, may remain unchanged while the pronunciation is changed indefinitely. But by means of dialectal pronunciations in our own day, of remarks in old Chinese dictionaries, of transcriptions of Sanskrit words made by Chinese Buddhists, of rimes in ancient poetry, of phonetic or partly phonetic elements in the word-characters, etc., is has been possible to demonstrate that Chinese pronunciation has changed considerably, and that the direction of change has been, here as elsewhere, towards shorter and easier word-forms. Above all, consonant groups have been simplified.

In 1894 I ventured to offer my mite to these investigations by suggesting an explanation of one phenomenon of pronunciation in present-day Chinese. I refer to the change sometimes wrought in the meaning of a word by the adoption of a different tone. Thus *wang* with one tone is ' king,' with another ' to become king ' ; *lao* with one is ' work,' with another ' pay the work ' ; *tsung* with one tone means ' follow,' with another ' follower,' and with a third ' footsteps ' ; *tshi* with one tone is ' wife,' with another ' marry ' ; *haδ* is ' good,' and *haó* is ' love.' Nay, meanings so different as ' acquire ' and ' give ' (*sheu*) or ' buy ' and ' sell ' (*mai*) are only distinguished by the tones. Edkins and V. Henry

---

[1] The examples taken from Gabelentz's *Grammar* and an article in Techmer's *Internat. Zeitschrift* I.

(*Le Muséon*, Louvain, 1882, i. 435) have attempted to explain this from gestures ; but this is palpably wrong. In the Danish dialect spoken in Sundeved, in southernmost Jutland, two tones are distinguished, one high and one low (see articles by N. Andersen and myself in *Dania*, vol. iv.). Now, these tones often serve to keep words or forms of words apart that but for the tone, exactly as in Chinese, would be perfect homophones. Thus *na* with the low tone is ' fool,' but with the high tone it is either the plural ' fools ' or else a verb ' to cheat, hoax ' ; *ri* ' ride ' is imperative or infinitive according to the tone in which it is uttered ; *jem* in the low tone is ' home ' and in the high ' at home ' ; and so on in a great many words. There is no need, however, in this language to resort to gestures to explain these tonic differences : the low tone is found in words originally monosyllabic (compare standard Danish *nar, rid, hjem*), and the high tone in words originally dissyllabic (compare Danish *narre, ride, hjemme*). The tones belonging formerly to two syllables are now condensed on one syllable. Although, of course, Chinese tones cannot in every respect be paralleled with Scandinavian ones, we may provisionally conjecture that the above-mentioned pairs of Chinese words were formerly distinguished by derivative syllables or flexional endings (see below, p. 373) which have now disappeared without leaving any traces behind them except in the tones. This hypothesis is perhaps rendered more probable by what seems to be an established fact—that one of the tones has arisen through the dropping of final stopped consonants (p, t, k).

However this may be, the death-blow was given to the dogma of the primitiveness of Chinese speech by Ernst Kuhn's lecture *Ueber Herkunft und Sprache der Transgangetischen Völker* (Munich, 1883). He compares Chinese with the surrounding languages of Tibet, Burmah and Siam, which are certainly related to Chinese and have essentially the same structure ; they are isolating, have no flexion, and word order is their chief grammatical instrument. But the laws of word order prove to be different in these several languages, and Kuhn draws the incontrovertible conclusion that it is impossible that any one of these laws of word position should have been the original one ; for that would imply that the other nations have changed it without the least reason and at a risk of terrible confusion. The only likely explanation is that these differences are the outcome of a former state of greater freedom. But if the ancestral speech had a free word order, to be at all intelligible it must have been possessed of other grammatical appliances than are now found in the derived tongues ; in other words, it must have indicated the relations of words to each other by something like our derivatives or flexions.

To the result thus established by Kuhn, that Chinese cannot have had a fixed word order from the beginning, we seem also to be led if we ask the question, Is primitive man likely to have arranged his words in this way ? A Chinese sentence, according to Gabelentz (Spr 426), is arranged with the same logical precision as the direction on an English envelope, where the most specific word is placed first, and each subsequent word is like a box comprising all that precedes—only that a Chinaman would reverse the order, beginning with the most general word and then in due order specializing. Now, is it probable that primitive man, that unkempt, savage being, who did not yet deserve the proud generic name of *homo sapiens*, but would be better termed, if not *homo insipiens*, at best *homo incipiens*—is it probable that this *urmensch*, who was little better than an *unmensch*, should have been able at once to arrange his words, or, what amounts to the same thing, his thoughts, in such a perfect order ? I incline to believe rather that logical, orderly thinking and speaking have only been attained by mankind after a long and troublesome struggle, and that the grammatical expedient of a fixed word order has come to Chinese as to European languages through a gradual development in which other, less logical and more material grammatical appliances have in course of time been given up.

We have thus arrived at a conception of Chinese which is *toto cœlo* removed from the view formerly current. The Chinese language can no longer be adduced in support of the hypothesis that our Aryan languages, or all human languages, started at first as a grammarless speech consisting of monosyllabic root-words.

XIX.—§ 5. Recent Investigations.

I have reprinted the above sketch of Chinese, with a few very insignificant verbal changes, as I wrote it about thirty years ago, because I think that the main reasoning is just as valid now as then, and because everything I have since then read about this interesting language has only confirmed the opinion I ventured to express after what was certainly a very insufficient study. Chinese pronunciation, including its tones, may now be studied in two excellent books, dealing with two different dialects—Daniel Jones and Kwing Tong Woo, *A Cantonese Phonetic Reader*, London, 1912, and Bernhard Karlgren, *A Mandarin Phonetic Reader in the Pekinese Dialect*, Upsala, Leipzig and Paris, 1917 (Archives d'Études Orientales, vol. 13). Karlgren is also the author of *Études sur la Phonologie Chinoise* (ib. vol. 15, 1915–19), in which he deals with the history of Chinese sounds and the reconstruction of the old pronunciation in a thoroughly scholarly manner on the basis of an intimate knowledge of spoken and written Chinese, and in *Ordet och pennan i mittens rike* (Stockholm, 1918), he has given a masterly popular sketch of the structure of the Chinese language and its system of writing.

Of the greatest importance for our purposes is the same scholar's recent brilliant discovery of a real case distinction in the oldest Chinese. In classical Chinese there are four pronouns of the first person (I, we) which have always been considered as absolutely synonymous. But Karlgren shows that the two of them which occur as the usual forms in Confucius's conversations are so far from being used indiscriminately that one is nearly always a nominative and the other an objective case ; the exceptions are not numerous and are easily explained. The present Mandarin pronunciation of the first is [u], of the second either [uo] or [ŋo]. But if we go back to the sixth century of our era we are able with certainty to say that the pronunciation of the former was [ŋuo], and of the latter [ŋa]. This, then, constitutes a real declension. Now, in the second person Karlgren is also able to point out a distinction of two pronouns, though not quite so clearly marked as in the first person, the objective showing here a greater tendency to encroach on the nominative (Karlgren here ingeniously adduces the parallel from our languages that the first person has retained the suppletive system *ego* : *me*, while the second uses the same stem *tu* : *te*). The oldest Chinese thus has the following case flexion :

	1st Per.	2nd Per.
Nom.	ŋuo	nźiwo
Obj.	ŋa	nźia

(See " Le Proto-chinois, langue flexionnelle," *Journal Asiatique*, 1920, 205 ff.).[1]

XIX.—§ 6. Roots Again.

To return to roots. The influence of Indian grammar on European linguists with regard to the theory of roots extended also to the meanings assigned to roots, which were all of them

---

[1] I must also mention A. Conrady, *Eine indochinesische Causativ-denominativ-bildung* (Leipzig, 1896), in which Lepsius's theory is carried a great step further and it is demonstrated with very great learning that many of the tone relations (as well as modifications of initial sounds) of Chinese and kindred languages find their explanation in the previous existence of prefixes which are now extinct, but which can still be pointed out in Tibetan. Though I ought, therefore, to have spoken of prefixes instead of 'flexional endings ' above, p. 371, the essence of the contention that prehistoric Chinese must have had a polysyllabic and non-isolating structure is thus borne out by the researches of competent specialists in this field.

of verbal character, and nearly always highly general or abstract, such as 'breathe, move, be sharp or quick, blow, go,' etc. The impossibility of imagining anybody expressing himself by means of a language consisting exclusively of such abstracts embarrassed people much less than one would expect : Chinese, of course, has plenty of words for concrete objects.

The usual assumption was that there was one definite root period in which all the roots were created, and after which this form of activity ceased. But Whitney demurred to this (M 36), saying that E. *preach* and *cost* may be considered new roots, though ultimately coming from Lat. *præ-dicare* and *con-stare* : these old compounds are felt as units, "reducing to the semblance of roots elements that are really derivative or compound." As Whitney goes no further than to establish the *semblance* of new roots, he might be taken as an adherent rather than as an opponent of the theory he objects to. But, as a matter of fact, new words *are* created in modern languages, and if they form the basis of derived words, we may really speak of new roots (*pun—punning, punster*; *fun—funny*; etc.). Why not say that we have a French root *roul* in *rouler, roulement, roulage, roulier, rouleau, roulette, roulis*? This only becomes unjustifiable if we think that the establishment of this root gives us the ultimate explanation of these words ; for then the linguistic historian steps in with the objection that the words have been formed, not from a root, but from a real word, which is not even in itself a primary word, but a derivative, Lat. *rotula*, a diminutive of *rota* 'wheel.' (I take this example from Bréal M 407). To the popular instinct *sorrow* and *sorry* are undoubtedly related to one another, and we may say that they contain a root *sorr-* ; but a thousand years ago they had nothing to do with one another, and belonged to different roots : OE. *sorg* 'care' and *sārig* 'wounded, afflicted.' If all traces of Latin and Greek were lost, a linguist would have no more scruples about connecting *scene* with *see* than most illiterate Englishmen have now. Who will vouch that many Aryan roots may not have originated at various times through similar processes as these new roots *preach, cost, roul, sorr, see*?

The proper definition of a root seems to be : what is common to a certain number of words felt by the popular instinct of the speakers as etymologically belonging together. In this sense we may of course speak of roots at any stage of any language, and not only at a hypothetical initial stage. In some cases these roots may be used as separate words (E. *preach, fun*, etc., Fr. *roul* = what is spelt *roule, roules, roulent*) ; in other cases this is impossible (Lat. *am* in *amo, amor, amicus* ; E. *sorr*) ; in many cases because the common element cannot, for phonetic reasons, be easily pronounced, as when E. *drink, drank, drunk* or *sit, sat, seat, set* are naturally felt to belong together, though it is impossible to state the root except in some formula like *dr.nk, s.t*, where the dot stands for some vowel. Similar considerations may be adduced with regard to the consonants if we want to establish what is felt to be common in *give* and *gift* (*gi +* labiodental spirant) or in *speak* and *speech*, etc.; but this need not detain us here.

In my view, then, the root is something real and important, though not always tangible. And as its form is not always easy to state or pronounce, so must its meaning, as a rule, be somewhat vague and indeterminate, for what is common to several ideas must of course be more general and abstract than either of the more special ideas thus connected ; it is also natural that it will often be necessary to state the signification of a root in terms of verbal ideas, for these are more general and abstract than nominal ideas. But roots thus conceived belong to any and all periods, and we must cease to speak of the earliest period of human speech as ' the root period.'

XIX.—§ 7. The Agglutination Theory.

According to the received theory (see above, § 1) some of the roots became gradually attached to other roots and lost their independence, so as to become finally formatives fused with the root. This theory, generally called the agglutination theory, contains a good deal of truth ; but we can only accept it with three important provisos, namely, first, that there has never been one definite period in which those languages which are now flexional were wholly agglutinative, the process of fusion being liable to occur at any time ; second, that the component parts which become formatives are not at first roots, but real words ; and third, that this process is not the only one by which formatives may develop : it may be called the rectilinear process, but by the side of that we have also more circuitous courses, which are no less important in the life of languages for being less obvious.

In the process of coalescence or integration there are many possible stages, with may be denominated figuratively by such expressions as that two words are placed together (that is—in non-figurative language—pronounced after one another), tied together, knit together, glued together (' agglutinated '), soldered together, welded together, fused together or amalgamated. What is really the most important part of the process is the degree in which one of the components loses its independence, phonetically and semantically.

As 'agglutination' is thus only one intermediate stage in a continuous process, it would be better to have another name for the whole theory of the origin of formatives than 'the agglutination theory,' and I propose therefore to use the term 'coalescence theory.' The usual name also fixes the attention too exclusively on the so-called agglutinative languages, and if we take the formatives of such a language as Turkish, as in *sev-mek* 'to love,' *sev-il-mek* 'to be loved,' *sev-dir-mek* 'to cause to love,' *sev-dir-il-mek* 'to be made to love,' *sev-ish-mek* 'to love one another,' *sev-ish-dir-il-mek* 'to be made to love one another '— who will vouch that these formatives were all of them originally independent words ? Those who are most competent to have an opinion on the matter seem nowadays inclined to doubt it and to reject much of what was current in the description of these languages given by the earlier scholars ; see, especially, the interesting final chapter of V. Grønbech, *Forstudier til tyrkisk lydhistorie* (København, 1902).

XIX.—§ 8. Coalescence.

The various degrees of coalescence, and the coexistence at the same linguistic period of these various degrees, may be illustrated by the old example, English *un-tru-th-ful-ly*, and by German *un-be-stimm-bar-keit*. Let us look a little at each of these formatives. The only one that can still be used as an independent word is *ful*(l). From the collocation in 'I have my hand full of peas ' the transition is easy to 'a handful of peas,' where the accentual subordination of *full* to *hand* paves the way for the combination becoming one word instead of two : this is not accomplished till it becomes possible to put the plural sign at the end (*handfuls*, thus also *basketfuls* and others), while in less familiar combinations the *s* is still placed in the middle (*bucketsful*, two *donkeysful* of children, see MEG ii. 2. 42). In these substantives -*ful* keeps its full vowel [u]. But in adjectival compounds, such as *peaceful*, *awful*, there is a colloquial pronunciation with obscured or omitted vowel [-fəl, -fl], in which the phonetic connexion with the full word is thus weakened ; the semantic connexion, too, is loosened when it becomes possible to form such words as *dreadful*, *bashful*, in which it is not possible to use the definition 'full of . . .' Here, then, the transition from a word to a derivative suffix is complete.

English -*hood*, -*head* in *childhood*, *maidenhead* also is originally an independent word, found in OE. and ME. in the form *had*, meaning 'state, condition,' Gothic *haidus*. In German it has two forms, -*heit*, as in *freiheit*, and -*keit*, whose *k* was at first the final sound of the adjective in *ewigkeit*, MHG. *ewecheit*, but was later felt as part of the suffix and then transferred to cases in which the stem had no *k*, as in *tapferkeit, ehrbarkeit.*

The suffix *-ly* is from *lik*, which was a substantive meaning 'form, appearance, body' ('a dead body' in Dan. *lig*, E. *lich* in *lichgate*); *manlik* thus is 'having the form or appearance of a man'; the adjective *like* originally was *ge-lic* 'having the same appearance with' (as in Lat. *con-form-is*). In compounds *-lik* was shortened into *-ly*: in some cases we still have competing forms like *gentlemanlike* and *gentlemanly*. The ending was, and is still, used extensively in adjectives; if it is now also used to turn adjectives into adverbs, as in *truthful-ly, luxurious-ly*, this is a consequence of the two OE. forms, adj. *-lic* and adv. *-lice*, having phonetically fallen together.

It may perhaps be doubtful whether the G. suffix *-bar* (OHG. *-bari*, OE. *bære*) was ever really an independent word, but its connexion with the verb *beran*, E. *bear*, cannot be doubted: *fruchtbar* is what bears fruit (cf. OE. *æppelbære* 'bearing apples'), but the connexion was later loosened, and such adjectives as *ehrbar, kostbar, offenbar* have little or nothing left of the original meaning of the suffix. The two prefixes in our examples, *un-* and *be-*, are differentiated forms of the old negative *ne* and the preposition *by*, and the only affix in our two long words which is thus left unexplained is *-th*, which makes *true* into *truth* and is found also in *longth, health*, etc.

XIX.—§ 9. Flexional Endings.

There can be no doubt, therefore, that some at any rate of our suffixes and prefixes go back to independent words which have been more or less weakened to become derivative formatives. But does the same hold good with those endings which we are accustomed to term flexional endings? The answer certainly must be in the affirmative—with regard to *some* endings.

Thus the Scandinavian passive originates in a coalescence of the active verb and the pronoun *sik*: Old Norse (*þeir*) *finna sik* ('they find themselves' or 'each other'), gradually becomes one word (*þeir*) *finnask*, later *finnast, finnaz*, Swedish (*de*) *finnas*, Dan. (*de*) *findes* 'they are found.' In Old Icelandic the pronoun is still to some extent felt as such, though formally an indistinguishable part of the verb; thus combinations like the following are very frequent: *Bolli kvaz þessu ráða vilja = kvað sik vilja*; "Bolli dixit se velle: B. said that he would have his own way" (Laxd. 55). In Danish a distinction can sometimes be made between a reflexive and a purely passive employment: *de slås* with a short vowel is 'they fight (one another),' but with a long vowel 'they are beaten.'

A similar coalescence is taking place in Russian, where *sja* ' himself ' (myself, etc.) dwindles down to a suffixed *s* : *kazalos* ' it showed itself, turned out.'

A similar case is the Romanic future : It. *finiro*, Sp. *finire*, Fr. *finirai*, from *finire habeo* (*finir ho*, etc.), originally ' I have to finish.' Before the coalescence was complete, it was possible to insert a pronoun, Old Sp. *cantar-te-hé* ' I shall sing to you.'

A third case in point is the suffixed definite article, if we are allowed to consider that as a kind of flexion : Old Norse *mannenn* (*manninn*) accusative ' the man,' *landet* (*landit*) ' the land ' ; Dan. *manden*, *landet*, from *mann*, *land* + the demonstrative pronoun *enn*, neuter *et*. Rumanian *domnul* ' the lord,' from Lat. *dominu(m) illu(m)*, is another example.

XIX.—§ 10. Validity of the Theory.

Now, does this kind of explanation admit of universal application—in other words, were all our derivative affixes and flexional endings originally independent words before they were ' glued ' to or fused with the main word ? This has been the prevalent, one might almost say the orthodox, view of all the leading linguists, who may be mustered in formidable array in defence of the agglutination theory.[1]

Against the universality of this origin for formatives I adduced in my former work (1894, p. 66 f., cf. *Kasus*, 1891, p. 36) four reasons, which I shall here restate in a different order and in a fuller form.

(1) Nothing can be proved with regard to the ultimate genesis of flexion in general from the adduced examples, for in all of them the elements were already fully flexional before the coalescence (cf. ON. *finnask, fannsk* ; It. *finirð, finirai, finira* ; ON. *maðrenn, mannenn, mansens*, etc.). What they show, then, is really nothing but the growth of new flexional formations on an old flexional soil, and it might be imagined that the fusion would not have taken place, or not so completely, if the minds of the speakers had not been already prepared to accept formations of this character. I do not, however, attach much importance to this argument, and turn to those that are more cogent.

(2) The number of actual forms proved beyond a doubt to

---

[1] Madvig Kl 170, Max Müller L 1. 271, Whitney OLS 1. 283, G 124, Paul P 1st ed. 181, repeated in the following editions, see 4th, 1909, 350 and 347, 349; Brugmann VG 1889, 2. 1 (but in 2nd ed. this has been struck out in favour of hopeless skepticism), Schuchardt, *Anlass d. Volapüks* 11, Gabelentz Spr 189, Tegnér SM 53, Sweet, *New Engl. Gr.* § 559, Storm, *Engl. Phil.* 673, Rozwadowski, *Wortbildung u. Wortbed.*, Uhlenbeck, *Karakt. d. bask. Gramm.* 24, Sütterlin WGS 1902, 122, Porzezinski, Spr 1910, 229.

have originated through coalescence is comparatively small. It is true that not a few derivative syllables were originally independent; still, if we compare them with the number of those for which no such origin has been proved or even proposed, we find that the proportion is very small indeed. In the list of English suffixes enumerated in Sweet's *Grammar*, only eleven can be traced back to independent words, while 74 are not thus explicable. Anyone going through the countless suffixes enumerated in the second volume of Brugmann's *Vergleichende Grammatik* will, I think, be struck with the impossibility of any great number of them being traced back to words in the same way as *hood*, etc., above: their forms and, still more, their vague spheres of meaning, and on the whole their manner of application, distinctly speak against such an origin.

As to real flexional endings traceable to words, their number is even comparatively smaller than that of derivative suffixes; the three or four instances named above are everywhere appealed to, but are there so many more than these ? And are they numerous enough to justify so general an assertion ? My impression is that the basis for the induction is very far from sufficient.

(3) This argument is strengthened when we are able to point out instances in which, as a matter of fact, flexional endings have arisen in a way that is totally opposed to the agglutinative, which then must renounce all claims to be the *only* possible way for a language to arrive at flexional formatives. See below (§ 13) on Secretion.

(4) Assuming the theory to be true, we should expect much greater regularity, both in formal (morphological) and in semantic (syntactic) respect than we actually find in the old Aryan languages; for if one definite element was added to signify one definite modification of the idea, we see no reason why it should not have been added to all words in the same way. As a matter of fact, the Romanic future, the Scandinavian passive voice and definite article present much greater regularity than is found in the flexion of nouns and verbs in old Aryan.

XIX.—§ 11. Irregularity Original.

It will be objected that the irregularity which we find in these old languages is of later growth, and that, in fact, flexion, as Schuchardt says, is "anomal gewordene agglutination." Whitney said that "each suffix has its distinct meaning and office, and is applied in a whole class of analogous words" (L. 254), and in reading Schleicher's *Compendium* one gains the impression that the old Aryan sounds and forms were like a regiment of well-trained soldiers marching along in the best military style, while all irregularities were the result of later decay in each language separately. But the trend of the whole scientific development of the last fifty years has been in the direction of demonstrating more and more irregularity in the original forms : where formerly only one ending was assumed for the same case, etc., now several are assumed (See, e.g., Walde in Streitberg's *Gesch.*, 2. 194, Thumb, ib. 2. 69.) And as with the forms, so also with the meanings and applications of the forms. Madvig as early as 1857 (p. 27, Kl 202) had seen that the signification of the grammatical forms must originally have been extremely vague and fluctuating, but most scholars went on imagining that each case, each tense, each mood had originally stood for something quite settled and definite, until gradually the progress of linguistics made away with that conception point by point. In place of the belief that the original Aryan verb had a definite system of tense forms, it is now generally assumed that different ' aspects ' (' aktionsarten '), somewhat like those of Slav verbs, were indicated, and that the notion of ' time ' differences was only afterwards developed out of the notion of aspect : but if we compare the divisions and definitions of these aspects given by various scholars, we see how essentially vague this notion is ; instead of being a model system of nice logical distinctions, the original condition must rather have been one in which such notions as duration, completion, result, beginning, repetition were indistinctly found as germs, from which such ideas as perfect and imperfect, past and present, were finally evolved with greater and greater clearness.

Similar remarks apply to moods. All attempts at finding out, deductively or inductively, the fundamental notion (grundbegriff) attached to such a mood as the subjunctive have failed : it is impossible to establish one original, sharply circumscribed sphere of usage, from which all the various, partly conflicting, usages in the actually existing languages can be derived. The usual theory is that there existed one true subjunctive, characterized by long thematic vowels -ē-, -ā-, -ō-, and distinct from that an optative, characterized by a formative -iē- : -ī-,[1] and that these two were fused in Latin. But, as Oertel and Morris have shown in their valuable article " An Examination of the Theories regarding the Nature and Origin of Indo-European Inflection " (*Harvard Studies in Classical Philol.* XVI, 1905) it is probably safer to assume for the Indo-European period substantial identity of meaning

---

[1] Two explanations of this formative element were given by the old school: according to Schleicher C § 290, it was the root *ja* of the relative pronoun ; according to Curtius and others it was the root *i* ' to go,' Greek *fer-o-i-mi* being analyzed as ' I go to bear,' whence, by an easy (?) transition, ' I should like to bear,' etc.

in the modal formatives *iē* : *i* and the long thematic vowels -*ē*-, -*ā*-, -*ō*-, which were then continued undifferentiated in Latin, while on the one hand the Gothonic branch has practically discarded the forms with long thematic vowel and confined itself to the *i* suffix, and on the other hand two branches, Greek and Indo-Iranic, have availed themselves of the formal difference and separated a 'subjunctive' and an 'optative' mood.

XIX.—§ 12. Coalescence Theory dropped.

In the historical part I have already mentioned some instances of coalescence explanations of Aryan forms which have been abandoned by most scholars, such as the theory that the *r* of the Latin passive is a disguised *se*, which would agree very well with the Scandinavian passive, but falls to the ground when one remembers that corresponding forms are found in Keltic, where the transition from *s* to *r* is otherwise unknown : these forms are now believed to be related to some *r* forms found in Sanskrit, but there not possessed of any passive signification, this latter being thus a comparatively late acquisition of Keltic and Italic : these two branches turning an existing, non-meaning consonant to excellent use in their flexional system and generalizing it in the new application.[1]

The explanation of the 'weak' Gothonic preterit from a coalescence of *did* (*loved = love did*) was long one of the strongholds of the agglutination theory, Bopp's original collocation of these forms with other forms which could not be thus explained (see above 51) having passed into oblivion. Now we have Collitz's comprehensive book *Das schwache Präteritum*, 1912, in which the formative consonant is shown to have been Aryan *t*, and the close correspondence not only with the passive participle, but also with the verbal nouns in -*ti* is duly emphasized.

The impossibility of explaining the Latin perfect in -*vi* from composition with *fui* has been demonstrated by Merguet (see Walde in Streitberg's *Gesch.*, 2. 220). Instead of this rectilinear explanation, scholars now incline to assume an intricate play of various analogical influences starting from a pre-ethnic perfect in *w* in isolated instances.

Many have explained the case ending -*s* as a coalesced demonstrative pronoun *sa* or, as it is now given, *so* ; the difficulty that the same *s* denotes now the nominative and now the genitive was got over

---

[1] Cf. Sommer, Lat. 528, and on Armenian and Tokharian *r* forms MSL 18. 10 ff. and Feist KI 455. But it must not be overlooked that H. Pedersen (KZ 40. 166 ff.) has revived and strengthened the old theory that *r* in Italic and Keltic is an original *se*.

by Curtius (C 12) by the assumption that *sa* was added at two distinct periods, and that each period made a different use of the addition, though Curtius does not tell us how one or the other function could be evolved from such a pronoun. The latest attempt at explanation, which reaches me as I am writing this chapter, is by Hermann Möller (KZ 49. 219): according to him the common Aryan and Semitic nominative ended in *o* and the genitive in *e*, but to this was added in the masculine, and more rarely in the feminine, the pronoun *s* as a definite article, so that the primitive form corresponding to Lat. *lupus* meant ' the wolf ' and *lupu* ' (a) wolf ' ; later the *s*-less form was given up, and *lupus* came to be used for both ' the wolf ' and ' wolf ' (similarly presumably in the genitive, if we translate the presumed original forms into Latin *lupis* ' the wolf's ' and *lupi* ' (a) wolf's,' later *lupi* in both functions). In Semitic, inversely, an element *m*, corresponding to the Aryan accusative ending, was added as an *in*definite article, the *m*-less form thus becoming definite, but in the oldest Babylonian-Assyrian the distinction has been given up, and the form in *m* is (like the Latin form in *s*) used both definitely and indefinitely. Ingenious as these constructions are, the whole theory seems to me highly artificial, and it is difficult to imagine that both Aryans and Semites, after having evolved such a valuable distinction as that between ' the wolf ' and ' a wolf,' expressed by simple means, should have wilfully given it up—to evolve it again in a later period.[1] Fortunately one is allowed to confess one's ignorance of the origin of the case endings *s* and *m*, but if I were on pain of death to choose between Möller's hypothesis and the suggestion thrown out by Humboldt (Versch 129), that the light (high-pitched) *s* symbolized the living (personal) and active (the subject), and the dark (low-pitched) *m* the lifeless (neutral) and passive (the object), I should certainly prefer the latter explanation.

Hirt (GDS 37) also thinks that the *s* found in Aryan cases is an originally independent word, only he thinks that this *se*, *so* was not originally a demonstrative pronoun, but the particle, which with the extension *i* is found in Gothic *sai* ' ecce,' and as it can thus be compared with the particle *c* in Lat. *hic*, it is clear that it might be added in all cases—and as a matter of fact Hirt finds it in six different cases in the singular and in all cases in the plural except the genitive. Hirt makes no attempt at explaining how these various case-forms have come to acquire the signification (function) with which we find them in the oldest documents; " the *s* element had nothing to do with the denotation of any case, number or gender, and only after it had been added to some cases

---

[1] If *s* was a definite article, why should it be used only with some stems and not with others ? Why should neuters never require a definite article ?

and not to others could it come to be distinctive of cases " (p. 39). In other words, his explanation explains just nothing at all. The same is true with regard to the ' particles ' *om* or *em, e, o, i,* which he thinks were added in other cases, and when he ends (p. 42) by saying that " this must be sufficient to give a glimpse of the way in which Aryan flexion originated," the only thing we have really seen is the haphazard way in which this flexion is formed, and the impossibility at present of arriving at a fully satisfactory explanation of these things. I should especially demur to the two suppositions underlying Hirt's theory that Aryan had at one period a completely flexionless structure, and that the same sound when occurring in various cases must have had the same origin : it seems much more probable to me that the *s* of the nominative and the *s* of the genitive were not at first identical.[1]

That item of the coalescence theory which probably appealed most to the fancy of scholars and laymen alike was the explanation of the personal endings in the verbs from the personal pronouns : we have an *m* in the first person of the *mi*-verbs (*esmi*) and in the pronoun *me*, etc., and we have a *t* in the third person (*esti*) and in a third-person pronoun or demonstrative (*to*) ; it is, therefore, quite natural to think that *esmi* is simply the root *es* ' to be ' + the pronoun *mi* ' I,' and *esti es* + the other pronoun, and to extend this view to the other persons. And yet not even this has been allowed to stand unchallenged by later disrespectful linguists, headed by A. H. Sayce (Techmer's *Zeitschr. f. allg. Sprwiss.* 1. 22) and Hirt. As a matter of fact, the theory is based exclusively on the above-mentioned correspondence *in* the first and third persons singular, while the dual and plural endings do not at all agree with the corresponding personal pronouns and the endings of the second person can only be compared with the pronoun through the employment of phonological tricks unworthy of a scientific linguist. Even in the first person the correspondence is not complete, for besides -*mi* we have other endings : -*m*, which cannot be very well considered a shortened -*mi* (and which agrees,

---

[1] While it is difficult to see the relation between a demonstrative pronoun or a deictic particle and genitival function, it would be easy enough to understand the latter if we started from a possessive pronoun (ejus, suus), and, curiously enough, we find this very sound *s* used as a sign for the genitive in two independent languages, starting from that notion. In Indo-Portuguese we have *gobernadors casa* ' governor's house,' from *gobernador su casa* (above, Ch. XI § 12, p. 213), and in the South-African ' Taal ' the usual expression for the genitive is by means of *syn*, which is generally shortened into *se* (*s*) and glued enclitically to the substantive, even to feminines and plurals : *Marie-se boek* ' Maria's book,' *di gowweneur se hond* ' the governor's dog ' (H. Meyer, *Die Sprache der Buren*, 1901, p. 40, where also the confusion with the adjective ending -*s*, in Dutch spelt -*sch*, is mentioned. For the construction compare G. *dem vater sein hut* and others from various languages; cf. the appendix on E. *Bill Stumps his mark* in ChE 182 f.).

as Sayce remarks, much more closely with the accusative ending of nouns), -o and -a, neither of which can be explained from any known pronoun. There is thus nothing for it except to say, as Brugmann does (KG § 770) : "The origin of the personal endings is not clear"; cf. also Misteli 47 : "The relations between personal endings and the independent personal pronouns must be much more evident to justify this view. . . . The Aryan language offers direct evidence against the assumption that a sentence has been thus drawn together, because it uses in the verbal forms of the first and third person sg. pronominal stems which are otherwise employed only as objects, and, moreover, would here place the subject after the predicate, though in sentences it observes the opposite order." Meillet expresses himself very categorically (*Bulletin de la Soc. de Ling.* 1911, 143) : "Scarcely any linguist who has studied Aryan languages would venture to affirm that *-*mi* of the type Gr. *fēmi* is an old personal pronoun."

The impression left on us by all these cases is that many of the earlier explanations by agglutination have proved unsatisfactory, and that linguists are nowadays inclined either to leave the forms entirely unexplained or else to admit less rectilinear developments, in which we see the speakers of the old languages groping tentatively after means of expression and finding them only by devious and circuitous courses. It is, of course, difficult to classify such explanations, and the agglutination or coalescence theory has to be supplemented by various other kinds of explanation ; but I think one of these, which has not received its legitimate share of attention, is important and distinctive enough to have its own name, and I propose to term it the ' secretion ' theory.

XIX.—§ 13. Secretion.

By secretion I understand the phenomenon that one portion of an indivisible word comes to acquire a grammatical signification which it had not at first, and is then felt as something added to the word itself. Secretion thus is a consequence of a ' metanalysis ' (above, Ch. X § 2) ; it shows its full force when the element thus secreted comes to be added to other words not originally possessing this element.

A clear instance is offered in the history of some English possessive pronouns. In Old English *min* and *þin* the *n* is kept throughout as part and parcel of the words themselves, the other cases having such forms as *mine, minum, minre*, exactly as in German *mein, meine, meinem, meiner*, etc. But in Middle English the endings were gradually dropped, and *min* and *þin* for a short time became the only forms. Soon, however, *n* was dropped before substantives beginning with a consonant, but was retained in other positions (*my* father—*mine* uncle, it is *mine*); then the former form was transferred also to those cases in which the pronoun was used (as an adjunct) before words beginning with vowels (*my* father, *my* uncle—it is *mine*). The distinction between *my* and *mine*, *thy* and *thine*, which was originally a purely phonetic one, exactly like that between *a* and *an* (*a* father, *an* uncle), gradually acquired a functional value, and now serves to distinguish an adjunct from a principal (or, to use the terms of some grammars, a conjoint from an absolute form); *my* came to be looked upon as the proper form, while the *n* of *mine* was felt as an ending serving to indicate the function as a principal word. That this is really the instinctive feeling of the people is shown by the fact that in dialectal and vulgar speech the same *n* is added to *his, her, your* and *their*, to form the new pronouns *hisn, hern, yourn, theirn* : " He that prigs what isn't hisn, when he's cotch'd, is sent to prison. She that prigs what isn't hern, At the treadmill takes a turn."

Another instance of secretion is *-en* as a plural ending in E. *oexn*, G. *ochsen*, etc. Here originally *n* belonged to the word in all cases and all numbers, just as much as the preceding *s* ; *ox* was an *n* stem in the same way as, for instance, Lat. (homo), hom*inem*, hom*inis*, etc., or Gr. ku*ōn*, ku*na*, ku*nos*, etc., are *n* stems. In Gothic *n* is found in most of the cases of similar *n* stems. In OE. the nom. is *oxa*, the other cases in the sg. *oxan*, pl. *oxan* (*oxen*), *oxnum, oxena*, but in ME. the *n*-less form is found throughout the singular (gen. analogically *oxes*), and the plural only kept *-n*. Thus also a great many other words, e.g. (I give the plural forms) *apen, haren, sterren* (stars), *tungen, siden, eyen*, which all of them belonged to the *n* declension in OE. When *-en* had thus become established as a plural sign, it was added analogically to words which were not originally *n* stems, e.g. ME. *caren, synnen, treen* (OE. *cara, synna, treow*), and this ending even seemed for some time destined to be the most usual plural ending in the South of England, until it was finally supplanted by *-s*, which had been the prevalent ending in the North ; *eyen, foen, shoen* were for a time in competition with *eyes, foes, shoes*, and now *-n* is only found in *oxen* (and *children*). In German to-day things are very much as they were in Southern ME. : *-en* is kept extensively in the old *n* stems and is added to some words which had formerly other endings, e.g. *hirten, soldaten, thaten*. The result is that now plurality is indicated by an ending which had formerly no such function (which, indeed, had no function at all) ; for if we look upon the actual language, *oxen* (G. *ochsen*) is = *ox* (*ochs*) singular + the plural ending *-en* ;

only we must not on any account imagine that the form was originally thus welded together (agglutinated)—and if in G. *soldaten* we may speak of *-en* being glued on to *soldat*, this ending is not, and has never been, an independent word, but is an originally insignificative part secreted by other words.

A closely similar case is the plural ending *-er*. The consonant originally was *s*, as seen, for instance, in the Gr. and Lat. nom. *genos*, *genus*, gen. Gr. *gene(s)os*, *genous*, Lat. *generis* for older *genesis*. In Gothonic languages *s*, in accordance with a regular sound shift in this case, became *r* (through *z*) whenever it was retained, but in the nom. sg. it was dropped, and thus we have in OE. sg. *lamb*, *lambe*, *lambes*, but in the pl. *lambru*, *lambrum*, *lambra*. In English only few words show traces of this flexion, thus OE. *cild*, pl. *cildru*, ME. *child*, *childer*, whence, with an added *-en*, our modern *children*. But in German the class had much more vitality, and we have not only words belonging to it of old, like *lamm*, pl. *lämmer*, *rind*, *rinder*, but also gradually more and more words which originally belonged to other classes, but adopted this ending after it had become a real sign of the plural number, thus *wörter*, *bücher*.

There is one trait that should be noticed as highly characteristic of these instances of secretion, that is, that the occurrence of the endings originating in this way seems from the first regulated by the purest accident, seen from the point of view of the speakers : they are found in some words, but not in others, whereas the endings treated of under the heading Coalescence are added much more uniformly to the whole of the vocabulary. But as a similarly irregular or arbitrary distribution is met with in the case of nearly all flexional endings in the oldest stages of languages belonging to our family of speech, the probability is that most of those endings which it is impossible for us to trace back to their first beginnings have originated through secretion or similar processes, rather than through coalescence of independent words or roots.

XIX.—§ 14. Extension of Suffixes.

A special subdivision of secretion comprises those cases in which a suffix takes over some sound or sounds from words to which it was added. Clear instances are found in French, where in consequence of the mutescence of a final consonant some suffixes to the popular instinct must seem to begin with a consonant, though originally this did not belong to the suffix. Thus *laitier*, at first formed from *lait* + *ier*, now came to be apprehended as = *lai(t)* + *tier*, and *cabaretier* as *cabare(t)* + *tier*, and the new suffix was then used to form such new words as *bijoutier, ferblantier, cafetier* and others. In the same way we have *tabatière*, where we should expect *tabaquière*, and the predilection for the extended form of the suffix is evidently strengthened by the syllable division in frequent formations like *ren-tier, por-tier, por-tière, charpen-tier*. In old Gothonic we have similar extensions of suffixes, when instead of *-ing* we get *-ling*, starting from words like OHG. *ediling* from *edili*, ON. *vesling* from *vesall*, OE. *lytling* from *lytel*, etc. Consequently we have in English quite a number of words with the extended ending : *duckling, gosling, hireling, underling*, etc. In Gothic some words formed with *-assus*, such as *piudin-assus* 'kingdom,' were apprehended as formed with *-nassus*, and in all the related languages the suffix is only known with the initial *n*; thus in E. *-ness* : *hardness, happiness, eagerness*, etc.; G. *-keit* with its *k* from adjectives in *-ic* has already been mentioned (376). From *criticism, Scotticism*, we have *witti-cism*, and Milton has *witticaster* on the analogy of *criticaster*, where the suffix of course is *-aster*, as in *poetaster*. Instead of *-ist* we also find in some cases *-nist* : *tobacconist, lutenist* (cf. *botan-ist, mechan-ist*).

To form a new word it is often sufficient that some existing word is felt in a vague way to be made up of something + an ending, the latter being subsequently added on to another word. In Fr. *mérovingien* the *v* of course is legitimate, as the adjective is derived from Mérovée, Merowig, but this word was made the starting-point for the word designating the succeeding dynasty : *carlovingien*, where *v* is simply taken over as part of the suffix ; nowadays historians try to be more ' correct ' and prefer the adjective *carolingien*, which was unknown to Littré. *Oligarchy* is *olig* + *archy*, but for the opposite notion the word *poligarchy* or *polygarchy* was framed from *poly* and the last two syllables of *oli-garchy*, and though now scholars have made *polyarchy* the usual form, the word with the intrusive *g* was the common form two hundred years ago in English, and corresponding forms are found in French, Spanish and other languages. *Judgmatical* is made on the pattern of *dogmatical*, though there the stem is *dogmat-*. In jocular German *schwachmatikus* 'valetudinarian,' we have the same suffix with a different colouring, taken from *rheumatikus* (thus also Dan. *svagmatiker*). Swift does not hesitate to speak of a *sextumvirate*, which suggests *triumvirate* better than *sexvirate* would have done ; and Bernard Shaw once writes " his equipage (or autopage) "— evidently starting from the popular, but erroneous, belief that *equipage* is derived from Lat. *equus* and then dividing the word *equi* + *page*. Cf. *Scillonian* from *Scilly* on account of *Devonian* as if this were *Dev* + *onian* instead of *Devon* + *ian*.

XIX.—§ 15. Tainting of Suffixes.

It will be seen that in some of these instances the suffix has appropriated to itself not only part of the sound of the stem, but also part of its signification. This is seen very clearly in the case of *chandelier*, in French formed from *chandelle* ' candle ' with the suffix -*ier*, of rather vague signification, ' anything connected with, or having to do with '; in English the word is used for a hanging branched frame to hold a number of lights ; consequently a similar apparatus for gas-burners was denominated *gaselier* (*gasalier*, *gasolier*), and with the introduction of electricity the formation has even been extended to *electrolier*. *Vegetarian* is from the stem *veget-* with added -*ari-an*, which ending has no special connexion with the notion of eating or food, but recently we have seen the new words *fruitarian* and *nutarian*, meaning one whose food consists (exclusively or chiefly) in fruits and nuts. Cf. *solemncholy*, which according to Payne is in use in Alabama, framed evidently on *melancholy*, analyzed in a way not approved by Greek scholars. The whole ending of *septentrionalis* (from the name of the constellation *Septem triones*, the seven oxen) is used to form the opposite : *meridi-onalis*.

A similar case of ' tainting ' is found in recent English. The NED, in the article on the suffix -*eer*, remarks that " in many of the words so formed there is a more or less contemptuous implication," but does not explain this, and has not remarked that it is found only in words ending in -*teer* (from words in -*t*). I think this contemptuous implication starts from *garreteer* and *crotcheteer* (perhaps also *pamphleteer* and *privateer*); after these were formed the disparaging words *sonneteer*, *pulpiteer*. During the war (1916, I think) the additional word *profiteer* [1] came into use, but did not find its way into the dictionaries till 1919 (Cassell's). And only the other day I read in an American publication a new word of the same calibre : " Against *patrioteering*, against fraud and violence . . . Mr. Mencken has always nobly and bravely contended."

XIX.—§ 16. The Classifying Instinct.

Man is a classifying animal : in one sense it may be said that the whole process of speaking is nothing but distributing phenomena,

---

[1] Cf. Lloyd George's speech at Dundee (*The Times*, July 6, 1917): " The Government will not permit the burdens of the country to be increased by what is called ' profiteering.' Although I have been criticized for using that word, I believe on the whole it is a rather good one. It is *profit-eer-ing* as distinguished from *profit-ing*. Profiting is fair recompense for services rendered, either in production or distribution ; profiteering is an extravagant recompense given for services rendered. I believe that unfair in peace. In war it is an outrage."

of which no two are alike in every respect, into different classes on the strength of perceived similarities and dissimilarities. In the name-giving process we witness the same ineradicable and very useful tendency to see likenesses and to express similarity in the phenomena through similarity in name. Professor Hempl told me that one of his little daughters, when they had a black kitten which was called *Nig* (short for Nigger), immediately christened a gray kitten *Grig* and a brown one *Brownig*. Here we see the genesis of a suffix through a natural process, which has little in common with the gradual weakening of an originally independent word, as in -*hood* and the other instances mentioned above. In children's speech similar instances are not unfrequent (cf. Ch. VII § 5); Meringer L 148 mentions a child of 1.7 who had the following forms: *augn, ogn, agn,* for 'augen, ohren, haare.' How many words formed or transformed in the same way must we require in order to speak of a suffix ? Shall we recognize one in Romanic *leve, greve* (cf. Fr. *grief*), which took the place of *leve, grave* ? Here, as Schuchardt aptly remarks, it was not only the opposite signification, but also the fact that the words were frequently uttered shortly after one another, that made one word influence the other.

The classifying instinct often manifests itself in bringing words together in form which have something in common as regards signification. In this way we have smaller classes and larger classes, and sometimes it is impossible for us to say in what way the likeness in form has come about: we can only state the fact that at a given time the words in question have a more or less close resemblance. But in other cases it is easy to see which word of the group has influenced the others or some other. In the examples I am about to give, I have been more concerned to bring together words that exhibit the classifying tendency than to try to find out the impetus which directed the formation of the several groups.

In OE. we have some names of animals in -*gga* : *frogga, stagga, docga, wicga,* now *frog, stag, dog, wig. Savour* and *flavour* go together, the latter (OFr. *flaur*) having its *v* from the former. *Groin,* I suppose, has its diphthong from *loin*; the older form was *grine, grynd(e). Claw, paw* (earlier *powe*, OFr. *pol*). *Rim, brim. Hook, nook. Gruff, rough (tough, bluff, huff—miff, tiff, whiff). Fleer, leer, jeer. Twig, sprig. Munch, crunch (lunch). Without uttering or muttering a word. The trees were lopped and topped.* In old Gothonic the word for 'eye' has got its vowel from the word for 'ear,' with which it was frequently collocated : *augo(n), auso(n),* but in the modern languages the two words have again been separated in their phonetic development. In French I suspect that popular instinct will class the words *air, terre, mer* together as names of what used to be termed the 'elements,' in spite of the different spelling and origin of the sounds. In Russian *kogot'* ' griffe ' (claw), *nogot'* ' ongle ' (fingernail), and *lokot'* ' coude ' (elbow), three names of parts of the body, go together in flexion and accent (Boyer et Speranski, *Manuel de la l. russe* 33). So do in Latin *culex* ' gnat ' and *pulex* ' flea.' *Atrox, ferox.* A great many examples have been collected by M. Bloomfield, " On Adaptation of Suffixes in Congeneric Classes of Substantives " (*Am. Journal of Philol.* XII, 1891), from which I take a few. A considerable number of designations of parts of the body were formed with heteroclitic declension as *r-n* stems (cf. above, XVIII § 2): 'liver,' Gr. *hēpar, hēpatos,* ' udder,' Gr. *outhar, outhatos,* ' thigh,' Lat. *femur, feminis,* further Aryan names for blood, wing, viscera, excrement, etc. Other designations of parts of the body were partly assimilated to this class, having also *n* stems in the oblique cases, though their nominative was formed in a different way. Words for ' right ' and ' left ' frequently influence one another and adopt the same ending, and so do opposites generally : Bloomfield explains the *t* in the Gothonic word corresponding to E. *white,* where from Sanskr. we should expect *th, çveta,* as due to the word for ' black ' ; Goth. *hweits, swarts,* ON. *hvítr, svartr,* etc. A great many names of birds and other animals appear with the same ending, Gr. *glaux* ' owl,' *kokkux* ' cuckoo,' *korax* ' crow,' *ortux* ' quail,' *aix* ' goat,' *alopex* ' fox,' *bombux* ' silkworm,' *lunx* ' lynx ' and many others, also some plant-names. Names for winter, summer, day, evening, etc., also to a great extent form groups. In a subsequent article (in IF vi. 66 ff.) Bloomfield pursues the same line of thought and explains likenesses in various words of related signification, in direct opposition to the current explanation through added root-determinatives, as due to blendings (cf. above, Ch. XVII § 6). In Latin the inchoative value of the verbs in *-esco* is due to the accidentally inherent continuous character of a few verbs of the class : *adolesco, senesco, cresco* ; but the same suffix is also found in the oldest words for ' asking, wishing, searching,' retained in E. *ask, wish,* G. *forschen,* which thus become a small group linked together by form and meaning alike.

XIX.—§ 17. Character of Suffixes.

There seems undoubtedly to be something accidental or haphazard in most of these transferences of sounds from one word to another through which groups of phonetically and semantically similar words are created ; the process works unsystematically, or rather, it consists in spasmodic efforts at regularizing something which is from the start utterly unsystematic. But where conditions are favourable, i.e. where the notional connexion is patent and the phonetic element is such that it can easily be added to many words, the group will tend constantly to grow larger within the natural boundaries given by the common resemblance in signification.

I have no doubt that the vast majority of our formatives, such as suffixes and flexional endings, have arisen in this way through transference of some part, which at first was unmeaning in itself, from one word to another in which it had originally no business, and then to another and another, taking as it were a certain colouring from the words in which it is found, and gradually acquiring a more or less independent signification or function of its own. In long words, such as were probably frequent in primitive speech, and which were to the minds of the speakers as unanalyzable as *marmalade* or *crocodile* is to Englishmen nowadays, it would be perhaps most natural to keep the beginning unchanged and to modify the final syllable or syllables to bring about conformity with some word with which it was associated ; hence the prevalence of suffixes in our languages, hence also the less systematic character of these suffixes as compared with the prefixes, most of which have originated in independent words, such as adverbs. What is from the merely phonetic point of view the ' same ' suffix, in different languages may have the greatest variety of meaning, sometimes no discernible meaning at all, and it is in many cases utterly impossible to find out why in one particular language it can be used with one stem and not with another. Anyone going through the collections in Brugmann's great *Grammar* will be struck with this purely accidental character of the use of most of the suffixes—a fact which would be simply unthinkable if each of them had originally one definite, well-determined signification, but which is easy to account for on the hypothesis here adopted. And then many of them are not added to ready-made words or ' roots,' but form one indivisible whole with the initial part of the word ; cf., for instance, the suffix -*le* in English *squabble, struggle, wriggle, babble, mumble, bustle*, etc.

XIX.—§ 18. Brugmann's Theory of Gender.

As I have said, man is a classifying animal, and in his language tends to express outwardly class distinctions which he feels more or less vaguely. One of the most important of these class divisions, and at the same time one of the most difficult to explain, is that of the three ' genders ' in our Aryan languages. If we are to believe Brugmann, we have here a case of what I have in this work termed secretion. In his well-known paper, " Das Nominalgeschlecht in den indogermanischen Sprachen " (in Techmer's *Zs. f. allgem. Sprachwissensch.* 4. 100 ff., cf. also his reply to Roethe's criticism,

PBB 15. 522) he puts the question : How did it come about that the old Aryans attached a definite gender (or sex, geschlecht) to words meaning foot, head, house, town, Gr. *pous*, for instance, being masculine, *kephalē* feminine, *oikos* masculine, and *polis* feminine ? The generally accepted explanation, according to which the imagination of mankind looked upon lifeless things as living beings, is, Brugmann says, unsatisfactory ; the masculine and feminine of grammatical gender are merely unmeaning forms and have nothing to do with the ideas of masculinity and femininity ; for even where there exists a natural difference of sex, language often employs only one gender. So in German we have *der hase, die maus*, and *der weibliche hase* is not felt to be self-contradictory. Again, in the history of languages we often find words which change their gender exclusively on account of their form. Thus, in German, many words in *-e*, such as *traube, niere, wade*, which were formerly masculine, have now become feminine, because the great majority of substantives in *-e* are feminine (*erde, ehre, farbe*, etc.). Nothing accordingly hinders us from supposing that grammatical gender originally had nothing at all to do with natural sex. The question, therefore, according to Brugmann, is essentially reduced to this : How did it come to pass that the suffix *-a* was used to designate female beings ? At first it had no connexion with femininity, witness Lat. *aqua* ' water ' and hundreds of other words ; but among the old words with that ending there happened to be some denoting females : *mama* ' mother ' and *gena* ' woman ' (compare E. *quean, queen*). Now, in the history of some suffixes we see that, without any regard to their original etymological signification, they may adopt something of the radical meaning of the words to which they are added, and transfer that meaning to new formations. In this way *mama* and *gena* became the starting-point for analogical formations, as if the idea of female was denoted by the ending, and new words were formed, e.g. Lat. *dea* ' goddess ' from *deus* ' god,' *equa* ' mare ' from *equus* ' horse,' etc. The suffix *-iē-* or *-ī-* probably came to denote feminine sex by a similar process, possibly from Skr. *strī* ' woman,' which may have given a fem. *wḷqī* ' she-wolf ' to *wḷqos* ' wolf.' The above is a summary of Brugmann's reasoning ; it may interest the reader to know that a closely similar point of view had, several years previously, been taken by a far-seeing scholar in respect to a totally different language, namely Hottentot, where, according to Bleek, CG 2. 118-22, 292–9, a class division which had originally nothing to do with sex has been employed to distinguish natural sex. I transcribe a few of Bleek's remarks : " The apparent sex-denoting characte which the classification of the nouns now has in the Hottentot language was evidently imparted to it after a division of the nouns into classes [1] had taken place. It probably arose, in the first instance,, from the possibly accidental circumstance that the nouns indica‑ ting (respectively) man and woman were formed with different derivative suffixes, and consequently belonged to different classes (or genders) of nouns, and that these suffixes thus began to indicate the distinction of sex in nouns where it could be distinguished " (p. 122). " To assume, for example, that the suffix of the m. sg. (-p) had originally the meaning of ' man,' or the fem. sg. (-s) that of ' woman,' would in no way explain the peculiar division of the nouns into classes as we find it in Hottentot, and would be opposed to all that is probable regarding the etymology of these suffixes, and also to the fact that so many nouns are included in the sex-denoting classes to which the distinction of sex can only be applied by a great effort. . . . If the word for ' man ' were formed with one suffix (-p), and the word indicating ' woman ' (be it accidentally or not) by another (-s), then other nouns would be formed with the same suffixes, in analogy with these, until the majority of the nouns of each sex were formed with certain suffixes which would thus assume a sex-denoting character " (p. 298).

Brugmann's view on Aryan gender has not been unchallenged. The weakest points in his arguments are, of course, that there are so few old naturally feminine words in -a and -i to take as starting-points for such a thoroughgoing modification of the grammatical system, and that Brugmann was unable to give any striking ex‑ planation of the concord of adjectives and pronouns with words that had not these endings, but which were nevertheless treated as masculines and feminines respectively It would lead us too far here to give any minute account of the discussion which arose on these points ; [2] one of the most valuable contributions seems to me Jacobi's suggestion (Compositum u. Nebensatz, 1897, 115 ff.) that the origin of grammatical gender is not to be sought in the noun, but in the pronoun (he finds a parallel in the Dravidian languages)—but even he does not find a fully satisfactory explana‑ tion, and the Aryan gender distinction reaches back to so remote an antiquity, thousands of years before any literary tradition, that we shall most probably never be able to fathom all its mysteries. Of late years less attention has been given to the problem of the feminine, which presented itself to Brugmann, than to the distinc‑ tion between two classes, one of which was characterized by the

[1] Bleek is here thinking of classes like those of the Bantu languages, which have nothing to do with sex.
[2] For bibliography and criticism see Wheeler in Journ. of Germ. Philol. 2. 528 ff., and especially Josselin de Jong in Tijdschr. v. Ned. Taal- en Letterk. 29. 21 ff., and the same writer's thesis De Waardeeringsonderscheiding van levend en levenloos in het Indogermaansch vergel. m. hetzelfde verschijnsel in Algonkin-talen (Leiden, 1913). Cf. also Hirt GDS 45 ff.

use of a nominative in -s, which is now looked upon as a 'transitive-active' case, and the other by no ending or by an ending -m, which is the same as was used as the accusative in the first class (an 'intransitive-passive' case), and an attempt has been made to see in the distinction something analogous to the division found in Algonkin languages between a class of 'living' and another of 'lifeless' things—though these two terms are not to be taken in the strictly scientific sense, for primitive men do not reason in the same way as we do, but ascribe or deny 'life' to things according to criteria which we have great difficulty in apprehending. This would mean a twofold division into one class comprising the historical masculines and feminines, and another comprising the neuters.

As to the feminine, we saw two old endings characterizing that gender, a and i. With regard to the latter, I venture to throw out the suggestion that it is connected with diminutive suffixes containing that vowel in various languages : on the whole, the sound [i] has a natural affinity with the notion of small, slight, insignificant and weak (see Ch. XX § 8). In some African languages we find two classes, one comprising men and big things, and the other women and small things (Meinhof, *Die Sprachen der Hamiten* 23), and there is nothing unnatural in the supposition that similar views may have obtained with our ancestors. This would naturally account for Skr. *vṛk-i* 'she-wolf' (orig. little wolf, 'wolfy') from Skr. *vṛkas*, *napt-i*, Lat. *neptis*, G. *nichte*, Skr. *dēv-i* 'goddess,' etc. But the feminine -a is to me just as enigmatic as, say, the d of the old ablative.

XIX.—§ 19. Final Considerations.

The ending -a serves to denote not only female beings, but also abstracts, and if in later usage it is also applied to males, as in Latin *nauta* 'sailor,' *auriga* 'charioteer,' this is only a derived use of the abstracts denoting an activity, sailoring, driving, etc., just as G. *die wache*, besides the activity of watching, comes to mean the man on guard, or as *justice* (Sp. *el justicia*) comes to mean 'judge.' The original sense of *Antonius collega fuit Ciceronis* was ' A. was the co-election of C.' (Osthoff, *Verbum in d. Nominalcompos.*, 1878, 263 ff., Delbrück, *Synt. Forsch.* 4. 6).

The same -a is finally used as the plural ending of most neuters, but, as is now universally admitted (see especially Johannes Schmidt, *Die Pluralbildungen der indogerm. Neutra*, 1889), the ending here was originally neither neuter nor plural, but, on the contrary, feminine and singular. The forms in -a are properly collective formations like those found, for instance, in Lat. *opera*, gen. *operæ*, 'work,' comp. *opus* '(a piece of) work'; Lat. *terra* 'earth,' comp. Oscan *terum* 'plot of ground'; *pugna* 'boxing, fight,' comp. *pugnus* 'fist.' This explains among other things the peculiar syntactic phenomenon, which is found regularly in Greek and sporadically in Sanskrit and other languages, that a neuter plural subject takes the verb in the singular. Greek *toxa* is often used in speaking of a single bow; and the Latin poetic use of *guttura*, *colla*, *ora*, where only one person's throat, neck or face is meant, points similarly to a period of the past when these words did not denote the plural. We can now see the reason of this -*a* being in some cases also the plural sign of masculine substantives: Lat. *loca* from *locus*, *joca* from *jocus*, etc.; Gr. *sita* from *sitos*. Joh. Schmidt refers to similar plural formations in Arabic; and as we have seen (Ch. XIX § 9), the Bantu plural prefixes had probably a similar origin. And we are thus constantly reminded that languages must often make the most curious *détours* to arrive at a grammatical expression for things which appear to us so self-evident as the difference between he and she, or that between one and more than one. Expressive simplicity in linguistic structure is not a primitive, but a derived quality.

CHAPTER XX

SOUND SYMBOLISM

§ 1. Sound and Sense. § 2. Instinctive Feeling. § 3. Direct Imitation. § 4. Originator of the Sound. § 5. Movement. § 6. Things and Appearances. § 7. States of Mind. § 8. Size and Distance. § 9. Length and Strength of Words and Sounds. § 10. General Considerations. § 11. Importance of Suggestiveness. § 12. Ancient and Modern Times.

XX.—§ 1. Sound and Sense.

THE idea that there is a natural correspondence between sound and sense, and that words acquire their contents and value through a certain sound symbolism, has at all times been a favourite one with linguistic dilettanti, the best-known examples being found in Plato's *Kratylos*. Greek and Latin grammarians indulge in the wildest hypotheses to explain the natural origin of such and such a word, as when Nigidius Figulus said that in pronouncing *vos* one puts forward one's lips and sends out breath in the direction of the other person, while this is not the case with *nos*. With these early writers, to make guesses at sound symbolism was the only way to etymologize ; no wonder, therefore, that we with our historical methods and our wider range of knowledge find most of their explanations ridiculous and absurd. But this does not justify us in rejecting any idea of sound symbolism : abusus non tollit usum !

Humboldt (Versch 79) says that "language chooses to designate objects by sounds which partly in themselves, partly in comparison with others, produce on the ear an impression resembling the effect of the object on the mind ; thus *stehen, stätig, starr*, the impression of firmness, Sanskrit *li* 'to melt, diverge,' that of liquidity or solution (des zerfliessenden). . . In this way objects that produce similar impressions are denoted by words with essentially the same sounds, thus *wehen, wind, wolke, wirren, wunsch*, in all of which the vacillating, wavering motion with its confused impression on the senses is expressed through . . . *w*." Madvig's objection (1842, 13 = Kl 64) that we need only compare four of the words Humboldt quotes with the corresponding words in the very nearest sister-language, Danish *blæse, vind, sky, ønske, to*

see how wrong this is, seems to me a little cheap : Humboldt
himself expressly assumes that much of primitive sound symbolism
may have disappeared in course of time and warns us against
making this kind of explanation a 'constitutive principle,'
which would lead to great dangers ("so setzt man sich grossen
gefahren aus und verfolgt einen in jeder rücksicht schlüpfrigen
pfad "). Moreover *blœse* (E. *blow*, Lat. *flare*) is just as imitative
as *wind*, *vind* : no one of course would pretend that there was
only one way of expressing the same sense perception. Among
Humboldt's examples *wolke* and *wunsch* are doubtful, but I do
not see that this affects the general truth of his contention that
there is something like sound symbolism in *some* words.

Nyrop in his treatment of this question (Gr IV § 545 f.) repeats
Madvig's objection that the same name can denote various objects,
that the same object can be called by different names, and that
the significations of words are constantly changing ; further, that
the same group of sounds comes to mean different things according
to the language in which it occurs. He finally exclaims : " How
to explain [by means of sound symbolism] the difference in
signification between *murus*, *nurus*, *durus*, *purus*, etc. ? "

XX.—§ 2. Instinctive Feeling.

Yes, of course it would be absurd to maintain that all words
at all times in all languages had a signification corresponding
exactly to their sounds, each sound having a definite meaning
once for all. But is there really much more logic in the opposite
extreme, which denies any kind of sound symbolism[1] (apart from
the small class of evident echoisms or ' onomatopœia ') and sees
in our words only a collection of wholly accidental and irrational
associations of sound and meaning ? It seems to me that the
conclusion in this case is as false as if you were to infer that because
on one occasion X told a lie, he therefore never tells the truth.
The correct conclusion would be : as he has told a lie once, we
cannot always trust him ; we must be on our guard with him—
but sometimes he may tell the truth. Thus, also, sounds may in
some cases be symbolic of their sense, even if they are not so in
all words. If linguistic historians are averse to admitting sound
symbolism, this is a natural consequence of their being chiefly
occupied with words which have undergone regular changes in
sound and sense ; and most of the words which form the
staple of linguistic books are outside the domain of sound
symbolism.

[1] " Inner and essential connexion between idea and word . . . there
is none, in any language upon earth," says Whitney L 32.

There is no denying, however, that there are words which we feel instinctively to be adequate to express the ideas they stand for, and others the sounds of which are felt to be more or less incongruous with their signification. Future linguists will have to find out in detail what domains of human thought admit, and what domains do not admit, of congruous expression through speech sounds, and further what sounds are suitable to express such and such a notion, for though it is clear—to take only a few examples—that there is little to choose between *apple* and *pomme*, or between *window* and *fenster*, as there is no sound or sound group that has any natural affinity with such thoroughly concrete and composite ideas as those expressed by these words, yet on the other hand everybody must feel that the word *roll, rouler, rulle, rollen* is more adequate than the corresponding Russian word *katat', katit'*.

It would be an interesting task to examine in detail and systematically what ideas lend themselves to symbolic presentation and what sounds are chosen for them in different languages. That, however, could only be done on the basis of many more examples than I can find space for in this work, and I shall, therefore, only attempt to give a preliminary enumeration of the most obvious classes, with a small fraction of the examples I have collected.[1]

XX.—§ 3. Direct Imitation.

The simplest case is the direct imitation of the sound, thus *clink, clank, ting, tinkle* of various metallic sounds, *splash, bubble, sizz, sizzle* of sounds produced by water, *bow-wow, bleat, roar* of sounds produced by animals, and *snort, sneeze, snigger, smack, whisper, grunt, grumble* of sounds produced by human beings. Examples might easily be multiplied of such 'echoisms' or 'onomatopœia' proper. But, as our speech-organs are not capable of giving a perfect imitation of all 'unarticulated' sounds, the choice of speech-sounds is to a certain extent accidental, and different nations have chosen different combinations, more or less conventionalized, for the same sounds; thus *cock-a-doodle-doo*, Dan. *kykeliky*, Sw. *kukeliku*, G. *kikeriki*, Fr. *coquelico*, for the sound of a cock; and for *whisper*: Dan. *hviske*, ON. *kvisa*, G. *flüstern*, Fr. *chuchoter*, Sp. *susurar*. The continuity of a sound is frequently indicated by *l* or *r* after a stopped consonant: *rattle, rumble, jingle, clatter, chatter, jabber*, etc.

[1] I have learnt very little from the discussion which followed Wundt's remarks on the subject (S 1. 312–347); see Delbrück Grfr 78 ff., Sütterlin WSG 29 ff., Hilmer Sch 10 ff.

XX.—§ 4. Originator of the Sound.

Next, the echoic word designates the being that produces the sound, thus the birds *cuckoo* and *peeweet* (Dan. *vibe*, G. *kibitz*, Fr. pop. *dix-huit*).

A special subdivision of particular interest comprises those names, or nicknames, which are sometimes popularly given to nations from words continually occurring in their speech. Thus the French used to call an Englishman a *god-damn* (*godon*), and in China an English soldier is called *a-says* or *I-says*. In Java a Frenchman is called *orang-deedong* (*orang* 'man'), in America *ding-dong*, and during the Napoleonic wars the French were called in Spain *didones*, from *dis-donc*; another name for the same nation is *wi-wi* (Australia), *man-a-wiwi* (in Beach-la-mar), or *oui-men* (New Caledonia). In Eleonore Christine's *Jammersminde* 83 I read, "Ich habe zwei *parle mi franço* gefangen," and correspondingly Goldsmith writes (Globe ed. 624): "Damn the French, the *parle vous*, and all that belongs to them. What makes the bread rising ? the *parle vous* that devour us." In Rovigno the surrounding Slavs are called *čuje* from their exclamation *čuje* 'listen, I say,' and in Hungary German visitors are called *vigéc* (from *wie geht's ?*), and customs officers *vartapiszli* (from *wart' a bissl*). Round Panama everything native is called *spiggoty*, because in the early days the Panamanians, when addressed, used to reply, "No spiggoty [speak] Inglis." In Yokohama an English or American sailor is called *Damurutsu H'to* from 'Damn your eyes' and Japanese H'to 'people.' [1]

XX.—§ 5. Movement.

Thirdly, as sound is always produced by some movement and is nothing but the impression which that movement makes on the ear, it is quite natural that the movement itself may be expressed by the word for its sound: the two are, in fact, inseparable. Note, for instance, such verbs as *bubble*, *splash*, *clash*, *crack*, *peck*. Human actions may therefore be denoted by such words as to *bang* the door, or (with slighter sounds) to *tap* or *rap* at a door. Hence also the substantives a *tap* or a *rap* for the action, but the substantive may also come to stand for the implement, as when from the verb to *hack*, 'to cut, chop off, break up hard earth,' we have the noun *hack*, 'a mattock or large pick.'

Then we have words expressive of such movements as are not to the same extent characterized by loud sounds ; thus a great

---

[1] Schuchardt, KS 5. 12, *Zs. f. rom. Phil.* 33. 458, Churchill B 53, Sandfeld-Jensen, *Nationalfølelsen* 14, Lentzner, *Col.* 87, Simonyi US 157, *The Outlook*, January 1910, *New Quarterly Mag.*, July 1879.

many words beginning with *l*-combinations, *fl-* : *flow, flag* (Dan. *flagre*), *flake, flutter, flicker, fling, flit, flurry, flirt; sl-* : *slide, slip, slive; gl-* : *glide.* Hence adjectives like *fleet, slippery, glib.* Sound and sight may have been originally combined in such expressions for an uncertain walk as *totter, dodder,* dialectical *teeter, titter, dither,* but in cases of this kind the audible element may be wanting, and the word may come to be felt as symbolic of the movement as such. This is also the case with many expressions for the sudden, rapid movement by which we take hold of something ; as a short vowel, suddenly interrupted by a stopped consonant, serves to express the sound produced by a very rapid striking movement (*pat, tap, knock,* etc.), similar sound combinations occur frequently for the more or less noiseless seizing of a thing (with the teeth or with the hand) : *snap, snack, snatch, catch,* Fr. *happer, attraper, gripper,* E. *grip,* Dan. *hapse, nappe,* Lat. *capio,* Gr. *kaptō,* Armenian *kap* 'I seize,' Turk *kapmak* (*mak* infin. ending), etc. (I shall only mention one derivative meaning that may develop from this group : E. *snack* 'a hurried meal,' in Swift's time called a *snap* (*Journ. to Stella* 270) ; cf. G. *schnapps,* Dan. *snaps* 'glass of spirits.') F. *chase* and *catch* are both derived from two dialectically different French forms, ultimately going back to the same late Latin verb *captiare,* but it is no mere accident that it was the form ' catch ' that acquired the meaning ' to seize,' not found in French, for it naturally associated itself with *snatch,* and especially with the now obsolete verb *latch* ' to seize.'

There is also a natural connexion between action and sound in the word to *tickle,* G. *kitzeln,* ON. *kitla,* Dan. *kilde* (*d* mute), Nubian *killi-killi,* and similar forms (Schuchardt, *Nubisch. u. Bask.* 9), Lat. *titillare* ; cp. also the word for the kind of laughter thus produced : *titter,* G. *kichern.*

XX.—§ 6. Things and Appearances.

Further, we have the extension of symbolical designation to things ; here, too, there is some more or less obvious association of what is only visible with some sound or sounds. This has been specially studied by Hilmer, to whose book (Sch) the reader is referred for numerous examples, e.g. p. 237 ff., *knap* 'a thick stick, a knot of wood, a bit of food, a protuberance, a small hill; *knop* ' a boss, stud, button, knob, a wart, pimple, the bud of a flower, a promontory,' with the variants *knob, knup.* . . . Hilmer's word-lists from German and English comprise 170 pages !

There is alsc ↲ natural association between high tones (sounds with very rapid vibrations) and light, and inversely between low tones and darkness, as is seen in the frequent use of adjectives

like ' light ' and ' dark ' in speaking of notes. Hence the vowel
[i] is felt to be more appropriate for light, and [u] for dark, as
seen most clearly in the contrast between *gleam, glimmer, glitter*
on the one hand and *gloom* on the other (Zangwill somewhere
writes : " The gloom of night, relieved only by the gleam from
the street-lamp ") ; the word *light* itself, which has now a diphthong
which is not so adequate to the meaning, used to have the vowel
[i] like G. *licht* ; for the opposite notions we have such words as
G. *dunkel*, Dan. *mulm*, Gr. *amolgós, skótos*, Lat. *obscurus*, and with
another ' dark ' vowel E. *murky*, Dan. *mörk*.

XX.—§ 7. States of Mind.

From this it is no far cry to words for corresponding states
of mind : to some extent the very same words are used, as *gloom*
(Dowden writes : " The good news was needed to cast a gleam
on the gloom that encompassed Shelley ") ; hence also *glum,
glumpy, glumpish, grumpy, the dumps, sulky*. If E. *moody* and
sullen have changed their significations (OE. *modig* ' high-spirited,'
ME. *solein* ' solitary '), sound symbolism, if I am not mistaken,
counts for something in the change ; the adjectives now mean
exactly the same as Dan. *mut, but*.

If *grumble* comes to mean the expression of a mental state of
dissatisfaction, the connexion between the sound of the word and
its sense is even more direct, for the verb is imitative of the sound
produced in such moods, cf. *mumble* and *grunt, gruntle*. The
name of Mrs. *Grundy* is not badly chosen as a representative of
narrow-minded conventional morality.

A long list might be given of symbolic expressions for dislike,
disgust, or scorn ; here a few hints only can find place. First we
have the same dull or dump (back) vowels as in the last paragraph :
*blunder, bungle, bung, clumsy, humdrum, humbug, strum, slum,
slush, slubber, sloven, muck, mud, muddle, mug* (various words,
but all full of contempt), *juggins* (a silly person), *numskull* (old
numps, nup, nupson), *dunderhead, gull, scug* (at Eton a dirty or
untidy boy). . . . Many words begin with *sl-* (we have already
seen some) : *slight, slim, slack, sly, sloppy, slipslop, slubby, slattern,
slut, slosh*. . . . Initial labials are also frequent.[1] After the
vowel we have very often the sound [ʃ] or [tʃ], as in *trash, tosh,
slosh, botch, patch* ; cf. also G. *kitsch* (bad picture, smearing),
patsch(e) (mire, anything worthless), *quatsch* (silly nonsense),
putsch (riot, political *coup de main*). E. *bosh* (nonsense) is said
to be a Turkish loan-word ; it has become popular for the same

[1] *F*, for instance, in *fop, foozy, fogy, fogram* (old), all of them more or
less variants of *fool*.

reason for which the French nickname *boche* for a German was widely used during the World War. Let me finally mention the It. derivative suffix *-accio*, as in *poveraccio* (miserable), *acquaccia* (bad water), and *-uccio*, as in *cavalluccio* (vile horse).

XX.—§ 8. Size and Distance.

The vowel [i], especially in its narrow or thin variety, is particularly appropriate to express what is small, weak, insignificant, or, on the other hand, refined or dainty. It is found in a great many adjectives in various languages, e.g. *little, petit, piccolo, piccino,* Magy. *kis,* E. *wee, tiny* (by children often pronounced *teeny* [*ti·ni*]), *slim,* Lat. *minor, minimus,* Gr. *mikros ;* further, in numerous words for small children or small animals (the latter frequently used as endearing or depreciative words for children), e.g. *child* (formerly with [i·] sound), G. *kind,* Dan. *pilt,* E. *kid, chit, imp, slip, pigmy, midge,* Sp. *chico,* or for small things : *bit, chip, whit,* Lat. *quisquiliæ, mica,* E. *tip, pin, chink, slit. . . .* The same vowel is found in diminutive suffixes in a variety of languages, as E. *-y, -ie* (*Bobby, baby, auntie, birdie*), Du. *-ie, -je* (*koppie* 'little hill '), Gr. *-i-* (*paid-i-on* 'little boy '), Goth. *-ein,* pronounced [i·n] (*gumein* 'little man '), E. *-kin, -ling,* Swiss German *-li,* It. *-ino,* Sp. *-ico, -ito, -illo. . . .*

As smallness and weakness are often taken to be characteristic of the female sex, I suspect that the Aryan feminine suffix *-i,* as in Skr. *vṛkī* 'she-wolf,' *naptī* 'niece,' originally denotes smallness ('wolfy '), and in the same way we find the vowel *i* in many feminine suffixes ; thus late Lat. *-itta* (*Julitta,* etc., whence Fr. *-ette, Henriette,* etc.), *-ina* (*Carolina*), further G. *-in* (*königin*), Gr. *-issa* (*basilissa* 'queen '), whence Fr. *-esse,* E. *-ess.*

The same vowel [i] is also symbolical of a very short time, as in the phrases *in a jiff, jiffy,* Sc. *in a clink,* Dan. *i en svip ;* and correspondingly we have adjectives like *quick, swift, vivid* and others. No wonder, then, that the Germans feel their word for 'lightning,' *blitz,* singularly appropriate to the effect of light and to the shortness of duration.[1]

It has often been remarked [2] that in corresponding pronouns and adverbs the vowel *i* frequently indicates what is nearer, and other vowels, especially *a* or *u,* what is farther off ; thus Fr. *ci, là,*

[1] The preceding paragraphs on the symbolic value of *i* are an abstract of a paper which will be printed in *Philologica,* vol. i.
[2] Benfey Gesch 791, Misteli 539, Wundt S 1. 331 (but his examples from out-of-the-way languages must be used with caution, and curiously enough he thinks that the phenomenon is limited to primitive languages and is not found in Semitic or Aryan languages), GRM 1. 638, Simonyi US 255, Meinhof, Ham 20.

E. *here, there*, G. *dies, das*, Low G. *dit, dat*, Magy. *ez, emez* 'this,' *az, amaz* 'that,' *itt* 'here,' *ott* 'there,' Malay *iki* 'this,' *ika* 'that, a little removed,' *iku* 'yon, farther away.' In Hamitic languages *i* symbolizes the near and *u* what is far away. We may here also think of the word *zigzag* as denoting movement in alternate turns here and there ; and if in the two E. pronouns *this* and *that* the old neuter forms have prevailed (OE. m. *þes, se*, f. *þeos, seo*, n. *þis, þæt*) the reason (or one of the reasons) may have been that a characteristic difference of vowels in the two contrasted pronouns was thus secured.

XX.—§ 9. Length and Strength of Words and Sounds.

Shorter and more abrupt forms are more appropriate to certain states of mind, longer ones to others. An imperative may be used both for command and for a more or less humble appeal or entreaty ; in Magyar dialects there are short forms for command : *irj, dolgozz* ; long for entreaty : *irjál, dolgozzál* (Simonyi US 359, 214). Were Lat. *dic, duc, fac, fer* used more than other imperatives in commands ? The fact that they alone lost *-e* might indicate that this was so. On the other hand the imperatives *es, este* and *i* had to yield to the fuller (and more polite) *esto, estote, vade*, and *scito* is always said instead of *sci* (Wackernagel, *Gött. Ges. d. Wiss.*, 1906, 182, on the avoidance of too short forms in general). Other languages, which have only one form for the imperative, soften the commanding tone by adding some word like *please, bitte*.

An emotional effect is obtained in some cases by lengthening a word by some derivative syllables, in themselves unmeaning ; thus in Danish words for 'lengthy' or 'tiresome' : *langsommelig, kedsommelig, evindelig* for *lang(som), kedelig, evig*. (Cf. Ibsen, *Når vi døde vågner* 98 : Du er kanske ble't ked af dette evige samliv med mig.—Evige ? Sig lige så godt : evindelige.) In the same way the effect of *splendid* is strengthened in slang : *splendiferous, splendidous, splendidious, splendacious*. A long word like *aggravate* is felt to be more intense than *vex* (Coleman)—and that may be the reason why the long word acquires a meaning that is strange to its etymology. And " to disburden one's self of a sense of contempt, a robust full-bodied detonation, like, for instance, *platitudinous*, is, unquestionably, very much more serviceable than any evanescing squib of one or two syllables " (Fitzedward Hall). Cf. also *multitudinous, multifarious*.

We see now the emotional value of some ' mouth-filling ' words, some of which may be considered symbolical expansions of existing words (what H. Schröder terms ' streckformen '), though others

cannot be thus explained ; not unfrequently the effect of length
is combined with some of the phonetic effects mentioned above.
Such words are, e.g., *slubberdegullion* ' dirty fellow,' *rumbustious*
' boisterous,' *rumgumption, rumfustian, rumbullion* (cf. *rum-
puncheon* ' cask of rum ' as a term of abuse in Stevenson, *Treas.
Isl.* 48, " the cowardly son of a rum-puncheon "), *rampallion*
' villain,' *rapscallion, ragamuffin* ; *sculduddery* ' obscenity ' ; *can-
tankerous* ' quarrelsome,' U.S. also *rantankerous* (cf. *cankerous,
rancorous*) ; *skilligalee* ' miserable gruel,' *flabbergast* ' confound,'
catawampous (or *-ptious*) ' fierce ' (" a high-sounding word with no
very definite meaning," NED) ; Fr. *hurluberlu* ' crazy ' and the
synonymous Dan. *tummelumsk*, Norw. *tullerusk*.

In this connexion one may mention the natural tendency to
lengthen and to strengthen single sounds under the influence of
strong feeling and in order to intensify the effect of the spoken
word ; thus, in ' it's very cold ' both the diphthong [ou] and the [l]
may be pronounced extremely long, in ' terribly dull ' the [l] is
lengthened, in ' extremely long ' either the vowel [ɔ] or the [ŋ]
(or both) may be lengthened. In Fr. ' c'était horrible ' the trill
of the [r] becomes very long and intense (while the same effect
is not generally possible in the corresponding English word, because
the English [r] is not trilled, but pronounced by one flap of the
tip). In some cases a lengthening due to such a psychological
cause may permanently alter a word, as when Lat. *totus* in It.
has become *tutto* (Fr. *tout, toute* goes back to the same form, while
Sp. *todo* has preserved the form corresponding to the Lat. single
consonant). An interesting collection of such cases from the
Romanic tongues has been published by A. J. Carnoy (*Mod. Philol.*
15. 31, July 1917), who justly emphasizes the symbolic value of
the change and the special character of the words in which it
occurs (pet-names, children's words, ironic or derisive words,
imitative words . . .). He says : " While to a phonetician the
phenomenon would seem capricious, its apportionment in the
vocabulary is quite natural to a psychologist. In fact, reduplication, be it of syllables or of consonants, generally has that character
in languages. One finds it in perfective tenses, in intensive or
frequentative verbs, in the plural, and in collectives. In most
cases it is a reduplication of syllables, but a lengthening of vowels
is not rare and the reinforcement of consonants is also found.
In Chinook, for instance, the emotional words, both diminutive
and augmentative, are expressed by increasing the stress of consonants. It is, of course, also well known that in Semitic the
intensive radical of verbs is regularly formed by a reduplication
of consonants. To a stem *qatal*, e.g., answers an intensive : Eth.
qattala, Hebr. *qittel*. Cf. Hebr. *shibbar* ' to cut in small pieces '

[cf. below], *hillech* ' to walk,' *qibber* ' to bury many,' etc.   Cf.
Brockelmann, *Vergl. Gramm.*, p. 244."

I add a few more examples from Misteli (428 f.) of this Semitic
strengthening : the first vowel is lengthened to express a tendency
or an attempt : *qatala jaqtulu* ' kill ' (in the third person masc.,
the former in the prefect-aorist, the latter in the imperfect-
durative, where *ja, ju* is the sign of the third person m.), *qātala
juqātilu* ' try to kill, fight '; *faXara jufXaru* ' excel in fame,'
fāXara jufāXiru ' try to excel, vie.'   Through lengthening
(doubling) of a consonant an intensification of the action is denoted :
Hebr. *šāβar jišbōr* ' zerbrechen,' *šibbēr ješabbēr* ' zerschmettern,'
Arab. *ḍaraba jaḍrubu* ' strike,' *ḍarraba juḍarribu* ' beat violently,
or repeatedly '; sometimes the change makes a verb into a causative
or transitive, etc.

I imagine that we have exactly the same kind of strengthening
for psychological (symbolical) reasons in a number of verbs where
Danish has *pp, tt, kk* by the side of *b, d, g* (spirantic) : *pippe pibe,
stritte stride, snitte snide, skøtte skøde, splitte splide, skrikke skrige,
lukke luge, hikke hige, sikke sige, kikke kige, prikke prige* (cf. also
sprække sprænge).   Some of these forms are obsolete, others
dialectal, but it would take us too far in this place to deal with
the words in detail.   It is customary to ascribe this gemination to
an old *n* derivative (see, e.g., Brugmann VG 1. 390, Streitberg Urg
pp. 135, 138, Noreen UL 154), but it does not seem necessary to
conjure up an *n* from the dead to make it disappear again immediately, as the mere strengthening of the consonant itself to
express symbolically the strengthening of the action has nothing
unnatural in it.   Cf. also G. *placken* by the side of *plagen*.   The
opposite change, a weakening, may have taken place in E. *flag*
(cf. OFr. *flaquir*, to become flaccid), *flabby*, earlier *flappy*, *drib* from
drip, *slab*, if from OFr. *esclape*, *clod* by the side of *clot*, and possibly
cadge, bodge, grudge, smudge, which had all of them originally -*tch*.
But the common modification in sense is not so easily perceived
here as in the cases of strengthening.

I may here, for the curiosity of the thing, mention that in
a ' language ' coined by two English children (a vocabulary of
which was communicated to me by one of the inventors through
Miss I. C. Ward, of the Department of Phonetics, University
College, London) there was a word *bal* which meant ' place,' but
the bigger the place the longer the vowel was made, so that with
three different quantities it meant ' village,' ' town ' and ' city '
respectively.   The word for ' go ' was *dudu*, " the greater the
speed of the going, the more quickly the word was said—[dœ·dœ·]
walk slowly."   Cf. Humboldt, ed. Steinthal 82 : " In the southern
dialect of the Guarani language the suffix of the perfect *yma* is

pronounced more or less slowly according to the more or less remoteness of the past to be indicated."

XX.—§ 10. General Considerations.

Sound symbolism, as we have considered it in this chapter, has a very wide range of application, from direct imitation of perceived natural sounds to such small quantitative changes of existing non-symbolic words as may be used for purely grammatical purposes. But in order to obtain a true valuation of this factor in the life of language it is of importance to keep in view the following considerations :

(1) No language utilizes sound symbolism to its full extent, but contains numerous words that are indifferent to or may even jar with symbolism. To express smallness the vowel [i] is most adequate, but it would be absurd to say that that vowel always implies smallness, or that smallness is always expressed by words containing that vowel : it is enough to mention the words *big* and *small*, or to point to the fact that *thick* and *thin* have the same vowel, to repudiate such a notion.

(2) Words that have been symbolically expressive may cease to be so in consequence of historical development, either phonetic or semantic or both. Thus the name of the bird *crow* is not now so good an imitation of the sound made by the bird as OE. *crawe* was (Dan. *krage*, Du. *kraai*). Thus, also, the verbs *whine, pipe* were better imitations when the vowel was still [i·] (as in Dan. *hvine, pibe*). But to express the sound of a small bird the latter word is still pronounced with the vowel [i] either long or short (*peep, pip*), the word having been constantly renewed and as it were reshaped by fresh imitation; cf. on Irish *wheen* and dialectal *peep*, XV § 8. Lat. *pipio* originally meant any ' peeping bird,' but when it came to designate one particular kind of birds, it was free to follow the usual trend of phonetic development, and so has become Fr. *pigeon* [piʒɔ̃], E. *pigeon* [pidʒin]. E. *cuckoo* has resisted the change from [u] to [ʌ] as in *cut*, because people have constantly heard the sound and fashioned the name of the bird from it. I once heard a Scotch lady say [kʌku·], but on my inquiry she told me that there were no cuckoos in her native place ; hence the word had there been treated as any other word containing the short [u]. The same word is interesting in another way ; it has resisted the old Gothonic consonant-shift, and thus has the same consonants as Skt. *kōkiláḥ*, Gr. *kókkux*, Lat. *cuculus*. On the general preservation of significative sounds, cf. Ch. XV § 8.

(3) On the other hand, some words have in course of time become more expressive than they were at first ; we have some-

thing that may be called secondary echoism or secondary symbolism. The verb *patter* comes from *pater* (= *paternoster*), and at first meant to repeat that prayer, to mumble one's prayers ; but then it was associated with the homophonous verb *patter* ' to make a rapid succession of *pats* ' and came under the influence of echoic words like *prattle, chatter, jabber* ; it now, like these, means ' to talk rapidly or glibly ' and is to all intents a truly symbolical word; cf. also the substantive *patter* ' secret lingo, speechifying, talk.' *Husky* may at first have meant only " full of husks, of the nature of a husk " (NED), but it could not possibly from that signification have arrived at the now current sense ' dry in the throat, hoarse ' if it had not been that the sound of the adjective had reminded one of the sound of a hoarse voice. Dan. *pöjt* ' poor drink, vile stuff ' is now felt as expressive of contempt, but it originates in *Poitou*, an innocent geographical name of a kind of wine, like *Bordeaux* ; it is now connected with other scornful words like *spröjt* and *döjt*.

In E. *little* the symbolic vowel *i* is regularly developed from OE. *y, lytel*, whose *y* is a mutated *u*, as seen in OSax. *luttil* ; *u* also appears in other related languages, and the word thus originally had nothing symbolical about it. But in Gothic the word is *leitils* (*ei*, sounded [i·]) and in ON. *lítinn*, and here the vowel is so difficult to account for on ordinary principles that the NED in despair thinks that the two words are " radically unconnected." I have no hesitation in supposing that the vowel *i* is due to sound symbolism, exactly as the smaller change introduced in modern E. ' leetle,' with narrow instead of wide (broad) [i]. In the word for the opposite meaning, *much*, the phonetic development may also have been influenced by the tendency to get an adequate vowel, for normally we should expect the vowel [i] as in Sc. *mickle*, from OE. *micel*. In E. *quick* the vowel best adapted to the idea has prevailed instead of the one found in the old nom. forms *cwucu, cucu* from *cwicu* (inflected *cwicne, cwices*, etc.), while in the word *widu, wudu*, which is phonetically analogous, there was no such inducement, and the vowel [u] has been preserved : *wood*. The same prevalence of the symbolic *i* is noticed in the Dan. adj. *kvik*, MLG. *quik*, while the same word as subst. has become Dan. *kvæg*, MLG. *quek*, where there was no symbolism at work, as it has come to mean ' cattle.' I even see symbolism in the preservation of the *k* in the Dan. adj. (as against the fricative in *kvæg*), because the notion of ' quick ' is best expressed by the short [i], interrupted by a stop ; and may not the same force have been at work in this adjective at an earlier period ? The second *k* in OE. *cwicu*, ON. *kvikr* as against Goth. *qius*, Lat. *vivus*, has not been sufficiently explained. An [i], symbolic of smallness, has been introduced in some comparatively recent E. words : *tip* from *top*, *trip* ' small flock ' from *troop, sip* ' drink in small quantities ' from *sup, sop.*

Through changes in meaning, too, some words have become symbolically more expressive than they were formerly ; thus the agreement between sound and sense is of late growth in *miniature,* which now, on account of the *i,* has come to mean ' a small picture,' while at first it meant ' image painted with minium or vermilion,' and in *pittance,* now ' a scanty allowance,' formerly any pious donation, whether great or small. Cf. what has been said above of *sullen, moody, catch.*

XX.—§ 11. Importance of Suggestiveness.

The suggestiveness of some words as felt by present-day speakers is a fact that must be taken into account if we are to understand the realities of language. In some cases it may have existed from the very first : these words sprang thus into being because that shape at once expressed the idea the speaker wished to communicate. In other cases the suggestive element is not original : these words arose in the same way as innumerable others whose sound has never carried any suggestion. But if the sound of a word of this class was, or came to be, in some way suggestive of its signification—say, if a word containing the vowel [i] in a prominent place meant ' small ' or something small—then the sound exerted a strong influence in gaining popular favour to the word ; it was an inducement to people to choose and to prefer that particular word and to cease to use words for the same notion that were not thus favoured. Sound symbolism, we may say, makes some words more fit to survive and gives them considerable help in their struggle for existence. If we want to denote a little child by a word for some small animal, we take some word like *kid, chick, kitten,* rather than *bat* or *pug* or *slug,* though these may in themselves be smaller than the animal chosen.

It is quite true that Fr. *rouler,* our *roll,* is derived from Lat. *rota* ' wheel ' + a diminutive ending *-ul-,* but the word would never have gained its immense popularity, extending as it does through English, Dutch, German and the Scandinavian languages, if the sound had not been eminently suggestive of the sense, so suggestive that it seems to us now *the* natural expression for that idea, and we have difficulty in realizing that the word has not existed from the very dawn of speech. Or let me take another example, in which the connexion between sound and sense is even more ' fortuitous.' About a hundred years ago a member of Congress, Felix Walker, from Buncombe County, North Carolina, made a long and tedious speech. " Many members left the hall.

Very naïvely he told those who remained that they might go too ; he should speak for some time, but 'he was only talking for Buncombe,' to please his constituents." Now *buncombe (buncome, bunkum)* has become a widely used word, not only in the States, but all over the English-speaking world, for political speaking or action not resting on conviction, but on the desire of gaining the favour of electors, or for any kind of empty ' clap-trap ' oratory ; but does anybody suppose that the name of Mr. Walker's constituency would have been thus used if he had happened to hail from Annapolis or Philadelphia, or some other place with a name incapable of tickling the popular fancy in the same way as *Buncombe* does ? (Cf. above, p. 401 on the suggestiveness of the short *u*.) In a similar way *hullaballoo* seems to have originated from the Irish village *Ballyhooly* (see P. W. Joyce, *English as we speak it in Ireland*) and to have become popular on account of its suggestive sound.

. In loan-words we can often see that they have been adopted less on account of any cultural necessity (see above, p. 209) than because their sound was in some way or other suggestive. Thus the Algonkin (Natick) word for ' chief,' *mugquomp*, is used in the United States in the form of *mugwump* for a ' great man ' or ' boss,' and especially, in political life, for a man independent of parties and thinking himself superior to parties. Now, no one would have thought of going to an Indian language to express such a notion, had not an Indian word presented itself which from its uncouth sound lent itself to purposes of ridicule. Among other words whose adoption has been favoured by their sounds I may mention *jungle* (from Hindi *jangal*, associated more or less closely with *jumble, tumble, bundle, bungle*); *bobbery*, in slang ' noise, squabble,' " the Anglo-Indian colloquial representation of a common exclamation of Hindus when in surprise or grief—*Bap-rē !* or *Bap-rē Bap* ' O Father ! ' " (Hobson-Jobson); *amuck* ; and U.S. *bunco* ' swindling game, to swindle,' from It. *banco*.

XX.—§ 12. Ancient and Modern Times.

It will be seen that our conception of echoism and related phenomena does not carry us back to an imaginary primitive period : these forces are vital in languages as we observe them day by day. Linguistic writers, however, often assume that sound symbolism, if existing at all, must date back to the earliest times, and therefore can have no reality nowadays. Thus Benfey (Gesch 288) turns upon de Brosse, who had found rudeness in Fr. *rude* and gentleness in Fr. *doux*, and says : " As if the sounds of such words, which are distant by an infinite length of time from the time when language originated, were able to contribute ever so little to explain the original designation of things." (But Benfey is right in saying that the impression made by those two French words may be imaginary; as examples they are not particularly well chosen.) Sütterlin (WW 14) says : " It is bold to search for such correspondence as still existing in detail in the language of our own days. For words like *liebe, süss* on the one hand, and *zorn, hass, hart* on the other, which are often alleged by dilettanti, prove nothing to the scholar, because their form is young and must have had totally different sounds in the period when language was created."

Similarly de Saussure (LG 104) gives as one of the main principles of our science that the tie between sound and sense is arbitrary or rather motiveless (immotivé), and to those who would object that onomatopoetic words are not arbitrary he says that " they are never organic elements of a linguistic system. Besides, they are much less numerous than is generally supposed. Such words as Fr. *fouet* and *glas* may strike some ears with a suggestive ring ;[1] but they have not had that character from the start, as is sufficiently proved if we go back to their Latin forms (*fouet* derived from *fagus* ' beech,' *glas* = *classicum*) ; the quality possessed by, or rather attributed to, their actual sounds is a fortuitous result of phonetic development."

Here we see one of the characteristics of modern linguistic science : it is so preoccupied with etymology, with the origin of words, that it pays much more attention to what words have come from than to what they have come to be. If a word has not always been suggestive on account of its sound, then its actual suggestiveness is left out of account and may even be declared to be merely fanciful. I hope that this chapter contains throughout what is psychologically a more true and linguistically a more fruitful view.

Though some echo words may be very old, the great majority are not ; at any rate, in looking up the earliest ascertained date of a goodly number of such words in the NED, I have been struck by the fact of so many of them being quite recent, not more than a few centuries old, and some not even that. To some extent

---

[1] I must confess that I find nothing symbolical in *glas* and very little in *fouet* (though the verb *fouetter* has something of the force of E. *whip*). On the whole, much of what people ' hear ' in a word appears to me fanciful and apt to discredit reasonable attempts at gaining an insight into the essence of sound symbolism; thus E. Lerch's ridiculous remark on G. *loch* in GRM 7. 101 : " *loch* malt die bewegung, die der anblick eines solchen im beschauer auslöst, durch eine entsprechende bewegung der sprachwerkzeuge, beginnend mit der liquida zur bezeichnung der rundung und endend mit dem gutturalen *ch* tief hinten in der gurgel."

their recent appearance in writing may be ascribed to the general character of the old literature as contrasted with our modern literature, which is less conventional, freer in many ways, more true to life with its infinite variety and more true, too, to the spoken language of every day. But that cannot account for everything, and there is every probability that this class of words is really more frequent in the spoken language of recent times than it was formerly, because people speak in a more vivid and fresh fashion than their ancestors of hundreds or thousands of years ago The time of psychological reaction is shorter than it used to be, life moves at a more rapid rate, and people are less tied down to tradition than in former ages, consequently they are more apt to create and to adopt new words of this particular type, which are felt at once to be significant and expressive. In all languages the creation and use of echoic and symbolic words seems to have been on the increase in historical times. If to this we add the selective process through which words which have only secondarily acquired symbolical value survive at the cost of less adequate expressions, or less adequate forms of the same words, and subsequently give rise to a host of derivatives, then we may say that languages in course of time grow richer and richer in symbolic words. So far from believing in a golden primitive age, in which everything in language was expressive and immediately intelligible on account of the significative value of each group of sounds, we arrive rather, here as in other domains, at the conception of a slow progressive development towards a greater number of easy and adequate expressions—expressions in which sound and sense are united in a marriage-union closer than was ever known to our remote ancestors.

CHAPTER XXI

THE ORIGIN OF SPEECH

XXI.—§ 1. Introduction.

MUCH of what is contained in the last chapters is preparatory to the theme which is to occupy us in this chapter, the ultimate origin of human speech. We have already seen the feeling with which this subject has often been regarded by eminent linguists, the feeling which led to an absolute tabu of the question in the French Société de linguistique (p. 96). One may here quote Whitney : " No theme in linguistic science is more often and more voluminously treated than this, and by scholars of every grade and tendency ; nor any, it may be added, with less profitable result in proportion to the labour expended ; the greater part of what is said and written upon it is mere windy talk, the assertion of subjective views which commend themselves to no mind save the one that produces them, and which are apt to be offered with a confidence, and defended with a tenacity, that are in inverse ratio to their acceptableness. This has given the whole question a bad repute among sober-minded philologists " (OLS 1. 279).

Nevertheless, linguistic science cannot refrain for ever from asking about the whence (and about the whither) of linguistic evolution. And here we must first of all realize that man is not the only animal that has a ' language,' though at present we know very little about the real nature and expressiveness of the languages of birds and mammals or of the signalling system of ants, etc. The speech of some animals may be more like our language than most people are willing to admit—it may also in some respects be even more perfect than human language precisely because it is unlike it and has developed along lines about which we can know nothing; but it is of little avail to speculate on these matters. What is certain is that no race of mankind is without a language which in everything essential is identical in character with our own and that there are a certain number of circumstances which have been of signal importance in assisting mankind in developing language (cf. Gabelentz Spr 294 ff.).

First of all, man has an upright gait; this gives him two limbs more than the dog has, for instance : he can carry things and yet jabber on; he is not reduced to defending himself by biting, but can use his mouth for other purposes. Feeding also takes less time in his case than in that of the cow, who has little time for anything else than chewing and a *moo* now and then. The sexual life of man is not restricted to one particular time of the year, the two sexes remain together the whole year round, and thus sociability is promoted ; the helplessness of babies works in the same direction through necessitating a more continuous family life, in which there is also time enough for all kinds of sports, including play with the vocal organs. Thus conditions have been generally favourable for the development of singing and talking, but the problem is, how could sounds and ideas come to be connected as they are in language ?

What method or methods have we for the solution of this question ? With very few exceptions those who have written about our subject have conjured up in their imagination a primitive era, and then asked themselves ; How would it be possible for men or man-like beings, hitherto unfurnished with speech, to acquire speech as a means of communication of thought ? Not only is this method followed, so to speak, instinctively by investigators, but we are even positively told (by Marty) that it is the only method possible. In direct opposition to this assertion, I think that it is chiefly and principally due to this method and to this way of putting the question that so little has yet been done to solve it. If we are to have any hope of success in our investigation we must try new methods and new ways—and fortunately there *are* ways which lead us to a point from which we may expect to see the world of primitive language revealed to us in a new light. But let us first cast a rapid glance at those theories which have been advanced by followers of the speculative or *a priori* method.

XXI.—§ 2. Former Theories.

One theory is that primitive words were imitative of sounds : man copied the barking of dogs and thereby obtained a natural word with the meaning of ' dog ' or ' bark.' To this theory, nick-named the *bow-wow* theory, Renan objects that it seems rather absurd to set up this chronological sequence : first the lower animals are original enough to cry and roar ; and then comes man, making a language for himself by imitating his inferiors. But surely man would imitate not only the cries of inferior animals, but also those of his fellow-men, and the salient point of the theory is this : sounds which in one creature were produced without any meaning, but which were characteristic of that creature, could by man be used to designate the creature itself (or the movement or action productive of the sound). In this way an originally unmeaning sound could in the mouth of an imitator and in the mind of someone hearing that imitation acquire a real meaning. In the chapter on Sound Symbolism I have tried to show how from the rudest and most direct imitations of this kind we may arrive through many gradations at some of the subtlest effects of human speech, and how imitation, in the widest sense we can give to this word— a wider sense than most advocates of the theory seem able to imagine—is so far from belonging exclusively to a primitive age that it is not extinct even yet. There is not much of value in Max Müller's remark that " the onomatopœic theory goes very smoothly as long as it deals with cackling hens and quacking ducks ; but round that poultry-yard there is a high wall, and we soon find that it is behind that wall that language really begins " (*Life* 2. 97), or in his other remark that " words of this kind (*cuckoo*) are, like artificial flowers, without a root. They are sterile, and unfit to express anything beyond the one object which they imitate " (ib. 1. 410). But *cuckoo* may become *cuckold*(Fr. *cocu*), and from *cock* are derived the names Müller himself mentions, Fr. *coquet, coquetterie, cocart, cocarde, coquelicot*. . . . Echoic words may be just as fertile as any other part of the vocabulary.

Another theory is the interjectional, nicknamed the *pooh-pooh*, theory : language is derived from instinctive ejaculations called forth by pain or other intense sensations or feelings. The adherents of this theory generally take these interjections for granted, without asking about the way in which they have come into existence. Darwin, however, in *The Expression of the Emotions*, gives purely physiological reasons for some interjections, as when the feeling of contempt or disgust is accompanied by a tendency " to blow out of the mouth or nostrils, and this produces sounds like *pooh* or *pish*." Again, " when anyone is startled or suddenly astonished, there is an instantaneous tendency, likewise from an intelligible cause, namely, to be ready for prolonged exertion, to open the mouth widely, so as to draw a deep and rapid inspiration. When the next full expiration follows, the mouth is slightly closed, and the lips, from causes hereafter to be discussed, are somewhat protruded ; and this form of the mouth, if the voice be at all exerted, produces . . . the sound of the vowel *o*. Certainly a deep sound of a prolonged *Oh !* may be heard from a whole crowd of people immediately after witnessing any astonishing spectacle. If, together with surprise, pain be felt, there is a tendency to contract all the muscles of the body, including those of the face, and the lips will then be drawn back ; and this will perhaps account for the sound becoming higher and assuming the character of *Ah !* or *Ach !* "

To the ordinary interjectional theory it may be objected that the usual interjections are abrupt expressions for sudden sensations and emotions ; they are therefore isolated in relation to the speech material used in the rest of the language. " Between interjection and word there is a chasm wide enough to allow us to say that the interjection is the negation of language, for interjections are employed only when one either cannot or will not speak " (Benfey Gesch 295). This ' chasm ' is also shown phonetically by the fact that the most spontaneous interjections often contain sounds which are not used in language proper, voiceless vowels, inspiratory sounds, clicks, etc., whence the impossibility properly to represent them by means of our ordinary alphabet : the spellings *pooh, pish, whew, tut* are very poor renderings indeed of the natural sounds. On the other hand, many interjections are now more or less conventionalized and are learnt like any other words, consequently with a different form in different languages : in pain a German and a Seelander will exclaim *au*, a Jutlander *aus*, a Frenchman *ahi* and an Englishman *oh*, or perhaps *ow*. Kipling writes in one of his stories : " That man is no Afghan, for they weep ' Ai ! Ai ! ' Nor is he of Hindustan, for they weep ' Oh ! Ho ! ' He weeps after the fashion of the white men, who say, ' Ow ! Ow ! ' "

A closely related theory is the nativistic, nicknamed the *ding-dong*, theory, according to which there is a mystic harmony between sound and sense : " There is a law which runs through nearly the whole of nature, that everything which is struck rings. Each substance has its peculiar ring." Language is the result of an instinct, a " faculty peculiar to man in his primitive state, by which every impression from without received its vocal expression from within "—a faculty which " became extinct when its object was fulfilled." This theory, which Max Müller propounded and afterwards wisely abandoned, is mentioned here for the curiosity of the matter only.

Noiré started a fourth theory, nicknamed the *yo-he-ho* : under any strong muscular effort it is a relief to the system to let breath come out strongly and repeatedly, and by that process to let the vocal chords vibrate in different ways ; when primitive acts were performed in common, they would, therefore, naturally be accompanied with some sounds which would come to be associated with the idea of the act performed and stand as a name for it ; the first words would accordingly mean something like 'heave' or 'haul.'

Now, these theories, here imperfectly reproduced each in a few lines, are mutually antagonistic : thus Noiré thinks it possible to explain the origin of speech without sound imitation. And yet what should prevent our combining these several theories and using them concurrently ? It would seem to matter very little whether the first word uttered by man was *bow-wow* or *pooh-pooh*, for the fact remains that he said both one and the other. Each of the three chief theories enables one to explain *parts of language*, but still only parts, and not even the most important parts—the main body of language seems hardly to be touched by any of them. Again, with the exception of Noiré's theory, they are too individualistic and take too little account of language as a means of human intercourse. Moreover, they all tacitly assume that up to the creation of language man had remained mute or silent ; but this is most improbable from a physiological point of view. As a rule we do not find an organ already perfected on the first occasion of its use ; it is only by use that an organ is developed.

XXI.—§ 3. Method.

So much for the results of the first method of approaching the question of the origin of speech, that of trying to picture to oneself a speechless mankind and speculating on the way in which language could then have originated. We shall now, as hinted above (p. 413), indicate the ways in which it is possible to supplement, and even in some measure to supplant, this speculative or deductive method by means of inductive reasonings. These can be based on three fields of investigation, namely :

(1) The language of children ;
(2) The language of primitive races, and
(3) The history of language.

Of these, the third is the most fruitful source of information.

First, as to the language of children. Some biologists maintain that the development of the individual follows on the whole the same course as that of the race ; the embryo, before it arrives at full maturity, will have passed through the same stages of development which in countless generations have led the whole species to its present level. It has, therefore, occurred to many that the acquisition by mankind at large of the faculty of speech may be mirrored to us in the process by which any child learns to communicate its thoughts by means of its vocal organs. Accord-

ingly, children's language has often been invoked to furnish illustrations and parallels of the process gone through in the formation
of primitive language. But many writers have been guilty of an
erroneous inference in applying this principle, inasmuch as they have
taken all their examples from a child's acquisition of an already
existing language. The fallacy will be evident if we suppose for
a moment the case of a man endeavouring to arrive at the evolution
of music from the manner in which a child is nowadays taught to
play on the piano. Manifestly, the modern learner is in quite
a different position to primitive man, and has quite a different
task set him : he has an instrument ready to hand, and melodies
already composed for him, and finally a teacher who understands
how to draw these tunes forth from the instrument. It is the same
thing with language : the task of the child is to learn an existing
language, that is, to connect certain sounds heard on the lips of
others with the same ideas that the speakers associate with them,
but not in the least to frame anything new. No ; if we are seeking
some parallel to the primitive acquisition of language, we must
look elsewhere and turn to baby language as it is spoken in the first
year of life, before the child has begun to 'notice' and to make
out what use is made of language by grown-up people. Here,
in the child's first purposeless murmuring, crowing and babbling,
we have real nature sounds ; here we may expect to find some
clue to the infancy of the language of the race And, again, we
must not neglect the way children have of creating new words
never heard before, and often of attaching a sense to originally
meaningless conglomerations of sound.

   As for the languages of contemporary savages, we may in some
instances take them as typical of more primitive languages than
those of civilized nations, and therefore as illustrating a linguistic
stage that is nearer to that in which speech originated. Still,
inferences from such languages should be used with great caution,
for it should never be forgotten than even the most backward
race has many centuries of linguistic evolution behind it, and that
the conditions therefore may, or must, be very different from those
of primeval man. The so-called primitive languages will therefore
in the following sections be only invoked to corroborate conclusions
at which it is possible to arrive from other data.

   The third and most fruitful source from which to gather information of value for our investigation is the history of language
as it has been considered in previous chapters of this work. While
the propounders of the theories of the origin of speech mentioned
above made straight for the front of the lion's den, we are like
the fox in the fable, who noticed that all the traces led into the den
and not a single one came out ; we will therefore try and steal

into the den from behind. They thought it logically correct, nay necessary, to begin at the beginning; let us, for variety's sake, begin with languages accessible at the present day, and let us attempt from that starting-point step by step to trace the backward path. Perhaps in this way we may reach the very first beginnings of speech.

The method I recommend, and which I think I am the first to employ consistently, is to trace our modern twentieth-century languages as far back in time as history and our materials will allow us; and then, from this comparison of present English with Old English, of Danish with Old Norse, and of both with 'Common Gothonic,' of French and Italian with Latin, of modern Indian dialects with Sanskrit, etc., to deduce definite laws for the development of languages in general, and to try and find a system of lines which can be lengthened backwards beyond the reach of history. If we should succeed in discovering certain qualities to be generally typical of the earlier as opposed to the later stages of languages, we shall be justified in concluding that the same qualities obtained in a still higher degree in the earliest times of all; if we are able within the historical era to demonstrate a definite direction of linguistic evolution, we must be allowed to infer that the direction was the same even in those primeval periods for which we have no documents to guide us. But if the change witnessed in the evolution of modern speech out of older forms of speech is thus on a larger scale projected back into the childhood of mankind, and if by this process we arrive finally at uttered sounds of such a description that they can no longer be called a real language, but something antecedent to language—why, then the problem will have been solved; for transformation is something we can understand, while a creation out of nothing can never be comprehended by human understanding.

This, then, will be the object of the following rapid sketch: to search the several departments of the science of language for general laws of evolution—most of them have already been discussed at some length in the preceding chapters—then to magnify the changes observed, and thus to form a picture of the outer and inner structure of some sort of speech more primitive than the most primitive language accessible to direct observation.

XXI.—§ 4. Sounds.

First, as regards the purely phonetic side of language, we observe everywhere the tendency to make pronunciation more easy, so as to lessen the muscular effort; difficult combinations of sounds are discarded, those only being retained which are pronounced with ease (see Ch. XIV § 6 ff.). Modern research has shown that the Proto-Aryan sound-system was much more complicated than was imagined in the reconstructions of the middle of the nineteenth century. In most languages now only such sounds are used as are produced by expiration, while inbreathed sounds and clicks or suction-stops are not found in connected speech. In civilized languages we meet with such sounds only in interjections, as when an inbreathed voiceless *l* (generally with rhythmic variations of strength and corresponding small movements of the tongue) is used to express delight in eating and drinking, or when the click inadequately spelt *tut* is used to express impatience. In some very primitive South African languages, on the other hand, clicks are found as integral parts of words ; and Bleek has rendered it probable that in former stages of these languages they were in more extensive use than now. We may perhaps draw the conclusion that primitive languages in general were rich in all kinds of difficult sounds.

The following point is of more far-reaching consequence. In some languages we find a gradual disappearance of tone or pitch accent ; this has been the case in Danish, whereas Norwegian and Swedish have kept the old tones ; so also in Russian as compared with Serbo-Croatian. In the works of old Indian, Greek and Latin grammarians we have express statements to the effect that pitch accent played a prominent part in those languages, and that the intervals used must have been comparatively greater than is usual in our modern languages. In modern Greek and in the Romanic languages the tone element has been obscured, and now ' stress ' is heard on the syllable where the ancients noted only a high or a low tone. About the languages spoken nowadays by savage tribes we have generally very little information, as most of those who have made a first-hand study of such languages have not been trained to observe and to describe these delicate points ; still, there is of late years an increasing number of observations of tone accents, for instance in African languages, which may justify us in thinking that tone plays an important part in many primitive languages.[1]

---

[1] It may not be superfluous expressly to point out that there is no contradiction between what is said here on the disappearance of tones and the remarks made above (Ch. XIX § 4) on Chinese tones. There the change wrought in the meaning of a word by a mere change of tone was explained on the principle that the difference of meaning was at an earlier stage expressed by affixes, the tone that is now concentrated on one syllable belonging formerly to two syllables or perhaps more. But this evidently presupposes that each syllable had already some tone of its own—and that is what in this chapter is taken to be the primitive state. Word-tones were originally frequent, but meaningless ; afterwards they were dropped in some languages, while in others they were utilized for sense-distinguishing purposes.

So much for word tones ; now for the sentence melody. It is a well-known fact that the modulation of sentences is strongly influenced by the effect of intense emotions in causing stronger and more rapid raisings and sinkings of the tone. " All passionate language does of itself become musical—with a finer music than the mere accent ; the speech of a man even in zealous anger becomes a chant, a song " (Carlyle). "The sounds of common conversation have but little resonance ; those of strong feeling have much more. Under rising ill-temper the voice acquires a metallic ring. . . . Grief, unburdening itself, uses tones approaching in *timbre* to those of chanting ; and in his most pathetic passages an eloquent speaker similarly falls into tones more vibratory than those common to him. . . . While calm speech is comparatively monotonous, emotion makes use of fifths, octaves, and even wider intervals " (H. Spencer).

Now, it is a consequence of advancing civilization that passion, or, at least, the expression of passion, is moderated, and we must therefore conclude that the speech of uncivilized and primitive men was more passionately agitated than ours, more like music or song. This conclusion is borne out by what we hear about the speech of many savages in our own days. European travellers very often record their impression of the speech of different tribes in expressions like these : " pronouncing whatever they spoke in a very singing manner," " the singing tone of voice, in common conversation, was frequent," " the speech is very much modulated and resembles singing," " highly artificial and musical," etc.

These facts and considerations all point to the conclusion that there once was a time when all speech was song, or rather when these two actions were not yet differentiated ; but perhaps this inference cannot be established inductively at the present stage of linguistic science with the same amount of certainty as the statements I am now going to make as to the nature of primitive speech.

As we have seen above (Ch. XVII § 7), a great many of the changes going on regularly from century to century, as well as some of the sudden changes which take place now and then in the history of each language, result in the shortening of words. This is seen everywhere and at all times, and in consequence of this universal tendency we find that the ancient languages of our family, Sanskrit, Zend, etc., abound in very long words ; the further back we go, the greater the number of *sesquipedalia*. We have seen also how the current theory, according to which every language started with monosyllabic roots, fails at every point to account for actual facts and breaks down before the established truths of linguistic history. Just as the history of religion does not pass

from the belief in one god to the belief in many goas, but inversely
from polytheism towards monotheism, so language proceeds from
original polysyllabism towards monosyllabism : if the development
of language took the same course in prehistoric as in historic times,
we see, by projecting the teaching of history on a larger scale back
into the darkest ages, that early words must have been to present
ones what the plesiosaurus and gigantosaurus are to present-day
reptiles. The outcome of this phonetic section is, therefore, that
we must imagine primitive language as consisting (chiefly at least)
of very long words, full of difficult sounds, and sung rather than
spoken.

XXI.—§ 5. Grammar.

Can anything be stated about the grammar of primitive languages ? Yes, I think so, if we continue backwards into the past
the lines of evolution resulting from the investigations of previous
chapters of this volume. Ancient languages have more forms
than modern ones ; forms originally kept distinct are in course
of time confused, either phonetically or analogically, alike in
substantives, adjectives and verbs.

A characteristic feature of the structure of languages in their
early stages is that each form of a word (whether verb or noun)
contains in itself several minor modifications which, in the later
stages, are expressed separately (if at all), that is, by means of
auxiliary verbs or prepositions. Such a word as Latin *cantavisset*
unites in one inseparable whole the equivalents of six ideas :
(1) ' sing,' (2) pluperfect, (3) that indefinite modification of the
verbal idea which we term subjunctive, (4) active, (5) third person, and (6) singular. The tendency of later stages is towards
expressing such modifications analytically ; but if we accept the
terms ' synthesis ' and ' analysis ' for ancient and recent stages,
we must first realize that there exist many gradations of both :
in no single language do we find either synthesis or analysis carried
out with absolute purity and consistency. Everywhere we find
a more or less. Latin is synthetic in comparison with French,
French analytic in comparison with Latin ; but if we were able
to see the direct ancestor of Latin, say two thousand years before
the earliest inscriptions, we should no doubt find a language so
synthetic that in comparison with it Cicero's would have to be
termed highly analytic.

Secondly, we must not from the term ' synthesis,' which etymologically means ' composition ' or ' putting together,' draw the
conclusion that synthetic forms, such as we find, for instance, in
Latin, consist of originally independent elements put together

and thus in their turn presuppose a previous stage of analysis. Whoever does not share the usual opinion that all flexional forms have originated through coalescence of separate words, but sees as we have seen (in Ch. XIX) also the reverse process of inseparable portions of words gaining greater and greater independence, will perhaps do well to look out for a better and less ambiguous word than *synthesis* to describe the character of primitive speech. What in the later stages of languages is analyzed or dissolved, in the earlier stages was unanalyzable or indissoluble ; ' entangled ' or ' complicated ' would therefore be better renderings of our impression of the first state of things.

XXI.—§ 6. Units.

But are the old forms really less dissoluble than their modern equivalents ? This is repeatedly denied even by recent writers, on whom my words in *Progress*, p. 117, cannot have made much impression, if they have read them at all ; and it will therefore be necessary to take up this cardinal point. Let me begin with quoting what others have said. " Historically considered, the Latin *amat* is really two words, as much as its English representative, the final *t* being originally a pronoun signifying ' he,' ' she ' or ' it,' and it is only reasons of practical convenience that prevent us from writing *am at* or *ama t* as two and *heloves* as one word. . . . The really essential difference between *amat* and *he loves* is that in the former the pronominal element is expressed by a suffix, in the latter by a prefix " (Sweet PS 274, 1899). " It is purely accidental that the Latin form is not written *am-av-it*. To the unsophisticated Frenchman *il a aimé* is neither less nor more one unit than *amavit* to a Roman. . . . When the locution *il a aimé* sprang up, each element of it was still to some extent felt separately ; but after it had become a fixed formula the elements were fused together into one whole. As a matter of fact, uneducated French people have not the least idea whether it is one or three words they speak " (Sütterlin WGS 11, 1902). " In some modern languages the personal pronoun is, just as in archaic Greek, beginning to be amalgamated with verbs so as to become a mere termination (*sic* : *désinence* ; prefix must be what is meant): Fr. *j'don'*, *tu-don'*, *il-don'* (je donne, tu donnes, il donne) and E. *i-giv'*, *we giv'*, *you-giv'*, *they-giv'*, correspond exactly to Gr. *dido-mi*, *dido-si*, *dido-ti*, only that the personal particle is in a different place " (Dauzat V 155, 1910). " If French were a savage language not yet reduced to writing, a travelling linguist, hearing the present tense of the verb *aimer* pronounced by the natives, would transcribe it in the following way : *jèm, tu èm, ilèm, nouzémon, vouzémé, ilzèm*. He would be

struck particularly with the agglutination of the pronominal
subject and the verb, and would never feel tempted to draw up
a paradigm without pronouns : *aime, aimes, aime, aimons,* etc.,
in which traditional spelling makes us believe. . . . He would
even, through a comparison of *ilèm* and *îlzèm*, be led to establish
a tendency to incorporation, as the only sign of the plural is a *z*
infixed in the verbal complex " (Bally LV 43, 1913).

In these utterances two questions are really mixed together,
that of the origin of Aryan flexional forms and that of the actual
status of some forms in various languages. As to the former
question, we have seen (p. 383) how very uncertain it is that *amat*
and *didosi,* etc., contain pronouns. As to the latter question,
it is quite true that we should not let the usual spelling be decisive
when it is asked whether we have one or two or three words ; but
all these writers strangely overlook the really important criteria
which we possess in this matter. Bally's traveller could only have
arrived at his result by listening to grammar lessons in which the
three persons of the verb were rattled off one after the other, for
if he had taken his forms from actual conversation he would have
come across numerous instances in which the forms occurred
without pronouns, first in the imperative, *aime, aimons, aimez,* then
in collocations like *celui qui aime, ceux qui aiment,* in which there
is no infix to denote the plural ; in *le mari aime, les maris aiment,*
and innumerable similar groups there is neither pronoun nor infix.
If he were at first inclined to take *ilaaimé* as one word, he would
on further acquaintance with the language discover that the elements were often separated : *il n'a pas aimé, il nous a toujours
aimés,* etc. Similarly with the English forms adduced : *I never
give, you always give.* This is the crucial point : the French and
English combinations are two (three) words because the elements
are not always placed together ; Lat. *amat, amavit,* are each of
them only one word because they can never be divided, and in the
same way we never find anything placed between *am* and *o* in
the first person, *amo.* These forms are as inseparable as E. *loves,*
but E. *heloves* is separable because both *he* and *loves* can stand
alone, and can also, in certain combinations, though now rarely,
be transposed : *loves he.* Some writers would compare French
combinations like *il te le disait* with verbal forms in certain Amerindian languages, in which subject and direct and indirect object
are alike ' incorporated ' in a ' polysynthetic ' verbal form ; it is
quite true that these French pronominal forms can never be used
by themselves, but only in conjunction with a verb ; still, the French
pronouns are more independent of each other than the elements
of some other more primitive languages. In the first place, this
is shown by the possibility of varying the pronunciation : *il te*

le disait may be either [itlədizɛ] or [itəldizɛ] or even more solemnly
[iltələdizɛ] ; secondly, by the regularity of these joined pronominal
forms, for they are always the same, whatever the verb may be ;
and lastly, by their changing places in certain cases : *te le disait-
il ? dis-le-lui*, etc.

Nor can it be said that English forms like *he's=he is* (or *he has*),
I'd = I had (or *I would*), *he'll = he will* show a tendency towards
' entangling,' for however closely together these forms are generally pronounced, each of them must be said to consist of two words,
as is shown by the possibility of transposition (Is he ill ?) and of
intercalation of other words (I never had) ; it is also noteworthy
that the same short forms of the verbs can be added to all
kinds of words (the water'll be . . ., the sea'd been calm). In
the forms *don't, won't, can't* there is something like amalgamation of the verbal with the negative idea. Still, it is important
to notice that the amalgamation only takes place with a few
verbs of the auxiliary class. In saying ' I don't write ' the full
verb is not touched by the fusion, and is even allowed to be
unchanged in cases where it would have been inflected if no
auxiliary had been used ; compare *I write, he writes, I wrote* with
the negative *I don't write, he doesn't write, I didn't write*. It will
be seen, especially if we take into account the colloquial or vulgar
form for the third person, *he don't write*, that the general movement
here as elsewhere is really rather in the direction of ' isolation '
than of fusion ; for the verbal form *write* is stripped of all signs
of person and tense, the person being indicated separately (if at
all), and the tense sign being joined to the negation. So also in
interrogative sentences ; and if that tendency which can be observed
in Elizabethan English had prevailed by using the combination
I do write in positive statements, even where no special emphasis
is intended, English verbs (except a few auxiliaries) would have
been entirely stripped of those elements which to most grammarians constitute the very essence of a verb, namely, the marks
of person, number, tense and mood, *write* being the universal
form, besides the quasi-nominal forms *writing* and *written*.

Now, it is often said that the history of language shows a sort
of gyration or movement in spirals, in which synthesis is followed
by analysis, this by a new synthesis (flexion), and this again by
analysis, and so forth. Latin *amabo* (which according to the old
theory was once *ama* + some auxiliary) has been succeeded by
amare habeo, which in its turn is fused into *amerò, aimerai*, and the
latter form is now to some extent giving way to *je vais aimer*. But
this pretended law of rotation is only arrived at by considering a
comparatively small number of phenomena, and not by viewing
the successive stages of the same language as wholes and drawing

general inferences as to their typically distinctive characters (cf. above, p. 337). If for every two instances of new flexions springing up we see ten older ones discarded in favour of analysis or isolation, are we not entitled to the generalization that flexion or indissolubility tends to give way to analysis ? We should beware of being under the same delusion as a man who, in walking over a mountainous country, thinks that he goes down just as many and just as long hills as he goes up, while on the contrary each ascent is higher than the preceding descent, so that finally he finds himself unexpectedly many thousand feet above the level from which he started.

The direction of movement is towards flexionless languages (such as Chinese, or to a certain extent Modern English) with freely combinable elements ; the starting-point was flexional languages (such as Latin or Greek) ; at a still earlier stage we must suppose a language in which a verbal form might indicate not only six things, like *cantavisset*, but a still larger number, in which verbs were perhaps modified according to the gender (or sex) of the subject, as they are in Semitic languages, or according to the object, as in some Amerindian languages, or according to whether a man, a woman, or a person who commands respect is spoken to, as in Basque. But that amounts to the same thing as saying that the border-line between word and sentence was not so clearly defined as in more recent times ; *cantavisset* is really nothing but a sentence-word, and the same holds good to a still greater extent of the sound conglomerations of Eskimo and some other North American languages. Primitive linguistic units must have been much more complicated in point of meaning, as well as much longer in point of sound, than those with which we are most familiar.

XXI.—§ 7. Irregularities.

Another point of great importance is this : in early languages we find a far greater number of irregularities, exceptions, anomalies, than in modern ones. It is true that we not unfrequently see new irregularities spring up, where the formations were formerly regular ; but these instances are very far from counterbalancing the opposite class, in which words once irregularly inflected become regular, or are given up in favour of regularly inflected words, or in which anomalies in syntax are levelled. The tendency is more and more to denote the same thing by the same means in every case, to extend the ending, or whatever it is, that is used in a large class of words to express a certain modification of the central idea, until it is used in all other words as well.

Comparative linguistics did not attain a scientific character till the principle was established that the relationship of two languages had to be determined by a thoroughgoing conformity in the most necessary parts of language, namely (besides grammar proper) pronouns and numerals and the most indispensable of nouns and verbs. But if this domain of speech, by preserving religiously, as it were, the old tradition, affords infallible criteria of the near or remote relationship of different languages, may we not reasonably expect to find in the same domain some clue to the oldest grammatical system used by our ancestors ? What sort of system, then, do we find there ? We see such a declension as *I, me, we, us* : the several forms of the ' paradigm ' do not at all resemble each other, as they do in more recently developed declensions. We find masculines and feminines, such as *father, mother, man, wife, bull, cow* ; while such methods of derivation as are seen in *count, countess, he-bear, she-bear*, belong to a later time. We meet with degrees of comparison like *good, better, ill, worse*, while regular forms like *happy, happier, big, bigger*, prevail in all the younger strata of languages. We meet with verbal flexion such as appears in *am, is, was, been*, which forms a striking contrast to the more modern method of adding a mere ending while leaving the body of the word unchanged. In an interesting book, *Vom Suppletivwesen der indogermanischen Sprachen* (1899), H. Osthoff has collected a very great number of examples from the old Aryan languages of different stems supplementing each other, and has pointed out that this phenomenon is characteristic of the most necessary ideas occurring every moment in ordinary conversation : I take at random a few of the best-known of his examples : Fr. *aller, je vais, j'irai,* Lat. *fero, tuli,* Gr. *horaō, opsomai, eidon,* Lat. *bonus, melior, optimus.* Osthoff fully agrees with me that we have here a trait of primitive psychology : our remote ancestors were not able to see and to express what was common to these ideas; their minds were very unsystematic, and separated in their linguistic expressions things which from a logical point of view are closely related : much of their grammar, therefore, was really of a lexical character.

XXI.—§ 8. Savage Tribes.

If now it is asked whether the conclusions we have thus arrived at are borne out by a consideration of the languages of savage or primitive races nowadays, the answer is that these cannot be lumped together; there are among them many different types, even with regard to grammatical structure. But the more these languages are studied and the more accurately their structure is described, the more also students perceive intricacies and anomalies in their grammar. Gabelentz (Spr 386) says that the casual observer has no idea how manifold and how nicely circumscribed grammatical categories can be, even in the seemingly crudest languages, for ordinary grammars tell us nothing about that. P. W. Schmidt (*Die Stellung der Pygmäenvölker*, 1910, 129) says that whoever, from the low culture of the Andamanese, would expect to find their language very simple and poor in expressions would be strangely deceived, for its mechanism is highly complicated, with many prefixes and suffixes, which often conceal the root itself. Meinhof (MSA 136) mentions the multiplicity of plural formations in African languages. Vilhelm Thomsen, in speaking of the Santhal (Khervarian) language, says that its grammar is capable of expressing a multiplicity of *nuances* which in other languages must be expressed by clumsy circumlocutions; the native speakers go beyond what is necessary through requiring expressions for many subordinate notions, the language having, so to speak, only one fine gold-balance, on which everything, even the simplest and commonest things, must be weighed by the adding-up of a whole series of minutiæ. Curr speaks about the erroneous belief in the simplicity of Australian languages, which on the contrary have a great number of conjugations, etc. The extreme difficulty and complex structure of Eskimo and of many Amerindian languages is so notorious that no words need be wasted on them here. And the forms of the Basque verb are so manifold and intricate that we understand how Larramendi, in his legitimate pride at having been the first to reduce them to a system, called his grammar *El Imposible Vencido*, ‘The Impossible Overcome.’ At Béarn they have the story that the good God, wishing to punish the devil for the temptation of Eve, sent him to the Pays Basque with the command that he should remain there till he had mastered the language. At the end of seven years God relented, finding the punishment too severe, and called the devil to him. The devil had no sooner crossed the bridge of Castelondo than he found he had forgotten all that he had so hardly learned.

What is here said about the languages of wild tribes (and of the Basques, who are not exactly savages, but whose language is generally taken to have retained many primeval traits) is in exact keeping with everything that recent study of primitive man has brought to light : the life of the savage is regulated to the minutest details through ceremonies and conventionalities to be observed on every and any occasion; he is restricted in what he may eat and drink and when and how ; and all these, to our mind, irrational prescriptions and innumerable prohibitions have to be observed with the most scrupulous, nay religious, care : it is the same with all the meticulous rules of his language.

XXI.—§ 9. Law of Development.

So far, then, from subscribing to Whitney's dictum that "the law of simplicity of beginnings applies to language not less naturally and necessarily than to other instrumentalities" (G 226), we are drawn to the conclusion that primitive language had a superabundance of irregularities and anomalies, in syntax and word-formation no less than in accidence. It was capricious and fanciful, and displayed a luxuriant growth of forms, entangled one with another like the trees in a primeval forest. "Rien n'entre mieux dans les esprits grossiers que les subtilités des langues" (Tarde, *Lois de l'imitation* 285). Human minds in the early times disported themselves in long and intricate words as in the wildest and most wanton play. Nothing could be more beside the mark than to suppose that grammatical and logical categories were in primitive languages generally in harmony (as is supposed, e.g., by Sweet, *New Engl. Grammar* § 543) : primitive speech cannot have been distinguished for logical consistency ; nor, so far as we can judge, was it simple and facile : it is much more likely to have been extremely clumsy and unwieldy. Renan rightly reminds us of Turgot's wise saying : "Des hommes grossiers ne font rien de simple. Il faut des hommes perfectionnés pour y arriver."

We have seen in earlier chapters that the old theory of the three stages through which human language was supposed always to proceed, isolation, agglutination and flexion, was built up on insufficient materials ; but while we feel tempted totally to reverse this system, we must be on our guard against establishing too rigid and too absolute a system ourselves. It would not do simply to reverse the order and say that flexion is the oldest stage, from which language tends through an agglutinative stage towards complete isolation, for flexion, agglutination and isolation do not include all possible structural types of speech. The possibilities of development are so manifold, and there are such innumerable ways of arriving at more or less adequate expressions for human thought, that it is next to impossible to compare languages of different families. Even, therefore, if it is probable that English, Finnish and Chinese are all simplifications of more complex languages, we cannot say that Chinese, for instance, at one time resembled English in structure and at some other time Finnish. English was once a flexional language, and is still so in some respects, while in others it is agglutinative, and in others again isolating, or nearly so. But we may perhaps give the following formula of what is our total impression of the whole preceding inquiry :

THE EVOLUTION OF LANGUAGE SHOWS A PROGRESSIVE TEN-
DENCY FROM INSEPARABLE IRREGULAR CONGLOMERATIONS TO
FREELY AND REGULARLY COMBINABLE SHORT ELEMENTS.
The old system of historical linguistics may be likened to an
enormous pyramid ; only it is a pity that it should have as its
base the small, square, strong, smart root word, and suspended
above it the unwieldy, lumbering, ill-proportioned, flexion-encum-
bered sentence-vocable. Structures of this sort may with some
adroitness be made to stand ; but their equilibrium is unstable,
and sooner or later they will inevitably tumble over.

XXI.—§ 10. Vocabulary.

On the lexical side of language we find a development parallel
to that noticed in grammar ; and, indeed, if we go deep enough
into the question, we shall see that it is really the very same
movement that has taken place. The more advanced a language
is, the more developed is its power of expressing abstract or
general ideas. Everywhere language has first attained to expressions for the concrete and special. In accounts of the languages
of barbarous races we constantly come across such phrases as
these : " The aborigines of Tasmania had no words representing
abstract ideas ; for each variety of gum-tree and wattle-tree,
etc., they had a name ; but they had no equivalent for the
expression ' a tree ' ; neither could they express abstract qualities,
such as ' hard, soft, warm, cold, long, short, round ' " ; or,
The Mohicans have words for cutting various objects, but none
to convey *cutting* simply. The Zulus have no word for ' cow,'
but words for ' red cow,' ' white cow,' etc. (Sayce S 2. 5, cf.
l. 121). In Bakaïri (Central Brazil) "each parrot has its special
name, and the general idea ' parrot ' is totally unknown, as well
as the general idea ' palm.' But they know precisely the qualities
of each subspecies of parrot and palm, and attach themselves so
much to these numerous particular notions that they take no interest
in the common characteristics. They are choked in the abundance
of the material and cannot manage it economically. They have
only small coin, but in that they must be said to be excessively
rich rather than poor " (K. v. d. Steinen, *Unter den Naturvölkern
Brasiliens*, 1894, 81). The Lithuanians, like many primitive
tribes, have many special, but no common names for various
colours : one word for gray in speaking about wool and geese,
one about horses, one about cattle, one about the hair of men and
some animals, and in the same way for other colours (J. Schmidt,
Kritik d. Sonantentheorie 37). Many languages have no word
for ' brother,' but words for ' elder brother ' and ' younger brother ' :

others have different words according to whose (person and number) father or brother it is (see, e.g., the paradigm in Gabelentz Spr 421), and the same applies in many languages to names for various parts of the body. In Cherokee, instead of one word for ' washing ' we find different words, according to what is washed : *kutuwo* ' I wash myself,' *kulestula* ' I wash my head,' *tsestula* ' I wash the head of somebody else,' *kukuswo* ' I wash my face,' *tsekuswo* ' I wash the face of somebody else,' *takasula* ' I wash my hands or feet,' *takunkela* ' I wash my clothes,' *takutega* ' I wash dishes,' *tsejuwu* ' I wash a child,' *kowela* ' I wash meat ' (see, however, the criticism of Hewitt, *Am. Anthropologist,* 1893, 398). Primitive man did not see the wood for the trees.[1]

In some Amerindian languages there are distinct series of numerals for various classes of objects ; thus in Kwakiatl and Tsimoshian (Sapir, *Language and Environment* 239) ; similarly the Melanesians have special words to denote a definite number of certain objects, e.g. *a buku niu* ' two coconuts,' *a buru* ' ten coconuts,' *a koro* ' a hundred coconuts,' *a selavo* ' a thousand coconuts,' *a uduudu* ' ten canoes,' *a bola* ' ten fishes,' etc. (Gabelentz, *Die melan. Spr.* 1. 23). In some languages the numerals are the same for all classes of objects counted, but require after them certain class-denoting words varying according to the character of the objects (in some respects comparable to the English twenty *head* of cattle, Pidgin *piecey* ; cf. Yule and Burnell, Hobson-Jobson s.v. Numerical Affixes). This reminds one of the systems of weights and measures, which even in civilized countries up to a comparatively recent period varied not only from country to country, sometimes even from district to district, but even in the same country according to the things weighed or measured (in England *stone* and *ton* still vary in this way).

In old Gothonic poetry we find an astonishing abundance of words translated in our dictionaries by ' sea,' ' battle,' ' sword,' ' hero,' and the like : these may certainly be considered as relics of an earlier state of things, in which each of these words had its separate shade of meaning, which was subsequently lost and which it is impossible now to determine with certainty. The nomenclature of a remote past was undoubtedly constructed upon similar principles to those which are still preserved in a word-group like *horse, mare, stallion, foal, colt,* instead of he-horse, she-horse, young horse, etc. This sort of grouping has only survived in a few cases in which a lively interest has been felt in the objects or animals concerned. We may note, however, the different terms employed

---

[1] On the lack of abstract and general terms in savage languages, see also Ginneken I.P 108 and the works there quoted.

for essentially the same idea in a *flock* of sheep, a *pack* of wolves, a *herd* of cattle, a *bevy* of larks, a *covey* of partridges, a *shoal* of fish. Primitive language could show a far greater number of instances of this description, and, so far, had a larger vocabulary than later languages, though, of course, it lacked names for a great number of ideas that were outside the sphere of interest of uncivilized people.

There was another reason for the richness of the vocabulary of primitive man : his superstition about words, which made him avoid the use of certain words under certain circumstances— during war, when out fishing, during the time of the great cultic festivals, etc.—because he feared the anger of gods or demons if he did not religiously observe the rules of the linguistic tabu. Accordingly, in many cases he had two or more sets of words for exactly the same notions, of which later generations as a rule preserved only one, unless they differentiated these words by utilizing them to discriminate objects that were similar but not identical.

XXI.—§ 11. Poetry and Prose.

On the whole the development of languages, even in the matter of vocabulary, must be considered to have taken a beneficial course ; still, in certain respects one may to some extent regret the consequences of this evolution. While our words are better adapted to express abstract things and to render concrete things with definite precision, they are necessarily comparatively colourless. The old words, on the contrary, spoke more immediately to the senses—they were manifestly more suggestive, more graphic and pictorial : while to express one single thing we are not unfrequently obliged to piece the image together bit by bit, the old concrete words would at once present it to the hearer's mind as a whole ; they were, accordingly, better adapted to poetic purposes. Nor is this the only point in which we see a close relationship between primitive words and poetry.

If by a mental effort we transport ourselves to a period in which language consisted solely of such graphic concrete words, we shall discover that, in spite of their number, they would not suffice, taken all together, to cover everything that needed expression ; a wealth in such words is not incompatible with a certain poverty. They would accordingly often be required to do service outside of their proper sphere of application. That a figurative or metaphorical use of words is a factor of the utmost importance in the life of all languages is indisputable ; but I am probably right in thinking that it played a more prominent part in old times than now. In the course of ages a great many metaphors have lost their freshness and vividness, so that nobody feels them to be metaphors any longer. Examine closely such a sentence as this : " He *came* to *look upon* the low *ebb* of morals as an *outcome* of bad *taste*," and you will find that nearly every word is a dead metaphor.[1] But the better stocked a language is with those ex-metaphors which have become regular expressions for definite ideas, the less need there is for going out of one's way to find new metaphors. The expression of thought therefore tends to become more and more mechanical or prosaic.

Primitive man, however, on account of the nature of his language, was constantly reduced to using words and phrases figuratively : he was forced to express his thoughts in the language of poetry. The speech of modern savages is often spoken of as abounding in similes and all kinds of figurative phrases and allegorical expressions. Just as in the literature transmitted to us poetry is found in every country to precede prose, so poetic language is on the whole older than prosaic language ; lyrics and cult songs come before science, and Oehlenschläger is right when he sings (in N. Møller's translation) :

> Thus Nature drove us ; warbling rose
> Man's voice in verse before he spoke in prose.

XXI.—§ 12. Emotional Songs.

If we now try to sum up what has been inferred about primitive speech, we see that by our backward march we arrived at a language whose units had a very meagre substance of thought, and this as specialized and concrete as possible ; but at the same time the phonetic body was ample ; and the bigger and longer the words, the thinner the thoughts ! Much cry and little wool ! No period has seen less taciturn people than the first framers of speech ; primitive speakers were not reticent and reserved beings, but youthful men and women babbling merrily on, without being so very particular about the meaning of each word. They did not narrowly weigh every syllable—what were a couple of syllables more or less to them ? They chattered away for the mere pleasure of chattering, resembling therein many a mother of our own time, who will chatter away to baby without measuring her words or looking too closely into the meaning of each ; nay, who is not a bit troubled by the consideration that the little deary does not understand a single word of her affectionate eloquence. But

---

[1] Of course, if instead of *look upon* and *outcome* we had taken the corresponding terms of Latin root, *consider* and *result*, the metaphors would have been still more dead to the natural linguistic instinct.

primitive speech—and we return here to an idea thrown out above—
still more resembles the speech of little baby himself, before he
begins to frame his own language after the pattern of the grown-
ups ; the language of our remote forefathers was like that ceaseless
humming and crooning with which no thoughts are as yet connected, which merely amuses and delights the little one. Language
originated as play, and the organs of speech were first trained in
this singing sport of idle hours.

Primitive language had no great store of ideas, and if we consider
it as an instrument for expressing thoughts, it was clumsy, unwieldy and ineffectual ; but what did that matter ? Thoughts
were not the first things to press forward and crave for expression ; emotions and instincts were more primitive and far
more powerful. But what emotions were most powerful in producing germs of speech ? To be sure not hunger and that which
is connected with hunger : mere individual self-assertion and
the struggle for material existence. This prosaic side of life was
only capable of calling forth short monosyllabic interjections,
howls of pain and grunts of satisfaction or dissatisfaction ; but
these are isolated and incapable of much further development ;
they are the most immutable portions of language, and remain
now at essentially the same standpoint as thousands of years ago.

If after spending some time over the deep metaphysical speculations of a number of German linguistic philosophers you turn to
men like Madvig and Whitney, you are at once agreeably impressed by the sobriety of their reasoning and their superior clearness
of thought. But if you look more closely, you cannot help thinking
that they imagine our primitive ancestors after their own image
as serious and well-meaning men endowed with a large share of
common-sense. By their laying such great stress on the communication of thought as the end of language and on the benefit
to primitive man of being able to speak to his fellow-creatures
about matters of vital importance, they leave you with the impression that these " first framers of speech " were sedate citizens
with a strong interest in the purely business and matter-of-fact
side of life ; indeed, according to Madvig, women had no share
in the creating of language.

In opposition to this rationalistic view I should like, for once
in a way, to bring into the field the opposite view : the genesis
of language is not to be sought in the prosaic, but in the poetic
side of life ; the source of speech is not gloomy seriousness, but
merry play and youthful hilarity. And among the emotions
which were most powerful in eliciting outbursts of music and of
song, love must be placed in the front rank. To the feeling of love,
which has left traces of its vast influence on countless points in

28

the evolution of organic nature, are due not only, as Darwin has shown, the magnificent colours of birds and flowers, but also many of the things that fill us with joy in human life ; it inspired many of the first songs, and through them was instrumental in bringing about human language. In primitive speech I hear the laughing cries of exultation when lads and lasses vied with one another to attract the attention of the other sex, when everybody sang his merriest and danced his bravest to lure a pair of eyes to throw admiring glances in his direction. Language was born in the courting days of mankind ; the first utterances of speech I fancy to myself like something between the nightly love-lyrics of puss upon the tiles and the melodious love-songs of the nightingale.[1]

XXI.—§ 13. Primitive Singing.

Love, however, was not the only feeling which tended to call forth primitive songs. Any strong emotion, and more particularly any pleasurable excitement, might result in song. Singing, like any other sort of play, is due to an overflow of energy, which is discharged in " unusual vivacity of every kind, including vocal vivacity." Out of the full heart the mouth sings ! Savages will sing whenever they are excited : exploits of war or of the chase, the deeds of their ancestors, the coming of a fat dog, any incident " from the arrival of a stranger to an earthquake " is turned into a song ; and most of these songs are composed extem-

[1] From the experience I had with my previous book, *Progress*, from which this chapter has, with some alterations and amplifications, passed into this volume, I feel impelled here to warn those critics who do me the honour to mention my theory of the origin of language, not to look upon it as if it were contained simply in my remarks on primitive love-songs, etc., and as if it were based on *a priori* considerations, like the older speculative theories. What I may perhaps claim as my original contribution to the solution of this question is the *inductive* method based on the three sources of information indicated on p. 416, and especially on the ' backward ' consideration of the history of language. Some critics think they have demolished my view by simply representing it as a romantic dream of a primitive golden age in which men had no occupation but courting and singing. I have never believed in a far-off golden age, but rather incline to believe in a progressive movement from a very raw and barbarous age to something better, though it must be said that our own age, with its national wars, world wars and class wars, makes one sometimes ashamed to think how little progress our so-called civilization has made. But primitive ages were probably still worse, and the only thing I have felt bold enough to maintain is that in those days there were some moments consecrated to youthful hilarity, and that this gave rise, among other merriment, to vocal play of such a character as closely to resemble what we may infer from the known facts of linguistic history to have been a stage of language earlier than any of those accessible to us. There is no ' romanticism ' (in a bad sense) in such a theory, and it can only be refuted by showing that the view of language and its development on which it is based is erroneous from beginning to end.

pore. "When rowing, the Coast negroes sing either a description of some love intrigue or the praise of some woman celebrated for her beauty." The Malays beguile all their leisure hours with the repetition of songs, etc. "In singing, the East African contents himself with improvising a few words without sense or rime and repeats them till they nauseate." (These quotations, and many others, are found in Herbert Spencer's *Essay on the Origin of Music*, with his Postscript.) The reader of Karl Bücher's painstaking work *Arbeit und Rhythmus* (2te aufl. 1899) will know from his numerous examples and illustrations what an enormous rôle rhythmic singing plays in the daily life of savages all over the world, how each kind of work, especially if it is done by many jointly, has its own kind of song, and how nothing is done except to the sound of vocal music. In many instances savages are mentioned as very expert in adapting the subjects of their songs to current events. Nor is this sort of singing on every and any occasion confined to savages; it is found wherever the indoor life of civilization has not killed all open-air hilarity; formerly in our Western Europe people sang much more than they do now. The Swedish peasant Jonas Stolt (ab. 1820) writes: "I have known a time when young people were singing from morning till eve. Then they were carolling both out- and indoors, behind the plough as well as at the threshing-floor and at the spinning-wheel. This is all over long ago : nowadays there is silence everywhere ; If someone were to try and sing in our days as we did of old, people would term it bawling."

The first things that were expressed in song were, to be sure, neither deep nor wise ; how could you expect it ? Note the frequency with which we are told that the songs of savages consist of or contain totally meaningless syllables. Thus we read about American Indians that "the native word which is translated 'song' does not suggest any use of words. To the Indian, the music is of primal importance; words may or may not accompany the music. When words are used in song, they are rarely employed as a narrative, the sentences are not apt to be complete " (Louise Pound, Mod. Lang. Ass. 32. 224), and similarly : "Even where the slightest vestiges of epic poetry are missing, lyric poetry of one form or another is always present. It may consist of the musical use of meaningless syllables that sustain the song; or it may consist largely of such syllables, with a few interspersed words suggesting certain ideas and certain feelings ; or it may rise to the expression of emotions connected with warlike deeds, with religious feeling, love, or even to the praise of the beauties of nature " (Boas, *International Journ. Amer. Ling.* 1. 8). The magic incantations of the Greenland Eskimo, according to

W. Thalbitzer, contain many incomprehensible words never used outside these songs (but have they ever been real words ?), and the same is said about the mystic religious formulas of Maoris and African negroes and many other tribes, as well as about the old Roman hymns of the Arval Brethren. The mere joy in sonorous combinations here no doubt counts for very much, as in the splendid but meaningless metrical lists of names in the Old Norse Edda, and in many a modern refrain, too. Let me give one example of half (or less than half) understood strings of syllables from "The Oath of the Canting Crew" (1749, Farmer's *Musa Pedestris*, 51):

> No dimber, dambler, angler, dancer,
> Prig of cackler, prig of prancer ;
> No swigman, swaddler, clapper-dudgeon,
> Cadge-gloak, curtal, or curmudgeon ;
> No whip-jack, palliard, patrico ;
> No jarkman, be he high or low ;
> No dummerar or romany . . .
> Nor any other will I suffer.

In the cultic and ceremonial songs of savage tribes in many parts of the world this is a prominent trait : it seems, indeed, to be universal. Even with us the thoughts associated with singing are generally neither very clear nor very abstruse ; like humming or whistling, singing is often nothing more than an almost automatic outcome of a mood ; and "What is not worth saying can be sung." Besides, it has been the case at all times that things transient and trivial have found readier expression than Socratic wisdom. But the frivolous use tuned the instrument, and rendered it little by little more serviceable to a multiplicity of purposes, so that it became more and more fitted to express everything that touched human souls.

Men sang out their feelings long before they were able to speak their thoughts. But of course we must not imagine that " singing " means exactly the same thing here as in a modern concert hall. When we say that speech originated in song, what we mean is merely that our comparatively monotonous spoken language and our highly developed vocal music are differentiations of primitive utterances, which had more in them of the latter than of the former. These utterances were at first, like the singing of birds and the roaring of many animals and the crying and crooning of babies, exclamative, not communicative—that is, they came forth from an inner craving of the individual without any thought of any fellow-creatures. Our remote ancestors had not the slightest notion that such a thing as communicating ideas and feelings to someone else was possible. They little suspected that in singing

as nature prompted them they were paving the way for a
language capable of rendering minute shades of thought; just
as they could not suspect that out of their coarse pictures of
men and animals there should one day grow an art enabling men
of distant countries to speak to one another. As is the art of
writing to primitive painting, so is the art of speaking to primitive
singing. And the development of the two vehicles of communication of thought presents other curious and instructive
parallels. In primitive picture-writing, each sign meant a whole
sentence or even more—the image of a situation or of an incident
being given as a whole; this developed into an ideographic
writing of each word by itself; this system was succeeded by
syllabic methods, which had in their turn to give place to alpha-
betic writing, in which each letter stands for, or is meant to
stand for, one sound. Just as here the advance is due to a further
analysis of language, smaller and smaller units of speech being
progressively represented by single signs, in an exactly similar
way, though not quite so unmistakably, the history of language
shows us a progressive tendency towards analyzing into smaller
and smaller units that which in the earlier stages was taken as an
inseparable whole.

One point must be constantly kept in mind. Although we
now regard the communication of thought as the main object
of speaking, there is no reason for thinking that this has always
been the case; it is perfectly possible that speech has developed
from something which had no other purpose than that of exercising
the muscles of the mouth and throat and of amusing oneself and
others by the production of pleasant or possibly only strange
sounds. The motives for uttering sounds may have changed
entirely in the course of centuries without the speakers being at any
point conscious of this change within them.

XXI.—§ 14. Approach to Language.

We get the first approach to language proper when com-
municativeness takes precedence of exclamativeness, when sounds
are uttered in order to 'tell' fellow-creatures something, as
when birds warn their young ones of some imminent danger. In
the case of human language, communication is infinitely more
full and rich and elaborate; the question therefore is a very
complex one: How did the association of sound and sense come
about? How did that which originally was a jingle of meaningless
sounds come to be an instrument of thought? How did man
become, as Humboldt has somewhere defined him, "a singing
creature, only associating thoughts with the tones"?

In the case of an onomatopoetic or echo-word like *bow-wow*
and an interjection like *pooh-pooh* the association was easy and
direct ; such words were at once employed and understood as
signs for the corresponding idea. But this was not the case with
the great bulk of language. Here association of sound with sense
must have been arrived at by devious and circuitous ways, which
to a great extent evade inquiry and make a detailed exposition
impossible. But this is in exact conformity with very much
that has taken place in recent periods ; as we have learnt in previous
chapters, it is only by indirect and roundabout ways that many
words and grammatical expedients have acquired the meanings
they now have, or have acquired meaning where they originally
had none. Let me remind the reader of the word *grog* (p. 308),
of interrogative particles (p. 358), of word order (p. 356), of
many endings (Ch. XIX § 13 ff.), of tones (Ch. XIX § 5), of the
French negative *pas*, of vowel-alternations like those in *drink,
drank, drunk*, or in *foot, feet*, etc. Language is a complicated
affair, and no more than most other human inventions has it
come about in a simple way : mankind has not moved in a
straight line towards a definitely perceived goal, but has muddled
along from moment to moment and has thereby now and then
stumbled on some happy expedient which has then been retained
in accordance with the principle of the survival of the fittest.

We may perhaps succeed in forming some idea of the most
primitive process of associating sound and sense if we call to mind
what was said above on the signification of the earliest words,
and try to fathom what that means. The first words must have
been as concrete and specialized in meaning as possible. Now,
what are the words whose meaning is the most concrete and the
most specialized ? Without any doubt proper names—that is,
of course, proper names of the good old kind, borne by and denoting
only one single individual. How easily might not such names
spring up in a primitive state such as that described above !
In the songs of a particular individual there would be a constant
recurrence of a particular series of sounds sung with a particular
cadence ; no one can doubt the possibility of such individual
habits being contracted in olden as well as in present times.
Suppose, then, that "in the spring time, the only pretty ring
time " a lover was in the habit of addressing his lass " with a hey,
and a ho, and a hey nonino." His comrades and rivals would
not fail to remark this, and would occasionally banter him by
imitating and repeating his " hey-and-a-ho-and-a-hey-nonino."
But when once this had been recognized as what Wagner would
term a person's ' leitmotiv,' it would be no far cry from mimicking
it to using the " hey-and-a-ho-and-a-hey-nonino " as a sort of

nickname for the man concerned ; it might be employed, for instance, to signal his arrival. And when once proper names had been bestowed, common names (or nouns) would not be slow in following ; we see the transition from one to the other class in constant operation, names originally used exclusively to denote an individual being used metaphorically to connote that person's most characteristic peculiarities, as when we say of one man that he is a ' Crœsus ' or a ' Vanderbilt ' or ' Rockefeller,' and of another that he is ' no Bismarck.' A German schoolboy in the 'eighties said in his history lesson that Hannibal swore he would always be a *Frenchman* to the Romans. This is, at least, one of the ways in which language arrives at designations of such ideas as ' rich,' ' statesman ' and ' enemy.' From the proper name of *Cæsar* we have both the Russian *tsar'* and the German *kaiser*, and from *Karol* (Charlemagne) Russian *korol'* ' king ' (also in the other Slav languages) and Magyar *király*. Besides being designations for persons, proper names may also in some cases come to mean tools or other objects, originally in most cases probably as a term of endearment, as when in thieves' slang a crowbar or lever is called a *betty* or *jemmy* ; E. *derrick* and *dirk*, as well as G. *dietrich*, Dan. *dirk*, Swed. *dyrk*, is nothing but *Dietrich* (*Derrick*, *Theodoricus*), and thus in innumerable instances. In the École polytechnique in Paris there are many words of the same character : *bacha* ' cours d'allemand ' from a teacher, M. Bacharach, *borius* ' bretelles ' from General Borius, *malo* ' éperon ' from Captain Malo, etc. (MSL 15. 179). *Pamphlet* is from Pamphilet, originally *Pamphilus seu de Amore*, the name of a popular booklet on an erotic subject. Compare also the history of the words *bluchers*, *jack* (boot-jack, jack for turning a spit, a pike, etc., also *jacket*), *pantaloon*, *hansom*, *boycott*, *to burke*, to name only a few of the best-known examples.

XXI.—§ 15. The Earliest Sentences.

Again, we saw above that the further back we went in the history of known languages, the more the sentence was one indissoluble whole, in which those elements which we are accustomed to think of as single words were not yet separated. Now, the idea that language began with sentences, not with words, appears to Whitney (*Am. Journ. of Philol.* 1. 338) to be, " if capable of any intelligent and intelligible statement, *a fortiori*, too wild and baseless to deserve respectful mention " (cf. also Madvig Kl 85). But the absurdity appears only if we think of sentences like those found in our languages, consisting of elements (words) capable of being used in other combinations and there forming other sentences : this seems to be what Gabelentz (Spr 351) imagines ; but it is not so wild to imagine as the first beginning something which can be *translated* into our languages by means of a sentence, but which is not ' articulated ' in the same way as such a sentence ; we translate or explain the dental click (' *tut* ') by means of the sentence ' that is a pity,' but the interjection is not in other respects a grammatical ' sentence.' Or we may take an illustration from the modern use of a telegraphic code : if *suzaw* means ' I have not received your telegram,' or *sempo* ' reserve one single room and bath at first-class hotel '—we have unanalyzable wholes capable of being rendered in complete sentences, but not in every way analogous to these sentences.

Now, it is just units of this character (though not, of course, with exactly the same kind of meaning as the two code words) whose genesis we can most easily imagine on the supposition of a primitive period of meaningless singing. If a certain number of people have together witnessed some incident and have accompanied it with some sort of impromptu song or refrain, the two ideas are associated, and later on the same song will tend to call forth in the memory of those who were present the idea of the whole situation. Suppose some dreaded enemy has been defeated and slain ; the troop will dance round the dead body and strike up a chant of triumph, say something like ' Tarara-boom-de-ay ! ' This combination of sounds, sung to a certain melody, will now easily become what might be called a proper name for that particular event ; it might be roughly translated, ' The terrible foe from beyond the river is slain,' or ' We have killed the dreadful man from beyond the river,' or, ' Do you remember when we killed him ? ' or something of the same sort. Under slightly altered circumstances it may become the proper name of the man who slew the enemy. The development can now proceed further by a metaphorical transference of the expression to similar situations (' There is another man of the same tribe : let us kill him as we did the first ! ') or by a blending of two or more of these proper-name melodies. How this kind of blending may lead to the development of something like derivative affixes may be gathered from our chapter on Secretion ; it may also result in parts of the whole melodic utterance being disengaged as something more like our ' words.' From the nature of the subject it is impossible to give more than hints, but I seem to see ways by which primitive ' lieder ohne worte ' may have become, first, indissoluble rigmaroles, with something like a dim meaning attached to them, and then gradually combinations of word-like smaller units, more and more capable of being analyzed and combined with others of the same kind. Anyhow, this theory seems to explain better than any other the great part which fortuitous coincidence and irregularity always play in that part of any language which is not immediately intelligible, thus both in lexical and grammatical elements.

Primitive man came to attach meaning to what were originally rambling sequences of syllables in pretty much the same way as the child comes to attach a meaning to many of the words he hears from his elders, the whole situation in which they are heard giving a clue to their interpretation. The difference is that in the latter case the speaker has already associated a meaning with the sound ; but from the point of view of the hearer this is comparatively immaterial : the savage of a far-distant age hearing some syllables for the first time and the child hearing them nowadays are in essentially the same position as to their interpretation. Parallels are also found in the words of the *mamma* class (Ch. VIII § 9), in which hearers give a signification to something pronounced unintentionally, the same syllables being then capable of serving afterwards as real words. If one of our forebears on some occasion accidentally produced a sequence of sounds, and if the people around him were seen (or heard) to respond appreciatively, he would tend to settle on the same string of sounds and repeat it on similar occasions, and in this way it would gradually become ' conventionalized ' as a symbol of what was then foremost in his and in their minds. As in agriculture primitive man reaped before he sowed, so also in his vocal outbursts he first reaped understanding, and then discovered that by intentionally sowing the same seed he was able to call forth the same result. And as with corn, he would slowly and gradually, by weeding out (i.e. by not using) what was less useful to him, improve the quality, till finally he had come into possession of the marvellous, though far from perfect, instrument which we now call our language. The development of our ordinary speech has been largely an intellectualization, and the emotional quality which played the largest part in primitive utterances has to some extent been repressed ; but it is not extinct, and still gives a definite colouring to all passionate and eloquent speaking and to poetic diction. Language, after all, is an art—one of the finest of arts.

XXI.—§ 16. Conclusion.

Language, then, began with half-musical unanalyzed expressions for individual beings and solitary events. Languages composed of, and evolved from, such words and quasi-sentences are clumsy and insufficient instruments of thought, being intricate, capricious and difficult. But from the beginning the tendency has been one of progress, slow and fitful progress, but still progress towards greater and greater clearness, regularity, ease and pliancy. No one language has arrived at perfection ; an ideal language would always express the same thing by the same, and similar things by similar means ; any irregularity or ambiguity would be banished ; sound and sense would be in perfect harmony ; any number of delicate shades of meaning could be expressed with equal ease ; poetry and prose, beauty and truth, thinking and feeling would be equally provided for : the human spirit would have found a garment combining freedom and gracefulness, fitting it closely and yet allowing full play to any movement.

But, however far our present languages are from that ideal, we must be thankful for what has been achieved, seeing that—

> Language is a perpetual orphic song,
> Which rules with Dædal harmony a throng
> **Of** thoughts and forms, which else senseless and shapeless were.

INDEX

Dialogues of

ALFRED NORTH WHITEHEAD

Other Books by Lucien Price

WINGED SANDALS

WE NORTHMEN

LITANY FOR ALL SOULS

Photograph by Richard Carver Wood

Alfred North Whitehead

" . . . his face, serene, luminous, often smiling, always benign . . ."

Dialogues of
ALFRED NORTH WHITEHEAD

as recorded by

LUCIEN PRICE

Max Reinhardt : London

First published 1954

Set in Baskerville
MADE AND PRINTED IN GREAT BRITAIN BY
WILLIAM CLOWES AND SONS LTD.,
LONDON AND BECCLES

" . . . *from this source we have derived philosophy, than which no greater good ever was or ever will be given by the gods to mortal man.*"

Plato: TIMAEUS

" . . . *and this place is sacred, to all seeming—
thick set with laurel, olive, vine; and in its heart
a feathered choir of nightingales makes music.
So sit thee here on this unhewn stone . . .*"

Sophocles: OEDIPUS AT COLONUS

CONTENTS

INTRODUCTION

BY

SIR DAVID ROSS

BOSWELL set an example for all time of the possibility of recording for posterity the very words of a venerated master; he has had few successful followers, but Mr. Price must be numbered among these.

To be worthy of mention in the same breath as Boswell's *Johnson*, a book must fulfil two conditions. In the first place, the man depicted must be worthy of depiction. Whitehead *was* worthy of it. He had a wide and well-stored mind, deeply interested not only in the fields of mathematics, physical science, and philosophy, to which his books are devoted, but, as the following pages testify, also in history, in politics, and in literature. He was trained in an old and old-fashioned school; and his magazine article on Sherborne is one of the best of all defences of the English public-school system. He never lost his love of the classics, and his devotion to Plato grew as his life advanced, and never failed. But in the years spent in Cambridge, England, his mind settled down to its main interests, in mathematics, in logic, and in physical science. This was a time when new ideas were stirring, both in logic and in physical science, and both at Cambridge and in the years (1910–24) which he spent in London Whitehead played a large part in the development and statement of these ideas. When he was sixty-three, an age at which most people begin to think of retirement, there came the dramatic invitation to begin a new life in America. He accepted the invitation with enthusiasm. There have been other British subjects—Lord Bryce and Lord Lothian are examples—who have been singularly at home in the American scene, but no one has ever been

[ix]

more so than Whitehead. He wrote copiously—too copiously, perhaps, for his reputation, for it is often difficult to follow the precise sequence and content of his ideas—but always suggestively. His home became a centre of simple but charming hospitality (in which his wife played almost as great a part as himself), both to colleagues and to students. I suppose that it would be true to say of him that he never made an enemy nor lost a friend.

The second requirement for a successor (I will not go so far as to say a rival) to Boswell's *Johnson* is the finding of a fit person to tell the story. This requirement Mr. Price satisfies to the full. It is clear from the book that, like Boswell, he elicited many of the best remarks made by his hero. His training as a journalist-reporter, and his habit of writing down his notes at the earliest possible moment, enabled him to give an exact and lively account of Whitehead's conversation. Those who wish to find an appreciation of Whitehead's scientific and philosophical thought will look elsewhere—to Lord Russell's account (in *Mind* for 1948) of Whitehead's share in the writing of *Principia Mathematica*, to Professor Quine's article in *The Library of Living Philosophers*, to Professor Emmet's account of Whitehead in *The Proceedings of the British Academy for 1947*, and to Professor Broad's discriminating essay in *Mind* for 1948. But of Whitehead as a man, a man of wide interests, a man whose conversation was always wise and sometimes witty, Mr. Price's account is a masterly one.

PROLOGUE

THE century between 1850 and 1950 is peopled with careers which no writer of fiction could have invented. Such extravagant vicissitudes are generally associated with men of action, but they can equally befall men of thought, and the revolution in thought during the past century has, if anything, been the more violent. What novelist could have imagined a career so intricated with an epoch so explosive as Whitehead's? Anthony Trollope? Trollope could have managed the start of it, for the story begins in an English parsonage, but as soon as it leaves the neighbourhood of Canterbury Cathedral and Archbishop Tait, who used to drive over for Sunday dinner to the vicarage of St. Peter's, Trollope's imagination would not have been up to it and neither would his intellect. It is almost as if Whitehead himself was aware of this, for has he not said:

> *Literature must in some sense be believable, whereas experiences of human beings in fact develop beyond all powers of conjecture. Thus Social Literature is conventional, while History exceeds all limitations of common sense.*

*   *   *

Whitehead's is a three-volume life. Volume I, Cambridge University; Volume II, London; Volume III, Cambridge, Massachusetts. He also said that he had a sense of having lived three lives in three successive epochs; the first, from 1861 to 1914; the second, during the war of 1914–1918; and the third, after that first world war.

This "Tale of Three Cities" begins quietly. He is son and grandson of schoolmasters, then his father becomes a parson. As parson he is an *Old* Testament man, and his prophetic

[1]

thunders reverberate under the barrel vault of a Norman church. The whole scene is picturesque—Ramsgate, fronting the Narrow Seas between England and the Continent, those narrow seas which "are the parents of all free governments in the world—Holland, England, the United States. The Pilgrim Fathers were their offspring." Not far away are the grim walls of Richborough Castle, built by the Romans; a mile inland from Ebbes Fleet beach, where the Saxons had landed, is the spot where Augustine preached his first sermon; and only sixteen miles away is Canterbury Cathedral, where ninety years ago, as still today, a little boy could look on the very spot where Thomas à Becket was murdered, and see the armour worn by the Black Prince. History for this lad was not something learned out of a book; he rubbed elbows with it every day and took it in at eyes and nostrils.

Although Whitehead always regarded himself as the East Anglian that he so typically looked and was—fair, ruddy, blue-eyed—there was one of those slight mixtures in the stock which, as he had observed time and again in history, provide a variant. One of his grandmothers was Welsh, her maiden name had been Williams, and he was so different from his brothers that it was attributed to the Celtic strain.

He was born on February 15, 1861. A frail child, he was taught at home by his father and spent much of his time out of doors with an old gardener to whom he retained a lifelong gratitude for having first let him see the light that can shine in obscurity. Winters he would visit his grandmother in London. She was the widow of a military tailor and lived in a town house, 81 Piccadilly, from whose windows overlooking the Green Park he used to see Queen Victoria, then a middle-aged widow and not too well liked, go by in her carriage. His grandmother was a wealthy woman, but, said he, "She made the mistake of having thirteen children," which somewhat reduced their several inheritances. She also must have been a redoubtable character, for the linch-pin who held the family together was the housekeeper, Jane Whychelow, and she it was who read aloud the novels of Dickens to the little boy as he sat on a hassock hugging his knees beside her grate fire.

His schooling is not less picturesque. He was sent to Sherborne as an adolescent lacking four months of his fifteenth birthday. In 1941 that school celebrated its twelve-hundredth anniversary. It dates from Saint Aldhelm and claims Alfred the Great as a pupil. The monastery buildings are still used and its abbey is one of the most magnificent in existence, with tombs of Saxon princes extant. During his last two years here young Whitehead's private study was a room reputed to have been the abbot's cell and he worked under the sound of the abbey bells—"the living voices of past centuries"—brought from the Field of the Cloth of Gold by Henry VIII and given by him to the abbey.

The curriculum, he remarked in after years, struck him as having been about right for that period and place. "We read Latin and Greek as the historical records of governing peoples who had lived close to the sea and exerted maritime power. They were not foreign languages; they were just Latin and Greek; nothing of importance in the way of ideas could be presented in any other way. Thus we read the New Testament in Greek. At school—except in chapel, which did not count—I never heard of anyone reading it in English. It would suggest an uncultivated religious state of mind. We were religious, but with that moderation natural to people who take their religion in Greek." English grammar he never studied; that was learned out of the grammars of Greek and Latin.

These boys were not overworked. There was time for athletic sports and private reading, which with him meant poetry, in especial Wordsworth and Shelley, but also much history. He was a good athlete and finally a prefect. As Head of the School, he was called upon to cane a boy who had stolen money. "Either he had to be caned before the school or expelled. I don't say that I did right, but I caned him."

[3]

Whitehead's classical training stuck; it was cultivated by him for the rest of his days, and as the twentieth century went on and so many men of science were found to be lamentably lopsided, this benign balance in him between science and humanism became one of his unique distinctions. It was a common saying that "Whitehead has both."

*   *   *

At the age of nineteen, when he went up to Cambridge University, he was already a good mathematician. The method of instruction at Cambridge in those days was largely Platonic, free discussion among friends, and he has said that he learned as much from conversation as from books. Once when asked how he was able to write *Science and the Modern World*, one chapter each week during the academic year while carrying his regular teaching schedule at Harvard, he replied, "Everything in the book had been talked over for the previous forty years."

He becomes a fellow of Trinity in 1885, at the ripe age of twenty-four—Trinity College, Cambridge, one of the most splendid educational foundations on earth. And now comes the great experience in which he found that rare jewel, true humility.

For the previous two centuries it had been comfortably supposed that Sir Isaac Newton had discovered the laws of the physical universe for ever. Then befell the thing. Let me try to quote Whitehead's own words as nearly as I can remember:

"We supposed that nearly everything of importance about physics was known. Yes, there were a few obscure spots, strange anomalies having to do with the phenomena of radiation which physicists expected to be cleared up by 1900. They were. But in so being, the whole science blew up, and the Newtonian physics, which had been supposed to be fixed as the Everlasting Seat, were gone. Oh, they were and still are useful as a way of looking at things, but regarded as a final description of reality, no longer valid. Certitude was gone."

It still is. But how many others have learned? This collapse of certitude where certitude was supposed to be least assailable affected his thinking for the rest of his days. Gone was the Everlasting Seat, yet he noticed how repeatedly even men of science themselves who knew this story would come forward with discoveries in the tone of, "Now at last we have certitude!"

In due season he formulated his reply:

> *The Universe is vast. Nothing is more curious than the self-satisfied dogmatism with which mankind at each period of its history cherishes the delusion of the finality of its existing modes of knowledge. Sceptics and believers are all alike. At this moment scientists and sceptics are the leading dogmatists. Advance in detail is admitted; fundamental novelty is barred. This dogmatic common sense is the death of philosophic adventure. The Universe is vast.*

We thus arrive at what he termed "the fallacy of dogmatic finality." It is one of the least popular of his doctrines. When tried out in conversation or in the public prints, its heresy is sensed with astonishing celerity, for people who do not know what it is that they don't like, do know that they don't like it . . . bristle and growl at the sensed presence of spooks.

*   *   *

Next scene, Dickens's "Bleak House." By no means imaginary, it is a flint-stone mansion which stands on the seaward-thrusting headland at Broadstairs; it *is* bleak, and its walls shake to the thundering shock of surges in winter storms. Here Alfred Whitehead encountered Evelyn Wade, daughter of an Irish military family. Reared in Brittany, she had been schooled in a convent and had come in girlhood to live in England. They were married in December 1890 and lived in Cambridge for the next twenty years. Eight of these, from 1898 to 1906, were

[5]

in the Mill House at Grantchester, a seventeenth-century farmhouse with thatched roof, seated at its ease in a lovely garden. Near it is a pool mentioned in Chaucer.

Here was no cleavage between town and gown. Their participation in the life of the village was lively; they took a flier in setting an example of teetotalism, for at that time the village was rather drunken, and they accepted quite a measure of responsibility for the needy and for their own servants, which savoured of a lingering eighteenth-century squiredom even stretching on back towards feudalism. This experience let Whitehead into an understanding of English character and folkways which he was able to relate to his wider philosophical generalizations and which helped to humanize his abstract thinking. He was also in the thick of liberal politics. "It was exciting work. . . . Rotten eggs and oranges were effective party weapons and I have often been covered with them. But they were indications of vigour, rather than of bad feeling."

"At what period of your life," he was once asked, "did you begin to feel that you had a grasp of your subject?"

He replied, somewhat brusquely for him, "Never."

It then appeared that for sixteen years at Cambridge he had had a constant tussle with insomnia, and each September after a summer's sojourn in the English countryside, in Kent, or in some little village by the sea, he would wonder whether he could ever again sustain a year's teaching. The insomnia never affected his work, however, and in London it diminished and finally ceased. At the same time, during eight of these years in Cambridge, he was reading theology. This was all extracurricular, but so thorough that he amassed a sizable theological library. At the expiry of these eight years he dismissed the subject and sold the books. A Cambridge bookdealer was willing to give quite a handsome figure for the collection. It then appeared that the pay must be taken in books at his shop. So he went on an orgy of book-buying until he had overdrawn his account.

*   *   *

In mid-career and with three children, he and his wife deliberately pulled up stakes and moved to London. This was a venture of faith without definite prospects. "I took a bottle-washing job," said he, "at London University." This lasted three years, then a professorship was made for him, and a dozen years later he was president of its senate.

This experience of the problems of London, extending for fourteen years (1910 to 1924), transformed my views as to the problems of higher education in a modern industrial civilization. It was then the fashion—not yet extinct—to take a narrow view of the function of universities. There were the Oxford and Cambridge type, and the German type. . . . The seething mass of artisans seeking intellectual enlightenment, of young people from every social grade craving for adequate knowledge, the variety of problems thus introduced—all this was a new factor in civilization. But the learned world is immersed in the past.

The nineteenth century ended on August 4, 1914. The Whiteheads' two sons, North and Eric, were in the first world war and the younger, Eric, an aviator, was killed. Their daughter, Jessie, entered the Foreign Office. Only as one came to know them gradually year after year did one even remotely understand how Eric's loss was felt. Finally they could talk of him eagerly and with laughter, but Whitehead once said that the most vivid wordings of grief or attempts at consolation by those masters of speech, the English poets, to him "only trivialized the actual emotions." It was the end of Volume II.

* * *

His invitation to Harvard came in 1924, a complete surprise. The letter was handed him by his wife on an afternoon which was dismal without and within. He read it as they sat by their fire, then handed it to her. She read it, and asked, "What do

[7]

you think of it?" To her astonishment he said, "I would rather do that than anything in the world."

The manner of their having come is not yet generally known. Mr. Lowell, of course, as president issued the invitation, but the idea had originated with Lawrence Henderson and the funds for Whitehead's professorship were furnished by the Henry Osborn Taylors. This was not known to the Whiteheads themselves until many years afterward.

Now comes Volume III. In 1924, at the age of sixty-three, Alfred North Whitehead in a new land begins a new life and by far the most brilliant and productive part of his career. How quietly, how gently this great light rose over Harvard. The sky begins to shine with the white radiance of eternity. Once more the department of philosophy is spoken of as it had been two decades earlier in the *floruit* of William James, Josiah Royce, George Santayana, and Hugo Münsterberg. Then began appearing one major work after another: *Science and the Modern World* in 1925, *Process and Reality* in 1929, his most difficult but the one which he said he had "most wanted to write," *Adventures of Ideas* in 1933, in which admittedly there is more of Whitehead the man than in any other, and, in 1938, *Modes of Thought* . . . the list of published works is of course much longer.

At Harvard it was expected that he would write but not do much teaching. He did both. His lectures came thrice weekly, and instead of allowing his students a twenty-minute conference, he gave them a whole afternoon or a whole evening. "From that inspiration a man comes back with a changed tone." And the traffic was two-way, for Whitehead felt that he needed contact with young minds to keep his own springs flowing. "It is all nonsense," he said, "to suppose that the old cannot learn from the young."

More than professorial, this association was also personal. For at least thirteen years beginning midway in the 1920's and lasting into the 1930's, one heard of "evenings at the Whiteheads'," one night a week of open house to students, although anyone was welcome. These entertainments were of the simplest: conversation, hot chocolate to drink, and cakes to nibble. The students helped make and serve the chocolate, the conversation was their own, skilfully encouraged by host and hostess. In fine, the evenings were theirs, not the Whiteheads'; they began coming timidly in pairs for mutual protection, then by the half-dozen. They were asked to bring their girls, and brought them. Finally they came by the score, from sixty on up to ninety-eight of an evening. So here was a salon in the eighteenth-century French meaning of that term, brought off in an academic town with young men and women on cookies and hot chocolate. But there was also decanted that heady vintage which exhilarates but does not inebriate, conversation with the Whiteheads, and that means both Whiteheads, for he himself once said, "By myself I am only one more professor, but with Evelyn I am first-rate."

★   ★   ★

One May morning in 1932 my telephone rang. Mrs. Thaddeus DeFriez, whose husband, a young victim of the wartime pestilence in an army camp in 1918, had been managing editor of the *Boston Globe*, spoke:

"I am having the Whiteheads to dinner tomorrow. Could you come?"

"Sorry, but I am all packed and ready to leave for the Berkshires."

"They are frail, and getting on in years. You had better change your mind." (I changed my mind.)

The acquaintanceship with Whitehead developed slowly. For its first half-dozen years, 1932 to 1938, I was merely one of scores, even hundreds, who came and went in that dwelling. He once said that conversation should begin on a quiet note: "People should be allowed to talk commonplaces until they have got the temperature of the room. Climate is a good topic. The weather will do." Some deliberation of that sort is mirrored

[9]

in the opening pages of these dialogues; the reader, too, is growing acquainted with Whitehead gradually.

But after about two years his personality exerted a peculiar force. He and his ideas seemed to permeate everything. By an odd quirk of imagination he became identified with one of the noble passages in music, those pages in the finale of Brahms's Fourth Symphony, that great *passacaglia*, where the theme is sounded by horns in goldenly glowing sustained notes above sonorous arpeggii in the darker registers of the string choir, violoncelli and violas (the measures from 113 to 129). Apparently there was no other connection except that of grandeur.

Then *he* disappeared. Oh yes, there remained his voice, clear, resonant, kindly, deliberate and perfectly articulated, British in tone and accent; there was his face, serene, luminous, often smiling, the complexion pink and white, the eyes brilliant blue, clear and candid as a child's yet with the depth of the sage, often laughing or twinkling with humour. And there was his figure, slender, frail, and bent with its lifetime of a scholar's toil. Always benign, there was not a grain of ill will anywhere in him; for all his formidable armament, never a wounding word. But his physical presence had become, as it were, only a transmitter, so intense was preoccupation with his ideas. He, the thinker, seemed to have vanished in the vastness of his own thought. Had this happened only once . . . but it happened so often, happened invariably. And something else happened too: time after time, going over to Cambridge after a day's work and feeling too fatigued to sustain a consecutive conversation, I would come away at midnight after four or five hours' lively interchange with him, exhilarated as with a raging flame of life. Did he emanate an electricity of the spirit?

It used to puzzle me that other guests could take that flood of powerful and original ideas, to all appearances, so coolly. Was he, then, merely one of many, and was nothing unusual going on? Could they pick up such conversation in a hundred other places? For my part, neither in America nor in Europe had I heard its like, and scarcely expect to hear its like again. If it was in books, what were the titles of the books? It was not in books, not even, as he later said, in his own books.

But, "What is so very wonderful here?" someone asks after having read these dialogues. I suggest that Whitehead's thinking makes its effect slowly. It is like a maxim of conduct, of no value unless put into practice; or like music, silent unless performed; or like seeds, sterile unless planted and cultivated. People say of Whitehead's books, "I read him, am stirred and interested, but afterwards I can't remember what he said." The same is true of Beethoven's *Diabelli Variations* and the *Republic* of Plato.

★   ★   ★

Be warned. Some of the matter in these dialogues is acutely controversial. There are books in which there is something to please everyone, and let us hope this will not prove entirely displeasing, yet I think it may be said with becoming modesty that in the following pages will be found something to annoy everybody, including myself. A frontiersman does not enjoy at one and the same time the zest of adventure and the placid comfort of a settled community. If some do not care for Whitehead's critiques of Christian theology or his dissent from Hebraic thought, no more do I care for some of his judgments about music and poetry, which happen to be *my* religion; for it makes a difference whose religion is gored. But for his part, he moved at a serene altitude above controversy:

Mine be some figured flame that blends, transcends them all.

He was not there to dogmatize—dogmatic finality he held in abhorrence—and I was not there to dispute Whitehead (which in any case I was totally incompetent to do). My function was to help keep the conversation moving and the ideas flowing. Never a dispute, "the worst of dispute is that it spoils a good discussion." In consequence, if some of the ideas which ensue are found offensive, I can only say with Todger Fairmile in *Major Barbara* (as reported by Bill Walker):

> "'*E looks up at the sky and sez, 'O that I should be fahned worthy to be spit upon for the gorspel's sake!' 'e sez.*"

And besides, to record the conversation of an eminent man is likely to be a thankless task. Even those who have done it best have earned, the one two hundred years, the other one hundred years of such epithets as flunkey, valet, toady, ass. Add to this that nowadays everybody is supposed to be as good as everybody else—if not better—and hence a becoming deference argues deficiency in self-respect. From any such presumed equality I emphatically dissent. Your informant was *not* as good as Whitehead, and the intellectual disparity was quite as pronounced.

My posture was that of a sixteen-year-old English lad, deck-hand on the Leyland Line freighter *Devonian*, which used before the war of 1914–1918 to dock at East Boston near St. Mary's House for Sailors. A Londoner by birth, his name was Charles Bailey (pronounced Choles Beyley), and so well bred was he that when on closer acquaintance it was permissible to ask, the question was put:

"Charles, you tell me your parents are poor and that you grew up on the docks of East London. Then how did this happen?"

And Charles, with becoming modesty, replied:

"I was taught to mind me manners in the presence of me betters."

Those golden words are still as shining as the day they were issued from the mint. When we come now to the Dialogues—

"Choles, let me mind me manners in the presence of me betters."

*   *   *

Dialogues is merely a convenient title, though the obvious one. Any notion of its challenging the Platonic precedent would be absurd. The two are, on the contrary, antithetical; Plato's dialogues are contrived to sound like spontaneous conversation, Whitehead's actually are spontaneous conversation, even to the several speakers often obeying the Socratic injunction to "follow the argument where it leads." Even here some of Whitehead's remarks must be read in the strict historical context of the exact date on which they were uttered, and this is one of the points he explicitly made, that what interests a later age in such conversations is how people felt and what they thought about events while they were still going on and before any final judgment was possible. This is something which seldom gets told, for the human race, being denied foresight, dearly loves prophetic hindsight; and more than one highly qualified historical scholar, reading some of these pages in typescript, promptly fell into that trap, protesting:

"He really should have known better than that!"

"But did you, in 1934, or in 1944?"

This element is, however, not large because for the more part Whitehead did not talk of ephemera. His interest in daily events ignited his mind and he always thought freshly as the event turned up, but the true wave length of his thinking was one which opened centuries.

It will be noticed that certain themes run through these dialogues from beginning to end. They are easily identifiable. Repetitions these returns of theme are not; at each recurrence the idea is seen in some novel aspect. It would have been easy enough to combine these recurrences into a single comprehensive statement of the idea; to have done so would have been inexcusably to falsify the document. Instead, the themes are allowed to return, each time in a different key and varied as to rhythm, harmony, tempo, figuration. This quasi-musical form, though quite unpremeditated, is even more pronounced. (There would be a preliminary beating-up of the game, any game, then the hunt was up and off it would go.) Themes and counter-themes would be stated, as in a sonata movement, then a moment would come when Whitehead's mind would take over, as in free fantasia or as a cadenza for the solo instrument. In this the whole movement would come to a climax, after which the accompanying instrument, or instruments, would strike in again to a gradual subsidence and a quiet close.

A visual metaphor was supplied by Mrs. Whitehead: "His thinking is a prism. It must be seen not from one side alone but from all sides, then from underneath and overhead. So seen, as one moves around it, the prism is full of changing lights and colours. To have seen it from one side only is not to have seen it." One-sided seeing is what Whitehead called "half-truth"— "There are no whole truths; all truths are half-truths. It is trying to treat them as whole truths that plays the devil." (The arithmetical quips to which this lends itself were all made long ago.)

The notion that such return of themes is mere vain repetition is thus excluded. My function was not to cut, hack, and mutilate, but to record what was said.

Very well then, what was said? How authentic is this text? In the practice of writing down dialogue from memory as nearly verbatim as one can, the first thirty years are the hardest. My practice began as a schoolboy on January 1, 1901; it continued as a shorthand reporter of lectures, then as a newspaper reporter (who soon discovers that if he produces pencil and paper within view of a person unaccustomed to being interviewed, the unfortunate creature promptly congeals); and after that, years of saving the discourse of all sorts and conditions of men, eminent and obscure. Then by 1932, when this association with Whitehead began, the recording of conversation had become merely some more of the same thing, though it might be well to add that memory is likely to be more exact forty-eight hours later than it is after twenty-four hours—as though the longer interval gave the matter time to strike bottom and rise again to the level of consciousness. This is like the experience of a listener at a concert; immediately afterward, the themes may be hard to recall; the next day or the next after that they return of themselves. But Whitehead, foreseeing that the accuracy of these records (which I do not guarantee to be one hundred per cent) might be questioned, said on one of the last evenings when we were together:

"You had better insert a remark to say that these have been read by us and that they correspond to what was said. Otherwise, people might not believe it. I wouldn't have believed it myself. . . ."

Then just how accurate do I myself think they are? In the run of general conversation where it is merely an affair of picking up cues and following the train of thought, albeit with an ear for characteristic idiom, they are often verbatim; when it comes to Whitehead's longer speeches, his use of language had such flavour of mathematical precision, his command of English was so masterly, and the thinking itself was so compact that moments would come when I listened with secret consternation: "How can I retain all that? How can I hope to get it written with anything like the distinction he is giving it in oral delivery?" The answer is that often I do not. My appeal is to the sign that was posted up in the dance hall of a western mining camp:

Don't shoot the pianist. He is doing his best.

$$\star \qquad \star \qquad \star$$

So it went for nine years, 1932 to 1941, and the book was half written before anybody, including the writer, knew it was to be a book. The Whiteheads did not know I was recording their conversation and there was no reason why they should. "Thrift, Horatio." The conversationally baked meats did furnish forth the journalistic tables. When they did, a copy of the editorial was duly sent him (his name was never mentioned in print), this partly in order to play fair and partly to learn whether the matter had been accurately retained and properly understood.

Then came the second war. Their son and his wife were in London under the bombing, and their grandson also in England was, as Mrs. Whitehead said, "for it." As a diversion these dialogues up to the autumn of 1941 were typed and sent them. Nothing was said about publication until the December of that year. The philosopher's view of their possible value will be found in the conversation of that date. Did the knowledge that they were to be saved impair spontaneity? It was never given a thought. There was too much else that was more interesting.

After his retirement, in 1937, the number of their guests had to be restricted. A good many callers still came, some from far corners of the earth, but advancing years and deafness made entertainment on the previous scale impracticable. And yet, although the larger gatherings may have elicited more aspects of his thought and revealed more sides of his personality, as time went on and the dialogues were among four or even three, he seemed to delve deeper into the ideas which were peculiarly his own. As touching subject matter, he had never liked to be quizzed about his published works. There they were, in print, to be read. He had done his best to make them intelligible. Let us go on to something new.

He was now in his eighties. There was not the least evidence that his intellectual powers were waning. In fact, the current was being stepped up. During those final years at their apartment in the Hotel Ambassador, when our sessions might begin as early as seven-thirty in the evening and last until after midnight, he would finish fresher than he began. The name of the hotel often made me think of Henry James's novel *The Ambassadors*, for ambassador in the highest sense Whitehead surely was.

The retention of his power he owed to moderation in all

things. His abstemiousness was marked. He ate sparingly. Table wine was admissible. No smoking. He seemed never to have craved stimulants. The sight of this ruddy octogenarian, clear-eyed, clear-skinned, without a mark of the customary male indulgences, was, as time went on, not the least of his impressiveness. Another and greater impression was the spectacle of his living, in a four-room apartment, a larger life, more free, more spacious of spirit and intellect than most others could have lived in affluence. One grows accustomed in filial piety to indulging the aged in crotchets and caprices. In him there was nothing to excuse. His calm, his magnanimity, the vastness of his concepts reduced the trivialities of daily living to their true dimensions, yet at the same time abstract principles were raised into issues which must be stood up for stoutly. He was not above the battle, but the battle was on higher ground. This gave him a peculiar quality. He had met and solved more problems than most of us are aware of as existing at all. One felt that here was a man who was not afraid—not afraid of those common enemies of mankind: illness, poverty, old age, misfortune, death; and then he was not afraid of the vast enigmas of human destiny or the immensities of the universe. In those awesome spaces he was at home and at his ease. This is what it means to be a philosopher, to have made friends with the enemy and to have domesticated the infinite in one's own soul. People sensed in him the habit of victory, and all those victories, long since forgotten by him, were there beside him invisibly working and fighting, and lo! his mountain was full of chariots and horsemen.

He once said that the Bible, instead of ending with the Revelation of Saint John, should have closed with the Funeral Speech of Pericles. Two sentences from that speech belong, the one at the beginning of these dialogues, the other at the end of his life:

We have no black looks or angry words for our neighbour if he enjoys himself in his own way.

And:

> *The whole earth is the sepulchre of famous men; and their story is not graven only on stone over their native earth, but lives on far away, without visible symbol, woven into the stuff of other men's lives.*

For a figure worthy of the Periclean Age had walked into our epoch.

The Dialogues

I

SEVENTEENTH anniversary of the United States's entrance into the first world war. The declaration of war came on a Good Friday, a historic irony which no one seemed to notice at the time. This had occupied us at editorial conference and was still in my thoughts as I went out to Canton to dine with the Whiteheads. Their youngest son, Eric, an aviator, had been killed in the war.

By telephone I had understood that dinner was to be at six. Having hustled out to Mattapan Square by train, and by taxi up to their house on Canton Avenue overlooking the Blue Hills, I was informed that dinner was not until seven. They relieved my embarrassment tactfully. A young Dr. Nichols, physician at some big hospital in London, who with his wife had landed in this country for the first time only the day before, met me—relatives of the Whiteheads, I gathered. Presently a message came.

"Won't you go into the study and chat with Mr. Whitehead till dinner-time?"

He was seated at his writing table beside two windows, his head ruddy and luminous from late-afternoon sunshine which poured over him. Rising, he said:

"How fortunate that you did come early! My afternoon was broken up and I was just loitering till dinner-time."

We chose two armchairs by the fire. He talked about newspapers.

"American newspapers give a totally wrong impression by their headlines. When one comes to read their small print, he

[19]

finds that they are written by very sensible people, and in their space allotments they are much more fair to political opponents than English ones. English papers are better written as a whole, but when the writing in American papers does rise, I think it rises higher."

"That coincides with some experience of mine. Last summer I was writing an article on the exhibition of Wagner's manuscript scores at Bayreuth for the London *Times*. It was not as well written as it would have been for the *Boston Globe*. The *Times* wants all the colour washed out of the style."

It appeared that he, too, was aware that the day was an anniversary, and spoke of how far wide of reality are the books by professors about the World War:

"They conscientiously examine state papers, but what have state papers to do with it? The condition of fear that reigned from 1900 to 1914 was unspoken, almost subconscious. People forbore to mention it, hoping thereby not to detonate the explosive, but the dread was always there. Only for a few years after 1870, when it was evident that France would not attack, was there a sense of security in England. The real history does not get written, because it is not in people's brains but in their nerves and vitals."

"Suppose our American culture were wiped out: whom have we produced so far who would stand as a lasting contribution to the world?"

"Walt Whitman."

"Not Emerson?"

"I read Emerson a good deal when I was younger, but if my good neighbours, the Forbeses, will pardon me for saying so," (they are grandsons of Emerson) "he was not so original. But Whitman brought something into poetry which was never there before. Much of what he says is so new that he even had to invent a form for saying it. Whitman seems to me to have been one of the few very great poets that have ever lived. He can stand easily beside the really great European poets. . . . If

English civilization had perished prior to the year 1500, the loss would not have been great. Chaucer is not of the stature of Dante or Homer, and though we have some fine cathedrals, English Gothic is not really as good as French Gothic; but if you destroyed the English civilization from 1500 to 1900, you would make the world much poorer, for it did add something important to the development of the human spirit."

"At Winchester College last summer I noticed something which struck me as a bit of measurement," I said. "Reginald Coupland had taken Sam Morison and me down from Oxford to show us where he went to school, and, in passing those cubicles of the top-form boys I noticed on their study tables texts of Aeschylus, Thucydides, and others of the Great Age, not 'study' texts, edited for schoolboys, but the Teubner *Opera*, the regular brass-knuckled article. 'Are these boys studying the fifth-century dramatists and historians already?' I asked Coupland. He said, 'No. They're reading them on their own.' In Harvard, you were doing well if you read those authors in the original by your sophomore or your junior year. I was flabbergasted."

"You must remember," Whitehead cautioned, "that at Winchester the boys are a selected group, with a very special kind of training to which they are well adapted. In that groove they acquire astonishing proficiency, but they would be quite ignorant out of it. They would know a great deal about Roman customs in the period of the Punic Wars, but very little, perhaps nothing, about urgent problems of their own land and time. They do well at the universities and make names in the professions and as colonial administrators and civil servants. The creative arts? I do not think you will find many of them excelling there. They write well, but not very imaginatively. American students are less well-informed but more eager to learn; English boys are less eager but more informed. The American boy knows less about what interests him more, the English boy knows more about what seems to interest him less." He said this with a laughing twinkle in his bright blue eyes.

"Yes," I conceded, "but all over Europe the cultural soil is so much deeper."

"You place too much stress on soil. It isn't soil. You are the same people as Europeans. You have access to the whole of European history. Americans are too diffident."

"It strikes me that our writers don't *know* enough."

"It is true that most great writers did know quite a lot. But it is possible to know too much. What is wanted is an immense *feeling* for things. And the danger in old civilizations is that the teaching may be *too* good. It damps students down. They know too much about what has been done, they write well, but without freshness. It is so fatally easy for a good period in art to die down into scholasticism and pedantry, for the life to go out of it. Oxford has taught the classics for centuries, and for centuries Cambridge virtually refused to teach literature and taught mathematics, and yet twice as many poets came out of Cambridge as out of Oxford."

"At least, no one can complain that our epoch doesn't provide plenty of excitement to write about. The trouble with history is that there is too much of it."

"If you want a striking parallel of our time," said Whitehead, "read Neale's life of Queen Elizabeth.[1] Point for point it is like ours: uncertainty, no one could have the least idea of what would happen, and Elizabeth's chances of assassination were excellent; and then there was Mary Stuart, for if she survived Elizabeth, either she would become queen and the work of the Reformation be undone, or else there would be the worst of civil wars. And yet that age put forth its astounding achievement."

"Are ages of upheaval favourable to creation?"

"I fancy they are, if not too prolonged and too violent. In the Elizabethan there would have been quiet weeks when nothing

[1] *Queen Elizabeth*, John Ernest Neale, Astor Professor of English History, University of London. Jonathan Cape, 1934.

much was happening and a poet could be at his play-writing. And then there is the incentive of any one great figure doing good work. It sets off a lot of others."

"How about the possibility of one or two great artists exhausting an epoch or an art-form? The Renaissance takes a drop after Michelangelo, and grand opera since Wagner has been a 'Tristan, Junior.' "

"That does happen. Such figures come at the end of an epoch. The danger is when the great themes have been superlatively well done, and the later workers come to secondary themes or refinements or niceties, and art or thought gets drawn off into shallows. That is fatally easy. I mean such themes as a mother's love for her child, something so universal that to express it sounds trite, and yet the medieval sculptors and Renaissance painters could express it with unbelievable beauty: but it is no good trying to imitate them. I have the feeling that the very greatest art gets created only in periods and about subjects as to which there is the very greatest enthusiasm and unanimity and popularity. It speaks to the common people, and when art begins to break up into coteries I do not think it is of much significance. When these coteries begin saying, 'This is too fine for the vulgar to understand,' I doubt if it is very good or great art.

"Our own time is a period of break-up and perhaps our thinkers haven't yet got their bearings in the new era. That may be what is putting them off. The assumptions of the nineteenth century are shaken, and one of the symptoms of it is satirical biography. Lytton Strachey, whom I knew and enjoyed, writes with amazing gusto and familiarity of the Victorians, but when a party of contemporaries says, 'Let us sit down and have a quiet laugh over those stuffy creatures, Dr. Thomas Arnold and Queen Victoria,' he may be very amusing, and may be getting at their weak spots, but he isn't writing about what gave them their moral energy or what carried their century along. And your second crop of such scoffing is likely to be a sorry one.

I think your generation caught the break-up harder than the one now growing up. They never knew a different world, but yours did. Take such a fifteen-minute conversation as we are having now: we are talking earnestly. Their attitude is, 'What is there to choose between one fifteen minutes and another, so long as it is enjoyable? Why should there be any difference? What is the purpose? What is the value? What is the goal?' "

"But you and I do *not* believe that this fifteen minutes is no more important than any other fifteen minutes," I said with some emphasis.

"That is because we belong to a generation which did feel that certain experiences were more valuable than others, and did have a sense of whither it was bound."

The question arose whether science, or a scientific age, was hostile to poetry. He said:

"I think if some of the great poets had lived in our time they might have been not poets but scientists. Shelley, for example; I think it quite possible that he could have been a chemist or physicist. Take Professor Ames of Dartmouth, a man whose discoveries in the field of psychology and optics have made him eminent in Europe and America. If you were to talk with him you would at once discover that you were speaking with a poet and a mystic."

(It struck me that just that thing does happen in the play *Wings Over Europe* by Robert Nichols and Maurice Browne. The scientist is a young Shelleyan poet-idealist.)

Here Mr. George Agassiz was shown in, and while he and Professor Whitehead discussed briefly some affairs of Harvard University, of which Mr. Agassiz is an overseer, there was time to take in the room. It is a large chamber with a peaked roof carried on open beams, and there is a brick fireplace wide enough for three-foot logs. This study is walled with books. The upholstery for the hearth settee and armchairs is a pale green, cool and restful, but the log fire was a grateful warmth against the lingering chill of April. The writing table and secretary are well daylighted, but his working place is evidently the deep armchair beside a south-west window, with a writing board to be held across his lap.

From that window one looks over a wide vista of rolling hills, meadows, and woodland. It was now past sunset, and under a clear sky of early spring, the interfolding hill contours against the horizon were twilight purple.

★   ★   ★

Mrs. Whitehead was in the living-room on her chaise longue. A good deal had happened. Their daughter, Jessie, while skiing on Mt. Washington had broken her neck. For weeks her life had hung as by a thread. When this siege was over, Mrs. Whitehead had had a heart attack. She was pale, but still had her sparkle. Tall, slender, white-haired, and gowned in black, she looked much more the *grande dame* than the invalid, though her dinner was brought on a tray. We others went out to the table, but the door was open so that she could join the conversation, which she did at intervals.

Before dinner was announced she was reading aloud with great gusto some of the opening parts of *John Brown's Body*, which they had all read and liked. Mrs. Nichols came in and was introduced, a handsome young Englishwoman of the black-haired, blue-eyed type, frank and friendly.

At the table, since the three English people continued the theme of American literature as it seemed to me out of courtesy, a shift was negotiated by someone's saying that Dickens's *Bleak House* is one of the few novels which (like the long catalogues of occupations in Whitman's poems) does give some sense of the immense range and variety of social life.

"Yes, all but at the top," said Dr. Nichols.

"Dickens was good at the bottom and middle," said Mr. Agassiz, "but poor at the top; Thackeray was good at the top but poor below the middle."

"In my time at Cambridge (I went up in '83) no one

read Dickens," said Whitehead. "He was considered beneath notice."

"Because poorly written?" asked Mrs. Nichols.

"Largely, I think."

"Of course, Thackeray can write."

"But," she was reminded, "you remember Chesterton's remark about him: that he thought a good many things were going to last which *weren't* going to last. 'He didn't know enough ignorant people to have heard the news.'"

"Dickens," said Whitehead, "didn't begin to be generally read by the university people and the cultivated classes, I think, until along in the 1890's."

"What carried him then? Did the socialists help him?"

"No, not a bit, I should think."

"I was thinking of the Fabians. Their tracts began in 1884."

"No. He came in on his own, along with poor-law relief and housing reform."

The talk veered to slum clearance, the victory at the polls of the Socialists for control of the London County Council, and its frightening the government to put out a huge slum-clearance scheme "which," said the professor, "they had been dangling but didn't really mean to do anything about"; comparison of London and New York slums, London having at least the advantages of more durable buildings and little or no fire risk. They spoke of how strange it seemed to see wooden houses but thought they fitted into our landscape more naturally, and Professor Whitehead added, "One of the first distinctive notes in the American city I noticed is the prominence of the fire brigades."

"Before we leave the novelists, what has happened to George Eliot?" I asked.

"She *has* tumbled off, hasn't she?" said the professor. "I wonder why. *Middlemarch* is a great book."

Mrs. Whitehead spoke from the living-room:

"Have you tried reading her lately?"

"Yes," said I.

"So have I. As I remembered it, she was rather gorgeous, and so she is still in spots, but didn't you find long intervals very prosy and ponderous?"

"What an awkward question! Yes, I did. But there was a time in my twenties when I swore by her, and now one sword at least her right shall guard."

"It was the same with me," said Mrs. Whitehead, "and I had to stop enthusiastically urging my friends to read her."

"That's dangerous," said Whitehead. "For years I have been extolling the Old Testament prophets. True, I hadn't read them recently, but as I remembered, they were quite sublime. Then I tried reading Isaiah. I couldn't go him."

"What was wrong? Did the JEPD,[1] the way the different versions of the Old Testament are cut and pasted, put you off?"

"No. It was the ranting, and wandering from the point. I found that when talking of the Old Testament prophets I should have to change my line."

"Do you remember what Strachey says about prophets?"

"No."

"It is in his essay on Carlyle. He says Carlyle had a low opinion of artists and would have preferred to be remembered as a prophet. Now to be a prophet one must have three qualifications, a loud voice, a bold face, and a bad temper. (Strachey got that joke from Aristophanes, but it's none the worse for that.) But, asks Strachey, who, in any case, remembers prophets? Isaiah and Jeremiah, perhaps, but then they have had the extraordinary good fortune to be translated into English by a committee of Elizabethan bishops!"

"Tell them about Strachey's remark at our house on Jane Austen," said Mrs. Whitehead.

[1] JEPD: Jahvist, Elohist, Priestly, and Deuteronomist elements in the Old Testament. "That is to say, in an average chapter of Genesis we may read a verse written in the ninth century, followed by one written in the fifth, a gap of four hundred years. And sometimes the gap will occur in the middle of a verse."—*The Rise of the Greek Epic*, Gilbert Murray. Oxford University Press, 3rd ed., 1924, page 109.

"It was when we were living in Cambridge, along toward the end of our time there and Strachey was down staying with us. He said he had been reading Jane Austen. 'You?' said I. 'What is there in Jane Austen for you?'—'Passion!' says Strachey."

"All the same," said Mr. Agassiz, more as one thinking aloud, "satire is the soured milk of human kindness."

"How singularly humourless the Bible is," remarked the doctor. "I wonder why."

"You would be gloomy, too," said Whitehead gravely, "if you had Jehovah hanging over you."

"But what a contrast with the Greeks and their laughter," said Mr. Agassiz.

"Where does it come in?" asked Mrs. Nichols.

"Aristophanes."

"Yes," said Whitehead, "but I think humour is a bit later than the stage to which the prophets belong. I think humour is a later thing, and Aristophanes is a bit special. Is there any, or much, humour in Homer?"

"Besides," said the doctor, "the Jewish scriptures were religious literature."

"Yes," said Whitehead, "and when writing is new, men don't set down what they regard as trivialities, and mischances they do regard as trivial even now in primitive tribes. Some of our fellows who were out in Africa with the Negroes during the war tell of how the Negroes went down to a stream for something and came back roaring with laughter. What was the joke? Why, a crocodile had suddenly popped out of the water and snatched one of their fellows off. One of *their* fellows, mind you; not a white."

This came as we were rising from the table. A spring shower was falling. It could be heard making a musical patter overhead, for the living-room roof, like that of the study, is carried on oak beams stained black, with white plaster in the intervals. Glass doors in three pairs open to a terrace that fronts westward, giving view across lawn and garden to the Blue Hills from which Massachusetts takes its Indian name. The room is large and cheerful with its huge fireplace, some quite choice mahogany chairs and lounges upholstered in a French-gray satin, a suggestion of the Empire style, and flowers on side tables and mantelshelf, tulips, jonquils, narcissuses, and lilies of the valley.

"When you were speaking at table of Lytton Strachey," said Mrs. Whitehead, whom the return to the living-room had brought back into the conversation, "I wanted to quote those verses by Miss Wordsworth of Lady Margaret Hall:

If all the good people were clever
And those that are clever were good,
This world would be nicer than ever
We dreamed that it possibly could.

But it seems as though seldom if ever
Do the two hit it off as they should,
The good are so harsh to the clever,
The clever so rude to the good.

"Then should clever portrait painters," asked Mrs. Nichols, "flatter good but stupid and perhaps homely sitters?"

"When John Sargent's portraits of some wealthy but disagreeable sitters were being exhibited in New York," observed Mr. Agassiz, "a Harvard professor murmured at my ear, 'Imitations of Immorality.'"

"Sitters, too, have their rights," said Mrs. Whitehead, and told of their recent adventures with a portrait painter. "He first did one of me. Eleven mortal mornings I sat, until he asked if I wished to see how he was getting on. Of course I knew that such first views aren't altogether happy, so I did not expect too much. He asked what I thought of it. I said, 'Well, of course, one never knows how one looks.' He worked some more. He all but counted the hairs of my head. When it was finished he showed it to his wife. She said, 'It is frightful! Why it isn't even a likeness. What are you planning to do with it?' 'I am going to have it framed and give it to Mr. Whitehead, keepsake style.' 'You are not,' said she, 'you are going to tear it up.' Whatever became of it I never did learn but some time afterwards he confided to me, 'You see, I wasn't really interested in the subject: what interested me was the medium!' "

"And what about the one he painted of me?" asked Mr. Whitehead.

"It looks," said Mrs. Nichols, "as if you were about six years old."

"Yes," said Mrs. Whitehead, "and he still had that same look twenty years later when I married him and for a good many years after that." She smiled with reminiscent, and slightly grim, relish. "I learned to know what it meant and to keep quiet!"

"When he was painting it," said the philosopher blandly, "I chatted along to him, but he kept stopping to scribble notes on paper till I wanted to ask, 'I say, are you an artist or an amanuensis?' And then he wanted to involve me in a controversy of his. You see he went abroad and brought home an Italian tomb, quite a beautiful one, I thought, and he had it put up in the middle of the museum, but then he went away again for a year and when he came back it was gone, quite disappeared. He finally found it down in the basement. But he couldn't get it up again. He tried to get me in on his side. He said, 'If only you will come in with me I think your influence will be tremendous, sufficient to get it restored to its rightful place of dignity.' 'But what good would I be?' I asked. 'I know nothing about art. All I know is that your tomb is quite beautiful.' 'That's all you need to know.' (He was taking Keats's line, you see.) 'Come and say that.' 'But I can say that here without coming to the museum. And besides it wouldn't help you, for the department leans toward archaeology and your tomb could be as beautiful as it liked but if it can't prove it is within a decade of the right period, it will never get out of the cellar!' "

"But don't mistake us," said Mrs. Whitehead. "He is a dear and we are very fond of him."

The talk then veered to the Buchman sect, which was just then coming into prominence, and was articulate, not to say vociferous.

"What is it about that movement," someone asked, "that makes a reticent person wince?"

Whitehead said what it was in no uncertain terms.

"Have you heard," said Mrs. Whitehead, "of Dr. and Mrs. Richard Cabot's visit to the group confessional?"

"No."

"At the proper moment Mr. Buchman, not knowing who they were, nodded, signifying that it was their turn to testify. Dr. Cabot rose and said sternly, 'I am Dr. Richard Cabot, a physician, and professor of sociology in Harvard College.' His wife followed": (she dropped her voice to a mere wisp) " 'My name is Ella Cabot. I am an earnest seeker after truth,' and *she* sat down. That was all."

"It seems to be a kind of upper-class Salvation Army," said I. "A time of social confusion jolts people loose from old beliefs and they catch at straws. Sex-confession is one of the selling points."

"So with the psychoanalysts. Isn't it inevitable that they should develop a taste by all this digging, digging, digging, for unconscious secrets?" asked Mrs. Whitehead. "I should think they ended by digging simply for the fun of digging. And what is there in it for the poor, who must need it as badly if not worse than the rich if there is anything in it? I don't notice any free psychoanalyst clinics. It strikes me that regular physicians are often paid rather meagrely and these psychoanalysts are doing themselves rather well. Isn't it something of a craze for prying into other people's minds and getting you to tell what perhaps you ought to tell, but perhaps not to the prier who is trying to get you to tell?"

Mrs. Dr. Nichols defended the absent profession rather ably, and seemed to know a good deal about it.

"Of all the branches of Protestant sectarianism that I know of," said the philosopher, "King's Chapel in Boston is unique. They will let anybody come there and preach to them—even myself, for instance. It is incredibly respectable. Do you know of any place more respectable," he appealed to me, "even in Boston?"

"None except Mt. Vernon Street. Doesn't Henry James call it the most respectable street in America?"

"I am afraid that doesn't help us," said the philosopher, "for King's Chapel is, as I understand it, owned by people who live on Mt. Vernon Street. It's extraordinarily select. There is a King's Chapel religion, the only one of its kind in existence. I believe it is *the* correct place to be married from."

"You see," explained Mrs. Whitehead, "we went into this venerable place and all sat down, and Altie climbed into a high pulpit, and one naturally expected that we would sing a hymn or begin a litany, but nothing of the sort happened; and then Altie spouted, I must own, in his best manner . . ."

"It's all quite liberal," said he, "almost as much so as Harvard. Did you know that Harvard has an endowed lecture dating back to the eighteenth century, the lecturer being expected to descant on 'the damnable errors of the Church of Rome'? They have even invited a Catholic priest to deliver it."

"How do they get around the terms?"

"Oh, quite easily! Perhaps the lecturer can't discover any damnable errors in the Church of Rome; he then isn't expected to descant on them."

"How that would be relished by one of my old friends. He is now a priest but was formerly a professor of history in Harvard, and with a distinguished career. We were undergraduates together and got on famously, both being from the Midwest and our fathers doctors. He was even then recondite of High Church Anglican lore."

"He must be the man I frequently meet in the library," said the philosopher. "We are just on the point of nodding."

"Do nod, next time."

"His clericalism dates a good way back?"

"Even thirty years ago I used to wonder, in my theological illiteracy, how he kept his High Church Anglicanism and German transcendental philosophers in logic-tight compartments."

"I fancy," said the philosopher, "that isn't as hard to do as it sounds. We all do a bit of that. The hard thing is to keep them in the same compartment."

II

April 22, 1934

ANOTHER fortnight of spring, and along the four miles from Mattapan to the Whiteheads' a veil of green leaf-buds had been spun over the woodlands of that hill country. My arrival this time was a little before seven, and the taxicab driver was asked, as before, to return at nine-forty, out of regard for Mrs. Whitehead's frail health; an order which was later to be rescinded.

She was just being brought to her chaise longue in the living-room by a wheel chair. Professor Whitehead, in his seventies, performing that act vigorously, and then bustling about under her direction arranging chairs and lights.

They chaffed me for leaving so early the previous time.

"Altie said, 'Have we been too much for him? Has he had all he can stand of us?' I told him you probably had an article to write for the morrow. One expects that when a journalist comes to dinner. But Grace DeFriez tells me you have to go early to bed."

"But Grace DeFriez told me *you* had to go early to bed—or something equivalent. It took all my self-abnegation to order that cab for nine-forty."

"Then don't do it again!"

C

"I just have done it again."

"Then undo it."

It was undone by telephone.

"The wife of Professor Morgan is coming." She briefed me a little. "(He, poor fellow, can't be here. He is in the hospital. His tuberculosis, as you know.) The others are Mrs. Nichols, whom you met here last time (the doctor is out at Ann Arbor studying), Professor Rosenstock-Huessy, a German, and Mr. and Mrs. Agassiz. He, too, was here last time. She is a dignified New England gentlewoman, the perfection of her type, and he, I tell him (it is a standing joke between us), *looks* like a Parisian *boulevardier* and *is* a correct Puritan Bostonian, and of course, a member of the Board of Overseers of Harvard. His sense of humour is quite equal to the antithesis, and he even improves upon it: 'When I am in Paris I have a Puritan conscience, and when in Boston my conscience is Parisian, but that won't go in Boston. In consequence, I am always at a disadvantage.' "

They arrived presently. Dinner was served to Mrs. Whitehead and Mr. Agassiz at a small table in the living-room; the rest of us went out to the dining-room.

"I understand," said one of the guests to the host, "that you have compared President Roosevelt with Augustus Caesar. I am a Republican. I can't bear the man."

Whitehead turned to the speaker with a look of glistening hesitancy, then replied in his urbane tones:

"I know of only twice in history when there was a gentleman on the throne."

" 'Throne' ought to satisfy any Republican animus," said Mrs. Nichols genially, being a British subject.

"But wasn't King Edward VII a gentleman?" inquired Rosenstock-Huessy, not unmindful of Edward's kinsman Wilhelm, a Hohenzollern.

"Far from it, I should say," replied the philosopher. "He was very badly brought up. He couldn't get on with the kaiser."

"But no one could get on with the kaiser," said Mrs. Agassiz,

[34]

"and besides he was the kaiser's uncle. It was a family matter. The uncle-nephew relationship made it impossible."

"That isn't the point. It was Edward's *job* to get on with the kaiser. That is what we paid him for, and paid him handsomely, jolly well too much. No, he was ill-bred! When he went out to India as Prince of Wales he blew up an old general who came to a review in the wrong uniform. 'You old fellows out here get into loose habits,' he stormed. 'Including this one, your Majesty!' said the old soldier, tapping his wooden arm with his remaining good hand."

"As if Edward were the one to talk about loose habits," remarked Mrs. Morgan.

"I could forgive him that. After all, his mother *was* a bit stuffy. But he should have minded his manners in public. I'm afraid I didn't care much for him. They knew their royal manners better in the eighteenth century. There was a powerful magnate named Tom Coke, who had great estates and hated George III. At a big public dinner someone proposed a toast to the king, and Tom Coke exploded, 'I won't drink the health of a bloody tyrant!' It was quite shocking and everybody wondered what would happen. But as the throne was just then a bit shaky, all that happened was Tom Coke got a letter from his sovereign saying that no offence was taken because His Majesty understood the *spirit* in which the remark was made!"

Conversation moved to Granville-Barker's production of *The Trojan Women* of Euripides in the Harvard Stadium in 1915, and there was a sudden tacit rallying of the table's talk to shield the German present from the discomfort of what was in every mind at the time, that it had been a contemporaneous performance of *The Belgian Women*, for that was why it was given. Someone said, "The tragedy gave a feeling of the shared guilt of all wars."

"Did anyone here see it?" asked Whitehead.

"Yes. And one of my old professors in the Greek department, who sat next to me, said, 'This is a complete knockdown for me.

I have read *The Trojan Women* repeatedly, and taught it; and if you had asked me this morning, I would have told you that it was full of faults and not really a very good play: and now here it is, overwhelming. You don't know a play until you have seen it acted.' "

"And yet," said Mr. Agassiz from the living-room, "the power of that performance was said to be twenty-five per cent Euripides and seventy-five per cent Granville-Barker."

"I should have put it the other way round," said Mrs. Agassiz.

"Knowing Euripides," said Whitehead, "I should say it was 'fifty-fifty.' "

We adjourned from the table to the living-room for coffee. The talk got headed toward how to get a good government. Someone had been saying that there have been plenty of Power States; indeed, of one sort or another, there has never been any other kind; but why not a Culture State, replacing government by the acquisitive persons with government by the creative people?

"That's so!" said Professor Whitehead. "The acquisitive, being interested in material concerns, do manage to get hold of government."

"Isn't that why they, in general, run it so badly," I asked, "why we get selfish governing classes, why they do such ruthless acts, care so little for the arts, and follow low-minded policies? After all, they are merely expressing the acquisitive instincts. How can we get the creative impulses running a state?"

"It would have to be made amusing," said Whitehead. "I fancy statecraft at present isn't amusing enough to keep a poet or an artist interested. It would need to be as interesting as poetry."

"I know of only one poem that has to do with such subjects," said Rosenstock-Huessy, "and that is by Goethe, and it has never been translated into English that I know of. In it he recites his pleasure in the administrative work he has done at Weimar, the road-building, military reorganization, metallurgy and so on."

"What is its title?" I asked.

"*Ilmenau.*"

"Wasn't it written for one of the Duke Karl August's birthdays?"

"Yes. You have read it?"

"As it happens, quite recently. But there is a difficulty. Goethe enjoyed administration and did it well, but *too* well. He got enmeshed in it to the detriment of his poetizing. That is why he ran away to Italy."

"What I think we want," said Whitehead, "is a head of state reasonably secure, but not *too* secure."

"How about the Antonine emperors?"

"They gave excellent administrations. It was a peculiar system of adoptive successors ratified by a military oligarchy. And singularly enough, the one who has the most credit deserves the least. I mean Marcus Aurelius, for he departed from the rule by appointing his own son Commodus, which happened to be a bad appointment. Marcus would have fared very ill with posterity if he hadn't written those amiable memoirs, which, however edifying and delightful, had nothing to do with the point. His job was to find a good successor."

"How would Pericles qualify?"

"Admirably. There you had the head of the state chosen by means of a political free fight and removable the same way."

"Altie dear, the reason you are down on Marcus is because he intruded into your pet preserve of philosophy where he didn't belong," his wife chaffed him.

"No, I don't say he didn't belong. I should like to venture as far afield from philosophy if *I* had plenty of lifetimes in which to experiment."

"Where, for instance?"

"Well, for one, I would like to be head of a great department store."

"You? Running Jordan Marsh's?"

"Oh. I don't say in Boston. Say London."

"Competing with Selfridge."

"Not necessarily. Mr. Selfridge might be considerate enough to die and leave me to manage the store."

"But, pettie, he *has* died, hasn't he, and here you are not running his store!"

"No. I don't think he is dead. Let me consult *Who's Who*." He went to his study for the volume.

"Oh, you!" Mrs. Whitehead fired after him. "You want to handle silks and satins. You'd *love* it."

"I assure you, my dear, my aspirations to management are much more impersonal."

Presently he returned with *Who's Who*, open to the page.

"He's still alive. Here he is. 'Gordon Selfridge,' " and he read excerpts.

"But that's the son, isn't it?" said Mrs. Whitehead.

"But it *would* be, wouldn't it, my dear?"

"What I'd like to know, Professor Whitehead, is what effect on a public you would try for in a department store?"

"Taste. Household economy. How to get along with fewer things and better."

"Then your shark competitors would devour you."

"I don't think so. That would be part of the fascination—keeping out of their maws."

III

January 24, 1935

THE Whiteheads have moved from Canton back to their former apartment in Radnor Hall on Memorial Drive overlooking the Charles River in Cambridge.

It was the day after a heavy snowstorm. The sky had cleared, an icy wind blew from the north-west, and snow lay heaped in the thoroughfares two and three feet deep. No paths had been shovelled between Harvard Square and the Charles. I waded and floundered, thinking of David McCord's variant of Robert Louis Stevenson:

> *In Boston when it snows at night*
> *They clean it up by candle light.*
> *In Cambridge quite the other way:*
> *It snows, and there they leave it lay.*

Dinner was at seven-fifteen. Only the family were present, Professor and Mrs. Whitehead, Margot, their daughter-in-law (Mrs. North Whitehead), and Eric, the grandson, a blond, blue-eyed lad of thirteen or fourteen years. Mrs. Whitehead was more vigorous and walked in and out of the library several times.

At the table the talk was of their life in Cambridge, England, as contrasted with this in Cambridge, Massachusetts, and of the English stage as they had known it in London. They had seen one of the first performances of Pinero's *The Second Mrs. Tanqueray* with Mrs. Patrick Campbell, who of course *was* Paula Tanqueray, in the title part, and they said that everyone came out of the theatre stunned and almost speechless at what was then considered its outspokenness, and yet, half a dozen years ago when it was revived and very well played by an excellent company, it fell flat and audiences actually laughed. What was all the row about? What was there in the situation that couldn't have been unscrambled in two hours' talk with a competent psychiatrist?

After dinner we separated, the women to the library, Professor Whitehead and I to the sitting-room, where coffee was brought. He talked a little about journalism, and we came to the subject of reputations made by machine publicity, and why fame, which used to be an oak, taking eighty years to grow, should now be a summer squash.

"Is there anything in spiritual law," I asked him, "to

compensate the truly fine pianist for two concerts a year as against the professional showman-virtuoso's two hundred?"

"I am inclined to think that is one of the permanent tragedies of life," said he, "that the finer quality doesn't prevail over the next less fine."

He asked why newspaper headlines are so sensational.

"They are billboards to sell the article."

"Often they give a wrong idea of what is inside the paper."

"Do they? There are days when my impression is that they are our modern substitute of the colosseum martyr-and-wild-beast show."

He looked grave and did not dispute the remark.

We returned to the library. The heavy curtains of black velours had been drawn across the tall windows which looked toward the river and Soldiers Field, and a wood fire burned on the andirons under a black chimney piece of panelled wood in a classic design. The long, wide room, walled with books on three sides, was cheerfully lamplighted. It is the philosopher's study, and his reading chair and writing table are established in a comfortable nook.

As conversation went on there was an opportunity to ask if they had noticed a sterility in the creative arts among the Bostonians. It was soon evident that they had.

"Has their loss of political control something to do with it?" suggested Mrs. Whitehead a shade diffidently.

"Frederic Stimson, a Boston lawyer, novelist, and sometime our ambassador to the Argentine," I said, "has dealt with that in his autobiography, *My United States*. It was published about four years ago. He says that immense wealth had been accumulated in Boston in the first sixty years of the republic, but the wealthy men, instead of trusting their sons and sending them out at their own risks on life's seas as they themselves had done, tied up their fortunes in trust funds so that they could not be squandered by their heirs. The effect was to choke off their initiative."

"Among the few wealthy men I come in contact with," said the professor, "I find a state of funk over what the Roosevelt administration is (quite wisely, I think) doing, and no equipment for understanding it."

"That was evident when the class war struck us in 1912 with the first Lawrence strike," I said. "It was a large-scale revolt and they were too frightened to understand it."

"Their women are timid," said Mrs. Whitehead. "It shows in their houses. Every house is furnished alike. No one dares be different. The monotony is so deadly that every time I go into one more such, I could scream."

He agreed. "In England, the houses would present more instances of vulgar taste, but it would be at least individual. The interior could express the personality. Here the shops do not keep the articles necessary for individual variety. You must take what you can get."

"The notable exception," said she, "is Grace DeFriez. In that house you have taste and individuality."

A question rose whether a common language is a help or a hindrance to Anglo-American understanding. Both Whitehead since he has come to Harvard, and Gilbert Murray when he was last here from Oxford in 1926, have expressed the opinion that it betrays both people into supposing they are alike, when they are profoundly different, and actually promotes misunderstanding.

"I have been reading John Buchan's *Cromwell*," said he, "and the point he makes is that both Cromwell and Charles I were beaten. There was a transition period from 1680 to about 1737 when there is rather a cultural blank; then England finds its footing again and is off into its eighteenth century. But it follows an aristocratic, land-owning tradition which lasts on and merges into the nineteenth-century industrialism, the old aristocracy intermarrying with the new. But your American history stems from the dissenter, the Puritan middle class with a strong democratic tinge. The Cromwellian revolution was undefeated

c*

in America, so the two countries have developed along quite different lines. Yet see what a curious science sociology is! In England, owing to the difficulty of individual talents finding their way up through class strata, people stay with their class, bring their class along, and we have a labour movement ably led by working-class men, *so* ably that in 1924, and again in 1929, when we had Labour governments, they were well qualified to carry on all the ministries of empire, including foreign affairs."

"Our labour movement is still a long way from that."

"Yes, and isn't that one reason why your exceptional talents can rise rapidly through the class strata?" said Whitehead. "*They* rise, but they leave their class behind. Thus, English aristocracy is creating a genuine democracy, and American democracy is creating an aristocracy."

He told of being consulted by a young graduate student in the Divinity School, on what early Church Fathers he should read.

"I asked how long his ancestors had been in this country. He replied that he had come here from Norway at the age of thirteen. His father was a country parson, too poor to give him a secondary-school education, so he was sent to Wisconsin or Minnesota, merely to an acquaintance, who got him a place to work on a farm for a year. Then he went to high school, did well, worked his way through a small college, obtained a scholarship, and came to Harvard, and here he was consulting about Origen and Thomas Aquinas. I understand he is being considered for an instructorship in the university. Of course there was some luck in it: there is an enormous element of luck in human lots; but he must also have been treated with great kindness. My point is that I know of no other place in the world where quite such a thing could happen."

He said that he thought the instrumentality of the monasteries in giving the more sensitive and imaginative types of humanity expression by protecting them in the Middle Ages had never been adequately explored. "The outer world was violent, yet here was this world of thought going on concurrently and it had enormous influence. Humble and impecunious scholars found harbourage in them. And then I observe how institutions run their course. From about the turn of the fifth century into the sixth, when St. Benedict founded his order, up until the fourteenth—nearly a thousand years—if any intellectual work was to be done it had to be under monastic protection. Yet by the time you come to Erasmus, he can hardly mention a monk without going out of his way to utter an expression of contempt. And I wonder how long our universities will keep their edge. Just now they have an enormous vogue and influence. Teaching can be too good. It can perpetuate a tradition and lose the spirit. I reflect that the University of Cambridge, which has done best at teaching mathematics, is the one from amongst whose graduates have come more of the English poets, while Oxford, which has specialized in the humanities, has tended to turn out writers who have attained, on the whole, a high level of mediocrity. I suppose by the time a man has discussed literature with a learned and witty tutor two or three times a week over a period of years he has rather talked it out instead of writing it. Then he knows too well how much good work has been done and how good it is, and is too respectful toward it: 'Who am I that I should do better?' "

We amused ourselves trying to see whether English poets derived sectionally, predominating in certain geographical regions. It seemed to run from the Lakes down through the Midlands east of a central vertical axis, and over into East Anglia, focusing of course in London.

He then discussed American universities in their broad functions: "I disagree with Abraham Flexner's idea that there ought to be separate institutions dotted over the land each giving a specific kind of training.[1] It seems to me that you do

---

[1] "The University in American Life," *Atlantic Monthly;* May, 1932: Vol. 149. "Failings of Our Graduate Schools." *Atlantic Monthly;* April, 1932: Vol. 149. *Universities, American, English, German.* Oxford University Press, 1930.

much better with a more flexible system in which a man taking a technological training can get cultural courses also if he wants and needs them. Your big midwestern universities seem to me to be doing this passably well. This flexibility gives the student a chance to look around and get his breath. Minds don't classify as easily as some of my colleagues appear to think. I am profoundly suspicious of the 'A'-man. He can say back what you want to hear in an examination, and since the examination is roughly a means of test, you must give him his A if he says it back; but the ability, not to say the willingness, to give you back what is expected of him argues a certain shallowness and superficiality. Your 'B'-man may be a bit muddle-headed, but muddle-headedness is a condition precedent to independent thought, may actually be independent creative thought in its first stage. Of course it may get no farther than muddle-headedness. But when my colleagues chaff me for giving more A's than they are willing to do and tax me with tender-heartedness, I reflect that I would rather not have it on my head that I was the one who discouraged an incipient talent."

IV

March 25, 1935

TEA with Professor and Mrs. Whitehead in Cambridge. The sycamores in double row along Memorial Drive are not yet in bud, but there was a goldenly hazed sun of early spring, the air though not warm was still and mild, the river glassy-blue where it was not stirred by college oarsmen.

Tea was served in their living-room. They brought out two old volumes of letters, *Three Generations of English Women*, Mrs. John Taylor, Mrs. Sarah Austin, and Lady Duff-Gordon, edited by Janet Duff-Gordon. The professor said:

"I think you get a truer picture of a period from intimate letters written spontaneously and without a thought of publication than you do from its fiction and often better than from its historians."

"And women write better than men in that vein," said his wife.

"Certainly better than authors writing letters to each other with an eye to future publication," he agreed.

"Edmund Gosse used to complain that while the letters Robert Louis Stevenson wrote him were works of art and literature they didn't tell him what he wanted to know about his friend—which touched off Carolyn Wells to write that ballade with the refrain, 'They *must* look well in print!' "

The professor read aloud a passage in remarkably prophetic vein about Bismarck, written by Sarah Austin to M. B. St. Hilaire, July 7, 1856 (volume 2, page 42):

> . . . *for these small (German) kingdoms, so admirably governed, are destined to disappear, and the reign of armed force inaugurated by the French Revolution and the wars which followed will soon be universal. Your pupil, Prussia, will beat you with your own arms. M. de Bismarck will not hesitate at violence, fraud, or baseness. He will be at least on a par with all you have. Our stupid Liberals insist on seeing liberty in Prussia, despotism in Austria; there is but one word—and name—for such people.*
>
> *Alas, my predictions are being realised. The small independent States will be annihilated and eaten up by the monsters who only know the law of the strongest.*

He laid down the book and said:

"All this has come strictly true, and it is not mere vague prophecy of disaster but a specific forecast of events by a liberal at the very zenith of nineteenth-century liberalism. The reverse of '48 had occurred, but few realized how serious it was."

"Janet Duff-Gordon Ross, who edited these letters, comes in like an old acquaintance," I remarked. "She was the young friend of George Meredith, is the 'lady' in *Modern Love*, Rose Jocelyn in *Evan Harrington*, and Janet Ilchester in *The Adventures of Harry Richmond*, but she had some less amiable qualities than those heroines of poetry and fiction."

"Wasn't there an episode with Ouida?" asked Mrs. Whitehead.

"She horsewhipped that novelist in Bond Street. Evidently she was one of those redoubtable characters of nineteenth-century England who did what they pleased, and were accepted."

"They were by no means rare," said Mrs. Whitehead. "Those great liberal families, though often poor, managed to go everywhere in England and on the Continent and knew everyone in the liberal movement. Ideas were the passports, and that condition to some extent still exists."

"When you get a distinguished liberal," said he, "you generally find nonconformists behind him: often quite humble people, tradesmen and such. To change the subject: we have been reading with great pleasure two articles by you, one signed, in the *Yale Review*, about Sibelius, the other unsigned in the *Globe*, about Hitler's move for rearmament, which we think took a very sensible view of it. I am not a musician, though my wife is; but you managed to interest me in Sibelius to a very lively degree. You took that significant figure and interpreted him in such terms as to universalize him, and your sociology was expressed in such concrete language that it made the whole study alive."

What so touched him off in conversation was that we both knew Eckermann's *Conversations with Goethe* forwards and back. He had gone to that book for help.

"You were doing a difficult thing universalizing a particular figure. It reminded me of how the aesthetic sense in that range of border peoples from the Balkans north, between Germany and Russia on up into Scandinavia, predominates over their administrative sense. They are little in politics but much in art. Finland's political history is brief, yet she produces this great artist. In East Anglia, that part of England where I was born and brought up as a boy, our executive abilities were good but our aesthetic powers were almost nothing. Our coasts face the Low Countries, which were the transmitters of the Renaissance, but more on the side of its political liberties, and it was from East Anglia that most of your New England colonists came. The west of England is more Norman and looked toward France; the tradition was more monarchical and mediaeval, and the Plantagenet kings looked across the Channel to their French provinces of Anjou and Aquitaine. The University of Cambridge was comparatively insignificant beside Oxford for generations after its founding and I do not consider it an accident that Charles I found Anglican and monarchical Oxford loyalist and that Cromwell was a Member of Parliament from Cambridge. East Anglia is largely Dane and Saxon: the west of England, between the Midlands and Wales, was more Norman French, and much more aesthetic in its tastes."

"New England inherited the non-aesthetic strain from East Anglia, then?"

"It was a series of precipitates," said he. "East Anglia, New England, and your Middle West. Midwesterners have something in them which I think New England would be better off if it had more of; and your New Englanders again have something for which East Anglia today would be better."

"How odd. Dr. Harvey Cushing said something almost identical—leaving out East Anglia. One Sunday afternoon in July 1932, over in Brookline before Harvard let him go back to Yale, we were talking about enthusiasm, how the tendency around here is to frown it down. He said, 'Nothing great or new can be done without enthusiasm.' He has plenty, and this community never damped it down, but he comes from the Midwest and can't be understood without that fact. He said he thought that, beginning in colonial times, the 'outgoing' people, who found the atmosphere of the Massachusetts Bay Colony a bit oppressive, moved on to Connecticut and Rhode Island—Hartford, New Haven, Providence—and that in turn

[47]

those who found Connecticut a bit slow moved on after the Revolution to the Western Reserve in Ohio, where he came from, and he said he had picked up further footprints of this long trek in Bloomington, Indiana, and somewhere else on out in Iowa."

"I think that was it," said Whitehead; "the vivid people keep moving on, geographically and otherwise, for men can be provincial in time, as well as in place."

"When you lived out Milton way they must have told you how one of Cameron Forbes's aunts said—or is said to have said—during his long absence as governor general of the Philippines, that she 'hoped Cam wouldn't get out of touch with Milton.' I'm not suggesting that you are; but how does it seem to be back here in the thick of things?"

"We had exhausted that experience," said he. "It was delightful while it lasted—five years; but we are better off here."

"Near our friends," Mrs. Whitehead added. "To live in the country when you can't walk or go out of doors is absurd."

"I think it is a mistake," he continued, "to cling to a region because it has given you a delightful experience once. You merely accumulate dead possessions. Don't cling to the old because it made you glad once: go on to the next, the next region, the next experience. We have left behind us the most extraordinary succession of delightful dwelling-houses each of which in turn once meant everything to us, but not one of which we now regret having left."

V

April 5, 1935

PROFESSOR Whitehead had had to go to a meeting of the Senior Fellows. While waiting for him, Mrs. Whitehead and I were in her little sitting-room, which overlooks the court of Radnor Hall, and the river, through the sycamores which are now beginning to bud. Her own books are in here on shelves from floor to ceiling.

"Mostly French memoirs," she explained, "in double rows, with Saint-Simon at the top 'for reference.' I have a hook by which I can pull the volumes down. France, as Altie was saying at tea the last time you were here, had the misfortune to lose a large proportion of her potential liberal intellectuals at the Revolution and that, I think, accounts for the low tone of her early nineteenth-century literature. I never could read it, and that is why I took up memoirs and letters."

He came in seasonably before the dinner hour, and we adjourned to the library beside the fire, for the April evening was sharp.

"I am a firm believer," said the philosopher, "in letting guests start off on commonplaces till they have shaken down and got the temperature of the room." He smiled expansively. "Even the weather, or the climate, is an unfailingly good topic."

One of the guests was to be Professor Ralph Barton Perry, a colleague of Whitehead's in the department of philosophy, and the biographer of William James. When I was an undergraduate in Professor George Herbert Palmer's course in the history of philosophy, Perry, a dark, brilliant-looking young fellow, occasionally gave one of the lectures for Palmer. Now past middle life, he has lost none of his edge nor his good looks. He was a little late, and, just before he arrived, our host was saying:

"When other Western nations perpetrate anything especially disgraceful at least they don't boast of it, but Germany seems to be peculiar in that the more atrocious the act the more vehement the Germans are in affirming its righteousness."

We all agreed that just so surely as a liberal in some other country defends them, they let him down with a crash. This happened to us repeatedly at the paper in 1914–1917, until we had had enough of it.

At table we were the Whiteheads, North, their son, now on the faculty of the Harvard School of Business Administration on the opposite bank of the Charles, and Professor Perry. The talk started on alcohol, since the maid had, to the dismay of the hostess, deposited a huge decanter on the table, *so* huge that it all but elbowed off the bouquet of spring flowers.

"A good many years ago," said Whitehead, "we lived in rather a drunken village, so in the hope of setting a good example we went teetotal, because the cathedral people were running a crusade. The result was we noticed the effects of drinking on others when we went to dinner parties. At last I said to one of my hosts, 'Look here, do you realize that although after everybody has had two glasses of champagne there is a good deal of laughter, the jokes aren't *really* very witty; you only think they are?' His reply quite dashed me. He said, 'Yes, but that's a definition of wit: a joke is funny if you think it is!' "

"Kittredge used to say," I remarked, "that everything is a joke when people are in high spirits."

"Yes," said North, "but isn't there a difference between wit and high spirits? I used to know an old bargee who was never sober but never quite drunk. He discoursed at large on politics, always keeping to the magnificent generalities but never getting down to brass tacks. He wasn't really witty, but when I had had a drink I noticed that his jokes sounded better and his wisdom more sublime."

"Has it ever been made clear why Northmen prefer hard liquor to wine?"

Whitehead thought it was to keep out the chill and damp.

"Could it be because the grape does not grow in the north?"

"I think it might be largely that," Perry agreed, adding, "but the fermentation of juice is as old as civilization."

"Are you suggesting alcohol as a criterion of civilization?" North Whitehead teased him.

"If so," replied Professor Perry smiling grimly, "the United States had a very low form of civilization in the 1920's!"

"The Norsemen were heavy drinkers as long as a thousand years ago," I remarked. "It was a recognized way of disposing of your enemies to wait until they were all drunk then burn their hall and them in it. Saga after saga records this amiable custom, and they even carried it over into Scotland."

"But did they drink at sea?"

"Apparently not."

"But active sailors can eliminate alcohol."

"As they can coffee."

"And there are the rations of rum."

"Don't take them too seriously," said North. "They are quite pathetically small."

"Discipline in that respect on English ships seems quite strict . . . not much drinking at sea, unless it be at Christmas."

By one of those swift transitions which occur in a conversation, the theme moved from the rarity of drunkenness in Latin countries south of the "wine line," to the comparative reliability and seamanship of Latin sailors. Someone said:

"They must have been good once, for most of those daring fifteenth- and sixteenth-century voyages were made by Portuguese, Spaniards, and Italians."

"That was quite a while ago," said Mrs. Whitehead, and she told of being aboard an Italian steamship coming out of Naples. "The pilot, who was disembarking, got into difficulty with the painter of his skiff. The captain, who happened to be standing near a stewardess, screamed and flung his arms around her: she screamed, and a general scream went up from all the crew. The pilot managed to disengage himself, but it was scarcely a reassuring way to start the voyage."

"If you want an example of the excellence of British seamanship, and a very recent one, here it is," I said. "A boy who was saved from the burning of the S.S. *Morro Castle*, a young Phelps from Philadelphia, related the affair to John Richards, who had been one of his schoolmasters at St. Paul's. He got hold of a rope which hung over the steamer's rail and clung to it four hours, wondering if the fire would burn it off, and *then* what? The two American ships steamed up, did little or nothing, then steamed away again. Finally, at daybreak came the British ship, and *three times*, said John, this American boy, without realizing that he was repeating, told of the effect on him of the calm efficiency and discipline of that English crew. The ships were so close that he could hear the creak of davits and the rattle of blocks, then the calm, cold voice of the first officer sounding over the water as he said to the man in charge of one of the lifeboats: 'Mr. Hawkins, your boat is slow. Lower away, damn you.' "

This story seemed to please Professor Whitehead immensely, but he said, "I think perhaps a fiery Latin might have screamed an order that would have got equal results."

Thence the talk moved to the Yankee clipper ships in the nineteenth century and the Gloucester fishing schooners in the twentieth having each in their turn reached a culminating point where they were works of art, only to be superseded, the clippers by steam, the schooners by the internal combustion engine.

"As I remember," said Whitehead, "perfection just precedes a change, and signifies the approaching end of an epoch."

This discussion was carried over from the table to coffee in the living-room, where it was presently being remarked by the host that "American inventiveness is not as primarily originative as it often gets the credit of being, but is frequently in the secondary inventions that diffuse the article into general use. You didn't really lead off with the automobile," he continued. "The French did that. What you did was adapt it to the multitude."

"Yes, and doesn't most of this inventiveness come down in the end to apparatus for the transportation of bodies and the transmission of thought, not thought itself? How about original thought? If these United States were engulfed, like the fabled continent of Atlantis, what would we have left by which to be remembered?"

"Your diffusion of literacy and average comfort and well-being among the masses, in my opinion, is one of the major achievements in human history," said Whitehead. "In previous lands and times, even under the best conditions, the diffusion of culture was to only a small stratum at the top, never more than twenty per cent at the most. I think this extending to the multitude of at least a decent standard of living is an enormous contribution to civilization."

"What is it more than mere material well-being, creature comforts?" I asked, and Professor Perry agreed.

"The real arts," said Perry, "are aesthetics, science and philosophy. The others are secondary achievements, not major ones."

"You Americans!" exclaimed Mrs. Whitehead. "Perpetually denigrating yourselves!"

"It is only of late that we have arrived at the stage of self-criticism," I said. "Perhaps we overdo it. But why, when the comfort was more widely distributed than ever before or since —from 1919 to 1929—did that tone of anger, bitterness, and exasperation so permeate our public prints? Don't you remember what a painful impression it made? Was it disenchantment with the war, or a sense of our temporary political impotency? The well-being came to the average lower-middle-class or worker's household in the form of a radio, a cheap car, a parchment lampshade, cretonne curtains, an armchair, and household short cuts for labour saving. Was it because comfort and leisure came to people unschooled to use them, and were withdrawn before they had had time to learn?"

"They were always looking forward to the time when they would have more material comforts," said Perry, abetting me. " 'Never were, but always to *be* blest': and so remained discontented."

"You are in too great a hurry," said Mrs. Whitehead. "You have only had three hundred years. Europe has had three thousand."

"But the Greeks had had only about three hundred years."

"Yes, but they bothered themselves singularly little about Egypt and Persia, if you will notice," interpolated Whitehead. "True, they picked up a few principles of civilization from Crete and Mycenae and Asia Minor, and not very much from Egypt —as you will remember, the Egyptian priests in Plato's story told Solon: 'You Greeks are only boys.' The point is, they did it on their own. And like America, they were rather violent. I can imagine the Persians and Egyptians saying to one another, 'I say, isn't it shocking how many murders get committed in Greece? Their society must be fearfully insecure.' But the murders didn't stop things from getting done. I fancy the place I have been in that was most like Greece was a gathering of university scholars at Chicago! The city was disorderly but very much alive. The Greeks weren't studying the best models to be had abroad. They were making their own. That, I fancy, is the most Greek thing a man can do. As for the value of studying the language in the original, I think most of the good can be got out of translations. As a young man I read the New Testament in the original. The Greek, as Greek, was quite beneath contempt and the translation into early seventeenth-century English is far superior. Ninety per cent of good old Herodotus can be got in translation, and sixty or seventy per cent of Thucydides. Even the sainted Plato doesn't lose so much. I have to teach several of his best Dialogues to successive classes of students, and I often ask myself what value there is to the ideas in them that would justify a man for the labour of going to get up the language. It being forty years since I read Greek fluently I now take a Loeb translation with the English on a parallel page, but with the help of Liddell and Scott's lexicon I can generally tell where old Jowett is making a fool of himself, which is about every other sentence. . . ."

"Altie, dear!" his wife stemmed the tide of his waxing eloquence. "Oxford, you know!"

"Yes, my dear . . . What I mean is"—he obediently moderated his pitch—"I question the value to the average student of

[54]

digging out the niceties of meaning from the texts. The Greeks themselves wouldn't have done such a thing. And when Greek scholars tell me, 'Yes, but what our author *really* meant was . . .' they aren't helping along the thought. They say any other method is anachronistic. I'm not sure the true anachronism isn't the other way round. This backward-looking traditionalism came in at the Renaissance. It wasn't Greek. My own department, philosophy, has been especially a sufferer from it. That is why I have attempted to invent new terminologies for new concepts. There is a jargon of thinking which gets in the way of thought itself. It is as bad as this archaeologizing of American art. In the great period of Renaissance painting the princes bought pictures that were being painted *then,* not centuries before. If your millionaires would spend their money not on collecting old masters but on contemporary paintings, your American art would have a better flourishing. The essence of your life here in America is that it looks not back but forward. If aesthetic history is all you want, then of course it is all to nothing in favour of Europe. But if it is forward-looking creation that you want, then you Americans must rely on yourselves and it is all to nothing in your favour."

A suspicion flickered in my left eye that the good philosopher was leaning a little in the other direction to correct the excess of my Hellenizing zeal, but I was busy laying the lesson to heart for all that, and presently I had a joke on him. He and Perry were talking of the combat in faculty meeting over dropping the Latin requirement for the degree of Bachelor of Arts. The name "Rand" suddenly caught my ear—this would be Edward Kennard Rand, Pope Professor of Latin in Harvard University, who put me through Livy and Horace as an undergraduate.

"Ken Rand made the principal speech on behalf of the Latin requirement," recited Perry, "and a very good speech it was: just the right arguments and just the right seasoning of wit, and, by the by, you came into it," he addressed Whitehead.

"*I?*"

"Yes. He quoted liberally from one of your essays in *Aims of Education*."

"Then he didn't quote all of my points, for not all of them would have been in his favour."

"Enough of them were in his favour to make a devastating loss in *our* ranks, Alfred. There were a good many members who did not say much, but when it came to vote—young men, too, whom you wouldn't have expected to be on that side— they voted with Rand—and you."

"I say," said Whitehead, "this is extraordinary—and a lecture I delivered years ago."

"It was one of your very best, Altie," said Mrs. Whitehead.

"Yes, but . . ."

"Not so extraordinary, sir," I decided to come out with it, "when I confess. A few weeks ago there was a dinner at Sam Morison's to collect ammunition for the defence of Latin. I found that they didn't know about that chapter in your *Aims of Education*, so I put them on it."

Perry looked startled. An enemy battery unmasked at his elbow! But I had calculated it before speaking and Whitehead's eyes sparkled with amusement. Whether he did or did not relish the result, he could see the fun.

Professor Perry's sense of humour was also equal to the occasion. When we left, he carried me in his car to Harvard Square, where we parted with mutual assurances of continued esteem.

VI

August 25, 1935

TEA and dinner with the Whiteheads in Cambridge. They had read my "Hellas and All Souls" and "Realms of Gold" in the "Oxford Rondo" of *We Northmen*, the typescript of which chapters had been submitted to Professor Whitehead because he is quoted frequently and at length, in part from his published works and in part from the conversation of April 5, 1935. He had read this typescript, he said, three times, and it precipitated a general discussion.

"The Jews," said the professor, "are singularly humourless."

"In America, at least, they get off some very good jokes—including jokes on themselves," I objected, "and some of the Jewish comedians are among the funniest people on earth."

"Yes, but their laughter is generally ironic. Heine is the type of Jewish humour. In that path between the Babylonian and Egyptian Empires, they were a people in a desperate position, feeling that they were not getting their rights, and thus from the beginning to end of their thought there is always a chip-on-shoulder."

"When all the usual historical explanations have been entertained," I asked, "what, after all, does explain the hold that this Hebraic thought gained over us Northern Europeans—for that is what we are?"

"It is peculiar," he said. "I think we must remember that it was a view of life that came in through the slave and proletarian populations. It was *their* view of how life may be well lived even though you are an underdog. And of course that view has coloured all subsequent European history. It is much more Paul's than that of Jesus. There is no evidence that Paul ever saw Jesus, and he seems to have had rather a patronizing view of his entourage. . . ."

"Like an Oxford don . . ." interpolated Mrs. Whitehead.

"Yes, one would have thought Paul would have gone to the apostles and said, 'Come now, tell me all you can remember about him. Just how was it?' But no: instead, he says, 'Now you sit there and I'll tell you what it all meant.' Jesus would appear to have been one of those winning persons to whom good things get attributed, so that when those oppressed classes were making up a scheme of life whereby existence would be tolerable to them, it clustered round the figure of Jesus. . . . But now curiously the Hellenic element which came into Christianity was an approach to the same problem from exactly the opposite end; namely, that the Greek thinkers had seen that 'the mailed fist' is the vulgar thing. They called it 'barbarian.' They had seen, as aristocrats, that kindness, graciousness, is the true ornament of life. And these two coalesced. But it must be remembered that Christianity came into Europe through 'the lower orders.' "

"Doesn't the chip-on-shoulder signify the state of mind of not having risen superior to your occasion?" I asked.

"Certainly, and you are quite right in your definition of Protestantism in America."

"I said it had no older tradition to temper it."

"That is its difference from Europe. In England, I think, after *The Tempest* got itself written, let us say after 1610, the vivid and sensitive people, the artistic type, got their satisfaction no longer out of aesthetic creation but out of religious experience, at least for the next fifty years. You will notice a distinct falling off in art, architecture, and poetry (Milton's *Paradise Lost* is an anachronism) until after the reign of Queen Anne. The literature is good, even work of genius, but not as good; the architecture has elegance but lacks power. Now I think religious experience lacks something which is got out of artistic expression: it stirs but it does not soothe. Perhaps it is that it lacks the intellectual discipline of artistic expression. When people watch a gorgeous sunset, for example, they are excited but they are also soothed, and when you add to this the element of order which the artist introduces into his creation, which must also be grasped by the enjoyer, there is mental effort required in co-operation with the artist in order to produce the effect. The Catholic Church knows this and has managed its affairs better. The confessional stirs the feeling which is aroused in man by not having come up to his own best standards and then soothes it by sending people off reassured and comforted. I don't say it isn't open to grave abuses; but compare it with Calvinism, in which the man undergoing conversion cannot be sure whether he is one of God's elect or marked for eternal damnation, and there is nothing he can do about it. Even good works will not save him, they are 'the filthy rags': the conception is as of God, an omniscient, all-wise, all-powerful Being who has created this world exactly as he wanted it, even with the evil pre-ordained, and although they throw in a few sentences to mitigate its severity, it does not really get them out of the rigid situation they have let themselves in for."

"What, do you suppose, is the difference between religious experience and aesthetic experience which seems so often to make the second—our response to an art-form or to aesthetic feeling—so much more wholesome? (An intellectual discipline is involved, too.)"

"I should say it was just that: aesthetic experience soothes as well as excites: religious experience is more apt to leave one suspended in mid-air, the emotions aroused but not satisfied."

"The preternatural solemnity of a good many of the professionally religious is to me a point against them."

"I have always noticed," said he, "that deeply and truly religious persons are very fond of a joke, and I am suspicious of those who aren't. The strain of solemnity becomes unbearable, because unnatural. The Athenians, you remember, after their tragedies always had a satyr play."

"Yes, and often the satyr play ridiculed the theme, if not the characters, in the tragedy."

"In *Science and the Modern World*, I have dealt with the 'necessity of irreverence.'" He got down the volume from the shelves, and found the passage in Chapter XIII, which we read aloud together.

Is it that nothing, no experience good or bad, no belief, no cause, is, in itself, momentous enough to monopolize the whole of life to the exclusion of laughter? Laughter is our reminder that our theories

*are an attempt to make existence intelligible, but necessarily only
an attempt, and does not the irrational, the instinctive burst in to
keep the balance true by laughter?*

"It often seems to me," Whitehead resumed, "that European
man was at his best between 1400 and 1600. Since then our
appreciation of beauty has become too overlaid with intellectualizing. We educated people have our aesthetic sense too
highly cultivated and do not come to beauty simply enough.
It is possible that the feeling for beauty is much more true and
strong in unschooled people than in ourselves. The early
cathedral builders—even the Norman and Romanesque—did
not theorize: they *built*; and the poets went to work much more
directly. We of today over-elaborate. The only place I see where
another great flowering of European culture might come is in
the American Middle West, where the start could be fresh and
from the ground up. You, in your chapter, have dealt sensibly
with the problem as between Americans and Europe. Americans must not copy Europe. They must be themselves, must
create *de novo*. These American imitations of Europe will always
lack interest and vitality, as all derivations do. Let Americans
study Europe and see what has been done. But when it comes
to creation, God bless my soul! then forget everything that has
ever been done before, and create!"

"In the deeper reaches of creation, there is nothing else you
can do," I said, "Your learning may help you, but it can't save
you."

"It can only help you, even," said he, "by having been so
assimilated as to have become unconscious and forgotten. As
you have written, there is something backward-looking in most
universities dealing with literature: it is not—'What is to be
done?' It is what has been done: and it is apt to be unctuous
and deferential. I have a horror of creative intelligence congealing into too-good teaching—static ideas: '*This* is the correct
thing to know'; passive acceptance of polite learning, without
any intention of doing anything about it. Teachers should be

acutely conscious of the deficiencies in the matter taught. What they are teaching may be quite lacking in the necessary ingredients of nutriment. They should be on their guard against their materials and teach their students to be on their guard against them. Once learning solidifies, all is over with it. These college faculties are going to want watching. The danger is that education will freeze, and it will be thought, 'This and this are the right things to know': and when that happens, thought is dead. I am immensely annoyed by the smugness of a certain kind of talk which goes on among my colleagues, scornful talk about no theory being good that is 'only half tested,' and the meticulous assembling of facts. Also, the aloofness of the university from practical life: not only the federal and state governments, but even municipal affairs. There is a great function which awaits the American universities, and that is to civilize business: or better, to get business men to civilize themselves by using their power over the practical processes of life to civilize their sociological functions. It is not enough that they should amass fortunes in this way or that and then endow a college or a hospital. The *motive* in amassing the fortune should be *in order* to use it for a socially constructive end."

"Would a man with so altruistic a motive ever be able to amass a fortune?"

"It would probably be given away as fast as he amassed it. What I mean is, law has been civilized—that was done by the Greeks and the Romans, Justinian and that lot;—medicine has been taken out of magic; education has been getting rid of its humbug; and next it is time to teach business its sociological function; for if America is to be civilized, it must be done (at least for the present) by the business class, who are in possession of the power and the economic processes. I don't need to tell you that there is a good deal of sniffing on this, the Harvard College and graduate schools side of the Charles River, sniffing at the new Harvard School of Business Administration on the opposite bank. That strikes me as snobbish and unimaginative. If the American universities were up to their job they would be taking business in hand and teaching it ethics and professional standards."

He said that he thought the interpretation of history by economic determinism was a singularly deficient method, and that even such an attempt at the unification of the world as Alexander's Hellenization of Eastern Asia, "success though he made, and muddle though he left," was a nobler effort and a more effective agent.

We talked of why the middle class has made such a sorry fist of it, and he thought it is because it was a highly selected group who happened to do well because qualified for the limited function of *entrepreneur* in a given epoch, though not really superior people, but merely that class of talent which changing circumstance throws uppermost. "But in England when that class is sincerely touched by the nonconformist religious feeling you get very valuable people, who have been of great historic significance."

"Is it that the middle class divides into two groups; one, which is accessible to religious emotion, or to aesthetic—which takes some of the curse off their economic function—and, on the other hand, those accessible mainly or only to the 'possessive impulses'?"

"Yes, I think that would go far to explain it. In England the aristocracy and the working class are found to have much more in common, and a better understanding of each other than either of those classes with the middle class. They get acquainted through their sports, and both are closer to the realities and the soil. Here in America I think your middle class is superior, and far more effective than ours. I can't see that your trade-union movement is politically responsible or fit to govern yet, and of aristocracy, in the European sense of a responsible governing class, of course you have none."

"The word 'aristocracy' in this country has a black eye. In

the Midwest, when I was a boy, one generally heard it coupled with the term 'codfish.' That had travelled out there from New England and, in especial, meant Boston. The New England aristocracy, if that is what we are to call it, seem to me to have lost or abandoned their leadership, imported hordes of Southern Europeans to work for them, then, frightened at their numbers, restlessness and potential power, gone into a funk and given up the task of trying to govern. The old stock make good doctors and professors, but a lot of them live on inherited money and social position."

"Any aristocracy that shirks its leadership," said he, "is done for. Its only excuse for existence is that it takes the lead. The Yankee upper classes in Boston and New England are, individually, among the kindest people I have ever met. Personally they are cultivated and charming: but when immigrants began flooding in here from Europe in the nineteenth century, they did nothing for them except in certain forms of philanthropy. The result is that two generations later, when they are now outnumbered and outvoted, they find themselves politically at the mercy of people who feel no loyalty towards them or their institutions." A moment later he remarked, "The nonconformist merchant families marrying into the English landed aristocracy in the nineteenth century brought a moral seriousness into an aristocratic class which I do not think ever quite existed before in history."

Earlier in the evening I noticed an instance of Whitehead's watchful kindness: he was speaking of Catholicism and lowered his voice, saying, "Our maid is a Catholic and we are devoted to her." What he had been saying was:

"The synoptic gospels are the thinking of vigorous people: the disciples pluck corn on the sabbath, and are chidden by the mayor and the village council. They reply brusquely": (he roughened his voice to asperity) " '*What does it matter?*' But the official religion which begins at about the second century, that is, the Catholic theology, is a philosophy of life as of a man who had lived dissolutely, tried everything, had a lot of sexual excitement, and suddenly, at the age of thirty-five, turned exactly around the other way, and thrown it all over."

"Why confine it to official Christianity?" said I. "Haven't you been describing our old friend Leo Tolstoy?"

"Not far off," said he, smiling.

This led into the subject of authorship. He said:

"A man really writes for an audience of about ten persons. Of course if others like it, that is clear gain. But if those ten are satisfied, he is content. A certain amount of encouragement is necessary."

I raised the question why the creation of an art-work exhausts the experience for its creator, but is infinitely potent of repeated stimulations in the enjoyer.

"Perhaps," he said, "it is because all human effort is directed towards the achievement of an end, whether it is satisfied or not, and the artist's end, although never quite the result he hoped for, is largely attained, and therefore finished for him; the point at which he ends is where the enjoyer begins."

"I would accept that, in the main; but I think it likely that Beethoven, Wagner, Brahms, and Goethe felt fairly well content with what they had brought off in the Ninth Symphony, *Tristan*, the Violin Concerto, or *Faust*—not that they didn't wish the work had been better; but did feel that it was as good as they could make it, so there was nothing left to bother about."

At table we talked about the intrusions upon personal privacy by American journalism. He said:

"An English publisher can appeal to a fairly compact public with taste who are easy to get at, so that the people interested in a really notable book hear about it in sufficient numbers to make its publication profitable; but here the discriminating public is widely scattered, the country is still sparsely populated, publishers must send agents in person vast distances to remote places, and in their advertising they seem to feel it necessary to make the book sound more exciting than it is. In America

everything has to be 'pepped up,' made exciting. Your potential public is greater than ours; but in proportion to your total
population, far smaller: ours is perhaps twenty-five thousand.
Yours is bigger but distributed. The result is that the publishers
of newspapers especially, instead of appealing to a select group
who will take excellence, must dilute and distribute their article
so that it will appeal to all classes, and that results in a levelling
down to some lower common denominator. Add to that, they
have got into a fix where their news is so expensive that they
are dependent on advertising to pay for it, and that impairs
their independence."

We also talked of the cleavage between youth and its elders
since the war. They said it was far less pronounced in England.
I asked what he thought it was that had happened here.

"The generation now at the age of fifty or thereabouts," he
said, "seems to me to have had its upbringing terribly bungled.
When I address an assemblage of youths under the age of thirty,
I am aware of feeling a hearty respect for them.

"I think," he continued, "it came from their parents having
lost their own belief but going on insisting on the dead formulae
of conduct in order to keep their children 'good,' when they
no longer believed in these formulae themselves. The children
eventually found it out, deceived their parents in turn, and it
resulted in deceit all round. They knew their old religion was
empty but were not honest with themselves nor with their
children about it. Their children, in those years between
eighteen and twenty-four, when one is experiencing for the
first time vital necessities, emotional and physical, were left in
total ignorance of the social consequences of certain types of
conduct."

This was said as we were returning from dinner to the library,
and when we were companionably settled there, a question was
put which had long been pending:

"Why has science kept advancing with such strides since 1900
when so much else has retrograded?"

"One reason," said he, "is the great advance of mathematics between 1700 and 1900. Men of science have thus had a delicate and precise instrument with which to explore their new worlds."

"But why such an advance in the past two centuries, when mathematics had been highly developed by the Greeks at least twenty-six centuries ago?"

"Man's earlier discoveries in mathematics were made by observation of his physical surroundings, as contradistinguished from abstract reason," said he, "On the plains of Chaldea he noticed the stars swinging round and round, deduced the conception of the circle, and finally arrived at the wheel. Now the wheel is not such an obvious invention as it sounds. As late as the fifteenth century, when America was found by the Europeans, the wheel had not been discovered in this hemisphere. Geometry, 'earth-measurement,' γεωγραφία, was developed by the Egyptians from their need to redraw boundaries obliterated in annual inundations of the Nile.

"But between these earlier discoveries, deduced from physical experience, and the later ones, only to be arrived at by abstract reason, occurred a long gap. Roman numerals were clumsy, and the Arabic numerals, easier to manage, did not reach Europe until the twelfth century. When they did, their simpler patterns, more readily seized by the eye, laid mathematics within the grasp of a wider variety of minds. By the end of the seventeenth century, this advance, begun at the Italian Renaissance, culminated in Newton and Leibniz—logarithms, trigonometry, and algebra were developed, and the period closed with, if not the invention, certainly the perfecting of the integral calculus. The road was now open, from 1700 onward, for that excursion into applied mathematics which has equipped scientists with a complex and sensitive medium for creating thought-patterns with which to interpret their explorations of sensory phenomena."

"Even when allowance has been made for the historical vicissitudes, the collapse of the Roman Empire, the Dark Ages, and so on . . . it still seems odd that that long lapse should have occurred after such a hopeful start in the ancient world," I remarked.

"You get a lot of hopeful starts," said he, "and then one or another will lead through. It will take two hundred years to follow out into all their ramifications the leads which scientists have started. This can be done by really rather second-rate men, men with nippy minds who can follow assigned procedures within a limited field. But they are not original minds. Their achievement may wear the look of originality yet be so limited that it may not represent one one-thousandth of experience. Science has reached a point where it can transmit this facility of investigation; but it is of secondary worth. It takes no Shakespeare to do."

"Are you suggesting that genuine scientific originators come as rarely as Shakespeares?"

"I am suggesting that a good many of the people, including prominent ones, who are now regarded as scientists are really little more than technicians. Only once in a great while do we get a really swagger scientist."

"How is experience to be brought to the level of consciousness and transmitted into an art-form out of the subconscious?"

"You are speaking too mentally. It is first an aesthetic experience, powerfully felt—emotional experience with mental perceptions—then it demands a definite artistic form. The trouble with creators of today is that they try to substitute a mental idea for the aesthetic experience. They think: 'Look here, wouldn't it be exciting to try it this way: a way no one else has ever tried it before?' But the novelty is of no significance. All that has any significance is the depth and validity of an experience out of which the art comes; and if it comes out of mere consciously clever ratiocination, it is foredoomed. You are dealing in secondary perceptions and relatively shallow experience: it does not bear the stamp of deepest truth."

"A while back you spoke of our Midwest, something to the effect that . . ."

He took it up vigorously:

"My remark was that the only place I know where European man can still create civilization on the grand scale is in the American Midwest."

"Between the Appalachians and the Rockies?"

"Yes. Roughly, the Mississippi Basin."

"Why not the coastal regions, Atlantic and Pacific?"

"They are rather transmitters of cultures, and their cultures are likely to be more derivative. In the Midwest, climate, soil, and food—those three preconditions to a flourishing civilization —are favourable. Man's earliest essays in recorded civilizations occur in hot climates where food is abundant and clothes and shelter next to needless. Rice, in large part, sustained the civilization of India; in Mesopotamia a civilized society arose on grain; in Egypt the food staple was mainly the date; in Central and South America among the Aztecs and Incas it was maize and the banana. But over-population, made possibly by cheap food, cheapens labour and opens the way to political despotism; and although the wealth, and hence the leisure requisite for culture may result from cheap labour, the consequent loss of liberty stultifies the intellect. Thus it was that in Europe, a colder climate, where food, clothes, and shelter are harder to get, and where proliferation of the human species is not so exuberant but individuality is more pronounced, our northern civilization ventured into rational thought, thought less shackled by religious superstition, and finally produced that energetic and self-reliant creature, European man."

"Nearly every variety of European man is somewhere in our Midwest."

"It has a human soil further favourable to a new civilization: not only is it a self-selected stock; the country people and the people in small towns still hold a favourably large proportion, as compared with the population of cities. Man's best thinking is done either by persons living in the country or in small communities, or else by those who, having had such environment in early life, enrich their experience by life in cities; for what is wanted is contact with the elemental processes of nature during those years of youth when the mind is being formed."

"How often I have noticed that as between country boys or boys from small towns, and city boys or boys brought up in the suburbs," I said, "how much more self-reliant and resourceful the country-bred lads are. Suppose they lose their jobs: the city or suburban boy, who is usually from the white-collar class, is generally upset and feels rather helpless; your country boy will be cool as a cucumber. What of it? He has earned his living by working with his hands, and he could do it again if necessary."

"Urbanization," Whitehead continued, "is a weakness in much of our modern thinking, especially about social problems. Thought is taken primarily for the cities when perhaps it isn't the cities that so much matter. Smart plays are written for blasé audiences in a metropolis; eccentric poetry and clever novels are concocted about dwellers in crowded streets who, poor souls, are cut off through most of the year from contact with the soil, the woods, and the sea, and who perhaps never did a day's hard manual labour in their lives; and to whom the very changes of the weather are but feebly perceptible. They are deprived of that discipline which is imposed by daily contact with the leisurely growth of crops, by the anxiety that those crops should be so at the mercy of nature's caprice, and yet also the reassuring experience of nature's bounty in the long term."

"Not long ago I was rereading the tavern scenes in the two parts of *Henry IV*," I remarked. "Those two plays come in the full flush of Elizabethan England, and I couldn't but keep noticing how gorgeous the sheer vocabulary is, and it comes from the commonest life; much of it from the country, and some of it from the barnyard. Having had a good deal to do with barnyards as a boy, I thought the barnyard smells in Shake-speare's vocabulary very wholesome. Anyhow, as you were saying, such writing had to come out of the countryside. It could have come from no other place."

"Yes," Whitehead assented, "and what is more, I don't believe Shakespeare ever had to grope for a word. Can you imagine him chewing the end of his quill pen until he could think of the right one? There is such exuberance in him that I believe once he had clearly imagined a scene, the words came of themselves, in a rush. You must remember that that immense vigour pervaded the whole of Tudor England. If we ever find ourselves in Cambridge together I would like to take you to the combination room of Trinity College. Here are the portraits of the college officers from the start—it was founded by Henry VIII—first you get the vivid Tudors and Eliza-bethans, then the dour Puritans, then the animated eighteenth-century people: in the nineteenth century you get the scholar and the gentleman; then in the twentieth century you have the scholar, and drop the gentleman. . . ."

Mrs. Whitehead made a wry face, but he wouldn't take it back!

"The intellectual drill of the Tudor monarchs must have sharpened their minds for ruling. Elizabeth's education was the broadest that Europe could afford. She was at home in Greek and Latin on her visits to the universities of Oxford and Cambridge. She had read Greek every morning with her tutor, Roger Ascham, beginning the day with the Greek Testament and then reading and translating such classical authors as Isocrates, Sophocles and Demosthenes. The afternoons were given over to Latin, and she read almost all of Cicero and a great part of Livy. When the Polish ambassador, wishing to insult her, made her an affronting speech in Latin, which he knew she could comprehend, but to which he did not suppose she could reply in kind, she delivered him a terrific counterblast which lasted half an hour—in Latin!"

VII

March 19, 1936

AT dinner, where we were but three, they asked me what I thought of the European broil. I said: "Not war—at least, not for the present."

"German diplomacy is operatic," the professor said. "They see themselves as romantic heroes. In 1914 they had the world outdistanced without fighting, yet they must try it. I imagine their industrialists knew it was folly, but yielded when the military men were able, as they thought, to show that it would be an affair of six weeks, or of six months at the most. I say, does it occur to you that half a century of Wagner's music may have had a lot to do with the mischief? Plato knew what he was talking about when he said there was 'immoral music.' It is *a*-moral. I was once taken to a performance of *Carmen* by a delightful little girl for her birthday party and when it was over, she stupefied me by asking, 'Was *Carmen* a really nice woman?' The question had never occurred to me. One enjoys the music and discards his moral prepossessions. The Germans are emotional and musically susceptible. Wagner appeals to their pride of race. I venture to think that if you had in England a series of really stunning grand operas with gorgeous music and pageantry glorifying England from the Tudors up to 1914, that in a generation they could wreck the English genius for political self-government."

"The idea is disquieting," was about as far as I wanted to assent to that, but in the interests of candour, went on. "As you know, I was at the festival in Bayreuth in July 1933, the fiftieth anniversary of Wagner's death. 'And Satan came also . . .' Hitler was there. He came for the six performances in eight days, the four operas of the *Ring*, *Meistersinger*, and *Parsifal*; sat in Wagner's box in the *Festspielhaus* with Frau Winnifred, the widow of Siegfried. He had only been in power since January, nazidom was still in its honeymoon; he came and went between the theatre and restaurant between double rows of Germans, any one of whom could have thrust a dirk between his ribs, and had his *hochs* and *heils*. He was a fresh-complexioned, brown-haired fellow. You never would have noticed him in the street. There he sat in the opera house, day after day, at performance after performance, and I wondered at the time what he would be making out of it."

"A year later," said Whitehead, "we saw his first blood-purge."

Since artists are not to be blamed for what is done with their works, Wagner was allowed to drop for the time being.

After dinner we returned to the library. The heavy black velours hangings had been drawn before the windows and a wood fire was burning on the hearth under the black chimney piece. Mrs. Whitehead, dressed in her customary black and white, looked handsome and distinguished.

Whitehead was speaking of how to identify talent, and what to do with it when you have identified it. I said:

"Aren't certain ages and civilizations favourable to the development of a given type of talent? Isn't it desirable to create a civilization that would be favourable to *all* types?"

"The most we can ask of a civilization, I think," said he smiling wickedly, "is that it shall not crush *every* type of talent."

"Aren't we Nordics of the late-blooming variety?" I asked. "Or, if you don't like 'Nordic' (and in the hands of certain people the word has begun to smell), let us say the Northern Europeans—don't we mature more slowly? When we are young, at least, the young Jews seem able to beat us all hollow."

They both agreed, and we discussed precocity awhile.

"But," said Whitehead, "when you meet them as students, it is very hard to know just what sort of handicaps to impose so as to equalize the strains as between the precocious, and the perhaps deeper minds which mature more slowly. You need first to know the student yourself, then you need to know what others think of his capacities, and then you need to know those others to know why they think of him what they do."

"Is German scholarship," I asked, "for all its laborious erudition and its ponderosity, not a little lacking in imaginative insight?"

"Scholarship," said he, "can ask itself three questions: first, 'What exactly did an ancient author mean when he wrote certain words, and what exactly did those words mean to his contemporaries?' (That is what scholarship was doing pretty much throughout the nineteenth century.) Next, it can ask, 'What and where are these flashes of insight in the work of genius whereby he rises out of his own time into all time?'— Such flashes as are always anachronistic, in the sense that they are timeless. (And this is a realm in which scholars do not much move and where scholarship rarely finds itself at home.) And finally, 'How can we perpetuate and propagate these rare flashes of genius in which humanity, as nowhere else, has risen above itself?'"

"In that, English classical scholarship is enough better than ours. Here in Harvard in the first decade of the present century, we had some of our very best, especially in the Greek department. Herbert Weir Smyth was then the authority on Aeschylus. Four years they put me through it, and I was glad to be put through—poetry, history, philosophy, drama; but it wasn't until a dozen years later that I began to understand what the great Hellenic ideas meant, and then the people who told me were Murray, Livingstone, Zimmern, Cornford, Casson, and that group. You may retort that I've thrown my case away, that those Harvard professors sowed the seed, and that I, being an excessively late bloomer had to have another dozen or fourteen years; but the same thing happened to others that I know."

They rummaged for specimens of precocity among the Northern Europeans. Keats and Shelley, of course; then Mozart and Mendelssohn, but Whitehead thought that although

D*

interesting specimens, they could scarcely be classed as typical, partly because music and poetry do seem to lend themselves peculiarly to brilliant work by young persons.

Then he suddenly fired at me:

"I say, with all this passionate love of music amongst you Americans, *Where are your American composers?*"

The very form in which the question was asked would have spiked my guns, for if we had had any undeniably of the stature of the great Germans, he would not have asked it. What I did find to say was that this art of symphonic orchestration, which had been developing in continental Europe for the past two or three centuries, has been imported into America at the very peak of its complexities and that our composers, instead of beginning back where the Europeans began, in simplicity, have begun in complexity and tried to make it more complex. It is perhaps too soon to know whether this is a success or a failure.

VIII

May 8, 1936

DINNER with the Whiteheads. The spring is now far enough advanced for it to be a pleasure to walk from Harvard Square down to the river. Elms are budded and the little grass plots are green in front of Hicks House, that white, wooden, gambrel-roofed farm dwelling which was General Israel Putnam's headquarters during the siege of Boston in 1775–1776. Moved from its original site, it is now the library of Kirkland House. Next comes the big, formal, arched gateway of Kirkland House itself and its iron gates in a red-brick Renaissance façade, and after this, heading the corner of Boylston Street and Memorial Drive, another Renaissance façade, the library front of Eliot House, its tall westward-facing windows flanked by white pilasters.

The river banks, too, are now green, and the double row of sycamores along Memorial Drive is in bud. The river is glassing in a breathless calm, stirred only by a single crew who have just landed at the Newell float and swung their shell overhead for the march up the ramp into the boathouse. From the river comes a cool exhalation with the pleasant smell of fresh water. One begins, in the language of Schubert's song, to have *Frühlingsglaube.* . . .

Dinner was at seven, which means six, since we are now having what the farmers call "daylight-wasting." The other guests were North, Margot, and Sheila, son, daughter-in-law, and grand-daughter respectively, and Dr. Walter B. Cannon [1] and his wife Cornelia.[2] He is a rugged, ruddy Midwesterner with a hearty voice, simple, direct, and no nonsense. An authority in his subject, he is freighted with honours which he wears invisibly. His wife is a good deal like him, full of humour and kindness, learned, clever, witty, but sees no reason for putting on side. There was no need to waste time over social preliminaries.

Yellow rays from the westering sun, streaming over roofs, and spires and treetops of Cambridge, shone on the table making a glitter of silver, sparkle of glass, and lighting brilliantly the stalks of yellow iris in a tall vase at the centre. Mrs. Cannon was placed at one end of the table, Mrs. Whitehead at the other.

Dr. Cannon talked of Russia, Germany, and China where he had been on tour and in medical conventions last summer.

Ivan Pavlov, the Russian scientist ("conditioned reflexes"), was one of his old friends. During the early days of the revolution, he said, Pavlov, as was his wont, before beginning his regular series of academic lectures, commented on world events.

---

[1] Dr. Walter Bradford Cannon, physiologist. Born Prairie du Chien, Wis., 1871. A.B. Harvard 1896, M.D. 1900. George Higginson Professor in the Harvard Medical School since 1906. Died 1945.

[2] Cornelia James Cannon (Mrs. Dr. Walter Bradford Cannon), author. Born St. Paul, Minn., 1876. A.B. Radcliffe 1899, L.H.D. Wheaton 1928. Married June 25, 1901.

He was called before the Cheka. After they had questioned him awhile he drew out his watch and said:

"Gentlemen, you must excuse me. I have a lecture to deliver," and walked out.

"You can do that if you are a Pavlov," said Whitehead. "Otherwise you go to Siberia."

"Foreign diplomatists and consuls in Russia," said Dr. Cannon, "have no Russian friends. The Russians dare not be seen talking with foreign officials. A British consul in Leningrad, who cultivates gypsy lore, was rejoiced at the prospect of going there because the Russian authority on gypsies lives and teaches in that city, but in two years he has not been able to meet him. Friends of the Pavlovs, a young scientist and his wife, were arrested by the Cheka while their little boy, a seven-year-old, was asleep, and they were jailed separately incommunicado. The concierge saw them being taken away and notified the Pavlovs, who took the child. By acting through Moscow they obtained the release of the parents a week later, but the woman was shattered and probably will never recover. The boy is of necessity being brought up in an utterly abnormal atmosphere, goes guarded to school, and can have no playmates."

"The hounding of scholars," said Whitehead, "is one of the symptoms of social decay, it keeps cropping out in Western Europe as well. The dread must be always upon them."

"It is," said Dr. Cannon, "and they bring it with them. When Pavlov visited me here in Cambridge, it was a sultry day in July. My family was in New Hampshire and I took him down to Harvard Square. 'But where is your watchman?' he asked. 'I have none.'—'Your house will be robbed?'—'Oh, I don't think so.'—Then seeing my old Ford car in the back yard, he said, 'But your beautiful car will surely be stolen!'—'Oh, no.'—'No? Then how superior is the morality of Boston to New York!' "

Poor Pavlov had been robbed of twenty-three hundred dollars in the Grand Central station in New York, wanted to go home to Russia then and there, and was only persuaded to stay as guest of the Rockefeller Foundation.

"He 'conditioned' a word for me while he was here," continued Dr. Cannon. "We were going down to Woods Hole on the train, when he saw in the seat ahead of us a man reading a newspaper whose headline had in large type the word 'fizzle.' 'Fitzel?' quoth he. 'Was meint das? Fiasco?' "

Presently the doctor was describing an incident in Russia: he had seen a huge crane operated by a woman. "She lifted tons of metal about as though she were putting her baby to bed." He had obviously been more open-minded about the Soviet state than a good many who have gone there of late— conceded that it had improved the lot of the common people.

Of Germany he said that, meeting a professional friend of his in Munich, he was told that the spirit of the German universities, their intellectual freedom which had been built up through centuries, had been crushed. "A sadder man I never saw."

"A young Jew," he recounted, "—an eminent man—was removed from his professorship. His post was offered to a young friend of mine, a German. He replied that he would accept it only with extreme reluctance. His punishment was to be excluded from every library and every laboratory in Germany. . . . The idea of the Nazis seems to be that the universities exist not for intellectual advance but to foster 'comradeship.' This is the expressed dictum of Bernhard Rust, Reichsminister of Culture and Education, who governs them."

"How does this arise in Germany?" asked Whitehead. "Does a house-painter express the Germans because he *is* a house-painter? (They have plenty of house-painters!) Is this regimentation an utterance of the military spirit, or of the undermen? If there had been a glittering Napoleonic dictator as successor to the Hohenzollerns, it might be understood as militarism. This seems more like a revolt of the unintelligent."

"I think," said Dr. Cannon, "it is the young people, who see in Hitler a chance to get what they want in life, and they little care how or what higher values perish in the process. In fact, they do not know that such values are higher. The higher-minded men in the universities often resign on account of what they see being done around them. . . . We are getting a similar group of young people here, and for the same reason—chafing from denial of economic opportunity."

"As in Denmark," said Mrs. Cannon, "where Ph.D.'s sell shoestrings on the streets."

"I don't see why Ph.D.'s shouldn't sell shoestrings," said Whitehead. "They can also meditate on philosophical problems."

". . . like Spinoza polishing lenses!"

"That was rather a better job: but people are better schooled than unschooled, selling shoestrings or no."

"The trouble is," said Dr. Cannon, "that so many Americans want an education not for its own sake, but in the hope of getting a better job."

"Couldn't we rear up a generation," asked Mrs. Cannon, "which would see its value in and for itself? In six years the whole tone of the young people we meet has changed, from the Jazz Decade of the 1920's to a serious interest in social questions."

The talk veered to the excessively long time it takes to train a doctor. Cannon said it was due to Eliot's fiat of ruling pre-medical studies out of the liberal arts course, though, by taking science, the student could to some extent defeat the veto. Men coming from western universities with a B.S. can anticipate the first two years of medical school.

"Our boy," said Mrs. Cannon, "at the age of twenty-eight, an A.B. and a skilled surgeon, is now as an intern earning his first salary, the munificent sum of fifty dollars a month."

Whitehead thought that a boy should be able to begin his medical practice at twenty-six:

"Between the ages of nineteen and thirty-five the imagination is most active," he said, "and we mostly keep going thereafter on whatever 'fizz' we have experienced then. He ought to begin while his imagination is effervescent."

"Wasn't Eliot's purpose—as Mr. Lowell's was—to save the liberal arts college from nibbling from above by preprofessional studies?" I suggested.

"In Europe," said Whitehead, "much of the liberal studies is given in preparatory-school work. Here in Harvard the freshmen are still treated like high-school students, examined once a week to find out if they are working."

"Do you remember William James's definition of such 'tests'?" asked Dr. Cannon. "He said it amounted to little more than applying the stomach pump!"

There was a gale of laughter.

The discussion swung to whether the Philistine hostility of students to faculty is dissolving at Harvard. There is still a good deal of it, but it is relaxing.

"The students seem to take the position," said North, "that they have a 'cheek' to trespass on their instructors' time—as if that weren't our job!"

"Or," said his father, "to put it bluntly—what we are paid for!"

"We can only get them to our house twice a year," said Mrs. Cannon.

"Do you have a regular time?" asked Mrs. Whitehead.

"No. But poor Mr. Conant does, and the Conants think they have had a big party if they get thirty out of a group of six thousand."

"Of course the president can't expect to meet the six thousand," said Whitehead. "His teas are a gesture, a useful one, I grant you, but a gesture it must remain."

"They come better in the evening," said Mrs. Whitehead, "when their day's work is past."

"In other colleges," said North, "we hear that students who are friendly with their instructors incur the stigma of suspicion that they are 'sucking up' to get good grades."

"It is a primitive taboo and dies hard."

"Is there such a thing as 'voodoo death'?" asked North abruptly of Dr. Cannon, knowing evidently that he had investigated it.

Then followed learned discussion of "controlled" experiment, whether the medicine man secretly poisoned the victim. Examples were adduced from Australian and from ancient literatures. After this came the question of how the American aborigines reached this continent from Asia—via Behring Strait or across the Pacific from island to island. Mrs. Cannon recounted having been shown a newborn baby in Mongolia with the Mongolian "blue" patches (peculiar to that stock) on its little buttocks—said baby having been picked up at random by a nurse in a maternity ward—and Mrs. Cannon added that a Dane who had a baby by an Eskimo woman in Greenland observed the same phenomenon on his own offspring. It disappears soon after birth.

Since no one present seemed to know which way our American aborigines came, the sequel was provided some days later by Dr. Alfred Vincent Kidder, the archaeologist who explored the cave-dwellings in the American Southwest and the Maya ruins in the jungles of Guatemala.

"There is no question whatever," said he. "They came across Behring Strait about twenty-five thousand years ago, either dry-shod at the end of the glacial period, or on the ice or in boats. All sorts of animals crossed on foot. 'The Mongolian spot?' " He took up that question with relish. "I was at a dinner party in Guatemala, when someone asked about it. 'My cook,' said the hostess, 'has just had a baby.' She clapped her hands (the way they call servants there), and said, 'Ask Maria to bring in her baby.' The baby was accordingly brought, the hostess turned him upside down and exhibited his little rump. Sure enough, there was the 'spot'!"

★ ★ ★

In the library the window hangings had been drawn close and the candles lighted. The place was gay with vases of apple twigs in pink and white blossom, and in this simple but beautiful study of a scholar, I enjoyed watching Whitehead's serene and luminous face. He looked a little tired.

Here, over coffee, Dr. Cannon talked of his sojourn in China. One of his former pupils is Minister of Public Health in the Nanking government and induced him to speak to two hundred students who understand English.

"At the sight of those expressionless bronze Buddhas my heart sank, but I tried a funny story, they all laughed, and my saliva began flowing normally again. The Chinese laugh at the same jokes as we do but what the Japanese laugh at no one but a Jap knows."

"You Americans," said Whitehead, "have done a great service for the English language by your return of the Boxer indemnity."

"So I found! Our colleges are sending a steady stream of English-speaking Chinese back into China."

"English is destined to be the second world-language."

"Would Shakespeare have been able to understand the language of our advertising signs in the subway trains? 'Vitamin,' 'germ' . . . and so on?" asked the doctor.

"He would have picked it up in no time," said North, "and would have positively revelled in American slang."

"Especially the expletives," put in his father. "Can't you fancy him writing a scene of Falstaff bursting into the Boar's Head tavern shouting, 'Gee Whiz!' " Some of us thought the slang would have been stronger.

The doctor asked:

"What is the taboo on the word 'bloody'?"

"Because it is short for 'By 'r lady.' "

"The taboo," said North, "is not universally operative."

Dr. Cannon returned to the point of what the Chinese laugh at, saying, "When Howard Lindsay was playing *Life with*

Father in Philadelphia, a young Chinese came back after the performance to thank him 'for a delightful evening.' Lindsay's curiosity was aroused. What would there be in the life of an American family that would strike a Chinese as funny? Lindsay said, 'Do you mind telling me just what it was about the play that you enjoyed so much?'—'Why,' said the Chinese, 'my father used to fuss just like that at breakfast.'"

IX

April 19, 1937

THREE novels about Boston have appeared within a year. The latest of them, *Ward Eight* by Joseph Dinneen, is a study of municipal politics, with a lifelike portrait of Martin Lomasney, who was something between guardian and czar of the West End. It deals with the other three-quarters of the city not coped with, although noticed, in John Marquand's *The Late George Apley*. Santayana's *The Last Puritan*, of a wider range, ends with a period two decades earlier than the other two.

The Whiteheads had been reading *Ward Eight* and asked:

"Do you know the author?"

"Certainly. He is a reporter on the *Globe*."

They pounced: "Tell us more about him. How old is he?"—"Fortyish."—"Born in Boston?"—"Yes, and knows it well, from the inside."

"We gathered as much," said Whitehead, smiling amusedly. "But we were wondering if he had been made to feel uncomfortable in consequence of his book."

"Well, encountering him yesterday upstairs in the reporters' room, I asked him just that. He said, 'In certain places that you can guess I am made to feel as though I am an advanced case of leprosy.' Not that he looked at all downhearted."

"How well he understands his own people," said Mrs. Whitehead, who is Irish.

"That is part of the case against him. The verdict is not unanimous."

"Could you bring him to see us? Would he care to come?"

"One can't undertake to produce him, but I can try."

It proved easier than anticipated. We went. Both Whiteheads were in top form: perfection of handling: genial, considerate, interested, but uncompromising. It was amusing to see Joe shaken out of his attitude of indifferentism. He began with a general defence of the system; they demolished it by Socratic questioning: What service does the Boss perform? Employment agency? Yes. Humanizer of the ward? Yes. But isn't the tribute he exacts excessive? And how about selling their votes after they have paid him for jobs and the employers have paid him for getting the labourers? Is it finally defensible?

Dinneen took it gamely. Besides he knew that Mrs. Whitehead was emotionally in sympathy and that both of them admired the novel. He explained the graft all through society—in the labour unions, the unions expecting to be sold out by their elected agents who openly justify their having done so on the score of policy; then in business, finance, journalism; it is an enveloping climate.

The discussion moved to a comparative view of the two social systems, American and English.

"We in England," said Whitehead, "have a bad system inherited from mediaeval feudalism which oughtn't to work but which, as a matter of fact, does work rather well; whereas you, here in America, have an excellent system which ought to work very well but does, as a matter of fact, work rather badly."

"Your system," said I, "keeps the individual of the class in the class, but by so doing provides it with able leaders, which gradually elevates the class as a whole; ours allows the individual to rise, but by so doing deprives the class of its natural leaders and so tends to leave the class as a whole down."

"That's striking," said Dinneen. "I never thought of that before."

[83]

"Neither had I, Joseph, until Mr. Whitehead pointed it out to me a year ago, since when I have been thinking of it."

Resuming, Whitehead said of the class system in England:

"There, where awareness of it is more precise, along with relative homogeneity of race, people know that at a pinch they will be taken care of. I am speaking now of the village and country where squire and gentry adopt a definite responsibility for illness and disaster. After the reforms of 1830, for example, when the middle classes, newly come to power, stiffened the poor law and made it harsher, it was the Tory squires who resisted violently, although the new law would cost them less than the old. Here, wages may be higher and there is more comfort while things are going smoothly, but the consequences of a break in luck or of disaster are frightful. The fate of the poor seems to be nobody's business. . . . In England, class lines may be stiff in major social relationships, but are softened in minor ones . . . the farmers' sons play cricket with the squires' sons. Here, our superficial fraternizing between classes dulls our perception of the profound cleavages between them until the clash occurs."

"In the sit-down strike in Michigan," said Dinneen, "what do you think of the owners' appeal to legality?"

"As the law now stands, the sit-down strike is probably illegal. If they stay on the premises but won't work, they are trespassers. Whether that is how the law *ought* to stand is another matter. Strict application of the present conception of property rights ('doing what I like with my own') may work well enough with small units like shops on Mt. Auburn Street employing a few people, but when you come to great corporate industries which affect the lives of hundreds of thousands of people, it seems to me that the state must step in, if necessary, to direct that they be so managed as to serve the interests of the greater number. The best way to do this, I think, is to leave the actual management to private initiative so as not to destroy that motive, and let the government exercise a general supervisory authority. To do this is the one chance that I see for the capitalist system to survive.

"It isn't, you know, very old: only about three hundred years at most. And it often seems to me that Adam Smith did us a grievous disservice in emphasizing the economic motive. It is important of course. We must eat. But it isn't so important. Think what could be done by stressing the aesthetic motive. I can imagine a state of society, even under our existing system, in which parents wouldn't need to be so anxiously concerned that their children should earn a great deal of money—as they are now. I mean that nervous struggle of American parents to lift their children at all costs into a higher income class than their own, which is called, 'giving my children a better chance than I had': but a chance at what? At more money, or at the things of the mind and spirit?

"I can imagine a society, even under capitalism, in which it wouldn't greatly matter whether a family had much money: music—free concerts; the radio. (I know the radio isn't as good as a concert hall, one wants the music not coming at him from one direction out of a box: one wants it all round him; still, the radio does give access to good music.) Then halls where people could give their own plays; and lectures, and discussion groups, a radio speaker perhaps stating the question, then the group carrying it on; or state-provided moving pictures on a really grand scale, free to the public; and playgrounds for athletic sports; and public libraries such as we already have. Mind you, I don't mean that all this should be heavy and dull. There could be light music, and informal games, and amusing plays. But under such conditions the average person, without much money, would have access to the good life."

At ten hot chocolate was brought, and at ten-thirty we left. Dinneen had to go back to the *Globe* office, and, as he had brought me over to Cambridge in his car, he carried me back to Beacon Hill. On the way, at intervals between a discussion of *The Late George Apley*, which we had both been reading, we counted up our takings from the evening.

"Anything farther from the Apleys," said Dinneen, "I wouldn't know where to look for in the city of Boston."

"All the same, they are warm friends with a lot of Apleys, and respect their good qualities."

"That may be," assented Joseph, a shade absent-mindedly; then, as we drove along he came out with it: "What I bring away is this: more than anyone else I ever met, he seems to have the answers. You say his subject was originally mathematics?"

"Yes."

"He is a Higher Mathematician," said Dinneen.

X

May 24, 1937

THE afternoon was clearing after rain and the drenched turf and foliage of Memorial Drive along the river bank, fresh in May green, smelt delicious.

In their apartment at Radnor Hall the Whiteheads were waiting in their library. Their maid had been out for the day and they laughed over having enjoyed the privilege of doing things for themselves.

". . . doing them on the whole rather badly, and getting thoroughly tired doing them."

Mr. Whitehead wore formal afternoon dress, spike-tailed black coat and starched collar; probably there had been some academic function. Tea was brought. Conversation was on the subject of tolerance.

"There is no tolerance," said he, "unless there is something to tolerate, and that, in practice, is likely to mean something which most people would consider intolerable."

"Do you suppose that the persecuting temper is peculiar to

religions, or only to some religions? Hellenism, for instance, was not a persecuting religion."

"Religion carries two sorts of people in two entirely opposite directions," said Whitehead; "the mild and gentle people it carries towards mercy and justice; the persecuting people it carries into fiendish sadistic cruelty. Mind you, though this may seem to justify the eighteenth-century Age of Reason in its contention that religion is nothing but an organized, gigantic fraud and a curse to the human race, nothing could be farther from the truth. It possesses these two aspects, the evil one of the two appealing to people capable of naïve hatred; but what is actually happening is that when you get natures stirred to their depths over questions which they feel to be overwhelmingly vital, you get the bad stirred up in them as well as the good; the mud as well as the water. It doesn't seem to matter much which sect you have, for both types occur in all sects. . . ."

"Does the fact of certain religions pretending to a closed system, one which sets up to have an answer for every question, have anything to do with it?"

"Wouldn't that be more or less included in my previous definition: that when people do feel strongly on a subject, they consider such questions closed?"

"Is impartial aloofness from such controversy (supposing it is tolerated) an effective position?"

"It depends on what you mean by 'effective.' In general, the 'effective' people are expected to act, and action lands you in conflict."

"Then here we are, at the question of violence. I remember you to have said in your *Adventure of Ideas* (one of the few books I was ever able to read on shipboard) that the only justification in the use of force is to reduce the amount of force necessary to be used."

"If there is a young fellow," said he, "who makes an infernal nuisance of himself going up and down stairs drunk in this building, annoying the twelve families who occupy suites in tihs entry, we either write a letter to the newspaper about it or telephone for the police: one is a mild form of persuasion, the other is potential force. If he then persists, we have him put away. That is restraint." He grinned engagingly.

We got into the question of non-resistance: does it make its appearance except as the last weapon of otherwise defenceless people: Czarist Russia, British India, the American anti-slavery agitators, pacifists in wartime?

This was taken by Mrs. Whitehead as a challenge to British imperial policy in India, which she proceeded to justify till I explained that the subject was adduced purely on its psychological merits, and quoted the chapter in Webb Miller's *I Found No Peace* on the clubbing of non-resisters in India as showing that non-resistance seems to increase the brutality of the attackers. As this topic was not especially congenial (which I might have known beforehand) it was dropped in favour of another, namely, how fares talent in different types of society.

"Aristocracies," said Whitehead, "welcome talent. Burke had neither money nor birth, yet they were glad to have him and he always had a seat in Parliament, for they knew he was a genius. The monarchy was, as the house of Hanover has been all along, healthily unpopular, allowing the government to be run by a committee of parliamentarians who could always hold over their kings the threat that if they didn't behave they could be sent home where they came from. Consequently a career was open to talents. Even the middle classes were privileged up to the time of the World War; we didn't realize it, but we were. My father was rather well off for a country parson. Yet my education was virtually paid for by scholarship funds up to and through my university training, not because we couldn't have paid, but because we weren't asked to. That is now changed. The scholarship funds, I believe, are supposed to go only to students who need them."

The telephone kept ringing. Mrs. Whitehead kept rising and

going into her sitting room to answer it. Finally, returning she seated herself on the arm of her husband's deep chair to say:

"Altie, it's the (she named the dean of a men's college in Massachusetts, and his wife). They 'must' see you. How about Thursday night?"

"For dinner?"

"No. After. It mustn't be for dinner. You must have your rest."

"Then let me look at my book."

He produced a tiny black-leather engagement book with gilt edges from his pocket and peered into its pages.

"Thursday will do."

"He will entreat you for lectures next year. You must be firm."

"I know."

"Remember he is a German. He will talk and talk and talk. You must just sit still, and not be talked over."

"I shan't be talked over."

She looked at me and smiled over this domestic duologue. He was quite unperturbed.

Again the telephone rang. This time it was a secretary in the School of Business Administration, whose father, a country parson from Maine, "dearly wishes to call," Mrs. Whitehead grumbled, "as if you were deity itself! (Imagine you, as deity!)" It was decided to have them, but the girl herself couldn't be persuaded to come.

" 'Why not?' "

" 'I have nothing to bring.' What nonsense! How sad it is. Where does this self-denigration come from?"

"It is the 'sense of sin,' " said Whitehead. "The worst blight that ever fell on man."

This domestic interlude being disposed of, we resumed a discussion of the correspondences between the principles governing diverse art-forms; various devices resorted to by artists to comment on their themes, the choric odes in Greek drama for one, and for another those symbolic figures on the Medici tombs by Michelangelo.

"It is human history speaking in the four recumbent figures," said Whitehead, "and the Medicis are rather lost out of it."

"Apparently Michelangelo knew it at the time," I said. "When it was complained that the statues of Julian and Lorenzo did not look like them, Michelangelo replied, 'Who will see that ten centuries hence?' "

"As for the choric odes in Greek tragedy," said Whitehead, "there it is as though the poet ceased and human nature, the great elemental truths of life, began speaking through him."

"Is it fair to say, as so many do say, that there is more milk of human kindness in Hebraic thought than in the Hellenic?"

His answer was in *oratio obliqua*, so blandly given, so disarming:

"I think there should be an Eleventh Commandment, '*Always make friends with people who do you a service.*' "

XI

March 17, 1938

THE usual holiday celebrating the evacuation of Boston by the British; but no holiday for a newspaper since there is always a big parade in South Boston, where Washington's cannon from Fort Ticonderoga were planted.

Evening with the Whiteheads. It was just after the Germans' seizure of Austria and they were feeling glum. He said he thought the situation was very bad, and she that it meant another war sooner or later. We talked about the composition of the British Cabinet. He said:

"Foreign policy has been run by a Tory group who wanted peace, it is true, but wanted it for the wrong reasons—in order that they might keep their havings. I'm not suggesting that they were treasonable."

"They wouldn't need to be," I said. "Classes identify the interests of their nation with those of themselves."

"That," said Mrs. Whitehead, "is as true of Labour as it is at the Tory end."

"The Labour people," resumed Whitehead, "have been shouting against rearmament whenever anybody mentioned a gun, and directly we began to come into collisions—as with Italy in the Abyssinian affray, they cried, 'This wouldn't have happened if we had been armed.'"

"I often wondered what Labour would have done had they suddenly been given the responsibility."

"Tories and Labour, both have been following one half of a wrong policy," he replied, "Labour opposing rearmament, Tories trying to conciliate dictators."

"It begins to look as though the one thing democracy has that is worth saving is the freedom of the individual."

"I would say," remarked Whitehead, "two: the freedom of the individual is one. But your knowledge of history will remind you that there has always been misery at the bottom of society: in the ancient world, slavery; in the mediaeval world, serfdom; since the development of machine technique, industrial proletariates. Our own age is the first time when, if this machine production is sensibly organized, there need be no material want. Russia has relieved the suffering of the masses at the price of the individual's liberty; the Fascists have destroyed personal liberties without really much alleviating the condition of the masses; the task of democracy is to relieve mass misery and yet preserve the freedom of the individual."

"Are aristocracies, so-called, of much use to us?"

"If they are kept alive. I would have inheritance taxes high enough so that a family of lazy aristocrats wouldn't survive. But I wouldn't have a dead level of income. Families with wealth are free to experiment. And the rich man's fad of one generation becomes the poor man's necessity of the next; from Rolls-Royce motor-car to the Ford car. Without rich

[91]

families you couldn't get your privately endowed universities in America, and it is Harvard, Yale, Princeton, Chicago, and such places, that set the pace for the state universities, without which they might be badly stagnant."

At nine the doorbell rang and Grace DeFriez arrived, animated and handsome, gowned, like Mrs. Whitehead, in black, which becomes them both. The week before, being in Nantucket, I had gone up on the moors' edge to the grave of her young husband, Thaddeus, who had been managing editor of the *Globe*. Nantucket, having been a family home of the DeFriezes for four generations, was mentioned briefly; the talk shifted to sea fogs which beset that island, and thence to the "dew ponds" of the Wiltshire Downs, where the Whiteheads had spent their summers for many years. When the conversation had regained momentum, I brought up his remarks of a year ago about grand opera. He corrected my memory:

"I don't say that Wagner isn't magnificent or that I didn't enjoy him. What I say is that an ideal of power and glory appealing to racial saga is fatally easy to misconstrue and has, as a matter of fact, *been* misconstrued. Struggle, ambition, heroic energy—these are noble, as potentially noble as anything in man; but when they decline into a mere love of domination they are evil."

"When I try your remark that such a series of music dramas could have wrecked the political genius of the English people in a generation, they say, 'Shakespeare!' "

There was a good deal of laughter and I got chaffed. In fact, I chaffed myself.

"Last summer they got me into the Memorial Theatre at Stratford-on-Avon for a performance of *King Henry V* and, at the end of three hours, three centuries of history had been so obliterated that I didn't care whether I was an American or an Englishman. You may say that it is the music that repeals the ethical sense, but I say Shakespeare's poetry can be just as insidious."

[92]

For a while we talked of small-town, suburban, or country people as desirable human types. Mrs. Whitehead described a Seattle woman who has brought up four handsome, manly sons:

"She talks platitudes—*and* yet she is the salt of the earth."

"How has she done it?"

"By being kind, and full of fun, and keeping them at home. She comes here and we talk platitudes—you should hear me grind them out—but it doesn't matter. The woman is as good as there is."

"How I would like to hear you talking platitudes!" cried Grace, laughing delightedly.

"I wouldn't want you to. It couldn't be true then. But vis-à-vis her only, it is perfectly genuine. We don't say a thing, and yet we understand each other perfectly."

"There you are," said she, "at your very best; and you couldn't be better!"

At ten, in came a tea cart with whisky, soda, ginger ale, and ice. A light fire of logs was burning on the hearth.

In a discussion of war, Whitehead said:

"The absolute pacifist is a bad citizen; times come when force must be used to uphold right, justice, and ideals."

This struck me as rather extreme. Is it as simple as all that?

Grace left at a little before eleven. Mrs. Whitehead had told me that she would, and had asked me to stay a little longer. At eleven they turned on the radio to hear the news:

"One must take the advertisements along with it," said he, "for it is a flash of news and advertisements alternately. They have got us quite depraved. We no longer mind it much, if any. Ask us and we can tell you all about Hecker's ale and some-body's toothpaste which is far and away the best."

They turned it on. Sure enough! A voice came out of the void:

"Snoodledicker's ale is made of toasted barley . . ."

"There," said Mr. Whitehead, grinning, "that's new! I didn't know that before."

Then came news; it was ghastly enough; the bombing of Barcelona; nine refugee Austrians arrived by plane in England, and, denied admission, one took poison at the airport. . . .

They looked at me inquiringly—as though I knew any more about it than they did! All I could find to say was:

"Allow for distorted emphasis. Mornings, as I walk downtown, the headlines fill me with dismay, old hand at it though I am; but at the office when I sit down to the papers for a careful reading, the scares seem to evaporate. This has been going on for the last dozen years, time after time it has looked like another explosion—only it didn't explode. Of course the danger is that we may grow desensitized."

XII

April 28, 1938

ONE of those spring days of sudden summer heat, the thermometer only half a degree under ninety, steam still on in office buildings, and effect, general exhaustion. Nothing and nobody could have induced me to go out for the evening except the Whiteheads, and even there I arrived in a state of wilt at eight o'clock.

The formality of last names has been discarded, and dinner is now a removable feast; conversationally we move faster and farther by ourselves. With windows open to the spring night, we forgot all about the oppressive day.

They talked of their life at Grantchester when Whitehead was a Fellow of Trinity College, Cambridge. They lived in the old Mill House and showed me a coloured picture of it in the *National Geographic* magazine for September 1936. The life of the village went on in all its Chaucerian looseness and in bland indifference to its near neighbour, the university; a bastard child was merely "a little mistyke." The easy-going, good-natured people relied instinctively on the gentry, as they had done for centuries, and the gentry did not fail them—or, if they did, lost caste; and when a liberal candidate for Parliament made the error of denouncing the local squirearchy, there was a storm of anger and he had to be bundled out to avoid unpleasant consequences. The Mill House was charming and picturesque, all but one drawback, rats. They were resisted in various ways, but at times would stage a come-back and have "terrific fights" inside the walls of the ancient dwelling. One got the idea that life there was exciting. They told it with huge gusto, and we had a good deal of laughter.

Later we got on to what Whitehead called "Asking ourselves 'historical riddles' ": whether the Spaniards had maimed their intellect by expelling the Jews and Protestants. He added:

"The gold they brought from the Americas demoralized them. And the armies they sent over Europe drained off more of their best blood. No doubt the soldiers produced their proper number of babies—but not in Spain. The blight, however, did not extend to the arts."

"Did the expulsion of the French Huguenots postpone the French Revolution?"

"Perhaps *caused* it," said he.

"That suggests the German 'forty-eighters.' After the failure of their revolutions, multitudes of Germans got up and came over here."

"You Americans have been fortunate in them. I fancy you got the Germans who could not go it in a stuffy political atmosphere. Note that emigration is always selective, in *some* sense: people must have a strong reason for moving. The reasons may vary from high moral grounds to steamship agents importing cheap labour from southern Europe. . . . If we English had found gold mines in North America instead of arable land and trade, it might have ruined us. Even as it was, after the vivid people had been drawn off by emigration in the seventeenth century, our eighteenth-century people, compared with those of the sixteenth, were a dull lot. . . . And, since we are asking ourselves historical riddles, here is one: didn't the younger Pitt, instead of letting Europe's worn-out dynasties tumble down when they deserved to, promote the present collapse of Europe by getting up a war to beat Napoleon and put them back in power for a hundred years during which things got too bad to manage? Didn't Pitt have one of the greatest decisions to make in the history of humanity, and make it wrong? . . . listening to Burke and that lot, instead of to the liberals?"

Later in the evening he said, "I have been meditating on the relation of technique to art, and have a theory; whether it can be sustained I am not sure. It is that in the early stages of an art, technique comes in as a means of expression for the burning conviction that is in the artists. It is often ragged. Take the cathedrals: you get something profoundly moving, and, at elbows with it, something clumsy but which does not detract from it. Then as the art matures and the technique gets established and transmissible by teaching, the bright boys are picked out who can learn the technique readily, to the neglect of the boys who have magnificent dreams. The work is clever and finished but lacks depth."

We started rummaging among the arts to test it. He thought Raphael was one of the clever technicians who appear at the moment when the profundity begins to be lost, and Milton another; and the flamboyant style in Gothic a further example.

"English Gothic," said he, "runs through about four centuries, 1100 to 1500, and through four successive styles—Romanesque, Early English, Decorated and Perpendicular—each style lasting, roughly, about a century, up to the sixteenth when it begins to peter out. What was happening in those four centuries was that new aspects of the idea of Gothic architecture were being discovered and developed. Its possibilities of novelty looked endless, but by the 1500's they began to look used up, I don't say that they *were* used up. Then you get a complete break. Builders go back to the architectural style of Greece and

Rome, 'Renaissance': they adapt that style for every usage in the modern world from church to railroad station, so that in London you get instead of a Gothic abbey, St. Paul's Cathedral, and in New York, the Pennsylvania railroad station, which is modelled after the baths of Caracalla in Rome."

We tried this theory on the art of Greek tragedy, and sure enough! here was the same life cycle: Aeschylus has burning moral convictions, his technique in *The Persians* is little more than that of a cantata or an oratorio; but in the *Agamemnon* it is highly advanced. In the extant plays of Sophocles you have the balance of a middle period: there is still strong conviction, the ideas are expressed with tremendous force, and at the same time with a technical mastery which releases their power to the full. In this group are the *Antigone* and the two *Oedipus* plays. By the time Euripides arrives, technique is so well understood that it can be juggled; but while there is still strong conviction and the ideas are powerful, the spirit is one of sceptical criticism.

We found that what we were discussing in terms of techniques were the life cycles of art-forms. Such cycles can be traced in Greek sculpture, in Renaissance painting, and in modern music, beginning three centuries ago and coming on down to the twentieth, when the technique of symphonic orchestration is so well understood that it can now be taught to the bright boys. . . .

"Some of these bright boys," Whitehead's theory had let in a flood of light, "put on dazzling shows of technical fireworks, brilliant flashes and bangs; they can astonish the natives with previously unheard-of combinations of sounds, can shock the daylights out of the old folks by using the naughty four-letter words of harmonic dissonance and atonality; but believing in nothing they have nothing to say, and the once-powerful idea is stone dead."

"Yet it may have a resurrection," cautioned Whitehead. "There are ideas which have lain in their tombs for centuries, then rising again, have revolutionized human society. Some boy who is more than merely bright gets hold of an idea which has long been supposed to be dead, and it comes to life in his hands. For when a young man is all in a glow over the discovery of a great idea, it is not so much the particular idea he has discovered that is important, as it is his glow over it. There you have the sense of adventure, of newness, the old idea has been seen freshly in some new aspect. For the vitality of thought is in adventure. *Ideas won't keep.* Something must be done about them. When the idea is new, its custodians have fervour, live for it, and, if need be, die for it. Their inheritors receive the idea, perhaps now strong and successful, but without inheriting the fervour; so the idea settles down to a comfortable middle age, turns senile, and dies; but the institutions organized around it do not stop; they go on by sheer force of acquired momentum, or like the dead knight borne along on his horse."

He did not particularize.

XIII

January 17, 1939

WHITEHEAD is now professor emeritus. He is in his seventy-ninth year, and since his retirement, owing to reduced income, they have moved from Radnor Hall to a four-room apartment in the Hotel Ambassador on Cambridge Street. On the fifth floor, their windows look out over the treetops southward, and westward to green dooryards and shade trees, and the delta where stands that red-brick, secular cathedral, Memorial Hall.

Most of his library had been fitted in here; a study where books are shelved from floor to ceiling on four sides, interrupted only by one door and one large window, and in the dining-room three more walls of them, where they have been treated so decoratively that one is hardly aware of them as an intrusion. The living-room is fairly spacious, and here the arrangement of furniture is so skilful and the effect so pleasing that although there is no fireplace, it is not much missed, and when conversation starts it is not missed at all. Again, as at Radnor Hall, the walls are tinted a shade just off black, and instead of being gloomy, it is restful.

Since it is no longer practicable for them to give dinner parties, guests are invited in after dinner for conversation. Robert Cunningham had driven down from Exeter, and we were dining in evening dress at Durgin-Park in the market district, which is nothing unusual since men and women go down there to dine before the opera in full regalia, the attraction being that you get a better dinner than you would in a swagger hotel, and at marketmen's prices.

One of Cunningham's former pupils at Exeter, now a freshman at Harvard, seeing us, came over and spoke. Here was his schoolmaster all dressed up and dining in the market, where was he going? The boy was all excitement and devoured with curiosity.

"Is it a date?" he asked.

"Yes," said Cunningham, "heavy."

He was aching to know. Finally Cunningham said:

"We are going to Professor Whitehead's for conversation."

Nick was as wise as before.

With the Whiteheads we found Mr. and Mrs. Richard Gummere, he being chairman of the Committee on Admissions for Harvard College. They were Philadelphians, Quaker in their religious sympathies, and he was formerly headmaster of Penn Charter School. Presently we were joined by Mr. W. G. Constable, curator of paintings at the Boston Museum of Fine Arts, whither he had come from the National Gallery in London. He is an Englishman of wide experience, learning, and cultivation, and such pleasant company that one always rejoices to see him. Last came Grace DeFriez, in black furs and black velvet, her usual sparkle of geniality and high spirits a little heightened by having just come in out of the winter night.

Whitehead talked of the differences between the seventeenth and eighteenth centuries in England. He thought the seventeenth-century Englishmen had more depth: "Their dominant interest was religion, as against the 'debunking' of the eighteenth-century rationalists. 'Debunking' is a good thing to have done, but is comparatively shoal water. Johnson, a sturdier figure, was still in essence of the seventeenth century. If he and Voltaire had met, they wouldn't have had much to say to each other. One trouble with the eighteenth century was that so many of the earnest people had emigrated to the colonies, leaving only the other kind to predominate. They had pale monarchs, shadowy figures from the Restoration till the Guelphs, whose dynasty was that of tame kings holding tenure at good behaviour, the country being managed by a committee from the aristocratic class. George III, the only masterful one, bungled badly our affairs with the American colonies; and we never should have fought Napoleon. What had we in common by that time with continental monarchism? We should have kept quiet and watched them."

"How much of such epochs, do you think, are caused collectively, and how much brought about by exceptional individuals?" asked Cunningham.

"The surrounding social conditions for a great age have to be present, but much, if not all, depends on the chance of there being a powerful personality to set it going. Lacking that, the occasion peters out. John Wesley was such a figure. He ignited two others, and they roused the serious part of the nation. But in times which are ripe, when such dynamic personalities do not appear, the opportunity is lost. Much depends on the chance production of a great man whose powers are adapted to the needs of his age. He voices those needs."

"Who would you say," asked Cunningham, "are the ablest people in England today?"

"The upper artisan class."

This did not surprise some of us, but Cunningham, a former

Rhodes scholar at Queen's College, Oxford (by way of Princeton), wanted it a little more precise:

"Not the intellectuals then?"

"I never can sufficiently get my friends to understand that the intellectuals do not speak for the country," said Whitehead. "If you want to hear that voice and watch it act, wait for the back streets, the quiet people of the middle and working class. When they act, the intellectuals are brushed aside."

"They are the 'respectable,' " said Mrs. Whitehead lightly. "And I honour them for it. Their religious life is lived once a week."

"But does religion cramp the style of the artisans?" asked Richard Gummere.

"Quite the contrary," said Whitehead smiling blandly. "They are nonconformists, 'chapel people,' and the first thing they think is that the Church of England should be disestablished. That makes them aggressive!"

He asked me where I thought American liberals mainly come from. I postponed the question, but asked why doctors are so reactionary in their social thinking.

"When I was in Cambridge, at Trinity," said he, "the question came up whether to award degrees to women. On the one side were men who worked in laboratories, and on the other, including physicians, those who worked with human beings. Almost to a man those in favour of granting degrees to women were the people who dealt with lifeless matter, while those who dealt with women as living creatures were opposed. In London I saw a good deal of physicians. After their day's work when they picked up their book or paper they were too spent to think on what they read."

"In this country," said Mr. Gummere, "doctors are scientifically acute and humanely sympathetic, but you must not expect them to understand social questions."

"Does a doctor see all of a human being?" asked Grace.

"No," said Whitehead. "When a man is full of beans he

doesn't say, 'Look here, let's go and see a doctor.' The doctor is the last person he is thinking of. He only sees us when we are a bit off our feed, and with the psychiatrist it is even worse; he only comes in when our friends are beginning to be worried about us. Taken as a whole, I think the professional classes are bad judges outside of their professions."

"This brings us back to your question about American liberals. Before the war, and perhaps still, many of the best of them came from fairly comfortable middle-class families where there had been good schooling and religious instruction. Then they either saw poverty by living in some social settlement house, as Jane Addams or Lillian Wald, or encountered some dynamic personality like Brand Whitlock, or as Newton Baker did in Tom Johnson of Cleveland. Then there were the radical journalists who became authors, the group which included Ida Tarbell, Ray Stannard Baker, and Lincoln Steffens."

"What happened to their religious faith?" asked Grace.

"It turned to social service."

The question was raised whether any equivalent class is in prospect now.

"When I first lectured in American colleges," said Whitehead, "—roughly, from 1924 to 1929—in those five years, I soon saw if I used a quotation from the Bible that not one of my students had ever read it, ever intended to, or had the least idea what I was talking about, and if they sensed that I was speaking of religion they leaned back until I should have got on to something else; but in the years from 1929 to my retirement, the last seven years of my active teaching, this attitude changed, and when I spoke of religion there was an attentive leaning forward."

"I see it among the young men I encounter at the museum," said Constable. "Their work, with them, is passionately felt as a religious mission. This acts irrespective of income; the sons of the wealthy feel it the same as those who have hardly enough money to get along on."

"Might this mean," I asked, "that the religious spirit of our time, which seems to be subsiding from the churches, may be going to reincarnate in the form of artistic and creative activities?"

No one cared to pick this up. For a diversion the talk veered to the subject of interior decoration. Mr. Constable said:

"One of my duties at the National Gallery in London when estates were being broken up was to go and see if they contained anything of national importance. Often I went into rooms where the masters themselves had never been; it was not only my right but my function. One found the oddest things. In a great house where the top story of a wing had been partitioned off for maids' rooms in the eighteenth century, I went along the corridor and found a complete dozen of Chippendale chairs, two in a room (the rooms were six), where they had been apportioned perhaps a century before. All I had to do was set the chairs out in the corridor. Down below, in the mansion's rooms of state, was Victorian black walnut."

"When I see English furniture," said Whitehead, "it looks as though its origin had generally been a comfortable but not pretentious house somewhere near the middle of the social scale. From there it might move in either direction, up or down; but generally kept its distinctive quality of comfort. In France . . . (My wife, who has lived there, will correct me if I am in error." —"Not publicly, my dear," said she, rising to pass the sandwiches.) ". . . wherever I see furniture," he resumed, "it always strikes me as an imitation, good or bad, of something in a palace."

The three English people fell whimsically to comparing their impressions of the British royal palaces.

"I have never been at Buckingham," said Mrs. Whitehead to Constable. "Have you?"

"Yes. Much of it is about what you might expect, pretty awful: lambrequins, and long fringe around the bottoms of the chairs; but even in the big rooms of state there is always some concession to comfort, some suggestion of human beings making themselves at home there."

Mrs. Whitehead laughed, "Exactly the same at Windsor."

Conversation veered back to the subject of religious enthusiasm.

"Religion in England," said Mrs. Whitehead, "isn't a thing to be enthusiastic about. That wouldn't be respectable!"

"No," said Mr. Whitehead, "we get our enthusiasm done for us by the Welsh and Scots."

"And the religious spirit of both gets into politics. Lloyd George, for example, came out of a Welsh chapel."

The death of Yeats had been announced and it led to a discussion of the Celtic revival.

"I think the attempt to revive the language itself was a mistake," said Whitehead. "The Irish have made a distinct contribution to English with the sounds they give it and the Gaelic is something only a few would understand. It resulted in many being taught Gaelic but remaining illiterate in English."

"When the Abbey Theatre first came on tour to Cambridge," said Mrs. Whitehead, "I had Alfred give them lunch at the college. Yeats was the *poseur*; tousled hair, adoring females in attendance, one permitted to carry his muffler, another his raincoat. He had written some splendid poetry, but certainly was conceited. There was one young man, shabbily clad, who said almost nothing and coughed dreadfully. After lunch someone took them the rounds of the college, but this young man stayed behind with Alfred and me. And then! Three hours, he talked brilliantly. We hadn't got his name. But after they were gone, we told each other, 'No matter who he is, the man is extraordinary.' At that time he had published nothing. Later we found out that his name was Synge! We hugged ourselves that we hadn't had to be told."

The group broke up at about eleven. While Cunningham and I stayed to replace the chairs and carry off the plates and tumblers, we talked of Celtic dialects in Breton and Irish, about Celtic racial types and of where the most beautiful human beings are to be seen. Northern Italy, they thought, especially the blond Italians up into the Italian cantons of Switzerland. English? "No," said Whitehead. "They are wholesome and rugged but seldom beautiful." There was another vote for certain parts of Southern Italy, where the people still seem to look like the old Greeks of Magna Graecia.

They were in high spirits. The evening had gone well. Before leaving, Grace DeFriez had said to me privately:

"A dinnerless party that went better than most dinner parties."

XIV

February 27, 1939

In the *Atlantic Monthly* for March, which was already on the news-stands, was Whitehead's "An Appeal to Sanity," occasioned by the excitement over Czechoslovakia; but Whitehead's discussion so transcended the immediate issues that one finished it feeling in a larger world. An editorial précis of his essay had been published in the *Globe*.

That evening he said genially:

"We have been reading each other."

"Mine is only to advertise the existence of yours. Also, I have sent a copy to Barrington-Ward of the London *Times*."

"It was written last November," said he. "Everybody has forgotten Czechoslovakia by now."

"That is precisely its value. The immediate occasion may be fading, but the historical processes you relate it to don't fade at all."

"Originally," said Mrs. Whitehead, "it was started as a letter to Felix Frankfurter. He was pressing us on the subject, and rather vigorously."

E*

"With his keen sense of justice these times must be peculiarly painful to him."

"Then, too," she said, "there is a strain of the crusader in Felix."

"The way he spent himself trying to get a fair trial for Sacco and Vanzetti," I said, "strikes me as something more abiding than mere crusading zeal."

"I always think of him as a Viennese," she said affectionately. "He has their gaiety, although, God knows! there hasn't been much to inspire it in the past half-dozen years."

"The day his appointment to the Supreme Court was announced," said Whitehead, "Evelyn and I happened to hear it on the radio broadcast. We called a cab and drove over to congratulate him. A few of his students from the law school were already there. It was quite charming: they were immensely pleased and one saw in them what young men are at their best, gracious and kindly."

From here the discussion detoured to a discussion of crusading zeal, and Whitehead remarked of professional crusaders that "their old age is likely to be a melancholy affair; they go from 'cause' to 'cause.' "

"Where, precisely, should a man's crusading zeal abate?" I asked. "When his blood cools?"

"With the professionals," said he, "it never does."

"Your spirited vindication of the Jews in the *Atlantic* prompts me to ask why they are, as you have remarked, so often unpopular."

"They are acute, and their acuteness often takes a form which excites envy, namely, the form of doing well in trade. It is not always depth. In picking men you must guard against the brilliancy of the young Jew. They mature at nineteen or twenty and can seem dazzling, but they do not always fulfil the expectations of them based on their superiority to others at that age."

"Furthermore," added Mrs. Whitehead, "they have not

had the experience of ruling other peoples, or even a state of their own."

"That gives them," said he, "a certain helpful preoccupation with the ideal. They are singularly deficient in humour, or were till they lived among the Europeans. The Bible is quite humourless. After their tragedies they never seemed to have a farce by Aristophanes."

"Situated as they were between military empires, perhaps there was nothing to laugh about."

"The Jew is naturally melancholy," said Whitehead. "And they don't get credit for their enormous achievement, the influence they have had on the development of Europe. Allowing for three centuries to get going, the Bible has been a best seller for fifteen hundred years, and is still. But the Jews get no credit for having produced the most influential book on earth because they insisted that every word of it had been dictated by God."

We discussed their achievements in the creative arts; for example, in music, since that is the dominant art-form of our epoch, or was until the 1920's. In music they give us some first-rate composers, from Mendelssohn to Ernest Bloch, and a great many executants, brilliant performing artists, especially in the past few decades, violinists, pianists, orchestral conductors. Whitehead said they produced good mathematicians.

Watching my chance I asked him how he thought the future would appraise the achievement of Lawrence Lowell.

"His predecessor, what was his name . . . ?"

"Eliot."

"Eliot did a very useful thing; he broke up the classical tradition in the American college. It never could have had the meaning here that it has in Europe because you are too far away from its sources; not only have you no direct geographical contact with the ancient Graeco-Roman civilization, but also none with the mediaeval world which transmitted it. Besides, the humanities, as taught in universities and derived from

Greece and Rome, have a divorcement of the life of contemplation from the practical world that comes of a slave society. The slaves did far too much of the manual work; the hand and brain need to be trained together. Eliot opened the whole field of study for choice, and left it open for quite a while. Finally, in due season, came Lowell, to give it some co-ordination. He came after about the right interval. What he did was very daring and difficult."

"President-emeritus Eliot 'is said to have said,' " I told him, "that after he had devoted his life to turning Harvard from a college into a university, President Lowell was devoting his to turning it from a university back to a college. He may never have said it, and probably the antithesis isn't fair."

"Lowell also," said Whitehead, "took good care of the graduate schools, and did something else that wanted doing; there was the matter of housing the young men."

"Mr. Lowell once told me with pride," said Mrs. Whitehead, "that when he was a boy of sixteen here in Harvard, walking down there on the then undeveloped river flats, he told himself, 'If I ever get power here, I shall do two things: bring the college down to the river, and break the Gold Coast' [1]—and he added, 'I have done both.' "

"In the nineteenth century," said I, "we modelled our university system after the Germans': in the twentieth, we appear to have begun copying the English. I wonder what our own is to be. . . ."

"I am not one of those who look down on what is being done at the big state universities in the Mid and Far West. There you get more attempt at co-ordination between learning and practical life. I think Hutchins, at Chicago, was quite wrong in ridiculing them for their courses in practical techniques. Some of the courses he named 'household techniques' may have been silly courses—that I don't know—but the principle is not. Here, in the East, the sciences do better than the humanities because

---

[1] Dormitories on Mt. Auburn Street for rich men's sons.

there is laboratory work, something to be done, tested, made accurate, not left hanging in the air. . . ."

"Mr. Lowell's pronounced fostering of the 'Department of History and English,' is, as I understand it, an attempt to do something of the sort Oxford does in 'Greats,' in English. But the question remains, how to relate it to practical life."

"Mind you," said he, "I don't say that Greek and Latin aren't excellent for those who can catch hold of their meaning; but I do say that, in America, where you are so removed from immediate contact with the ancient and mediaeval civilizations, it takes more imagination—to get the substance of those older worlds out of books—than all but a few students have. Your friends in Oxford—Sir Richard Livingstone, for example —read Greek and Latin always with an eye to 'How does this affect our life of today? How can we utilize it for the modern world?' "

"Sir David Ross, who was here at Christmas, was speaking of someone's strictures against the American universities— Abraham Flexner's I think—and said that he wrote and thought as though universities exist for research scholars alone, or, if not that, then to produce them—whereas, said he, the number of students who come to a university who are qualified to become research scholars or scientists are very few; and is the whole university system to be designed for the few?"

The question of Mr. Lowell's deficiencies arose.

"He has defects," said Whitehead. "I have known him very well for years and I can see them. One is, that he doesn't understand timid men. He thinks timidity is cringing."

". . . and barks at the man," supplied Mrs. Whitehead. "Altie, tell Lucien that experience you had with a certain modest gentleman who wanted to lay a case before Lowell. . . ."

Fearing that he would not, she did. The man had come to Whitehead saying, "I can't take this to Lowell. He will shout me down. Could you?" "No," said Whitehead, "but I will go with you." He did. Three times, Lowell, irritated by the visitor's timidity, began bawling at him, and thrice did White-head raise his hand and say, "Wait!" The visitor finally got his case stated, and, the mentor being Whitehead, Lowell did not take offence.

"He is the queerest of democrats," said Mrs. Whitehead. "He cannot practise democracy personally but he does believe in it passionately."

"And," continued her husband, "his judgments are states-manlike."

This led into a discussion of Boston as a dwindling Yankee island in an Irish sea.

"They don't mix—these Yankees," said Whitehead, his eyes twinkling with inward amusement. "Only this very afternoon I was in a group of them, including Lawrence Lowell, Lawrence Henderson, and John Livingston Lowes—the last a New Englander at least by assimilation—and you never would have imagined, *you never would have imagined*, from a single word they uttered that they were living in the midst of a community of a million and a half people, at least seventy per cent of whom are Irish Catholics."

I told him how Brüning, sometime Chancellor of Germany, had said during a conversation at Dr. Hans Zinsser's that education should be reserved for an elite.

"Until fifty years ago in England," said Whitehead, "it was confined to a small upper layer, and no one thought it amiss that the mass of the people should be illiterate. Now we take literacy for granted. My father had the running of the village school when schooling was first made compulsory. He encountered the stiffest opposition. The villagers had not been educated and they did not want their children to be educated."

"There was a sudden and immense trek to education in this country after the World War, which has continued ever since," I remarked. "By 1926 it was unmistakable, and it kept right on through the depression. With it has come a higher regard for the teacher."

"In the early nineteenth century in America, as I understand it," said Whitehead, "the teacher, and scholar, and professor were looked up to. They were Unitarians and had a nimbus of religious awe. But as the century wore on, that wore off. Unitarianism was a religion not of 'one God,' but of 'one God at most,' if not of 'one God, if that. . . .'"

"And also," said I, "as the continent was opened, the feeling was at the turn of the century that if a man was what he ought to be, he would make a fortune. This was what made William James call success the 'Bitch Goddess.' That worship is not as prevalent now."

"There are still 'escapists' in your faculties," said Mrs. Whitehead.

"I don't deny that. But men of first-rate ability now not only go into teaching, but are respected for so doing."

A paragraph in Whitehead's "Appeal to Sanity" prompted me to ask again if any state had ever permitted adequate expression to the creative impulses of man. Time and again we see the heads of states, themselves humane men, acting on behalf not of a society's creative impulse but its possessive instincts:

"Herbert Hoover, a Quaker, fed milk to Belgian babies; Herbert Hoover as President of the United States had the war veterans of the Bonus Army bombed out of Washington by tear gas. What is this profound dichotomy?"

"The milk for Belgian babies didn't necessarily imply humanitarian sentiments on his part," said Whitehead. "It was merely an organization job which the sentiment of his time had adjudged had to be done and he was engaged to do it. Quaker, yes; but unimaginative. In his original function as an engineer, his job was to get minerals from mines somewhere in the interior down to tidewater. Such men don't think in terms of human values or human well-being; those items, if they enter at all, come in incidentally to the main object, namely: that of taking up the metal from one place and laying it down in another. They keep their minds fixed on that. . . . When it came to getting the Bonus Army out of Washington, there you had a situation that wanted to be handled very delicately, and he showed how heavy-handed he really was. . . ."

"Then let me cite another instance. In 1914, we had an 'incident' with Mexico. Something provocative happened in the harbour at Tampico, first a squabble, then a dispute over an 'insult' and a demand that the Mexicans apologize and salute our flag. The affair kept worsening, the North Atlantic fleet was ordered to the coast of Mexico, public feeling was inflamed (or, at least, the press vociferated) and President Wilson ordered the Navy to attack and capture Vera Cruz. They did, and seventeen boys were killed, sixteen marines and one sailor. (Two more died of wounds a few days later.) Only half a dozen years before that, Mr. Wilson, instead of being President of the United States, had been a college president, at Princeton, a humane gentleman, like any of your colleagues here, who would have been distressed if seventeen boys in his freshman class had died of an epidemic. The bodies were brought to the Brooklyn Navy Yard on an armoured cruiser, and the coffins each covered with a flag were rolled out on the parade ground on caissons. The President came from Washington to deliver the funeral speech. He said he envied those dead young men. It was Wilson the official who had given the order for them to attack; it was Wilson the man who had to look at the seventeen coffins. Remember, this was in May 1914, and next to no one foresaw the World War; our world hadn't then been calloused by years of mass slaughter; such events were still felt normally, and Mr. Wilson was heart-broken. My point is that as President he was required to act on behalf of collective property interests in a manner which, as a man, he never would have entertained. Only a part of the man was acting, as President, because only a part of man is organized in the state."

Whitehead replied that inside the state men pursue numerous

corporate enterprises which do express other aspects of their natures: educational, charitable, creative, artistic, social; and that perhaps the function of the state thus far is to provide conditions of sufficient tranquillity within which those more varied forms of activity can proceed. Already many of them, such as science and education, are international, and supervene the state boundaries.

What he had said in his "Appeal to Sanity" was:

> *Each human being is a more complex structure than any social system to which he belongs. Any particular community life touches only part of the nature of each civilized man. If the man is wholly subordinated to the common life, he is dwarfed. . . . Communities lack the intricacies of human nature. . . . War can protect; it cannot create.*

Later, in our discussion of this, he said:

"The task of government is not to satisfy everybody, but at least to satisfy *somebody*. If it satisfies one reasonably influential class, or perhaps two, they will try to keep it in power; and the more classes it can satisfy the solider it will be. . . . Civilization doesn't break up when only one major activity, or two, go awry. But in our age economics have swollen into these huge corporate enterprises which bring a new form of oppression that wants coping with; and nationalism has got out of hand; and religious faith has gone to pieces . . . and between the lot of them our civilization does seem to be in a bad way."

"The Emperor Domitian's reign gets a bad press from Tacitus, and no doubt deserved it," I said, "but although it is clear that the emperor's ferocity paralysed Roman thought for nearly a generation and none of the patricians could be sure of their lives, still the wheels of common life were kept rolling. Perhaps it was none of his doing, but it was done."

"Tacitus," said Whitehead, "who so abhorred him, I have always suspected of being a conservative who, on behalf of his class, resented Domitian's raising to positions of administrative authority a lot of social nobodies, clever Greek freedmen and the like. , . .''

"If the Jews have done little laughing until comparatively modern times, how about the Romans? One doesn't hear them laughing either, at least not until the second century B.C. In the earlier centuries they were for ever fighting, now with the Celt, again with the Carthaginian; and when the laughter does come; that is, when you begin to get it in their literature, isn't it satirical, or '*Schadenfreude*'? "

"The Romans"—began Whitehead—"They were a queer people . . ." He thought of it, then decided to give it up!

"The Greek gift for laughter, including laughter at themselves," I said, "begins to look the more remarkable, since there was apparently so little laughter in the ancient world."

"But there is less occasion in America," said Mrs. Whitehead, "for you to study the Greeks, for you are like the Greeks yourselves—creating a new world."

"Quite so," said Whitehead. "The last thing the Greeks would have done would have been to read about what another people thought, or said, or did."

By way of a little laughter for ourselves, we fell to recalling our earliest conscious memories. Hers was of "Biting my father's ear and getting well thwacked for it"; his was as a child of three at a Swiss table d'hôte, being very thirsty and drinking glass after glass of water, till an old gentleman sitting opposite said, "Little boy, you shouldn't drink so much water."—"Whereupon I picked up a spoon, threw it, and hit him in the mouth! My father, quite sensibly, did not punish me. Partly he was amused, and partly, I suspect, he thought it served the old fellow right." Whitehead instanced this as an example of "false memory." "It was being retold in my hearing as I grew up until by the time I was nine I could picture the whole scene perfectly, and thought I remembered it."

I told them they must have been violent children.

XV

July 17, 1939

As respite from the sultriness of midsummer in Cambridge, the Whiteheads were staying with Mr. and Mrs. Edward Pickman at Dudley Farms in Bedford. Trained in the law, a naval lieutenant in the war, Pickman is of the family of the historian Motley and has himself turned to the writing of history, *The Mind of Latin Christendom*, published two years ago.

Dudley Farms has belonged to the family since before the Revolution. There is a brick farmhouse, hip-roofed and with the usual four tall chimneys, two each in the end walls, dating from 1795, and the simplicity of the building has been retained although wings and guest houses have been added. The drive to it from the highway is through seemingly interminable woodlands and meadows, a pine grove here, a pond there, and what Concord people call a "bog garden," all amounting to a New Englandish wild park. Up the river to Concord are similar estates almost boundary to boundary along its bank. These neighbours are known as "the river families."

Theodore Spencer was there. This tall, fair, mild-mannered scholar had just figured in an adventure story typical of our time, when anything can happen to anybody. Along with several other members of the Harvard faculty he was suddenly informed by President Conant that his assistant professorship in English, which he had held on a three-year appointment, would not be renewed. Feeling ran high. One of the ablest academic heads in the country had said, "I may not know much about administration, but I doubt if you can break ten men's lives in a forenoon and expect your institution to go on as before," a doubt which events in the next three years justified. The sequence was dizzying. Professor Spencer had been appointed visiting lecturer in English of the University of Cambridge for 1939–1940. When the second world war began, that university, having a visiting lectureship to fill at Harvard, reappointed Spencer to fill it. Back in the bosom of alma mater. Tableau! At the moment, however, this comedy, known to Spencer's friends as one of Life's Little Ironies, had progressed only to the end of Act I. His sense of humour was quite equal to it, though at moments he found it a bit grim.

There were a dozen of us at dinner. The dining-room is an eighteenth-century kitchen, cavernous fireplace and brick ovens. On its outer side the room opens to a lawn, a garden with a round pool under elms, and a peaceful vista of pastures sloping to the placid current of the river, which Whitehead said he was never tired of contemplating.

Conversation was brisk, but since there were many speakers and it went so fast, it can, at the start, only be summarized. What was being said was that in any assemblage of alleged eminence hereabouts you were likely to find that most of them owed their prestige to being not so much creators on their own account as administrators of cultural institutions—a college, a university, a publishing house, a museum, a conservatory of music, a state government, a library, a hospital, a religious society—and the question was raised whether civilization in America had reached a point where it could identify and utilize administrative ability, but not yet genuine "power of origination," Whitehead's phrase.

From here, since the household is musical and there were musicians at the table, the discussion moved to the singular but little-regarded fact that so many, if not most, of the European composers of first rank, from the youth of Bach to the death of Brahms, a span of two hundred years, were men who not only wrought for the most part outside of institutions, but also owed little to formal institutional instruction. This was the more striking since music is the one art-form in which our world, since 1700, has excelled every other epoch. In consequence, well, what? Apparently, that the spring may decline to bubble up through the marble basin prepared for it, and that the wind of creative spirit bloweth whither it listeth.

At this point someone remarked that the year 1859 was a climax of the nineteenth century. The table started rummaging for verifications and brought out quite a list. Darwin's *Origin of Species*; an essay on political economy by Karl Marx; Dickens's *Tale of Two Cities*; George Eliot's *Adam Bede*; George Meredith's *Ordeal of Richard Feverel*; Thackeray's *The Virginians*; Tennyson's *Idylls of the King*; Fitzgerald's *Rubáiyát*; Wagner's *Tristan und Isolde* . . .

(Pause, while the twentieth century tries to match that score.)

Then ensued a discussion of something which seems to fascinate the people of this country—namely, the superiority of uneducated persons. Pickman, from his experience in the navy, had been immensely struck by it, but thought their three weak points were, generally, an inability to see a long way ahead, to take a line and stick to it over a period of years, and a tendency to confuse public questions with personal ones.

"The mass of people probably determines the general direction of society, but its great men give that direction its precise aim," thought Whitehead. "I put it in the metaphor of a ship; the masses are vessel and crew, genius is captain. . . . The supply of babies in any one year in a land as large as the United States must cover a spread of all the potential talents necessary for any kind of cultural development."

"Any *one* year?" asked Mrs. Pickman genially.

"I'll say five," replied Whitehead smiling. "That will make my argument stronger. . . . But obviously conditions may prevent certain types of talent coming to fruition; that of a musical composer, for instance, in the western states during the past century. Clearly, a general has no chance in peace times."

"Grant," said Spencer, "was a failure, addicted to drink, and living in a log cabin outside St. Louis as late as 1859, in that same climacteric year of the nineteenth century. Four years later he was hero of Vicksburg, and nine years later President of the United States."

"There was more than luck in it, though," said Pickman, addressing Whitehead. "Alfred, you have often spoken of the element of luck in careers. . . . Lee had been an honours man at West Point; he had studied the same textbooks as the Northern generals, knew what moves they were likely to make, and beat them. But Grant was unpredictable."

The dinner-table session adjourned to the living-room. This is contrived a triple debt to pay, being also music room and library. It is quite large and high, open beams supporting a stucco ceiling. Draperies are few, so as not to deaden the sonorities, and there is a grand pianoforte. The bookshelves are well-populated, about four thousand volumes. At the inner end is a large fireplace with the usual assemblage of settees, armchairs, and small tables on opposite sides of the hearth; while the walls east and south open to the grounds by large French windows.

Conversation had moved to why nineteenth-century England should have been a time peculiarly favourable to writers of prose fiction, and what a powerful influence they had in imparting to people the unwritten laws.

"*Middlemarch*," said Spencer, "was the first novel I read as a youth which gave me the feeling that I was being treated as a man and paid the compliment of being talked to without sentimental deceit."

"What parts of it?" asked Mrs. Whitehead.

"The Lydgate-Vincy theme, that disastrous marriage."

"We knew them in Cambridge," said she.

"*Knew* them?" (It was a knockdown for me.) "I never heard that she had taken those characters from life!"

"Oh, but didn't she!" Mrs. Whitehead named names. "Everybody knew it."

Spencer raised the question whether George Meredith's one-time pre-eminence is destined to last.

"I think not," said Whitehead.

"What will defeat him?"

"He lived in a high-grade literary set, rather out of the current of events, and evolved those figures out of his cogitations. When a good writer fails, it is likely to be from too great pre-occupation with clever literary ideas to the exclusion of the broad common human themes. Take Shakespeare, there is hardly an idea or a situation that isn't commonplace, but the language and imagination make them into something that is superb. There should be broad human subjects of interest to everyone, vividly treated."

"We read aloud in our family," said Mrs. Pickman, "and I find that my young people aren't interested in Meredith, but are in Henry James. They don't find his involved sentences difficult to understand and do follow the involutions of his thought. Within the limits of the smaller field that he tilled, evidently he delved deeper. He explores the individual."

"When first," someone asked, "in history does the individual begin to be prized for his own sake?"

"I would have thought our old friends the apostles," said Whitehead. "But no, that won't do, they were subordinated to a theology."

"Can the Greeks serve us here? That remark of Pericles in the Funeral Speech, 'We have no hard words or black looks for people who enjoy themselves in their own way.' Where does the concept of liberty first arise?"

This flowed into a general discussion, but without much agreement, perhaps because too many disputants were in it. Whitehead remarked that among the eighteenth-century thinkers there was a clear prevision that the tyranny of a majority might be more onerous than that of a despot.

Continuing, Whitehead said, "Historians never sufficiently credit the man who *averts* a catastrophe. I am thinking of Augustus Caesar. It has always been a marvel to me that Rome could produce, just when they were most wanted, two such men of genius as Julius and Augustus. People must have wanted order and civilization in their hearts, for the legions were mostly at the frontiers. Not many troops were required to suppress revolts at home."

"The Romans had had more than enough of that in the hundred years of civil war," I remarked. "People were in despair; they had been caught in those terrific duels, first between Marius and Sulla, then between Caesar and Pompey, and finally between Antony and Augustus, and it was by no means certain that they could ever be stopped."

"The effort was risen to and they finally were stopped," said Pickman to Whitehead. "I have heard you say, 'Because the Romans were not yet bored with their civilization.'"

"I stick to that," responded Whitehead. "That we are seated here, in the clothes we wear, and uttering some of the thoughts we do, is in part thanks, I believe, to Augustus. He found a way to keep the empire in being by the principate. He gave men of all parties responsible tasks to which they responded. Gaul was quiet, but Germany" (he smiled), "then as now, was the problem."

"They never did pacify it," I said, "and no wonder. The German forest was nine days' march from one end to the other —dark, damp, no roads, no towns, and the tribesmen always ready to pounce. Gaul was culturally centuries ahead of the Teutons. . . ."

"Had the Gauls a literature then?" asked Whitehead.

"I don't remember any. Unless you want to credit the Gauls with Caesar's *Commentaries*. The difference was that in Gaul, Caesar had roads to travel, crops to live on, and cities and property which the inhabitants were forced to make a stand and fight for; but in Germany, the legions had to make their own roads, and carry their own provisions."

"And then," said Whitehead, "came that fearful disaster in Germany, Varus had perished and with him three of the best legions of the Roman army."

" '*Quintili Vare, legiones redde,*' " Pickman quoted the despairing cry of Augustus ("Quintilius Varus, give me back my legions.") and added smiling, "We are still suffering from the loss of those Roman legions in Germany by Varus?"

"I should think it quite probable," replied Whitehead gravely.

XVI

July 18, 1939

THIS morning at ten the Whiteheads were to return to their apartment in the Hotel Ambassador in Cambridge for a night until North came to take them to "Battleship Island" in Lake Sebago, Maine.

Before leaving, Whitehead, coated and hatted, wanted to step out into the field slope above the river for another look at the scene which he has grown so to love. Pickman and I went with him. Standing in the field and looking across the placid landscape, to the sleepy current of the Concord, conversation turned to the question of a poet's rewards.

"It lies in getting down his thought," said Whitehead. "Something which was unformulated, formulated into a stanza, and he thinks, 'There! I have it!' "

"Is applause of much value to the poet?"

"They must have it, I suppose," said he. "How else are they to know if they are effectual? It is idle to pretend that a man lectures as well if half his audience are drowsing. The response is necessary."

"It can also be an intoxicant."

"It is necessary for the secondary artists; the performers and executants," rejoined Whitehead. "But the poet has his in the doing of it. He *knows* when it is good. . . . And how miraculous it is! Even in common speech. I do not mean thoughts we have first carefully formulated in our minds and then given words. I mean quite unconscious thoughts which spring instantaneously from the unconscious into words without any intermediary process being operative that we know of; that is the most amazing thing. It has never been explained, no one knows the connection between these unconscious meditations and their sudden translation into speech."

The talk turned to Goethe:

"It has been occurring to me of late," said Whitehead, "that Goethe's thinking is too special, and that the world would be better off for the sound, sane, sensible, second-rate sentiments of Schiller. They never rise beyond a certain level but they are safe and serviceable."

"Our friend Livingstone," I remarked, "once said to me that he did not care for Goethe because 'he was not a gentleman.' Three years later, in Oxford, I taxed him with it; he burst out laughing, 'Did I say that? I wonder what I meant.' "

"Goethe uncommonly indulged himself in romantic emotions," said Whitehead, "for which specifically I doubt if the world is much better off."

The drive to Cambridge was through a radiant summer morning. They spoke of their regret at having had to give up their Sunday evenings for the students.

"When we first came to Harvard," she explained, "Altie's colleagues in the department said, '*Don't let the students interfere with your work!* Ten or fifteen minutes is long enough for any conference with them. . . .' "

"Mind you," he supplied, smiling with relish, "they were mostly graduate students, with complex psychological problems to discuss."

"How did you get around it?"

"Altie replied in his most mellifluous tones, which always come out when he is particularly determined to have his own way, 'My habits are too formed. I'm afraid I am too old to change my ways. You will have to be patient with me.' "

"I heard of your Sunday evenings years before I knew you, and longed to come."

"Why didn't you?" said she. "We were told no one *would* come. And the first time no one did—except one Chinese, who stayed till after midnight. We nearly perished! But then they began coming in squads of six, for mutual protection, I suppose. Finally one night they heard me dispute the oracle—on a point where I knew Altie was wrong. We had it back and forth, and finally Altie admitted he was wrong. For some reason —we never knew what—the fame of that travelled. They began to come. I never had more than ninety-odd on any one evening. Next, the Jews heard of it and came in droves. The gentiles stayed away. This lasted two years, we and the Jews having a good time without the gentiles, then the gentiles came again and all was as before. Felix was a great help. He did not talk, but made everyone else talk. My friends couldn't believe that I would not forgo our Sunday evenings for their dinners to famous foreigners, but we never once failed our students."

We had reached the Hotel Ambassador.

"You will come in, won't you?" they asked.

The apartment was in curlpapers for the summer; literally, for during their absence the faithful Mary and John, who have been with them, she for nineteen years, and he for nearly a decade, had dusted all the books and put them back on their shelves covered over with newspapers. Everything smelt fresh and clean. They went around sniffing and exclaiming their pleasure.

"You will stay and have a chop with us?" she asked.

Getting back from the country to an apartment on a July day which by now was sultry turned into a festive occasion. While the promised chops were being cooked by Mary, we sat in his study, a light breeze blowing through.

Europe's fever chart grows steadily worse, and we fell to comparing the behaviour of the fascist dictators to the mad tyrants in Greek tragedy:

"Hitler never would have heard of the Greek doctrine of 'Hybris' and 'Nemesis,' " I said, "and it would mean nothing to him if he had, but the other man has read."

"He has read Machiavelli," said Whitehead, "and

[123]

Machiavelli wrote the rules for a short-term success, of from five to fifteen years."

This led to a discussion of the life span of institutions, and he said:

"The universities are now having a great period, but universities may make themselves as great nuisances as did the monasteries, and for much the same reasons."

"They already have the choice sites," said his wife.

We talked about the abuse of "research" and I cited John Burnet's address on March 12, 1904, at St. Andrews; that the people who talk most about "research" are not those who have done any; it has vulgarized the word and made it offensive to many people. We hear of the "environment of research," "research scholarships," and the like, as if it were all a question of money, but he doesn't suppose that any of the greatest discoveries have ever been paid for at all, and certainly they have all been made by men who had no thought of being paid for them.

"You have heard me criticize the timidity of scholars," said Whitehead. "I think the value of textual criticism is about used up—the immense labour that has gone on since the Renaissance to clear up the classical texts. That has been done. We know now about what the man said. But they will go on re-re-refining, when there is no more value in it."

"Why should science be able to take such leaps, as it has done in the last century, even the last forty years, when the humanities advance so slowly? Are we really much ahead of Plato and Aristotle there?"

"In the eighteenth century," he answered, "(I speak of England where I know what I am talking about) you could follow Rome and Greece of their best ages. The social structures were similar enough for historical precedents to be of some practical value: you still had the mob and the aristocrats. If it was a question of governing a colonial empire, India, you could still follow your Roman model; if a colonial governor was

brought to trial for maladministration—Warren Hastings—
you had Cicero's orations against Verres for his rapacious
governorship in Sicily. . . . Even in the nineteenth century
the Graeco-Roman model could still be fairly closely patterned
after. But now, in the twentieth, this new technology has so
altered the moral values, or the social relationships, that a
much more searching and subtle readjustment of the traditional classic models to modern needs is wanted."

"Well, what is the effect of these scientifically schooled men
on governing the British Empire likely to be?"

"We are sending out as colonial administrators men trained
not in the old humanistic tradition, but products of the scientific schooling. They are just as good intellects, but is their
training as happy? I doubt if they will bring as sensitive an
understanding to the emotional set-up of the peoples they
must rule."

"The Roman Catholic Church is an instance," said I, "of
an institution with an immense experience in governing which
has profited by the learning of the ancient world."

"It is an institution which has learned how to manage
successfully in a monarchical society ruled by an aristocracy,
and when it is proposed to alter that society, to liberalize it on
the side of republicanism or democracy, the Church is generally
found resisting the change. Just now, when certain European
governments are off their heads, the Church sees, or thinks
it sees, an advantage on the side of the fascist dictatorships
as against the kind represented by Stalin. I think they are
mistaken."

"A sociologist of my acquaintance (he is distinctly on the
socialist side) has told me that he believes Catholicism will
survive communism either by adjustment with it or by winning
over it, and this largely because the Marxists wilfully blind
themselves to the emotional needs of average humanity, which
the Church does gratify."

"Catholicism," said Whitehead, "is successful in producing

[125]

rather a fine type of woman, but is not so happy with the men. The men have a need to shake off something which the Church hangs on them, and unless they do, they are ineffective as thinkers. If they remain within the Church dogmas they are always fearful of thinking some thought that will conflict with them. The Church, I think, could safely be more venturesome with its list of permitted books than it is. Emerson would really do their people no harm."

XVII

December 15, 1939

MEANWHILE, the second world war had begun. This was my first evening with the Whiteheads since that event in September. One still approached the subject cautiously with anybody, for feeling ran high and unpredictably. Not here, however. We came to it at once:

"I am firmly convinced," said he, "that America should keep out. You need about fifty years to settle and adjust certain domestic problems which you now seem well on your way to do. If you came in and were deeply involved, it might result in a permanent injury to the future of the world. If we won through your help, as the last time, the settlement arrived at through your presence might lose equilibrium after your withdrawal; it is better for Europe to find its own equilibrium."

"But if we are beaten," said she, "you are bound to come in, for otherwise you will have the Nazis in Canada and South America."

"I doubt," said he, "if the world has ever had suffering on such an enormous scale as this."

"You surprise me. Not Rome under the bad emperors?"

"The suffering and anxiety there were largely confined to the upper classes; but, well, yes, I suppose the suffering of the immense slave population on which that society rested must have been enormous."

"The historian Priscus tells of his visit to the camp of Attila's Huns, passing through territories where whole communities had committed suicide at their approach, arrived at their camp, finding those selfsame warriors full of enthusiasm and singing songs about their own virtues. . . ." (I had intended to relate this to the quantitative aspect of human suffering, when my mind lost the thread. I said so, and said it had been happening to me frequently of late.)

"I am relieved to hear you say so," said he, "for mine does the same and I was attributing it to my age."

"It is fatigue, rather, I think. The consciousness of the war is always there; we are forced to rethink ordinary thoughts with reference to it; often we do this unconsciously, but the effort after a while is exhausting. It is a subconscious drag."

"For a while after the war started," said he, "I was able to do nothing; it was constantly in my thoughts, but now of late I have absorbed it into my mental processes, and I am beginning to work again."

"Scott Nearing, who breakfasted with me this morning (he is one of the war-horses of American liberalism), says the problem of our time is how to live well in a decaying society. I am not so sure. Certainly we do live in a contracting economy, but may not the impact of this scientific technology, and the violence and confusion engendered by it, bring about a re-integration of our society? Better not despair prematurely— not that I suggest that any of us are likely to do so. But every great age, fifth-century Athens, Augustan Rome, the Renaissance, the Reformation, the French Revolution, was preceded or accompanied by violence and upheaval; Persian war in Greece, Roman civil wars before Augustus, and so on. . . . Isn't it too soon to judge? And can we be surprised at what has happened when we think of the mechanical and intellectual changes since the turn of the century?"

"I have lived three distinct lives in this single span," said Whitehead; "one from childhood to the first world war; one from 1914 to my residence in America in 1924; and a third here since 1924. The first seems the most fantastic; in those years from the 1880's to the first war, who ever *dreamed* that the ideas and institutions which then looked so stable would be impermanent?"

"Although I was a little boy when you were already a man grown, that world of the 1890's seems to swim in a golden haze of mythological idyl."

"Fifty-seven years ago it was," said he, "when I was a young man in the University of Cambridge. I was taught science and mathematics by brilliant men and I did well in them; since the turn of the century I have lived to see every one of the basic assumptions of both set aside; not, indeed, discarded, but of use as qualifying clauses, instead of as major propositions; and all this in one life-span—the most fundamental assumptions of supposedly exact sciences set aside. And yet, in the face of that, the discoverers of the new hypotheses in science are declaring, '*Now at last, we have certitude*'—when some of the assumptions which we have seen upset had endured for more than twenty centuries."

"Is that a reason why you are at pains to use a new terminology for your own concepts?"

"You have noticed that, then?"

"I have noticed that I can understand the first third and the last third of your *Adventures of Ideas* and of your essay on the Harvard Tercentenary, but that in the middle third I bog down. Is the middle third over the head of a layman who is willing to keep rereading it?"

"No. I don't think so. I write for the layman, and in so doing I avoid the technical language usual among philosophers."

"The philosophers don't like him for it," said his wife, "though they have been very sweet about it."

"But I am convinced," said he, resuming, "that what

philosophers should do is relate their thoughts to the needs of common life. And there is another thing they need to do. When you consider how at pains men of science are to base their hypotheses on carefully criticized assumptions—how they set up tests to control experiments—then consider how the fundamental concepts of even the greatest philosophers in the past must have been largely conditioned by the necessarily ephemeral environmental relationships in which they lived. The scandal is how unhesitatingly later thinkers have accepted their conclusions without pausing to re-examine them in terms of changed social conditions."

"A striking example of it," said I, "is Aristotle's *Politics*. They must have been based on the fundamental assumption that the city-state is the regnant political form, and that, too, in an age when it was already being outmoded and about to be supplanted by military monarchies on a model derived from the conquests of Alexander the Great, his own pupil."

"That is an excellent example of what I mean. There is an enormous need for philosophies to be rethought in the light of the changing conditions of mankind."

"How much of this can be done by intellect alone?"

"I doubt if we get very far by the intellect alone. I doubt if intellect carries us very far. I have spoken of direct insights. The longer I live the more I am impressed by the *enormous*"— he urged his voice into emphasis, and narrowed his eyelids— "the unparalleled genius of one philosopher, and that is Plato. There seems hardly an insight that he has not had or anticipated; and even after you have allowed, as I was saying a moment ago, for the modifications introduced by changed social conditions since he thought and wrote, and the consequent variations which must be made, still in essence the most of it stands. He came face to face with these realities, truths not directly apprehensible by the average man, then by a marvel of subtlety and dialectic, whittled them down to a form in which they could be grasped by the educated Athenian of his day."

F

It was by now about half past ten. The tray of hot chocolate was brought in. We got on the question whether English Methodism had had any economic determinant.

"Not a bit, I think," said Whitehead. "In John Wesley you had that very unusual combination; a man of spiritual insight coupled with great organizing ability. He organized as naturally as he breathed. I owe to my friend Elie Halévy one of the most penetrating observations on English history that I have ever heard; namely, that the French revolutionary ideas, especially Jacobinism, were prevented from crossing the English Channel by the religious idea of the Wesleyans, who looked upon the Jacobins as godless. The revolutionaries were, as you remember, deists—Robespierre, Saint-Just, and that lot—but to a Methodist that was as good as nothing at all. Then when, at the development of the industrial age, the rich middle-class families began to marry into the aristocracy, it did a singular thing—that mixture gave an aristocracy, almost for the first time in history, a religious tinge which coloured the whole of English political life in the nineteenth century."

"Romain Rolland in *Jean-Christophe*[1] makes someone say that what has made the English so formidable is that they have been for centuries a nation of Bible-readers."

"That sounds more like a literary idea than a historical force." He considered it doubtfully, then said, "The Bible excels in its suggestion of infinitude." Suddenly he stood and spoke with passionate intensity, "*Here we are with our finite beings and physical senses in the presence of a universe whose possibilities are infinite, and even though we may not apprehend them, those infinite possibilities are actualities.*" He remained standing a moment,

---

[1] "England makes me shudder when I think that her people have for centuries been nourished on the Bible. . . . I'm glad to think that there is the dike of the Channel between them and me. I shall never believe that a nation is altogether civilized as long as the Bible is its staple food."

"In that case," said Christophe (a German), "you will have to be just as much afraid of me, for I get drunk on it. It is the very marrow of a race of lions. Stout hearts are those that feed on it. Without the antidote of the Old Testament the Gospel is tasteless and unwholesome fare. The Bible is the bone and sinew of nations with the will to live."—*Jean-Christophe: The House*, Romain Rolland.

absorbed in his own thought, then reseating himself continued, "The trouble with the Bible has been its interpreters, who have scaled and whittled down that sense of infinitude into finite and limited concepts, and the first interpreter of the New Testament was the worst, Paul."

"Do you happen to have read Nietzsche's *Antichrist*?"

"No."

"It sounds more violent than it is, though it is vigorous enough. To my astonishment, he is rather tender toward Jesus, says there was only one Christian and he died on the cross. But Saint Paul certainly does catch it."

"One has to speak of the end of Christianity in terms of a thousand years," he said, smiling, "but it has assumed so many forms in its history that I often speculate on its taking a new and perhaps final form here in America, coalescing with your democratic idea of life. With all its limitations, life in America is better and kinder than anywhere else on earth that I have ever heard of in history. But the clergy have lost their hold. In America a man in trouble now goes to his doctor, he would not think of telling his parson, saving here or there when his parson is an exceptional individual. In England the man people went to in trouble was the old family solicitor; you get that in English fiction; he is a familiar figure there. The problem in religion is to link finitude to infinitude. It is significant that people no longer believe in heaven."

"What would *you* find to do in a Christian heaven?"

"I would far rather go to Limbo, where I could meet the Greek philosophers and Roman statesmen and exchange ideas."

"How," asked Mrs. Whitehead, "could a person beguile the mortal tedium of heaven? At least as it is generally depicted, an oratorio in costumes."

"Something needs to be found to take its place," said he.

"Might not some form of creativity be what is wanted?"

We discussed that. He said:

"Sir Richard Livingstone wrote me that to him the most significant sentence in my *Aims of Education* was the one that says the common man needs to be convinced of the importance of the work he is doing."

"Of his function, not the importance of himself," said Mrs. Whitehead.

"Similarly, the central problem in modern philosophy is how to relate the one and the many," Whitehead resumed. "Plato talks about that. He was right about so many things and sometimes also dreadfully wrong. The modern tendency is to say, 'I am happy *now*. The future does not matter!' but the 'now' is meaningless without a significant future. What is wanted is to relate all the 'nows' with the future."

"What," asked Mrs. Whitehead, "is the distinction between intelligence and ability? I have the idea that we are all delighted to find intelligence in a child or an adolescent but that if we are still admiring it in an adult there is something wrong."

"Isn't there a character in one of Dickens's novels who is always, to the end of his days, spoken of as 'a promising young man'? I suggest that intelligence is quickness to apprehend as distinct from ability, which is capacity to act wisely on the thing apprehended. But what I have been burning to ask is, What do we mean when we say that a person has depth? We know what we mean but can't put it into words."

"Precisely not," said Whitehead, "for depth is the power to take into account all those factors in a situation which cannot be adequately verbalized."

"When they are verbalized," said she, "they flatten out. It is the ability to see around things, and to see them in all their relationships."

"Are we to suppose that it is inherited or acquired?"

"Acquired? No," said she. "Inherited, yes; but developed."

"You get the best ability," said Whitehead, "from children reared in an economic status without luxury, which admits them at an early age to the society of people responsible for a community. The community may be a big one but needn't be; merely responsible persons doing public work. That is one. The other needn't even be in a comfortable economic position, but the child must be born with or reared in ideas strongly moral or religious."

"Your moral and religious senses are what have served you, Altie. You got them from your parson father."

"America," said he, "was founded by people of both these groups, with social responsibility and moral sense. It has often seemed to me that that was why the eighteenth century in England was so flat, the vivid people had come over here in the seventeenth. France did better in the eighteenth. And the principal result of the French Revolution was the American Revolution. It failed in France but in America it succeeded."

This led to a remark about the lack of enthusiasm in Harvard, as distinguished from the tone of the Midwest, and especially among Harvard undergraduates, where enthusiasm was socially bad form. He said it was lacking from the Boston and New York sons of prosperous families and in one-third of the undergraduates, that another, the middle third, are neutral as always, but that the final third have it, boys largely from smaller towns and more remote places. As for the faculty he admitted that the tone of many of them was set up by the upper-class boys. He thought they do not have voice enough in the government of American universities, but they never have had, in contradistinction to England, where they *are* the governing body. Here, it is every professor for his department; at Trinity you had some of that too, but at the bottom they were all one in wanting Trinity to be a place of lively educational value. When London University was being assembled from schools widely sundered, one of the stipulations was that the faculty have a voice in the management of the institution.

"England has evolved its university system. I often wonder how long will it take us to evolve one peculiarly adapted to our own needs."

"The university system in England has changed momentously since 1900," he said. "Before that, you had Oxford, Cambridge, Edinburgh, Glasgow and St. Andrews. Since then all these others have sprung up." He named half a dozen.

Into the discussion then came the question of how to keep thought from freezing into static ideas, and how easy it is for scholarship to wither into dead learning. When the Senior Fellows were last choosing from among the candidates for the Junior Fellowships, he said a young archaeologist had read a learned paper to the committee on whether a certain excavated pillar was dated wrongly three years one way or the other!

"(And Ferguson sat chin-on-left-hand scowling concentration,
(and Chase sat chin-on-right-hand scowling concentration,
(and Lowes sat chin-on-both-hands scowling concentration,
(and all the while it didn't matter one way or the other.) But a young fellow named Charles Moore [1] presented a paper on Sophocles which was so good that if it wasn't true of Sophocles, it *ought* to have been."

"How old is he?"

"About twenty-two, I should say."

"That seems young to understand so much about Sophocles."

"Perhaps he doesn't; but two of us said he should get in if over our dead bodies."

From here Whitehead turned the subject to Boston newspapers:

"The *Herald*," said he, with a slightly heightened sparkle, "gives the point of view of the prosperous businessman admirably—perhaps too admirably—but if you want to know what New England of all classes is thinking—and I do want to know —it is the *Globe* that you must read. We hazard a guess that a good many of the editorials on foreign relations, especially those about British foreign policy, are written by an irate Irishman."

[1] Mr. Charles Moore did understand some very remarkable things about Sophocles.

"They are."

"He is quite within his rights; only he gives undue importance to a phase of Tory influence which annoys him."

"His grandfather was knocked down and beaten by British troops in Ireland. The memory was still vivid with his grandmother when she told him about it. He is a man of extraordinary ability, with high principles which are kept in daily working order."

Without asking who had written it, they spoke of the editorial on music published November 24th. In it I had said that great music, even more than great literature, is intelligible to children, since it speaks directly to the emotions, the imagination, and the intuitions, faculties which in childhood are often more acute than they are when we have grown up, and that no blunder could be more stupid than to suppose children do not sense grandeur in the arts. While agreeing with it in the main, he said:

"Not all children respond to music. About fifty per cent, I should say. It would have been better to qualify. Mind you, I agree with your main contention, that all children have a right to be presented to these major experiences, in literature, the arts, nature; they can then select those which will be fruitful to them. I was especially struck by your remark that the charm of good music is that it surprises the ear by the unexpected interval, and that the element of surprise is permanent, no matter how familiar the music may become. It is a principle which carries over into other affairs of life; what we crave is the element of freshness, and some of the most vivid experiences seem to have in them an element of freshness which is perpetual. This carries over, too, into related areas of experience, so that when we are freshened in one area it freshens us for others."

"My home environment," I said, "a small town, was so aesthetically barren that we were forced upon books and music (apart from friends, and what beauty of nature there was) in order to keep our souls alive."

"His, too," said Mrs. Whitehead, "a country parsonage, was a milieu where the aesthetic was not only absent, but held in contempt."

"Your saying that this freshening of the whole nature by a novel experience, of which music is an example, carries over into other affairs of life reassures me after what Bliss Perry [1] said about this same subject: 'I don't see how you can transform sound-patterns from music into moral concepts.' "

"But that is exactly what music does do," said he, "revivifies the whole nature."

"How can anybody be the same person after a close knowledge of Beethoven's last quartets that he was before?"

This led Whitehead to speak of the striking difference between the seventeenth-century poets in England and those of the eighteenth. "With the eighteenth-century men you never find anything in their poetry that you don't think you could have written yourself; but the charm of the seventeenth-century English poetry is that you come upon something totally unexpected and say, 'There! It is inconceivable that I could ever have thought of this!' "

It was growing late, and for a little while by tacit consent we let the conversation drift.

His *Aims of Education* is out of print in America, and I told him that people I know keep complaining to me that they cannot obtain it. He said it was not out of print in England, "But Macmillan burned their unsold copies without offering me an opportunity to take them off their hands, a performance which made me indignant."

"For a distinguished firm, they certainly do some strange things—the mud-coloured binding, for example, of the *Cambridge Ancient History*, whose English edition is nobly bound.

---

[1] Bliss Perry, university professor, author. Born Williamstown, Mass., 1860. A.B. Williams College 1881, A.M. 1883. Professor of English at Williams 1886–1893, Princeton 1893–1900; editor *The Atlantic Monthly* 1899–1909; professor of English literature Harvard 1907–1930.

I bitterly regret not having bought mine in the English format."

"I am considering republishing my *Aims of Education*. Tell me what you think of omitting those last two chapters."

"Considering that I couldn't understand them I am a poor one to ask."

"On the contrary, you are just the one."

"The first eight chapters are electrifying. How many of my friends have told me so, Livingstone, for one. Why not omit the last two and substitute your essay on the Harvard Tercentenary?"

"I had thought of that, too; but would the book be long enough?"

"Haven't you something else that would fit in?"

"I have a good deal of unpublished work. . . ."

Mrs. Whitehead suggested various papers that might fit.

"I also have an idea of a volume of reminiscences," said he.

We discussed format, and that it might be wise to keep an eye on publishers about cover designs, in view of some dire experiences.

"When the cover Macmillans were going to put on his *Adventures of Ideas* arrived," said Mrs. Whitehead, "I was aghast."

"What was it?"

"A moon, and stars, and rays of light."

"What was the notion?"

" 'Adventures,' I suppose, and cosmic space."

"Jazzing Whitehead!" said I. "Do you suppose the designer had read the book?"

"Probably no more than heard the title," said she.

As the evening drew to a close he returned to the influence of the Bible, and to its interpreters:

"Two strains seem to run through Hebrew thought; one, mild, gentle, gracious, sympathetic, and full of insight: Isaiah, Amos, Jesus; the other, harsh, vengeful, humourless, treacherous: the very characteristics of the oriental despot. Both

[137]   F*

are in Paul, but the second comes out strongly. The Semites are harsh. I often wonder if there wasn't an infiltration of Hellenic blood in the Galileans to account for the graciousness of those peasants and Jesus. For if you follow the interpretation of the Gospels in their first four or five centuries, you will find that the Christian thinkers on the African shore of the Mediterranean and on to Spain, who were mainly under Semitic influence, are gloomy and harsh; but that the Italian and Gallic interpreters, Gregory the Great and Martin of Tours, were remarkably tolerant. When the issue of persecution of their own sectaries was first raised, these men saw and said that persecution would do more harm than heresy. These two strains in the Hebrew are greed for material gain, and gentleness of spirit; sometimes, in great Jews, you find both strains in one nature. It is the *interpreters* of Christianity that have been its misfortune."

XVIII

April 22, 1940

WHITEHEAD had asked me to one of the regular Monday evening dinners of the Junior Fellows at Eliot House. On the drive down there from the Hotel Ambassador in a taxi, I asked if he had read the narrative by the British seaman from the destroyer that was sunk at Narvik.

"No," said he, "in a time like this, news that is a week old might as well be about the battle of Marathon." He said it genially, but the remark shows how keenly aware he is of situations affected by changes wrought through time.

At Eliot House we crossed a court and entered by a side door under a bracket lamp held in a wrought-iron lantern. The spring evening was mild and a fine mist was falling, borne in by an east wind off the sea. The forsythia shrubs were in golden blossom.

President Emeritus Lowell and Lawrence Henderson [1] were already there in the common-room with Sam Morison,[2] who considerately let me read a list of the twenty-four Junior Fellows and their subjects of study. Twenty-four names and twenty-four subjects of study are not memorized at a glance, but some of it at a pinch may come back.

"Go easy on the preprandial sherry," Morison warned me *sotto voce*, "it's not much good. Go strong on the Burgundy during dinner. Henderson chose it and he knows wine. Shun the after-dinner port. Lowell gave it, and he knows nothing about wine. It is merely a fortified California port, but the Fellows must drink it up. There are two views about it: one is to drink it up at once and get it over with; the other is to go slow, because Lowell might give us some more."

Mr. Lowell is of course quite deaf, and, as he finds it easier to speak than to be spoken to, conversation with him is, if he likes, allowed to become a monologue.

He was discussing how the English manage their political opposition:

"Party lines are much stricter there, and if you are in the government you must vote with it. The historian Lecky told me, 'I am perfectly free to vote against the government of which I have been a member for eighteen years.' I asked him, 'How often have you voted against it?'—'Twice,' said Lecky."

Continuing the subject of a political opposition Mr. Lowell adduced the Report on German Atrocities in Belgium headed by Lord Bryce which, by a singular coincidence, was made public by the British government on May 12, 1915, five days

---

[1] Lawrence Joseph Henderson, biological chemist. Born Lynn, Mass., 1878. A.B. Harvard 1898, M.D. 1902; Sc.D. Cambridge 1934. Lecturer biol. chem. Harvard 1904–1905, instructor 1905–1910, asst. prof. 1910–1919, professor since 1919. Senior fellow, Society of Fellows, Harvard since 1933. Died 1942.

[2] Samuel Eliot Morison, historian. Born Boston, Mass., 1887. A.B. Harvard 1908, Ph.D. 1912, Litt.D. 1936; M.A. Oxford 1922. Instructor and professor of American history at Harvard since 1915. Author, *Maritime History of Massachusetts*, 1921; *Oxford History of the U.S.*, 1927; *Tercentennial History of Harvard Univ.*, 1930–1936; *History of U.S. Naval Operations in World War II*, 1947——Rear Admiral U.S.N. (retired).

after the sinking of the S.S. *Lusitania* by a German submarine, when public opinion in the United States was acutely inflamed. He said the report was an example of the mischief that could result from not appointing "an *advocatus diaboli*. . . . You don't get at the truth without a cross-examination of the evidence," he concluded.

(Mindful of Sacco and Vanzetti, I thought, "Nor sometimes with it.")

He moved on to the advisability of due postponements before naming avenues and public places after the illustrious. One of the young men said:

"Didn't the French have a rule not to name a street after a personage until he had been dead ten years?"

"The Catholic Church," said Mr. Lowell, "is even more deliberate: before canonizing it may wait a hundred. . . ."

A gong was struck. It was a signal to go into the dining-room.

The rooms are rather sumptuous. I had first seen them when they were being built, in 1930, but at that time their destined use was not allowed to be known, since the money was not yet available for the foundation of the society. (When Mr. Lowell died in 1943 it was revealed that he had endowed it: ". . . there being no visible source of the necessary funds, I gave it myself, in a kind of desperation, although it took nearly all I had.") As organized on December 8, 1932, there are two-dozen Junior Fellows and nine Senior Fellows. The Junior Fellows are men between twenty and thirty years old, chosen by the Senior Fellows from among the recent graduates of American universities for their promise of exceptional ability to enrich knowledge and thought. They are elected for three years, with prospect of renewal for another three. Given their board and lodging, they are paid a stipend and set at liberty to pursue any intellectual adventures that they find interesting and important. The plan [1] originated by a species of spontaneous combustion

---

[1] It is fully explained in *The Society of Fellows* by George C. Homans and Orville T. Bailey, published by Harvard University, Cambridge, Massachusetts.

with Lawrence Henderson, Alfred Whitehead, and President Lowell, and it derives somewhat from the prize Fellows of Trinity College in Cambridge University and at All Souls College, Oxford, and the *Fondation Thiers* in Paris.

Both rooms are panelled in oak from floor to ceiling, their tall windows flanked by fluted Ionic pilasters and draped with heavy brocades in a colour to harmonize. The chimney-pieces are similarly framed in pilasters with overmantel panels and ornate carving. The oval table from which sherry is served before dinner is the Breakfast Table at which the Autocrat presided, and on the walls hang oil portraits of eighteenth-century worthies, one by John Singleton Copley.

The dining table is *U*-shaped and, with ease of conversation in mind, narrow enough to permit of give and take across its candle-lighted board. The silver candlesticks are of a design which Lawrence Henderson found at Névache, France, at the time when he first began thinking of the plan of such a society. Mr. Lowell, as chairman, sits at the head of the table in a high-backed chair of carved oak, the other diners have arm-chairs of the traditional Harvard design. The port coasts along the board in two decanters set in a little silver wagon, suggested perhaps by the silver galleon which sails laden with port over the mahogany at All Souls.

One of the unwritten decrees is that guests and Senior Fellows do not sit side by side. This mixes the Junior Fellows with the older men. Thus in Whitehead's immediate group were Harry Levin,[1] George Homans,[2] Conrad Arensberg,[3] and George Hanfmann,[4] a young German who has been through two revolutions and said it was not until he had been in this country two years that he could believe he was actually safe in saying what he thought.

[1] Professor of English, Tutor in the Department of English, and Senior Fellow of the Society of Fellows, Harvard University.
[2] Associate Professor of Sociology, Harvard University.
[3] Associate Professor of Sociology, Columbia University.
[4] Associate Professor of Fine Arts, Harvard University.

The five of us, who were within speaking-range of Whitehead, were discussing whether it would ever again be possible for a single mind to grasp the sum of human knowledge, at least to the extent that Aristotle, Da Vinci, or Goethe grasped that of their own time.

Whitehead said he thought such a grasp necessitated too much reliance on the reports of others and brought it down to a mediocre level:

"Aristotle did harm by allowing people to suppose they knew and understood all about the subjects he discussed, and he certainly didn't help Plato."

"Gilbert Murray said something highly similar about Aristotle—especially when Aristotle came to drama," I recalled. "He was talking about the ecstatic element in the *Bacchae* of Euripides, the Dionysian 'possession,' and said, 'After all, isn't μηδὲν ἄγαν (nothing too much) the motto of a Philistine?'"

"That is it," said Whitehead. "To get really into a subject takes more energy than 'nothing too much,' and a man has to ignore much to get on with something. A certain element of excess seems to be a necessary element in all greatness." And, as an example of the opposite he quoted a remark about someone "who knew forty-one languages and had nothing to say in any of them."

Then he and two physicists fell to discussing the alertness and intuition necessary to a good experiment—how it is "competent work plus a 'happy chance,' or even being aware that something is wrong with the result, the discovery following from having asked, 'What?'"

"The heavy hydrogen," continued Whitehead, "was on several men's plates before another man discovered it. Error itself may be the happy chance."

It was suggested that we were here in the problem of how to keep thought active and living, as in his essay on the Harvard Tercentenary in the September *Atlantic* for 1936. He said:

[142]

"I put the things for the rather simple people at the start, and repeated them at the end, but the serious matter in the middle. And the best thing in it came by accident. The editor sent it back saying that it was a little too short for the run-over page and would I add about a hundred and fifty words? With a transitional sentence I found I had added one hundred and sixty-eight words, about the length of a sonnet, and it was the best in the work. I wonder if you could identify the passage."

"Do you challenge me?"

He smiled and nodded:

"Yes."

"Meanwhile, until I shall have had a chance to re-read it, what do you think of Robert Hutchins's reply to it in the following November issue?"

"Hutchins—whom (mind you) I admire—nevertheless treated me like a lawyer, separated certain of my remarks from their context, and then attacked them. I had admitted that a lot of vocational rubbish is taught, and dismissed it."

There was a lively discussion of how long a man can sustain various forms of mental labour effectually. Evidence came in from first and secondhand. Some of the tall tales about scholars working all hours suggested mere acquisitive learning, since certainly most creative artists seem obliged to content themselves with three or four at a stretch.

One of the Junior Fellows (I think it was George Homans) steered the subject to the writing of history. "Gibbon," said Whitehead, "had the best education of any historian excepting Thucydides; he had belonged to a regiment, captain of Hampshire Militia, and knew what that felt like; he knew the London literary set, Johnson and that lot; he had travelled and knew the Continent; and had been in Parliament and heard the talk of men who governed."

"But they didn't govern very well," said Homans. "The prime minister was Lord North, who lost the American colonies."

[143]

"I submit," said Whitehead smiling, "that a man who lost a war was the very most valuable acquaintance for a man who was going to write the *Decline and Fall of the Roman Empire*."

A question arose of what is the difference between active and static thought.

"Static thought," said Whitehead, "is knowing exactly where Shakespeare bagged all his plots, and identifying all his borrowings from Plutarch and Holinshed."

Anxious glances swept round toward Professor Livingston Lowes, as Whitehead had humorously intended they should. Lowes had withdrawn. Then Homans discreetly observed:

"Exit Kittredge!" and everybody laughed.

Kittredge is, of course, the autocrat of that Shakespearean breakfast table, and I have heard Bliss Perry,[1] who knew him for years and liked him, say, "I never knew anyone whom words interested so much and ideas so little."

From static ideas the debate moved to that besetting question, whether the modern world is utterly at the mercy of its novel technological inventions.

"I believe Europe would have got on about as well with its inland waterways and canals as it has with railways," said Whitehead, "but for America the railway came at exactly the right moment to enable you to subdue the continent."

"We had not got very far with it before that," said Homans.

"The railroad was your decisive factor."

"How about the airplane?"

"It will revolutionize life in the backward regions, like interior Asia, the east of Africa, and places like that; your American far north. A new technology first destroys half of an old society then assists at its rebuilding into a new. Its first effect is, however, violently destructive. . . . I say," he broke off, "what do people mean by talking about the future being obliged to pay for the wars of the present?" He drew into it a

[1] See footnote on page 136.

handsome, blond young fellow named Paul Samuelson,[1] of whom he was obviously proud and fond. They went into a learned and fascinating duologue on it, but much too fast to take down by memory.

"It is a metaphor, no more," concluded Whitehead, "and if one were writing a poem on economics, as Lucretius did in *De Rerum Natura*, the metaphor would be superb; but in any economic connotation all that you are saying when you refer to the future as paying for wars of the present is that you are bequeathing to posterity a changed form of society."

The group had lingered until nearly eleven o'clock. One of the Junior Fellows, who drives Mr. Lowell home to Boston, where he is now back in his own town house on Marlboro Street, carried Whitehead and me to the Hotel Ambassador. Lowell got out and assisted Whitehead, a bit officiously, I thought. Evidently someone else thought so too, for when we were back upstairs and settled in our chairs over a pitcher of hot chocolate, Whitehead remarked to his wife, with the faintest twinkle of a smile, and in his most demure tones:

"Lowell helped me out of the car."

"Yes?"

"Do you suppose he thought I needed it?"

"No," said she, with genial asperity. "He was trying to prove that he is a better man than you are, and he's not!"

XIX

November 2, 1940

EVENING with the Whiteheads at the Hotel Ambassador. There were no other guests. The strain of the war had been wearing them. When I arrived, at eight-thirty, Professor Whitehead was having a nap in his study. Mrs. Whitehead told me they had had occasional cablegrams from North, who is in

[1] Professor of Economics, Massachusetts Institute of Technology.

the Foreign Office at Whitehall and has been bombed badly twice.

"We live a double life," said she; "when guests are here, we live in this country; when they are gone, we live in the war."

A few minutes later Whitehead came out. He looked a little dim at first, more bent in figure, and more frail, but after about half an hour's conversation was burning as brightly as ever. I told him:

"Since last September the readers of the *Boston Globe*, though they don't know it, have been getting *Science and the Modern World* morning, noon, and night."

"Tell him how you wrote that book, Altie."

"All my life, from young manhood at Cambridge, then in London, I had been a lecturer on mathematics. At the age of sixty-three in 1924, I came to Harvard to lecture on philosophy for the first time. Of course in all the intervening years I had heard and participated in the philosophical discussions at Cambridge and London and read an occasional paper before the Royal Society; so it was mostly in my head. Then in the autumn of 1924 I was asked, in addition to all my regular lecturing which was in a sense new, to deliver the Lowell Lectures. Three-fourths of the volume as it stands are those lectures; they were written at the rate of one a week as wanted for delivery. . . ."

"At white heat," interjected Mrs. Whitehead.

"And I was never more than one week ahead."

"Do you rewrite much?"

"No. But I write very slowly and elide a good deal."

"Am I right in thinking that such sentences are written only by a mathematician? Your prose is totally unlike anyone else's."

"I do not think in words. I begin with concepts, then try to put them into words, which is often very difficult."

"A corresponding effect is had on the reader; after the meaning of the words has been grasped, their content next seems to lead an existence independent of the printed page, and almost a palpable one. But how had you in your head such material as that striking galaxy of great men in the early 1600's —your 'Century of Genius'?"

He laughed. "Ever since I was a young man, and still, as you may have noticed, if a great name is mentioned which is unfamiliar to me, I look it up, memorize the dates and his form of activity, and thus for any period of history I have an accurate image of the sort of activity which was going on in that time and place. Mind you, it had better be accurate; you had better know exactly whether Marlowe was older than Shakespeare and how *much* older. I discovered, for example, that five of the principal figures in English history overlap in lifetimes: Elizabeth and Cromwell; Pitt, Wellington, and Victoria. . . ."

"Altie, show him your little book," prompted Mrs. Whitehead.

He went into his study and returned with a small volume bound in brown calfskin, the back cover of which was missing. This was presented with an expression of whimsey:

"I picked this up at a bookshop in Cambridge when I was a young man. My only criticism of it is that it includes too many second-rate Englishmen."

I read: *A Brief Biographical Dictionary*, by Rev. Charles Hole, Macmillan & Co. 1866. Its pages presented merely the full name, calling, and dates of birth and death. From it he produced sheets of yellow paper on which he had listed the philosophers from Ionia to modern times, the Roman emperors, "and here," said he, "is a table of the English kings."

"Do you people buy books from catalogues or by seeing them?"

"One goes into a bookshop," said Mrs. Whitehead, "and comes out with a book."

He told of an episode early in their wedded life when they had read a great many books on theology. This study went on for years, eight of them, I think he said. When he had finished with the subject, for he *had* finished with it, he called in a

Cambridge bookseller and asked what he would give for the lot. The figure the bookseller named was so handsome that they felt quite affluent until, at the door, he said, "I shall, of course, credit them to your account." So they went on an orgy of book-buying, and discovered after a while that they had spent about twice what their credit was!

This bookseller was one of those oddities which academic towns still harbour. He was very able, but amusingly conceited, and once told them:

"I have been in Oxford recently and don't think their bookshops are up to ours. I went the rounds and looked them all over —*incog* of course!"

"Nowadays when people have quirks," Whitehead took it up, "they are locked up and the quirks diagnosed by pseudo-scientific names, but we used to have just as many queer people and we called them 'characters' and were proud of them. Take old so-and-so who used always to walk along the street sidewise, hop up, pluck a leaf off a tree, and go on nibbling it." Rising, he impersonated the ancient worthy doing that very thing. "If he had been locked up we should have lost one of our best astronomical textbooks."

This led into the subject of the unsuspected powers in common people.

"As you know," he said, "I admire your American democracy and believe our class-lines in England are a great evil. However, they work in unexpected reversals. I believe there is more genuine respect as between persons of different classes in England (excepting the commercial middle-class pusher, or the social 'bounder') than in America, for there you *know* that your gardener or housemaid hasn't a chance in the world to rise, but here you are so accustomed to the idea that everyone has equal opportunity, whether they have or haven't (and mostly they haven't), that unless you are imaginatively on your guard, you automatically assume, when thinking of a supposed inferior, 'If he were any good he would have done as well as

I have,' which doesn't follow at all. What lets a man up to what is popularly known as the 'top' is often a very narrow range of ability which happens to be wanted in a particular place or time and which is compensated accordingly, but this may have little or no relation to the higher capacities of the human being or even the better powers of the individual so elevated. . . . Very few people are adequately drawn out—some are never drawn out at all, and remain, to all purposes, idiotic; though no one knows what their latent powers might have been. Others are about half drawn out; some happy encounter, some favouring condition elicits their peculiar abilities, but the waste of undeveloped faculties must be tremendous. For the powers of the individual are unique and unpredictable. This has been one of the great discoveries of the human race and it is still proceeding very slowly. It was dimly in the mind of Plato, it was being made by the ancient Hebrews and came into articulation by Christianity. But the Christians did not do much with it for a thousand years, because they thought so many people would be going to hell in the natural course of events that it didn't much matter, and they thus failed to grasp the full implication of the idea."

"In speed and force," I remarked, "a great idea suggests a glacier."

"The average length of time it takes, I think," said he, "for any great discovery in the realm of ideas to pass into general currency or to receive any practical effectuation is a thousand years. This idea of the unique value of the individual hardly obtained any political expression until the eighteenth century and it was then given by the framers of your American Constitution, and has become, I believe, the basic unifying idea of your nation. Writing was an invention which took about two thousand years to make its effect felt. Do you recall how, even in Plato's dialogues, the discussions are seldom if ever about what the participants have 'read' but almost invariably about what they 'remember'? The amount of memorizing must have been tremendous, and one reason for the popularity of verse was that the rhythmical cadence is an aid to memory. But for a long time after writing had been invented it was little more than a keeping of accounts; a business of kings and bankers, promulgating orders and computing moneys. Only when men began putting down their thoughts did the effect of the written word begin to be felt on the intellectual progress of mankind."

"The terrific blackout after the fall of Rome suggests how dependent on written words we had become. It took nearly a thousand years to get some of them back."

"That textual criticism of the classics had to be done from the Renaissance on if the modern world was ever to repossess the culture of the ancient one," said Whitehead, "and done it has been in the five hundred years since 1400 . . . whether Sophocles wrote 'he-she-or-it.' But as to transmitting that possession, I used occasionally in London to go to meetings of the Royal Society, and for dogmatism I may say that I thought them the modern equivalents of the mediaeval Schoolmen."

Somewhat later in the evening when speaking of the Roman Republic in the period of the Civil Wars Whitehead said, "To all appearances that was a society that was going to pieces. If a man, not knowing what the issue of the event was, were to want a period to study in which a civilization was disintegrating, that one would appear to have all the symptoms, and yet there came an Augustus who was able to pull it together. He saw the one class which still had the integrity to administer its affairs, namely the small squires. It wasn't easy to enlist them or to get them accepted by the old patricians, but he was able to effect both."

"Isn't it singular," I said, "how little there is culturally to show for the more tranquil centuries which followed? Isn't Tacitus almost the last great name? Under the Antonines probably the world was better administered than it has ever been before or since, yet in creative achievement it was poor. I suppose there wasn't much liberty."

"Periods of tranquillity," said Whitehead, "are seldom prolific of creative achievement. Mankind has to be stirred up."

At eleven or thereabouts we had chocolate. At parting they said, "Do come often." For a whole evening we had been interested and not thinking of the war.

XX

June 17, 1941

A RADIANT morning in late spring. The windows of their apartment in the Hotel Ambassador were opened wide and a scent of fresh greenery from lawns and foliage swung in on a light breeze. We sat in Whitehead's study, where sunshine poured in cheerfully. Keeping off the subject of the war had gradually become a tacit manoeuvre by common consent. Otherwise, it occupied us throughout most of our waking hours.

He said that the Frankfurters had been there yesterday.

"Whose idea do you suppose it was, the Oxford degree for President Roosevelt?" I asked.

He reflected, "I suppose it was the Halifax-Frankfurter connection."

"'Tell him the joke about Halifax that is going around Washington," suggested Mrs. Whitehead.

"Halifax," said he, "is very pious, and they say he spends three days a week with the Almighty, but comes back misinformed!"

A turn of the conversation brought up the topic of what valid basis we have for our concept of human equality. We know that mortals are unlike and unequal, yet we crave that sense of equality.

"It is founded on the infinite potentialities of human beings," said he. "In many the powers are never elicited, or only partly elicited. Yet they are there and we never can be sure what they are. I will give you an example: our maid's husband. He is of

Scots Highland stock, was a highly skilled workman in the General Electric, some skill which required a most delicate manipulation of machinery, and, as such, one of the highest-paid manual workers in America. Suddenly an invention which could do the same task reduced him to the lowest. He came to us. We discovered that he also had remarkable aesthetic sense."

"When we lived in the house at Canton," said Mrs. Whitehead, "I could send him in town to select draperies and fabrics for me. He worked in our flower garden until ten at night, when I had to forbid him on pain of discharge. He always arranged the flowers in my vases."

Whitehead took it up:

"These qualities are latent until circumstances bring them out. Mind you, I don't say there isn't a lot of stupidity—but imaginative people in the presence of those infinities of possibility prefer to reserve judgment. The combinations haven't been explored."

"The way I phrase it to myself is, that the things we, as human beings, do not have in common, are as nothing to the things that we do have in common."

"That glances in the same direction," said he.

"Coming from a small town to a metropolis, when my bewilderment had subsided, I observed two main facts; one, that the first-rate people were all through society, at bottom and middle as well as top, and regardless of education; and the other, that if they had not been at heart peaceable, there were and are not enough police in the United States to keep them from mutual extermination. Doesn't it suggest that most are men of good will and ask only a set of rules to go by?"

"Men of good will is well put in, for there is a vicious element, both in men and in societies," said he. "It is puzzling enough to know what to do with the individuals; it is enough worse when a whole society becomes infected with evil and runs amuck. Even in a peaceable state we all live under police protection, and force is used to restrain evil-doers. But you notice that when we want to word the issue we resort to extreme cases: the poor girl who is kidnapped and outraged by some ruffian. But who shall say in the borderland cases exactly where the force shall be applied, exactly *where* along the series the police shall be called in, exactly where the law shall be invoked?"

"I have seen my own clan, the middle class, foully in error on that point."

"In England, we get our best morality, our better standards, class for class, from the upper strata of the workers and from the conscientious or the gifted members of the aristocracy. In between, a good many in the professional and commercial classes are unkind, unjust, greedy, crass, and inferior in any true sense of morality. I am very proud of the way England is standing up to this ordeal. North writes me that when the news placards appeared in London saying that Roosevelt's speech of three weeks ago would 'strengthen British morale,' people on the streets merely looked at one another and grinned . . . as if a speech by the American President could affect it. They are fighting either Thermopylae or Marathon: they don't yet know which, but in either case there is not a thought of yielding. And when it is over I think you will see the middle-class morality replaced by a fusion of the other two and a result vastly superior."

"If you asked me where our American morality comes from I would have hard work to answer; we are so diverse of races and traditions."

"I will tell you one thing you do have here," said he, "kindness. The presumption is that all people will treat one another kindly. I have never been in a place where kindness was so general, and I do not know of any society ancient or modern where a similar state of things existed. I would not hesitate to say that the United States is the finest society on a grand scale that the world has thus far produced."

"Let me dispute that: Gilbert Murray said much the same thing to me down here by the Charles in the fall of 1926, and

Livingstone said it to me at New Haven in 1934. To both I
made the same reply: we are not under the population pressure,
and hence not the economic pressure, of Europe. Kindness costs
less here. It is no especial credit to us."

Whitehead replied smiling:

"I state it merely as a fact.

"One mistake I think your Protestant sects did make," he
continued; "they were too anxious that nothing be taught that
was not so. Now of the thirty-odd sects that have come down to
us in the form of religions from the Graeco-Semitic origins, I
would take vigorous exception to certain elements in all of
them; nevertheless there would remain solid substrata, or, if
you like, confluent streams which, blended into a general
ethical code, would be invaluable to teach the young. I think
the moral unity of England today is based on a few such simple
concepts, which are accepted by everyone. The school does
best when it inculcates moral precepts which are also accepted
and taught in the home. They don't need to be very many nor
very complicated; hardly more than rules of thumb so they are
basically sound. And that, I think, for the time being has been
lost here."

"There is no doubt of it," I said. "One sees it in two obvious
ways: the generation now growing up does not recognize either
quotations from or allusions to the Bible; and the classical
tradition is equally on the wane."

"Poor things," said Mrs. Whitehead, "they know so little
about what has happened in the world before them, what
people have borne and put up with and lived through, and
conquered, that when something goes wrong in their own little
lives, they think the universe is shattered and that the only
remedy is suicide, however much misery that act may spread
around them. . . . A moment ago when you two men were
discussing the bases for our craving for human equality, I
wanted to exclaim: 'I love you both, but you are both miserable
sinners. And it is the usual male sin against the Holy Ghost of

trying to reduce the infinite to a neat intellectual formula.'
Oh, you strange creatures; will you never learn that our
craving for equality comes from the sense of the pathos, the
grotesquerie, the humour, the tragedy, the inexplicability of
human nature? It won't reduce to a formula. It is simply *there*.
We can do nothing about it. We *are* fantastic, we *are* pathetic,
we *are* comical, we *are* tragic, we *are* human; and all we can do,
if we have an iota of sense, is recognize the fact in a sentiment
of equality."

"But that is just what I *was* saying, Evelyn."

"Yes, in your precise logic—when there is nothing logical in
it." She shook her head at us severely. "That's how we are all
at bottom equal!"

XXI

June 28, 1941

SUMER *is icumen in*, and, going over to Cambridge I had taken
to the Whiteheads, for her, two boxes of roses from a neighbour's
garden in Marblehead, and to him Sir Richard Livingstone's
newly published *The Future in Education*, in which his *Aims of
Education* is admiringly quoted.

He was seated in his study. They had been out, over to
Harvard Square, to buy a *winter* suit, on the hottest day in June,
"and could not get one."

When I confessed to having got one last month, "not a
minute too soon," the tailor assured me, he said genially:

"We were a minute too late."

They leave for the month of July with the Pickmans in
Bedford. Mrs. Whitehead remarked:

"The atmosphere of the place just suits me, a Catholic
household where something is being done about religion, but
not by me. It is like that in which I was brought up in Brittany,
among Catholics but not a Catholic myself."

"It sounds a little like going to church by radio."

"There must be a place in the next world *in between*," said he, "for such people; not too hot nor too cold; nor as melancholy as Limbo."

"You must mean Laodicea, abhorred by the zealots as 'neither cold nor hot.' "

Returning to church-by-radio, he thought the sonorous voices came over best, though divested of all the ecclesiastical trappings which do lend impressiveness.

"The two most impressive religious services I remember," said he, "were, one, a Low Mass in a cathedral in a city—how bothersome it is to forget names!—on the edge of the Black Forest in Germany. There was an immense concourse of devout people, you couldn't hear a thing that was being said, and it was perfect. You had a sense that the religious office was going on, and you shared it with all those pious people. The other was Quaker; only that service must not go on too long. It was at a school near Birmingham. Several of us had gone down there to deliver lectures, which began at nine o'clock, and every morning for a quarter of an hour before nine, the head of the school gathered us in his study, which was commodious, we had a time of quiet meditation, then, just at the end, he spoke briefly. It had exactly the right effect."

"You are not including the Anglican."

"It is admirable for its purpose; the beautiful ritual, the music, the architecture, the good voices—it has everything except religion. It is not religious, it is sociological."

"Ralph Emerson was exceedingly annoyed by it. He says why in *English Traits*."

"Mind you; I think the Protestant sects lack even that. The Anglican service is a symbol of the aristocracy's responsibility for governing a nation. It was not originally in Christianity. The Jewish peasants, out of whose profound moral intuitions Christianity came, had no idea of managing a complex society. Even Christ himself said practically nothing about it, except,

'You had better pay your taxes,' but that is not a civil constitution exactly."

"The rest—responsibility for a scheme of society—was a later accretion?"

"Yes. And the paradox is that this idea, so new in the world at its inception—the worth of the individual—which you still see so strikingly affirmed in any Catholic church by the sight of a solitary worshipper kneeling in the shrine of a saint—has been fostered by an institution, namely the Catholic Church, which has done so much to suppress individuality. There is always in religion an element of brutality, and it is generally the work of sincere men trying to conserve a state of society. I suppose it has seldom been any worse than the Inquisition in Spain or the persecution of the Huguenots in France. It is surprising that the separation of the English Church in the sixteenth century under the Tudors was accomplished with so comparatively little brutality. There were, of course, burnings and beheadings but nothing like the quantity you would have had on the Continent in a similar situation. Whatever the reform was, however, it wasn't religious. I don't know what Henry VIII or Elizabeth had to do with religion."

"Trevelyan's pages on the dissolution of the monasteries make close reading," I said. "The issues weren't as clear-cut as we of today are prone to suppose."

"The expropriations," said Whitehead, "were harsh, but not half as harsh as the wars of religion that devastated the Continent. I know of only two occasions in history when the people in power did what needed to be done about as well as you can imagine its being possible. One was the framing of your American Constitution. They were able statesmen, they had access to a body of good ideas; they incorporated these general principles into the instrument without trying to particularize too explicitly how they should be put into effect; and they were men of immense practical experience themselves. The other was in Rome and it undoubtedly saved civilization for, roughly, about four hundred years. It was the work of Augustus and the set around him. He saved Rome from the Romans—I mean the city Romans—from the bankruptcy of the republican form of government, and the desiccated ideas of the old patrician class. Somehow, he found a way to call in, first, the Italian country squires, the 'new men' of new ideas, then, as the centuries went on, came the provincials, people like the Spanish Caesars. It prolonged the life of Rome up to the middle of the third century A.D.—about the time when it began to go to pieces. He left the senate enough power to preserve its self-respect, and, for the rest, the government was in the hands of civil authorities plus the military. It was one of the great achievements in human history and I doubt if, after all the legalistic analysis has been done, anybody quite understands how the thing was accomplished."

He was presently saying that historically the best civilizations seem to come from racial mixtures: the Normans with the French, the Norman-French with the Anglo-Saxons, the Dorian invaders in Attica with τοῖς αὐτόχθονες "the people sprung from land itself."—"Where the racial strain is 'pure' they are likely to be pretty stupid people until their blood is mingled with a more vivid strain. I suspect there was a largish mixture of Semitic with Ionian, which produced that brilliant mainland culture.

"Behind all this," he continued, "is the problem of how to keep a society from stagnating. It is the hardest thing in the world to do. You might have a social system that would run along smoothly enough for centuries, but if it lacks the element of novelty, of progressivism, it is a dead thing. I dare say the ants and the bees have smoothly working systems, but they do not change. This element of novelty is what makes the difference between man and the animals. Man sees a future in the present; there is a vision of what can be done with the materials of what is. A dog sees the present as a present and nothing else. And, mind you, I don't say that it isn't quite possible for man to come to the end of his powers of origination. Not that those powers themselves might fail, but that he might get into a planetary situation of static society where they would have no scope—and 'there an end to man.' His society, creature for creature, would be of no more worth than the ants."

"Artists" (it had occurred to me while he was speaking) "seem to recognize this power of origination as something which they do not command, but which commands them. It is true, they develop a technique through which it can work, but technique no more creates than a mechanical tool—it merely aids creation. Goethe is quite explicit about this to Eckermann; he as good as says that a masterpiece is a gift from on high when the artist has had 'a good day'; but that the force acts from outside himself."

"I suggest," Whitehead took it up, "that that society prospers best which can provide the conditions necessary for artists to give freest scope to their capacities for novelty—not eccentricity, not the bizarre—but origination in the furtherance of an artistic tradition; a carrying forward of what has been its new achievement."

"And Plato, in *The Laws*, the work of his old age—wasn't he very severe about the admission of novelty in the arts?—at least in the art of tragedy."

"Look here: let me show you a passage in Plato. . . ." He rose, peered along his shelves, and finally chose a volume in the Loeb edition, opening to Chapter 51 of the *Timaeus*. The translation was amended here and there by his own pen: he spoke of it: "This translator turns φυσέως into 'substance.'"

"But it means 'nature,' doesn't it? Or more exactly 'growth,' or 'the process of growth.'"

"Yes. Now here Plato is speaking of 'the receptacle'; the idea is vast, and a little vague." He went on through two or three pages summarizing as he read, until he reached Chapter 54. "And now here, you see, he reduces the idea to *commonplace*—to geometry!"

"But wasn't that often his method; to take the infinite, which he alone was capable of tackling, and reduce it to a finite form which average mortals, 'the educated man of ancient Athens,' as you once said, could understand?"

"This relationship between the infinite and the finite is what I was coming to. Our minds are finite, and yet even in these circumstances of finitude we are surrounded by possibilities that are infinite, and the purpose of human life is to grasp as much as we can out of that infinitude. I wish I could convey this sense I have of the infinity of the possibilities that confront humanity—the limitless variations of choice, the possibility of novel and untried combinations, the happy turns of experiment, the endless horizons opening out. As long as we experiment, as long as we keep this possibility of progressiveness, we and our societies are alive; when we lose them, both we and our societies are dead, no matter how externally active we and they may be, no matter how materially prosperous they and we may appear. And nothing is easier to lose than this element of novelty. It is the living principle in thought, which keeps all alive."

"How much validity do you give that sense of oneness which we sometimes have—that sense of our individuality being merged into the all? One is anxious not to talk moonshine about this, the more if, like me, he is neither a metaphysician nor a psychologist. And yet I know that those moments are so memorable, the sense of it is so strong, that years later, ten, perhaps, one can reach back into it as if it were only yesterday or today and create out of it something living and new."

"Mysticism," said Whitehead, "leads us to try to create out of the mystical experience something that will save it, or at least save the memory of it. Words don't convey it except feebly; we are aware of having been in communication with infinitude and we know that no finite form we can give can convey it. . . ."

"Music," I ventured, "may come nearer it than words.

Sometimes, during a good performance of the very greatest music one has a sense that he is in the presence of infinitude somewhat similar to what the composer must have felt when he was having to choose between one concept and another in the hope of expressing it. The definite concepts are there, in tones or phrases, but all around them hover the infinitudes of possibility—the *other* ways in which this vastness might have been expressed."

"Out of this effort to save the mystical experience," said Whitehead, "in the hope of creating a form which will preserve the experience for ourselves and possibly for others, comes clarification—in a thought or perhaps an art-form; and that clarification is then turned into some form of action. . . . Mysticism, clarification, action; I have never put it in that form before; but that is the order in which I would state it."

He said that a static quality appeared in the Buddhist religion as evidenced by the history of India and China, that their rate of advance retarded or stopped, and that since the year 1800 B.C. very little change had come in China until modern times, except minor ones in small living arrangements. He was illustrating how subtle a possession dynamic thought is, and how easy it is to lose.

This led to a discussion of the vitality of thought in the medical profession in our own time, how rapidly their science is moving, and yet they will tell you they know very little. He said:

"One of the most advanced types of human being on earth today is the *good* American doctor."

"Because in him science is devoted to the relief of suffering?"

"I would place it on more general grounds: he is sceptical toward the data of his own profession, welcomes discoveries which upset his previous hypotheses, and is still animated by humane sympathy and understanding."

"But for their advance," said I, "I would have been dead twenty years ago, of appendicitis. In 1892 the victims died. Now it is rated a 'minor' operation."

"But for a discovery in medicine only three years old," said Whitehead, "I would have been dead six weeks ago." He had had pneumonia and been saved by the new drug.

Mrs. Whitehead brought in some of the roses arranged in a glass bowl. So I then produced *The Future In Education* by Livingstone.

"I have a high respect for him," said Whitehead, "I once served on a royal commission with him to study the place of the Graeco-Roman classics in English education. I liked him immensely."

Turning to page 30, I indicated the passage quoted. He read it:

In one of the really good books on education, Professor Whitehead has spoken of the danger of

. . . inert ideas, that is to say, ideas that are merely received into the mind without being utilised or tested or thrown into fresh combinations . . . Education with inert ideas is not only useless; it is, above all things, harmful . . . Except at rare intervals of intellectual ferment, education in the past has been radically infected with inert ideas . . .

*　　*　　*

For good measure I added that Livingstone had written me months ago that *Aims of Education* was one of the few books he had ever read on the subject which struck him as having been written by someone who knew something about it.

In the little time remaining they talked of the newly published biography of *Catherine of Aragon* by Garrett Mattingly, which Whitehead praised highly.

"It makes historical figures human and alive," said he. "The descriptions are quoted from intimate family letters, and you hear such things as how Henry VIII looked on a particular morning. . . . I say, what tortures mediaeval medicine inflicted on dying monarchs! Everybody thought they were doing their best and nobody knew much of anything. Of course the tortures of the common people were just as bad, only no record of them remains. You get, too, from this volume a very different idea of Cranmer than the usual one of martyrdom. He was perfectly willing to recant to save himself, but when he found he was going to be burnt anyhow, he recanted his recantation."

"We used to think that life in those periods was exposed to fearful risks. And *now* look at us!"

"I know it. One is almost ashamed to say that the day is hot, or the soup is cold, it seems such a trifle to endure. The world is so upset, that even our most platitudinous concepts, things that would once have been accepted by everyone, require to be looked at a second time."

XXII

August 30, 1941

A GOLDEN summer morning. By previous appointment, as always with the Whiteheads, my arrival was timed for eleven-thirty. By now Professor Whitehead was well recovered from his bout with pneumonia, and he looked uncommonly well. I said so.

"People tell me that I do," said he, "but the effects of the illness still linger."

"That should teach you not to have pneumonia."

"Yes," he assented to the chaffing, "there must be a lesson to everything."

"Nietzsche, who specialized in disagreeable remarks, has an observation that suffering may deepen a man but doesn't make him better."

"Anxiety," said Whitehead, "may give one an aspect of brightness, purely because it sharpens all the faculties. It

[163]

makes all one's impressions more intense. . . . I have been thinking, of late, about custom; how it varies with time and place, but comes, in the end, to much the same thing. Now in England if something goes wrong—say, if one finds a skunk in the garden—he writes to the family solicitor, who proceeds to take the proper measures; whereas in America, you telephone the fire department. Each satisfies a characteristic need; in the English, love of order and legalistic procedure; and here in America, what you like is something vivid, and red, and swift. . . ."

"And noisy! One day in State Street I watched the fire apparatus pass; about six pieces. The streets cleared; the traffic policeman flexed his knees with the tension; the crowds stopped to watch; the speed and din were terrific—everybody was quite happy—and, after all, there wasn't any fire."

"That is my point," Whitehead took it up. "One method works just as well as the other, and the reason is that ninety per cent of the difficulty is psychological. As soon as we are assured that the properly constituted agents are taking the necessary measures about skunks in gardens, we go along contentedly about our business."

"Since 1910," I said, "in this country at least, we would have to admit a new agent, called psychiatrist. But how much of the psychiatrists' knowledge is actually new?"

"Some of it the Catholics have had all along in their confessional," said Whitehead. "I have been reading, or rereading, E. J. Boyd Barrett's *The Jesuit Enigma*. He criticized the order for what he calls their 'false psychiatry.' I looked him up in *Who's Who*, and find he has some achievement to his record, but he concedes very little good to the Jesuit order. My opinion is that it must have more in it than he concedes to have flourished as it has."

"Wouldn't that be an instance of the two-sidedness of nearly everything, from a truth to an institution? Phrased one way, it is intolerable; phrased another, it could be accepted gladly."

"It is the rigid dogma that destroys truth; and, please notice, my emphasis is not on the dogma but on the rigidity. When men say of any question, 'This is all there is to be known or said of the subject; investigation ends here,' that is death. It may be that the mischief comes not from the thinker himself but from the use made of his thinking by late-comers. Aristotle, for example, gave us our scientific technique (he also did some useful work in ethics); but in the main, it was he who devised our methods of scientific investigation (and of observation, too); yet his logical propositions, his instruction in sound reasoning which was bequeathed to Europe, are valid only within the limited framework of formal logic, and, as used in Europe, they stultified the minds of whole generations of mediaeval Schoolmen. Aristotle invented science, but destroyed philosophy."

"Would you say that Plato's distinctive contribution to the technique of thought is the willingness, as he makes Socrates call it, 'to follow the argument where it leads'? This sounds so simple, yet how few people understand how to play the game. In his *Dialogues*, for example, a question is beaten flat and round, several people have a go at it—"

"The German scholars who worked on Plato in the early part of the nineteenth century, to my mind, missed the point," said Whitehead. "Their view seems to have been that a lot of rather foolish people put forward somewhat nonsensical opinions until finally Socrates steps in and sets everything right. I do not believe that is it at all. When you get a group of diverse professional people in a discussion, their experience is so varied that you are sure to get novel contributions to the idea. None of them may be final, some of them may not be valid, but all of them will make some contribution to the subject, and while perhaps they cannot be accepted, they will bear study. I venture to suppose that in a newspaper office like yours there are a good many such discussions. . . ."

"That is what our daily editorial conferences are; and, over a period of years, the give-and-take grows uncommonly like a Platonic dialogue. I think perhaps that is where I first began to comprehend the Platonic method of dialectic."

"By that method the subject is explored, various opinions are given their weight, and the participants feel that they have spent their energies to good purpose, even though no definite conclusion emerges."

"Do you suppose that method existed in Athens before Plato?"

"I should think it likely. The prime of Athens came a little before Plato, in the period of the three great tragic dramatists, yes, and I include Aristophanes too. I think a culture is in its finest flower before it begins to analyse itself; and the Periclean Age and the dramatists were spontaneous, unselfconscious."

"The analytical spirit gets going in Euripides, the last of the three; and also rather more of the discussion method, the dramatist putting forth this or that point of view, not as anything final, but only so that it may 'have its say.' "

"How many people saw those plays?"

"In Athens about twenty thousand, though the citizenry itself was much more, probably one hundred and fifty thousand. Imagine them sitting there from dawn to dark on a March day of the Greater Dionysia watching three tragedies followed by a farcical satyr play, by each of three competing poets, and one of those trilogies would have been the *Oresteia* of Aeschylus. Where in our modern world is an audience that could take such a 'helping'? "

"Print has had a damaging effect," said Whitehead. "Before the mind had the assistance of the page it was given much harder work to do. When you remember that Athenian prisoners of the Syracusan expedition were given their liberty because they could recite choric odes from Euripides, obviously it was not mere snippets of the text which they had memorized."

"Do you ever find the sight of library stacks disconcerting? What if one knew everything in those volumes: would he be any better off—or worse off? Or the question comes, Can excessive reading actually enfeeble one's thinking apparatus?"

"I read very slowly," said Whitehead. "Sometimes I see myself referred to as 'a well-read man.' As a matter of fact, I have not read a great quantity of books; but I think about what I read, and it sticks."

(Remembering the size of his library in the house at Canton, again in the apartment at Radnor Hall, and even here in the Hotel Ambassador, books overflowing from study to dining-room, to limit the case even to those present-and-voting, his remark about not having read a great quantity of books was to be taken relatively.)

"What do you think of this modern emphasis on *speed* of reading?"

"Speed is not for me. On the other hand, some of my reading is 'skippy.' Last night, for example, I was rereading that book in your lap on the Jesuits, but finding, at the beginnings of successive chapters that he was still on the same aspect of a subject whose point I had already grasped, I did not hesitate to skip."

We were next discussing the kind of book about which one must do something, if there is to be any benefit from the reading. The *Meditations* of Marcus Aurelius can be read through in a matter of hours, but to incorporate those precepts into thought and action may be a life's work. Then I asked:

"Living and working as you have and do in academic communities, does it ever strike you that acquisitive scholarship can be overdone?"

"The universities," said he, "are like any other necessary implement—like a gun. We must have them, the work of civilization could scarcely be carried on without them; but while they are very valuable, they can also be very dangerous. The reason Harvard has kept its place at the top as a capital of thought is the graduate schools, where knowledge is wedded to action."

"An idea which has been occupying me of late I would like to put up for criticism. It is that in nineteenth-century America the influence of religious thinking was still very powerful; that at the turn of the nineteenth into the twentieth, the rise of science and then the first world war so impaired that influence that leadership passed to the educationists, say after 1920; but that now numerous signs seem to indicate that in another generation or so, the germinating power in American civilization may be the artists—using that term in its broadest sense—the creators."

"Your dates confuse me a little," said he. "I would have said that you have already had two very happy periods of flourishing in this country; one in New England during the first half of the nineteenth century, when you really enjoyed one of the world's great ages, though it is not yet as famous as it deserves to be; and the other in the late eighteenth century, with the framing of your American Constitution. I am not suggesting that these framers were acting entirely on original initiative; some of their ideas were a hundred years old—going back to Locke, for example—or much older; but they were unique in laying down, not details of procedure but general principles for the conduct of a great democratic state. I know of only two instances when a work of such magnitude was accomplished consciously. The other was done according to principles which would not have satisfied either your or my ideals of liberty, and yet it certainly saved civilization and bequeathed a point of view, even to the Middle Ages, which enabled the monastic foundations to transmit the ancient heritage; I mean when Augustus Caesar appealed from the narrow patricians and the unreliable plebs to the solid middle class, first of Rome and Italy and later of the empire. Nobody could admire the English governmental system more heartily than I do; but equally nobody could say at exactly what point the idea of a limited monarchy came in. The growth was unconscious. It was not an idea which originated with any person or at any specific time.

But the Augustan Principate and your Federal Constitution were the results of conscious effort. The English system, too, is very difficult to copy, and it has been copied successfully only by people of English stocks setting up colonial societies, in places like Australia, Africa, or North America."

"You are evidently using 'artist' in the sense of creators of great states."

"And you are using the word 'creative' in a sense which I give to the word 'novelty,' " resumed Whitehead. "A hundred thousand years ago—or sometime—nobody knows when—there came a turn in the development of man which brought about a very rapid advance. It was man's capacity for origination, his capacity for novelty, his curiosity, his liking for investigation. My fear for humanity is that they may lose it. One of the few places where it is still free is here in the United States. I don't say there aren't ways in which you could improve. I think there are regions where you would do well to reduce your rate of murders—but even allowing for Chicago at its worst, in the 1920's, before your authorities stepped in and put a stop to it, life in general, your life, my life, is less subject to interference and less in danger here than any place else on earth. It is only in certain happy ages and lands that conditions are favourable to the development of talent—Greece in the fifth and fourth centuries B.C. was one; Rome in the first century A.D. was another; and even then the range of talent elicited by the temporarily favourable conditions is a limited one, not nearly the whole range of potential talents or of gifted individuals receives the needed encouragement. And when those fortunate times do come, we don't know how to keep them going."

"How short-lived the Elizabethan drama was," I remarked; "in full bloom between 1590 and 1612, then by the 1620's it had begun to thin out."

"I was thinking of that very period," said he. "Art flourishes when there is a sense of adventure, a sense of nothing having been done before, of complete freedom to experiment; but when caution comes in you get repetition, and repetition is the death of art. Here in America you had a good period up to about 1860; then the idea came in that nothing was any good unless it came from Europe."

"Yes, men like Emerson and Thoreau can be seen pushing it away from them; but after the middle of the century it does descend like a blight."

"The two world wars," said he, "have destroyed Europe and liberated America."

"Unless we are thwarted by our loss of racial homogeneity?"

"On the contrary, you have gained by that loss. I know of no other situation in history similar to yours, in having assembled the vivid and adventurous spirits of numerous races in an environment favourable to the creation of a great culture, except in the Mediterranean Basin of the fifth and fourth centuries B.C. (its most brilliant period), when Greeks and Phoenicians and Italians and heaven knows who else were bobbing about in rowboats, mixing races and founding new societies. It will be strange if you don't profit by your situation."

"I am not quite sure I understand what you mean by 'repetition is the death of art.'"

"Then take architecture. I was brought up in a part of England where everybody landed that *did* land, from Caesar on through the missionaries, the Danes, the Normans, and the rest. My father's church was one example, and Canterbury Cathedral was another. (I can see it now, the spot when Thomas à Becket was murdered, and the armour of the Black Prince in the south aisle of the chancel.)—I have read and don't hold at all with T. S. Eliot in his view of what went on in Canterbury Cathedral. Mind you, I don't pretend to know a great deal about it, but I feel sure it wasn't like *that*.—All the successive ages are embedded in those buildings; walls of the early churches, then the heavy Norman arches, then the lighter and more fanciful Gothic of the middle period, and finally the too-fanciful late Gothic; but no repetition; only the very slightest reliance on what went before, always some novel departure."

"A while back," I said, "you were speaking of the death of truth which results when men attempt to codify it into some dogma or institution which they hope will conserve it for posterity. Even Plato, in his old age at least, seems unwilling to let his ideal society take its chances (possibly, it is true, because he had seen the disaster to Athens); but isn't the difficulty with all such attempts that the sum of existence is larger than any system, however large?"

"The desire for a pattern of existence," said he, "is a natural and very common wish that our experience should have some meaning, some order, that it should make sense. The hypotheses of science are the same. The pattern may not represent anything more than our conception of our lives, as we would like to believe them to be, or our hypothesis of a scientific process, but it steadies us. If we are speaking of naïveté, it is the scientists who are naïve. For years they have been welcoming hypotheses which destroy their previous assumptions, and welcoming them as a condition of advance; whereas the theologians—and I consider Christian theology to be one of the great disasters of the human race –if they admitted that their assumptions had been upset, would consider it a major defeat for themselves (when all the while their position has been shaken and so altered that the tenets of today would, in certain intellectual levels, be hardly recognizable as those of the same or similar people seventy years ago). But much the same is true in science, and whether the scientists realize it or not, their 'advance' has been upset."

"Kirsopp Lake [1] once remarked in my presence that his father, a physician, being asked late in life what had done the

---

[1] Kirsopp Lake, theologian. Born Southampton, England, 1872. Lincoln College, Oxford. Professor of early Christian lit. Harvard 1914–1919, Winn professor of ecclesiastical history 1919–1932, professor of history 1932–1938.

should be listened to and that these 'silly questions' ought to be asked, you will instantly be pestered with letters from three thousand idiots whose questions *are* silly!"

"That is true," said I, "for I *have* said it in print and *have* been pestered with letters from three thousand idiots."

"But the point is," he resumed, "that the 'silly question' is the first intimation of some totally novel development. Suppose we admitted this principle in the sphere of morals. What is morality in any given time or place? It is what the majority then and there happen to like, and immorality is what they dislike. But the 'silly question' as applied to morals would open the way to a discovery of the few ultimacies behind *all* systems of morals, a region in which very little has as yet been done."

XXIII

September 10, 1941

EARLY in the summer I had told Professor Whitehead that I had been keeping his conversations in my Note Books since 1933. He knew that I had occasionally used parts of them transcribed almost verbatim in the editorial columns of the *Globe*, for when I did, a copy was always sent him. The immediate reason for speaking of it was that North, Margot, and Eric, his son, daughter-in-law, and grandson, were in England, and two of them, North and Margot, in London under repeated bombings. Beyond this personal anxiety was his concern for England, for Europe, and the future of civilization. He suffered from the war with a peculiar intensity, for, more than most, he understood what was at stake for the future of mankind.

There had been no thought of publication. My idea was to offer him some novel diversion, however brief, from this daily strain, which had clearly begun to tell. Copies of these conversations in typescript had begun to be made in midsummer and sent to him as fast as finished. This had progressed to about the first hundred pages, for the years from 1933 to 1937, and was to continue through the autumn until they were brought up to date.

It was now Wednesday, September 10, 1941, and I went to Cambridge to see him late in the forenoon. In the College Yard the elms were yellowing somewhat earlier than usual, although it was still a sultry summer day.

The apartment at the Hotel Ambassador, being five floors up, was cool and airy; the Venetian blinds keeping out the glare. It was Whitehead's day to be spent in bed, so I was received in that chamber, a cheerful room, bright with sunshine, its walls tinted a light blue. He sat propped on pillows, a reading table by his side, looking cool and comfortable.

He had been reading the typescripts of the Dialogues, was satisfied that they were in substance what was said, and asked:

"How can you remember so accurately?"

I told him what my previous experience had been; shorthand reporter as a youth, and thirty years' practice of recording the conversation of others.

He turned pages of the typescript, pausing here and there.

"Your prospects of getting these published," he said, "aren't for the present very bright. I come of a long-lived family. When my grandfather died, at the age of eighty-seven, his old friend Sir Moses Montefiore sighed, 'Poor Whitehead, cut off in the prime of life!'"

"If I would swap you for a book about you," I told him, "I would be a poor hand at a bargain."

"You have suppressed your own remarks more than I wish you had."

"My purpose in writing was to remember yours."

He suggested that in future, if I went on recording the conversations, the remarks of the other speakers be reported more fully. We understood each other without more words; but what was understood was this: the ideas advanced by the other speakers were necessary to the flow of the thought, even though they might not be particularly important in themselves. Dialogues are interchange and I divined that he did not care to be represented as indulging in monologues or monopolizing a conversation, neither of which he ever did. Being dialogues, they proceed on the principle which he has already noted in the *Dialogues* of Plato, various speakers setting forth different points of view but without any attempt at dogmatic finality.

"About our discussions of Hellenism and Hebraism," I said apologetically, "you may think I brought that subject up too often. My only excuse is, if it *is* an excuse, I had been studying for years the relationship of those two main forces in Western civilization, and you are one of the few persons who would be of any value to me. You have read the books and done the thinking. Perhaps our repeated discussions have had this advantage—like 'sonata form' in music, the theme keeps returning with enriched development."

"The Jews," said he, "as a race, are probably the most able of any in existence. Now when a gifted person is charming and uses his exceptional ability generously, he is a paragon and people adore him; but in the same way, if a person with unusual ability is disagreeable, his ability makes him just so much the more disagreeable, and thus the disagreeable individuals in that race are the more conspicuous."

"They are not one bit more disagreeable than the Anglo-Saxons," said Mrs. Whitehead. "Having been brought up in Brittany, then taken to England, I came fresh to both, and I know."

"There is a type of well-to-do Englishman," he said, "who has been well established as to property and family for two or three generations, the product of a rather narrow training, and with very limited sympathies, whose reputation for being a disagreeable person is world-wide."

"He is even a figure in literature," said I.

"Yes, and even in the literature of his own country," said Mrs. Whitehead.

[176]

"On the other hand," said the professor, "you get a type of rather impecunious second or third sons of well-to-do families who are cut off from inheritance by our law of primogeniture, and they go out to the colonies, behave pretty well, are much respected and use their talents constructively."

I returned to the question of America and the artist in the present century, which I rather thought had been misdirected in our previous conversation.

"I didn't mean to have you think," said he, "that the artist isn't an immensely important figure in America today. As a matter of fact, you are in a situation here now much like that of the Mediterranean world, centring in the Aegean, say, roughly, between 1000 B.C. and 100 A.D. There was remarkable ease of water transportation, assisted by a lot of convenient islands; it promoted the movement of ideas and the mixing of gifted races. A 'pure' race is likely to be stupid—the Lacedaemonians —but mix the native Attic stock with Dorian invaders or the Ionians with Asiatics, and the results are brilliant. I think the one place where I have been that is most like ancient Athens is the University of Chicago. You see, I am looking for your American equivalent of the Aegean, and I believe it is the Midwest."

"Geographically, the Midwest may be our Aegean," said I, "but our trireme is the motor-car."

"Great events," said he, "points of new departure in human history, are seldom if ever the product of a single cause; they come when two or three causes coalesce. Add to your motor-car the collapse of Europe. (It is no longer considered necessary for your scholars to go to Berlin or London to find out what is happening; in fact, it is impossible.) Then to those two, namely, the collapse of Europe and the motor-car, add a third factor, the blending here of strains from several superior races, the gifted individuals of which are already beginning to appear. And we mustn't forget the means of rapid communication and transport, airplane and wireless, which have unified life on this planet, while placing America at the top of modern civilization."

Returning to the artist's place in our national development, he said, "In the arts, too, you get a great departure when naïve people, because they are keenly interested in the important things, treat an old subject in some novel aspect. The Midwesterners have the great advantage of being naïve. In New York, for example, your type tends to be blasé; they have heard everything, and consider that the simple subjects are hackneyed. So they are. But great art is a dealing with simple subjects freshly. What could be more hackneyed than Shakespeare's plots? True, he set them here or there in time or place, but his characters are all Englishmen of Elizabeth's time viewing these old and simple problems in the light of contemporary life. Why, the plot of *Hamlet* was an old story three thousand years before Shakespeare took it up. But the naïve people view everything freshly, and so they take old things and make them new."

"You remember Goethe, late in the eighteenth century when people were beginning to flock to America, making someone return from America to Europe and say, 'Here, or nowhere, is America'?"

"The situation is reversed; Europe has collapsed; civilization is in your hands, and now," said Whitehead, " 'here, or nowhere, is America.' "

He spoke of the part the Catholics may have in our future.

"The United States looks to be about the only promising field they have left. England, in the seventeenth century; France, in the eighteenth; Germany and Italy in Fascist hands, Spain in revolt, Mexico Communist, South America not very profitable. I wonder how influential American bishops are in Rome? Marxism is now considered to be their chiefest enemy, the stressing of the economic motive. Over the centuries see how they have yielded inch by inch. From 1000 A.D. to 1500 A.D. the pope was, I suppose, the most powerful individual

[178]

in Europe. Then he was defied by the Tudor monarchs in England. Since then the papacy has lost the support of the Bourbons, the Hohenzollerns and the Hapsburgs; and the Church takes second place to the national state. But the Catholic clergy accommodate themselves to changed externals."

Before I left we were discussing methods of composition and whether the typewriting machine would permanently worsen the writing of English prose.

"People compose," said he, "in one or the other of two ways. I first observed this when collaborating on a book with Bertrand Russell. He loved words, and words actually satisfied his craving for expression. He admitted this. But people compose either in words directly, the words satisfying their ideas of things, or they compose in concepts and then try to find words into which those concepts can be translated. I may add that my own method is the second."

XXIV

November 19, 1941

THANKSGIVING Eve I dined with the Whiteheads in Cambridge. As the evening went on we discussed whether there was much help in the Bible for people like us during the present world tumult. He said there was no longer much of anything in it for him. I mentioned the Beatitudes, some of the sayings of Jesus, and the saga of Elijah on Mount Carmel.

"That is a great saga," said he, "but no more."

"The two who have never failed me," I said, "are Beethoven and Plato."

"Plato is the great one," he answered quietly.

I asked what he was reading.

"In my curious overwrought state," said he, a little wearily, "it is hard to tell. I have to try now one thing, now another."

"It is hit or miss," said she.

[179]

We were speaking of the Protestant clergy, and he remarked that a group of Congregational parsons who once came to him struck him as very able people, "liberal, open-minded, equipped to cope with situations. I thought they were, as a group, superior to the Harvard faculty."

It was an inquiry among us three:

Who prop, thou ask'st, in these bad days, my mind?

He had given up the Bible. I said the beauty of nature gives me occasional moments of peace, the crystalline green of a curling breaker which flashes the instant before it foams; it will be equally beautiful a hundred-thousand years hence; it is good, it is true, it asks nothing of me. I am merely permitted to partake of its quality of eternity.

"Some of my utmost sustainment," said he, "I have got out of English poets; not the eighteenth-century people, certainly not Pope, though I like the Churchyard man, what is his name? Gray—but the nineteenth- and seventeenth-century men. My experiences since the first world war, however"—he spoke wearily—"have been such that I find it hard now to read poetry. If you have had the feelings they try to depict, and have really felt deeply, the poetry doesn't verbalize them."

XXV

December 10, 1941

IT was two days after the undeclared attack by the Japanese on our fleet at Pearl Harbour. After dinner at the Faculty Club with Louis Lyons, who had just returned from Washington with a budget of not-very-cheerful news (he is curator of the Nieman Foundation at Harvard), I telephoned to ask the Whiteheads if I could come and call for half an hour.

By good luck no one else was there. Since our minds had been full of nothing else but Pearl Harbour for the past two days, there was a tacit agreement to keep off that subject.

Mr. Whitehead sat with an envelope containing the whole sheaf of my typescripts thus far. He wore his spectacles and dipped into the pages for some correction here and there.

"It is very unusual," he said, "to get authentic records of conversation from the past."

"None occur to me at the moment," I replied, "except Boswell's *Johnson*, and Eckermann's with Goethe, and Eckermann's are seldom general conversation so much as monologues by Goethe, valuable though they are."

"The novelists," said he, "don't help us much here, for they must always be getting on with their story; although occasionally a mediocre novelist like Anthony Trollope does bring back exactly the kind of talk I heard amongst my father's friends when I was a small boy, the provincial clergy with an occasional dean and archbishop."

"Later than that," said she. "It was still going on when I arrived at your house. I remember it well."

"The letters of authors seldom give it to you," said he, "for they always know, whether they admit it or not, that their letters will be printed. What posterity really want to know is what people talked about when they got together, and there's very little of it. I should think these pages of yours might be more valuable a hundred years from now than they are now."

"Before they can be printed," said Mrs. Whitehead, smiling, "there will have to be a few 'demises,' including our own. We talk with you completely off guard."

"I know that, and therefore nobody has seen them except my sister, who typed them. She has said that they make an "Introduction to Whitehead"—that abstract ideas which the average reader might find it difficult to get from your published works, here come out in casual conversation, quite easy to grasp. Most of the matter, it seems to me, is new. I don't remember much, if any, of it in your books."

"No, it is not in any of them. . . . I was trying to think of the name of that Roman banker to whom Cicero wrote letters,

[181]

Atticus. There you have a semblance of conversation from the ancient world—at least the topics in which educated men were interested; and you get some of it in Plato, though of course not even the educated man of Athens was up to Plato all, or even most, of the time."

"Occasionally, though, you do get a bit in Plato that must have come straight out of life. I am thinking," said I, "of that comic anecdote in the *Laches* about a naval battle where a marine, fighting with a scythe-spear, stuck it into the rigging of the other vessel and couldn't pull it out again; and so as the two vessels wore past each other he ran along his own ship hanging to the end of the scythe handle till he had to let go. The crews of both ships knocked off fighting to laugh and applaud the act. His scythe-spear was waving in the air on the other vessel. It was evidently a yarn that went all over Athens."

"You get those homely touches in the earlier *Dialogues*," said Whitehead, pleasantly reminiscent, and cited one or two more, but he resumed:

"Writing only brings out comparatively superficial experiences. Man has had it a relatively short time—shall we say about four thousand years?—first in the form of chipping pieces of stone for the decrees and boasts of monarchs; then on papyrus. For only about three thousand years, or less, have men written down their thoughts; let us say from Homer's time. Now for ages before that you had immense quantities of human experience accumulating in men's bodies. The body itself was, and still is, an immense experience; the sheer harmony of its properly functioning organs gives us a flood of unconscious enjoyment. It is quite inarticulate, and doesn't need to be articulate. But in bulk, and perhaps in significance, it far outweighs the scope of the written word. That, by comparison, is mostly trivial."

"Even with the very greatest masters of the written word," I remarked, "Dante, Goethe, Aeschylus . . . one is left aware of how pale the statement is in comparison with the experience itself; Goethe can only suggest the misery and horror of the Gretchen tragedy; Dante's *Inferno* can be only a shadow of what he imagined; or the murder of Agamemnon, and the agony which came before it and after. What perhaps the written word *can* do is recall to us our own experiences, or give us intimations of experiences which we are likely to have. But since you say the written word is comparatively superficial, what is it that does come first as conscious experience, after these floods of sheer bodily self-enjoyment?"

"The moral values, I should say," he replied, after a longish pause for reflection. "Even dogs have them, in the form of simple-minded affection and loyalty."

"Even that 'subtle-soul'd psychologist,' William James," said I, "was immensely interested in the behaviour of dogs and touched by their affection. He sometimes used them as illustrations when he was lecturing."

"Dogs do better than cats," observed Mrs. Whitehead. "Have you noticed how people divide in their likings, the one sort for cats, the other for dogs? Cats are selfish and self-centred," she added, leaving the inference to be drawn, but he supplied it, smiling:

"If a dog jumps up into your lap, it is because he is fond of you; but if a cat does the same thing, it is because your lap is warmer."

"Are you ever aware of human beings having a predominance of 'cat qualities' or of 'dog qualities'—canine personalities as distinct from feline personalities? Among the felines I would class the person who 'doesn't like people.' Precisely what does that phrase signify?" I asked.

"Self-centredness," suggested Mrs. Whitehead, "and a nature that broods over 'never having had its due.' One, I should think, produces the other."

"After the moral values developing in early men (since we are speculating on origins), what," I asked, "would you say came next?"

"The aesthetic," said Whitehead. "When a nightingale sits up all night singing to his wife, and singing very well, too, you can't make me believe that aesthetic values of a very high order are not present."

"Tell him about our poor nightingale in Surrey," prompted Mrs. Whitehead. As he looked a little at a loss for the episode, she supplied the setting:

"We had a cottage in Surrey in the early spring, and, believe it or not, on the first of May, after the nightingales had arrived, there was a fall of snow. The poor dear caught cold, but went right on singing; and he never did get back to proper pitch all that summer."

"Yes," said Whitehead, smiling, "we had the experience of hearing a nightingale sing out of tune."

"I would rather hear a performance with heart in it," said I, "than an impeccable technique."

"And mind you," said Whitehead, "the same holds for personalities; they make their effect more by what they are than by anything they say. Even when you are using words effectively, they gain a great deal from the physical presence of the speaker; warmth, accent, emphasis, are emanations from body and spirit."

"Of course the very best writing is an attempt to convey in printed words some of those overtones which are sounded by the voice and emanated from the physical personality."

"Yes," said he, "and occasionally with surprising success. That is a property of the very best writing."

"In what you have just said, you 'countenance' me in a perception toward strangers of which I have been aware for years," said I. "It is not necessarily an intuitive perception of beauty or goodness, although it often takes that form; rather, it seems to be an unconscious emanation from the face and body and spirit of a total stranger which one's wireless somehow picks up and signals that, in one sort or another, there is interest and vitality in that person."

"There is nothing surprising in it to me," said Mrs. White-head. "We have just been reading Mrs. Margaret Deland's autobiography (it's there on the little stand at your elbow) and —did you know her?"

"No. I wasn't so fortunate. She was one of my mother's favourite contemporary authors. Didn't she and her husband stand a little aside from social Boston?"

"That is what I meant," said she, ". . . their taking into their home unmarried mothers, to save them from suicide and degradation and steady them by letting them reorganize their lives around the love for the child until they would get on their feet. *There* you have that sense of the interest and worth of a stranger even under a cloud." And she went on to speak of an experience she had had rescuing a beautiful girl, ". . . with that hectic glow of the consumptive. I drove to eleven places in London before I found one that would take her in. First, a Church of England home. 'We don't take second offenders' . . . and so on till we came to—what do you suppose?"

"The Salvation Army?"

"Right. We were received as long-awaited friends and taken in as if we were week-end guests. I asked how much it would cost to maintain her there. 'Nothing,' was the answer. 'If you can afford to pay, of course we shall expect you to do so, but only so that we can take in someone else.' The girl stayed there fifteen months of her own choice and was quite happy."

"What finally became of her?"

"She married a greengrocer, but being consumptive, she died young."

"How good a rating would you give the Salvation Army as Christians?" I asked Whitehead.

"Excellent," said he; "they take their Christianity simply."

"As simply as Francis of Assisi?"

"Oh, much more simply than he. They aren't nearly as encumbered with a bad theology."

"You *do* consider the theology a bad one, then?" I baited him.

[185]

"The trouble," said he, "comes from intellectualizing upon a religion. Jesus was not very intellectual; what he had was a profound insight. Humanity in the Eastern mediterranean between 500 B.C. and 200 A.D. began to write down their intimate thoughts and a great age resulted. I am speaking of course of the exceptionally gifted men who wrote down their thoughts. Paul comes as quite a drop from Jesus, and although his followers included many estimable persons, their idea of God, to my mind, is the idea of the devil."

"How about Buddhism?"

"It is a religion of escapism. You retire into yourself and let externals go as they will. There is no determined resistance to evil. Buddhism is not associated with an advancing civilization."

XXVI

April 5, 1942

SPRING at last, one of the first mild evenings, with a vague stir of exhilaration in the air, robin song, the brilliant yellow of the forsythia and pink of the flowering almond blossoming in the College Yard. Having dined at the Faculty Club, I telephoned Mrs. Whitehead, asking if I might call.

"Come ahead!" said she. "You'll meet nobody but Grace DeFriez."

The Ambassador is only five minutes' walk from the club. Over the elmtops in the west the sky still glowed a burning umber. I had not seen the Whiteheads since February, such is the heartless pace of this city in winter. She was looking tired, but bright as ever. His study door was shut and we sat a little while conversing in the living-room, where she had a vase of English violets on her chair-side table, which diffused their fragrance in the room. She spoke about women she knew who could dismiss all thoughts of the war:

"They 'mustn't be depressed; happiness is necessary to their

[186]

health.' . . . They 'must have complete new outfits, or they might look shabby.' How do such minds work? They're beyond me. Theoretically I envy such insensitivity; actually, I would rather die than be so obtuse to events around me."

"Since you've confessed, so will I. I have one of those theoretical envies: he is a real-estate dealer, quite a fine fellow—the world as it is exactly suits him and he is exactly suited to it. I doubt if he ever wanted anything but what he has: a big house, a tennis-court, wife, family, good income. In low moments I say to myself, 'Why couldn't you have been like him?' "

"But you don't mean it for an instant."

"Of course not, How is Alfred weathering the season?"

"Working too hard, some days better than others, but nothing serious."

She rose, opened the study door, and said quietly:

"Lucien is here."

His voice within made a cordial exclamation.

I went in. He was sitting in one of the big armchairs with a leg-rest, reading a large typescript under a study lamp.

"This tells," said he rising, "how to bring about a world order in three hundred years, if enough people could understand what he is talking about."

I remarked that most of such blueprints assume that the world's entire population is of the same mentality as a college professor.

"Yes," said he, "and that would take a good deal *more* than three hundred years, besides being of doubtful desirability."

The doorbell rang. He answered. It was Grace DeFriez.

"We are going to have a good time," said he delightedly.

Someone quoted a nursery rhyme and a question arose of their antiquity.

"I believe some of them go back to Egypt," said he. "They get new trimmings as they come down the ages, but essentially they are the same."

"Children are your true die-hard conservatives; they pass along the oral folk-lore—including naughty words—undeviatingly from crop to crop," said I. "And some of the words are sharply regional. There is one I used to hear as a boy in the Midwest which I never heard east of the Alleghenies, until a Montana boy who was visiting me used it: 'helleshen,' or 'hellishin.' It's probably some local variant of 'hellish.'"

"My children," said Grace, "bring home the same stories and jokes I used to hear and repeat when I was their age. I hadn't thought of them for years."

"The one place where my Americanism breaks down," said Whitehead, "is on the jokes in *The New Yorker*. I can generally see the humour of the pictures, but the captions are often too much for me."

"Oh, you needn't feel sensitive about that," said Grace. "My children often have to explain the jokes to me. It makes me realize how out of date I must be."

"And you needn't feel sensitive about *that*, either," I offered comfort, "for a good many of the jokes are sharply regional— New Yorky."

Mrs. Whitehead said, "I can understand the jokes about the fat women—"

"Helen Hokinson's?"

"Yes. But I don't think fat women are funny. I feel sorry for them, poor things."

"You are like Sir Richard Livingstone's son, Rupert, a kindly boy, who used to see *The New Yorker* on some reading table in Oxford. He said, 'I laugh at the jokes, but I have a feeling that I oughtn't.'"

"My feeling is," said Mrs. Whitehead, "that such excess flesh must be a glandular affliction and shouldn't be laughed at."

"Then I can relieve your conscience. Come in to Huyler's on Tremont Street any afternoon at three o'clock and I will show you scores of women mowing away sweet cakes with sugar frosting filled with whipped cream."

"Oouff!" says she, with a grimace. "Don't expect me!"

By some transition—as to whether weight, like hanging and wiving, goes by destiny—we came to the question of free will. Mrs. Whitehead thought we have very little; occasional margins of deflection, although within those limits we might exercise considerable control.

"I think," said Whitehead, "that although in the final act we are so conditioned by unconscious previous thought that it looks automatic, as a matter of fact we have been determining that act by an enormous amount of rejection and selection. It all depends on what ideas are entertained and how we entertain them; some may be dismissed at once as horrible and repugnant, others dwelt upon as pleasant. After this rejection and selection has gone on for a sufficiently long period, the final act *is* conditioned, but we have had a large share in doing it."

"May I follow the process a little farther upstream?" I proposed. "Behind what is selected or rejected haven't we the economic position, which may determine whether one has easy access to superior standards; then the inherited disposition, which may be congenial to certain types of choice and hostile to others?"

"Yes," he assented, "the area of choice seems to exist between those antecedent determinants and the final, seemingly automatic act. But you can catch yourself entertaining habitually certain types of ideas and setting others aside; and that, I think, is where our personal destinies are largely decided."

"If you two could have got out to see the film of Shaw's *Major Barbara* I would have haled you there," said I. "Grace saw it and we have already discussed it at length. The point is that Shaw has rewritten that feeble last scene, at the armament factory, and now seems to be saying, 'These forces of nature are in themselves neither good nor bad; all depends on how they are used; and the unique function of man is to learn how to use them properly, though the moral values we lend them are entirely of our own devising; if they promote comfort and harmony, we term them "good"; if the reverse, "evil." The great mystery remains, how did any life come into being on this planet capable of conceiving such values at all?' "

"Whoever would have dreamed," said Whitehead, "when this earth was a mere molten mass, of any such forms of life as have appeared? The method of nature seems to be by the production of novelty—some totally unexpected turn of origination. By and by the earth cooled, and the seas appeared; aeons later, plant life and animals."

"And what hideously fantastic animals!" said Mrs. Whitehead.

"And finally, man," he resumed, "after perhaps a million years. And who that watches the heavens can doubt that forms of life just as amazing exist on other planets? The nebulae, too, have their life cycles; come into being, are obliterated, and pass into some other form. Where do the moral ideas first appear? Actually, they appear *before* man; animals have them; birds know when they have done wrong."

"Dogs," said Mrs. Whitehead, "are far more moral than most human beings; they are more self-effacing and more self-sacrificing. Watch a dog try to help someone he loves; the beast puts us to shame."

"I think that our power of conscious origination is where free will comes in," said Whitehead. "We are continually choosing between the good and the less good, whether aware of it or not. Even children do so before they can hardly speak. When one of our boys was little (he wasn't punished, for he did nothing to be punished for) he evidently had a code of his own which he sometimes violated. The only way we would know it was that he would crawl under the bed. When we saw his little shoes sticking out from under the bed, we always knew he was guilty, though we never knew of what, nor asked, for he couldn't have told us. He wouldn't come out unless dragged by the heels. That done, all was expiated. Being dragged out by the heels he evidently considered a full atonement."

Grace said she wished she knew some way to get dragged out from under the bed by the heels, it would simplify so many complicated problems of ethics.

"And mind you," Whitehead continued, "children must have such ideas long before they can talk. This child called himself 'Goo,' and one day I heard him passing under the open window of my study murmuring to himself, 'Goo can walk now. Goo can talk now.'"

"Something similar happened when Ivins was little," said Grace. "He was a heavy baby, not light on his feet like Polly, but a little ice wagon. One day he suddenly discovered that he could stand. He was terribly excited and cried, '*tan! tan!*' He kept tumbling down, but getting up on his legs again. I suppose they see larger persons doing these wonderful things and, long before they can talk, resolve to do them too."

"An enormous part of our mature experience, also," said Whitehead, "cannot be expressed in words."

"Dr. McFee Campbell, the professor of psychiatry in the Harvard Medical School, said something similar a few evenings ago," said I, "—that words are clumsy, or quite inadequate to express certain experiences or emotions."

"That is what poetry at its best does," said Whitehead, "—comes somewhere near capturing in a net of words one of those powerful, evanescent moments, of happiness or pain. After all, a word is only a sound, and the relationship between that sound and an experience is very artificial and arbitrary. Look up the poet's words in the dictionary, and you will find that the meanings there given do not total the poet's; he has *added* to their meaning by emotional overtones, so that in some cases you follow the accretions of meaning which successive poets have added to words. But always in the poetry itself is a fragrance of experience which the poet alone has been able to capture, though we recognize it as also our own."

"Don't we all have some such moments of intense being," I

asked, "when we are peculiarly and uniquely alive? And there they remain, eternal springs, into which we can lower our buckets time after time, and years later, without exhausting them."

"Yes. But it is not *the* experience," corrected Mrs. Whitehead. "It is a *memory* of the moment when we lived so intensely. You see that mirror on the inner wall? Bernardine gave it me. It came from Florence, and I have never happened to see another. It is a 'black' mirror. If it were white, the persons and scenes reflected in it would be mere fresh aspects of their daylight selves; but seen in this curious black medium, they look disembodied; they are 'memories.' My black mirror is the world of memory. And what the poets are able to do with words to save these intense moments of ecstasy or pain from oblivion is a black mirror."

"When first I came to see you," said Grace, "when you lived down by the river, that mirror was the first object that I noticed in your living-room."

"It is different every hour of the day," said Whitehead, "and, being hung where it is, it reflects the sunsets. The effect is extraordinary; again, as Evelyn says, they look like the *memory* of a sunset—or of a very abstruse idea that escaped one. Whenever I hear, as sometimes I do, one of my colleagues say that there are no ideas which cannot be expressed clearly in simple language, I think, 'Then your ideas must be very superficial.'"

"You once said to me," I reminded him, "that certain writers, philosophers among them, think in words; but that you think in concepts, then try to find words to express them. Now what happens between the concept and the word? How do you translate the one into the other?"

"God knows!" said he, fervently. "Sometimes the sentence comes, and sometimes it doesn't."

"He tears up a good many sheets of written paper," supplied his wife in parenthesis.

[192]

"Do you visualize your thought, even abstract ideas?"
I asked.

"I don't know. Do you?"

"First let me qualify my remark. I don't handle such high voltage of abstraction as you, and yet, having worked at it for a quarter of a century, I know how hard it is to translate even fairly simple abstractions into simple language."

"You handle difficult enough abstractions," said he reassuringly. "I have read your articles."

"Then I can answer. When concentration is at its most intense, the abstract idea seems to be a kind of disembodied substance floating in space; but directly underneath it is some totally irrelevant visual scene—generally from my childhood, say a meadow in summer sunshine."

"That is most singular. No. I don't think I visualize like that."

"Please explain to me," said Grace to the philosopher, "what you mean by concepts."

"I will tell you," said he, his eyes beginning to twinkle. "There opposite me sits Lucien Price. I have a concept of him; of his personality, of his appearance, of the kind of person I think he is, all very definite to me. But when I try to put him into words, what have I? Well, I can say, 'He is a valued friend. I am always glad to see him. His personal appearance is of such a sort. . . .' But I could say exactly the same of Lawrence Lowell."

The two women laughed much harder than I did.

"Alfred," said Grace, "this conversation has reached a climax. You will scarcely do better than that."

"Do you grasp the concept?" said he.

"Perfectly! But I don't think Lucien does. He looks dazed. Do you grasp it?" she appealed to me.

"I'm not sure that I want to."

"Have some ginger-ale," says she, "that will revive you."

After the fortissimo passage ending with Mr. Lowell, Whitehead resumed on a quiet note:

"Some of the finest moral intuitions come to quite humble people. The visiting of lofty ideas doesn't depend on formal schooling. Think of those Galilean peasants."

"Our Mary, who has done our housework for nearly twenty years," said Mrs. Whitehead, "has a little girl named Margaret. One Easter she asked about the story of Jesus and the Crucifixion; wanted it explained. So Mary sat down with her and went through it. 'And Jesus died on the Cross?' asked the child. 'Yes,' said her mother. 'And his mother was standing by all that time?' 'Yes.' 'But why didn't his mother die for him?' Mary was quite taken aback."

The question then arose why and how a noble or original idea, after having been promulgated, is debased almost beyond recognition. Inventions are turned from production to destruction; Christianity is made a pretext for persecution; the classics of symphonic music are hawked about night-clubs in garbled versions which are almost obscene. In its original form, does such an idea have to come to an exceptionally lofty nature; and is it necessarily debased by exposure to the commonalty? Whitehead took it up:

"Intuition may be an angel," said he, "but intellect can play the devil. Of course you must have intellect to manage the ideas that come through intuition; but the mischief enters when the ideas begin to be certified and classified and organized into rigid formulas. Christianity is a fearful example. The Jews had originally a barbaric morality which was gradually undergoing humanization at the hands of their finer spirits, although it was also from time to time rebarbarized by the coarser. I don't remember that the Buddhistic religion was ever guilty of such fearfully immoral ideas as the Hebrew theology in its earlier form or the Christian in its later: that mankind were to be either saved or damned, and damned to eternal torment. Rather, the Buddhist held that we are, all of us, so imperfect that we must keep returning lifetime after lifetime for purification through experience until we are worthy to lose our identity in the all. But the Jews, looking around them, saw always an Oriental despot, and so, looking over the world at large, thought there must be a despot over all, and the consequence was they conceived one of the most immoral Gods ever imagined."

"Fancy Jehovah telling Abraham to sacrifice his son!" said Mrs. Whitehead.

" 'An honest God is the noblest work of man,' " I quoted Samuel Butler.

"It is true," said Grace, "Jehovah did things which any one of us would have hesitated to do."

" 'Hesitated?' " said Mrs. Whitehead. "You mean horrified."

"Do you remember that remark of Thomas Hardy about the 'jealous God' in *Tess of the D'Urbervilles?*" I asked.

"No," said Whitehead. "What is it?"

"I remember it," said Mrs. Whitehead. "Quote it him."

" 'But although to visit the sins of the fathers upon the children may be a morality good enough for divinities, it is scorned by average human nature.' "

"How amiable the Grecian gods appear by comparison," said Mrs. Whitehead. "They may have had their crimes and follies, and have been no better than they should have been, but their offences were more urbane."

"Yes," I said. "Even if they, too, went to the devil in the end, they had a good time going. The point is, the Greeks always reserved the right to laugh at their gods."

"The total absence of humour from the Bible," remarked Whitehead, "is one of the most singular things in all literature."

"Goethe notices it in the Prologue to *Faust.* Mephistopheles is made to twit God with his lack of humour," I said,

> *My pathos would but move Your Grace to laughter,*
> *Had not you long since laughter quite abjured.*

"The absence of humour from the writings of the ancient Jews may be explained," said Whitehead, "by the fact of their always having been a depressed people. They were always being invaded, and overrun, and deported hither and yon. The Greeks, on the other hand, no matter what happened to them, or whether they really were on top or not, always regarded themselves as being on top."

We began comparing the *Iliad*, in which the gods laugh, with the Bible. The authors of the Bible conceived their function to be that of edification—if you didn't like it, you *ought* to; the authors (or author) of the *Iliad* considered themselves artists. If they failed to interest you, it was not your fault, but theirs.

"But has the *Iliad* had the effect of good that the Bible has had?" objected Grace. "I read the Bible stories at the right age and later their shine never came off."

"The *Iliad*," said Whitehead, "is probably the origin of our idea of the gentleman. But the gentleman is not a complete answer."

As the evening wore on we fell to discussing the relative merits of maple syrup and suet pudding.

"Maple syrup? That gluey substance?" said Mrs. Whitehead. "I abhor it."

"She walks out on the choicest article New England can produce!" I appealed to my fellow-Yankee.

"Go slow," says Grace. "I'm not too strong for maple syrup myself."

"If you really want to take me on my weak side," confessed Mrs. Whitehead, "try me with suet pudding!"

"Suet pudding!" exclaimed Grace. "*That* awful preparation?"

"It's not awful. It's quite heavenly. On that side I'm quite, quite unregenerate."

"So here we are," said Whitehead, "after having discussed the loftiest abstractions, down to suet pudding. The historic cycle is complete; it is the decay of a civilization, into suet pudding!"

XXVII

May 5, 1943

AN evening at the Whiteheads' with Edward Weeks. It had been planned for months, yet this was the first time it had been practicable for all of us. Since Whitehead's work has been appearing in the *Atlantic Monthly* for many years, both when Ellery Sedgwick was editor and since the editorship has been assumed by Mr. Weeks, they were well acquainted.

After having dined, we walked up Prescott Street to the Hotel Ambassador in the twilight of one of the few mild evenings in this painfully belated spring.

He had asked whether anybody else would be there except the Whiteheads. I didn't know, but hoped not. They were alone, to the great satisfaction of us both; lamps lighted, shades and blackout curtains drawn, and the living-room brightened with big bowls and vases of spring flowers.

Mrs. Whitehead had had a severe sprain to her ankle, almost a fracture. It was a surprise to find her walking on it.

"It hurts," said she, "but I have to do it. . . ."

Conversational preliminaries were then of the briefest. In the May *Atlantic* had appeared a leading article by President Conant of Harvard, "*Wanted: American Radicals.*" It proposed a third choice between the two old alignments, a radicalism that should be indigenous, Jeffersonian, with a good word for Andrew Jackson, Emersonian in the temper of his "American Scholar," with Walt Whitman for its poet; and respectful but aloof to Marx, Engels, and Lenin. It was addressed to planning for the post-war world: foreign policy, internal problems such as ownership or control of the tools of production, decentralization, attack on a stratified society, and an attempt to redefine culture in democratic and American terms.

"I say," Whitehead appealed to the editor of the magazine, "what response are you getting to Mr. Conant's article?"

"It is still a little early to judge."

"I should think you would get fifty letters in each morning's mail, denouncing him for writing and you for publishing it."

"What do *you* think of it?"

"His idea of having a redistribution of wealth every generation is challenging. I don't say it is new. But as presented by him it lacks practicality. You could do it by taxation, but that would merely come to the government's getting it. A certain amount of surplus wealth in the hands of private individuals is favourable to all sorts of experimentation."

"What is going to become of the English landed aristocracy?"

"It has already happened," Whitehead replied calmly. "They are ruined. The government takes their land, allows them to remain in the houses as custodians, but the land is turned over into cultivation, and trees are grown not as ornaments but as a crop. Old trees are being cut down for war purposes and small pines planted."

"My England!" sighed Mrs. Whitehead. "I am glad I shall never see it again."

"After the war," he continued, "I doubt if we shall ever again have as big a foreign trade, and that means we must do more in agriculture."

Mr. Weeks, who has just returned from a transcontinental tour, spoke of the sweeping industrialization of the West, from Texas on up the Pacific Coast to Puget Sound, at the expense of the inland agricultural states. The report was given in some detail and listened to intently, since it is all too recent to have been described very conclusively in print. This led to certain questions about the conduct of the magazine, due to curtailment of the paper supply, which he answered briefly but explicitly. He said that American publishers have been warned by English ones not to create a powerful competitor in the form of the government, with unlimited access to the paper pool and power to commandeer printeries.

There was a year in the 1920's, money still being flush, when it was told me at the Old Corner Book Store that in this country alone twenty thousand new books were published. I mentioned this, naming the year.

"You are wrong about that," Weeks corrected me. "About nine thousand were new. For the rest, they counted reprints."

"Even at nine thousand," (which was my point) "quantities of them must have been worthless."

"You look straight at a man who has published twelve books," said Whitehead, looking back at me, "and say that many of them can't have been worth printing!"

The conversation turned to whether men of exceptional intellect are successes as statesmen.

"They rarely get a chance to try," said Whitehead. "The kind of man who is wanted to run a state, and the kind of man who mostly does run it, is the one who, while he may not be exceptional intellectually, has a good nose for what needs to be done."

"Can we think of any exceptions?"

"Disraeli!" exclaimed Whitehead and Weeks in the same breath. "Thomas Jefferson would be another of my candidates," added Weeks, after a moment of reflection.

"The men who founded your republic," Whitehead continued, "had an uncommonly clear grasp of the general ideas that they wanted to put in here, then left the working out of the details to later interpreters, which has been, on the whole, remarkably successful. I know of only three times in the Western world when statesmen consciously took control of historic destinies: Periclean Athens, Rome under Augustus, and the founding of your American republic."

This raised an inquiry as to what extent statesmen in power at great historical crises can be alive to the magnitude of the destinies involved. Augustus—the ancient world was in the gravest peril when he took over Rome, yet could he remotely have envisaged what was at stake for the future of Europe and the West?

"No," said Whitehead. "Being a Roman, he wanted to save

the Roman Empire. In so doing, it resulted that the Roman Empire became the bottleneck through which the culture of the ancient world passed into Northern Europe and to the Western Hemisphere. And now, after five hundred years, the civilization of the Renaissance is crumbling. In great historical events you can seldom assign a single cause. Several causes coalesce. The Russians got sick of their fearfully wasteful czarist government; the Hapsburg monarchy was ready to fall; France was decaying far faster than we supposed; and Germany had that unstable monarch, Wilhelm II. Bismarck did his work too well. He would be horrified if he could see the lengths to which it has been carried. The collapse of the five-hundred-year-old Renaissance civilization was not caused by any one of these; and all of these are only a few of the causes. Add to these the industrial revolution and the new scientific techniques. The question was, would this machinery fall into the hands of the bad people or of the good people? At the start of the industrial revolution, a hundred years ago, the machinery fell, I should say, on the whole into the hands of fairly good people; they exploited the poor, but at least they used it for production. But in our time, these new technologies have fallen, temporarily let us hope and believe, into the hands of the bad people; predatory gangsters. All of these causes were cumulatively present; the separate events were results. I don't say that Europe is done for for ever; it will recover in time of course; but it is collapsed for a generation, if not longer. Three of the modern states with good societies which I hope will survive are Denmark, Norway and Sweden."

He went on to speak of the element of chance in history—how a British expeditionary force bound for China was diverted to Calcutta just in time to help quell the Sepoy Rebellion, and concluded humorously:

"Divine Providence seemed to be on our side."

"But Divine Providence plays no favourites," said Weeks laughingly, and cited that extraordinary succession of seeming coincidences on the Hudson River which revealed the plot of Benedict Arnold.

" 'As luck would have it,' " quoted Mrs. Whitehead, from Samuel Butler's *Erewhon*, " 'Providence was on my side.' "

But what *is* "coincidence," the question was resumed. Sometimes it appears beneficent; again, as with the Athenians before Syracuse, it looks maleficent, and in such a sequence as positively to suggest foreordination. What are we to suppose? Do the causes lie deeper than mere brute accidents?

"The causes, I am inclined to think," said Whitehead, "are there all along, and the events which we see, and which look like freaks of chance, are only the last steps in long lines of causation."

A tray was brought in. The little cakes were in a silver basket which, as an inscription on it read, had been presented to Mr. Whitehead's father, the vicar, in 1858.

As conversation was allowed to drift for a few minutes, there was space to enjoy the pictorial element. The three sat in shaded lamplight; Weeks, as usual, looking slim, trim and vigorous, though more than usually alert; Mrs. Whitehead stretched at her ease, the lamp beams falling more directly on her face, which gains expressiveness with age. An embroidered shawl was thrown over her knees, and beside her was a bowl of garden flowers. Occasionally she or Weeks smoked a cigarette. Whitehead's eyes retain their blue brilliancy undimmed, his complexion is still ruddy, his voice clear, strong, and melodious. As he speaks, he turns from one to another of us; his speech is deliberate, perfectly articulated, everything weighed, the qualifying clauses duly entered, the language precise and almost mathematically exact. The youth of his face is astonishing. This is often remarked by others. It is the illumination of thought within which gives him this glow and glisten. Also, it is communicated; one's own perceptions are heightened.

The discussion was resumed by Whitehead's saying:

"Americans care more for equality than they do for liberty.

You have it in a sense in which we do not, but you are much harder than we on the people who don't make good. Over here it is assumed that if a man doesn't make good it must of course be his own fault. There is much more fellow-feeling in England between the upper classes and the labouring people. With us, classes are more solidified, but while our class-lines run horizontally, our lines of friendship are vertical."

This called forth a remark that, especially since the present war has so shuffled our population, it is noticeable how people try to ease the situation for one another.

"The kindness of the American people," said Whitehead, in his gentlest tones, "is, so far as I know, something unique in the history of the world, and it is the justification of your existence. Your immigrants, before the 1880's when your immigration began to be commercialized by the steamship companies, came, in the main, because they liked the American idea. In fact, one cause of the collapse of Europe may be that so many of the abler people left Europe and came over here. Your German 'forty-eighters' are one of your best population strains."

"We didn't fare so badly, as it turned out, with most of those who came after the 1880's—" observed Weeks, rising to light Mrs. Whitehead's cigarette—"little as some of those who brought them over here may have intended the result. It is probable that their cheap labour affected the living standards of our workers for a generation, but their children went to our public schools and learned a lively sense of their civil rights."

"England, too, got some of the German forty-eighters," said Mrs. Whitehead. "You will find them among the wealthy manufacturers in places like Birmingham. And they have this peculiarity, that among them is, so far as I know, the only anti-Semitism in England."

"Anti-Semitism was very rare," assented Mr. Whitehead. "In my home village in Kent my father's old friend Sir Moses Montefiore was a Jew and no one ever gave it a thought."

"I fell in love with this place when I came here to live," said Mrs. Whitehead, "and where I love I'm not critical. But I do notice a hardness toward shop assistants by customers. It would be just as easy to be kinder when they haven't what one wants. In your streetcars the young and the old are treated royally. Grey hair never has to stand. But in between I have seen women standing who ought to have been seated—one, who looked as if she was about to have a child—that very day. . . . On the other hand, this is the sort of thing that can happen: one summer at a cottage in a Vermont village our plumbing went out. I was told the plumber was a very peculiar, independent man, and maybe he would fix it, and maybe he wouldn't. Anyhow, we sent for him. He didn't come. Late in the afternoon, while Alfred and North were off somewhere, and I was sitting on the porch, a man came in, dressed as we all are up there, in a sweater. I said my husband would be back shortly and asked if he wouldn't come up and wait. We chatted. He was interesting and well-read. By and by I asked him if he would have tea. He said he would. So I brought it. We had tea and I was growing more and more interested in what he had to say, when finally he said, 'Well, I guess I had better have a look at your plumbing.'"

"Had you no inkling who he was?"

"I suppose I might have had; but I hadn't."

"One thing we lack, though, and that is a visible, tangible past," said Weeks. "We try to invent it; we get it out of books, but it is always an effort. And this pastlessness is emphasized by our mobility. We not only never die in the house where we were born, but we move out of it before we are out of knee breeches, and when we go back to visit our birthplace, the house has been demolished and on its site stands a filling station. In the New Jersey town where I was brought up, and where the suburbs of New York were already reaching into that country-side, there was only one 'Great House.' We children of the town were never invited there to tea, though we were allowed to visit its gardens, but it stood for something in our life of the imagination."

"Our sense of the past in England," said Whitehead, "is so all-pervasive that it is quite unconscious with us. Everywhere we turn, the past is before us, in buildings, monuments, history, legend—five hundred years of it, a thousand years of it. And it enters, of course, into all that we think and do."

"How was this 'pastlessness' in the town where you grew up?" Weeks turned to me.

"We had less past than you. A building in the Western Reserve of Ohio that had stood seventy-five years was 'old.' But what we lacked in past we made up in equality."

"That would mean," asked Professor Whitehead, "that anyone who got rich went away?"

"No one went away rich. It was necessary to go away in order to get rich. Among those who stayed, there were a few shadowy class-lines, but at bottom everybody was felt to be about as good as anybody else, if he paid his debts."

"You have omitted one class-line of the American small town a generation ago," said Weeks.

"What is that?"

"It was not respectable to get drunk."

"That is true. The orgies of the 1920's had blurred my memory of it."

"Do you think there is any possibility of a re-enactment of Prohibition?" Mrs. Whitehead appealed to Mr. Weeks.

"The waves of that Prohibition movement are beating against the *Atlantic* office more heavily month by month. I hope there is no danger of a repetition. But arguments come in that are deaf and blind to every lesson of experience. How about liquor smuggling in England," he inquired of Whitehead, "when you lived on that Kentish coast? Was there an incentive to bringing it in, or was there nothing to bring in that couldn't be had just as easily at home?"

"On the marshes near the sea," said Whitehead, "stood a very old church. All I know about it is that a hundred and forty years ago, say in Napoleon's time, a great deal of very superior brandy and wine used to come up those marshes and was stored in the vaults of that church, with the approbation of the vicar. And more than once, when word was brought, during service, that officers were coming up the road, the whole congregation adjourned to get that liquor out of the way— assisted by the vicar! That is evidence," he concluded, beaming upon us, "of how intimately the Established Church shares the life of the nation."

XXVIII

June 3, 1943

EDWARD WEEKS and I play a return engagement with the Whiteheads. It was a day of summer heat which, coming suddenly after the cold, backward spring, took the gimp out of everybody. At 53 Chestnut Street, the house of Weeks was in curl-papers; they were to leave for their summer at Beverly Farms next morning.

Beacon Hill in June can look quite bridal. Flowers blooming in the little areas between iron fences and red-brick house walls; wisteria and ivy climbing house-fronts; fresh foliage and grass plots in dooryards and Louisburg Square. No sooner does the town turn beautiful than we go away and leave it.

There was a quick shift of scene from Boston to Cambridge. In order to reach the Whiteheads' at the appointed time, we took a taxicab. Their blackout curtains were drawn, but all the windows of all the rooms being open, a light breeze drafted through refreshingly. Some June garden had filled the vases of this living-room with irises, peonies, and yellow lilies.

No preliminaries.

"Your June number of the *Atlantic*," said Whitehead to Weeks, "is brilliant."

"Luck," said he, modestly, "but one is very thankful for it. Just the right things came in at the right moment."

(Among the right things were "Bring Back the Liberal Arts" by E. K. Rand, "The Unimagined America" by Archibald MacLeish, "Western Star" by Stephen Vincent Benét, and "The Hoover Frame of Mind" by Rebecca West.)

It appeared that Mr. Weeks had been in Washington, "where I had an hour's talk with Wavell, or rather, was talked to by him for an hour."

"How did he seem?"

"It was about Tobruk, Crete, and India; none of it too cheerful. He seemed worn and tired, not discouraged, but pretty well used up." (Weeks was softening this. It had come into the newspaper office that the impression Wavell made in Washington was of a man all but exhausted.) "What he told was interesting. He had taken over that command in Africa when it looked anything but hopeful; and they were as surprised as anybody at how fast and how far they were able to go."

The discussion swung to the situation in India. They said that Roosevelt was careful not to intrude on British colonial affairs.

"I admire him for that," said Mrs. Whitehead. "God knows we've made mistakes enough; but they must be corrected by ourselves. Are you for Roosevelt? . . ." She hesitated and made as if to draw back.

"Very much so," said Weeks. "I'm a Democrat."

"Good! One never knows which way people are going to jump on that question. We grow used to feeling our ground first. There ought to be some emblem we could wear so as to recognize one another," said she.

"A campaign button on our lapels," suggested Mr. Weeks. "But that might prove more awkward than none."

I remarked that it had sometimes brought good luck for people to be politically incommunicado, especially in touchy times.

"Indeed yes!" said Whitehead, smiling. "It was a piece of especially good luck for us that our first two kings of the Hanoverian dynasty couldn't speak English. When finally we got a third who could, he involved us in that trouble with you people, from which we have not yet fully recovered, and, to make matters worse, George III was an exemplary family man, well liked by the people: 'Farmer George,' good husband, kind father, that sort of thing: he had all the domestic virtues which gave fatal weight to his appalling political ineptitude."

"Even the Nonconformists," added Mrs. Whitehead, "respected him."

"Haven't you said," I asked him, "that the Hanoverian dynasty was only tolerated on good behaviour?"

"They were brought over by a group of Whig nobles," said Whitehead. "These nobles were the 'committee.' Had the first two Georges proved meddlesome, they could have been sent home. It was George III, in my opinion, who caused us to be on the wrong side when the French Revolution came along. Otherwise, I think we might have enacted the reforms of the 1830's in 1789. Had we done so, we should have got on much better with the French, and we would have gone into the Industrial Age of the next century without those dreadful urban slums."

As the conversation veered to the art of letters, Weeks asked Whitehead what shape he thought literature might take when this war ends.

Replying, Whitehead spoke of the tendency toward satire after a war, instancing Lytton Strachey after the last war, but said that such men, however amusing, are sterile and the ensuing crop is likely to be thin.

"Do you think," asked Mr. Weeks, "that we shall be repossessed by the Freudians in literature?"

"They are an example of what I mean by the naïve acceptance of a part of the truth as the whole truth," said Whitehead. "The ideas of Freud were popularized by people who only imperfectly understood them, who were incapable of the great effort required to grasp them in their relationship to larger truths, and who therefore assigned to them a prominence out of all proportion to their true importance."

"Add to that," said Weeks, "their popularity with a post-war generation which wanted to be told exactly what these incomplete interpretations of Freud seemed to say."

"You once remarked" (my question had been long pending) "that between the time when experience enters into us and when it is uttered forth again in language or in action there is a gap about which we know nothing. Have you gone any farther with it?"

"Last week during commencement," Whitehead replied, "a brain specialist was here. He said that our bodily experience is transmitted to the brain through the spinal column, and especially to that part of the brain at the back of our heads. I had often observed people with big bulges at the back of their skulls and thought, 'Isn't it a pity that they couldn't have had those bulges at the front of their skulls where it would have done them some good,' but it appears that I was quite mistaken. This surgeon informs me that a man can have quite a lot of his brain removed from here or here" (he pointed to his left and right temples) "and get on quite as well as ever; but if any serious disconnection takes place at the back of the neck, the man is an idiot. Philosophers have known for centuries that our senses are no reliable testimony to the existence of the outside world. That has been known not only since the seventeenth- and eighteenth-century men, but as far back as the Greeks. There was absolutely no reason to infer the existence of external reality from any evidence brought in to us by our senses. It is all subjective. The outer world may not be there at all. And yet, as a matter of fact, the only human beings who do not assume the existence of that outer world as a reality are in the lunatic asylums. But all the while, our knowledge of it is brought to us up our spinal columns through our bodily experience, the pleasurable functioning of our organs. For our bodies *are* a part of that external world, just as much as this chair in which my body is at present sitting. So I wouldn't advise you to let anything serious happen to the back of your neck. The front of your head; yes, you can be as careless with that as you like, and still get on fairly well; but if the back of your neck gets dislocated, then you are really in a bad way."

This led to some gaiety at the expense of masseurs. When the discussion sobered down again, we came to that passage in *Adventures of Ideas* (page 355) where a striking sentence seems to bear upon this mystery of what happens between the time when external experience impinges on body, spinal column, and brain, and the time when it is uttered forth again. That sentence is:

The process is itself the actuality.

This was quoted to him with the remark, "People have told me that once it gets into their heads, it won't come out. I think I know what it means; at least, I know what it means to me. But would you tell us what it means to you?"

"It took a long while, centuries in fact, for philosophers to get beyond the idea of static matter," said he. "Certain substances, like water or fire, could be seen to be changing rapidly; others, like rock, looked immutable. We know now that a piece of granite is a raging mass of activity, that it is changing at a terrific rate; but until we did know it, a rock seemed to possess little or no life, though it looked immensely permanent. But, since there was obviously quite a little mind about, the older philosophers brought it in from the outside. There seemed to be divisions between one part of the universe and another. But in the light of what we now know, there is no dividing line between the infinitely vast and the infinitely small. The element of time affects it too. Our human bodies change from day to day; certain external appearances of them are the same, but change is constant and sometimes visible. The constellations do not appear to change at all, though we know that they do, as we know that the nebulae have come into their present form but are also passing into another. Whether the change occurs in a minute or in billions of years, is merely a matter of human measurement; the fact of change is not affected by our using, as human beings, the only standards of measurement we have, which are necessarily affected by the limitations of our own lives. We exist here under certain conditions of space and time within which we have to function, and these conditions, unless watched, colour our judgments. . . . This little table by my side"—he tapped it with his fingers—"is in process of change. If you were to shut it up somewhere for ten thousand years and then went back to look at it, the change might be so pronounced that you would hardly know it had been a table; yet the process which would produce that so visible change is going on in it right now, although for all practical human purposes it is the same table you saw the last time you were here and the same one I have seen around for forty years. Change is constant, whether we measure it by minutes or millennia; we ourselves are a part of it; we have been brought into existence in a certain quarter of the universe in consequence of its processes, and there is no reason to suppose that other types of existence, unimaginable to us, have not been produced elsewhere in the universe. Those other lives could scarcely strike us as much more different from us than we now know ourselves to be different from our ancestors. Some of our more immediate ancestors would be quite congenial to us; but as they grow increasingly remote, your ancestors would be creatures which I doubt if you would like at all."

(He had been telling us in simple terms that our judgments are sharply conditioned by time and space, but that the actualities are outside of both, and that change is the process and is itself the actuality.)

"To what extent," I asked, "did mathematics let you into these secrets?"

"Mathematics," said he, "is essentially a study of types of order. In its earlier forms it had to do with number and quantity. That is its historical origin; the idea of mathematical logic is comparatively modern. But while mathematics is a convenience in relating certain types of order to our comprehensions, it does not, as used to be supposed, give us any account of their actuality. You have probably studied the Euclidean geometry, but I doubt if it diminished for you any of the mystery of life."

"I did study the Euclidean geometry, but, not being good at mathematics, it rather increased the mystery of life," I confessed.

"Euclid's geometry was once supposed to be an exact description of the external world. The only world of which it is an accurate description is the world of Euclidean geometry. When it began to be challenged in the eighteenth century, the ascertained deviations from it were at first considered, even by their discoverers themselves, to be errors."

"You once remarked that at the time when the discovery of the magnetic needle found its way into Europe, 'mathematics had been almost useless for a thousand years.' How useless?"

"Archimedes, when the Roman soldier stabbed him, knew as much mathematics as was known at any time until, say, the fourteenth century, when its advance was resumed."

"And we have no control over the process by which the arts or sciences advance or retrograde in one age or another?"

"Take it in our own time," he replied to the question out of his own experience. "I was in Cambridge in the 1880's, first as an undergraduate, later as one of the staff. If was from two hundred to two hundred and fifty years since mathematics had had its fresh impetus from men like Descartes and Sir Isaac Newton; there were certain borderlands where affairs in that science were considered indefinable, but in the main, mathematical physics looked sound and solid. . . . By the turn of the century, nothing, absolutely nothing was left that had not been challenged, if not shaken; not a single major concept.

This, I consider to have been one of the supreme facts of my experience."

"Could the same be said of religion and ethics?" I asked.

"Yes, with this difference, that philosophy and science welcomed these new hypotheses which upset their old ones, and thus profited by them; whereas, religion resisted the new ideas and has suffered in consequence."

"Can this rate of change be expected to continue?" asked Weeks.

"The consequences of these new ideas in science will continue to affect our lives profoundly, especially their techniques. We talk about the changes wrought on society by the 'Industrial Revolution' of, roughly, a century ago; beginning, say, about 1790, and coming on up into the nineteenth century. They are as nothing when compared to the scientific revolution which has been going on for the past fifty years; say, since 1890. But new techniques are easier to grasp and less important in their results than new discoveries; they are also illusory, for they give people an impression that advance is still going on when, as a matter of fact, its impetus may have already spent itself."

"In view of some of the uses that are being made of the new techniques," said Weeks, "we could perhaps afford to pause a little, until man catches up with them sociologically."

"It was in the nature of things, I suppose," said Whitehead, "that these new techniques should fall into the hands of bad people. . . . And then, too, the techniques in their turn assisted to fresh discoveries. But after one such experience in a lifetime of the impermanence of the most solid-seeming ideas, one is chary of overconfidence, and in the last words I have written (at the end of that essay which concludes the volume on my philosophy) I have said: 'The exactness is a fake.' "

"That looks bad for the editor of a magazine," observed Weeks. "How much exactness can be in *our* pages?"

"It looks worse for a daily newspaper," I added with corresponding candour.

"You can append notes at the bottoms of your leading articles," suggested Whitehead, by way of letting us down easily, "explaining that this is what looks true today but that tomorrow it may be something quite different."

"That is about the frame of mind in which my 'leading articles' *are* written. Nietzsche has remarked that nobody knows what news is important until a hundred years afterward."

"The life of an idea," Whitehead dealt with this, "varies widely. Some live two hundred years, others two thousand. Some last no longer than a year or two; and others have to wait centuries before they are taken up and put into effect. Here again, the element of time is capricious. But no period, I think, has ever seen such a complete overturn in the established modes of thought as this past half-century. There is one philosopher who would not have been surprised. In reading Plato today we have occasionally to say, 'Poor fellow, he didn't know this . . . or that'; but in the main he had anticipated most of these possibilities. Fewer allowances, on the whole, need be made for him than for anyone else. Aristotle now . . . Aristotle would have been horrified; for he divided and classified into separate genera and species. But Plato holds. I find myself more engrossed by his later work, embodying metaphysical ideas—like the *Theaetetus*—than in the earlier ones, where he is more concerned with sociology, some of which, to our notions, don't come off too well."

We joined in comparing this with what often happens from long study of some great artist—how we gradually find our preferences gravitating to his later works, as to the last quartets and pianoforte sonatas of Beethoven. . . .

"The works of Plato I return to again and again," said Whitehead, "are the ones which come after the *Republic*. His method is to announce his subject, then present it rapidly in numerous aspects, few of which had occurred to anybody else, and which arouse eager activity in the reader's mind. Those ideas are thrown out more or less at random: this done, he begins to relate them to the lives of those people living in his own time who would be most nearly able to grasp them; then, as he goes on, he 'commonizes' them until they seem to have been brought within the comprehension of the multitude; but, mind you, in so doing much of the virtue of the ideas will have evaporated."

"You once showed me a passage in the *Timaeus* which exactly conforms to your description of this process."

"When ideas are commonized, they tend to lose their force. That which relates them to the specific forms of life in any given period is necessarily ephemeral. Something of this ephemerality is also in the ideas themselves even in their purest and most powerful form. I have tried to allow for that fact when dealing with the ideas of philosophers in other periods; obviously their thinking, however abstract, was coloured to some extent by the land and time in which they lived, by the historical forces at work, by the intellectual climate, and all the peculiar conditions governing life when they thought and wrote. This point seems to have been missed by all, or most, of the people who have written about my work, and it invalidates much of what they have had to say. I have made my point clear, both in speech and writing; but if it isn't grasped, it isn't. One cannot go on repeating. There is an instance of what I mean in those last two lectures, at the end of the volume I mentioned. Plato's God is a God of this world. Augustine combined Plato's God with St. Paul's and made a fearful job of it. Since then our concept of this world has enlarged to that of the universe. I have envisioned a union of Plato's God with a God of the universe."

The clang of the big clock-bell in the tower of Memorial Hall striking the hour was a startling reminder of time in the midst of this contemplation of eternity. In through the open windows drifted the mild air of the sultry June evening. Mrs. Whitehead and I went out into the kitchenette to bring the tray of biscuits, whisky, and water. Their own drinks were temperate: for her, plain water without ice; for him, plain water with ice.

While we were breaking out ice cubes a burst of laughter sounded from the living-room.

"We're missing it," said I.

We hustled back.

"He was speaking," said Weeks, "of the modern gap between statesmanship and specialized learning, and I reminded him that the *Atlantic* had published his paper on that subject."

"And I reminded him," said Whitehead, blandly, "that he had cut the first four pages."

"Yes, and you were very wrong to do it," said she, standing over him, and shaking an accusatory forefinger. "We have regretted ever since that we gave our consent."

They had him at their mercy. He pulled the silk shawl over his head in mock terror. There was laughter and the episode was accepted as comedy.

"I considered those opening pages essential to my discussion," resumed Whitehead. "They distinguished between the arts and the sciences, between literature and history, and between a static and an active social system. I am magnanimous; I forgive you, even if you did suppress my thought, for I cannot print those ideas elsewhere now."

"They are printed in full," said I, "in '75-1, Proceedings of the American Academy of Arts and Sciences,' where you delivered the lecture, for I begged a dozen copies from the secretary to send to friends."

"Have you any left?"

"Yes."

"Could you let me have one?"

"You shall have it tomorrow."

There was another quarter of an hour before we had to go, during which the conversation came back from universals to particulars, such as the impending coal strike, and how far anyone would get if he tried to publish an impartial account of the issues. We left shortly after ten o'clock.

In the taxicab, Weeks explained why he had cut the opening pages: "It showed that it had been delivered as a lecture, and people prefer to read what appears to come to them as freshly written."

Next day I reread the opening pages of the lecture as published by the academy. It seemed to me that Whitehead had said in the opening three columns of that pamphlet more than most men can say in thirty.

XXIX

June 10, 1943

THERE had been another wartime commencement, and the College Yard, where I crossed it, was being cleared of scaffolding timber, which had been put up for the out-of-door ceremonies. The grass plot looked trodden into hard ground. Academic Cambridge, like any other academic town out of term-time seemed suddenly deserted.

It was a loury evening with rain in brew and a rising wind. The Whiteheads were alone and seemed more than usually at their ease. In no time at all we were out beyond the harbour jetties and into the conversational open water. It was about the gap between written and spoken language, between literature and vernacular.

"It is quite unlikely," said Whitehead, "that Cicero spoke to his friends in the language of his letters, to say nothing of his orations."

"A slave population complicates it, too," Mrs. Whitehead added. "No matter how vivid or picturesque the vernacular may be, if it is used by a servile class it is avoided by the educated."

I said that the gap seemed particularly wide in English.

"Not so wide as you might think," said he. "The London poorer classes, for example, have an extraordinary appreciation for Shakespeare. His language doesn't put them off at all; their sense of humour is about the same as his; they think the same things are funny. All this is not surprising for they were the sort of people for whom the plays were originally written. There is a school of technology in the East End for which I used to be on the visiting committee, and I saw a good deal of it. One evening a teacher was going over a page of literature in a textbook with his class, and asked the meaning of an unusual seventeenth-century word. One of the young men answered correctly. He was asked how he happened to know. 'I saw a play of Shakespeare's (he named the one) 'at the Old Vic last Thursday night, and that word was used in it in the same sense as here.' "

"The English sense of humour as it expresses itself in common vernacular," said Mrs. Whitehead, "is likely to be coarse; it is also very funny. It is not like French slang, which generally has a nasty innuendo behind it; the English slang is good, honest coarseness that hits you in the face."

"If I may say a good word for American slang," said I, "it is that, besides being fresh and vigorous, it is almost always sweet and clean, pure animal high spirits."

"That is true," he assented, "and very much to your people's credit."

"Slang is the bane of my writing life. Being in a newspaper office I hear it spoken continually, and for a newspaper-reading public complicated ideas need to be in seemingly simple language, but with the literary language to fall back upon at need. For this, slang looks like a short cut but isn't; it is a dead end, a blind alley."

"As a lit'ry gent," Mrs. Whitehead twitted me, "the vigour of a growing language makes you uncomfortable."

"Perhaps. But it also makes me uncomfortable to watch the

subjunctive and auxiliary verbs fade out of our commonly spoken language."

"I'll tell you what," said she suddenly, "as between your speech and ours, American and English, it is a difference in 'style.' If we have style in ours, even in the vernacular, it is because we can't help ourselves; we are unaware of it; but I think idiom and vocabulary, for the time being at least, are spread thinner over here. I often sense a paucity of words even with my friends here who have had most access to them, and if I do hear 'style' in speech, it has had to be acquired (however meritoriously) and that means it had to come out of books."

"A striking instance of that came under my notice in one of our Massachusetts small towns," I said. "He was a fourteen-year-old English boy brought over here to live. Parent for parent and class for class he was no different from the American boy scouts he played with; in fact, they had had, if anything, rather better advantages; and yet every time that English lad opened his mouth he shamed me with his beautiful speech, a natural English idiom. It was nothing he was aware of. He was speaking the only way he knew."

"You Americans have one great advantage which would scarcely have occurred to you," said Whitehead. "I mean Americans of the old English stock. It isn't generally realized, but English literature from the time of Charles II on up to the end of the eighteenth century was so much influenced by French that it lost its distinctive character. That is one reason it is so dull. Restoration comedy, for example, is more French than English."

"Brilliant though it is, it often smells to high heaven."

"The eighteenth-century poets, too," he continued, "are starched and go in the stiff brocades of imitation-French. Now you people in America escaped that. You were off over here maturing whatever it was that you were going to say, and although some of your great figures, like Jefferson and Franklin, were in France during the revolutionary ferment, which the

French felt from you and you from them, so that it is commonly *supposed* that the influence of France on America was considerable, nevertheless it was really much less serious than the influence of France on English thought. Coleridge, Wordsworth, and the later English Romantic poets, Byron, Shelley, Keats, were the reaction against it. On the other hand, when it comes to your use of the language itself, as distinguished from the thoughts you express with it, your situation is, it is true, enormously complicated by your influx of stocks other than English."

"That burden falls on our public-school teachers, and here in Boston, at least, they are meeting it valiantly. Down in Newspaper Row one hears Italian, Greek, Jewish, and heaven knows what other races, of little newsboys crying their wares in correct Bostonese, down to broad *a*'s and softened terminal *r*'s."

"The same need has produced the 'English' courses in your colleges. In the public school, Sherborne, in the west of England, where I was sent as a boy of fifteen, my father, the vicar, having tutored me until then, we never heard of such a thing, nor at Cambridge either until nearly a generation later. The training was Greek, Latin and mathematics. Ancient history came along in the course of Latin and Greek; English history we read because it interested us, and it might surprise you to know how actively we discussed the ancient civilization and how apposite the lessons of the Aegean islands and its adjacent mainlands seemed to us English boys of our own island in its relation to the larger seas and continents. Russia, in those days, was 'Persia' to our 'Greece.' English literature we read for pleasure, especially the poets. Two of Shakespeare's plays were 'taught' us—I can't remember which ones, but I *can* remember that I never cared to read those two plays again, although I read and reread the rest of Shakespeare with delight. Of the modern languages, German we took seriously; but the two subjects which were beneath our serious consideration at school were French and physics." He paused and said, smiling mischievously, "Of science just as little was taught as possible."

"Why not French?" I asked.

"What?" exclaimed Mrs. Whitehead. "Take a 'Froggy Frenchman' seriously in those days? Remember, I was brought up in France and spoke only French until I went to England when I was a girl of seventeen. I spoke English, only no one could understand me."

"The first evening we spent together," volunteered Mr. Whitehead in reminiscence, "I spent showing her pictures, because I couldn't understand what she said."

"Yes, but," said she, "I soon realized that I would not 'do' as I was, and however hard I may have worked to learn English, I worked harder to drop my French accent. One of our Cambridge friends, a delightful man, Theodore Beck, being out in the East somewhere met a Trinity man who had known me and said, 'Have you heard that Whitehead is married?' 'No. Who is she? What is she like?' 'Whitehead has made a great mistake,' said our friend to Beck. 'He has married out of his tripos (out of his subject).' "

"What puzzled me about the two of you for a long time, before I knew you, was that although you had lived, more or less perforce, on the cream of things, in the sense of mental interchange, in Cambridge and later in London, you weren't in the least 'choosy.' Although it never occurred to me in those days that I could come to your Sunday evenings, I was told that anybody over here might come who liked, and that you did get them in droves."

"Sixty to an evening," said she, with pride. "But they came out into the kitchen and helped me."

"I had known professorial families who had come here from other universities and had had, for a while, rather a hard time learning to feel at home in Cambridge. When you people came, it seemed to be a general love feast."

"Tell me," said she, "did we seem very 'foreign' at first?"

"At first, yes. I can remember when the change took place; it was between '34 and '35."

"What made the difference?"

"I loved you both."

She said that explanation sufficed.

"How long have we known each other?" asked Whitehead.

"Eleven years."

"Friendship abolishes time. I feel as though I had known you forty years."

"There is an English novelist whom I used to read and re-read, the reason being that his pages were my only access at that time to the world where you moved as a matter of course, a world where people understood ideas and handled them easily. I mean George Meredith."

"It is true, we did enjoy the society of Trinity and King's, the two colleges where we most naturally knew people," said he, "and by 'society' I do not mean, of course, a silly sense of elevation, but association with people of congenial minds. But in neither Cambridge did we ever pick and choose." He named over several of his colleagues, among whom my ear noted the name of Jebb.

"Jebb? He edited my Sophocles," I exclaimed. "Jebb was always at my elbow in a Greek text when I was here in college, and I often wondered what he was like; but this is the first time I ever picked up his tracks."

"He was a delightful fellow and had a charming wife. She was not exactly learned but you wouldn't have wanted her to be. Her husband had rather a fiery temper which was carried off by the charm of Mrs. Jebb."

"*Lady* Jebb," Mrs. Whitehead corrected him. "Don't rob her ghost. She loved the title."

"The place I came into collision with him," continued Whitehead, "was at elections of Fellows for Trinity, about which he felt very strongly. Each time we came out from such an election, Sir Richard was generally not on speaking terms with some one of his colleagues. I would have to say to my wife, 'I say, pet, do ask the Jebbs to dinner. Sir Richard isn't speaking to me at present.' One of his performances which I remember best and enjoyed most was the time he rode into the river on his bicycle."

"Lady Jebb was very kind to me when I arrived in Cambridge as a bride. 'My dear,' said she, 'have as many brothers as you like, but no cousins.' It was good advice and I followed it."

"To me," I said, "as an undergraduate, the editor of my Sophocles was an Olympian."

"Even to his temper!" agreed Mrs. Whitehead demurely.

"He also gave me one of my 'English' courses, about which you were speaking a moment ago. For I, like you, learned about English from Greek."

"Mind you!" Whitehead warned me—"those 'English courses' in American colleges are very necessary. If the ancient Greek and Latin classics aren't taught, then English must be, as best we can. Only I hope they won't make it too dull. Teachers, unless they are born to it, aren't the best persons to make young people love good literature."

"Can you tell me," asked Mrs. Whitehead suddenly, "why men make so much better teachers than women? As a whole, I mean. When a woman teacher *is* good (and I was one and wasn't) she is splendid, but an exception. With men, there is something about it which comes to them naturally (if at all), and they love doing it."

"Confining our remarks to persons not present," (I glanced at the teacher on my right) "it seems to 'take' men in the form of a desire to impart. Richard Wagner had it, knew that he had it, and said in a letter to Mathilde Wesendonck that that was how it took him. One sees the same thing in quite humble people, and it can be very touching: it is compounded of a genuine love of human beings, and a desire to help them . . ."

"Plus the pleasure of holding forth?" asked Mrs. Whitehead.

"Suppose we appeal to the member of the profession present. What can you say for them?"

"Only," said he, eyeing us blandly, "that being one myself, I consider them admirable people."

"The desire to dominate comes into it," his wife stuck to her guns.

"A distinction needs to be made, I think," said he, "between the desire for domination and a love of effective action. The world is always full—and never more so than now—of people who want to dominate"—he shook his clenched fist in the air and set his jaw grimly—"*for the sake of dominating*. But the beneficent people, people like the professional classes and men of creative imagination, want effective activity. You, for instance, when you write your articles, aren't moved by a desire to dominate . . ."

"Even if I were, the illusion of dominating would be impossible to maintain."

"I admit there is a very slender dividing line between the two," said Whitehead, "but it is the division that is important. On one side is sheer love of domination, on the other is the pleasure of effectuating some beneficent activity. . . . Take Wagner's operas, which you love. I don't believe they do you a bit of harm. To you, they are a world of poetic imagination; but to a good many Germans of today I am sure they mean, '*We looted you once, and we shall do it again!*' "

Again the italic was Whitehead's, both in look and in tone.

"Was there ever," I asked, "such a wholesale repudiation of moral principle by supposedly responsible people, as in modern Germany?"

"There have always been people animated by an unscrupulous will to dominate," said he, "among all nations. They were uppermost for longer or shorter periods. What is new about this situation in Germany is its extent and duration. It has been going on longer, with greater intensity, and with wider and more devastating effect."

"You mentioned Meredith, a moment ago," said Mrs. Whitehead. "How could he ever have put two such utterly irreconcilable natures into one woman as he put into Diana? The two could never have lived together in the same skin; they would have burst it!"

This led to a comparison of English and Russian novelists.

"The novel on the grand scale," said Whitehead, "seems to have been done best by the Russians—Tolstoy, Dostoevsky, Turgenev. Except in such hands, where the whole range of society is presented—the family, the political, military, and economic systems, and the clash of personalities and ideas—the novel is concerned largely with the prevailing social habits of a given place and time. This tends to restrict it to secondary range as an art-form, not quite up to those tremendous universal themes of the great Greek tragedies. But, have you noticed that there are a good many second-rate works of art which survive and have a long life—which they may not deserve as well as their betters—because they embody some continuingly popular subject? It is true, a widely popular subject is likely to be a good one, but for purposes of survival the work must appeal to a good many people."

"How our world would like to know whether the thirty-three Greek tragedies which we have are the best of the three hundred and nineteen known to have been written by the three great tragic poets," I said. "Gilbert Murray thinks that the ones which survived probably *are* the best. But if we are to speak of the novel as sociology, the work of fiction which I would read if I wanted a picture of middle-class England in the mid-nineteenth century is by a woman, and the title of it is *Middlemarch*."

"I'll tell you another novelist," said he, "who, I think, comes as close to it, if not closer to the reality, and that is Anthony Trollope."

"Only of you, dear, and your clerical family," said his wife, making him a comic grimace, and in her very sweetest tones.

"I don't deny," she added wickedly, "that the picture is a likeness."

"How about dialogue?" I asked. "How much of it in print or on the stage is a plausible likeness of the way people actually talk?"

"Hallo!" exclaimed Mrs. Whitehead. "Here we are, back at our question of the gap between written and spoken language."

"It is 'sonata form'— the return of themes. . . . Dialogue, as actually spoken, seldom goes into print effectively unless something has been done to it—often quite a little. It must sound the way people talk, but if you try setting down their talk verbatim, you may find that it doesn't seem as lifelike as it ought."

"Art," said Whitehead, coming to our rescue, "is the imposing of a pattern on experience, and our aesthetic enjoyment is recognition of the pattern. The mistake is to think of words as entities. They depend for their force, and also for their meaning, on emotional associations and historical overtones, and derive much of their effect from the impact of the whole passage in which they occur. Taken out of their context, they are falsified. I have suffered a good deal from writers who have quoted this or that sentence of mine, either out of its context or in juxtaposition to some incongruous matter which quite distorted my meaning, or destroyed it altogether."

"Is it something which professional philosophers would be likely to do?"

"I have a poor opinion of philosophers, as a class," said he. "The few first-rate philosophic minds need to be understood in relation to the times in which they lived and thought, and this is precisely what is not done. A philosopher of imposing stature doesn't think in a vacuum. Even his most abstract ideas are, to some extent, conditioned by what is or is not known in the time when he lives. What are the social habits around him, what are the emotional responses, what do people consider important,

I

what are the leading ideas in religion and statesmanship? Descartes, for example, was comparatively a simple man. I think he forgot the seventeenth century."

"So did those who lectured on Descartes here when I was an undergraduate, and it was the same when they came to Spinoza and Leibniz."

"Aristotle better illustrates my point," said Whitehead. "He founded modern science. His divisions of observed phenomena, which he supposed to be whole truths, have been ascertained to be no more than half-truths, if that. Aristotle's divisions into species and genera are true in the sense that we know a dog is different from a baboon, and that both are different from a man; but you and I and the dog and the baboon are all descended from minute particles of animate matter which originated somewhere at the edges of the sea and land millions or billions of years ago. And yet if we are to have science, what Aristotle did was exactly the right thing to do. In science you must have order, and for that you must isolate certain types of order for observation. But again, with science as with philosophy, the subject cannot be understood without studying it in relation to the life which surrounds it. We might just as well have had the Industrial Age in the time of Archimedes; everything necessary was known; the only things lacking were tea and coffee. That fact so affected the habits of people that the Industrial Age had to wait centuries until people in Scotland watched their kettles boil and so invented the steam-engine.

"There is one philosopher," he continued, "who provides his own environing sociological interpretation, and that is the greatest mind ever produced by Western man, Plato. He writes in the dialogue form, several persons are speaking, you get their various points of view, are given a notion of what sort of characters they are and by what surrounding social habits and political institutions their thinking has been affected—the city state, its industry, its economic system, its family life, and traditional customs. I said a while ago that words could not safely be treated as entities or ideas detached from their contexts. They acquire their true meanings from the momentum of the passage, as the beauty of a star is not only in its colour and brightness but also gains from the grandeur of its surrounding immensities."

This was going to require some time to sink in, and, since we were engaged in a conversation, not reading a book which one can lay down or reread for a paragraph, I said, in order to give myself twenty measures' rest:

"For the past year I have been spending evenings with the last quartets and piano sonatas of Beethoven, which are some of the most abstruse music ever written. I don't pretend that I understand them except in parts, but they, too, like the beauty of a star, gain from the grandeur of their surrounding immensities of thought. They plunge one for hours at a time into a world of abstract values, like higher mathematics, and I actually think they have made me better able to comprehend some of the higher mathematics of abstract thought which I hear from you. Music is of course highly mathematical and it is also abstract. It is peculiar, too, in having at one and the same time an emotional and an intellectual content. I do not presume to define music, but I do think that music is a mathematics of aesthetic."

"I would accept that definition," said he, "for I think we take in quite as much through our sense of hearing as by our sense of sight, perhaps more. Mind you, I don't mean to compare our dependency on the two senses, for we are more dependent on sight, since we have mobility. But I think we respond more to a solemn sound, to music, or to a great bell. It establishes the emotion almost instantaneously, and we think about it only later. Organ music much more easily conveys a devotional attitude than visual objects. Your national anthem, which I hear frequently over the radio, does not, fortunately, lend itself to being shouted by mobs in unison, but it admirably serves its purpose and, hearing it, I am more moved than I am by the sight of your flag. I say nothing," he smiled as he spoke, "about the relative merits of your national flag *as* a flag. The point I am making is that, with the sense of sight, the idea communicates the emotion, whereas, with sound, the emotion communicates the idea, which is more direct and therefore more powerful."

"Mr. Judd, the manager of the Boston Symphony Orchestra, and I were at a performance of Ibsen's *John Gabriel Borkman*," I remarked. "In the second act, someone plays Saint-Saëns's *Danse Macabre* behind the scenes. The play is powerful, but when the music stopped, we looked at each other and smiled. The music, though toned down so as not to blur the dialogue, had smashed the scene. It had done just what you said—spoken to the emotions directly."

"Ninety per cent of our lives," he replied, "is governed by emotion. Our brains merely register and act upon what is telegraphed to them by our bodily experience. Intellect is to emotion as our clothes are to our bodies: we could not very well have civilized life without clothes, but we would be in a poor way if we had only clothes without bodies."

The clock of Memorial Hall had struck nine. Mrs. Whitehead brought the tray of hot chocolate. In the time remaining we talked of a period in history which had looked very fortunate, one in which all three of us had, at varying lengths, lived.

"One of the happiest times that I know of in the history of mankind," said he, "was the thirty years, roughly, from 1880 to 1910. I am not suggesting that there were not a great many things which needed changing; but we intended to change them and had set about doing so. For people like us, moderately comfortable, the conditions were ideal—not too much money, engrossing work to be done, and a sense of purpose and progress in the world."

"We were working, too," said Mrs. Whitehead, "for ends which were often against the interests of our class."

"My wife, between the ages of twenty and twenty-five, had a

difficult time," said he. "She had her living to earn in London."

"I was young and unprotected and had to go alone to and from my work. My clothes exposed me to pestering, because they were not the right kind for a working girl, but I had to wear them, for they were the only ones I had."

"For myself," he continued, "I may say that all my life I have had perfect conditions. And in those years between 1880 and 1910, we often used to speak of what a wonderful world to live in our children would have."

XXX

June 19, 1943

AT the previous luncheon of the Saturday Club in May, Whitehead had been absent. He sent word that the edict forbidding the use of gasoline for going to social gatherings applied, so far as he was concerned, to taxicabs, and since the Cambridge subway was out of the question for him, he must stay away. The regret was general. I remarked:

"We ought to be ingenious enough to get him here. The Checker Taxi Company has horse-drawn cabs on the street."

"You and Alfred Kidder are appointed a committee to see what can be done," said the chairman.

This commission led me to the South End where, in the stable of the Checker Taxi Company, the nineteenth century is still going full blast. Here were ostlers, grooms, and at least thirty good horses, and vehicles that are now museum pieces: hansom cabs, victorias, landaus, broughams, barouches, surreys, traps, flys, and a tallyho. The very stable-smell itself was a museum piece; how it brought back the good old days! A one-horse brougham was chosen, very smart, upholstered with Morocco; bevelled plate-glass windows, speaking-tube, and side lanterns. It was forty years old, had belonged to some wealthy family whose name I forget, and used to be sent over the road to Washington every winter.

*   *   *

(The Saturday Club will arrive at its centenary in 1955. "Mr. Emerson very often left his study in Concord on a Saturday to go to the Athenaeum Library, call on friends, or see his publishers on business. He was likely to stop in at the original 'Corner Book Store' on the corner of Washington and School Streets." Six years before it was started Emerson was talking over with his friends a plan for a club where lonely scholars, poets, and naturalists, like those of Concord, might find congenial company when they came to the city. Two clubs actually resulted, and nearly at the same time. One, the Magazine Club, gave birth in 1857 to *The Atlantic Monthly*. The Saturday gradually displaced or absorbed it. Among the early members were Emerson, Hawthorne, Longfellow, Lowell, Holmes, Motley, Dana, Whittier, Prescott, Agassiz, and Parkman. Its luncheons were, and are, on the last Saturday of each month from September to June, with some skirmishing each June to meet the Harvard commencements. In those brave days of the nineteenth century they sat from three o'clock till nine, at the Parker House, in a large front room where long windows looked out on the bronze statue of Dr. Franklin—what a prized member he would have made!—in the green grounds of the City Hall. It now meets at the Union Club on Park Street, almost within a baseball's throw of those two original landmarks, the Athenaeum and the Old Corner Book Store, now moved to Bromfield Street. These facts and quotations are from the first of two plump volumes of its annals, *The Early Years of the Saturday Club*, by Edward Waldo Emerson.)

*   *   *

Luncheon was at one-thirty. The cab was ordered to be at the Hotel Ambassador in Cambridge at twelve-thirty. It was there on the tick, a brougham but not the one ordered. Later,

[230]

it appeared why. This one was a little seedy, the handle was off the door on its port side, it was upholstered in royal purple, and though it had various odours, including the horsy one, I could smell no traces of funeral wreaths about it. So we got in.

It was no motor-car. The seats, though cushioned, were hardish; knee-room was none too generous, hard rubber tyres on wooden wheels do not much mitigate the jolts of paving blocks (and all this used to be considered luxury); but the windows were open, it was a radiant June day with a fresh breeze and blazing sunshine. The shortest route to Park Street was down Cambridge through the factory district and over the Longfellow Bridge.

Our equipage attracted attention. William Hill, the cab driver, wore a high black silk hat, not as new as it had been once, and a blue coat, ditto, with brass buttons. Pedestrians seemed surprised. They first thought it was an advertising stunt, I think, and were looking for the sign. Since there was no sign, their next idea was that it might be a pair of undergraduates on a spree, and peered in to see who was riding. The occupants did not fit that theory. Everybody grinned and some laughed outright. As the cab rolled down through the factory district, the little boys playing in the streets, untroubled by inhibitions, shouted jeering remarks; and occasionally a passing taxicab driver would lean out and deliver a wisecrack to our cabby, "Step on it, Grandpa!"

All this was not much more than a subconscious accompaniment to the subject under discussion.

"We are," said Whitehead, "in the dissolution of that historical period which I date, roughly, from about 1450 A.D.; which, in turn, began with the break-up of the Middle Ages. I doubt if anyone in the thirteenth century realized what was already happening."

"Is it ever generally possible," I asked, "for people to grasp the fact of a major social break-up until it is upon them?"

"My own father will illustrate that," he replied. "He was born in 1827 and lived until 1898, a span of seventy-one years. He had watched, and taken as a matter of course, the first Industrial Revolution, the one which began late in the eighteenth century—the steam-engine, the factory system, and so on; but he never even faintly surmised the second and greater revolution by technology. He was a vicar, and the world in which he lived looked safe and solid. Yet it was almost at its end in the year of his death. . . . England's being the first to industrialize affected our history in a way curiously inverse. Instead of liberalizing us, at the period of the French Revolution, it made our government conservative and we resisted the advanced ideas of the eighteenth century instead of welcoming them."

I said that in epochs of rapid change a great deal, *too* much, depended on the sort of personalities that were brought uppermost into positions of power.

"It is a great pity that Erasmus was not a stronger character," said Whitehead. "His ideas were the right ones, and could have provided a much happier solution for the development of Christendom than the one which came. But he lacked the force; and the matter fell into the hands of Luther and Calvin, who made a fearful botch of it. The view of Erasmus was that of the sensible and enlightened people, and if it could have been effectuated by an able leader there never need have been an Ignatius Loyola, and a Council of Trent. Calvin and Luther made the egregious blunder of throwing away the whole aesthetic appeal of the Church, which was one of its best elements. You know how bleak the Protestant services are, little for the emotions, little or no appeal to beauty."

"You might be interested to know that our friend Livingstone, after having read a recent biography of Luther, wrote me that Luther seemed to him 'like a fouler-mouthed Hitler.' "

"Livingstone," said Whitehead, "is a man whose perceptions in such matters as these I would trust farther than anyone's.

What was wanted in that period of transition was someone to generalize the old conceptions and give them a liberal turn or a symbolical interpretation which could have made them acceptable to the forward-looking people. This was what was done for the old Greek religion of the Olympians in the fifth century B.C. by the great tragic poets, Aeschylus, Sophocles, and Euripides, and later by the philosophers, Plato principally. They were able to take the old gods, Zeus, Apollo, Pallas Athene and the rest, soften down the barbarities of the old theology, criticize it, turn the primitive myths into symbolism, and by carrying the people along with them—big, popular audiences at the public performances of their dramas—build a bridge from what they had formerly believed in but no longer could, to ideas which could gain acceptance by civilized men."

"Myth," I remarked, "is said to be the form in which people communicate their most deeply felt truths before they have arrived at the stage of general ideas, and those Attic dramatists, using mythical plots, had the enormous advantage of appealing at once to the emotions and to the intellect, both to the average citizens and to the educated, with the result that the two groups could feel and act more in harmony."

"Any system of thought based on this earth of ours," said Whitehead, "is extremely limited in its conceptions—either theology or philosophy—and most of them have been. We know now that our earth is an insignificant planet swinging round a second-rate sun in no very important part of the universe. The response to that knowledge of first-rate people talking together as you and I are talking—assumed," he said smiling, "that we *are* first-rate people—should be immeasurably larger than it is. I see no reason to suppose that the air about us and the heavenly spaces over us may not be peopled by intelligences, or entities, or forms of life, as unintelligible to us as we are to the insects. In the scale of size, the difference between the insects and us is as nothing to that between us and the heavenly bodies; and—who knows?—perhaps the nebulae are sentient entities and what we can see of them are their bodies. That is no more inconceivable than that there may be insects who have acute minds, though," he smiled again, "their outlook would be narrower than ours. My point is, that we are part of an infinite series and since the series *is* infinite, we had better take account of that fact, and admit into our thinking these infinite possibilities."

"As a young man you had the advantage of hearing and sharing what was talked over in the common-room of Trinity—"

"Add King's," said Whitehead.

"King's and Trinity then; this went on all through your twenties and thirties; those men were indubitably first-rate, there were many scientists among them as well as humanists. All this was in the 1880's and 1890's, on the eve of these tremendous social and technological changes which have burst upon us. It would seem as though they would have guessed that something was up, if anybody could. How much inkling do you think they had?"

"On the scientific side, certainly a good deal. I went up to Cambridge in 1880. For a boy of nineteen I was a good mathematician. My teacher was a pupil of Clerk Maxwell, who had died only a year or so before, and he, too, was eminent. The Newtonian conceptions were still in full force. Clerk Maxwell had worked at reconciling them with the then new discoveries in electricity; but in mathematical physics the work looked to be about done. The attempt was to explain away by mathematical interpretation some remaining discrepancies between what was understood and what wasn't—and in the attempt to do this, everything was upset. The people of Trinity between, say, 1885 and 1895, some of them men of genius, knew in general what was coming in the way of scientific advance, but what they could not, of course, foresee was what the social consequences of the new techniques would be. There is not a single concept of the Newtonian physics which was taught as a whole truth, that has not now been displaced. The

Newtonian ideas are still useful, as useful as they ever were, but they are no longer true in the sense in which I was taught that they were true. This experience has profoundly affected my thinking. To have supposed you had certitude once, and certitude about the solidest-*looking* thing in the universe, and then to have had it blow up on your hands into inconceivable infinities has affected everything else in the universe for me."

The cab had crossed the Longfellow Bridge and was heading up Cambridge Street instead of Charles.

"Which way do you suppose he is going?" asked Whitehead, peering out.

"These are the steep streets up the back side of Beacon Hill. He can't be going up any of these. I suppose he and his boss talked over the route and chose the one easiest on the horse," said I.

"The horse wanders about a good deal from side to side," said Whitehead. "He doesn't seem used to a carriage. I wonder if he could have been a saddle horse. His idea of making things easier for himself seems to be trying to turn into every side street."

(This was a shrewd guess. At the end of the trip, William Hill admitted to me that he had owned the horse only since last Monday.)

He drove up through Scollay Square, along Tremont Street past the Granary and King's Chapel Burial Ground to Park Street corner, thus avoiding any hill until the last hundred yards of the way, the first slant of Park Street up to the State-house. A horse-drawn vehicle halting at the Union Club again attracted a good deal of attention, the more so as it was headed into the alleyway between the club and the Ticknor mansion and had stopped plumb across the sidewalk. A motor-car blocked the inner end of the alley. The cabman asked me to get the people inside to move it.

He had done well. We entered the club at 1.25 P.M. I gave the cabman's message to the clerk at the desk. He looked as though he had been accosted in Choctaw. I repeated it: "Professor Whitehead has come to the luncheon of the Saturday Club in a brougham. The driver says he cannot hold the cab on the hill and wants to drive into your alleyway which is blocked by a car." The clerk looked just as blank. I said:

"Come on out. I'll show you."

He came. He laughed immoderately but moved the car and the cabman drove in, on level pavement, in shade for the horse, and out of traffic. (End of the first half, and our side ahead.)

William Phillips, under-secretary of state from 1933 to 1936, and ambassador to Italy from 1936 to 1941, is a member of the club and was present. He had quite recently come back from his mission to India as personal representative of the President with the rank of ambassador, and after luncheon talked about it by request for perhaps half an hour, then invited questions. Excepting some characterizations of Linlithgow, the viceroy, Auchinleck, the commander-in-chief, and Field-Marshal Wavell, he was careful to say little that could not have been given at a press interview; but he made it evident that the United States is very unpleasantly involved in that quarter, and that the British Government's repressive acts are giving the lie in Asia to our pretensions as liberators.

In the discussion which followed he was questioned by Whitehead, Professor Harlow Shapley, the astronomer of Harvard, Bliss Perry, Jerome Hunsaker, the aeronautical engineer and head of that department at the Massachusetts Institute of Technology, and Cameron Forbes, who, having been governor-general of the Philippines and ambassador to Japan, conversed on the terms of one who has had experience of his own as a diplomatist in Asia.

The room was cool and pleasant even though outside the afternoon was oppressively hot. It is long, high-ceiled, and has rather an ornate early nineteenth-century chimney-piece at one end, for the building was originally the town house of

Lawrence Lowell's parents and he once remarked that this room had been his mother's bedchamber. One looks out over the treetops of the Common, which are just now luxuriantly foliaged and richly green from the rainy spring. Above them was a sky of June blue, whitened by the strong sunlight, and full of silvery clouds in full flight before a south-west wind.

Before we left, Edward Forbes, the secretary of the club, asked me to have a look at "the book." There was only a moment, for the cab had been ordered for three-fifteen and it was now nearly three-thirty, but in that moment I saw the signatures of Francis Parkman, William James, and that of his and his brother Cameron's grandfather, R. W. Emerson.

Edward Pickman and Alfred Kidder went out to have a look at the cab. Remembering their college years, they said the episode would not have been complete if they hadn't, and that in order to live up to the tradition, the cabman ought to have been slightly drunk. He was not; but they were gratified to observe that he had been no teetotaller.

It being Saturday afternoon, and fine weather, the world and his wife and their little boy were in town, afoot, on the sidewalks, and most of them on Tremont Street, where we had a household errand to do at S. S. Pierce's: three heavy pasteboard cartons, already ordered by telephone, to be picked up, for gasoline rationing prevents them from delivering groceries in Cambridge. When the cab drew up at the curb in front of the store, the shoppers, mostly women, were hard put to it to mind their manners. At first glance they would look astonished, then amused, then bewildered, and then try not to laugh. They could see at a glance, of course, that we were ethically jumping the gun on gas rationing, but they weren't prepared to take the whole nineteenth-century regalia quite so literally.

"I think," said Whitehead, when the provisions were stacked, two cartons beside the cabman's knees and one beside him on the seat, "I think that if we leaned out of the windows and bowed, we would be received with cheers."

[237]

It wasn't so far off that, as things were. Sailors in Navy uniform turned their heads after us and grinned, boys in Army uniform stopped dead in their tracks to gawp; shoppers, with arms full of bundles, stopped and stared, obviously trying to figure us out. At stops for traffic lights, some of the bystanders' conjectures were audible. We could have had plenty of repartee from the sidewalks if we had wanted it.

What was more memorable than all this, however, was the splendour of the June day. Excepting the Granary and King's Chapel Burial Grounds, you don't see much greenery driving back as we did. It was the same way we came—through Scollay Square and out Cambridge Street across the Longfellow Bridge; but everywhere there *was* a tree or a wisp of grass-plot, it was fresh, luxuriant green, and the treetops were all bending and blowing in the sou'wester. In its June dress, under the blue June sky, the city for once looked beautiful.

We were jolting over the pavement-blocks of Cambridge Street. Whitehead was speaking of the varying general characteristics as between English and American women.

"American women," said he, "are conventionalized by the prevailing sameness of their education. The theory is that, being brought up with boys, playing with boys and boys' games, going to school with them, and often to college, too, they would gain in individuality. As a matter of fact, it is not as successful as you would expect it to be. I suppose the most successful women, *as women*, were in the eighteenth century. (I am speaking, of course, of those in the more fortunate classes.) There they seem to have wider scope for their innate and characteristic abilities. My wife is one of that type. She grew up in what was practically an eighteenth-century family, aristocrats; the aristocratic influence was modified by her having been obliged, as a young woman inadequately prepared, to earn her own living, and she did it! But if you want to know what the eighteenth-century woman was like, spend an evening with my wife."

[238]

"Having spent several of them," said I, "the same idea had already occurred to me."

"Mind you," he resumed, "I don't say that your American women aren't tremendously vital and effective. In many ways they are more liberated than our English women. But, taken as a class, among the more active ones, the kind that carry on public work besides running their own households and families and running them well, I think our English women have a wider scope. . . . I tell you what," he summarized abruptly, "if I were to be born a woman, I would want to be born in America and live here the first thirty years of my life, and after that, in England. In that way I think a woman would get the best of both worlds."

"Is your family's friendship with your servants, which I have noticed to be a deep and genuine thing, an individual affair, or typical?"

"Much more typical than individual," said he, "and I can tell you why. The employer and employee relationship, with us, is much more kept out of it—singular though that may seem—by our class system, with its vestiges of feudalism. Friendships between persons of different classes are much more possible because, knowing that it is a mere matter of luck which class you are born in, we don't look down on people for not having risen."

"In this country, until quite recently," I assented, "the assumption was that if people hadn't gotten on in the world, it *was* their own fault, and, especially in the Midwest where I was reared, until within this present generation, there was something in it. That is one of the great gaps between the previous generation and this: we did have, or thought we had, security; this present crop has never known it, and hasn't it to look forward to."

"Servants have always been my friends," said Whitehead. "As a child of six I used to trot around with our gardener as he went about his work, and he taught me the names of flowers and plants; again, as a child, I used to spend months at a time at the house of my maternal grandmother, overlooking the Green Park in London, and her housemaid, Jane Wychelow, read Dickens aloud to me: *Pickwick Papers* and *David Copperfield*. She made them tremendously alive. My mother's family, while socially somewhat better placed, hadn't the intellectual distinction of my father's, and they were very contentious people. When they fell out with one another, as they frequently did, they always took their case to Jane Wychelow and *she* patched it up. Jane was the cement which held the family together."

"There in the middle of London, with Dickens being read aloud by your grandmother's housemaid, did his characters," I asked, "strike you as whimsical caricatures?"

"No. Dickens's characters *are* the poorer classes of London. They aren't caricatures at all. That idea arises naturally enough among readers who do not know the Londoners, but to us, the delight of Dickens is that he is describing real people, the like of whom we have known. Their whimsey is most characteristic. I know of no place which produces it like London."

"We were speaking a few evenings ago about novelists who did and did not bring it off. Thackeray?"

"He sees too much of one class and not enough of the other. His attempts are ambitious but not quite brought off. Trollope's characters are much more real. I recognize them exactly, for I have lived among just such people."

"A moment ago when we were speaking of servants, I was going to say that in the Midwest when I was a boy, if you didn't make a friend of the 'hired girl,' as the servant was called, and have her at the family table, you just didn't have one!"

"The sense of human equality," Whitehead took it up again, "is affected by prevailing ideas of opportunity. Human abilities are infinitely varied; some are successfully elicited in a given environment, others are not elicited at all. The possible combinations of human abilities are as infinite a series as the possible environments which would be favourable for drawing them out, but it is largely a matter of luck whether the two fit. To assume, as it is so often assumed, that genuine ability consists in forms of aptitude which happen to be wanted in a given time and place, and forms, too, which lead to economic advancement, is totally an error. The faculties which respond to such opportunity are a very small range in the human scale."

"You have spoken more than once of the element of luck, even in the most determined lives," said I. "How about your own?"

"There were two vacancies at Cambridge, when I was a young man, that were most lucky for me. One was a Fellowship, the other was a lectureship. Had it not been for the second, I would probably have taken a teaching position in a Public School and never have gone much farther."

"Some people strike me," I suggested, "as carrying inside themselves the magnetism which creates their opportunity. It looks like luck, but I do not believe it is. Perhaps you were one of them."

"No. I never created my own opportunities," said he positively. "I have done fairly well, but there has been an element of luck in it."

"You have had a good deal of administrative work to do, at Trinity and later at London University—what amounted to living, simultaneously with your life of thought, a life of action. . . . Before I put my main question, let me ask an incidental one: What is your opinion of the University of London?"

For reply he described in some detail what its functions are and what some of his duties in its committee work had been, concluding, with a smile, "Being a part of it, I think we did a damned good job!"

"Which brings me to my second question: as between your life as scholar, and your life as executive, which developed you more?"

"I learned my profession out of books, of course; but the administrative work developed me quite as much; in fact, I should be inclined to say, more. But for the continual meeting and dealing and talking with people, I might have stuck in the ruts of an academic scholar. I am a great believer in conversation. Outside of the book-knowledge which is necessary to our professional training, I think I have got most of my development from the good conversation to which I have always had the luck to have access."

"At Trinity, yes; and later in London. But suppose yourself to have spent those years in a newspaper office. . . ."

"You, too," said he, "have had an immense advantage from your office conversations."

"The talk at the *Globe*, it is true, is much better than most academic people would suppose. In fact, if I were to confess, I would have to say that it is of a much higher voltage than I can get from a good many academic enclaves. They don't encounter as many kinds of life as we do. In a sense, too, newspaper men lead a life of action. It is no mere speculative existence, for even after we come in off the street as reporters, and write as I do, we must at least be able to say something in print about urgent questions and say it responsibly enough so that we will not get a brickbat through our office window next morning."

"I would call that 'a life of action,' " said Whitehead, "as well as a life of thought. And my own, now I come to think of it, goes back to my days as a schoolboy. I was a leader in games, and, though you might not guess it now, a good football player and a passable cricketer. Sherborne was a school of about four hundred boys, ninety of whom lived in the dormitory. As head boy of the school and captain of the playing teams, I had to keep order in the dormitory. So all my life I have had the discipline of having to run things. . . . I say, we must be nearly back." He had been glancing out of the cab window, where sidewalk pedestrians, now more numerous again as we rolled into the residential streets of Cambridge, eyed the outfit with astonishment, and then remembered themselves, perhaps, in time to smother a laugh.

The return trip was made in forty-five minutes. William Hill had got us there and got us back without incident, unless you consider the trip to have been one continuous incident. Upstairs in the apartment Edward Pickman was waiting to carry them off to Dudley Farms in Bedford and Mrs. Whitehead was smartly gowned, hatted, and gloved for the journey. She asked how our cab ride had gone.

"We went and came," said Whitehead, "in an atmosphere of considerable public attention."

"You mean 'derision,' " said she.

"Well," he conceded, "I would say 'smiles.' "

"The trip was much less uncomfortable and went much more quickly than I had expected," I remarked.

Whitehead didn't take up the question of comfort; as to the other he said genially:

"I have had a delightful afternoon, but I don't associate it with *speed*!"

XXXI

July 27, 1943

AFTER a busy and hot day in the city, it was a refreshment to go over to Cambridge and dine with the Whiteheads at six-thirty. No one else was there. A breeze had sprung up and was drawing pleasantly through their open windows five stories up and overlooking lawns and trees.

There had been joking about the dinner. Mrs. Whitehead had said:

"I'm not sure we can give you enough to eat. We ourselves dine on five butterflies and find it quite sufficient." I told her three butterflies would be enough for me in warm weather.

Professor Whitehead was in his study, so we went in there. Being dressed in white and without his coat (I was invited to shed mine, and did) he looked cool and uncommonly fit. Mussolini had just fallen, and I remembered that two summers before in this very room, Whitehead had said to me, "Machiavelli has written the rules of a short-term success, say from fifteen to twenty years." Also that there was an old Roman who had been legate of Upper Germany under the Emperor Domitian, and who though ill and racked by pain, clung to life "so that I can survive that brigand for one day at least." I said it was some satisfaction to have seen Mussolini go down.

"It is *good*!" said Whitehead.

" 'Brigand' for him!" said she. "He is a foul scorpion!"

I asked Mr. Whitehead if he was writing anything.

"No," said he, "but I have been reading what you have been writing."

At first I could not think what he meant, for I have written little daily journalism since April; then it occurred to me that the *Atlantic* for August, which was just out, contained my "Eye of the Hurricane."

There had been a conference between several headmasters of New England preparatory schools and members of the *Globe* editorial staff on the plight of liberal education in wartime as it affected boys below the conscription age of eighteen. The danger was of their education being abandoned, if not entirely to the military sciences, certainly to science at the expense of the humanities. There was no knowing how long the war would last, and if several successive crops of adolescents were denied their only access to general education and to those civilian habits of mind on which our society had depended for the transmission of its liberal traditions, our war might be a Mississippi steamboat race, stoking the furnaces with cargo and cabin furnishings to end with a victory won by a hulk empty of everything but its industrial boilers and military engines.

"You raise all of the right questions," said Whitehead, "but I could not agree with all of your conclusions. If in America, unlike England and some of the European continental countries, you undertake to give a good education not to a few but to all your people, the form it takes will need to be modified. I would be inclined to require universal education up to, say, the age of sixteen; then, between sixteen and nineteen, infuse it with the elements of practicality. After that there would need to be the widest possible access to opportunity for further study, both in institutions and outside of them, as by university extension lecturers, so that people could satisfy their curiosity about all sorts of subjects and find their special aptitudes. Their reading, too, would be enlivened by personal association with the lecturers. I would make some of this advanced education compulsory, and keep up the process of education to the age of ninety." This last he said smilingly; but all the same, he meant it. "Mind you," he resumed, "I doubt if these great universities with their high concentrations of specialized learning and societies of scholars so shut off from the daily lives of average people are altogether a good thing."

"The same idea has occurred to me, and repeatedly," said I. "My own phrase for it is that they grow intellectually dandified."

"There are numerous groups of professional people in this, in any city, whose instruction would be quite as valuable to the public as that of university lecturers," (we had been called to dinner and were walking out to the table) "and one of these groups are the newspaper men. They ought to lecture more than they do."

"One of the puzzles to me," (I had decided to come out with it) "is that after three centuries of Harvard's pumping supposedly and often really educated men into the city of Boston, more hasn't come of it. Oughtn't the city to have done much better than it has?"

"It *has* done well, uncommonly well," he replied with

emphasis. "Will you name me an American city which has done better? Your professional people maintain, on the whole, a very high standard, especially the medical profession. What do you expect of it?"

"A steady blaze of genius, I suppose, is all that would satisfy me; and also, perhaps I know too much of the city's seamy side."

We sat at a beautiful little Duncan Phyfe mahogany table set for three, the late-afternoon yellow of sunshine filtering in from the west through the slightly tilted shutters of the Venetian blinds, which, a few minutes later, the sun having set behind the tower of Memorial Hall, Mrs. Whitehead raised, letting in the still strong and clear but paler light of the afterglow, which fell full upon the philosopher's serene face. The "five butter-flies" for dinner was certainly understatement, for we dined, I thought, sumptuously (though Mrs. Whitehead said "simply"), with glasses of a chilled sauterne beside our plates. She explained how the fowl, the salad, and the apple pie had been done; the "sumptuousness" came from skilful touches in the cookery. She told me what they were, adding:

"Cookery is one of those tasks which are insupportable unless done for people one loves. But for that, I myself would be willing to live on bread and cheese and would vastly prefer to."

"People are unlikely to get good food, no matter how many cooks they have, or how much they pay for them," said White-head, "unless the cooks love the people for whom they cook."

I said the two best cooks I had ever known, one a Yorkshire woman, the other Irish, did come exactly in that classification, in addition to which they were both devout, one a Protestant, the other Catholic.

"Cooking," replied Whitehead demurely, "is one of those arts which most requires to be done by persons of religious nature."

"And a good cook," added his wife, "cooks to the glory of God."

[246]

We lingered at the table in the fading afterglow. By now the breeze which drew in at the large window was deliciously cool and refreshing. In that tranquil light it was one of those summer evenings which seem like a pleasant eternity.

We shifted scene to the living-room. Whitehead was saying that his leaving Cambridge at fifty and going up to London was one of the determinants in his development: "It plunged me into the *practicalities* of education. At Cambridge I had had experience in political work and organization, but the actualities of life in London were much broader." He told many of the things he had to do and how they carried him amongst all classes. "Our polytechnical schools," said he, "are a specimen of the kind of thing I meant when earlier in the evening we were discussing universal education. I know the system of popular education in London has been criticized as inadequate, but from close association with it, I think it is admirable. It gives all sorts of people access to studies useful to them in practical life and also in the arts; and you find people of all classes and all ages haunting them."

"As showing their 'classlessness,'" said Mrs. Whitehead, "a young man we knew, who was enormously wealthy, and had had the best instruction in painting on the Continent that money could buy, found on coming home the best instruction he had found anywhere was in one of these London polytechnics."

"I am hearing, again, a partial explanation of something which has puzzled me about you two ever since I have known you. Pickled in donnish society though you have been pretty much all your lives, you are the least donnish of dons."

"In what way do you notice it?" asked Mrs. Whitehead.

"Understanding of common life. Restrict the case to your sympathy with the working class: that is something which experience had taught me not to take for granted with the average college professor, at Harvard or anywhere else. Here and there a specialist? Yes, in sociology perhaps. They have limbered up somewhat in the past few years, possibly because their own security has been affected."

"One of the great fallacies of American thinking," said Whitehead, "is that human worth is constituted by a particular set of aptitudes which lead to economic advancement. This is not true at all. Two-thirds of the people who can make money are mediocre; and at least one-half of them are morally at a low level. As a whole, they are vastly inferior to other types who are not animated by the economic motives; I mean the artists, and teachers, and professional people who do work which they love for its own sake and earn about enough to get along on. This habitual elevation of the type of ability that leads to economic advancement is one of the worst mistakes in your American thinking and needs to be unceasingly corrected by people who speak to the public, as you do."

Some of it, I said, was a hangover from our pioneering days when the subduing of this continent did take courage and ability.

"Yes," said Mrs. Whitehead, "but even there, a fine distinction must be drawn. The swollen fortunes were seldom made by the pioneers; they were made by the men who came after."

"The mischief of elevating the type that has aptitude for economic advancement," said Whitehead, "is that it denies the superior forms of aptitude which exist in quite humble people. Who shall say that to live kindly and graciously and meet one's problems bravely from day to day is not a great art, or that those who can do it are not great artists? Aesthetics are understood in too restricted a sense. People who can live beautifully in humble environments have a most advanced understanding of aesthetics—compared with which the ability to paint pictures on canvas," (he did so in dumb show) "delightful as that may be, is a rudimentary form."

"You confirm me in a glow I often feel when meeting my neighbours on the village street, the carpenter, the postman, the lobster fisherman—their goodness and geniality warm me to my marrow, and I smile inwardly, thinking, 'Life comes before literature.' "

"Fifty thousand years ago," said Whitehead, "or five hundred thousand—I don't know how long—when man, perhaps suddenly, took a turn of development which produced his faculty of enjoyment, he produced something whose possibilities are infinite. A human being—you, Evelyn, I—has certain capacities for enjoyment developed, partly because inherent, partly by training. There is a good deal of luck in it. You, for example, besides your enjoyment of literature have the faculty and training for the enjoyment of music. Some have the faculty for enjoying mathematics, but it is latent, and has to be brought out by study. We aren't *born* with the faculty of enjoying mathematics. Others, though born with the latent faculty of enjoying music, either as listeners or as performers, aren't *born* as either performers or highly intelligent listeners; both must be developed. The range of our faculties for enjoyment is enormous and has been explored hardly beyond a fringe. Even the insects must have it, though I don't know enough about them to surmise what their forms of enjoyment are. . . . Now the singular part is that man, in his social systems, has so far given so little scope to the development of our faculties of enjoyment. There have been various fortunate periods. Turbulent as the Italian cities in the Renaissance were, they did occasionally have rulers with acute perceptions for various and new forms of human enjoyment, and the rulers of certain small German principalities in the late eighteenth and early nineteenth centuries, too, were successful in fostering certain forms, principally music and the theatre. Small states, I think, do it better than large ones. The small German states were able to produce excellent provincial opera throughout the nineteenth century, while the French Government, though it maintained an excellent theatre, tended to rigidity of classicism. There was little experiment, and ideas always require adventure."

[249]

"That 'time lag' between the individual and his social system throws me back upon your remark of last year about the relationship between man's infinite possibilities, and the limitations of finite form. States concern themselves with the organization of material existence, which is a very finite thing. You may remember how once, when you lived out in the Blue Hills, we talked about the fact that there has never been, except incidentally, a Culture State, only Power States with a little creativity on the side; and you remarked that you doubted whether the state was best competent to foster the creative arts."

"When big states attempt it," said he, "they tend to formularize men's faculties of enjoyment and creativity. That tends towards rigidity. I doubt if state supervision would be good for the arts in America. The vitality of thought is in adventure. That is what I have been saying all my life, and I have said little else. Ideas won't keep. Something must be done about them. The idea must constantly be seen in some new aspect. Some element of novelty must be brought into it freshly from time to time; and when that stops, it does. The meaning of life is adventure."

"It is an adventure to be born," said Mrs. Whitehead, gravely, "and a very dangerous one."

She spoke standing. Behind her was the wall tinted its peculiar shade just off black; she wore a black gown with white embroidery at the throat; her hair is white, and there in the tranquil summer twilight her aspect was that of a striking portrait canvas by some eminent painter. The glimpse was only instantaneous, the moment of pause required to deliver her remark, then she turned away to go into the dining-room.

"How about the adventurers," I asked, "whose adventures are, for all their good will, mistaken and mischievous?"

"They are damned fools," said Whitehead emphatically. "That is where learning comes in. Adventurers must use their reason and must know the past, so as not to go on repeating the mistakes of history. One of my anxieties about this war has been lest a rigid system be imposed on mankind and that fragile quality, his capacity for novel ideas, for novel aspects of old ideas, be frozen and he go on century after century, growing duller, more formularized until he and his society reach the static level of the insects. Asia has known something of this sort. Good things no doubt were being said in China a thousand years ago, but for at least two thousand years, each century was a little less interesting than the century before; and when people want to tell me what civilization owes to India they have to start back at about 500 B.C. You may have wondered at my coolness, not to John Dewey personally, whom I respect as a man and certain aspects of whose work I admire, but to his thought. The reason is that the emphasis of his thought is on security. But the vitality of man's mind is in adventure. The Egyptians in 500 B.C. obviously had an enormous history behind them, yet there was no adventure in it. Contrast with it the little they have bequeathed to Western man with the much in aesthetics and morals that we have inherited from the Greeks and the Hebrews."

"I was doing so as you spoke. That old Egyptian priest in Plato's story was unconsciously recognizing some contrast of the sort when he told Solon, 'You Hellenes are never anything but boys. . . . In mind you are all young.'—The boy is adventurous."

"My hope is," replied Whitehead, "that out of this war, America will take the leadership of humanity. America, as I see it, is the only hope. There is adventure here, and a welcome for novelty. You could do for the future of humanity what Greece and Judaea did for the modern world as against Asia and Europe. The Jews had certain moral ideas but these would not have come to much without the Greeks."

"What would you say was the contribution of the Greeks?"

"The aesthetic view of life."

"I noticed a moment ago when you used those two words,

'aesthetics' and 'morals,' in connection with Hellas and Israel, that 'aesthetics' came first."

"Properly so," said he.

"Beauty is 'a wider and more fundamental notion than truth'?"

"Yes. Apart from beauty, truth is neither good nor bad."

"That was how the Puritans tumbled overboard," said Mrs. Whitehead, who had returned during the discussion. "They cast out beauty. They began well, by believing they were made in the image of God. They ended by making God in their own image."

"And how fast such cream can curdle: it is less than a century from the Plymouth Colony and William Bradford to Cotton Mather."

"The idea," said Whitehead, "was losing its vitality. It had ceased to adventure. The inheritors of it inherit the idea without inheriting the fervour. Their progenitors would have gone to the stake for it, and some of them did. Perhaps there was no longer any stake for its inheritors to go to; they knew how strongly their forebears believed, felt that they ought to feel the old fervour and tried to or pretended to, and so gave the impression of being hypocrites."

"Your own parents," Mrs. Whitehead reminded him, "didn't believe as strongly as they thought they did."

"They *thought* they still believed strongly," he took it up, "and *their* parents had been strong believers; but by the time mine came along, the idea had cooled off to a point where, today, the attitude of my parents might have been regarded as hypocritical. Mind you, I don't say it was. They were quite sincere. Only, the attitude had changed, and they represented their religion to us chiefly as a means of keeping order—order in the family and order in society. But that is something quite different from religious conviction."

"One sees a similar change in the Cathedral of Strassburg," I remarked. "Nobody had prepared me for it and it was a great surprise. The nave and aisles are late Gothic, light and graceful in its elegant logical perfection; the older parts at the chancel end are Romanesque, from an age of strong belief, and their effect is so powerful that they dim the force of the nave, beautiful though it is."

"Architecture," said Whitehead, "is a good illustration of the life cycle in adventures of ideas. It happens that it is one of the art-forms in which I am most interested. Let me take English Gothic. You start with early Norman, Romanesque, and go on century by century through, roughly, the four successive styles to the fifteenth century when it comes to an end. What was happening in those four successive centuries was that the new aspects of the idea were being discovered and developed; successive elements of novelty were being introduced and explored —the abundant fenestration, the height of the piers, beauty of tracery, and the like—until there seemed nothing more to be done. The possibilities of novel aspect had been used up, the Gothic idea comes to a full stop, and you get a complete break. They go back to the architecture of Greece and Rome, adapt it to the changed world of the Renaissance, and you get, instead of a Gothic abbey, St. Paul's. But the classic style of ancient architecture brought into the modern world has, I think, this peculiarity: although it does lend itself admirably to a host of purposes and can generally, in the hands of a good craftsman, be made to look well, it lacks that . . . that final something . . . What shall I call it? . . ."

"Transcendence," suggested Mrs. Whitehead.

"Yes," he accepted the word, "that final 'transcendence.' I mean that it doesn't produce the building which I would take a four-hour railway journey to see. A new material, as well as a new way of looking at the idea, may give it the happy turn," he resumed, "as when your early New England settlers brought the English house to these shores but had to build it of wood. It was the same style but with fresh and delightful modifications. With your stone houses I doubt if you have done so well. . . ."

"We hardly got round to them until the 1840's and 1850's, 'Gothic revival'; and you know how short a time that lasted. . . ."

"I don't think they are considered very successful."

"It was an attempt to return to the Gothic style without the Gothic tradition."

"The greatness of Lawrence Lowell included this perception of the difficulty in keeping an idea vital," Whitehead suddenly opened his own idea into a novel aspect, "and this form of his greatness is not yet generally appreciated. He had seen that what is wanted is a certain period of systematized instruction for young men, then that they be allowed to explore for themselves, with or without professional guidance, various areas of learning or achievement. To this he saw the need of adding the oldest form of entertainment and instruction known to the human race; namely, conversation. If you will notice, his foundation of the Junior Fellows is on these principles. They are chosen as nearly as possible for merit from all over this continent and their pursuits are as varied as the arts and sciences. They have had a certain amount of systematized training and some achievement to their credit. Their association is so organized that they meet to dine and spend an evening together at least once a week in conversation with one another and with a wide variety of notable guests drawn from all the professions. There is no 'departmentalism.' The men studying literature are at elbows with men studying biology or mathematics. In the Harvard faculty itself I notice a good deal of departmentalism. You would think the men in one department had nothing to learn from their colleagues in another, or else that"—his eyes twinkled roguishly—"they were protecting themselves from contamination. I consider it a monstrous presumption that university lecturers should think themselves competent to go on talking year after year to young men, students, while holding themselves aloof from the opportunity of learning from eager youth, which is one of the most valuable things on earth. . . ."

"Lecturers," observed Mrs. Whitehead, "are licensed to brag!"

"When you use the expression, 'eager youth' as 'one of the most valuable things on earth,' will you explain more explicitly what you mean by it?"

"I mean—" he hesitated, pondering his definition—"the glow of a young man . . . (I'm afraid I shall have to use a portentous expression, but it isn't portentously meant) . . . I mean the glow of a young man who has just discovered some great work of literature. It isn't the book which he has discovered which is so important: it is his glow over it. There you have the sense of adventure, of newness, the old idea seen freshly in some new aspect. It is this which university instructors should be on the watch for, and should respect wherever it appears, instead of being a trifle irritated at over-eager young men."

"Coming as I did from the Midwest, I had the feeling that in New England enthusiasm was bad form. Harvey Cushing, who came from out there, had noticed it and said that, for himself, the resistance of inert mind and matter to any innovation, surgical or other, was so heavy that a man who had (as he had) anything new and difficult to accomplish must have great enthusiasm as a flywheel to carry the saw of his idea through knots in the log."

"Coming from England to New England, as we did," said Mrs. Whitehead, "we experienced not a drop in temperature, as you did coming from the Midwest, but a rise. After the social climate of England, that of New England seemed a blast from a furnace."

"New England's intellect," I said "(a good many strangers have noticed it) often makes a better first impression than New England's heart."

"Had it occurred to you," asked Mrs. Whitehead, "that New Englanders may be timid?"

"No. It hadn't. But they often are, the best of them. And if I hadn't liked them, why did I stay? I admire the people, and the scenery, and the mellowed culture, and the libraries, and the orchestra, and I can hardly remember having heard good conversation among young men until I came here."

"There is a club in Cambridge," said Whitehead, "to which I had access as a young man. Tennyson and his friend Hallam, the one who died young, were among its founders. They called themselves 'the Apostles.' The members are undergraduates and when you have graduated you 'take wings' and become an 'Angel.' The new members are chosen entirely by undergraduates and on the ground that they are likely to prove interesting. At each meeting—they were on Saturday nights—some member presents a paper setting forth ideas for discussion. This takes about twenty minutes. The members have previously drawn lots for the order of their speaking after the initial presentation of ideas. Each one is expected, when his turn comes, to stand on the hearth and say whatever is in his mind. The understanding is that nothing of what is said here shall ever be repeated outside as having come from any member. In fact, no one is supposed to know who the members are, though, as a matter of fact, they are sometimes guessed. Quite a number of distinguished men have come through the 'Apostles,' and once a year they have a dinner in London which the 'Angels' attend. The chairman, who sits at the head of the table, is an 'Angel,' and the latest-chosen 'Apostle,' who sits at the other end of the table, is vice-chairman. Members of Cambridge colleges are not permitted to enter another college after ten o'clock, but we used to congregate just before ten o'clock, our number being restricted to twelve, and our conversations went on into the small hours. The quality of it held up surprisingly well—at least until the war."

Twilight had deepened into dusk and dusk to darkness. The room was so cool and pleasant with the night breeze coming in at windows that we had continued sitting in the darkness, which seemed, if anything, to promote conversation. We continued speaking from the restful shadows.

"Mr. Lowell's foundation of the Junior Fellows," said Mrs. Whitehead, "received mention by the newspapers of course, but not in anything like the proportion that its importance to the future deserved. What *is* 'news'? If Mrs. Lowell had run away with the chauffeur, or if Mr. Lowell had been carrying on an affair with the housemaid, the newspapers would not have so restricted their space as they did about the Junior Fellows."

"You are asking," said I, "who is to blame. It depends on whom you ask. If you ask me, I think the necessity of a newspaper's paying its way as an article of commerce is at the bottom of it. What is needed is a Hippocratic Oath for journalists. What would a university be like, if it had to live by its fees?"

"It wouldn't exist," said Whitehead.

"In southern England," Mrs. Whitehead took it up, "there used to be very little music. The people there were supposed to be congenitally unmusical. Of late, since the B.B.C. has been broadcasting only good music, they have grown very fond of music, have started groups of village musicians, and want only the best music themselves. In England each owner of a radio set has to pay a small tax that supports the B.B.C. and no advertisements are allowed on the air. The damnable heresy is that people don't want the best. On that plea they are given whatever debased matter may be expected to sell and the tendency of this is steadily downward."

"Having combated that damnable heresy inside a newspaper office for more than half a lifetime and proved that it *is* a heresy—not without, it is only fair to say, some collaboration from its management and its owners—I am still astonished when I see decent-looking people in the public vehicles reading small type under the most blatantly vulgar headlines. They don't look like people who would care for that kind of thing."

Mrs. Whitehead suggested, "They may finally succumb and learn to like the poison after they have been sufficiently tainted. . . ."

K

"On the credit side," said Whitehead, "I notice that a large part of what is written for the serious columns of your newspapers is to set before the readers their responsibility for maintaining the social system. The aspects of this are various, but that in the end is what it all comes to: the readers are being reminded that the preservation of a social system depends on them. Now responsibility for a social system is the groundwork of civilization. Without a society in which life and property are to some extent secure, existence can continue only at the lowest levels—you cannot have a good life for those you love, nor can you devote your energies to activity on the higher level. Consequently, a sense of responsibility for the continuance of a social system is basic to any morality. Now this form of responsibility is almost entirely absent from Christianity. Jesus hardly mentions it, except for one or two remarks."

"And one of these," said Mrs. Whitehead, " 'Render unto Caesar,' was evasive."

"There were historical reasons for this lack, I grant you," he continued. "The Hebrews had no independent state to govern, and a man cannot be blamed for failing to consider what there was in his period no occasion for considering. He said what an able thinker might be expected to say. His historical situation did not elicit a code of ethics concerned with responsibility for a social system; but the absence of such responsibility has been a characteristic of the Jews for centuries. That is one reason for their unpopularity. You may say that the way they have been treated in many of the countries of their sojourn has not permitted such participation, and I quite agree. But that absence has involved Christianity in an almost perpetual self-contradiction. It held that the externals of life are not worth caring about and at the same time insisted on types of moral conduct which cannot be observed—without perishing—unless the externals of life are sufficiently well organized. A society run on strictly Christian principles could not survive at all."

"That kept appearing," I remarked, "in the social criticism

of the nineteenth century, especially among the Russians, like Tolstoy and Kropotkin; Christian anarchist, and philosophical anarchist. But in the other European (and American) nineteenth-century social critics, one keeps encountering this sense of puzzled exasperation: 'You call yourselves Christians and your society Christendom; then why don't you . . .?' What has appeared now, which hadn't then, is that the comparative social stability of the century from 1815 to 1914 had deluded even many of the ablest thinkers into regarding a stable social system as an assured thing."

"It was not until the unification of the modern world by scientific techniques," he replied, "that people realized that social stability would have to be one of the prerequisites of ethical behaviour. This has been forced on us by the types of men in control of the state machinery in certain countries, who have obliged us to fight them in order to be able to maintain any of the social decencies."

"Yet the moment we have admitted that," I raised the question, "what sort of morality do we want a stable social system to maintain? A few evenings ago I was startled by hearing an author, a man I very much respect, refer to someone, in a book or a public speech, as 'extolling all the bourgeois virtues.' Now I have heard the bourgeois criticized sharply enough and know some of the grounds for that criticism. But couldn't our world do with a few bourgeois virtues?"

"One of their virtues," said Whitehead, "is paying their debts. And a robust virtue it is. You can't have a stable society without it."

The clock in Memorial Hall had struck ten. Knowing that I had a train to catch, Mrs. Whitehead considerately rose and switched on a light. We had been sitting in the darkness for nearly an hour past.

Mr. Whitehead went out with me to the elevator. "I always feel," said he, "that I have two duties to perform with a parting guest: one, to see that he doesn't forget anything that is his; the other, to see that he doesn't take anything that is mine."

XXXII

January 13, 1944

THE first volume of Santayana's autobiography, *Persons and Places*, had just appeared. At the Whiteheads', where I was spending the evening, it prompted a discussion of irony.

"Not long ago," I reminded Whitehead, "you defined irony. I have remembered the words, but am not sure that I understand what you mean. You said, 'Irony is a depressive frame of mind.'"

"The connection in which I said it has escaped me," said Whitehead, "so I had better start afresh." He considered awhile, puckering his nose and knitting his fingers, elbows on the arms of his chair. "Irony, I would say," he brought out presently, "signifies the state of mind of people or of an age which has lost faith. They conceal their loss, or even flaunt it by laughter. You seldom get irony except from people who have been somehow more or less cleaned out."

"Lytton Strachey?"

"His name was just about to be on my lips," said Whitehead.

"He was a delightful person," said Mrs. Whitehead, "but a great sufferer."

"Bodily or mentally?"

"Not so much bodily, though he was always frail and often ailing. (He was the son of an elderly father.) But more, mentally. His personal appearance was ridiculous and he knew it. That portrait of him by Augustus John, which is often mistaken for a caricature, is not, but on the contrary, an excellent likeness. And his voice was high and squeaky. He suffered from being so unlike other people."

'Strachey's irony," said Whitehead, "was that of an intellectual set who have abrogated their responsibility for a social system. We in England were treated to a stiff dose of this after the previous war by what I may for convenience term 'the Bloomsbury set.' I grant you that some of them were able people. . . . But confining ourselves to the decent ones," he continued, "there were two whom I knew well as young men and often think of as together, however different they may have been. One was Logan Pearsall Smith and the other was Strachey. Both were men of learning and cultivation but there was this great difference between them, at least as I saw them: Pearsall Smith was determined to write and to write well— and he did; but Strachey wrote because he had to. It was in him and had to come out. And yet the paradox of it is that while Pearsall Smith had no followers, for he lacked the originality of the other man, Strachey, who did have followers, was the cause of their doing a great deal of harm."

"And also," added she, "some of them were plain rotten. . . ."

"Strachey came at the end of what had been a robust age," continued Whitehead. "I grant you he was able and witty, but he was immediately imitated by a host of writers who lacked both his wit and his ability, and they did a great deal of harm. How would you define Santayana's irony?"

"Denigrating and destructive," replied his wife promptly. She told of meeting him repeatedly at the rooms of an Oxford undergraduate who was a close relative of his who admired Santayana and was always having him in for tea. "Santayana was for ever treating the young man ironically. The youth was no heavy intellectual, but I saw what was going on and thought it shabby. It is the irony of one who, lacking faith himself, tries to destroy it in the young—which *I* think devilish!"

"We Americans are often spoken of as incorrigibly naïve," I replied, "but after reading this volume of Santayana's autobiography, admiring its superb prose and flashes of insight, and laughing at his digs at us, I found myself doubting whether all of us are so dense as not to know when we are being sneered at from behind a veil of irony."

"Your people would take that good-humouredly, as they take a joke on themselves," said Mrs. Whitehead, "but let no one suppose that you wouldn't understand what was going on. You have a contemporary novelist of your own in our midst who sneers at you that way; it is taken good-naturedly, but he doesn't fool anybody. And his sneers come from unbelief, beginning as sneers generally do, from unbelief in himself."

"That suggests a puzzle in Santayana. He writes lyric prose about Catholicism; but is it possible, knowing all that he knows—I mean everything from ancient folk-lore to modern psychology—that he can still number himself among the true believers?"

"Catholicism," said Whitehead, "lends itself to being beautifully written *about*! It is very old, it is hugely diversified, picturesque, has its poetical and aesthetic aspects, and can be made very entertaining. A man wouldn't need to be much of a believer to do that, and I dare say that a non-practising Catholic like Santayana, who, as a writer, is a great artist, has done so charmingly. . . . When it comes to his philosophy, however, I confess to a different feeling. The interest of philosophy depends on the sincerity of the philosopher. He has looked at the universe in a certain way, has seen phenomena under some fresh aspect; he is full of his vision and anxious to communicate it. His value to other men is in what he has seen. Now most philosophers do intensely mean what they say, and all of the great ones do. With Santayana's philosophy, I have the feeling that he is merely playing with ideas, all is cool, detached, and almost indifferent. He just misses greatness and I believe it is because he is lacking in sincerity."

"What would you say about Socratic irony? Would that fall within the terms of your original definition?" I asked. "Or the dramatic irony of the Greek tragic poets? I mean the shuddery spectacle Sophocles makes of Oedipus unwittingly condemning

[262]

himself out of his own mouth, uttering speeches which mean
one thing to him and the exact opposite to the awestruck spec-
tators. Or the tragic irony which Aeschylus gives us in the
Agamemnon—such scenes as the king walking into his palace on
that purple carpet, which his queen has persuaded him to do as
a symbol that she will have success in murdering him. Greek
tragedy is drenched with such irony."

"That," said Mrs. Whitehead, "is irony of situation."

"With the Greeks, certainly," said he, "in the fifth century
B.C., which is of course the period of the great dramatists, you
certainly do not have decadence. It is doubtful whether anywhere or at any time men have lived so vividly or more widened
the scope of human faculties. But what you do get in that
century is a questioning of the older religious forms. They had
ceased to believe that the gods were supernatural personages, as
their ancestors had believed, but they saw that the gods could
still serve useful purposes as symbols. Then, with regard to the
irony of Socrates—whether you take him as an historical figure,
or a little under the aspect of his literary character in the
Dialogues of Plato—there had been, of course, lively sceptical
criticism of the traditional religion—by the Sophists and that
lot—but you also had in that society something similar to what
we have much more commonly in ours of today: namely, that
in one and the same period and region, you may get, as we in
London had in Bloomsbury, an intellectual movement that was
distinctly decadent, while just around the corner from it might
be the beginning of a fresh and vigorous life of the mind and of
society; so that you can seldom say that an age is all of a piece.
In every age of decay there may be a half a dozen seeds of the
future, as in the decline of the Roman Empire you have the rise
of Christianity, only—out of these half-dozen seeds, there is no
telling at the time which will die out and which will live to take
over what is left of the affairs of Rome. This makes a reason the
more for tolerance since there is no knowing out of which seed
the future will sprout. There is an admirable letter by the

Emperor Trajan[1] on this subject, about the Christians, who were considered a nuisance. Trajan says that rather than persecute them it is better, if you can, to pacify them and keep them quiet."

The question arose whether myth is the form in which primitive peoples express their general ideas before they possess a language of abstractions, with the result that later, the myths are perceived to have been abstract ideas. I had raised this question before, but I raised it again, thinking that something different might come out, and it did.

"The myth," said Whitehead confidently, "comes *before* general ideas exist. When it first arises, I think there is no thought of personalizing any abstract conception at all. Rather, the myth-makers see certain personalities clashing, with specific results, or see one force arising in the universe around them, to be opposed, or aided by another force, and these processes are personalized. Later, these myths are rethought by more philosophical minds and are seen to contain the germs of abstract ideas; just as, a moment ago, we were saying that when the Greeks ceased to believe in their gods as superhuman beings, they saw that they still contained aspects of symbolic truth."

"Some biographer of Shelley," said I, "Clutton-Brock, I believe, said that Shelley is one of the few myth-makers who have survived into the modern world."

"Shelley is a very great poet," said Whitehead, "and I used

---

[1] "The method you have pursued, my dear Pliny, in the proceedings against those who were denounced to you as Christians, is extremely proper; as it is not possible to lay down any fixed plan by which to act in all cases of this nature. But I would not have you officiously enter into any enquiries concerning them. If indeed they should be brought before you, and the crime is proved, they must be punished; with the restriction, however, that where the party denies himself to be a Christian, and shall make it evident that he is not, by invoking our gods, let him (notwithstanding any former suspicion) be pardoned upon his repentance. Informations without the accuser's name subscribed ought not to be received in prosecutions of any sort, as it is introducing a very dangerous precedent, and by no means agreeable to the equity of my government."—Book X, *Letters*, Gaius Plinius Caecilius Secundus (Pliny the Younger). Mommsen suggests as date for Book X 108 or 109 A.D.

to read him a great deal at one time, when I read poetry. I do not read it now."

"The reason I raise the question is this: most great literatures have had a folk mythology behind them. We Americans seem to have none—at least in this sense, that most of our past on this continent takes place in the full glare of historical record."

"You Americans are creating your myths now," said Whitehead.

This led to a lively discussion of what some of our myths are.

"One of them is democracy," replied Mrs. Whitehead wickedly.

"The political concepts on which your American society is founded," said Whitehead, "are a kind of myth, and yours have a long history. Starting in fairly modern times (I mean, leaving out their Graeco-Roman and Hellenic-Hebraic origins) they stem from Locke in the English seventeenth century, come on down to the great Frenchmen of the eighteenth century, but are never given practical effectuation until they come to the founders of your republic. The purport of that political myth is to improve and safeguard the lot of the common man. In your nineteenth century, however, that myth in America undergoes a serious reversal. The right of the common man to a good life is interpreted as the right of a few exceptional individuals, say one in a thousand—or less—to exploit the resources of a new continent in such a way as to make themselves inordinately rich. When I say 'exceptional' I do not wish to be understood as meaning that they are superior. In every other relationship of life besides the making of money they may be, and quite often are, inferior. But as the nineteenth century proceeded on this continent, they were the ones who ran away with your political myth, and with them it degenerated into the false and vulgar idea that anybody in America could get rich if he were willing to set his mind to it. In this present century you are having to rescue the original conceptions of your political myth

K*

from those few individuals controlling corporate wealth who falsified it."

"You set me wondering," I said, "how the future will rank the Victorian Age."

"Socially," said Whitehead, "it was stuffy, and stuffiness marred a good deal of its literature, since literature is sharply conditioned by the social forms amidst which it arises. The eighteenth-century people, in England and France at any rate, were much more lively and vivid than the nineteenth—though when you say that you must always remember that you are speaking only of the fortunate few at the top of society. Where the nineteenth century excels is in its concern for the common people. That is new. The concern was clumsy and fumbling for a start, did not by any means reach all of them, but it was genuine and it sets the nineteenth century off from every one that has preceded it. And when this present world conflict dies down, that is the side of our modern age which, if it can be saved, will be most worth saving."

"Culturally how do you think the Victorian Age will be ranked?"

"It will be ranked among the world's few great ages, but as the least of them."

"Can you give me an idea of where and how?"

"Yes. Somewhat like that period of the Roman Empire after Tacitus, when life is fairly safe and sound, but not very brilliant; an age of silver, not of gold."

"What dates are you taking as the Victorian Age?" asked Mrs. Whitehead.

"Nineteenth century would be a better term, he replied," "and I should begin the nineteenth century in 1830, ending it of course at 1914. In 1830 most of the men who made the greatness of that century were still in college."

"Tell me," asked Mrs. Whitehead abruptly, "what English poet or poets of the nineteenth century do you still read, if any? . . . Shelley?"

As her question was addressed to me, I confessed to quite a list of them, including Tennyson.

"What poems?"

"*The Holy Grail* at Christmas, *The Passing of Arthur* at New Year, and *In Memoriam* at frequent intervals."

"*In Memoriam*," said she, "doesn't come off. To have been successful it would need to have been the outpouring of a soul in torment, and it wasn't."

Knowing that her husband thought considerably better of it than that and has discussed it as one of "those great serious poems in English literature," the case was carried to him.

"Tennyson," said he, "was a great poet with a mediocre subject. His subject was Victorian England."

"I give you the nineteenth-century English novelists," said she. "Some are good; others less good; but didn't that century do well in science? There's Darwin . . ."

Whitehead didn't take this up, and I thought I knew why; because in science the nineteenth century, certainly until toward its close, would have made a poor showing in comparison with the seventeenth, "The Century of Genius," as he has called it in *Science and the Modern World*. At that point I tried to get Goethe and Beethoven in, only to be reminded that our nineteenth century was deemed to have begun in 1830, whereas Goethe died in 1832 and Beethoven in 1827.

"But while this concern for common people distinguishes our period and is one of its admirable traits," Whitehead resumed, "there is the question whether more widely diffused opportunity will not depress talent and genius to less exalted levels. The eighteenth century had its means of identifying talent and fostering it, inadequate though the means often were. How will exceptional ability—I don't mean ordinary talents, but really exceptional powers—be identified in a completely democratic society?"

"There I disagree with you," said Mrs. Whitehead decidedly, emphasizing her conviction by rolling up her ball of yarn more and more vigorously. "The levelling will release talents where they were never released before, and *raise* standards by diffusing opportunity. I will give you an example of how this process is already at work. From the nineteenth century only the best novels have survived; they were published among more having less merit or none; but when a good one appeared in the nineteenth century it was an event. Today, while the number of novels, bad, good, indifferent, which are being turned out, is much greater, the publication of a good novel isn't so much of an event, for there are quite a good many of them."

"As one who doesn't read enough contemporary novels to have any right to an opinion," I said, "it strikes me that Tolstoy, Dostoevsky, Turgenev, Tchekov and Gorki, who wrote novels under the czarist autocracy, at least haven't been surpassed by any writers known to us since the Revolution of 1917."

"But would you call Soviet Russia a democracy," asked Mrs. Whitehead.

"We English and Americans," answered Whitehead, "are singularly unimaginative in our interpretations of the term 'democracy'; we seem unable to admit under our definition any form of society which does not conform closely to our own. See the way their armies fight in this war. The whole Russian people is evidently unified in the determination to free their soil of the Germans. No question arises but that that shall be done. Their unity for defence is complete, because they are defending a social system which they feel to be their own. I believe that the two great powers which will emerge from this war will be Russia and America, and the principles which animate them will be antithetical: that of Russia will be cohesion; that of America will be individualism."

"Do you see anywhere in contemporary political thought any new idea as daring as the discoveries in science and the resulting inventions have been in the past fifty years?"

"There is Marx, of course; though I cannot speak of him with any confidence."

"Lenin put him to work."

"Yes, and it is a singular fact that the prophet of proletarian revolt found the first practical effectuation of his ideas in a society predominantly agrarian."

"Only," offered Mrs. Whitehead as correction, "because it was rottenest and ready to fall."

"I wonder," said Whitehead, "if Lenin didn't die at about the right time. Hadn't he accomplished his work, and wasn't a man of a less theoretical and more practical talent the man wanted?"

"How do you think Trotsky would have done?"

Whitehead said he doubted if Trotsky would have been of much use as head of a socialist fatherland, or to speak more explicitly, Soviet Russia. I remarked that "when Trotsky was being deported from Russia by Stalin, he said, as I remember, that Stalin was intellectually a fearful come-down after Lenin, and that Russia would be ruled not by a great thinker but by a man with the political mentality of a ward boss."

"His peculiar abilities," said Whitehead, smiling blandly, "seem to be finding useful scope at present."

"You remind me—and I shall remind you—of what you said to Constable at the Saturday Club when it was being discussed whether Churchill's boots could, if necessary, be filled by Anthony Eden, Churchill having just had pneumonia. Constable, who had known Eden, said, 'He is not a brilliant man, but he is a thoroughly decent fellow,' and you said . . ."

"What did he say?" asked Mrs. Whitehead mischievously.

"He said, 'Churchill is a better prime minister flat on his back in bed with pneumonia than any other man in England up in his boots. Eden may be a decent fellow but this is no time for decency!'"

(It had set the table in a gale of laughter.)

The tray of chocolate came in next, it being now about ten o'clock. The chocolate was, if possible, better than ever, or else we were all hungrier than usual, and meanwhile the conversation had shifted somehow to school discipline.

"As head boy at Sherborne," said Whitehead, "I once had to thrash a boy. He was guilty of stealing money. The headmaster said, 'Either you must thrash him in the presence of the school or I must expel him.' That left no choice, I had to go ahead with it. The masters, of course, were not present; it was done only in the presence of the boys."

"How did you feel about it?"

"I didn't like it; but I had to do it, and in those days, the late 1870's, flogging was still an accepted part of the discipline. The headmaster, who was an exceptionally kind-hearted man, occasionally had to do it himself, and after having thrashed a boy, we could see him bury his head in his arms and weep. You could have heard a pin drop!"

"Were you ever thrashed by your parents when you were a child?"

"No. When I needed to be punished they would give me a dose of medicine and tell me they were sorry I wasn't feeling well."

"My parents thrashed *me*," said Mrs. Whitehead rebelliously, "and it didn't do a bit of good. It was the Breton rearing, which was stern. As children we were brought up on the mediaeval folk tales which were still rife in the countryside, and I remember, once when something went wrong with me, being told—like the wounded knight in the tourney, who said, 'I thirst'—being told, I say, in the words of the king, '*Bois ton sang, Beaumanoir, et tu n'auras plus soif.*' "

We were peering through an album of old photographs, looking for two of the cricket teams at Sherborne when Whitehead was a youth in his teens. They were taken in front of what seemed to be an ancient Gothic gateway. I said it looked very old.

"The school," said Whitehead, "celebrated its twelve-hundredth anniversary in 1941, and is supposed to go back to

King Alfred. One of its buildings was an abbey and the little room I occupied in my last year was supposed to have been the abbot's."

"Can you pick him out of that group of young men?" asked Mrs. Whitehead.

There were two group photographs in the same spot from two successive years; and he was more easily identifiable in the second, or elder, group than in the younger.

"A singular thing about our schooling there," said Whitehead, "and it was by no means confined to Sherborne, but was characteristic of all English schooling of that time—we studied the literature and history of the Greeks, but took from it only those aspects which seemed to resemble our English life and affairs. Thus, Athens was a naval power, and England had a navy, and, the larger aspects of modern naval power not yet having been grasped, we thought of it as being mainly applied to the coasts of Europe, as the Athenian naval power was applied to the coasts and islands of the eastern Mediterranean. Mind you, nobody realized that this was going on. We were merely taking from the ancient world what seemed applicable to ourselves. And similarly, when it came to Rome, although we read the great authors of the late republican period and in the time of Augustus, the part of Roman history which seemed analogous to our own were those later centuries after the literature has lost its greatest names—I should say Tacitus was the last—say the three centuries following the year 70 A.D. when it was a question of Rome's maintaining its ascendancy by wise statesmanship, and able civil administration. . . . As between the Greek and Roman authors of their respective great ages, namely the fifth century in Greece and the Augustan Age in Rome, I find the Greek immeasurably superior to the Roman. The ideas are immensely more original and vital. In fact, the only Roman author whom I find at all comparable with the Greeks in those qualities of vital and original ideas is one who may surprise you. He is Lucretius."

"Lucretius has something to say to the people of our time. *That* doesn't surprise me," I replied, "for I remember how Arnold Toynbee found the lines from a passage in Lucretius which argue that death destroys personality running in his head during the spring of 1918. They were written about one hundred and fifty years after Hannibal evacuated Italy, but the horror of that invasion was still so vivid in men's minds that Lucretius thought its mere memory made oblivion seem preferable to personal immortality. . . . And this brings up a question which I have been wanting to open with you. It isn't a very cheerful one, and I shall find it hard to phrase precisely, for it doesn't come from any single piece of evidence but, rather, from a thousand scattered impressions; what I read, what I see, what I hear, what I experience, and what I am left to infer. The effect is cumulative and the only way I know how to word it at last may sound banal, dreadful though it is. It is this: that we live amid a steady disintegration of what people are accustomed to call 'civilized life.' "

"I don't consider that banal," said he, "and I do consider it true. And I am afraid our old friend Adam Smith had something too much to do with it; not in the sense that one man's words can effect such vast consequences, but in the sense that he gave expression to a half-truth which was already lurking in men's minds, which, in fact, is always lurking there, and they took it as a whole truth and proceeded to act on it. I mean the idea of the predominance of the economic motive in man. Now I don't deny that the economic motive is there, but what plays the devil in human affairs is mistaking a half-truth for a whole truth. This elevated the material motive into good repute and allowed people to act on it with what they took to be good conscience. But no period of history has ever been great or ever can be that does not act on some sort of high, idealistic motives, and idealism in our time has been shoved aside, and we are paying the penalty for it."

"The very word 'idealism,' " I said, "has been a term of

derision since the first world war. Writing for readers of the daily press one grows very sensitive to what sort of ideas are and are not acceptable, and how the unacceptable ones must be rephrased to make them go down. And at about the same time it began to be noticed that there was a marked decline in the influence of Christian theology."

"Christian theology," said Whitehead, "took a fearfully wrong turning."

"Buddhist theology, though very elaborate, in fact too elaborate for me, does nevertheless strike me as being intellectually respectable," I remarked.

"The Hindus," added Whitehead, "had, among other things, grasped the resemblances between us and the animals and incorporated it into their religious thought, but you can hardly call it an equalitarian idea, for they considered that it was the job of all of us alike to get rid of our damned personalities." (He said this smilingly, but immediately turned serious again.) "As for the Christian theology, can you imagine anything more appallingly idiotic than the Christian idea of heaven? What kind of deity is it that would be capable of creating angels and men to sing his praises day and night to all eternity? It is, of course, the figure of an Oriental despot, with his inane and barbaric vanity. Such a conception is an insult to God. . . . I will tell you, though, that on its emotional and aesthetic side, Christianity plays an enormous part in the lives of people who are not over-intellectualized; women especially, and it gives them a sustainment which is often quite touching. One of the worst pieces of luck that has befallen Europeans was that when it came time to reform the Church, the new forms were set by Martin Luther, who threw away the aesthetic and emotional appeal, and left only the dry bones of theology."

German theology led to a discussion of German scholarship and its distinctive qualities as viewed beside the scholarship of France and England. Whitehead presently generalized the three impartially by remarking:

"German scholarship shares a defect which I find common to most scholarship. Scholars insist upon using words as though the meanings of those words existed in a vacuum. They will say, 'This man said *that* about *this*,' as though the words themselves were all there were to it, and quite ignoring the emotional content of those words in the historical environment in which they were first uttered. What was the total emotional connotation of those terms when they were originated, and how have the historical changes which have occurred since altered our understanding of them?"

" '*Er hat zu viel gelesen*,' was the verdict of a young German who came out from a lecture by one of the eminent savants at Berlin, with Bliss Perry when he was a young student there. Bliss heard Mommsen, whom he did admire, and von Treitschke, whom he admits he didn't see through at the time, and also many of the university bigwigs of that period, and he was left thinking that a good many of them had also 'read too much.' And men who read too much are likely to be contented with half-truths."

"Most propositions are that," said Whitehead. "Under one aspect it may be false; and under another, true. Whether it is true or false will depend upon its relevancy. In the aspect in which it is relevant we call it true, and in the aspect in which it is irrelevant, untrue. Actually it is neither, and it is both, depending upon the relevancy in which it is seen. A half-truth, you see. And it is taking these half-truths for whole truths that raises the mischief."

"Do you consider that the economists have been any worse offenders with half-truths than historians?"

"The more history I read," he replied, "the less I think of historians. Most of them strike me as men who presume to write authoritatively about events which they are not qualified to understand. Or else they accept the official documents of an epoch at their full value, omitting to reflect that its real significance lay in the emotional atmosphere which activated its people and the general ideas under whose sway they lived. I make two exceptions: Gibbon is one and the other is Thucydides. Gibbon had had some practical experience of managing men in that regiment of his, the Hampshire Volunteers; he had had experience in politics; he had known an interesting set of literary men in London; and then just at the right moment, he emigrated to Geneva where he came into contact with the point of view of travelled and cultivated people on the Continent. These, with his other qualifications, gave him an equipment for the writing of history which is unique among modern historians. As for the ancient one, Thucydides was a general who had been a part of the life and times which he depicts."

XXXIII

May 9, 1944

ONE of those oddities which keep happening in wartime occurred on my way to dine with the Whiteheads. Each spring on fine evenings the Harvard and Radcliffe choirs sing from the steps of Widener Hall, the university library, in what is generally known as the Sever Quadrangle. These massive stone steps mount to an imposing classical façade of red-brick academic Georgian with Corinthian columns. They are spacious enough for several hundred persons, and they face a somewhat similar portico of the Memorial Church across a greensward and elm grove, making a pleasant out-of-door concert hall. The church was built to commemorate the Harvard men who were killed in the first world war.

Half a dozen undergraduates, three of them in uniform, were trundling a small cabinet pianoforte on a wheeled carrier toward the steps; people were already assembling; evidently it was for a Yard concert. The boys did not know what the programme was going to be, but just then Professor Wallace Woodworth, the choirmaster, arrived and told me: they were to sing three movements from Brahms's *German Requiem*. We agreed that it was a piece of historic irony which might be taken in any one of several ways.

The May evening was golden of late sunlight behind the fresh green of the budding elms, a pink dogwood tree was in full flower over by the church, and the robins were already choiring.

At the Hotel Ambassador the Whiteheads were sitting beside their westward windows, which were wide open; for in four warm days spring had come at a bound. We dined beside another window opening westward, still in the late rays of the setting sun, and dined scrumptiously, albeit without a single rationed item on the table, unless it were a few snicks of butter or sugar. As the meal went on, Whitehead spoke of what the sudden access of wealth had done to Spain in the sixteenth century.

"That influx of gold from the West Indies and South America ruined Spain in about the span of two lifetimes," said he. "As soon as they had exhausted what the natives had accumulated, there it ended. Not that the Spanish people saw much of it, for Charles V used the gold to finance his European wars and political manoeuvres. No new industries were started and so the stream of bullion from the New World created no lasting wealth. Food and manufactured goods were largely imported, and it has been said that the only articles of export were 'soldiers and priests.' Now the true prosperity of a country is derived from its *internal* industrial activities. Of course, the fruits of these activities must be more or less equitably distributed. But if the wealth comes from outside and without any particular exertion from the most of your people, its effects are ruinous. A nation flourishes and survives by its internal activity. Even if your loans to other nations are never paid after this war—and I don't suppose they will be—you still have in this country your immense industrial equipment, your agrarian productivity, and your people with technical skill; and by these your recovery is sufficiently assured."

"The Spaniards had two other misfortunes at about the same time," I remarked. "There is a striking page in Gilbert Murray's *Tradition and Progress* in which he says that persecution, however disastrous its remoter consequences, may be a complete political success, instancing the treatment of the Protestants and the Jews in Spain, where 'the blood of martyrs' was certainly *not* 'the seed of the church.'"

"Toleration," said Mrs. Whitehead, "pays such immense returns. The Jews have done a great deal for England and, *as* Jews, I would say, are tending to disappear. You need your Jews in this country. They make an admirable ingredient in your population—are more acute and more subtle than our Anglo-American stock. Your Negro problem, on the other hand, is a real problem. When English people deplore their having been brought here, I want to ask them, 'Who began it?' Your Southern planters and Northern shipowners continued on a larger scale what the English started, and it is all very well for us to point out that we abolished it legally by the year 1833, but black slavery was never in *our* islands. It was a colonial problem."

"Bringing them in was so fearfully short-sighted in the first place," said Whitehead. "A little imagination should have warned anybody what was being incurred. The immediate motive of individual profit is of too limited a range to serve as foundation for a stable society—and so, for that matter, is the immediate advantage of any single nation, as I should think we should all have learned by now."

"Do you ever see Dr. Brüning?" asked Mrs. Whitehead.

"Only now and then, and not with much opportunity for personal conversation."

"He was here once, and he and I spoke together by ourselves," she replied. "One thing he said was that he could have succeeded as chancellor of Germany if Britain and America had supported him! What kind of government is it that needs to be sustained by two other governments?"

"Once, at Dr. Hans Zinsser's, where we were only five at table," I said, "and probably because Zinsser was of German descent, Dr. Brüning spoke very freely. What he told in detail of Hitler's rise to power sounded like melodrama; Brüning seemed to have known what was going on and what Hitler intended, yet he seemed to have been powerless to stop it."

"Brüning is a very devout man," observed Whitehead, "but a man may be devout without being good. He may be a man of conscience, but his conscience may be a damned *bad* conscience, for conscience presupposes that its promptings are socially beneficent."

Dinner ended, Mr. Whitehead and I were shooed into the living room, where we sat by the open window in the soft twilight until Mrs. Whitehead had cleared the table. He asked what I thought of the government's eviction of Sewell Avery from the offices of Montgomery Ward in Chicago.

"The most eloquent comment on it," I thought, "was the newspaper photograph of Avery being carried out, cat's-cradle fashion, by the two soldier boys. It was much worse than if the boys had been laughing; for they were gentlemen and trying hard to keep their faces straight. But I will tell you who *were* indignant about it—the small business people and every little property-holder hanging on for dear life to what property he has in the midst of a world war in which the young men, who have not yet lived, are dying."

"The idea," said Whitehead, "of supposing that in the midst of the greatest crisis in the history of mankind, people should not be disturbed in their accustomed procedures and routines! I would have liked to be there in order to kick Avery!"

"It was a carnival for the Roosevelt-haters," I observed.

"To hear them talk," said Whitehead, "you would think that Mr. Roosevelt had entered the Presidency in an era of unprecedented prosperity."

"I am patient with their dialectic," said I.

"It is not dialectic," said Whitehead, "it is ranting."

Before settling down for the evening we roamed around the living-room a little, looking at its various pieces of Spanish mahogany, now no longer obtainable, Mrs. Whitehead remarked.

"The desk," said Whitehead, "is a museum piece. One of those Jacobean chairs is a bad Victorian imitation. The other is genuine Jacobean."

One of the pieces had a family genealogy of four generations, having been transmitted from a ninety-year-old great-grandmother to a grandmother, who in turn lived to the age of ninety or more. Taking one of her dining-room chairs into Boston for repairs, Mrs. Whitehead had asked its value. "How many of these have you?" inquired the dealer. "Half a dozen," said she for reply, for some of them are in her children's house. "Two hundred and fifty dollars," says the dealer. "For the half-dozen?" she asked. "No. Apiece."

"So I am having them insured," she said in epilogue.

Midway in a discussion of how our world has been jolted loose from what it thought were its most impregnable ideas, not alone in theology but even in physics, Whitehead remarked, "I have been rereading Huxley's *Letters*, especially the second volume. He strikes me as one of those men who fall just under the first rank, immensely able but not great. Darwin, on the other hand, is truly great, but he is the dullest great man I can think of. He and Huxley had grasped the principle of evolution in material life, but it never occurred to them to ask how evolution in material life could result in a man like, let us say, Newton."

"There was one man who saw that omission very early, and said so. He was Samuel Butler."

"They didn't like him," said Whitehead.

"Like him? They tried to ignore him, but he was a hard man to ignore."

"Darwin's dismissal of the transmission of acquired characteristics is another lapse. Who knows where our bodies begin or end, or how characteristics may be transmitted otherwise than by heredity? There may be a thousand predispositions in a child due to the occupations of his immediate forebears. A certain type of activity may have been going on in the family for generations, and the child is predisposed to it. Is that 'environment' or is it heredity?"

"Harvey Cushing came of four generations of doctors, first in this state, then in Ohio," I remarked. "Clevelanders can't remember a time when there wasn't a Dr. Cushing, and he couldn't remember a time when Cushings weren't doctoring someone. How vastly that must have increased his initial momentum."

"My father," said Whitehead, "my grandfather, and my uncles all had to do with education or local administration, or both. And so have I."

"You are a changeling, though, all the same," Mrs. Whitehead remarked, "as different from the others as could be imagined. I have always attributed the Celtic fire in you to that Welsh grandmother of yours, Mary Williams."

"That supine reliance on heredity," continued Whitehead, "had a bad effect. People felt safe in neglecting environment. 'Heredity would take care of all that.' If you want a civilization to progress, there are two or three things you must do. The forces that are constantly playing in upon our minds and bodies are inconceivably innumerable—for instance, rays from some star millions of light-years away from us—forces as fantastic as that . . . and the forms of life which might be lived on other stars millions of light-years away and millions of years hence could be infinite and admit every possibility that the imagination could conceive. The thousand thoughts that drift through a man's mind day by day he should entertain and turn over and consider in every aspect, give them their share of consideration. We need to entertain every prospect of novelty, every chance that could result in new combinations. But at the same time we need to entertain those with sceptical examination, and subject them to the most impartial scrutiny, for the probability is that nine hundred and ninety-nine of them will come to nothing, either because worthless in themselves or because we shall not know how to elicit their value; but we had better entertain them all, however sceptically, for the *thousandth* idea may be the one that will change the world!"

"People in our time, having seen the incredible achieved so often," I said, "are prepared to admit that possibility in the world of scientific discovery, but not yet in the larger world of general ideas."

"I will give you an example," said he, "of how unpredictable these chances of novel origination are. Seated in this room with an apparatus, we can convey thought to someone seated in another room in Boston or farther away. But seventy years ago if you wanted to communicate quickly with Tokyo you had to telegraph. Today you can speak to somebody in Asia who has with him an apparatus no larger than that one in the other room. Marconi thought that such communication might be possible; at the start, of course, he couldn't be sure. But there were plenty of first-rate men of science who could tell him that it wouldn't work, and could tell him why; the vibrations, instead of continuing around the earth, would go up into the stratosphere and disperse. They did go up into the stratosphere, but instead of being dispersed they were reflected back down to the earth, and so we have wireless communication. No one foresaw that fact which made it possible; not even Marconi at the outset. Something unknown and unpredictable—a mere chance, if you care to call it that—determined the success of this still almost incredible means of human communication. Now some general idea, equally inconceivable to people now living, might change our manner of life on this planet even more than wireless has affected intercommunication."

"Europe, for all its ructions," said I, "has produced no lack of novel origination—at least since the Renaissance, and for centuries before the fall of Rome. But if enough young men are slaughtered in these wars, and civil societies are repeatedly disrupted, I wonder where the impetus for novel ideas will come from."

"Russia is a possibility," said he.

"But tinged with the Asiatic: don't forget that," said Mrs. Whitehead. "That makes it not quite the same thing."

"There is not much reason thus far to suppose that the impetus would come from South America," continued Whitehead. "I look for it to come from you, here in the United States, in North America. If you people cannot produce it, I think the world will be in a bad way. You may need another century to coalesce your races; and I believe you will gain by the admixture of the brilliant southern European strains. Left to itself the old Anglo-American stock is a little too stolid."

"This fusing of races," I said, "is only just beginning. As yet, it is likely to take the form of gifted individuals rising spectacularly. The races are mixing but we don't yet know what the result will be. It might be brilliant—or it might be stupid."

"I have never ceased to entertain the idea," said he, "that the human race might rise to a certain point and then decline and never retrieve itself. Plenty of other forms of life have done that. Evolution may go down as well as up. In Asia we have seen how life can stagnate for centuries. A part of that stagnation seems to come from religious mysticism. 'Never mind about this world,' or 'Our misfortunes are our karmas incurred in previous incarnations, and must be expiated' or 'The overruling purposes of the universe are inscrutable, and who are we that we should question them?'"

"The West, in contrast," said I, "has seldom hesitated 'to take arms against a sea of troubles.'"

"Static religions are the death of thought," said Whitehead.

"Would that be because they presume to answer all questions before they have been asked?"

"Any dogmatic system of thought does that. When a priesthood becomes dominant in a society, freedom of inquiry is discouraged; and if their dominance continues long enough, the level of general intelligence is depressed."

XXXIV

August 29, 1944

SUMMER ending, the Cambridge elms already beginning to look like September with brown leaves fallen on the greenswards. It was seven-forty when I rang the bell of the Whiteheads' apartment. They were both looking uncommonly well. "But then," as I told them, "why shouldn't you? Back from a month on your island in Maine, and then this deluge of favourable war news? You must wonder, as we all do, whether we are living in the same world as that of 1940–1942."

"It is true, these events are staggering," said Whitehead.

"Are they really unprecedented," I asked, "or are they only on a larger scale physically?"

"Nothing like it that I know of has happened in a thousand years, and when it did it took a hundred years to happen, while this takes only a matter of months. Formerly the magnitude of such events could be seen only afterwards, and then mainly by historians and scholars, but these can be seen happening by everybody, from day to day, almost from hour to hour."

"I come to you almost blind from reading newspapers or hanging over the office teletype, and this since June 6th. As you read these events, what, in essence, do you think it is that is happening?"

"Two things. First, sheer self-preservation. We have been forced to defend ourselves against not now one, but two types of German military men (acting, of course, as agents for people in the background); one, the regular German army officers of the old aristocratic class; and two, these new, low-class adventurers. They both thought, 'Wouldn't it be great to enslave the whole of Europe!' And they threatened us with a slavery of a new and horrible kind. Most previous conquerors have been willing to leave regional cultures fairly intact! . . ."

"The Romans preferred to," said I. "Conquered territories were easier to govern that way."

"But these Germans," said he, "set to work extirpating all that. I'm not sure they meant to 'rule the world'; at least not yet, but if they had won they would have made plenty of trouble for you acting through South America. The other thing that is happening, as I see it, is this: you cannot wage a war of such magnitude as this without inaugurating a new epoch. We have been fortunate in Churchill. He is an admirable leader to arouse the patriotism of his people in a desperate war; but he doesn't think sociologically in terms of a new epoch. I doubt if he would be so admirable in the making of the peace."

"Churchill thinks in terms of the eighteenth century," said Mrs. Whitehead positively. "He has two sides to his nature; on one side he is a British statesman of the type one knows, and, in many aspects, admires. But I knew his mother—a lighter-headed young thing . . . and on that side he is a back-slapping Rotarian, singing jovial songs with 'the boys.' "

"You are more fortunate in your man," continued Whitehead. "Mr. Roosevelt does, I believe, think largely in terms of a new epoch. It was shown before this war began in his domestic policies, which so infuriated some of our wealthy friends. Let us hope he lives to have a large hand in the shaping of the peace. And in the epoch to come, again, I look to Russia."

"When I think of the 'bad press' Russia has had in America for twenty-five years, to see ourselves now locked in fraternal embrace . . ."

"You Americans, it seems to me, are rather narrow-minded in your views about the excellence and general applicability of your own form of government," Whitehead spoke slowly, weighing his thoughts. "How is it that the Russians have been able to do what they have? For the previous century, or century and a half, before their Revolution, whenever they came into the affairs of western Europe it was usually to support the wrong side, as they did Metternich at the Congress of Vienna. There were, it is true, charming and gifted people at the top of their society of whom one knew, and they did well in the arts—literature (those novels of Tolstoy, Dostoevsky, and Turgenev, that are so much better than ours of the same period), and drama, music, and painting. . . ."

"Don't omit the dance. . . ."

"Also," said he, "their defeat of Napoleon—as such great events usually are—was an advance notice of what was to come. But it is not until our own century that the world has seen the true greatness of which Russia is capable."

"Where do you date it? November 1917?"

"Rather, from the departure of Trotsky and the arrival of Stalin in power."

"Lenin," observed Mrs. Whitehead, "being a revolted aristocrat, had it in for his class, as such rebel sons usually do. But Stalin is a man of the people and much more representative."

"Stalin's being a Georgian, I think, does have a good deal to do with it," agreed Whitehead. "He has had this concept that Russia, with its enormous diversifications and extent, could be coalesced into one great people. And how this vast array of talents has been elicited from the masses of the Russian people in such a short time is worth looking into. Take their generals in this war; they are mostly a young set. Presumably someone had to pick them, and I don't suppose Stalin chose them by chance. It is a main function of society to release the widest possible spread of talents, and this appears to have been being done in Russia. When great departures come in the lives of peoples they are generally the result of two or more causes coming together; but although one man cannot initiate such great changes, once these changes are in motion, one man may be able to give them their direction, this way or that. Napoleon rode into power on the ideas of the French Revolution,

[285]

but he never, at heart, was interested in those ideas. One reason was that he was too good a general; the application of military science interested him more; the revolutionary ideas stoked, as it were, his war-machine."

"Would you agree that Napoleon's star rose as long as he subserved the great ideas of the French Revolution and began to decline when he supplanted them with his own imperial ego?"

"Yes. And we English were on the wrong side all along. Our ruling classes and landed aristocracy were frightened by the Terror and the beheading of the king."

"As if the English hadn't beheaded a king . . ."

"Yes," said Mrs. Whitehead, "but that was 'different.' "

"Haven't I heard that there was some religious revulsion in it, too; that the English nonconformists regarded the deism of the French *philosophes* and revolutionary leaders as sheer atheism?"

"That would have placed our people solidly behind our aristocracy," said Mrs. Whitehead, "where, as a matter of fact, they were."

"And yet, to think of our American War of Independence having had, from start to finish, a sizable block of favourable votes in your British House of Commons."

"I do," said Mrs. Whitehead, "but I wish I could convince some of my American friends that that was the fact."

"Is it only when people have gone through some fearful personal or social ordeal that they can sufficiently universalize their minds to identify the movements for human liberation on whichever side of a national frontier they may be?"

"It doesn't always follow," said Whitehead. "Take the type of Frenchman so often produced by complete opposition to the Church; that type strikes me as unfortunate. The Reformation was one of the most colossal failures in history; it threw overboard what makes the Church tolerable and even gracious; namely, its aesthetic appeal; but kept its barbarous theology."

"What oppresses me," said Mrs. Whitehead gravely, "is where we are to find, since Christianity is losing its hold, a place where humanity can collectively express its good will. I don't deny the fearful suffering that Christian theology has inflicted on the more sensitive and imaginative spirits. That has been shocking enough, God knows! But just as the family is the only place one can turn to when he has behaved disgracefully (and we are all capable of so behaving at some time in our lives, even unintentionally) so there needs to be a place where people can come together, not to do specifically this or that, but to remind themselves and one another of their benevolent intentions, their general good will. If I thought the church, or any form of organized Christianity, were still doing this, or could still do it, I wouldn't be saying what I am. The need still exists; how can it be filled?"

The objection that multitudes of church-goers might say that the churches are still filling just that need was not raised because, so often, what one solitary voice is saying today the multitude may be saying tomorrow. Instead, the question was raised whether aesthetic experience might not be a form of religious worship: "Are not aesthetics a form of ethics?"

"No," replied Whitehead, "the two move in different realms."

"Wait a moment; let me try to rephrase that. . . . Isn't there a high moral content in the work of great artists?"

"What do you mean by 'moral content'?"

"I mean the effect on the spectator or the listener of artists who have lived and worked at a consistently high level. Surely, it isn't stretching things to say that we are getting a higher voltage of the spirit when hearing good performances of music created by men of genius than when listening to the Reverend Doctor or the Reverend Father. . . . And I encounter a good many others who think the same way. How can the effect of such works be other than religious?"

"While you were speaking," said Whitehead, laughing at

me, "I was of two minds. One said, 'Yes, that sounds all right,' and the other said, 'What the devil does he mean?' No," he continued, "the only question in aesthetics is: is the work of art good or bad? If you and I were enjoying together, say, a fine sunset, I wouldn't nudge you and ask, 'I say, what do you propose to do about this sunset?' We enjoy aesthetic experiences purely for their own sakes. That is all we have any right to expect of them."

"Well, perhaps what you have been hearing from me is the hang-over from two sets of dissenting grandparents: one, New England Puritans, the other Philadelphia Quakers."

"The artist," said Whitehead, "has, and must have, a continuous flow of fresh aesthetic experiences. These he translates into an art-form, and it is through these works that his experience passes into the lives of others." He let it go at that, but he knew, and I knew, that what he had said meant more than met the ear.

"So morals have nothing to do with good poetry?"

"Was Byron 'moral'?" he inquired, smilingly.

Of a sudden he had me on his side:

"This is one thing which ails so many of our American nineteenth-century poets. They are entirely too 'correct'—in their printed sentiments at least. Reading them now, one finds himself thinking: 'You didn't really believe that. It's not possible that you didn't know better. Only you didn't dare say so!' A sample in prose of that timidity is the feeble 'moral' which Hawthorne ventures at the end of *The Scarlet Letter*: 'Be true! Show freely to the world, if not your worst, yet some trait whereby the worst can be inferred!' Even as a boy, reading that, I knew it was evasive. 'If you can't be true, be as true as you can!' "

"The one of your poets who escapes all that," said Mrs. Whitehead, "is Whitman. And American poetry has never elsewhere reached such heights as in his elegy for President Lincoln."

From here the discussion moved to the impact of scientific technology on our modern world:

"These new techniques," said Whitehead, "have created a situation absolutely unprecedented. At the beginning of this evening you asked me if I thought these world events—the military action and the consequent social changes—are really more significant than similar crises in the past, or merely on a larger scale physically."

"Yes: are these events of today 'greater' or only 'bigger'?"

"They are probably no bigger and no greater than the collapse of Athens at the end of the Peloponnesian War seemed, or was, to the Greeks; and probably no greater or no bigger than the fall of Rome was to the Romans of the fifth century A.D.; but I will tell you what *is* new. In those earlier crises in the history of mankind, and in others like them, it took a hundred years to bring about changes which we have been watching in the past five years; even in the past five months. That *is* new, and the spectacle is terrific. For one thing, the apparatus for communication works with a rapidity which is almost instantaneous. Already we are all so accustomed to this that to mention the fact seems trite. Yet the fact itself is far from being trite. Again, the acceleration of new techniques is such that since 1900 the rate of technological innovation is double that between 1800 and 1900. I was born in the year 1861. And I would almost venture to say that the techniques of living have changed faster and more between 1861 and 1944 than they did, going backward, between 1861 and . . . "—he paused, smiling —"I was going to say—between 1861 and 61 B.C.!

"Furthermore," he continued, "the effects of these new techniques are interactive. Their alterations in our ways of daily living affect our moral ideas, and the alterations in our ways of thinking in turn react upon the uses to which we put our new techniques and, in turn, produce fresh novelties. As I have often told you, I can hardly think of a concept which was accepted as fundamental truth when I was a young man

L

in the 1880's, that has not been profoundly modified if not rendered obsolete by the changes of which we have been speaking. Thus our moral ideas are affected by these floods of change and the fluidity of ideas reacts upon the uses to which the new techniques are put."

"A while ago," said Mrs. Whitehead, "when we were speaking about the impulse of worship, I was asking myself, 'Where—finally—does it come from?' What is this moral sense that we have? A child has it, a mere baby, and feels guilty, poor lamb, when he thinks he has violated his little vision of the good."

"As you speak, I can see Eric's tiny boots sticking out from under the bed," said I.

"We never knew what he thought he had done that was wrong," said she. "Our first intimation of anything amiss was that only his heels were visible. I never pumped him. He was very glad to be taken by one foot and hauled out on his little tummy, but we never found out."

"He was the most fascinating human being I have ever known," said Whitehead absently. "His colonel came to see us afterwards, and told us a good deal that we hadn't known. He said, among other things, that while there was a good deal of bawdy talk at table, it was always moderated when Eric was there, not because Eric was a prig, for he wasn't, but out of deference to some quality in him. He was full of fun and if there was a 'rag' he would be one of the ringleaders."

"They couldn't believe," said Mrs. Whitehead, "that he spent his evenings on leave at home. 'I say, Whitehead, where do you go?' Directly he arrived home the telephone would start ringing. 'May I speak to Eric?' One evening it rang five times. I said, 'What ails them? Can't they let you alone for a single evening?' He explained: 'They are charming fellows. What they do doesn't seem to harm them in the least; it glides off them like water off a duck's back; but if I did the same, I couldn't look you in the face.' What sort of homes they had been reared in I don't know; perhaps their mothers were of the order of women who are too pure to discuss sex with their sons."

"That restraint on rough tongues in the presence of a well-bred boy is a mysterious process. I have seen it work but can't say I ever understood exactly what was going on. The Signet Society in Harvard when I was an undergraduate was a group of brilliant young men, and the first place I ever heard young men talk well; but there were two or three upperclassmen who were quite disagreeable. With the first Junior Seven came in a Philadelphia boy with, I judge, a personality somewhat like Eric's. Almost at once it was noticed that when he was at table the three disagreeables moderated their pitch. It wasn't that he ever said anything or perhaps even thought anything. But what *might* he think? And one wouldn't want to be thought badly of by Spencer Ervin."

"This awareness of worth in human beings," said Whitehead, "develops very early. Most attempts to formulate it in words fail."

"When I meet it, this quiet worth, where there is the most of it, in common life, I can see that it is a value above all other values, that it outranks all other ranks, and yet its dignity is totally unselfconscious. This was my first discovery when I went to work in a city. Boston in those years was a good deal wickeder than it is now. It was really grim, and there were places in it that were downright sinister. And yet . . . one kept encountering this silent, innate worth in the most unlikely places: on the docks, in police courts, in slum tenements; there was no name for it, yet there it was, and one always knew it when encountered. Truly, I may say to you that this is the only thing of any importance that I know; and, as you see, I cannot communicate it; all I can tell you is that I have 'seen something.' But there are no words for it."

"Words," said Whitehead, "do not express our deepest intuitions. In the very act of being verbalized they escape us. The trouble is that we are in the habit of thinking of words as fixed things with specific meanings. Actually the meanings of language are in violent fluctuation and a large part of what we try to express in words lies outside the range of language."

"Music often seems to come nearer expressing our deepest feelings."

"Another form of profound expression is sculpture," said he. "I am thinking more especially of ancient sculpture, for that, I think, was the principal art of the ancient world. They had their literatures, too, very great ones, and music, though we know little about that. . . ."

"Christianity," said Mrs. Whitehead, "—if we accept the historical figure of Christ, complicated and garbled though the historical records are—tried to express some of this idea of human worth."

"It did get some useful principles formulated," said Whitehead, "but in general it was too simple-minded and too ignorant."

"How shocked I was at myself, when I first began to realize that!"

"When was it?" asked Mrs. Whitehead.

"After the first war. The realization had been growing for several years before I knew what it was."

"Did it take specific form?"

"It took dozens of them. One that I remember best was, 'Christianity did not invent human worth.'"

"As this war goes on," said Whitehead, "and so many young men die before they have had time to live, I keep asking myself what it is that can inspire such heroism and devotion. If our side had failed in this war, life on our earth would not have been worth much, and multitudes have finally realized that fact. Manifestly most of these young men in uniform are not animated by complex political concepts, and only a small proportion, I suggest, consciously think of themselves as Christians. Their ideas are multiform, and, taking them by their millions, often conflicting. Yet there is one which they have in common, and, while it isn't verbalized by them, and while we have admitted that there are no words for it, it is, as nearly as we can come to a definition, the idea of human worth. They are dying for the worth of the world."

XXXV

November 14, 1944

WHEN I arrived, Mr. Whitehead was asleep in his study. It was eight o'clock of a mild autumn evening, with moist air and the residential streets smelling agreeably of fallen wet leaves:

> *All in a death-dumb, autumn-dripping gloom.*

Coming almost directly from the office my brain was full of the horrors of the Germans' massacre of the Greek village of Distomo, which had just been verified in detail and published in the final edition. The philosopher found Mrs. Whitehead and me threshing out the question of German cruelty half an hour later when he came out of his study. One remark he made was that in other cases anywhere remotely comparable, "cruelty has been practised for some purpose, but the Germans practise it for its own sake, and even when it is senseless, no advantage to be gained, and, as they retreat, merely making things worse for themselves."

"I have some good news for you" (it seemed to me a good idea to shift the subject), "and more edifying; our friend Livingstone has been made vice-chancellor of Oxford; 'admitted,' I believe, is the correct verb."

"Has he? I am pleased."

"He says he will read '(but with adequate humility, I hope) Plato's remarks about the return of the philosophers to the cave. However, Plato's philosophers had more power than vice-chancellors, and no doubt had the advantage of being better philosophers.' Will this office grind up much of his time and strength in administrative tasks?"

"Not excessively, I think. There is a committee of which he will be chairman, but nine-tenths of the administrative work is done by the heads of the colleges."

"I have been told the vice-chancellorship isn't considered any dizzying altitude, but that it is a demerit if you don't get it."

"Not as serious as that," said Mrs. Whitehead smiling, "only a hush-hush" (laying finger to her lips) "on the part of one's friends."

"The office," said he, "is passed around in rotation among the heads of the colleges, and each one has a turn at it unless he is considered incompetent. How old is Livingstone?"

"About sixty-one, I think."

"Isn't he older than that? I would have said seventy."

"Nonsense!" exclaimed his wife. "They were just young people when we first knew them."

"Let's look him up in *Who's Who*." He went into his library and returned with the volume. Holding it down to the lamp with a big, heavy-lensed reading glass, he scanned the page, and announced: "Sixty-four . . . and I say, what a lot he has done! vice-chancellor of the University of Belfast from 1924 to 1933, then president of Corpus Christi, Oxford, and a great deal of public work. I first came to know him well in 1920 when we were both on the prime minister's committee to look into the study of the classics, and respected him immensely."

"Add to that," said I, "all his books. They begin with *The Greek Genius* in 1911. That's a remarkable book to have been written by a man of thirty-one."

"I don't dispute the quality of the book," said Whitehead, "but the age at which it was written doesn't strike me as remarkable. It is not unusual for men to begin producing their best work at the age of thirty or thereabouts."

"You score off me: Beethoven, Goethe, Michelangelo."

"The basic ideas of a man's life-work may be well in his mind by the time he is thirty. He may give them widely different forms later, and more extended development; but their main outlines can be already present."

"Wouldn't you consider Livingstone's one of the solid contemporary English careers?"

"Yes. Since Murray is less active, I suppose Livingstone is his successor. What a useful book *Who's Who* is," he continued, turning over the thick, red-covered, closely printed volume in his hands. "If I were to be cast on that desert island and allowed to take only one book, I would certainly take *Who's Who*," he looked up at us laughing.

"It would last a good while," I conceded, "but the entertainment to be had from it presupposes your equipment."

"What is Lady Livingstone like?" asked Mrs. Whitehead. "I remember her only as a young thing, rather shy, when her second baby was in a pram."

"Quiet and effective. To know her is to admire. I could enlarge on this theme to some extent. Also, she is exactly the wife for the head of an Oxford college."

Midway in a discussion of Livingstone's books, Whitehead remarked:

"I am struck by the fact that mankind has not advanced morally, to speak of, for the past two thousand years."

"You could make it longer than that."

"Say, three thousand, then."

"I would have said about twenty-five or twenty-six hundred."

"Well, my own figures would come to about that."

"The period I was thinking of was the fifth century B.C. in Hellas, and the preceding sixth century in which its forces were gathering. If you say fifth-century Athens, then yes, it's not only a matter of modern man not having made an advance, but also a question of whether we have kept up to their mark." I cited certain undisputed historical facts as reasons for thinking so.

He weighed them awhile, then said:

"I consider it not at all impossible (though I hope improbable) that man might reach the apex of his intellectual powers and go into a deterioration lasting thousands of years. In fact, I have often thought that this war might be determining his future one way or the other. The momentum, the impetus of independent thought is so easy to lose. Men might sink into mere routine repetition of habitual acts and accustomed social processes at a fairly low level, almost brainless, as certain insects can run a stable society though they have no brains. . . . And, too, what a mess mankind has made of its religions!"

"Those who know their histories are apt to find themselves hesitating to use the very word religion."

"Have you considered how many of the great religious founders take their rise about in the fifth century B.C.?"

"I hadn't. Where does Buddha come?"

"About then, I think. Let's be sure." Again he went into his study and came back this time with a volume of the *Britannica*. Sure enough, fifth century.

"How about Moses?" I asked. Neither of us was sure—with good reason, as the event proved.

"Let's look him up, too."

"I don't want to make you a lot of work. Let me."

"No. I want to see for myself." He went for another volume of the *Britannica*.

"'Moses'; now where are his dates?" Holding the big volume to the lamp and scanning it with the reading glass, he could find none. I looked along with him. No dates.

"Why, this is queer!" said he. "They don't even give you any idea of where he comes within two centuries. 'Moses!'—in a vacuum."

"Suppose we try 'Exodus.'"

We tried it. Page after page, column after column, subheading after sub-heading, we peered together at the print, up and down, down and up. No dates. The co-authors whose initials were signed at the end of the article were certainly cagey. Perhaps they had heard, as I had, doubt cast on the idea that such a historical character as Moses ever existed, and that "the great character in fiction is Jehovah."

"I say, those men *must* be first-rate scholars," murmured Whitehead, "to give us so little help. Let's look up their initials in the front index and see who these asses are."

It was a bad knock-down for both of us.

"Cook!" said I. "A member of your own sainted Cambridge University, and co-editor of my sainted *Cambridge Ancient History*!"

He replaced the volume on its shelf.

"When I read history," said he, "I want to know where I am. The date should be at the top of each page."

"Trevelyan, at least, will do that for you in his one-volume *History of England*."

"When I was going through old Froude, as a young man," continued Whitehead, "I would read along page after page, almost chapter after chapter, and never a date."

"With a really swagger historian," said I, "perhaps dates are considered *infra dignitatem*. Lots of times in the *Cambridge Ancient History* you can find the event quite explicitly on one page, then have to read pages before and pages after to corner the exact year when it happened."

"They can't be bothered!" said Whitehead. "Dates interrupt the beautiful, even flow of the literary style."

"Tell me," I asked, "did you ever have much luck with Buddhism?"

"I can't say that I have. It all seems to lead in the end to an unfruitful passive meditation. Perhaps that enervating climate had something to do with it. In such a situation it is easiest to sit still and do nothing. But it leads to social stagnation, as the world has seen."

"It is said not to have made much headway in this country except with bored wives; but in the 1920's, when I was studying it—and very respectfully, I assure you—I thought the psychology often hit pretty close to the facts of life. But I hadn't spent the previous twenty years in coughing up one theology to swallow another whole."

"Never swallow anything whole," said Whitehead emphatically. "We live perforce by half-truths and get along fairly well as long as we do not mistake them for whole-truths, but when we do so mistake them, they raise the devil with us."

"That experience of yours as a young man, of seeing the Newtonian physics, which were considered fixed as eternity, blow up under you, must have made a powerful impression."

"It taught me," said he, "to beware of certitude. We supposed that, except for a few dark spots which might take a few years to clear up, everything was known about physics, and then, by 1900, it was found that while the Newtonian physics were still a useful and convenient way of looking at things, they were, in any absolute sense, gone. Now, as I have told you, this would have astonished Aristotle but it would not have surprised Plato. If you will let your mind run over his *Dialogues* —excepting the *Laws*, which, though they contain admirable matter, show him in his old age when his ideas have begun to harden—you will remember that when the Dialogue, whichever one it is, is ended, nothing is finally settled. Everybody has had his say, the subject has been examined from many sides, some of the aspects are more persuasive than others, but it is erroneous to identify Plato entirely with any single one of them. He is passing us around through various points of view, knowing that each of them has, more or less, some truth in it, but no single one the whole truth. The final effect of this on a receptive and flexible mind is about right; we are left with a fair working knowledge which we must then learn to apply for ourselves. Nothing is entirely true, but there is some truth in each aspect. That, if we understood ourselves better, is about the way we do deal with experience, unless we begin to dogmatize—when we immediately get into trouble. We do fairly well with half-truths so long as we remember that they *are* half-truths."

"And now, since we are speaking of certitude, what can you say in defence of the zealot?"

"He is a useful member of society."

"You surprise me. Time was when I thought he was our only hope. Today I look on him with suspicion!"

"The zealot gets things done. He cuts through established routine. A certain amount of zealotry is necessary to get habituated mortals out of their accustomed ruts. It is so easy, you know, to keep on doing and thinking the same things just because for generations those are the things that have been thought and done. And it is also very dangerous, because, left to itself, humanity has a tendency to keep grinding around in the same grooves. The zealot is one form of the element of novelty in life, and though his ideas may not be original (and, in fact, seldom are) his energy and persistence are one form that is taken by the power of origination."

"He has given me a sociological defence of zealotry," said I to Mrs. Whitehead. "Can you give me a personal justification of the zealot?"

"Yes. He makes the comfortable classes uncomfortable."

"That is what our abolitionists did. Some of them were intensely disagreeable—had congenital grouches which they indulged under the pretext of anti-slavery agitation; some were people who loved mercy and justice; and some were of the stuff of heroes."

"People come to accept the most shocking wrongs inflicted on others," resumed Mrs. Whitehead, "because it is customary, or not inconvenient to themselves, or through insensitiveness, or lack of imagination. The element of excess in the zealot is demanded by the lack of feeling in those he finds it necessary to rouse."

I said that sympathetic imagination was a rarer quality than those who have it are prone to suppose, and Whitehead added, smiling, "So is the power of origination. . . . You may recall a sentence of mine which Livingstone quotes in his book on education. . . ."

"I do recall it. 'Moral education is impossible without the habitual vision of greatness.' He adopts that as one of his main themes."

"Last Sunday morning"—Whitehead smiled with relish—"a man was calling on us who is a fellow of Livingstone's college; he had read the book and said, 'I have been trying to think where that sentence comes from. It sounded familiar. Where did you find it?' "

XXXVI

January 19, 1945

AT New Year Whitehead had been awarded the Order of Merit by King George VI. This was founded by Edward VII at his coronation and the number of British members is fixed at twenty-four. I had written about it in the *Globe* ("Philosopher and King") concluding:

> *One of Plato's remedies for the ills of this world was that philosophers should be kings. This was Plato's little joke, for philosophers are kings already. Kings rule only in the material world; but philosophers create that out of which worlds are created. This king has honoured himself in honouring a philosopher.*

"You patted me on the back," was Whitehead's greeting as he came out of his study. "It occurs to me that Livingstone might have had a hand in my receiving this."

"There are plenty of other people in England who would have seen to it besides Livingstone." (In Oxford, at Easter, 1947, Sir David Ross, then provost of Oriel and sometime vice-chancellor, told me that he had proposed Whitehead for the order. It is quite possible that they both had.)

"I don't know," Whitehead continued. "Livingstone is now quite important. The vice-chancellorship of Oxford sounds like second place, but it is really first. The chancellor is like the king, the vice-chancellor is prime minister."

"He writes to me interestingly about his administrative problems; that, like all other administrative work, it consists in being pushed by events, finding immediate answers to immediate questions, and the difficulty is, behind their urgency, to remain aware of anything ultimate, to avoid mortgaging the future. He says it makes him realize how much people live in the immediate present and how little any view of ultimate aims enters their minds."

"Those are unusual thoughts for an administrator, and that is why administrative work should be done by such men as Livingstone."

"By the way," said I, "your New Year's honour, I understand, won you a great success in the Basement." (The "Basement" is the lobby of the hotel, slightly below the surface-level of the street.)

"Oh, rather," says Mrs. Whitehead. "The manager told me, 'It was read to me before daylight this morning by the night-watchman, who sent word to Mr. Whitehead grandly, "Tell him he deserved every bit of it!"' And when I went down to the news-stand at ten o'clock, here was the news-stand woman reading it aloud to an admiring circle of our fellow-tenants. Knowing that I can't see to read, she offered to read it aloud to me. I explained that I had to rush away, so she sold me her last copy. Then that afternoon when Alfred went out to walk, the newsboy spoke to him about it, and said, 'and besides that, it was better written!' The reason the newsboy knew was that he is Jewish."

"They have been my best audience for thirty years. Hebraism and I kissed and made up long ago," said I. "We may disagree amicably, but I know my friends when I see them."

"How strange it was," said Whitehead, "that it should have

been Hebraic thought which went northward among the European peoples instead of Hellenic."

"We were barbarians," said she. "It represented something better than we had."

"Christianity was the form in which the intellectuality of Alexandria went north into Europe. Most of what we don't like in its content and its results," said Whitehead, "comes from its oriental tinge; its asceticism, its despotic quality, its rigidity of dogma. But without Alexandria we might never have received Hellenic thought at all. Alexandria systematized it; in being systematized it lost much of its force, but it wanted a certain amount of systematization to preserve it, for in its pure form it is fluid and evanescent. Alexandria gave us the clues by which centuries later we were able to recover its true content. But systematization is entirely alien, I don't say to Aristotle, but certainly to Plato. In the *Laws*, the work of his old age, it is true, there are elements of dogmatism—certain types of people, he says, are not to be tolerated—but in the work of his prime he is careful, as he says in one of his letters, that he does not give us a 'system' of Platonic philosophy. He says there is none, yet in the nineteenth century how the German classical scholars laboured to construct a Platonic system of philosophy! 'Now what, *exactly*, did Plato mean?' He was at pains *never* to mean anything exactly. He gave every side of a question its due. I have often done the same, advancing some aspect which I thought deserved attention, and then in some later work, presenting its opposite. In consequence I am accused of inconsistency and self-contradiction."

"Perhaps I can suggest a reason why. Your idea that all truths are necessarily half-truths took me months, perhaps I should say years, to grasp. Yes, I heard your words the first time, remembered what they were, wrote them down, and thought about them; but it is only gradually that a realization of what the idea means grows clear and becomes active in one's unconscious thinking. Ibsen, as I now realize, must have had the same idea. In the period of his social dramas, say from *Pillars of Society* on to the end, he would write one play, as he did *Ghosts*, to present one side of a case, and another, as he did *The Wild Duck*, to present the other. I believe the late plays move to a large extent in such pairs. . . . But why should it have been Hebraic thought that travelled northward through Europe and not Hellenic?"

"Hellenic thought has a way of becoming whatever the peoples who receive it are themselves. In Alexandria it became Alexandrian, in Rome it became Roman."

"But in neither was it truly Hellenic," I said.

"No. But they transmitted enough of it to us so that we could find its true form for ourselves. Alexandria provided the intellectual framework for Christian theology, and the man who, I suppose, did more than anybody else to distort and subvert Christ's teaching was Paul. I wonder what the other disciples thought of him—if they thought anything. Probably they didn't understand what he was up to, and it may well be doubted whether he did himself. It would be impossible to imagine anything more un-Christlike than Christian theology. Christ probably couldn't have understood it."

"Could Greek thought of the Great Age, do you suppose, ever have come into being without that matchless instrument of thought, the Greek language?"

"The same innate genius which begot one," said Whitehead, "begot the other."

"Its precision, its flexibility, its power of expressing exact shades of meaning, its sheer beauty of sound and splendour of resource, and, through all, its simplicity," said I, "are a never-ending amazement."

"How fortunate it would have been," said he, "had Greek become the language of Europe instead of Latin."

"We might have been spared a lot of confusion for one thing, for a Greek sentence generally means exactly what it says, and nothing else. Since the drill in the ancient classical languages

[303]

has been dropped out of our school curricula, the results are glaring in the work of contemporary writers. We used to learn our English grammar in Latin and Greek. If an English construction was grammatical in Greek or Latin, it was generally good English. But many of these people writing English today seem to be semi-illiterates."

"I was never taught English grammar at all," said Whitehead. "My father, who had been a schoolmaster before he became a clergyman, taught me at home until I was fourteen. He did not send me away to school until then because as a child I had been frail. He taught me my Greek grammar out of a Latin grammar. It was written entirely in Latin and I learned and recited its rules in Latin. Greek grammar, as such, I never studied at all; yet I read Greek as easily as English."

"One result of this abandonment of the classics is that English novels are now 'taught' in our secondary schools. I am properly respectful towards the men who teach them for they are able and devoted schoolmasters, but the idea of being 'taught' English!"

"When I was a schoolboy," said Whitehead, "we read novels, but we read them for fun."

"So did my generation. It would never have occurred to us to 'study' them. Tell me, where did your novel-reading begin?"

"With *Pickwick*, as a child of six, seated on a hassock beside a fire at the feet of my grandmother's maid, Jane Wychelow. . . . My grandmother was a wealthy woman. She made the mistake of having thirteen children, and by the time even a large fortune is divided among thirteen it is no longer large, and when it came to the grandchildren, not much came to me. But as a child I spent a good deal of time at my grandmother's house in London, and it was Jane Wychelow, reading to me by the hour, who first gave me my taste for literature, and it was *Pickwick* which gave me my first insight into the English social system."

"You don't consider it overdrawn then—caricature?"

"Bless you, no! Dickens's people were all around us; they were Londoners, or South of England. Pickwick, you notice, never goes very far north—as far as Norwich, say. . . . I am standing now at a window of my grandmother's house . . ." he mused.

"Eighty-one Piccadilly?" supplied Mrs. Whitehead, wistfully.

". . . looking out over the Green Park," he continued, "and there is Queen Victoria going by——"

"You would have seen her? . . ."

"Bless you, yes; and not once or twice but every day or so."

"Imagine your having seen the old queen as often as the grocer's delivery wagon!"

"She wasn't 'old' then; she was in the prime of life, and not very popular. It was only after the 1870's that she began to be popular, and she ended by becoming such an institution that when she died, we couldn't believe it."

"Even the poor went into mourning," said Mrs. Whitehead. "If they couldn't afford to buy black clothes, they dyed their ordinary clothes black. They were in mourning for the Victorian Age—though they didn't know that then," she added sombrely.

"We had grave apprehensions about Edward VII," continued Whitehead, "and he was far from popular when he came to the throne, but by the end of his reign he was well liked. The two Georges since (I think) have paid their way."

"Though George VI seems to me a somewhat colourless figure," said she, "after his father. George V had a temper."

"It's amazing that the monarchy has lasted until 1945," said I.

"Oh, no, it isn't," said Whitehead. "The English never abolish anything. They put it in cold storage. That has its advantages. If they should want it again, there it is!"

"If you will permit me to say so, sir, that also goes for their Established Church."

[305]

"As I have said to you before," remarked Whitehead, "the Reformation seems to me one of the calamities of history. If given more time, I think the Church would have reformed from within. Erasmus had about the right ideas and he was offered a cardinal's hat before his death, though he refused it. But the revolt of the Protestants hardened the Church's resistance; and the Protestants threw out precisely that part of the Church which makes it gracious and tolerable; namely, its aesthetic and emotional appeal. If I were to choose among present-day Christians, I would prefer the Unitarians, but I wish they had more influence. They are, I realize, close to the Congregationalists, and I think it would be well if they were closer, for it would not surprise me if in another hundred years the United States were predominantly Catholic."

"The one aesthetic and emotional appeal which the Protestants didn't throw overboard," I remarked, "was music."

"Religion," said Whitehead, "cannot exist without music. It is too abstract."

"That's so! Even the New England Puritans, who did away with church organs and instruments, kept their psalmody!"

"Music comes before religion," said he, "as emotion comes before thought, and sound before sense. What is the first thing you hear when you go into a church? The organ playing. What is the last thing you hear as you come out? The organ. And in the Catholic service, the mass itself is sung. Music comes aeons before religion. You can't tell me that the nightingale is singing to his mate out of anything but the joy of life, for the love of singing. These things lie deeper than thought, as sound strikes deeper in us than sight. When we were savages, I venture to suppose, we were much more impressed by the sound of thunder than by the flash of lightning."

"We can protect ourselves from sight by closing our eyes," remarked Mrs. Whitehead, "but we cannot close our ears. From sound we are defenceless. As a young woman when I went to the theatre, the love-making on the stage would some-times offend me by its exhibitionism. I had only to shut my eyes."

"You once said to me that you thought mankind had paid an overdue share of attention to the impressions that come to us by the eye."

"Our education does," he replied, "rely largely on what is written and printed."

"But sound evaporates; writing, print is fairly permanent. Pericles delivers the Funeral Oration, but we have it because Thucydides wrote it down."

"The oration is Thucydides, probably; not Pericles, you know," Mrs. Whitehead corrected me smilingly.

"If so, it is none the worse for that!"

"Perhaps better," says she.

"What has saved writing," assented Whitehead, "is the survival value of its relatively permanent form. But sound speaks to the emotions, the emotion then becomes thought, and the thought action."

"The emotion may become action without ever going through the stage of thought: remember that," corrected Mrs. Whitehead.

"I do," said he. "The relationship between sound and action may be much more direct than between sight and action. That which we see suggests, in general, thought; that which we hear, emotion. Music speaks directly to the emotions; it may, I admit, suggest thoughts, too. . . ."

"But if it suggests them too explicitly," said I, "it is likely to be not very good music."

"When the children were little," said Mrs. Whitehead, "I started them on Mozart. It was thought snobbish of me, but they never heard any trash at home, and when they did hear it, later, they knew it was trash and never cared for it."

"Music," said I, "is amoral. It is like any other great force of nature—in itself, neither good nor bad. All depends on how it is used. It energizes what is already in us; if bad, bad; if good, good."

"I don't agree that music is amoral," said she. "Wagner's music is often distinctly sensual. I don't consider it 'pure' music either aesthetically or morally. Mind you, I like it, at times; but I know what it is doing all the same."

"Music," said Whitehead, "can be both moral and immoral. Take Wagner, if you like. You Americans love his music, and I can't see that it has done you a bit of harm; but I think it has done immeasurable harm to the Germans. To them it suggests dreams of power which lead to violence."

"Wagner, I admit, can still be a controversial figure, but Beethoven must be exempted. Where is there a purer religion than the music of his last quartets? And it is pure sound, too."

"I am inclined to agree with you," said Whitehead, "and I think one of mankind's earliest emotions was in response to a solemn sound."

XXXVII

May 25, 1945

LUNCHEON of the Saturday Club. It was radiant spring weather, and since the interdict on taxicabs had been rescinded, Whitehead came in one. Bliss Perry brought as guest Professor Carl Weber of Colby College, who made that unique collection of memorabilia of Thomas Hardy. He told me, "I wanted to study Hardy and no collection existed, so I had to make one. Just now I am working at Cambridge and often, for wanted materials, I wish I were back at Colby."

About fifteen members were at table. Whitehead and I were at the lower end by ourselves. "You must be careful what you say to me from now on," said I. "I'm your boss, having been made one of the Visiting Committee for the Department of Philosophy."

"Oh, but so am I!" says he.

"In that case, we start over again."

By way of being careful what he said, he was next remarking, *sotto voce*, at my ear:

"Imagine a Being capable of creating a world for the express purpose of its creatures praising him!"

"Isn't it strange that although Christianity is occasionally criticized by capable men, the prevailing attitude is that, however indifferent people may be in practice, Christianity is immune from criticism. If anyone ventures to view it from the outside, it is regarded as a foolish eccentricity."

"The educated people who have been brought up as Protestants and then embrace Catholicism—as a few did in the 1920's and '30's," said he, "—strike me as people who have read history without understanding it, or else as people who do not know history. No one who had even meditated on the meaning of historic events, could knowingly so retrogress. Stagnation of thought is one of the pitfalls of mankind. It is easier to grasp from the history of mathematics than from theology. *Mathematics is the study of possibilities*. Beyond the immediate practical applications of the multiplication table, say at 12×12, mathematics in fifth-century Athens was useless. It was a form of speculation. Plato was immensely excited about the subject. His mind was full of mathematics; he used it as an instrument of thought, and it suggested to him all sorts of hitherto unguessed possibilities. If you had talked to Aristotle about him at that time, no doubt Aristotle would have remarked to you privately, 'Poor old Plato! All bogged down in those useless mathematical ideas.'" (He smiled drolly as he said this.)

"Now, as a matter of fact, in Plato's time those mathematical ideas *were* useless, and they remained useless for roughly sixteen or seventeen centuries. Then, beginning at about the twelfth century A.D. those mathematical ideas which had so excited Plato, made possible the modern world."

"Was there any specific reason that we know of for their

coming to fruition as they did between the Renaissance and, say, the seventeenth century in France and England?"

"No. Everything necessary for modern science and technology existed in the time of Archimedes. People think I am making an idiotic joke when I say it, but I am quite serious when I say to you as I have said before, apparently all that was lacking was that in Sicily or Magna Graecia people did not sit by their fires and watch the lids of their kettles lift from the steam of boiling water."

"Then we are here back at the *diffusion* of a given experience. As you have remarked to me, an experience needs to be widely diffused in order to elicit the response from the widest possible spread of talents—as you didn't get concert pianists from a western cattle ranch in the nineteenth century, no matter how brilliant the potential talent may have been. There wasn't any piano."

Until the chairman at the head of the table raps for order, conversation is usually in pairs, so Whitehead asked me what news had been coming into my office that morning. I told him, then remarked:

"Can you think of a single Western nation which has had access to the civilizing ideas of the past twenty-five centuries since ancient Greece which could have been made to do what the Germans are now shown to have been doing?"

"There is nothing new in their specific deeds," said he. "To be knocked down, robbed, and murdered, perhaps tortured, has always been going on somewhere to some extent. What is new with the Germans is the scale. It has never before been done on anything like such a scale as this."

"What would you give for the chances of their behaving themselves after this?"

"They knocked over the Roman Empire," said he. "They knocked over the system of the Middle Ages; and they have knocked over the civilization of modern Europe—and I mean the one which originated about five hundred years ago, say at the Renaissance. They will probably go on trying to knock things over, because they like to knock things over."

Here the chairman, Mark Howe, rapped the table and tossed the subject of Japan into discussion. Langdon Warner, who has lived and travelled widely in China and Japan, and Cameron Forbes, who has been ambassador to Japan as well as governor-general of the Philippines, carried most of the discussion, urged on by leading questions: What, in the event of victory, should be done with the Chinese treaty ports, Manchuria, Korea, island airplane bases? What sort of government for the Japanese home islands? . . . Cam thought the treaty ports should be returned to Chinese sovereignty but perhaps bases to Britain to save imperial face, all but Hong Kong, which he considered too centrally vital for anything less than inter-nationalization. Whitehead saw no reason why Britain should have back the treaty ports. "Singapore, however," said he, "is important to us on account of Australia and New Zealand."

"I am uncertain about the Chinese," continued Whitehead. "Their cultural development shows no continuity of process. From about 500 B.C. to 1200 A.D. there seemed to be no development to speak of; and in modern times, they appear to be trying to make themselves as much like Americans as possible. But suppose they do succeed in making themselves like twentieth-century Americans; when they have done so, have they the capacity to go on developing in their own way from there, or will they merely remain for centuries to come like twentieth-century Americans?"

Of the Chinese Communists, Cameron Forbes said, "They are so different from the Communists of Soviet Russia, the historic origins which condition them go back so far and are so peculiar to China, that when you use the word 'communist' of them, you are hardly talking about the same thing as what is understood by communism in Russia."

"What you say interests me," said Whitehead, "for people appear to think that when they have used the word 'communism,' they have designated something exactly, and know what they are talking about. Now, as a matter of fact, not only should there be, as you have suggested, half a dozen varying ideas and definitions of communism in people's minds when the subject comes up for discussion; there ought to be nearer six hundred varying definitions."

The party rose at about half past three. Whitehead and I hailed a taxi at Brimstone Corner, rolled up Park Street and down Beacon to Charles past the rich May greenery of the Common. "I never heard Cam speak with such admirable good sense," said he. "Generally, when he begins, one gets ready to disagree or make allowances or maintain a discreet silence. But to my astonishment, I found myself substantially in agreement with everything he said."

We rolled across the Longfellow Bridge and into Cambridge, which also is looking fresh and comely in its new May-green dress. There were stalks of pale-blue larkspur in the vases of Mrs. Whitehead's living-room and brilliant afternoon sunshine streamed in at the west windows. She was given some of the table talk at second hand, by request, and it went on into a discussion of the American social system.

"I tell you what," said Whitehead positively, "I believe the American social system to be, on the whole, the best that has ever existed. It has grave defects; the English system has points of superiority, but yours remains the best that has been done so far. The paradox is that you are not really a 'political' people. About one-third of your citizens I would say are genuinely first-rate; but they are not in politics. Of the remaining two-thirds, about half, I should say, are second-rate but still good. The other half" (he hesitated, then went on), "are criminal."

"Including many of our politicians," I supplied.

"Yes," said he.

It was decided to change the subject.

"I am invited to the party on June sixth," said I, "and

hastened to accept before they should have had time to take it back."

"One is supposed to go to Buckingham Palace to receive it, or, if in this country, from the hands of the ambassador," said Mrs. Whitehead, "but as Lord Halifax has plenty else to do, it is to be given by the British consul."

Whitehead was of the opinion that too much fuss might be made about it.

"Not from the point of view of the university," I remarked. "Whenever before has an American university had as its emeritus professor of philosophy a man with the Order of Merit?"

"That is nothing," said Whitehead.

"I know it is nothing. But this university has made some bad blunders in recent years. One was allowing Harvey Cushing to go away to Yale. Another was George Pierce Baker . . . ditto. There have been still others." I told them Harvey Cushing's account of that affair as he recited it to me one Sunday afternoon in the summer of 1932 when we were alone in his old house on Walnut Street in Brookline.

"This custom of retiring a man perforce in his sixties," said Whitehead, "is idiotic."

"With surgeons it is said to be a necessity," his wife corrected him. "I understand they can no longer be sure of a steady hand."

"Cushing didn't complain of the retirement age of sixty-three. He had set it himself when he organized the Peter Bent Brigham Hospital. In fact, he didn't complain of anything. He only said that devious financiers, whom he had trusted, had wiped out a large part of his estate, including his patrimony from old Dr. Cushing of Cleveland, which he had never touched, but salted down for his old age. As you remember, his health was gone, and, all this being well known, he was offered at Harvard a professorship without salary."

Whitehead looked grim.

"How old were you," I shifted gears, "when you first felt a sense of conscious mastery of your subject?"

"I have never felt it at all," said he.

"Then I have asked my question clumsily. Perhaps what I was trying to ask was, when did you first begin to feel an adequacy to your work?"

"I have never felt adequate to it."

"Good heavens!" said his wife. "Don't I know? Not a year went by bringing back September and the resumption of his teaching, that he didn't have a bad case of the jitters."

"You are a competent witness."

"I have only observed him for fifty-one years."

Whitehead, who had been listening absently, now said, "I will tell you what, about this custom of enforced retirement; it is idiotic, because, although a man may not think of anything new after he is sixty, he often finds new ways to use what he already knows."

XXXVIII

May 29, 1945

THERE was a party for the Whiteheads given by Mr. and Mrs. William James, at 95 Irving Street, in the big, comfortable house which Professor James had built in the 1890's, and where he lived until his death in 1910. I remembered the study from having gone there as an undergraduate to consult him about a thesis subject.

The guests had been asked to come "any time after half past eight." It was a mild May evening, Cambridge was quiet, and the fresh greenery of the elms and ivies in the College Yard was a temptation to loiter. When I arrived, the Whiteheads and several other guests were already in the study. There was a group around the hearth where a wood fire was burning, and others kept arriving until the room must have held thirty or forty persons. The guests were seated but the groups kept changing, and I noticed with what skill and tact the combinations were managed.

At intervals I was able to renew my acquaintanceship with this room. It was still walled with books, but William James, the second son, who joined me presently for a chat by ourselves over in a corner beside his father's study table, said: "They are not all the books, nor all his books, and they have been rearranged, largely by sizes and sets. His was a scholar's library, in which books of every size and shape stood side by side arranged according to subjects."

"That seems more as I remembered it; a good many paper-backed volumes, and pamphlets. . . . I notice up there on the next-to-the-top shelf a complete set of the Edinburgh Edition, Constable & Company, of George Meredith."

"That was Uncle Henry's. It was a present from Meredith."

On the fireplace mantelshelf was an excellent photograph, about four inches by eight, framed under glass, of the two brothers, William and Henry. The centre table was gone, and so was the green-shaded kerosene study lamp of other years, but here was the big black-walnut study table, long enough for a tall man to stretch out on as bivouac, and carried on two pedestals of black-walnut desk drawers. It looked, indeed, as though it might have antedated Professor James's tenancy, having perhaps belonged to his father. His son said:

"Father used to work on the other side of it, in that corner."

It was a sore temptation to forget the party and browse along those shelves taking notes of titles and authors, as I have once or twice been able to do in Whitehead's library. Beside the hearth Professor Ralph Barton Perry, the biographer of William James, was in conversation with Whitehead.

It was necessary for me to leave early. Out in the hall, when my coat and hat had been picked up, I ventured the remark to my host, who had come out with me:

"What are we going to do about an oil portrait of White-head?"

"Charles Hopkinson has made two sketches in oils," said he; "one not so good; the other, *very* good. Then, as so often happens with us painters, he took it along to his studio to 'finish' and some people think he spoilt it."

"I have seen the two sketches in his studio. One, I thought, was pretty close to it. I spoke to Charles about it a few days ago, and he said, with admirable modesty, 'I doubt if I am up to painting Whitehead.' . . . But are we going to let Whitehead get away from us without a good portrait? You owe it to yourself to have painted a portrait of Whitehead."

"When I was young," he replied, smiling, "I would ask anybody to sit for me. Now when I am trying to learn a language, I hesitate to ask a sitter until I shall have learned to speak that language."

As the front door of 95 Irving Street closed after me and I went out again into the May evening, I had a glimpse of that spacious dooryard to the south of the house, overlooked by the windows of the study. There, on a September afternoon in 1903, I had seen William James for the first time. My entrance examinations were safely passed, and I was not yet an under-graduate but in two days more I would be. It was two years since I had begun to read what William James had written, and, as a seventeen-year-old lad in a small town of the Midwest, two essays of his in especial had put heart and courage into me. I was grateful to him and loved him *in absentia*. Being in Cambridge at last, it had suddenly struck me that, after having gone to Concord and seen where Emerson and Hawthorne had lived, I could walk around and see where William James lived. A college directory gave the street and number. This time, the hunting was considerably better than a house. There in his dooryard seated in a lawn chair conversing with some callers was William James. Not a doubt of it! I had seen photographs of him. The tones of his voice, a genial tenor or high baritone, though not his words, carried out to the sidewalk. This was, I suppose, the first time I had ever seen an eminent man in the flesh. It is quite an eye-opener: had you not been told, you might not have guessed. He could easily have been supposed to be not much different from anybody else; and this was true, and at the same time, was not true. At any rate, there sat William James in a lawn chair chatting with his friends like an affable archangel, and if I had had to choose between being given a glimpse of an archangel or William James, I certainly would have chosen William James. I still think that choice valid.

XXXIX

June 6, 1945

WEDNESDAY afternoon at four o'clock in the Faculty Room at University Hall the Order of Merit—Badge and Grant of Dignity—was presented to Alfred North Whitehead, D.Sc., LL.D., S.D., F.R.S., F.B.A., and Professor of Philosophy Emeritus in Harvard University.

This was at three removes. Had he been in England he would have been expected to go to Buckingham Palace; were the British ambassador less preoccupied, it would have been presented by him either in Washington or Cambridge; things being as they are, the presentation was by the British consul-general at Boston. Considering the dimensions of the world Whitehead lives in, and those of the British Empire, the notion of bestowing dignity or merit upon him seemed like my Swampscott dory towing the S.S. *Queen Elizabeth*, and in fact Whitehead himself had dismissed the idea of its being of any intrinsic importance. I remembered too that George Meredith, who received the Order of Merit in 1905, said that what the letters *O.M.* meant was that he was an old man.

The scene, however, was picturesque. We had produced our

equivalent to a June day in England, a south-west wind with alternate sunshine and showers, and white-backed grey-breasted clouds tumbling about a pure blue sky. By four o'clock the afternoon sun was pouring in at the high-arched windows on the west side of the hall, while the faculty chairs, about two hundred, I should say, had been arranged to face the equally high eastern windows which look out into the green foliage of the Sever-Widener-Memorial Church Quadrangle.

The room has an aspect of reticent dignity. Its height is two stories, the second and third of University Hall, and its architect was Charles Bulfinch. The walls are tinted a pale green which, in certain lights, looks light blue, and between the arched windows white fluted Ionic pilasters rise from floor to cornice. From the ceiling hang four crystal chandeliers.

The marble busts on plinths around the dais which runs along the wall on the long dimensions of the hall were distracting my attention from most of the immediate company. There is an excellent one of Benjamin Franklin, by Houdon I think; another of President Eliot and another of my old friend and teacher Dean Briggs, startlingly real, almost to the twinkle in his eyes and to the least wrinkle in his lean Yankee jowls. The walls on all four sides are hung with portraits of Harvard presidents and eminent scholars from the past three centuries. Here was my old Greek grammarian, W. W. Goodwin, his crimson doctor's hood over his shoulder, his complexion fresh and rosy, his hair pure white, and his smile bland and unworldly. With certain notable exceptions, the men on the walls were more interesting than the people in the chairs.

On each chair was laid a programme bound in a heavy greenish-grey paper. "The Proceedings" were begun by President Conant, who said, among other things, that Whitehead, after a long and distinguished career in England, came to Harvard to give his first course of lectures in philosophy, and "the first lecture in a course on philosophy which you had ever attended was the one given by yourself."

The consul narrated the institution of the Order of Merit. Looking down the list of its present members, eighteen in number, I noticed the names of Gilbert Murray, G. M. Trevelyan, J. W. Mackail, Vaughan Williams, John Masefield, and Augustus John. It had often occurred to me that a good many eminent men in England would feel silly accepting feudal titles, and that perhaps this Order of Merit was tardily devised as a method of the government (including the monarchy) to climb aboard the bandwagon of continuing British genius.

A photographer flashed two bulbs while the consul was hanging the badge by a ribbon of the order around the philosopher's neck. As a decoration it is quite striking.

The participants in the ceremony, including Dean Buck of the faculty, who assisted as a benign presence, had been seated at a large round table, which looked as though it might have been the one around which William James, Josiah Royce, and George Herbert Palmer had their portraits painted sitting together.

Over on the north wall is a noble portrait of William James. He is standing beside his breast-high writing desk in his study at 95 Irving Street. Behind him are bookshelves and rows of brown-backed volumes. His writing desk is of brown walnut, he wears a brown suit, his hair and beard look brownish, touched with grey, the light in the study is an atmosphere of mellow autumnal brown, and his face is ruddy as if from a summer in the open at Chocorua, New Hampshire. He is made to look a bit more severe than his usual genial self. The canvas was well lighted by the late afternoon sunshine which poured in through those western windows. After the ceremonies, as I was admiring it, Professor Ralph Barton Perry, first his pupil, then his colleague, and finally his biographer, came over and spoke.

"When was it painted?" I asked.

"About 1908, I think," said he.

"How satisfactory is that portrait to you?"

"Very! Miss Ellen Emmet painted with bold strokes."

"Nineteen-eight was only two years before his death. He must have been frail" (in fact, we both knew that he was) "but here he looks robust and vigorous."

"He always looked more robust than he was," said Professor Perry, "perhaps because his mind was so vigorous."

I have noticed the same thing about Whitehead; he speaks, because he thinks, with the vigour of a young man.

After the presentation I had asked him if he had a copy of his response. Our interchanges have been so almost entirely oral that I had only two scraps of paper written in his hand. He said he would send me the MS. Next day it arrived. The text is as follows:

President Conant: It is impossible for me to express adequately the obligations of my wife and myself to the University over which you preside. Both as an institution and as a group of individuals, Harvard has made it possible for me to express ideas which had been growing in my thoughts for a lifetime. I wish to emphasize my admiration and personal affection for so many Harvard friends, some of whom are present today. During my life I have had the great happiness of teaching in two countries which have contributed so greatly to learning and to the dignity of mankind.

XL

June 19, 1945

IT had been a day of thunderstorms, two by the sea—one at Marblehead, another at Nahant—and a third on the editorial floors of the *Globe*, where one party was indignant at the publication in the paper of Ciano's diary, as Fascist whitewash, the other laughing at its exposure in all directions and giving the public credit for knowing a hawk from a handsaw.

The second view was shared by the Whiteheads. They were

in Cambridge passingly for a few days between their return from the Pickmans' at Bedford and a month in Maine, whither they go next Friday. All the windows of their apartment were wide open to the humid night air, a light breeze drawing through; huge white peonies nodded in the vases; all the rugs were up and the window hangings down, giving the rooms a cool, bare, refreshing look. With the June flowers scenting the air, these familiar rooms had taken on an unfamiliar aspect, looking summery.

We had been speaking of how the high polish of the now bare hardwood floor reflected the mahogany and white peonies, when Whitehead came in from his study.

"Why, our rugs are up, aren't they?" said he. "I hadn't noticed it."

"Yes," said she, laughing at him, "and me hustling around to get them off to the cleaners." She rose and went to a tall, mahogany cabinet, saying, "We have something to show you." It was in a dark-leather case and lay on velvet of an off-ivory shade. It was the badge of the Order of Merit. The Maltese cross is a rich amber-coloured enamel on gold, with a gold crown mounted above it, and a circle of pearls around the centre of royal-blue enamel on which the inscription, *For Merit*, is laid in gold. Around it is a wreath of laurel.

"They don't do it by halves, do they?" I remarked.

"Fortunately for us," she said, "it cost us nothing. Every other decoration, those given by the government, must be paid for by the person who receives it; but not this, which is a gift of the Crown."

"The Crown paid something, I should say. And I should also remark how neatly the university ran that ceremony; no long speeches, no fatigue, no fuss or feathers, and just about the right number of people. Tell me: was that a typical faculty audience of two hundred persons?"

"It was typical," said he smiling, "of those who were there. They were members of the philosophical department—"

"'Cock and hen,' of course," said she.

"–and the Junior and Senior Fellows–"

"Those I was able to identify, as I knew some of them–"

"–and, to my great satisfaction," he continued, "the secretaries of both departments, men and women who carry so much of the administration load."

"We had nothing to do with the invitations," explained she. "The only ones we invited were our John and Mary, who are, of course, a part of the family. *That* gave us a good deal of satisfaction. It wasn't certain until the last minute whether Alfred would be able to attend. He lay down all day, and finally got up to try it. The moment he arrived at University Hall, he felt all right. . . . Your invitation, by the way, came through your official connection with the department of philosophy."

"I have some good news for you": (it was now my turn to produce) "he didn't say I wasn't to tell, but I have told no one so far. Livingstone is coming over to lecture at Toronto next September."

"We would love to see him," said Whitehead. "Is there any prospect of his coming here?"

"I'm not sure. He says he spends his hours turning his mind from one university problem to another, and that he will lecture in Toronto if he can get the lectures written."

"When you write him," said Whitehead, "will you say that if we don't see him we shall be greatly disappointed?"

In some detail we discussed ways and means.

"His two booklets on education have been republished in this country in one volume by Macmillan's, and called just that—*On Education*. The salesmen at the Old Corner Book Store tell me it is going very well."

"It deserves to," said Whitehead. "I have read them in the English edition, and thought highly of them."

"When was your *Aims of Education* published?"

"Let me see. I've forgotten." He went into his library,

returned with the volume and read from the preface the dates of its various chapters. Most of them came between 1912 and 1922. "My writings on philosophy," he continued, "were all after I came to this country; but the ideas had been germinating in me for the better part of a lifetime. Some of them I had had when I was at school before ever I went up to the university. Education I had heard discussed continually since I was a little lad: my father and two uncles were in it. And at Cambridge I was, as you know, a member of The Apostles."

"This was somewhat unusual, wasn't it?" said she. "Weren't you the only mathematician in the group?"

". . . Perhaps because I was the only mathematician interested in general ideas," he replied.

It then transpired—"transpired" in the correct use of that verb—that Whitehead had only taken his examinations for the fellowship at Trinity as a chance shot (you are given three tries) and with so little expectation of being accepted that afterwards he went away for the summer without leaving his address.

"Until I first read *Aims of Education*, in 1933," I said, "I doubt if I had ever met such compactness of thought in English sentences. Is writing easy for you?"

"Yes," he said, "if it's something I want to write." His wife looked sceptical. "What would *you* say?" he asked of her.

"You are full of ideas," she reminded him, "and first you write them all down; everything is in it. But after that comes the rearranging and pruning–"

"With your help. . . ."

"Well, you read it aloud and I listen. . . . He has a wretched tendency," she imparted for my benefit, "of getting going on some particular word—'thereby,' or 'whereas'—and on every other page that damned word will turn up. . . ."

"Does he do that too? Tautologies are a species of self-hypnosis."

"I don't see how you can write as often as you do," she added, to me.

[323]

"Neither do I. And the answer is, I don't. Twice a week nowadays, or thrice at a pinch; but with absences of months to refuel. What do you do to protect yourself from exhaustion?" I asked Whitehead.

"Lectured twice a day for years, since I was twenty-four years old," he replied, smiling blandly at my discomfiture. "It is true, the summer vacation ran from late June to early October, and we also had four weeks at Christmas and five at Easter. The schedule was really not heavy."

"But it is also true," she reminded him, "that you never stopped working. If we travelled on the Continent, there was not a blank envelope-back in your pocket that wasn't written all over on your knee in railway trains or hotels as ideas occurred to you; and if we stayed in England somewhere in the country, you were always just the same, pursuing your private philosophical Boojum."

"You evidently," I addressed him, "don't think a man uses himself up and works himself out by continual expression— within limits of his time and vitality." (I was thinking of more than one academic scholar who appears to have talked out as lectures what might otherwise have been a good book; also of the exhaustion which I see around me among journalists who cannot or will not pause long enough.)

"No," Whitehead replied. "I think one gains by such expression. He brings vague ideas into precision by putting them into speech or writing; and by expression he develops his ideas and finds his way to new ones."

"Perhaps what I was trying to ask was, Do you *enjoy* writing?"

"Yes. I like being in that world."

"The compactness of thought in your style—do you suppose it comes from your mathematical training? You learned one technique of expression, and then moved on to another. It is as if, having had one severe intellectual discipline, you moved easily into the art of writing and speaking."

"William James had something of the same sort," said his

wife. "A hard intellectual discipline in medicine first; then he moved on into philosophy, psychology, and, one might almost say, *belles lettres*."

"At Trinity," said Whitehead, "and later, in a wide experience of educational problems at London University, I had the advantage of general discussions. It was precisely the kind of education that Plato approves. Mathematics must be studied; philosophy should be discussed."

This shot landed heavily. He saw it land and gave me breathing space to take it in.

"You must allow," he went on presently, "for the imprecision of language. It is a point I cannot make too emphatic. Again and again I return to it. The notion that thought can be perfectly or even adequately expressed in verbal symbols is idiotic. And that supposition has done philosophy immeasurable harm. Take the simplest statement of a fact: that we three are sitting in this room. Nearly everything of importance is left out. 'This room' presupposes a building, Cambridge, the university, the world around us of which we are a part, stellar systems of which our world is a part, the infinite past from which we have come, and the endless future which is streaming through us and out ahead of us. It presupposes our separate individualities, each quite different, and all that we know, we are, or have ever done. That verbalization of our sitting here means next to nothing; yet, in much more serious subjects and on a far more ambitious scale, we are constantly accepting statements of historic fact, and philosophical speculations which are much more lacking in accuracy or in any relationship with exact truth. When such over-simplified ideas are addressed to persons who cannot supply the omitted presuppositions, they mean nothing, are not comprehended, are not even taken in. . . ."

Two wine glasses, his and mine, stood on a little table at his left hand. He touched them, saying, " 'One and one make two.' One and one what? One glass, or one glass partly filled with wine? Or one and one where? On a table, in this room, or in this universe? But two glasses are not and cannot possibly be made exactly equal. Nor can they be filled with equal amounts of wine. Then do we mean 'one plus one' after all the necessary deductions and additions have been made? But the glasses are also raging with molecular activity, and, if we were not in the habit of measuring time by the ridiculously inadequate yard-sticks of our consciousness in this human life span, we should remember that those glasses are disintegrating before our very eyes. I refuse to be taken in by such monstrous inexactitude in the use of words."

This was quite a headful for one while. Circling around it a little, he asked, "Do you suppose the Greeks were the first people who ever wanted something reduced to exactitude in language? They wanted a correct version of Homer. When was that?"

"Probably somewhere in the sixth century B.C. It's supposed to have been done at the command of Peisistratus."

"About when would you say the great Hebrew literature begins?"

I spoke of the familiar JEPD, adding, "The Old Testament and the Homeric poems are both 'traditional books,' taking centuries to grow. In their editing, the one by the ancient Hebrews, the other by the ancient Greeks, how characteristic the differences of method and spirit are of the two peoples: one produced a manual of morals; the other, a work of art."

"How unique the Hebrew genius is," said he. "It was profoundly moral. The Hebrews were one of the most remarkable peoples that ever lived. And yet," he ruminated, "I don't think I would have cared to live among them. The Greeks were more reasonable."

"All the same," said I, "the Hebrews produced one of the greatest books in history. It has outsold the *Iliad*!"

"If you accept the divine authorship attributed to the Bible," said Whitehead, his eyes twinkling, "it seems a little odd that a person like Solomon, with his million wives and thousand concubines, should have been chosen to write parts of it."

"If he did, it must have been as a young man when he had only about ten wives, and was just getting started in life," I suggested.

"Before his heavy family responsibilities had begun," added Mrs. Whitehead demurely.

"David," I remarked, "is a much more 'sympathetic character.' His palace memoirs are certainly more candid than that class of literature generally is. Legions of gentile boys are still being named David—long after Hector has gone out of fashion. David is quite a beautiful name. As for Solomon, aren't his million-and-one wives merely a tall tale? After all, when telling a whopper, why not tell a good one?"

"Is there any reason to suppose," asked Whitehead, "that the surrounding nations took much notice of the ancient Hebrews—that is, before the period of the Roman conquests?"

I pleaded ignorance, but the impression was that there had been comparatively little.

"What I would like to know," he continued, "is to what extent, if at all, the Semites and the Hellenes re-expressed ideas which were generally current in that part of the ancient world—ideas that flowed down to them from older peoples and the surrounding nations. Of course we know that some of that did happen; some of the Eastern notions were known to Plato; and the older prophets anticipated, mostly, the ideas of Jesus."

"When I am asked, as I often am, how to account for the explosion of genius in Greece from the sixth century to the third B.C. I hardly know where to begin."

"The Eastern Mediterranean, you must remember," replied Whitehead, "was a remarkable place, and had been for a long time. Besides the Hellenes and Semites you have the Minoan-Mycenaean culture, the Phoenicians, and the three big empires of Babylonia, Assyria and Egypt."

This glance at the monotonous regularity with which empires collapse caused him to remark on how much faster our world of today is changing than it ever changed before.

"In fact," Mrs. Whitehead remarked in parenthesis, "if we can arrange it, Alfred and I have agreed to come back once in every fifty years and see what has happened."

"We only want to stay two months at any given time," said he.

"Like Tom Sawyer, you want to 'die temporarily.' "

"No. Three months," said she. "We would need that much time to assimilate what we can."

"Whether you date this acceleration of change from a hundred and fifty years ago, or from fifty years ago," Whitehead pursued the main theme, "the alteration in our society exceeds anything in history. The long-term views of human nature have not been changed; those have to do with how we think, feel, and act. What is new in our situation is"—he paused, smiling, then continued—"what I may call 'the dodges.' "

"Precisely what do you mean by 'the dodges'?"

"The names given to various devices of statecraft to make them go down more easily, the methods of meeting various sociological exigencies, the nomenclature of social change . . . that sort of thing."

"I will give you an example," interposed Mrs. Whitehead energetically. "When your government finds itself obliged to pursue imperialistic policies, you call it 'the good neighbour'; but you will keep the Pacific islands just the same—and so you should. They have cost you something. But when Britain does the same sort of thing, you call it 'spheres of influence.' "

"Do you believe," I appealed to Whitehead, "that the United States is imperialistic?"

"Certainly," said he calmly.

Having ascertained their opinions, I did not pursue the subject. Instead I returned to the definition of "dodges."

" 'The dodges,' then," said I, "are how people go around corners on two wheels without hitting the hydrant."

"They don't always miss the hydrant," said Whitehead.

" 'The dodges' are fairly familiar to me," I remarked. "They occupy by far the major portion of newspaper space. But about the long-term views of human nature—how we think and feel, why we behave as we do . . ."

"Those are fairly familiar to you also," said Whitehead. "They were written down by the Greeks. The singular thing about Greek literature is that it doesn't age. It is just as vital today as it was when it was written."

"It is more," said I. "We study it to understand things about ourselves which our own writers are not able to say as clearly."

"The mortality of literatures is a singular study," continued Whitehead. "Suppose Greek literature had perished completely, as it might easily have done; we would never have missed what we had never known and yet how immeasurably poorer all of our lives would have been! It was the university at Alexandria, I suppose, which saved it, preserved the papyri and diffused their influence and their contents widely enough for survival. Sometimes I ask myself what constitutes the survival value of a literature. The literature of the eighteenth century, for example, has already lost much, perhaps most, of its interest excepting in so far as one reads it in order to understand how people lived and thought during that period. And the rapidity and violence of social change in our own times is certain to condemn much other literature—including some of our esteemed contemporaries—to the discard. It is the *social* literatures, I think, that tumble overboard when the vessel has to be lightened to ride out a gale."

"I'm not quite sure what you mean by the social literatures."

"Literatures which presuppose the continuance of an existing social system—namely, the social system on which they are based."

M*

"That makes it clearer. Already, one can think of numerous highly respected nineteenth-century works of literature— actually first-rate in some instances—which social change in our epoch has pitched over the dam."

"The late sixteenth and early seventeenth-century writings are more durable," said he.

"You have also, I think, defined the durability of Greek literature. While it is based on a then-existing social system, that social system is subjected to such constant critical scrutiny from the sixth century to the fourth, its existence is so often in jeopardy, and its forms are so diverse and can change so rapidly, that most of the great Greek authors seldom, it seems to me, fall into the way of taking it for granted as a necessarily permanent fixture; and some of the greatest of them—Plato, Thucydides, and Aristophanes—toward the end of the fifth century have a pretty clear notion that their social system is threatened with dissolution."

"If you want another example of one of the 'dodges,' " said Whitehead, "I will give you the treatment of the big industrial corporations. We began by treating them as 'persons.' For England in the eighteenth century in its dealings with India that concept served well enough—though I wouldn't guarantee that the Indians found it equally satisfactory. But by the time you reach the end of the nineteenth century, that conception is obviously untenable. The corporations, for better or for worse, have reached into all corners of our lives, and to pretend that a corporation is a 'person' is nonsense. A person has feelings, emotions, desires, aspirations; a corporation is an impersonal entity. It is idle to suppose that they will not be brought more and more under public control."

Ten had long since boomed from the clock tower of Memorial Hall, which they see from their windows; and rain was falling.

By previous agreement, Mrs. Whitehead drew up a chair to the big six-drawered mahogany escritoire and began rummaging for the promised photograph of Alfred. This developed into a major operation: drawer after drawer was pulled out, contents turned over, or heavy manuscript packets dropped on the floor. Her manner of doing it, all in complete absorption, was interesting and a dash picturesque; totally unselfconscious and yet so watchable for its own sake that the idea, which has so often crossed my mind before, crossed it again: "That act would be effective on the stage: she is looking for something in an escritoire, the contents are rummaged out interestingly, some of them plumped on the floor, others examined in her lap: this woman could probably have been a fine actress. I get it by flashes." She was handsomely gowned, and earlier in the evening, while we were turning over his badge of the Order of Merit, had laid it against the texture of her dress to show how the colours blended; but hang it around her own neck? Not she!

I said, "Oh, give up the search. That's too hard work. Wait till some other time."

"If you wait," said she, "you'll never get it."

"That's true. I've already waited nine years."

Finally she produced what she was looking for—a photograph of Alfred in his study when they lived out in Canton. He is seated in his leather-upholstered chair with his writing-board laid across its arms and his hands folded on a heap of manuscript sheets. Behind him are rows of books on shelves and beside him on a low table one of those familiar cups in which we have so often had chocolate.

"I like this better than the Harvard Tercentenary photograph," said I, "because in that one he is looking down and one doesn't see the eyes."

"Let me show you the first picture that was ever taken of me," said he, and going into another room brought back an old album. Paging through it, "I can't find it," he said finally. "But here is the headmaster of Sherborne when I was there as a boy, one of the greatest schoolmasters I have ever known; and here is my grandfather."

[331]

"He looks the typical Victorian Englishman. Does he fall entirely in the nineteenth century?"

"Nearly. He was born in 1794 and lived well into his eighties. This photograph was taken when he was about eighty years old."

"If that face isn't nineteenth-century England . . . !"

"He ruled the town," said his grandson, in a tone of humorous reminiscence, "and as a mob orator he was without peer."

"How big was the town?"

"Twenty thousand."

"We call that a city. I was reared in a 'town' of three thousand."

"We call that a village."

"Here it is," said Mrs. Whitehead, suddenly producing from the penetralia of her escritoire a small photograph in an oval fillet of ormolu mounted on a faded but still-deep crimson velvet. It was framed and backed in embossed leather and equipped with a brass ring from which to hang it on the wall. He showed it me.

"That is my first picture," he said.

On the lap of a smiling matron who bends over him fondly is a year-old baby in a white muslin dress, with plump features, fair hair not yet long enough to cut, a strongly modelled head, firm features, and rather a determined expression. Had I been shown the picture and asked to guess, I think it would have been easy to guess that this baby was British.

They said they were off to Maine on Friday.

"What is your address?"

"Battleship Island, Little Sebago Lake, West Gray," said Mrs. Whitehead. "The island is about a quarter of an acre. It has the great advantage," she glanced sidewise at Alfred, "that one cannot go on too long walks."

XLI

In August, 1945

IN August the war of 1939–1945 was crashing to its close. Two of those detonations were the atomic bombs dropped, the first on Hiroshima on August 6, the second on Nagasaki on August 9. Preoccupation with public events had become so intense as to reduce one's personal affairs to the estate of a waking dream. The evening after the first atomic bomb was dropped, I was with the Whiteheads. Professor Henry Maurice Sheffer, of the department of philosophy in Harvard, was there. My expectation had been that Whitehead would discuss the possible social consequences of atomic fission; instead, after having politely noticed the subject, he dismissed it. A year or two later he did discuss it, but at that moment he was one of the few who knew enough to know what it was that could not yet be known.

Charles Hopkinson was painting his portrait. The two sketches had been trial trips. Now there were seven sittings of two hours each, from 11 A.M. to 1 P.M., about as long as Whitehead could sustain the sessions, which were lightened as far as practicable by conversation among the four of us. Most of this had to go unrecorded because of the pressure of public events, but fragments of it remain. Being asked, "Which are more important, facts or ideas?" Whitehead reflected a while, then said: "Ideas *about* facts."

During a discussion of William James's *Varieties of Religious Experience*, he said:

"The difficulty of communication in words is but little realized. If I had to write something about your personality, of course I could—but how much would remain that couldn't be put into words. So, when the rare balance of knowledge and perception appears, as in William James—one who could communicate so much more than most—it is perhaps an advantage that his system of philosophy remained incomplete. To fill it out would necessarily have made it smaller. In Plato's *Dialogues* there is a richness of thought, suggestion, and implication which reaches far. Later, when he came to be more explicit concerning some of those implications, we have a shrinkage.

"Something similar can happen in scholarship. There is, of course, great importance in scholarship—exact knowledge, rationalization—but a great many scholars are engaged in reducing men of genius to the commonplace.

"Consider John Dewey. In carrying on the philosophy of William James, I think he enormously narrowed it. With James the consciousness of the ever-present complexity and possibility in human experience is always implicit in his writing. Dewey is without it. William James's awareness of the wide scope and the interrelations of all questions made him one of the great philosophic minds in history. Furthermore, that awareness is so sensitive and so vibrant that even if he did not survive as a philosopher, he would survive as a man of letters. But his philosophic thought does have the quality of permanence. When I was passing examinations for my mathematical degree, the physical and mechanical aspects of the world were considered to be all known and settled, with the exception of a few out-of-the-way problems which were being worked on by capable persons and which would no doubt be solved before long. Then it all blew up. The character of William James's mind was such that he could stand the shock of that explosion, which was the death of many others."

Those conversations during the sittings for the portrait were sometimes gay as well as grave, for, yes, by now we did know that the slaughter was nearing an end, temporarily at least. The Whiteheads entertained us with stories of their young married life at Ramsgate and in Cambridge. One was of Lady Jebb and her irascible Sir Richard.

"She was playing chess in their library, with young Arthur James Balfour," recited Mrs. Whitehead. "Sir Richard kept going in and out of the room and it put them off their game.

Finally Lady Jebb rose and locked the door after him. He came back, tried it, rattled the knob, and then began kicking it. Whereupon Lady Jebb called out, 'Kick away, Dickie. It's your ain paint and your ain dure!' "

Whitehead was equally informative:

"My father's church at Ramsgate," said he, "was an ancient Norman building roofed by a barrel vault. It was more impressive as architecture than it was helpful with acoustics. If you sat in the rear of the church you could hardly distinguish one word in ten, but when my father preached, that didn't matter, his voice was so powerful and sonorous it rolled reverberating the length of that barrel vault freighted with such moral earnestness. He was an Old Testament man; the New didn't mean so much to him, but he had the fervour of the old prophets, and when you heard him, that depth of feeling penetrated in his tones. You didn't need to know the words; his tones were enough. What was so intensely moving was the sincerity of a solemn sound. Wasn't that so, Evelyn?"

"Entirely!" she agreed. "And 'the converse is also true.' When we were engaged you insisted on taking me to vespers at St. Mary's in Cambridge. I dressed in my best bib and tucker for I well knew that I would be under public inspection; in addition to which, quite as I had apprehended, we were led up almost prematurely to the altar and seated far forward, where there was no difficulty in hearing. And what do you suppose happened?" she appealed to me.

"Either something quite distressing or very amusing. It wouldn't have been anything halfway."

"It was both," said she decisively. "A young vicar preached. Toward the end of his sermon he said—that was once when the words didn't help the sound—he said, 'Finally, my brethren, for well-conducted people life presents no problems.' "

"He didn't!"

"He did. Alfred and I had exemplary control over our facial muscles, but when we were outside and beyond earshot, I said to him, 'Catholicism may have its defects, but at least in a Catholic church you would never hear anything like that,' and Alfred replied, 'My dear, even in a Protestant church one doesn't very often hear anything as good as that.'"

When he lived in London, being obliged to ride about on buses, Whitehead said he had made a practice of taking along with him one or another historic personage, seated at his side, usually on top of the bus. They held animated conversations, he explaining what was meant by what they could see from the bus-top and then listening to his companion's comments. Who were they? Well, he often took along Sir Isaac Newton, Aristotle, or Archimedes, but never Plato. But why not Plato? He never could be brought to say, perhaps didn't himself quite know, but Plato was never taken along.

This led to some chaffing about Europeans who come over here on a whirlwind tour, then go home and write a book explaining all about us.

"Oh, but," said Whitehead, "that's the only way to do it. Having lived here more than twenty years, I wouldn't dream of writing such a thing now, but if I had written my impressions of America after I had been here my first three months, *that* would have been the book of books!"

One forenoon we were speaking of revolutions, in especial, those of France and Russia.

"The real destructiveness of revolutions," said Whitehead, "is not their overthrow of a ruling class or the execution of a monarch. England got on quite well enough without Charles I and France could well spare Louis XVI. The Hohenzollerns were no great loss to Germany nor the Hapsburgs to Austria, let alone the Romanoffs to Russia. Even when it comes to the overthrow of ruling classes the social dislocation may not be serious. During the French Revolution, even under the Terror, life in Paris within a few streets of the Place de la Concorde and the guillotine flowed on much as usual. But the real destructiveness of revolutions comes in the displacement of the people who carry on the minor social services, those who do the day labour of carrying forward the normal processes of civilized life, and I do not mean the so-called learned professions, law, medicine, the clergy, but rather the teachers, the small civil servants, the skilled artisans, people who know how to do the unspectacular but necessary tasks. They are the cambium layer under the bark of the tree, and if that is girdled, the tree dies."

*   *   *

To bring Charles Hopkinson, then in his seventies, to those sittings had taken some manoeuvring. In summer he lives at "Sharksmouth," his place on the North Shore at Manchester, and the train ride to Boston followed by the subway journey to Cambridge would have brought him to his painting in an advanced state of August wilt. Fortunately the Marblehead Rationing Board saw the light and was gracious enough to grant the extra petrol necessary to carry him from the Salem railroad station to Cambridge and back. This went on until mid-August; then the surrender of Japan released supplies of petrol in their former flood. Besides, it had long been understood that petrol rationing had been primarily for the economizing not of petrol but of rubber for tyres.

The portrait was finished about September 1st. In a thunderstorm the painter and I drove over to the Boston Museum of Fine Arts to show it to Mr. Constable, the curator of paintings. Constable and Hopkinson went into an abstruse discussion of its merits. It was later exhibited in the rooms of the Society of Fellows at Eliot House.

As the month went on, Whitehead questioned our good faith about keeping our every next appointment for a sitting:

"I say, shall we expect you next Thursday forenoon punctually at eleven on the dot while the bell of Memorial Hall is striking the hour?"

"But why not?"

"The war may end any day, in which case you will be dancing in the streets, or standing on your heads."

On August 14th Japan surrendered and rejoicing was frenetic, though some of those who had seen the armistice in 1918 were not so sanguine. The war did end September 2nd with a formal surrender. Since then, peace has been defined as a pause between wars for enemy identification.

Yet that month of August, with those quiet forenoons of painting and conversation in the Whiteheads' living-room, sun shining on the treetops beneath their windows, the still, sultry air fragrant from white phlox in vases of gleaming black enamel, and the deep-voiced bell of Memorial Hall punctuating Whitehead's discourse first with the strokes of twelve, then with the stroke of one, and all this preceded by the drive from Salem to Cambridge through a countryside smiling with summer where the purple loosestrife blossomed in marsh meadows along the way, still remains an idyl of peace in a world of war.

XLII

September 11, 1945

So the war had ended, but people were still benumbed and not yet fully able to realize it. Summer was moving toward the threshold of autumn in a procession of days glowing with sungold and sea-blue. Since the slaughter had stopped it was once more possible to feel that the world was beautiful, and on the shores of Nahant Bay it is never more radiant than at summer's end.

In the midst of this, Sir Richard Livingstone had arrived from England by plane ("high priority" for a civilian) and had gone to spend two days at the Institute for Advanced Study in Princeton. His destination was Toronto, where he was to deliver four lectures at the university. For another two days of rest and quiet beside the sea he came to Swampscott; we then drove on Thursday forenoon into Cambridge for luncheon with the Whiteheads. As there was a strenuous fortnight awaiting him at Toronto before his return to England by plane, he had made no other engagements.

His younger son, Captain Rupert Livingstone, had been killed in this second war, as had Whitehead's in the first. This bond was present wordlessly.

The four of us sat in Whitehead's book-walled study. It was flooded by golden sunshine through a south window which stood wide open to the warm, still air, and in the trees outside the cicadas were shrilling. Scot and Englishman, the two are a contrast in type, Whitehead, the fair, florid Briton of Kent and East Anglia; Livingstone, tall, slender, sandy-haired and sandy-complexioned, though just now unwontedly reddened by exposure to the blazing sunlight and sea-glare of New England's September on the North Shore.

Their renewals of acquaintance were quickly disposed of; a brief pause, then Livingstone asked:

"What do you think has been the effect of science on our world?"

"Before I answer, what do you think?"

"Hasn't science abolished slavery?"

"If you had said that about the year 1900, yes. But the acceleration of change in the past, let me say, fifty years has altered the whole situation. I'm not speaking of the atomic bomb for the present, since it is only the latest in a series, and too recent to be appraised anyhow."

"When the atomic bomb was announced," said Livingstone, "the scientists, it seemed to me, were somewhat frivolous in their view of it, but the people were alarmed."

"I mean," resumed Whitehead, "that the conditions of our lives have been basically more altered in the past fifty years than they were in the previous two thousand—I might say three thousand. My answer to your first question would be, I think that we are on the threshold of an age of liberation, a better life for the masses, a new burst of liberated creative energy, a new form of society; or mankind may all but exterminate itself and desolate this planet."

"Suppose," said Livingstone, "some of the greatest Greeks were to come back and see us as we are now . . . Thucydides, Plato, Pericles, Aristotle?"

"Aristotle would be inexpressibly shocked at the way his generalizations have gone overboard. Mind you, I don't say his ideas—species, genera, and all that sort of thing—haven't proved vastly useful. Aristotle discovered all the half-truths which were necessary to the creation of science."

"Aristotle's *Ethics*, on the other hand," rejoined Livingstone, "seem to me to stand up better."

Whitehead looked dissent. "I grant you, they are admirably definite," said he. "Plato's ideas on that subject tend, in comparison, to be vague. But I prefer the vagueness."

"The Greeks didn't like vagueness," remarked Livingstone. "In that sense Plato may almost be said to be atypical. They liked outline to be distinct and subject matter to be clearly organized within definite form."

"I prefer Plato," Whitehead resumed. "He seems to me to have been the one man in the ancient world who would not have been surprised at what has happened, because his thought constantly took into account the unpredictable, the limitless possibilities of things. There is always more chance of hitting on something valuable when you aren't too sure what you want to hit upon."

He turned again to Livingstone, and continued, "There's something I want to ask you: am I right in thinking that German scholarship is quite wrong in trying to identify Plato with some explicit conclusion in his *Dialogues*, with some single speaker and a final point of view? It seems to me that was just what he was trying to avoid. Take his letters: assuming that he wrote them, and even if he didn't, they would state a prevailing frame of mind in ancient times about his work: namely, that there *is* no Platonic system of philosophy. What he did was explore various aspects of a problem and then leave us with them. . . . He seems to me to have had, more than anyone else, a supreme sense of the limitless possibilities of the universe."

"About German scholarship, I'm not at the moment prepared to say," replied Livingstone, "but all through Aristotle one can see his resistance to the influence of Plato, and all through him the influence of Plato's thought is inescapable."

"Let me speak personally for a moment," said Whitehead. "I had a good classical education, and when I went up to Cambridge early in the 1880's my mathematical training was continued under good teachers. Now nearly everything was supposed to be known about physics that could be known—except a few spots, such as electro-magnetic phenomena, which remained (or so it was thought) to be co-ordinated with the Newtonian principles. But, for the rest, physics was supposed to be nearly a closed subject. Those investigations to co-ordinate went on through the next dozen years. By the middle of the 1890's there were a few tremors, a slight shiver as of all not being quite secure, but no one sensed what was coming. By 1900 the Newtonian physics were demolished, done for! Still speaking personally, it had a profound effect on me: I have been fooled once, and I'll be damned if I'll be fooled again! Einstein is supposed to have made an epochal discovery. I am respectful and interested, but also sceptical. There is no more reason to suppose that Einstein's relativity is anything final, than Newton's *Principia*. The danger is dogmatic thought; it plays the devil with religion, and science is not immune from it. I am, as you see, a thorough-going evolutionist. Millions of years ago our earth began to cool off and forms of life began in their simplest aspects. *Where did they come from?* They must have been inherent in the total scheme of things; must have existed in potentiality in the most minute particles, first of this fiery, and later of this watery and earthy planet. Does it not strike you how absurd it is to start from the five and one-half or six feet of our own bodies as our scale of physical measurement?"

"Overdoing the idea," said Livingstone, quoting it in Greek, "that 'man is the measure of all things.' "

"Our notions of physical dimension," assented Whitehead, "are absurdly arbitrary. It doesn't strike me as at all impossible that the smallest pebble might contain within it a universe as complex as the one we know, and that the universe or universes which we have recently begun to apprehend may be as minute in the scale of what lies beyond as that in the pebble to the one we know; or that the vastness might be as much greater in the opposite direction—the direction of what we consider the infinitely small. . . . Development, I believe, goes by jumps. Fifty thousand years ago, let us say, there would have been a lucky jump; embodied in one man, or in one family, or in a few families, and, after an interval, another great advance following from that."

It was suggested that we may be living in the midst of one of those "jumps"—if it doesn't extinguish us.

Whitehead considered this, then said, "Why talk about 'the laws of nature' when what we mean is the characteristic behaviour of phenomena within certain limits at a given stage of development in a given epoch—so far as these can be ascertained?"

As the laughter subsided, he said to Livingstone, "But come, let's drop all this; I want to talk about your admirable books on education, especially adult education. How idiotic it is to dismiss children from school at sixteen, or even at eighteen, and consider them capable of coping with the complexities of life. . . ."

"My idea, as you know," said Livingstone, "is that education must continue throughout life for everybody, at the varying levels of ability and aptitude, and that that is the only way a modern democracy is workable or can continue to exist."

"What we want," said Whitehead, "is to elicit as nearly as possible all the latent capacities of human talent. No way of doing this adequately has ever been devised. A certain class of talents will be elicited under certain forms of social organization favourable to their development, but in a very limited range and in very limited conditions of space and time. We never seem to have found a way to elicit the complete spread of man's potential capabilities."

Mrs. Whitehead returned to the study. Luncheon was not quite ready, so seating herself on the cushioned leg-rest of her husband's arm-chair facing the two Englishmen, she plunged into a discussion of our two countries:

"The thing one mustn't do," she was addressing herself to Livingstone, "and it is so fatally easy, is to compare. They are not comparable; each is itself. We have lived here twenty-one years, and it is the differences which keep coming out. When we first came here after the other war, the hope that I saw in the faces was 'choky'—all these young things looking forward to life eagerly . . ."

"Having just arrived by airplane in Baltimore last Sunday afternoon," said Livingstone smiling, "I am in a perfect position to write a book about America."

"The longer one lives here, the less competent one feels to write it," said she. "But don't be put off by externals: to us, many of them are misleading. . . ."

"I'll tell you one of them," said Whitehead, "if Lucien will forgive me; the newspapers."

"I could damn them more specifically. But go on."

"To glance at their front pages," he continued, "you might suppose that a principal occupation was murdering one another."

"Remember, Altie," she cautioned him, "that when we used to go from England to the Continent, the crime on the Continent seemed tremendous, and *was* tremendous."

"I do remember, and the impression given by the front pages of the newspapers is quite fallacious. It isn't news when you ask a stranger, anybody in the whole scale of American life, the

direction to some place, and he goes out of his way two streets
to set you right, yet it is this that is absolutely typical among
these people who seem to me to possess more native kindness
than any people who ever lived on the face of the earth."

"Were you required to sign papers for admission to this country?" she asked of Livingstone.

"I don't recall anything unusual or formidable."

"Oh, but that is so; you wouldn't. It was when we were
coming over here to stay—this is what I mean by not being put
off by externals—Alfred and I were required to sign sworn
statements that we had never spent longer than ten months in
jail!"

"No, I don't remember signing anything like that," says
Livingstone.

"But Gilbert Murray does," I offered a correction. "When
he came over here in 1926, like you merely to deliver a series
of lectures, he said, foreigners had to sign a paper answering
the questions: Are you an anarchist? Are you a polygamist?"

"My God!" said Mrs. Whitehead.

Regaining her equanimity, she continued: "For nine years,
after we came here to stay, we used to have students in, one
evening a week. First and last, the number of boys and girls
who went through our rooms would have run into the hundreds.
They came from all sorts of homes, including the farms and
what you would call something next door to a slum, and yet
I tell you that the gentleness of their manners, their good taste,
and really good breeding was virtually invariable. That was in
the brave days of the Volstead Act, when people, and especially
older people, were filling up before ever they started out to
dine. And yet in all that time only one drunk came, and he,
if you please, a scion of Boston blue-blood! At the other extreme
was a boy who turned up from New York, the East Side.
About half-way through the evening he stretched himself,
sighed, and said, 'Isn't the world wonderful?' . . . 'What do
you mean?' I asked him. 'Why,' said he, 'a few weeks ago I

was rolling barrels in the streets of New York, and now here I am amidst luxury and all these books.' (Well, of course, our apartments down by the river were never anything special.) What he meant was that this was his first time in such surroundings—but not his last! He became one of Alfred's most brilliant pupils, and has done very well."

"The social constituency of English universities," remarked Livingstone, "has changed greatly." He cited instances: "The net incomes of the parents of our last year's scholars in Corpus were £400, £688, £361, £318, £1,065." (These figures have, of course, been made precise since that conversation.) "Two did not claim the extra emolument and therefore were well off; but there were two weekly wage-earners, £3 10s. 0d. per week, and £8 per week."

"It seems to me," said Whitehead, "that the English universities, Oxford and Cambridge perhaps in especial, are returning more nearly to their function in the Middle Ages, of training the gifted boys from the poorer classes. In the eighteenth century they trained young aristocrats at most, or the sons of country squires at least, with few scholars from the poorer classes, and in the nineteenth century, they drew largely from the more prosperous parts of the middle and professional classes—people like us, for example, for whom the world seemed to have been made fairly safe and enjoyable; but now they are beginning to get the children of the working class."

"From what you have been telling me," said Livingstone, "and from what I have observed here on previous visits and even a little on this one too, it seems to me that democracy in England is vertical, that is, an equalitarian feeling that runs from top to bottom of society, cutting through classes—and that in America, where classes are less defined, democracy is more horizontal." He indicated the two dimensions by gestures of his two hands.

"Let us give you an example of how horizontal it is here," Whitehead said. "Taxicab chauffeurs here in Cambridge and

Boston are good conversationalists; they have something really interesting to say. Quite recently we had one driving us home from Boston; he slowed down, and drove by side streets (explaining to us that he wasn't lengthening the distance, but only the time), conversing animatedly with us, and we with him, and when he let us out at our door, he said, 'This is the most enjoyable conversation I have had for a long time.' "

Luncheon was announced. We went out to the table. Conversation turned to English novelists.

"Women, it seems to me, write better novels than men," said Whitehead. "Men are too apt to go off in search of abstract ideas and try to fit life to them; women are more likely to give us the intimacies which make life and character vivid to us. How does it seem to you?" he appealed to Livingstone.

"As you spoke, I was thinking of Mrs. Gaskell, and I would agree."

"One exception I would make," Whitehead continued, "not a genius of the first rank, but an admirable talent for precisely what he did; present the average life and thought of his time through a fairly representative class, the clergy. I mean Anthony Trollope."

"You ought to know," exclaimed his wife. "Heavens, you were steeped in it and so was I, from my early twenties on. . . . And don't forget that it all but spoilt every member of your family in your generation except you. I grant you that Trollope does it well; only perhaps a trifle too well."

"At least, pettie, he got it right," said Whitehead, beaming across the table at her. "We agree about that! Reading him, I can hear my father and his clerical friends talking. Even the jokes sound natural. We lived near Canterbury and saw a good deal of the cathedral clergy."

"But women novelists don't draw men well," conceded Mrs. Whitehead. "When it comes to their favourite figures of men, something usually goes wrong."

The question arose whether men novelists drew women any

better, with comparisons between George Meredith and George Eliot.

"Thackeray," said Whitehead, "has immense art, but he is too narrowly confined to a class; he carries you all over England and the Continent, but in the end they are always about much the same kind of people."

"He was writing of a class, too," added she, "to which he didn't belong, and saw from the outside with a mixture of fascination and repugnance, never able to make up his mind."

"One nineteenth-century English novel that I think *will* last," said Livingstone, "is *Pickwick*." (In his *Greek Genius* he parallels the jollity of Christmas at Dingley Dell with the picture of country life in Attica in the *Peace* of Aristophanes [verses 1127–1171].) "*Pickwick*," he continued, "is not only literature; it is also history. That is what the English are really like."

"A moment ago," said Whitehead, "I was saying that I thought women wrote the best novels." (He paused and gave us a mischievous twinkle.) "I would almost say that Dickens was one of the best women novelists!"

"How about Galsworthy?"

Livingstone thought his people weren't very real.

"Galsworthy, like Thackeray," said Mrs. Whitehead, "was another 'outsider.'"

"As with novels, so with letters," Whitehead carried it forward. "Women write better letters than men. They put in what we want to know, how people felt about things, how they lived, what they ate and wore, what they worried about—all those immediacies which make the life of an epoch live again. History should be written more from letters. Who cares about the Battle of Crécy, dates, places, and all that we are crammed with in the name of history? What had they to do with it? History is from day to day; and it is not events, it is sociology; it is the progress of thought."

"The trouble with formal history, it seems to me," said

Livingstone, "is that it gives us the conclusions, the end results, without showing us how these results were arrived at."

"Precisely," assented Whitehead; "the clashes are only the last step in the process; what we need to know is the progress of ideas and ferments which produced the clashes."

"Another historical source which should be more used, though the French have made more use of it than the English, and effective use, too, is memoirs," said Mrs. Whitehead. "English literature is not very rich in memoirs and those we have are likely to be bleak and dreary. French memoirs, on the contrary, are vivacious and full of reality. It's true they often record scandalous escapades, but with such spirit that, while one does not condone, one is not depressed. The equivalents in English memoirs I find repellent, and the people unamiable."

They began casting about for those who could be said to have written history well in the nineteenth century in England:

"Not Macaulay," said Mrs. Whitehead, "with that much-touted 'style' . . . rhetorical periods, 'tum-te-tum-te-tum,' the sort of House of Commons speech that was effective in that epoch, and all quite superficial."

"Don't forget," says Livingstone, "that Macaulay managed to make the reading of history popular, no small achievement."

"So did Strachey," said she, "but that didn't make what he wrote *good* history."

"I don't like it," said Livingstone, "any better than you do, but it is often very good writing."

"That I grant you; and what he says is often very funny, but it is not funny when others try to say it like him."

We rose. Coffee was served in the living-room. Whiteheads and Livingstone, Cambridge and Oxford, began playing a kind of tennis game as between their two universities, comparing their whimsicalities, their contrasts, their merits and defects.

"I arrived there," said Mrs. Whitehead, "in the Year of the Thirty Brides, and I assure you, it was not an easy place for brides."

"There had just been a change in the university statutes," explained Whitehead, "permitting dons to marry. Before that, in order to marry, one had to take holy orders, and as most of them no longer believed in the Articles to which they were obliged to subscribe, they found ways of satisfying their consciences by all sorts of far-fetched interpretations of those theological concepts which, I should say, did the Broad Church no particular good. The result was, as Evelyn says, that thirty or forty brides arrived in Cambridge all at once, some of them, like her, quite young; others by no means young."

"But I learned fast," said Mrs. Whitehead. "Having been born and reared in France, I had read a good deal in French, but, being transplanted abruptly to England, hadn't read what one is expected to have read in English. One of the dons, seated next me at a dinner party, began questioning me about my English reading. Naturally, I didn't come off very well. 'I see that you read nothing!' said he, and ceased to attend to me for the rest of the evening. . . . And his lack of interest in me lasted some years. No, it was not an easy place for brides."

"Nor always for bridegrooms," added Whitehead. "You remember the Verralls and Jim Stephen?" he asked her.

She suddenly choked with laughter.

"But be sure and explain to Sir Richard," she cautioned him, "that that was before Stephen went 'off'."

"He was down visiting us at Cambridge," pursued Whitehead, "when we lived next the Verralls; our gardens adjoined—"

"Only a one-brick thickness of wall between them," Mrs. Whitehead put in.

"Now Verrall talked in a high, squeaky voice" (he mimicked it), "and Jim Stephen was a deadly mimic. He began mocking Verrall in an imaginary scene of Verrall proposing to his wife. Poor Evelyn was horrified and made frantic gestures to him to stop. 'They can hear; just over the wall,' said she in whispers. 'What of it?' says Stephen. 'Do them good!'"

As between the two universities, Livingstone questioned whether there was much to choose in man's inhumanity to man.

"At Cambridge," said Whitehead, "what civilization we got, came from outside. But at Oxford, you civilize your people inside the university."

"Oxford is more sociological," admitted Livingstone. "At Cambridge you train mathematicians and scientists."

"What saved me for civilization," said Whitehead, "were two things. One was The Apostles. It was a discussion club of twelve members, undergraduates."

"And what was the other?" asked Livingstone.

"Being taken out of Cambridge and plunged into the University of London for fifteen years."

"What do you think that did for you?" Livingstone inquired in a gently chaffing tone.

"Stirred me about among all sorts of people; and, added to that, was my experience in the university senate."

"The sociological cast of Oxford," observed Livingstone, "is generally accredited to the classical Greats. I say the classical Greats, because even the men who take modern Greats and do well in them admit that they aren't as effective, aren't as powerful."

"Just what do you conceive to be the effect on a man of the classical Greats?" inquired Whitehead.

"In Newman's *Nature of University Education* there is a definition of a gentleman," replied Livingstone. "It covers about three pages,[1] and comes nearer to defining what you inquire than anything else I know. It's all the more forceful since Newman doesn't approve of the type he is describing and leaves you in no doubt about it, for, as an example, he cites the Emperor Julian, 'the apostate from Christian Truth, the foe of Christian education,'" and he quoted, "'a gentleman's religion is of a liberal and generous character; it is based upon

[1] On the scope and Nature of University Education, John Henry Newman. Everyman's Library; pages 186–188.

[350]

honour; vice is evil, because it is unworthy, despicable, and odious.' "

"Poor Newman," exclaimed Mrs. Whitehead, "that sensitive, defenceless, skinless creature! *Ecorce*. Who could blame him?"

"I saw him once," said Whitehead.

"To speak with him?" asked Livingstone.

"Yes."

"Can you remember what he said?"

"It is too long ago." Whitehead looked preoccupied for a moment, then exclaimed suddenly, "There's a question I would like to ask of a Jesuit priest. . . ."

"Then ask it in your study," proposed Mrs. Whitehead, rising. The conversation was temporarily adjourned.

"There was a question you wanted to put to a Jesuit priest," prompted Livingstone, when we were again in the study.

"Yes. It is this: 'Is there laughter in Heaven?' The humourlessness of the Bible is amazing."

"I tried rereading the Old Testament a while ago," replied Livingstone. "Much of it is superb in every way; but bits are . . . Well, you remember Oscar Wilde's 'When I think of all the harm that book has done, I despair of writing anything to equal it.' "

"Had the Hebrews no sense of humour?" asked Whitehead.

"When something is very serious, don't we lose a bit of it by laughing about it? Doesn't laughter diminish it in value?"

"Suppose we consider the arts," proposed Whitehead. "Do we find humour there?"

Livingstone thought it might be hard to find in the greatest art, say religious painting of the Italian Renaissance. "I doubt," said he, "whether it goes with the greatest thought or art."

"There's plenty of laughter in the comedies of Aristophanes," I said, "and his works are both art and religion."

"Yes," said Livingstone, "but I always think Aristophanes is at his best in the parts where he isn't joking."

[351]

"Still, on the main issue, I challenge you: Laughter is a divine attribute. And the absence of laughter from the Hebraic religions is a serious matter to us of the Northern European races, for laughter plays a large part in our lives, and we are forced to do our laughing almost entirely outside of our religion."

"How could it be done inside religion?" asked Livingstone.

"It has been done. There is a liberal arts college in New England which had better be nameless, since things were going badly in it during the 1920's and 1930's."

"You are quite right about that," said Whitehead, to my consternation. "I was invited there to lecture in 1930, and I could see that for myself."

"Then you must be clairvoyant, for we mean the same college. The boys were out of hand; were required to attend daily chapel and church on Sundays, but if they didn't like the visiting preacher (and they mostly didn't) they would cough him down and no way could be found to stop them. But there was one preacher who came there repeatedly, whom the boys heard gladly. He was a man of intellect and of great moral earnestness, and he also had a lively sense of humour. Between his passages of earnestness he could keep the boys rocking with laughter. They adored him. . . . As for laughter in Greek religion, we needn't stop with Aristophanes. It begins as far back as Homer, the first book of the *Iliad* ends with gods laughing on Olympus."

"There is a fragment of a lost satyr play," Livingstone conceded, "in which Prometheus has stolen fire from heaven, and the satyrs think it so beautiful that they try to kiss it and get their beards singed."

"The Hebrews," resumed Whitehead, "had a most intense ethical perception, though within a very limited range. It is 'the beauty of holiness.' In that, no one else approaches them, but the range is narrow."

(Sometime afterwards we did come up with sundry examples

in Holy Writ of what, by stretching the definition, might be interpreted as humour. One was the prophet Elijah taunting the priests of Baal with the impotency of their god, though he also ordered them to be slaughtered by their late sectaries [I Kings 18 : 40]; another was the prophet Elisha conjuring bears to tear two and forty children who had taunted him with his bald head [II Kings 2 : 24]; a third was Haman hanged on the gallows fifty cubits high which he had had built for Mordecai [Esther 7:10]; and a fourth was Saint Paul's incident with the silversmiths of Ephesus, which is first-rate satire [Acts 19 : 24]. But it had to be admitted that none of these was the kind of hilarity which has audiences rolling in the aisles.)

"The Greeks," said Livingstone, in reply to Whitehead's last remark, "had everything which the Hebrews lacked."

"Touching this problem on its modern side," Whitehead continued, "the Unitarians, I think, come the nearest to having found a way to adapt the Christian ideas to the world we live in now—and with the Unitarians I group those other religious people who are so nearly like them, the Congregationalists. And by the way, a few days ago I even had a letter from an Episcopalian bishop commending me for my philosophy. I couldn't but think he was a good deal more like an eighteenth-century English bishop in respect to his breadth of religious thought than a twentieth-century one. . . . See here," he said abruptly, turning to Livingstone, "at the risk of being rude, I am going to ask you a personal question: you needn't answer it if you don't want to: how did you vote in the last election?"

"For Labour."

"Good! So would I have had I been there."

"It happened that our local candidate was a very good one."

"I would have voted for the Labour candidate, even if he had been a poor one, unless he had been *too* great an ass."

"Did you expect the result that came?" asked Mrs. Whitehead.

"No," said Livingstone. "The most that anyone seems to have expected was a sharp diminution of the Conservative seats."

"What went wrong with Churchill's campaign?" she asked.

"He is thought to have got into the hands of Beaverbrook."

"We've known Churchill and followed his career since the Boer War," she continued. "He seems to be one-half hero and the other half bounder. In a fight he is superb, but the moment the fighting stops, the bounder comes uppermost."

"It's greatly to the credit of the British electorate, I think," said Livingstone, "that there was no raking up of dead bodies and dead issues. Baldwin and Chamberlain were left out of the controversy. The only time I know of when one of them was brought in was during a discussion in the House of Commons about sending our iron railings off to war. 'Leave Baldwin his railings,' said a member. 'He'll need them to protect him from the people!' The remark was drowned in boos, and it was made by a Conservative member."

"There is no diminution of Churchill's popularity," resumed Mrs. Whitehead. "He is still 'good old Winnie!' and gets the more cheers when he appears in public, more than the Labour premier. The people admire him and honour him, but they won't vote for him. To me it seems an extraordinary manifestation of political good-sense on the part of the British electorate."

"Yes," said Livingstone, who, being a Platonist, is well acquainted with the valid criticisms of "the democratic man." "It makes one believe in democracy."

"What do you think are the chances of your getting a military man for President after this war?" Whitehead appealed to me.

"We have had two melancholy experiences in that kind which are pretty vividly remembered," said I.

"But General MacArthur is making a play for it," said Mrs. Whitehead.

"That may be. As a military man he is admirable, but he also has a sense of theatre and that, in American public life, doesn't wear too well."

"Eisenhower," said Whitehead, "is a really great figure. How about him?"

No one cared to predict.

"One great change in the American frame of mind which you must take into account," Mrs. Whitehead addressed Livingstone, "is that they now know that the world is not safe, even for them. We, for our part, never were safe, and we have mostly known it, unless it were for a brief period towards the end of the nineteenth century. What a comfortable—and vanished—world that was!—The world of Queen Victoria. What a figure of legend she is now!"

"Is Queen Victoria ever known to have made a joke?" asked Whitehead, suddenly reverting to our discussion of humour.

"'We are not amused,'" quoted Livingstone. "At least, she had a negative sense of humour; she knew what she thought was *not* funny."

"But she once said, 'Mr. Gladstone addresses me as if I were a public meeting.'"

"Yes," said Mrs. Whitehead, "but did she know that remark was funny?"

"Wasn't it disgraceful," said Whitehead, "the way 'Dizzy' sucked up to her. Disraeli's eminence is a striking instance of political detachment. They didn't like him, but they knew he had ability and accepted him as a political representative."

The clock in the tower of Memorial Hall struck a booming "Three"! There was an afternoon train for Toronto which Sir Richard must be aboard. We stood, to take our leave.

"Shall you," asked Whitehead genially, "feel let down when no one any longer walks before you carrying a poker?" The allusion was to the degree ceremony at Oxford, when the academic procession enters the Sheldonian Theatre, the vice-chancellor preceded by his staves as the symbols of authority.

"My children," replied Livingstone, "amuse themselves by asking why I don't turn around and walk in the opposite direction. At the same time our registrar, who has had long experience in it, says that the custom of standing when the vice-chancellor enters the Hebdomadal Council does have a good effect on getting to the business seriously. Ritual has a place in life. The deference may not be for a personality, or even for the institution; but it can be for the ideas embodied in the ceremony."

XLIII

November 11, 1947

ARMISTICE DAY. Evening with the Whiteheads, an autumn storm raging outside, with a gale of almost hurricane force and torrential rain.

At first they both seemed a little limp. This was scarcely to be wondered at, for their daughter-in-law, Mrs. North Whitehead, had died after a lingering and dreadful illness; and Mrs. Whitehead herself had had to go to Phillips House, Massachusetts General Hospital, for what threatened to be an emergency operation. She referred to it coolly as "knife work." Privately, before he came out of his study where he was having a nap, she said that it had been rougher on him than on her.

"He can meet these things when they happen, but he no longer has his endurance, and they take it out of him after they are over. Here I am, as usual—well, not *quite* as usual—but with him"—she paused and regarded me with a comic glance —"you might suppose I had been cremated and dispersed!"

The living-room was full of flowers, chrysanthemums, yellow, bronze, lavender, artistically arranged with fronds of green. I spoke of them. "Yes," said she, "I am being spoilt, and how I love it! You would think I was a film actress from the way flowers arrive."

Rising, she went to her big mahogany escritoire and took out a sheaf of letters.

"There is something I wish you to know," said she, "though nothing must be said about it at present." She kept opening letters and scanning them, speaking along as she did so.

"As you know, our income from England was cut down during the war. Financially for us it was quite a tight pinch. But I managed. What I want you to know is that three times during the war, the bank manager where we have our accounts received anonymous certified cheques to be deposited to our account. Each time the sum was the same, three hundred dollars. I asked if he knew who. He said he didn't but could communicate through the other bank. We couldn't accept anonymous gifts, of course, but I asked if it was possibly in payment of some forgotten debt or obligation. The answer came back, 'It might be considered so.' No. We're too old for that. Our hearty gratitude was conveyed but we couldn't accept. . . . I can't find the letter I'm looking for. Do you put things away and lose them?"

"Do I? Last spring I brought home as gifts some things from Oxford, which I put away carefully. It is now November and I haven't found them yet."

"You make me feel better. . . . I would have preferred you to read the letter; but can tell you. The college has had an anonymous gift of money for a scholarship, to be known as the Alfred North Whitehead Scholarship, the income of which is twelve hundred dollars a year, to be paid to Alfred during the remainder of his life and to me if I survive him; after that to the student holder of the scholarship. What impresses us both most is the generosity of it; also the tact and delicacy. It is paid to the college. That makes it quite different. We have no say in the matter. And what pleases Alfred most is that it leaves a permanent connection of his name with the college in a living form."

She added, "The endowment sum is thirty thousand dollars at four per cent."

No conjectures were offered as to who the donor might be, but there were two or three strong probabilities.

"Well, that is it." Rising, she put the papers back in the escritoire and, resuming her arm-chair, lighted a cigarette. The telephone rang. "Oh, damn!" says she, and answered it. Her surprise was a joyful one, for it was somebody she dearly loves. That conversation being ended, she knocked at the study door, went in softly, and spoke in a quiet voice: "Lucien is here. Now don't bound up: wait a few moments before you rise."

Presently he came out of the study, not quite fully awake. But after bathing his face in cold water, he came back feeling fit.

They were most entertaining. It seems that his publishers' envoys had been to call. This meant that a representative of the English firm had been brought by one from the American branch.

"The immediate occasion," said he, "is that they are planning an omnibus edition of my work."

"Will it include *Process and Reality*?"

"Some of it. . . ."

"We would have preferred," said she, "to have all or nothing of each work, instead of all the works with cuts by editors, and were quite let down when we found that the editors had taken it upon themselves to cut the works, in some cases whole chapters."

"Why, the colossal . . . what shall I call it?"

"And what do you suppose Alfred said?"

"Well, what did he say to anything like that?"

"'No doubt they've improved it' . . . !"

"I always said he is too good for this world. But it's wonderful news that *Process and Reality* is to be republished in any form. I can't get a single-volume edition. The Old Corner Book Store has been advertising for one for me these two months. I remember your telling me that it is the book you most wanted to write."

"In the preface to it," said he, "I wrote something which ought to have been repeated in the opening sentence of the first chapter, and repeated at frequent intervals all through the book: namely, how impressed I am with the inadequacy of any human being's attempt to express such philosophical ideas at all; how utterly beyond our scope are these universal processes. All one can do, in venturing on such subjects, is to *offer suggestions.*"

"Is it true that a single-volume edition of *The Aims of Education* has been reissued in England?"

"Yes," said she, "they sent us a copy."

"That is more good news, for at least half a dozen of my friends, headmasters and such, have been trying to obtain it."

"Look here," said he, "I'll give you this one."

He went to his study, brought it back, and laid it in my lap. The plates (it was an English firm) were obviously the original ones, but the dark-blue binding was different and in better taste than the crimson cover of the 1928 edition. Later in the evening he autographed it.

"We had a pleasant time with the publishers' representatives," said Mrs. Whitehead, "but there was one ghastly moment. What do you suppose the publishers wanted to do? *Print a photograph of Alfred on the cover of* Life *magazine!*"

"Good God!"

"Imagine Alfred's face being hawked about the streets," said she, grimacing.

"How did you get out of it?"

"I told them, most gently, that he had made it a lifelong rule not to give interviews and not to be photographed for the press —except at the Harvard Tercentenary, of course, when all the old boys were photographed."

"Imagine Alfred joining the publicity hounds!"

"The publishers' men were very kind about it," she resumed. "They agreed to drop it."

"When is the 'omnibus' to appear?"

"We don't know. They gave us no idea."

"My own guess is," said Whitehead, looking at me with a mischievous twinkle, "—mind you, I don't know, and perhaps I shouldn't say this; but my own guess is that they mean to postpone publication of this until shortly after I have quitted this earthly sphere."

"If that's the case," said his wife, "I question their judgment. If they want a 'Whitehead boom,' it is on now. Have you seen the new volume of excerpts?"

"Yes. So far, three copies have been sent me."

"What do you think of it?"

"It strikes me as very well done."

"*The Wit and Wisdom of Whitehead*," said she, "—what a title! I grant you the wit, and some of the wisdom, but—"

"The title is not exactly new. It was used for those excerpts from George Eliot during her lifetime, and again for George Meredith during his. No doubt the alliteration of the three *W*'s was an irresistible temptation. But looking it over I thought the selections were made with care and skill; a good many of them I recognized, but others I didn't, and the result is that I shall do what I expect the excerpts will cause a good many others to do—go back to the books themselves."

Dinner was quite sumptuous. The beating of wind and rain against the windows reminded them of "Bleak House" at Broadstairs, where they first met, for Alfred's Aunt Susan had lived in it; but long after Dickens's sojourn there. And bleak it was, for the building was high, narrow, and exposed, and although built of flint-stone, on nights like this it shook in the gales off the North Sea. They said there had been numerous shipwrecks on that headland.

From Bleak House they moved in imagination to the vicarage at Ramsgate.

"It was of brick," said Mrs. Whitehead. "There were fine trees, spacious grounds, and a lovely garden—under which, you are to understand, was a sizable cave."

"Rock-walled?"

"No. In the chalk."

"An entrance to a cavern yawning in your garden?"

"No," said Whitehead. "It was entered through the coach-house."

"It sounds a bit like sword-and-cape melodrama. Was the vicarage interior interesting?"

"Yes. Not impressive, you understand," said Mrs. Whitehead, "but interesting. There was a wide hall, though the staircase was not good. It was something new that had been added by a predecessor of Father's. But the old stairway was lovely; that had been moved back into the servants' wing. Of course the tone of the interior had to be ecclesiastical. The dining-room was properly dark. Dining-rooms were expected to be gloomy. The darkness set off the family silver, of which there was any quantity."

"What was that amusing tale you were telling Livingstone here at luncheon about Archbishop Tait and his son? So much went on in those four hours that I couldn't remember it all."

"That's Alfred's story," said she, laughingly. "He was there. I wasn't. Though I know it almost as well as if I had been."

"Tait was a very great man," said Whitehead. "He should have been Prime Minister of Great Britain; but Providence made a mistake; he went into the church instead and became Archbishop of Canterbury. Living so close by, he became a great friend of my father's and was often at our house. Sometimes he drove over after morning service from Canterbury for Sunday dinner at the vicarage. On this particular day he brought with him Bishop Gore of Oxford, a man who had found religion. Now, being eighteen years old by that time, I was well aware that Archbishop Tait had quite a name for peopling posts of good emoluments with his relatives, and when I heard Bishop Gore ask Mrs. Tait, by way of making table conversation, 'And what profession does your son seem inclined to enter?' I realized they were on thin ice. There was a pause. Gore leaned forward solicitously over the table, and I listened intently for the reply. 'We have considered a great many possibilities,' said Lady Tait, 'but it seems, after all, to come back to one thing—we think dear Gordon will take holy orders.' Another pause. Then Gore said, as if to himself, 'Quite!'"

When we rose they asked if the epidemic of war-scares in the newspapers had begun to subside. All I could say was that we hadn't had a war with Russia for thirty-six hours.

"If either this country or they start a war with these new instruments," said Whitehead, "civilization is done for. It won't wipe out the human race, but it will set civilization back thousands of years."

"Do you see any bulwark against such a disaster?"

"Only the appearance of half a dozen eminent men."

"Can you descry half a dozen such on the horizon?"

"They don't appear on the horizon; they appear in our midst and cannot at once be identified."

"Shall I confess? I go about my accustomed occupations, among my friends, amid my favourite scenery, all with a sense of unreality, a sense that all this may be blown to atoms within the next few years."

"So do I," said Mrs. Whitehead.

"This much I will say," said Whitehead. "When you consider the past history of Russia, who the Russians are, what they endured under the czars, and the vast extent of their territory and population, it seems to me that it has to be admitted that their present government is the best obtainable by them, and enough better than any they have ever had before. And this notion that in any part of the earth, no matter how barbarous its previous history or how backward its people, all you need do is give everybody the vote is idiotic."

He added that although modern weapons, especially since the atom bomb, had rendered all previous forms of warfare as obsolete as fists and cudgels, "this has not been grasped by the military people, for all their talk about it, or by hardly anybody else. Take this room; it looks solid, stable, and used to be thought so. As a matter of fact it is a raging welter of activity, nothing permanent about it at all; merely different rates of change, decay, disintegration, ranging from weeks to thousands of years, which in the time span is nothing. Almost no one has grasped the fact that our world has so changed since 1900 as to make any future utterly unpredictable, and any attempt to apply the standards of the past to the present very risky. The nineteenth century was dead by the 1880's; the 1870's was its last lush decade; 1914 was only the mace-blow, which confirmed the fact of its previous demise. But we are now in an epoch where change is far more drastic than that which slew the nineteenth century."

I asked, somewhat circuitously, if he had ever had a sense of being seized by a force not of himself, while writing.

"In all I have written," said he, "I have been trying to express common sense."

Discussing the "half-truths," he continued:

"People make the mistake of talking about 'natural laws.' There *are* no natural laws. There are only temporary habits of nature. . . .

". . . What is more, we are too stuck-up in our notions of size, measuring everything in proportion to our bodies. From what science has discovered about the infinitely small and the infinitely vast, the size of our bodies is almost totally irrelevant. In this little mahogany stand"—he touched it with his hand—"may be civilizations as complex and diversified in scale as our own; and up there, the heavens, with all their vastness, may be only a minute strand of tissue in the body of a being in the scale of which all our universes are as a trifle. Man has only just begun to understand, not this vastness, for we cannot grasp it, but that such vastness exists, and that it throws out all his previous calculations. Dead knowledge is the danger. It is the peculiar danger of scholarship, of universities; and it is

N2*

considered quite respectable. If you 'know' a great deal, that is supposed to suffice. Now what is wanted is 'activity in the presence of knowledge.' Novel viewpoints; knowledge applied to experience."

I asked him whether he thought he had learned more from books or from people. He said: "I have learned, I suppose, far more from people than from books."

As we discussed this, Mrs. Whitehead exclaimed:

"You two men talk like sated gluttons! If you had struggled all your lives under the handicap of not having had a formal scholastic training, you would speak of books more respectfully. The paralysing thing is the uncertainty, the never feeling quite sure of your ground. What the formal training with books does for you is enable you to organize what you know."

She had us, we knew it, and meekly retired from the fray. Whitehead resumed our theme in a different development:

"I am impressed by the inadequacy of language to express our conscious thought, and by the inadequacy of our conscious thought to express our subconscious. The curse of philosophy has been the supposition that language is an exact medium. Philosophers verbalize and then suppose the idea is stated for all time. Even if it were stated, it would need to be restated for every century, perhaps every generation. Plato is the only one who knew better and did not fall into this trap. When ordinary methods failed him, he gave us a myth, which does not challenge exactitude but excites reverie. Mathematics is more nearly precise, and comes nearer to the truth. In a thousand years it may be as commonly used a language as is speech today. Most of what we think and say with our conscious minds and speech is shallow and superficial. Only at rare moments does that deeper and vaster world come through into the conscious thought or expression; they are the memorable moments of our lives, when we feel—when we know—we are being used as instruments of a greater force than ourselves for purposes higher and wider than our own. Men of genius have the moments more often, but nearly everyone has had a few moments of such illumination. The poets are important here, because they express these vast intuitions in words, often better than most philosophers, and in words, however inadequate, that do nevertheless somehow stir in the reader or listener some corresponding sense of the infinitude of thought or feeling or experience which is being talked about. I mean of course only the very greatest poets."

"Should poets know a good deal?"

"Some poets should have known more (especially today); others would have been better poets had they known less. Shakespeare wrote better poetry for not knowing too much; Milton, I think, knew too much finally for the good of his poetry."

"You remember our old friend Walter Raleigh," said Mrs. Whitehead.

"Yes. You always said that he should have been a poet, not a university don."

"I stick to it. He did have just such glimpses of infinitude. There was a quatrain of his, it was published years ago, and I can remember where—in the *Westminster Gazette*—that has stuck in my memory ineradicably." She quoted it:

> Stand on the trestles of the world
> And view the humours of the fair
> Where knives and fiery balls are hurled
> And God leads round his starry Bear . . .

*   *   *

It was growing late, and later than I thought. The autumn gale was still pelting and pouring outside. As the evening went on, it had kept occurring to me that my first visit to them at Canton more than a dozen years ago had been on an April 6th, anniversary of our entrance into the first world war, and that this was Armistice Day, another such anniversary. The idea annoyed me a little, for of late each time I had seen him it had been to wonder if it might be the last. The notion was dismissed, for earlier in the evening though he had looked frail and tired, he was now speaking with the vigour of a young man, of the creative force in the universe.

"It was a mistake, as the Hebrews tried, to conceive of God as creating the world from the outside, at one go. An all-foreseeing Creator, who could have made the world as we find it now—what could we think of such a being? Foreseeing everything and yet putting into it all sorts of imperfections to redeem which it was necessary to send his only son into the world to suffer torture and hideous death; outrageous ideas. The Hellenic religion was a better approach; the Greeks conceived of creation as going on everywhere all the time *within* the universe; and I also think they were happier in their conception of supernatural beings impersonating those various forces, some good, others bad; for both sorts of forces *are* present, whether we assign personality to them or not. There is a general tendency in the universe to produce worth-while things, and moments come when we can work with it and it can work through us. But that tendency in the universe to produce worth-while things is by no means omnipotent. Other forces work against it.

"God is *in* the world, or nowhere, creating continually in us and around us. This creative principle is everywhere, in animate and so-called inanimate matter, in the ether, water, earth, human hearts. But this creation is a continuing process, and 'the process is itself the actuality,' since no sooner do you arrive than you start on a fresh journey. In so far as man partakes of this creative process does he partake of the divine, of God, and that participation is his immortality, reducing the question of whether his individuality survives death of the body to the estate of an irrelevancy. His true destiny as co-creator in the universe is his dignity and his grandeur."

EPILOGUE

Mrs. Whitehead speaks:

"On Christmas Eve I was putting up the holly and mistletoe around our living-rooms. Alfred was in a state of complete happiness, even of elation, holiday high spirits. You would have thought from his praise of our rooms that we had spent our previous years living in kennels. I said so. I said, 'This place isn't anything.' He said, 'I know it, but what does it matter?' What *did* it matter? He had long since ceased to live in it, perhaps never had lived in it at all. On Christmas Day we had our usual family gathering. The next day he wasn't so well, and on that day it came. I saw it happen. He raised his left hand and let it drop, to tell me that he knew, for it was already half paralysed. And I knew the end was not far off."

He lingered four days, but without regaining consciousness, and died December 30, 1947, in his 87th year.

Such was the end, Echecrates, of our friend; concerning whom I may truly say, that of all the men of his time whom I have known, he was the wisest and justest and best.

President Conant: It is impossible for me to express adequately the obligations of my wife and myself to the University over which ~~passide~~ you preside.

Both as an institution and as a group of individuals, Harvard has made it possible for me to express ideas which had been growing in my thoughts for a life-time.

I wish ~~more expressedly~~ to emphasize my admiration and personal affection for so many Harvard friends, some of whom are present today.

During my life I have had the great happiness of ~~learning~~ teaching in two countries which have contributed so greatly to learning and to the dignity of mankind.

Manuscript page in Alfred North Whitehead's handwriting

On the occasion of Whitehead's receiving the Order of Merit from the British Crown at University Hall, Cambridge, Massachusetts, June 6, 1945.

Books by

ALFRED NORTH WHITEHEAD

(1861–1947)

A Treatise on Universal Algebra (1898)

Principia Mathematica (with Bertrand Russell; 3 vols., 1910–1913)

Axioms of Projective Geometry (1906)

Axioms of Descriptive Geometry (1907)

An Introduction to Mathematics (1910)

The Organization of Thought (1916)

An Enquiry Concerning the Principles of Natural Knowledge (1919)

The Concept of Nature (1920)

The Principle of Relativity with Applications to Physical Science (1922)

* Science and the Modern World (1925)

* Religion in the Making (1926)

* Symbolism: Its Meaning and Effect (1927)

* The Aims of Education (1928)

* Process and Reality: An Essay in Cosmology (1929)

* The Function of Reason (1929)

* Adventures of Ideas (1933)

* Nature and Life (1934)

* Modes of Thought (1938)

* Essays in Science and Philosophy (1947)

* *Written in the United States.*

[369]

INDEX

ABILITY, where you get the best, 132; very narrow range of, 149
Acquisitive scholarship overdone, 168
Action lands you in conflict, 87
Active and static thought, difference between, 143
Actuality, process is itself the, 209; mathematics does not give any account of, 211
Adult education, 342
Adventure, meaning of life is, 250
Adventures of Ideas (Whitehead), 8, 128, 209–10: book he had most wanted to write, 8
Adventures of ideas, the life cycle in, 252
Advocatus diaboli, 140
Aeschylus, 182, 263
Aesthetic appeal of the Church, blunder of throwing away, 232
Aesthetic came after the moral values, 183–4
Aesthetic sense too highly cultivated, educated people have, 60
Aesthetic view of life, contribution of Greeks is, 251
Aims of Education, The (Whitehead), 132, 136, 137, 155, 162, 322, 323, 359
Air about us may be peopled by intelligences, 234
Alcohol as a criterion of civilization, 50–1
Alexandria systematized Hellenic thought, 302
America, life looks not back but forward in, 55; Protestantism in, 58; to be civilized by the business class, 61; potential public bigger (than England) in, but distributed, 65; life in, is kinder than anywhere else, 131; and the artist, 177; "pastlessness" in, 204; universal education in, 245; will gain by the admixture of the brilliant southern European strains, 282; democracy horizontal in, vertical in England, 345
American aborigines, how (they) reached this continent from Asia, 80

American democracy creating an aristocracy, 42
American history stems from the dissenter, 41
American inventiveness not primarily originative, 52
American journalism, intrusions upon personal privacy by, 64
American liberals, where (they) come from, 101
American Midwest, civilization on grand scale in the, 68
American myth, corruption of the, 265
American nation, basic unifying idea of, 149
American newspaper headlines, 19, 20
American people, kindness of, unique in history, 202–3
American slang, 217
American small town, one class-line of, 204
American social system the best that ever existed, 312
American students less well-informed than English, 21
American universities, in their broad functions, 43; to civilize business, 60–2
American women conventionalized by the sameness of their education, 238
Americans, must not copy Europe, 60; care more for equality than for liberty, 201; creating myths now, 265; unimaginative in interpretations of democracy, 268
Ancient world, conversation from, 181
Anglican service a symbol of aristocracy's responsibility, 156
Anglo-American stock, 282
Anglo-American understanding, common language a help or hindrance to, 41
Anti-Semitism rare in England, 202
Antonine emperors, adoptive successors to, ratified by a military oligarchy, 37
"Appeal to Sanity, An" (Whitehead), 105, 113

[371]

Buddhism, 161, 186, 194, 297; not associated with an advancing civilization, 186

Business, American universities to civilize, 61

Business class, America to be civilized by the, 61

Butler, Samuel, 195, 279

CADENCE OF VERSE is an aid to memory, 150

Caesar, Julius, 119; *Commentaries*, 120

Calvin, John, 232

Calvinism, man marked for eternal damnation by, 59

Cambridge, Massachusetts, Whitehead comes to, 1, 7–8. *See also* Harvard University

Cambridge Ancient History, 297

Cambridge and Oxford, returning more nearly to their function in the Middle Ages, 345; comparison of, 350

Cambridge University, 22, 43, 47; Whitehead's student days at, 4; Fellow of Trinity, 5–6; reminiscences of, 234, 247

Cannon, Dr. Walter B., 75–81

Capitalism, wouldn't greatly matter whether a family had much money even under, 85

Capitalist system, (its) one chance of survival, 85

Career was open to talents, 88

Careers, extravagant (1850–1950), 1

Carmen, was (she) a really nice woman, 71

Catastrophe, the man who averts a, 119

Catholic Church, 140, 157. *See also* Roman Catholic Church

Catholic confessional, 58–9

Catholic theology is a philosophy of life as of a man who had lived dissolutely, 63–4

Catholicism, 125, 262

Catholics, 178

Celtic revival 104

Certitude, gone, 5; now at last we have, 128; beware of, 298

Chance, freaks of, only the last steps in causation, 201; element in history of, 200

Change, perfection just precedes a, 52; is constant, 210

Chaucer, Geoffrey, 21

Chicago, university scholars at, most like Greece, 54

Children, "giving my, a better chance than I had," 85; are die-hard conservatives, 188

China, discussion of Communism in, 311

Chinese laugh at the same jokes as we do, 81–2

Choric odes in Greek tragedy, 89–90

Christian theology, 11, 171–3

Christianity, the Hellenic element came into, 58; came into Europe through "the lower orders," 58; the end of, 131; interpreters are (its) misfortune, 138, 172; had no idea of managing a complex society 156; theological disaster of, 173; involved in perpetual self-contradiction, 258; responsibility for continuance of a social system absent from, 258; deficiencies of, 292; did not invent human worth, 292

Church, blunder of throwing away the aesthetic appeal of the, 232

Church of Rome, "damnable errors" of the, 32

Churchill, Winston Spencer, 269, 284, 354

Cicero, 70

Civilization, new factor in, 7; alcohol as a criterion of, 50: on the grand scale in the American Midwest, 68; three preconditions to flourishing, 68

Civilized life, we live amid a disintegration of, 272

Class-line of American small town, 204

Classic models, readjustment of traditional, to modern needs is wanted, 125

Classical tradition on the wane, 154

Classics, textual criticism of, done, 150

Clergy have lost their hold, 131

Coincidence, what is (it), 201

Colosseum, modern substitute for, 40

Common language a help or a hindrance to Anglo-American understanding, 41

Common man, American political myth is to safeguard lot of, 265

Common people, greatest art speaks to, 23; unsuspected powers in, 148

Commonplaces, letting guests start off on, 49

Communication in words, difficulty of, 333

Communism ought to have six hundred varying definitions, 312

Conant, James B., 115; *Wanted: American Radicals*, 197

their force, 214; the life cycle in adventures of, 253

"If all the good people were clever," 29

Iliad, comparing with the Bible, 196; origin of our idea of the gentleman, 196; laughter in, 352

Imagination is most active between ages of nineteen and thirty-five, 78

"Imitations of Immortality," 29

Immoral God, the most, ever imagined, 195

Immoral music, 71

"In Boston when it snows at night," David McCord, 39

Incentive of any one great figure, 23

Independent thought, muddle-headedness a condition precedent to, 44

Individual, when does (he) begin to be prized, 119; powers of, are unique and unpredictable, 149

Individual profit too limited to serve as foundation for a stable society, 277

Individuality more pronounced in Europe, 68

Industrial Age, we might have had (it) in the time of Achimedes, 226

Inert ideas, 162

Infinite, relationship between the finite and the, 160

Infinite possibilities are actualities, 130–1

Infinite potentialities of human beings, 151

Infinite series, we are part of, 234

Infinitely vast, no difference between the infinitely small and the, 209

Inherit the idea without inheriting the fervour, 252

Insomnia, tussle with, 6

Institutions run their course, 43

Instruction, Platonic method of, 4

Instruments of a greater force than ourselves, we are being used as, 364

Intellect is to emotion as our clothes are to our bodies, 228

Intellectual enlightenment, artisans seeking, 7

Intellectualizing upon a religion, trouble from, 186

Intellectuals do not speak for the country, 101

Intelligence and ability, distinction between, 132

Intelligence congealing into too-good teaching, 60

Internal industrial activities, true prosperity of a country derived from, 276

Interpreters of Christianity, the trouble with, 172

Intimate letters, truer picture of a period from, 44

Intuition, necessary to a good experiment, 142; an angel—intellect, the devil, 194

Inventions, whether the modern world is at the mercy of its, 144

Irony, defined, 260; Strachey's, 261; Santayana's, 261; Socratic, 262; tragic, 263

Irreverence, necessity of, 59

Italian tomb, 30

JACOBINISM, 130

Japan, discussion on, 311

James, Henry, 32, 119; *The Ambassadors*, 16

James, William, 8, 79, 111, 183, 333–4; description of Cambridge (Mass.) home and study of, 314–15; an affable archangel, 317; portrait of, 319; *Varieties of Religious Experience*, 333

Jargon of thinking gets in the way of thought, 55

Jebb, Sir Richard, 221, 334–5

Jesuit order, 164

Jesus, was one of those winning persons, 57; no evidence Paul ever saw, 57; was not very intellectual, 186

Jew, brilliancy of the young, 106

Jewish comedians funniest people on earth, 57

Jews, 114, 195, 251; singularly humourless, 57; young, beat us all hollow, 72; characteristics and achievements of, 106–7; are ablest of any race, 176; in England, Spain and America, 277. *See also* Hebrews

Johnson, Samuel, 100

Joke, is funny if you think it is, 50; truly religious persons fond of a, 59

Journalists, Hippocratic Oath for, 257

Julian, Emperor, 350

KINGDOMS, "small (German), destined to disappear," 45

King's Chapel religion, 32

King's College, 234

Kittredge, George Lyman, 50, 144

Knowledge wedded to action, 167